D0883660

H = human capital
I = investment
INT = interest paid by the government
K = capital stock
KA = capital account surplus
L = quantity of land (Chapter 6)
L = real money demand function
M = money supply
$MC(I)$ = marginal cost of investment
$MB(I)$ = marginal benefit of investment
MPC = marginal propensity to consume
MP_K = marginal product of capital
MP_N = marginal product of labour
$MRS_{x,y}$ = marginal rate of substitution of x for y
$MRT_{x,y}$ = marginal rate of transformation of x for y
MU_C = marginal utility of consumption
N = employment
N = population (Chapters 6, 7, 8)
NFP = net factor payments
NX − net exports
P = price level
P^* = foreign price level
PPF = production possibilities frontier
Q = labour force
R = nominal interest rate
S = aggregate savings
S^p = private savings
S^g = government savings
T = current taxes
$TOT_{a,b}$ − terms of trade, or world price of a in terms of b
TR = aggregate transfers from the government
U = utility function (Chapters 4 and 17)
U = number of unemployed (Chapter 6)
V = present value of profits (Chapter 11)
V = velocity of money (Chapter 17)
X = credit card balances, in units of goods
W = nominal wage
Y = aggregate real income
Y_d = disposable income
Y_T = trend level of output
p = profits

Notes

- Primes denote future variables; for example, C' denotes the future level of aggregate consumption.
- A superscript d denotes demand; for example, N^d is labour demand.
- A superscript s denotes supply; for example, N^s is labour supply.
- In Chapters 7 and 8, lowercase letters are variables in per-worker terms.

FOURTH CANADIAN EDITION

MACROECONOMICS

STEPHEN D. WILLIAMSON

Washington University in St. Louis

PEARSON

Toronto

Vice-President, Editorial Director: Gary Bennett
Editor-in-Chief: Nicole Lukach
Acquisitions Editor: Claudine O'Donnell
Marketing Manager: Leigh-Anne Graham
Developmental Editor: Patti Altridge
Project Manager: Rachel Thompson
Production Editor: Sheena Uprety, Cenveo Publisher Services
Copy Editor: Rodney Rawlings
Proofreader: Julia Hubble
Compositor: Cenveo Publisher Services
Art Director: Julia Hall
Cover Designer: Anthony Leung
Interior Designer: Anthony Leung
Cover Image: Philippe Sainte-Laudy/GettyImages

Credits and acknowledgments for material borrowed from other sources and reproduced, with permission, in this textbook appear on the appropriate page within the text.

Original edition published by Pearson Education, Inc., Upper Saddle River, New Jersey, USA. Copyright © 2011 Pearson Education, Inc. This edition is authorized for sale only in Canada.

If you purchased this book outside the United States or Canada, you should be aware that it has been imported without the approval of the publisher or the author.

Copyright © 2013, 2010, 2006, 2002 Pearson Canada Inc. All rights reserved. Manufactured in the United States of America. This publication is protected by copyright and permission should be obtained from the publisher prior to any prohibited reproduction, storage in a retrieval system, or transmission in any form or by any means, electronic, mechanical, photocopying, recording, or likewise. To obtain permission(s) to use material from this work, please submit a written request to Pearson Canada Inc., Permissions Department, 26 Prince Andrew Place, Don Mills, Ontario, M3C 2T8, or fax your request to 416-447-3126, or submit a request to Permissions Requests at **www.pearsoncanada.ca**.

10 9 8 7 6 5 4 3 2 1 EBM

Library and Archives Canada Cataloguing in Publication

Williamson, Stephen D

    Macroeconomics / Stephen D. Williamson. — 4th Canadian ed.

Includes index.

ISBN 978-0-321-73397-9

    1. Macroeconomics—Textbooks. I. Title.

HB172 .5.W55 2012   339   C2012-903876-8

ISBN 978-0-321-73397-9

BRIEF CONTENTS

CONTENTS

CHAPTER 6   *Search and Unemployment*   172

PART 3   *Economic Growth   203*

PART 4   *Savings, Investment, and Government Deficits*   271

CHAPTER 9   *A Two-Period Model: The Consumption–Savings Decision and Credit Markets*   272

CHAPTER 10   *Credit Market Imperfections: Credit Frictions, Financial Crises, and Social Security*   317

PART 5 **Money and Business Cycles 393**

PART 6

International Macroeconomics 503

PREFACE

This book follows a modern approach to macroeconomics by building macroeconomic models from microeconomic principles. As such, it is consistent with the way that macroeconomic research is conducted today.

This approach has three advantages. First, it allows deeper insights into economic growth processes and business cycles, the key topics in macroeconomics. Second, an emphasis on microeconomic foundations better integrates the study of macroeconomics with approaches that students learn in microeconomics courses and in economics field courses. Learning in macroeconomics and microeconomics thus becomes mutually reinforcing, and students learn more. Third, in following an approach to macroeconomics that is consistent with current macroeconomic research, students will be better prepared for advanced study in economics.

Structure

The text begins in Part 1 with an introduction and study of measurement issues. Chapter 1 describes the approach taken in the book and the key ideas that students should take away. It previews the important issues that will be addressed throughout the book, along with some recent issues in macroeconomics, and highlights how these will be studied. Measurement is discussed in Chapters 2 and 3, first with regard to gross domestic product, prices, savings, and wealth, and then with regard to business cycles. In Chapter 3, we develop a set of key business cycle facts that will be used throughout the book, particularly in Chapters 13 and 14, where we investigate how alternative business cycle theories fit the facts.

Our study of macroeconomic theory begins in Part 2. In Chapter 4, we study the behaviour of consumers and firms in detail. In the one-period model developed in Chapter 5, we use the approach of capturing the behaviour of all consumers and all firms in the economy with a single representative consumer and a single representative firm. The one-period model is used to show how changes in government spending and total factor productivity affect aggregate output, employment, consumption, and the real wage. Then, in Chapter 6, we develop a one-period model of search and unemployment, so as to study in detail the macroeconomic determinants of labour market behaviour.

With a basic knowledge of static macroeconomic theory from Part 2, we proceed in Part 3 to the study of economic growth. In Chapter 7 we discuss a set of economic growth facts that are then used to organize our thinking in the context of models of economic growth. The first growth model we examine is a Malthusian growth model, consistent with the late-eighteenth century ideas of Thomas Malthus. The Malthusian model predicts well the features of economic growth in the world before the Industrial Revolution, but it does not predict the sustained growth in per capita incomes that occurred in advanced countries after 1800. The Solow growth model, which we examine next, does a good job of explaining some important observations concerning modern economic growth. Finally, Chapter 7 explains growth accounting, which is an approach to disentangling the sources of growth. In Chapter 8 we discuss income disparities across countries in light of the predictions of the Solow model, and introduce a model of endogenous growth.

In Part 4, we first use the theory of consumer and firm behaviour developed in Part 2 to construct (in Chapter 9) a two-period model that can be used to study consumption–savings decisions, the behaviour of credit markets, and the effects of government deficits on the economy. Credit market frictions, with a particular focus on applications related to the financial crisis, is the topic of Chapter 10. The two-period model is then extended to include investment behaviour in the real intertemporal model of Chapter 11. This model will then serve as the basis for much of what is done in the remainder of the book.

In Part 5, we include monetary phenomena and banking in the real intertemporal model of Chapter 12, so as to construct a monetary intertemporal model. This model is used in Chapter 12 to examine the effects of changes in monetary policy on the economy. Then, in Chapters 13 and 14, we study Non-Keynesian and Keynesian theories of the business cycle. These theories are compared and contrasted, and we examine how alternative business cycle theories fit the data and how they help us to understand recent business cycle behaviour in Canada.

Part 6 is devoted to international macroeconomics. In Chapter 15, the models of Chapters 5 and 11 are used to show what benefits accrue from international trade, how changes in the relative prices of imports and exports affect the economy, and what determines the current account surplus. Then, in Chapter 16, we show how exchange rates are determined, and we investigate the roles of fiscal and monetary policy in an open economy that trades goods and assets with the rest of the world.

Finally, Part 7 examines some important topics in macroeconomics. In Chapter 17, we study in more depth the role of money in the economy, the effects of money growth on inflation, and aggregate economic activity, banking, and deposit insurance. Finally, in Chapter 18, we see how central banks can cause inflation, either because they do not correctly understand the relationship between real macroeconomic activity and inflation, or because they cannot commit themselves to a low-inflation policy. We also demonstrate in this chapter how inflation has been reduced over the last twenty years in Canada, New Zealand, and Hong Kong.

Features

Several key features enhance the learning process and illuminate critical ideas for the student. The intent is to make macroeconomic theory transparent, accessible, and relevant.

REAL-WORLD APPLICATIONS

Applications to current and historical problems are emphasized throughout in two running features. The first is a series of "Theory Confronts the Data" sections, which show how macroeconomic theory comes to life in matching (or sometimes falling short of matching) the characteristics of real-world economic data. A sampling of some of these sections includes the comparison of unemployment, productivity, and real GDP in the U.S. and Canada during the 2008–2009 recession; consumption smoothing and the stock market, and interest rate spreads and macroeconomic activity. The second running feature is a series of "Macroeconomics in Action" boxes. These real-world applications relating directly to the theory encapsulate ideas from front-line research in macroeconomics and the history of economic thought, and they aid students in understanding the core material. For example, some of the subjects examined in these boxes are the empirical evidence on quantitative easing, and the origins of the financial crisis in the United States.

ART PROGRAM

Graphs and charts are plentiful in this book. They act as visual representations of macroeconomic models that can be manipulated to derive important results and show the key features of important macro data in applications. To aid the student, graphs and charts use a consistent two-colour system that encodes the meaning of particular elements in graphs and of shifts in curves.

END-OF-CHAPTER SUMMARY AND LIST OF KEY TERMS

Each chapter wraps up with a summary of its key ideas, followed by a glossary of key terms. The key terms are listed in the order in which they appear in the chapter, and they are highlighted in bold typeface where they are first explained within the chapter.

QUESTIONS FOR REVIEW

These questions are intended as self-tests for students after they have finished reading the chapter material. The questions relate directly to ideas and facts covered in the chapter, and answering them will be straightforward if the student has read and comprehended the chapter material.

PROBLEMS

The end-of-chapter problems will help the student in learning the material and applying the macroeconomic models developed in the chapter. These problems are intended to be challenging and thought provoking.

NOTATION

For easy reference, definitions of all variables used in the text are contained on the end papers.

MATHEMATICS AND MATHEMATICAL APPENDIX

In the body of the text, the analysis is mainly graphical, with some knowledge of basic algebra required; calculus is not used. However, for students and instructors who desire a more rigorous treatment of the material in the text, a mathematical appendix develops the key models and results more formally, assuming a basic knowledge of calculus and the fundamentals of mathematical economics. The Mathematical Appendix also contains problems on this more advanced material.

Flexibility

This book was written to be user friendly for instructors with different preferences and with different time allocations. The following core material is recommended for all instructors:

Chapter 1 Introduction

Chapter 2 Measurement

Chapter 3 Business Cycle Measurement

Chapter 4 Consumer and Firm Behaviour: The Work–Leisure Decision and Profit Maximization

Chapter 5 A Closed-Economy One-Period Macroeconomic Model

Chapter 9 A Two-Period Model: The Consumption–Savings Decision and Credit Markets

Chapter 11 A Real Intertemporal Model with Investment

Some instructors find measurement issues uninteresting and may choose to omit parts of Chapter 2, although, at the minimum, instructors should cover the key national income accounting identities. Parts of Chapter 3 can be omitted if the instructor chooses not to emphasize business cycles, but there are some important concepts introduced here that are generally useful in later chapters, such as the meaning of correlation and how to read scatter plots and time-series plots.

Chapters 7 and 8 introduce economic growth at an early stage. However, Chapters 7 and 8 are essentially self-contained. Given the recent keen interest of students in business cycle and financial issues, instructors may want to forego growth, in favor of search and unemployment (Chapter 6), and monetary and business cycle theory in Chapters 12–14. Though the text has an emphasis on micro foundations, Keynesian analysis receives a balanced treatment. For example, we examine a Keynesian coordination failure models in Chapters 6 and 13, and we study a New Keynesian sticky price business cycle model in Chapter 14. Instructors can choose to emphasize economic growth or business cycle analysis, or they can give their course an international focus. As well, it is possible to de-emphasize monetary factors. As a guide, the text can be adapted as follows:

FOCUS ON ECONOMIC GROWTH

Include Chapters 7 and 8, and consider dropping Chapter 6, or Chapters 13 and 14, depending on time available.

FOCUS ON BUSINESS CYCLES

Drop Chapters 7 and 8, and include Chapters 6, and 12–14.

INTERNATIONAL FOCUS

Chapters 15 and 16 can be moved up in the sequence. Chapter 15 can follow Chapter 11, and Chapter 16 can follow Chapter 12.

ADVANCED MATHEMATICAL TREATMENT

Add material as desired from the Mathematical Appendix.

What's New in the Fourth Canadian Edition

The first through third Canadian editions of *Macroeconomics* had excellent receptions in the market. In the fourth Canadian edition, I build on the strengths of the first through third Canadian editions while modifying and streamlining existing material and adding new topics, in line with the interests of students and instructors, new developments in macroeconomic thought, and recent events in the Canadian and world economies. As well, applications have been added to help students understand macroeconomic events that have occurred since the third edition was written, and the end-of-chapter problems have been expanded. In more detail, here are the highlights of the revision:

• In Chapter 5, there is new material on the optimal choice of government spending.

• Chapter 6 is **entirely new**, and is an innovation in the market for intermediate macroeconomics textbooks. This chapter contains an accessible treatment of the Diamond-Mortensen-Pissarides search model of unemployment, which has become a workhorse for research on labour markets and the macroeconomics of search and unemployment over the last 30 years. This model allows the student to understand recent events in labour markets in North America and the rest of the world, along with the key determinants of the unemployment rate, the vacancy rate, and labour force participation.

• Chapter 9 has been separated out as a chapter on credit market frictions related specifically to the global financial crisis and social security programs.

• The treatment of monetary economics in Chapter 12 has been streamlined, and material has been added on currently popular topics: nominal GDP targeting, the zero lower bound, liquidity traps, and quantitative easing.

• Chapter 13 includes new material on New Monetarist Economics, which models the role of assets in financial market exchange, and highlights novel effects of monetary policy that are important to the financial crisis and recent central banking interventions.

• Chapter 17 includes new features on the financial crisis and banking in the United States and Canada.

• **Macroeconomics in Action** and **Theory Confronts the Data** features have changed. Some have been dropped and others added to add contemporary relevance to the material.

• **New end-of-chapter problems** have been added.

Supplemental Materials

The following materials that accompany the main text will enrich the intermediate macroeconomics course for instructors and students alike.

CourseSmart FOR STUDENTS

CourseSmart goes beyond traditional expectations–providing instant, online access to the textbooks and course materials you need at an average savings of 60%. With instant access from any computer and the ability to search your text, you'll find the content you need quickly, no matter where you are. And with online tools like highlighting and note-taking, you can save time and study efficiently. See all the benefits at www.coursesmart.com/students.

INSTRUCTOR'S SUPPLEMENTS

The following instructor supplements are available for downloading from a password-protected section of Pearson Education Canada's online catalogue (www.pearsoned.ca/highered). Navigate to your book's catalogue page to view a list of those supplements that are available. See your local sales representative for details and access.

INSTRUCTOR'S MANUAL

This manual contains chapter key ideas, teaching goals, classroom discussion topics, outline, and textbook problem solutions.

TEST ITEM FILE

Available in Microsoft Word this test bank includes over 1000 multiple-choice questions and one essay question per chapter.

TestGen

A computerized test bank that enables instructors to view and edit the existing questions, add questions, generate tests, and print the tests in a variety of formats. Powerful search and sort functions make it easy to locate questions and arrange them in any order desired. TestGen also enables instructors to administer test on a local area network, have the tests graded electronically, and have the results prepared in electronic or printed reports. The Pearson TestGen is compatible with IBM or Macintosh systems.

PowerPoint Presentations cover the key concepts and figures in each chapter.

Image Library provides electronic versions of the figures and tables that appear in the text.

CourseSmart FOR INSTRUCTORS

CourseSmart goes beyond traditional expectations–providing instant, online access to the text-books and course materials you need at a lower cost for students. And even as students save money, you can save time and hassle with a digital eTextbook that allows you to search for the most relevant content at the very moment you need it. Whether it's evaluating textbooks or creating lecture notes to help students with difficult concepts, CourseSmart can make life a little easier. See how when you visit www.coursesmart.com/instructors.

TECHNOLOGY SPECIALISTS.

Pearson's Technology Specialists work with faculty and campus course designers to ensure that Pearson technology products, assessment tools, and online course materials are tailored to meet your specific needs. This highly qualified team is dedicated to helping schools take full advantage of a wide range of educational resources, by assisting in the integration of a variety of instructional materials and media formats. Your local Pearson Education sales representative can provide you with more details on this service program.

PEARSON CUSTOM LIBRARY

For enrollments of at least 25 students, you can create your own textbook by choosing the chapters that best suit your own course needs. To begin building your custom text, visit www.pearsoncustomlibrary.com. You may also work with a dedicated Pearson Custom editor to create your ideal text—publishing your own original content or mixing and matching Pearson content. Contact your local Pearson Representative to get started.

Acknowledgments

For this fourth Canadian edition, I am grateful to the following economists who provided formal reviews. Their observations and suggestions were very helpful.

Ahmet Akyol (York University)

Joseph DeJuan (University of Waterloo)

David Fuller (Concordia University)

Wai-Ming Ho (York University)

Hashmat Khan (Carleton University)

Robert F. Lucas (University of Saskatchewan)

Desmond McKeon (University of Western Ontario)

Diego Restuccia (University of Toronto)

Charlene Richter (British Columbia Institute of Technology)

Kenneth Stewart (University of Victoria)

Greg Tkacz (St. Francis Xavier University)

Special thanks go to Claudine O'Donnell, Patti Altridge, Rachel Thompson, and Rodney Rawlings at Pearson Canada who provided so much help and encouragement.

Stephen D. Williamson

ABOUT THE AUTHOR

Stephen Williamson is Robert S. Brookings Distinguished Professor in Arts and Sciences, Department of Economics, Washington University in St. Louis; a Visiting Scholar at the Federal Reserve Bank of Richmond; and a Research Fellow at the Federal Reserve Bank of St. Louis. He attended Merwin Greer Public School, Dale Road Junior High School, and Cobourg District Collegiate Institute East in Cobourg, Ontario; received a B.Sc. (Honours, Mathematics) and an M.A. in Economics from Queen's University in Kingston, Ontario; and received his Ph.D. from the University of Wisconsin–Madison in 1984. He has held academic positions at Queen's University, the University of Western Ontario, and the University of Iowa, and has worked as an economist at the Federal Reserve Bank of Minneapolis and the Bank of Canada. Professor Williamson has been an academic visitor at the Federal Reserve Banks of Atlanta, Kansas City, Minneapolis, Cleveland, and Philadelphia, at the Board of Governors of the Federal Reserve System in Washington, D.C., and at the Bank of Canada. He has also been a long-term visitor at the University of Tilburg, the Netherlands; the London School of Economics; the University of Edinburgh; Victoria University of Wellington, New Zealand; Seoul National University; Hong Kong University, and Fudan University. Professor Williamson has published scholarly articles in the *American Economic Review*, the *Journal of Political Economy*, the *Quarterly Journal of Economics*, the *Review of Economic Studies*, the *Journal of Economic Theory*, and the *Journal of Monetary Economics*, among other prestigious economics journals. His research, focused mainly on macroeconomics, monetary theory, and the theory of financial intermediation, has been supported by the National Science Foundation, the Lynde and Harry Bradley Foundation, and the Social Sciences and Humanities Research Council of Canada. Professor Williamson lives in Clayton, Missouri

Part

1

Introduction and Measurement Issues

Part 1 contains an introduction to macroeconomic analysis and a description of the approach in this text of building useful macroeconomic models based on microeconomic principles. We discuss the key ideas that will be analyzed and some current issues that the macroeconomic theory developed in Parts 2 to 7 will help us to understand. Then, to lay a foundation for what is done later, we explore how the key variables relating to macroeconomic theory are measured in practice. Finally, we analyze the key empirical facts concerning business cycles. These facts will prove useful in Parts 2 to 7 in showing the successes and shortcomings of macroeconomic theory in explaining real-world phenomena.

1

Introduction

This chapter frames the approach to macroeconomics that we take in this text, and it foreshadows the basic macroeconomic ideas and issues that we will develop in future chapters. We first discuss what macroeconomics is and then go on to look at the two phenomena of primary interest to macroeconomists—economic growth and business cycles—in terms of twentieth-century Canadian economic history. Then, we explain the approach this text takes—building macroeconomic models with microeconomic principles as a foundation—and discuss the issue of disagreement in macroeconomics. Finally, we explore the key lessons that we will learn from macroeconomic theory in this text, and we discuss how macroeconomics helps us understand recent and current issues.

What Is Macroeconomics?

Macroeconomists are motivated by large questions, by issues that affect many people and many nations of the world. Why are some countries exceedingly rich and others exceedingly poor? Why are most Canadians so much better off than their parents and grandparents? Why are there fluctuations in aggregate economic activity? What causes inflation? Why is there unemployment?

Macroeconomics is the study of the behaviour of large collections of economic agents. It focuses on the aggregate behaviour of consumers and firms, the behaviour of governments, the overall level of economic activity in individual countries, the economic interactions among nations, and the effects of fiscal and monetary policy. Macroeconomics is distinct from microeconomics in that it deals with the overall effects on economies of the choices that all economic agents make, rather than the choices of individual consumers or firms. Since the 1970s, however, the distinction between microeconomics and macroeconomics has blurred, for microeconomists and macroeconomists now use much the same kinds of tools. That is, the **economic models** that macroeconomists use, consisting of descriptions of consumers and firms, their objectives and constraints, and their inter-actions, are built up from microeconomic principles, and these models are typically analyzed and fit to data by using methods similar to those used by microeconomists. What continues to make macroeconomics distinct, though, is the issues on which it focuses, particularly **long-run growth** and **business cycles**. Long-run growth refers to the increase in a nation's productive capacity and average standard of living that occurs over a long period of time, whereas business cycles are the short-run ups and downs, or booms and recessions, in aggregate economic activity.

The approach in this text will be to consistently build up macroeconomic analysis from microeconomic principles. There is some effort required in taking this type of approach, but the effort is well worth it. The result will be that you better understand how the economy works and how to improve it.

Gross Domestic Product, Economic Growth, and Business Cycles

To begin our study of macroeconomic phenomena, we must first understand what facts we are trying to explain. The most basic set of facts in macroeconomics has to do with the behaviour of aggregate economic activity over time. One measure of aggregate economic activity is **gross domestic product (GDP)**, which is the quantity of goods and services produced within a country's borders during some specified period of time. GDP also represents the aggregate quantity of income earned by those who contribute to production in a country. In Figure 1.1 we show real GDP per capita for Canada for the period 1870–2010. This is a measure of aggregate output that adjusts for inflation and population growth, and the unit of measure is 2002 dollars per person.

The first observation we can make concerning Figure 1.1 is that there was sus-tained growth in per capita real GDP during the 140-year period 1870–2010. In 1870, the average income for a Canadian was about $2700 (2002 dollars), and this grew to more than $38 000 (2002 dollars) in 2010. Thus, the average Canadian became more than 14 times richer in real terms over the course of 140 years, which is quite remark-able! The second important observation from Figure 1.1 is that, while growth in per capita real GDP was sustained over long periods of time in Canada during the period 1870–2010, this growth was certainly not steady. Growth was higher at some times than at others, and there were periods over which per capita real GDP declined. These fluctuations in economic growth are business cycles.

Two key, though unusual, business cycle events in Canadian economic history that show up in Figure 1.1 are the Great Depression and World War II, and these events dwarf any other twentieth-century business cycle events in Canada since then, in terms of the magnitude of the short-run change in economic growth. Two other very signifi-cant events are the major recession in the early 1920s and the subsequent boom leading up to the Great Depression, but we will focus here on the Great Depression and World War II, as these were events of worldwide macroeconomic significance. During the Great Depression, real GDP per capita dropped from a peak of $8268 (2002 dollars)

FIGURE 1.1

**Per Capita Real GDP for
Canada, 1870–2010
(2002 dollars)**

Per capita real GDP is a
measure of the average
level of income for a Canadian resident. Two unusual,
though key, events in the
figure are the Great Depression, when there was a large
reduction in living standards
for the average Canadian, and
World War II, when per capita
output increased greatly.

Source: Adapted from the Statistics
Canada CANSIM database, Series
v3860085, V1, and from the Statistics
Canada publication *Historical Statistics
of Canada*, Catalogue 11-516, 1983,
Series F33–55, A1.

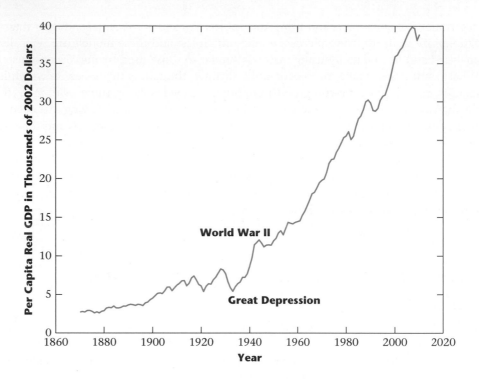

per person in 1928 to a low of $5366 (2002 dollars) per person in 1933, a decline of about 35%. At the peak of war production in 1944, GDP had risen to $12 026 (2002 dollars) per person, an increase of 124% from 1933. These wild gyrations in aggregate economic activity over a 16-year period are as phenomenal, and certainly every bit as interesting, as the long-run sustained growth in per capita real GDP that occurred from 1870 to 2010. In addition to the Great Depression and World War II, Figure 1.1 shows other business cycle upturns and downturns in the growth of per capita real GDP in Canada that, though less dramatic since the Great Depression or World War II, represent important macroeconomic events in Canadian history.

Figure 1.1 thus raises the following fundamental macroeconomic questions, which will motivate much of the material in this text:

1. What causes sustained economic growth?
2. Could economic growth continue indefinitely, or is there some limit to growth?
3. Is there anything that governments can or should do to alter the rate of economic growth?
4. What causes business cycles?
5. Could the dramatic decreases and increases in economic growth that occurred during the Great Depression and World War II be repeated?
6. Should governments act to smooth business cycles?

In analyzing economic data to study economic growth and business cycles, it often proves useful to transform the data in various ways, so as to obtain sharper insights. For economic time series that exhibit growth, such as per capita real GDP in Figure 1.1, a useful transformation is to take the natural logarithm of the time series. To show why this is useful, suppose that y_t is an observation on an economic time series in period t; for example, y_t could represent per capita real GDP in year t, where $t = 1870, 1871, 1872$, etc. Then, the growth rate from period $t - 1$ to period t in y_t can be denoted by g_t, where

$$g_t = \frac{y_t}{y_{t-1}} - 1.$$

Now, if x is a small number, then $\log (1 + x) \approx x$, that is, the natural logarithm of $1 + x$ is approximately equal to x. Therefore, if g_t is small,

$$\log (g_t + 1) \approx g_t$$

or

$$\log\left(\frac{y_t}{y_{t-1}}\right) \approx g_t$$

or

$$\log y_t - \log y_{t-1} \approx g_t.$$

Since $\log y_t - \log y_{t-1}$ is the slope of the graph of the natural logarithm of y_t between periods $t - 1$ and t, it follows that *the slope of the graph of the natural logarithm of a time series y_t is a good approximation to the growth rate of y_t when the growth rate is small.*

In Figure 1.2 we graph the natural logarithm of per capita real GDP in Canada for the period 1870–2010. As explained above, the slope of the graph is a good approximation of the growth rate of real per capita GDP, so that changes in the slope represent changes in the growth rate of real per capita GDP. It is striking that in Figure 1.2, except for the large fluctuations that occur from about 1920 to 1945, a straight line would fit the graph quite well. That is, over the period 1870–2007, growth in per capita real GDP has been "roughly" constant at about 2.0% per year.

A second useful transformation to carry out on an economic time series is to separate the series into two components: the growth or **trend** component, and the business cycle component. For example, the business cycle component of real per capita GDP can be captured as the deviations of real per capita GDP from a smooth trend fit to the data. In Figure 1.3 we show the trend in the log of real per capita GDP as a coloured line,[1] while the log of actual real per capita GDP is the black line. We then define the business cycle component of the log of real per capita GDP to be the difference between the black line and the coloured line in Figure 1.3. The logic behind this decomposition of real per capita GDP into trend and business cycle components is that it is often simpler and more

---

[1]Trend GDP was computed using a Hodrick-Prescott filter, as in E. Prescott, 1986, "Theory Ahead of Business Cycle Measurement," *Federal Reserve Bank of Minneapolis Quarterly Review,* Fall.

FIGURE 1.2

Natural Logarithm of Per Capita Real GDP

Here, the slope of the graph is approximately equal to the growth rate of per capita GDP. Excluding the period from 1920–1945, the growth rate of per capita GDP is remarkably close to being constant during this period. That is, a straight line would fit the graph fairly well.

Source: Adapted from the Statistics Canada CANSIM database, Series v3860085, V1, and from the Statistics Canada publication *Historical Statistics of Canada*, Catalogue 11-516, 1983, Series F33–55, A1.

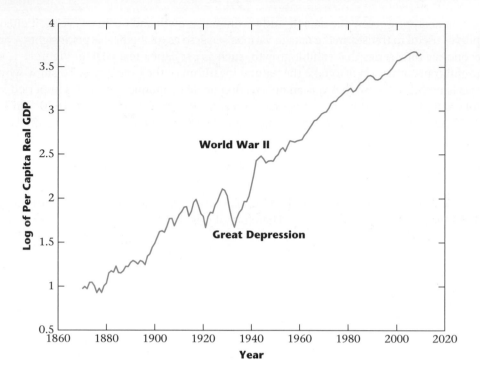

FIGURE 1.3

Natural Logarithm of Per Capita GDP and Trend

Sometimes it is useful to separate long-run growth from business cycle fluctuations. In the figure, the coloured line is the log of per capita GDP, while the black line denotes a smooth growth trend fit to the data. The deviations from the smooth trend then represent business cycles.

Source: Adapted from the Statistics Canada CANSIM database, Series v3860085, V1, and from the Statistics Canada publication *Historical Statistics of Canada*, Catalogue 11-516, 1983, Series F33–55, A1.

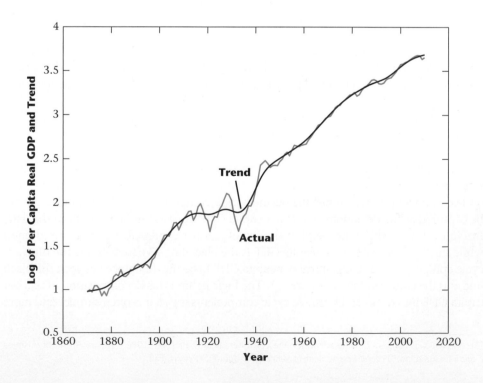

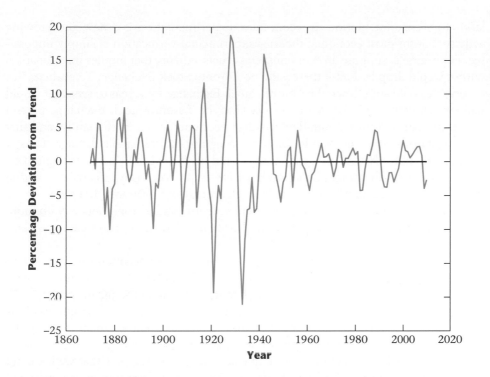

FIGURE 1.4

Percentage Deviations from Trend in Per Capita GDP
Note the reduction in the volatility of per capita GDP since World War II.

Source: Adapted from the Statistics Canada CANSIM database, Series v3860085, V1, and from the Statistics Canada publication *Historical Statistics of Canada*, Catalogue 11-516, 1983, Series F33–55, A1.

productive to consider separately the theory that explains trend growth and the theory that explains business cycles, which are the deviations from trend.

In Figure 1.4 we show only the percentage deviations from trend in real per capita GDP. Note in Figure 1.4 that the Great Depression and World War II represent enormous deviations from trend in real per capita GDP relative to anything else during the time period shown in the figure. During the Great Depression, the percentage deviation from trend in real per capita GDP was less than –20%, whereas the percentage deviation from trend was close to 16% during World War II. In the period after World War II, which is the focus of most business cycle analysis, the deviations from trend in real per capita GDP are at most about ±5%.[2]

Macroeconomic Models

Economics is a scientific pursuit involving the formulation and refinement of theories that can help us better understand how economies work and how they can be improved. In some sciences, such as chemistry and physics, theories are tested through

---

[2]Note that the extremely large deviation from trend in real per capita GDP in the late 1920s is principally a statistical artifact of the particular detrending procedure used here, which is akin to drawing a smooth curve through the time series. The presence of the Great Depression forces the growth rate in the trend to decrease long before the Great Depression actually occurs.

laboratory experimentation. In economics, experimentation is a new and growing activity, but for most economic theories experimental verification is simply impossible. For example, suppose an economist constructs a theory that implies that Canadian output would drop by half if there were no Toronto Stock Exchange. To evaluate this theory, we could shut down the Toronto Stock Exchange for a year to see what would happen. Of course, we know in advance that the Toronto Stock Exchange plays a very important role in helping the Canadian economy function efficiently, and that shutting it down for a year would likely cause significant irreparable damage. Thus, it is extremely unlikely that the experiment would be carried out. In macroeconomics, most experiments that might be informative are simply too costly to carry out, and in this respect macroeconomics is much like meteorology or astronomy. In predicting the weather or how planets move in space, meteorologists and astronomers rely on **models**, which are artificial devices that can replicate the behaviour of real weather systems or planetary systems, as the case may be.

Just like researchers in meteorology or astronomy, macroeconomists use models, which in our case are organized structures that explain long-run economic growth, business cycles, and the role economic policy should play in the macroeconomy. All economic models are abstractions. They are not completely accurate descriptions of the world, nor are they intended to be. The purpose of an economic model is to capture the essential features of the world needed for analyzing a particular economic problem. To be useful, then, a model must be simple, and simplicity requires that we leave out some "realistic" features of actual economies. For example, a road map is a model of part of the earth's surface, and it is constructed with a particular purpose in mind: to help motorists guide themselves through the road system from one point to another. A road map is hardly a realistic depiction of the earth's surface, as it does not capture the curvature of the earth, and it does not typically include a great deal of information on topography, climate, and vegetation. However, this does not limit the map's usefulness; it serves the purpose for which it was constructed, and does so without a lot of extraneous information.

To be specific, the basic structure of a macroeconomic model is a description of the following features:

1. The consumers and firms that interact in the economy

2. The set of goods that consumers want to consume

3. Consumers' preferences over goods

4. The technology available to firms for producing goods

5. The resources available

In this text, the descriptions of the above five features of any particular macroeconomic model will be provided in mathematical and graphical terms.

Once we have a description of the main economic actors in a model economy (the consumers and firms), the goods consumers want, and the technology available to firms for producing goods from available resources, we want to then use the model to make predictions. This step requires that we specify two additional features of the model.

First, we need to know what the goals of the consumers and firms in the model are. How will consumers and firms behave given the environment they live in? In all the models we will use in this text, it is assumed that consumers and firms **optimize**—that is, they do the best they can given the constraints they face. Second, we must specify how consistency is achieved in terms of the actions of consumers and firms. In economic models, this means that the economy must be in **equilibrium**. Several different concepts of equilibrium are used in economic models, but the one that we will use almost universally in this text is **competitive equilibrium**. In a competitive equilibrium, we assume that goods are bought and sold on markets in which consumers and firms are price-takers; they behave as if their actions have no effect on market prices. The economy is in equilibrium when market prices are such that the quantity of each good offered for sale (quantity supplied) is equal to the quantity that economic agents want to buy (quantity demanded) in each market.

Once we have a working economic model, with a specification of the economic environment, optimizing firms and consumers, and a notion of equilibrium, we can begin to ask the model questions.[3] One way to think of this process is that the economic model is an experimental apparatus, and we want to attempt to run experiments by using this apparatus. Typically, we begin by running experiments for which we know the answers. For example, suppose that we build an economic model so that we can study economic growth. The first experiment we might like to run is to determine, by working through the mathematics of the model, using graphical analysis, or running the model on a computer, whether in fact the model economy will grow. Further, will it grow in a manner that comes close to matching the data? If it does not, then we want to ask why and determine whether it would be a good idea to refine the model in some way or abandon it altogether and start over.

Ultimately, once we are satisfied that a model reasonably and accurately captures the economic phenomenon we are interested in, we can start running experiments on the model for which we do *not* know the answers. An experiment we might want to conduct with the economic growth model is to ask, for example, how historical growth performance would have differed in Canada had the level of government spending been higher. Would aggregate economic activity have grown at a higher or a lower rate? How would this have affected the consumption of goods? Would economic welfare have been higher or lower?

In keeping with the principle that models should be simple and designed specifically for the problem at hand, we will not stick to a single, all-purpose model in this text. Instead, we will use an array of different models for different purposes, though these models will share a common approach and some of the same principal building blocks. For example, sometimes it will prove useful to build models that do not include international trade, macroeconomic growth, or the use of money in economic exchange, whereas at other times it will prove crucially important for the issue at hand that we explicitly model one, two, or perhaps all of these features.

---

[3]The following description of macroeconomic science is similar to that provided by Robert Lucas in "Methods and Problems in Business Cycle Theory," reprinted in *Studies in Business Cycle Theory*, 1981, MIT Press, pp. 271–296.

Generally, macroeconomic research is a process whereby we continually attempt to develop better models, along with better methods for analyzing those models. Economic models continue to evolve in a way that helps us better understand the economic forces that shape the world we live in, so that we can promote economic policies that will make society better off.

Microeconomic Principles

This text emphasizes building macroeconomic models on sound microeconomic principles. Since the macroeconomy consists of many consumers and firms, each making decisions at the micro level, macroeconomic behaviour is the sum of many microeconomic decisions. It is not immediately obvious, however, that the best way to construct a macroeconomic model is to work our way up from decision making at the microeconomic level. In physics, for example, there is often no loss in ignoring micro behaviour. If I throw a brick from the top of a five-storey building, and if I know the force that I exert on the brick and the force of gravity on the brick, then Newtonian physics will do a very accurate job of predicting when and where the brick will land. However, Newtonian physics ignores micro behaviour, which in this case is the behaviour of the molecules in the brick.

Why is it that there may be no loss in ignoring the behaviour of molecules in a brick, but that ignoring the microeconomic behaviour of consumers and firms when doing macroeconomics might be devastating? Throwing a brick from a building does not affect the behaviour of the molecules within the brick in any way that would significantly change the trajectory of the brick. Changes in government policy, however, will generally alter the behaviour of consumers and firms in ways that significantly affect the behaviour of the economy as a whole. Any change in government policy effectively alters the features of the economic environment in which consumers and firms must make their decisions. To confidently predict the effects of a policy change in terms of aggregate behaviour, we must analyze how the change in policy will affect individual consumers and firms. For example, if the federal government changes the income tax rate, and we are interested in the macroeconomic effects of this policy change, the most productive approach is first to use microeconomic principles to determine how a change in the tax rate will affect an individual consumer's labour supply and consumption decisions, on the basis of optimizing behaviour. Then, we can aggregate these decisions to arrive at a conclusion consistent with how the individuals in the economy behave.

Macroeconomists were not always sympathetic to the notion that macro models should be microeconomically sound. Indeed, before the **rational expectations revolution** in the 1970s, which generally introduced more microeconomics into macroeconomics, most macroeconomists worked with models that did not have solid microeconomic foundations, though there were some exceptions.[4] The argument that macroeconomic policy analysis could be done in a sensible way only if

---

[4]See M. Friedman, 1968, "The Role of Monetary Policy," *American Economic Review* 58, 1–17.

microeconomic behaviour is taken seriously was persuasively expressed by Robert E. Lucas, Jr., in a journal article published in 1976.[5] This argument is often referred to as the **Lucas critique**.

Disagreement in Macroeconomics

There is little disagreement in macroeconomics concerning the general approach to be taken to constructing models of economic growth. The Solow growth model,[6] studied in Chapter 7, is a widely accepted framework for understanding the economic growth process, and newer **endogenous growth models**, which model the economic mechanism determining the rate of economic growth and are covered in Chapter 8, have been well received by most macroeconomists. This is not to say that disagreement has been absent from discussions of economic growth in macroeconomics, only that the disagreement has not generally been over basic approaches to modelling growth.

The study of business cycles in macroeconomics, however, is another story. As it turns out, there is much controversy among macroeconomists concerning business cycle theory and the role of the government in smoothing business cycles over time. In Chapters 6, 12, 13, and 14 we study some competing theories of the business cycle.

Roughly, business cycle theories can be differentiated according to whether they are **Keynesian** or **non-Keynesian**. Traditional Old Keynesian models, in the spirit of J. M. Keynes's *General Theory of Employment, Interest, and Money* published in 1936, are based on the notion that wages and prices are sticky in the short run, and do not change sufficiently quickly to yield efficient outcomes. In the Old Keynesian world, government intervention through monetary and fiscal policy can correct the inefficiencies that exist in private markets. The rational expectations revolution produced some non-Keynesian theories of the business cycle, including **real business cycle theory**, initiated by Edward Prescott and Finn Kydland in the early 1980s.[7] Real business cycle theory implies that government policy aimed at smoothing business cycles is at best ineffective and at worst detrimental to the economy's performance.

In the 1980s and 1990s, Keynesians used the developments in macroeconomics that came out of the rational expectations revolution to integrate Keynesian economics with modern macroeconomic thought. The result was two new strands of Keynesian thought—**coordination failures** and **New Keynesian** economics. In a coordination failure model of the business cycle, the economy can be stuck in a bad equilibrium, not because of sticky wages and prices, but because economic agents are self-fulfillingly pessimistic. Alternatively, New Keynesian models include sticky wages and prices, as

---

[5]See R. E. Lucas, 1976, "Econometric Policy Evaluation: A Critique," *Carnegie-Rochester Conference Series on Public Policy* 1, 19–46.

[6]See R. Solow, 1956, "A Contribution to the Theory of Economic Growth," *Quarterly Journal of Economics* 70, 65–94.

[7]F. Kydland and E. Prescott, 1982, "Time to Build and Aggregate Fluctuations," *Econometrica* 50, 1345–1370.

in traditional Old Keynesian models, but New Keynesians use the microeconomic tools that all modern macroeconomists use.

In Chapters 6, and 11 through 14, we will study a host of modern business cycle models, which show how changes in monetary factors, changes in productivity, or waves of optimism and pessimism can cause business cycles, and we will show what these models tell us about how macroeconomic policy should be conducted. In Chapters 6 and 13 we study two Keynesian coordination failure models, and in Chapter 14 we examine a New Keynesian sticky price model. Chapter 13 contains an examination of the real business cycle model, and two monetary business cycle models—the money surprise model and the New Monetarist model—are studied in Chapters 12 and 13, respectively.

In this text, we seek an objective view of the competing theories of the business cycle. In Chapters 6 and 12–14, we study the key features of each of the above four theories of the business cycle, and we evaluate the theories in terms of how their predictions match the data.

What Do We Learn from Macroeconomic Analysis?

At this stage, it is useful to map out some of the basic insights that can be learned from macroeconomic analysis, which will be developed in the remainder of this text. These are the following:

1. *What is produced and consumed in the economy is determined jointly by the economy's productive capacity and the preferences of consumers.* In Chapters 4 and 5, we will develop a one-period model of the economy, which specifies the technology for producing goods from available resources, the preferences of consumers over goods, and ways that optimizing consumers and firms come together in competitive markets to determine what is produced and consumed.

2. *In free-market economies, there are strong forces that tend to produce socially efficient economic outcomes.* Social inefficiencies can arise, but they should be considered unusual. The notion that an unregulated economy peopled by selfish individuals could result in a socially efficient state of affairs is surprising, but this idea goes back at least as far as Adam Smith's *The Wealth of Nations*, written in the eighteenth century. In Chapter 5, we will show this result in our one-period model and explain the circumstances under which social inefficiencies can arise in practice.

3. *Unemployment is painful for individuals, but it is a necessary evil in modern economies.* There will always be unemployment in a well-functioning economy. Unemployment is measured as the number of people who are not employed and are actively seeking work. Since all of these people are looking for something they do not have, unemployment might seem undesirable, but the time unemployed people spend searching for jobs is in general well spent from a social point of view. It is economically efficient for workers to be well matched with jobs, in terms of their skills, and if an individual spends a longer time searching for work, this

increases the chances of a good match. In Chapter 6, we explore a modern model of search and matching that can be used to make sense of labour market data and current phenomena.

4. *Improvements in a country's standard of living are brought about in the long run by technological progress.* In Chapters 7 and 8, we study economic growth models, which give us a framework for understanding the forces that account for growth. These models show that growth in aggregate output can be produced by growth in a country's capital stock, growth in the labour force, and technological progress. In the long run, however, growth in the standard of living of the average person will come to a stop unless there are continual technological improvements. Thus, economic well-being ultimately cannot be improved simply by constructing more machines and buildings; economic progress depends on continuing advances in knowledge.

5. *A tax cut is not a free lunch.* When the government reduces taxes, this increases current incomes in the private sector, and this might seem to imply that people are wealthier and may want to spend more. However, if the government reduces taxes and holds its spending constant, it must borrow more, and the government will have to increase taxes in the future to pay off this higher debt. Thus, future incomes in the private sector must fall. In Chapter 9, we show that there are circumstances where a current tax cut will have no effects whatsoever; the private sector is no wealthier, and there is no change in aggregate economic activity.

6. *What consumers and firms anticipate for the future will have an important bearing on current macroeconomic events.* In Chapters 11 and 12, we consider two-period models in which consumers and firms make dynamic decisions; consumers save for future consumption needs, and firms invest in plant and equipment so as to produce more in the future. If consumers anticipate, for example, that their future incomes will be high, they will want to save less in the present and consume more, and this will have important implications for current aggregate production, employment, and interest rates. If firms anticipate that a new technological innovation will come online in the future, this will make them more inclined to invest today in new plant and equipment, and this will in turn also affect aggregate production, employment, and interest rates. Consumers and firms are forward looking in ways that matter for current aggregate economic activity and for government policy.

7. *Money takes many forms, and having it is much better than not having it. Once we have it, however, changing its quantity ultimately does not matter.* What differentiates money from other assets is its value as a medium of exchange, and having a medium of exchange makes economic transactions much easier in developed economies. Currently in Canada, there are several assets that act as a medium of exchange, including Canadian currency, transactions deposits at banks, and travellers' cheques. In Chapters 12 and 17, we will explore the role of money in the economy. One important result in Chapter 12 is that a one-time increase in the money supply, brought about by the central bank, has no long-run effect on any real economic magnitudes in the economy; it will only increase all prices in the same proportion.

8. *Business cycles are similar, but they can have many causes.* In Chapter 3, we show that there are strong regularities in how aggregate macroeconomic variables fluctuate over the business cycle. In Chapters 6 and 12–14, we will study several theories that can explain business cycles. The fact that there are several business cycle theories to choose from does not mean that only one can be right and all the others are wrong, though some may be more right than others. Potentially, all of these theories shed some light on why we have business cycles and what can be done about them.

9. *Countries gain from trading goods and assets with each other, but trade is also a source of shocks to the domestic economy.* Economists tend to support the lifting of trade restrictions, as free trade allows a country to exploit its comparative advantage in production and thus make its citizens better off. However, the integration of world financial and goods markets implies that events in other countries can cause domestic business cycles. In Chapters 15 and 16, we will explore how changes in goods prices and interest rates on world markets affect the domestic economy.

10. *In the long run, inflation is caused by growth in the money supply.* **Inflation**, the rate of growth in the average level of prices, can vary over the short run for many reasons. Over the long run, however, the rate at which the central bank (the **Bank of Canada** in Canada) causes the stock of money to grow determines what the inflation rate is. We will study this process in Chapter 17.

11. *There may be a short-run tradeoff between aggregate output and inflation, but no such tradeoff exists in the long run.* In some countries and for some historical periods, a positive relationship appears to exist between the deviation of aggregate output from trend and the inflation rate. This relationship is called the **Phillips curve**, and in general the Phillips curve appears to be a quite unstable empirical relationship. The Friedman-Lucas money surprise model, discussed in Chapters 12 and 18, provides an explanation for the observed Phillips curve relationship. It also explains why the Phillips curve is unstable and does not represent a long-run *tradeoff* between output and inflation that can be exploited by government policymakers. In Chapter 18, we explore the importance of commitment on the part of central bank policymakers in explaining recent inflation experience in Canada.

Understanding Recent and Current Macroeconomic Events

Part of the excitement of studying macroeconomics is that it can make sense of recent and currently unfolding economic events. In this section, we will give an overview of some recent and current issues and how we can understand them better using macroeconomic tools.

PRODUCTIVITY GROWTH

A measure of productivity in the aggregate economy is average labour productivity, Y/N, where Y denotes aggregate output and N denotes employment. That is, we can measure aggregate productivity as the total quantity of output produced per worker. Aggregate productivity is important, as economic growth theory tells us that growth in aggregate productivity is what determines growth in living standards in the long run. In Figure 1.5 we plot the log of average labour productivity for Canada, measured as the log of real GDP (the quantity of goods and services produced within Canadian borders) per worker. Here, we show the log of average labour productivity because then the slope of the graph denotes the growth rate in average labour productivity. The key features of Figure 1.5 are that total factor productivity grew rapidly during the 1960s and 1990s. Growth in productivity slowed from the early 1970s until the early 1980s, and later, after 2000.

What causes productivity to grow at high rates, and what causes it to slow down? If we can understand this behaviour of aggregate productivity, we might be able to avoid productivity slowdowns in the future and bring about larger future increases in our standard of living. One potential explanation for productivity slowdowns is that they simply reflect a measurement problem. Estimates of economic growth can be biased downward for various reasons, which would also cause productivity growth to be biased downward. A productivity slowdown could also be symptomatic of the adoption of new technology. Modern information technology began to be introduced in the

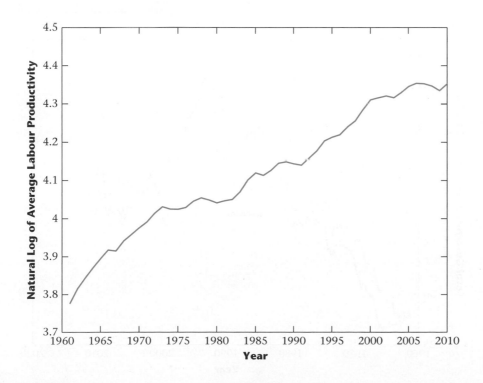

FIGURE 1.5

Natural Logarithm of Average Labour Productivity
Average labour productivity is the quantity of aggregate output produced per worker. Because the graph is of the log of average labour productivity, the slope of the graph is approximately the growth rate in average labour productivity. Productivity growth slowed from the early 1970s to the early 1980s, and later on, after 2000.

Source: Adapted from the Statistics Canada CANSIM database, Series v3860085, v2461119, v3822183, v1078498, and from the Statistics Canada publication *Historical Statistics of Canada*, Catalogue 11-516, 1983, Series D175–189.

late 1960s with the wide use of high-speed computers. While people were learning to use computer technology, there was a temporary adjustment period, which could have slowed down productivity growth from the early 1970s until the early 1980s. By the mid-1980s, however, according to this story, how to embody new information technology in personal computers had been discovered, and the 1990s saw further uses for computer technology via the Internet.

GOVERNMENT INCOME, GOVERNMENT OUTLAYS, AND THE GOVERNMENT DEFICIT

Figure 1.6 shows total government income (this primarily includes taxes) and government outlays (this includes government expenditures on goods and services, transfers, and interest on the public debt) by all levels of government (federal, provincial or territorial, and municipal) in Canada from 1961 to 2011 as percentages of gross domestic product. Note the broad upward trend in both income and outlays until the 1990s. Total income was about 27% of GDP in 1961, and this increased to a high of almost 45% of GDP in the early 1990s, while outlays rose from about 27% of GDP in 1961 to a high of more than 50% of GDP in the early 1990s. These trends generally reflect an increase in the size of government in Canada relative to the aggregate economy over this period. However, since the early 1990s, a decrease in the size of government is reflected in declines in outlays and income, with the decrease in outlays being quite substantial.

FIGURE 1.6

Total Government Income (coloured line) and Outlays (black line) in Canada, as Percentages of GDP

Of particular note is the gap that opens up between spending and taxes in the late 1970s, representing a government deficit. The gap closes in the 1990s, and in the late 1990s spending falls below taxes, so that there is a positive government surplus. A deficit opens up during the 2008–2009 recession.

Source: Adapted from the Statistics Canada CANSIM database, Series v498316, v498326.

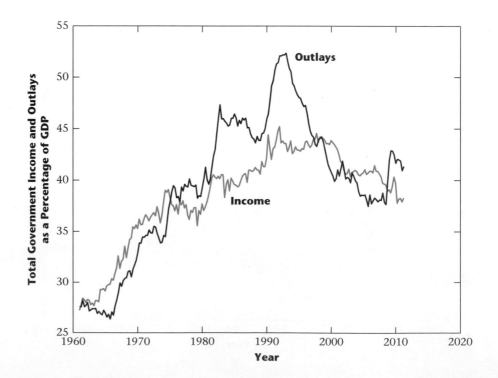

What ramifications does a larger government have for the economy as a whole? How does higher government spending and taxation affect private economic activity? We show in Chapters 5 and 11 that increased government activity in general causes a **crowding out** of private economic activity. That is, the government competes for resources with the rest of the economy. If the size of the government increases, then through several economic mechanisms, there is a reduction in the quantity of spending by private firms on new plant and equipment and there is a reduction in private consumption expenditures.

An interesting feature of Figure 1.6 is that governments in Canada sometimes spent more than they received, and sometimes the reverse was true. Just as for private consumers, the government can in principle spend more than it earns by borrowing and accumulating debt, and it can earn more than it spends and save the difference, thus reducing its debt. Figure 1.7 shows the total **government surplus** or total **government saving**, which is the difference between income and outlays. From the figure, the government surplus was positive from 1961 until the mid-1970s, but from 1975 until the late 1990s the surplus was negative. When there is a negative government surplus, we say that the government is running a deficit; the **government deficit** is the negative of the government surplus. The largest government deficit over this period was more than 8% of GDP, in the early 1990s. It was not until the late 1990s that there was again a positive government surplus. There was a positive government surplus from the late 1990s until the 2008–2009 recession, when the government again ran a deficit.

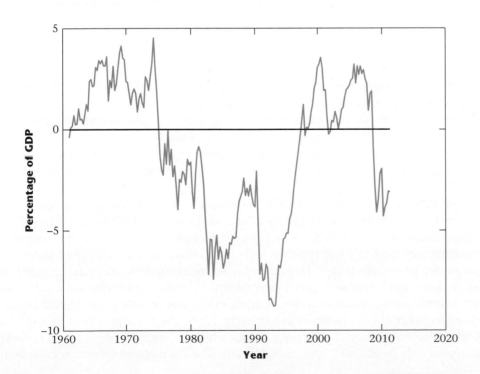

FIGURE 1.7

The Total Government Surplus in Canada, as a Percentage of GDP

Of particular note is the trend decrease that occurs in the government surplus until the early 1990s, with the government surplus being negative for most of the period since the mid-1970s. The government surplus increases through most of the 1990s and becomes positive in the late 1990s. A deficit opens up in the 2008–2009 recession.

Source: Adapted from the Statistics Canada CANSIM database, Series v498316, v498086.

What are the consequences of government deficits? We might think, in a manner similar to popular conceptions of household finance, that accumulating debt (running a deficit) is bad, whereas reducing debt (running a surplus) is good, but at the aggregate level the issue is not so simple. One principal difference between an individual and the government is that when the government accumulates debt by borrowing from its citizens, then this is debt that we as a nation owe to ourselves. Then, it turns out that the effects of a government deficit depend on what the source of the deficit is. Is the government running a deficit because taxes have decreased or because government spending has increased? If the deficit is due to a decrease in taxes, then the government debt that is issued to finance the deficit will have to be paid off ultimately by higher future taxes. Thus, running a deficit in this case implies that there is a redistribution of the tax burden from one group to another; one group has its current taxes reduced while another has its future taxes increased. Under some circumstances, these two groups might essentially be the same, in which case there would be no consequences of having the government run a deficit. This idea that government deficits do not matter under some conditions is called the **Ricardian equivalence theorem**, and we will study it in Chapter 9. In the case where a government deficit results from higher government spending, there are always implications for aggregate economic activity, as discussed earlier in terms of the crowding out of private spending. We will examine the effects of government spending in Chapters 5 and 11.

UNEMPLOYMENT

As explained previously, the phenomenon of unemployment need not represent a problem, since unemployment is in general a socially useful search activity that is necessary, though perhaps painful to the individuals involved. As macroeconomists, we are interested in what explains the level of unemployment and what the reasons are for fluctuations in unemployment over time. If we can understand these features, we can go on to determine how macroeconomic policy can be formulated so that labour markets work as efficiently as possible.

In Chapter 6, we introduce a model of search and unemployment based on the work of Nobel Prize winners Peter Diamond, Dale Mortensen, and Christopher Pissarides that allows us to explain the determinants of labour force participation, the unemployment rate, the vacancy rate (the fraction of firms searching for workers to hire), and market wages.

An interesting current feature of labour markets in North America is displayed in Figure 1.8, which shows unemployment rates in Canada and the United States since the beginning of 2008, when the most recent recession began. Before the recession, the unemployment rate was typically higher in Canada than in the United States, by one or two percentage points. That difference in unemployment rates can be explained by measurement error, more generous employment insurance benefits in Canada, and the different composition of sectoral output in Canada relative to the United States. However, after the recession began in early 2008, the unemployment rate in the United States rose about 5 percentage points, while the unemployment rate in Canada increased only by about 2.5 percentage points. The unemployment rate in Canada in

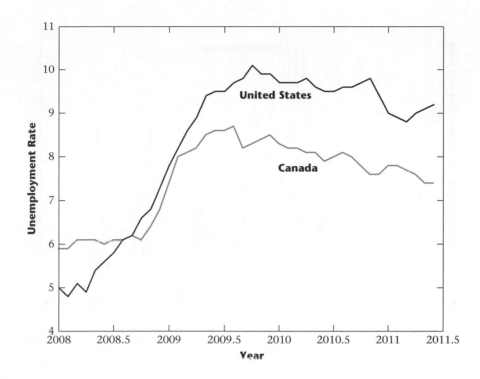

FIGURE 1.8
Unemployment Rates in Canada and the United States after the Beginning of 2008
The unemployment rate rose much more in the U.S. than in Canada in the recent recession.

Source: Adapted from Statistics Canada CANSIM database, Series v2062815. U.S. source: Bureau of Labor Statistics.

2011 was significantly lower than in the United States. This differing labour market behaviour in Canada and the United States is a very important feature related to the financial crisis and the recent recession.

INFLATION

Inflation, as mentioned earlier, is the rate of change in the average level of prices, where the average level of prices is referred to as the **price level**. One measure of the price level is the consumer price index, which is essentially the price of a set of goods bought by the "average" consumer. In Figure 1.9 we show the inflation rate, the black line in the figure, as the percentage rate of increase (from 12 months previously) in the consumer price index. The inflation rate remained low from 1956 until the early 1970s, and then began climbing, reaching peaks of more than 10% per year in the mid-1970s and early 1980s. The inflation rate then declined steadily, but has recently increased to just under 4% per year.

Inflation is economically costly, but the low recent rates of inflation we are experiencing are certainly not viewed by the public or by policymakers as worthy of much attention. However, it is certainly useful to understand the causes of inflation, its costs, and why and how inflation was reduced in Canada. There are good reasons to think that the inflation experience of the 1970s and early 1980s, or worse, could be repeated. As mentioned in the previous section, the inflation rate is explained in the long run by the rate of growth in the supply of money. Without money supply growth, prices

FIGURE 1.9

Inflation and Money Growth

Macroeconomic theory tells us that growth in the money supply causes inflation in the long run. The figure is broadly consistent with this, in that the money growth rate (coloured line) tracks the inflation rate (black line) reasonably well, at least until the mid-1990s. There is substantial short-run variation in the inflation rate and money growth that appears to be unrelated, and money growth is quite erratic after 1995.

Source: Adapted from the Statistics Canada CANSIM database, Series v735319, v37145.

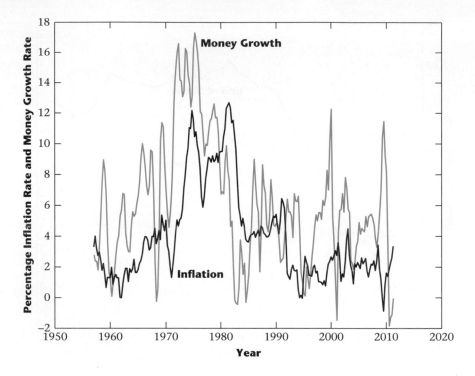

cannot continue to increase, and higher money supply growth implies that there is more and more money chasing a given quantity of goods. This will ultimately cause prices to be bid up at a higher rate. In Figure 1.9 we also show the rate of money growth (measured as the percentage rate of growth in the monetary base, a narrow monetary aggregate) from 1956 until 2011. Here, it is clear that the short-run relationship between the rate of inflation and the rate of money growth is not a tight one; there are many short-run ups and downs in the rate of money growth that are not reflected in similar movements in the inflation rate, and vice versa. Thus, there must be other factors that explain short-run movements in the rate of inflation, in addition to changes in the money growth rate. However, the broad trends in money growth in Figure 1.9 match the broad trends in the inflation rate. Money growth increases, on trend, until the mid-1970s and then falls, as does the inflation rate, though money growth behaviour is quite erratic from the mid-1990s on. The long-run effects of money growth on inflation are explored in Chapter 17, and we study the short-run effects of nonmonetary factors on the price level in Chapters 12 through 14.

Long-run inflation is costly, in that it tends to reduce employment, output, and consumption, as we will show in Chapter 17. However, because inflation is caused in the long run by money growth, the central bank determines the long-run inflation rate through its control of the rate at which the money supply grows. Why would the central bank want to generate inflation if it is costly? In Chapter 18, we explore the answer to this question, with recent experience in Canada as a backdrop.

Surprise increases in the rate of inflation can cause short-run increases in employ-ment and output, and the central bank might be tempted to generate these short-run surprises, either because it has not learned the consequences of long-run inflation, or because there is a failure of the central bank to commit itself to long-run actions. In Chapter 18, we will study the importance of central bank learning and commitment for the behaviour of inflation.

INTEREST RATES

Interest rates are important, as they affect many private economic decisions, particularly the decisions of consumers as to how much they will borrow and lend, and the deci-sions of firms concerning how much to invest in new plant and equipment. Further, movements in interest rates are an important element in the economic mechanism by which monetary policy affects real magnitudes in the short run. In Figure 1.10 we show the behaviour of the short-term **nominal interest rate** (the coloured line) in Canada over the period 1962–2011. This is the interest rate in money terms on three-month federal government Treasury bills, which are essentially riskless short-term government securities. In 1962, the short-term nominal interest rate was about 3%, but it rose on trend through the 1960s and 1970s, reaching a high of more than 20% in 1980. Since then, the nominal interest rate has declined on trend, and it was close to zero in 2009, as the result of accommodative monetary policy by the Bank of Canada.

What explains the level of the nominal interest rate? Observant readers will recall that the trends in the inflation rate discussed in the previous subsection were very similar over the period 1962–2011 to the trends in the nominal interest rate, and we have plotted the inflation rate (black line) in Figure 1.10 to show this. Observe also that several of the peaks in inflation, around 1970, in the mid-1970s, around 1980, and around 1990, are coupled with peaks in the nominal interest rate. Thus, the nominal interest rate tends to rise and fall with the inflation rate. Why is this? Economic decisions are based on real rather than nominal interest rates. The **real interest rate**, roughly speaking, is the nominal interest rate minus the expected rate of inflation. That is, the real interest rate is the rate that a borrower expects to have to repay, adjusting for the inflation that is expected to occur over the period of time until the borrower's debt is repaid. If Allen obtains a one-year car loan at an interest rate of 9%, and he expects the inflation rate to be 3% over the next year, then he faces a real interest rate on the car loan of 6%. Now, because economic decisions are based on real interest rates rather than nominal interest rates, market forces will tend to determine the real interest rate. Therefore, as the inflation rate rises, the nominal interest rate will tend to rise along with it. In Chapters 12 through 14, we will study the determination of real and nominal interest rates in the long run, and the relation-ship between real and nominal rates.

In Figure 1.11 we plot an estimate of the real interest rate, which is the nominal interest rate minus the actual rate of inflation. Thus, this would be the actual real inter-est rate if the inflation rate over the next three months were the same as the inflation rate over the previous year. Consumers and firms cannot correctly anticipate the actual inflation rate. However, given that inflation does not change too much from quarter to

FIGURE 1.10

The Nominal Interest Rate and the Inflation Rate

Macroeconomic theory tells us that the nominal interest rate and the inflation rate are positively related. In the figure, the nominal interest rate, which is the three-month Treasury bill rate (a short-term interest rate on federal government securities) tends to track the ups and downs in the inflation rate.

Source: Adapted from the Statistics Canada CANSIM database, Series v122531, v735319.

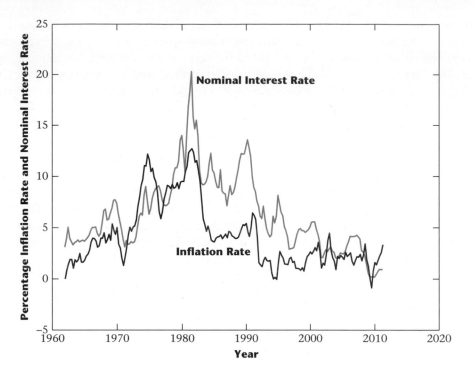

FIGURE 1.11

Real Interest Rate

The figure shows a measure of the real interest rate, which here is the short-term nominal interest rate minus the actual rate of inflation. Monetary policy can have a short-run effect on the real interest rate; for example, the high real interest rates in the 1980s are often attributed to tight monetary policy. Monetary policy has been quite accommodative since the last recession, with low or negative real rates.

Source: Adapted from the Statistics Canada CANSIM database, Series v122531, v735319.

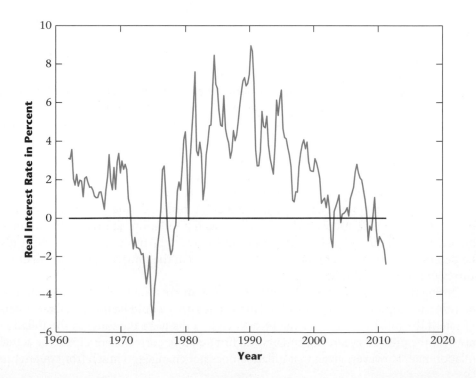

quarter, their forecasts will be fairly accurate, and our estimate of the real interest rate will have a reasonably small measurement error. Note that the real interest rate fluctuates a great deal over time. The real interest rate has sometimes been negative, falling as low as almost −5% in 1975. Since the late 1970s, the real interest rate has been positive, except around 2002 and recently when it has dipped below zero.

In the short run, the real interest rate is affected by monetary policy, though there is some disagreement among macroeconomists concerning why the central bank can control the real interest rate and for how long it can do so. We can give the following interpretation to the path of the real interest rate from the mid-1970s to 2011 in Figure 1.11. First, the real interest rate was low in the mid-1970s because the Bank of Canada was causing the money supply to grow at a high rate—that is, monetary policy was expansionary and accommodating. As a result of the high inflation caused by this high money growth, the Bank of Canada embarked on a contractionary course in the early 1980s, reducing money supply growth and causing the real interest rate to rise. Since the mid-1980s, the Bank of Canada has remained seriously concerned about the possibility that high inflation might re-emerge, and it has for the most part maintained a nonaccommodating monetary policy stance, which has caused the real interest rate to be historically high. Since the early 1990s, the real interest rate decreased on trend, indicating a more accommodating monetary policy, and in 2008 the real interest dropped significantly below zero, indicating a dramatic easing of monetary policy. In Chapters 12 through 14, we will study some theories of the business cycle that explain how the central bank might influence the real interest rate in the short run. While the rate of money growth may affect real interest rates in the long run, monetary policy is aimed not at setting the long-run real interest rate, but at determining long-run inflation while staying in tune with the short-run effects of monetary policy.

TRADE AND THE CURRENT ACCOUNT SURPLUS

As the technology for transporting goods and information across countries has advanced and government-imposed impediments to trade have been reduced, Canada has become a more open economy. That is, trade in goods and in assets between Canada and the rest of the world has increased. The change in the flow of goods and services between Canada and the rest of the world is shown in Figure 1.12, where we plot Canadian exports (the black line) and imports (the coloured line) as percentages of GDP from 1961 to 2011. Canadian exports increased from about 16% of GDP in 1962 to about 45% of GDP in 2005, and then decreased somewhat, while imports increased from about 16% in 1962 to about 44% in 2008. During the recent recession, imports fell and then rose again, while there was a dramatic decrease in exports. As mentioned in the previous section, more trade has a positive effect on general economic welfare, as it allows countries to specialize in production and exploit their comparative advantages. However, more trade could also expose a given country to the transmission of business cycle fluctuations from abroad, though this need not necessarily be the case.

Although the level of trade with the outside world is important in terms of aggregate economic activity and its fluctuations, the balance of trade also plays an important role in macroeconomic activity and macroeconomic policymaking. One measure of the

FIGURE 1.12

Exports and Imports of Goods and Services for Canada, as Percentages of GDP

The increase in both imports and exports reflects a general increase in world trade.

Source: Adapted from the Statistics Canada CANSIM database, Series v1992060, v1992063, v1992067.

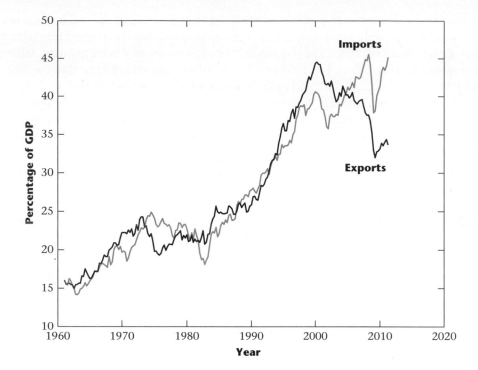

balance of trade is the **current account surplus**, which is **net exports** of goods and services (exports minus imports) plus **net factor payments** (net income from abroad). In Figure 1.13 we have graphed the current account surplus for Canada as a percentage of GDP for the period 1961–2011. Canada had a current account deficit for most of this period (the current account surplus was usually negative), but the current account moved into surplus in the late 1990s, with a deficit opening up again during the last recession.

Why is the current account surplus important? When the current account surplus in Canada is negative, there is a **current account deficit**, and the quantity of goods and services purchased abroad by domestic residents is greater than the quantity of domestic goods and services purchased by foreigners. To finance this current account deficit, residents of Canada and/or the Canadian government must be borrowing abroad. Is it a bad idea for a country to run a current account deficit? Not necessarily, for two reasons. First, just as it might make sense for an individual to borrow so as to smooth his or her flow of consumption over time, it might also make sense for a country to borrow in the short run by running a current account deficit so as to smooth aggregate consumption over time. Second, persistent current account deficits might make sense if the associated foreign borrowing is used to finance additions to the nation's productive capacity that will allow for higher future living standards.

What accounts for movements over time in the current account surplus? One important influence on the current account surplus is government spending. When the government increases its spending, holding taxes constant, this will increase the

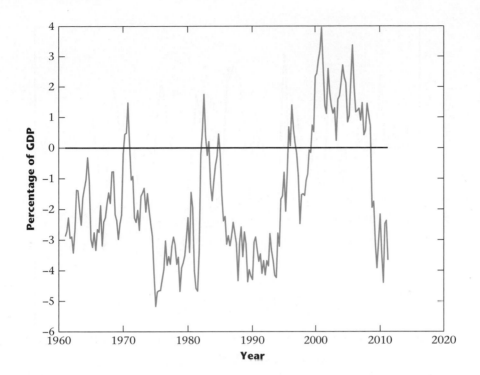

FIGURE 1.13

Current Account Surplus for Canada, 1961–2011

The figure shows the current account surplus for Canada from 1961–2011, which is exports of goods and services minus imports of goods and services plus net factor payments from foreigners, here plotted as a percentage of GDP. Canada ran a current account deficit for much of this period, but began to run a surplus in the late 1990s, with a deficit opening up in the 2008–2009 recession.

Source: Adapted from the Statistics Canada CANSIM database, Series v114421, v498086.

government deficit, which needs to be financed by increased government borrowing. Other important influences on the current account surplus are increases in domestic income, which tend to increase imports, and increases in foreign income, which tend to increase exports.

We will study international trade, the determinants of the current account surplus, and other issues associated with international business cycles and international financial relations in Chapters 15 and 16.

THE FINANCIAL CRISIS

A financial crisis that developed during 2008 in the United States quickly spread globally, and it had important effects in Canada because world financial markets are highly integrated and the United States is Canada's most important trading partner in both goods and services and financial assets. The first signs of trouble were in the market for mortgages in the United States, and problems spread from there to the banking sector and to credit markets throughout the world. These financial market problems were reflected in a deep worldwide recession of significant proportions.

In Figure 1.14, we show the percentage deviations of real GDP in Canada from trend. As is clear in the figure, the recession ended in 2009 in Canada, and the Canadian recovery from the recession has been strong, relative to other countries in the world. In particular, Figure 1.15 shows the performance of real GDP in Canada and the United States from the beginning of the recession in early 2008, scaling real GDP in Canada

FIGURE 1.14

Percentage Deviation from Trend in Real GDP

Source: Adapted from the Statistics Canada CANSIM database, Series v1992067.

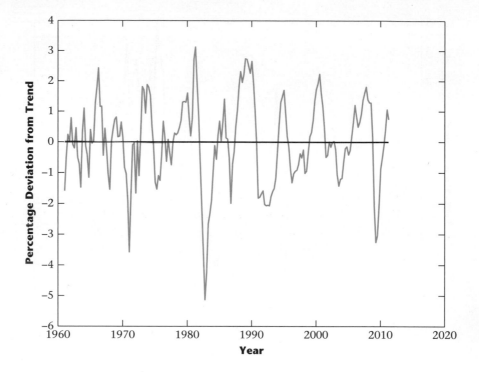

FIGURE 1.15

Real GDP in Canada and the U.S., 2008–2011

Source: Adapted from the Statistics Canada CANSIM database, Series v1992067. US source: Bureau of Economic Analysis.

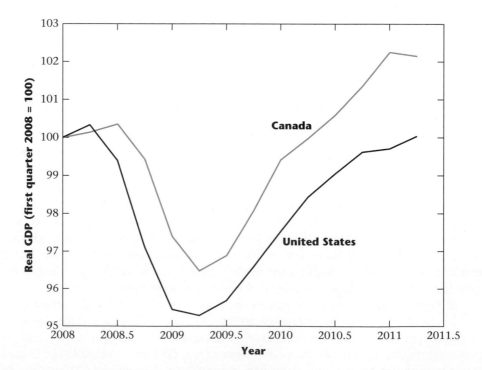

and the U.S. so that both quantities equal 100 in the first quarter of 2008. Figure 1.15 shows that the recovery from the recession has been much stronger in Canada than in the United States. Relative to the first quarter of 2008, real GDP is now 2% higher in Canada than in the U.S. One explanation for this is that the financial sector in Canada is better-regulated and more resilient than is the U.S. financial sector. We will discuss this in detail in Chapter 17.

Some conventional macroeconomic tools are extremely useful in analyzing the financial crisis, including our analysis of labour markets, credit markets, money, and banking in Chapters 6, 9, 10, 12–14, and 17. New to this fourth edition are an analysis of search and unemployment in Chapter 6, the study of liquidity traps and New Monetarist economics in Chapters 12 and 13, and further analysis of banking and the financial crisis in Chapter 17.

A key feature of the financial crisis that we wish to understand is the role of the government, both in potentially contributing to the advent of the crisis and in mitigating its effects. Government regulation possibly caused the crisis by setting up a moral hazard problem—a feature of regulation that causes financial market participants to engage in activities that are too risky relative to what is socially optimal. We study moral hazard in the banking sector in Chapter 17. The response of monetary and fiscal policy to the financial crisis appears to be motivated primarily by Keynesian arguments, so it is important to understand how Keynesian economists think and to evaluate the merits and demerits of Keynesian economics. Chapters 6, 13, and 14 contain an analysis of Keynesian coordination failure models and sticky price New Keynesian models that illustrate how modern Keynesians think and that show what motivates many policymakers in the current environment.

Chapter Summary

- Modern macroeconomics analyzes issues associated with long-run growth and business cycles, using models that are built up from microeconomic principles.

- Since 1870, Canada has experienced long-run sustained growth in per capita gross domestic product; we also observe that gross domestic product exhibits business cycle fluctuations about a smooth long-run trend.

- Two unusual but important events in twentieth-century Canadian economic history were the Great Depression and World War II.

- The primary questions of interest to macroeconomists involve the causes of long-run growth and business cycles and the appropriate role for government policy in influencing the performance of the economy.

- Macroeconomists rely mainly on abstract models to draw conclusions about how the world works, because it is usually very costly or impossible to experiment with the real economy. A good macroeconomic model is simple, while retaining all of the features essential for addressing the macroeconomic issue for which the model was intended.

- The models we construct and use in this text are ones in which price-taking consumers and firms optimize given the constraints they face and in which the actions of consumers and firms are consistent in a competitive equilibrium.

- Building models from microeconomic principles is important, because this will more often give us the correct answers to questions regarding the effects of changes in economic policy.

- There is relatively little disagreement among macroeconomists concerning approaches to modelling growth, but there are contentious issues in business cycle modelling between Keynesian macroeconomists and those who argue for non-Keynesian alternative explanations for business cycles.

- The issues discussed in this chapter, to be addressed later in the text, are: productivity growth; taxes, government spending, and the government deficit; unemployment; money growth and inflation; interest rates; the current account surplus; and the financial crisis.

Key Terms

economic model: A description of consumers and firms, their objectives and constraints, and how they interact.

long-run growth: The increase in a nation's productive capacity and average standard of living that occurs over a long period of time.

business cycles: Short-run ups and downs, or booms and recessions, in aggregate economic activity.

gross domestic product (GDP): The quantity of goods and services produced within a country's borders during some specified period of time.

trend: The smooth growth path around which an economic variable cycles.

models: Artificial devices that can replicate the behaviour of real systems.

optimize: The process by which economic agents (firms and consumers) do the best they can given the constraints they face.

equilibrium: The situation in an economy when the actions of all the consumers and firms are consistent.

competitive equilibrium: Equilibrium in which firms and households are assumed to be price-takers, and market prices are such that the quantity supplied equals the quantity demanded in each market in the economy.

rational expectations revolution: Macroeconomics movement that occurred in the 1970s, introducing more microeconomics into macroeconomics.

Lucas critique: The idea that macroeconomic policy analysis can be done in a sensible way only if microeconomic behaviour is taken seriously.

endogenous growth models: Models that describe the economic mechanism determining the rate of economic growth.

Keynesian: Describes macroeconomists who are followers of J. M. Keynes and who see an active role for government in smoothing business cycles.

Non-Keynesian: Alternatives to Keynesian models, developed mainly post-1970.

real business cycle theory: A theory, initiated by Finn Kydland and Edward Prescott, implying that business cycles are caused primarily by shocks to technology and that the government should play a passive role over the business cycle.

coordination failure theory: A modern incarnation of Keynesian business cycle theory positing that business cycles are caused by self-fulfilling waves of optimism and pessimism, which may be countered with government policy.

New Keynesian economics: A model in the tradition of Keynes, but with sticky prices and features consistent with modern Keynesian thought.

inflation: The rate of change in the average level of prices over time.

Bank of Canada: The central bank of Canada.

Phillips curve: A positive relationship between the deviation of aggregate output from trend and the inflation rate.

crowding out: The process by which government spending reduces private sector expenditures on investment and consumption.

government surplus: The difference between taxes and government spending.

government saving: Identical to the government surplus.

government deficit: The negative of the government surplus.

Ricardian equivalence theorem: Theory asserting that a change in taxation by the government has no effect.

price level: The average level of prices.

nominal interest rate: The interest rate in money terms.

real interest rate: Approximately equal to the nominal interest rate minus the expected rate of inflation.

current account surplus: Exports minus imports plus net factor payments to domestic residents from abroad.

net exports: Exports of goods and services minus imports of goods and services.

net factor payments: The payments received by domestic factors of production from abroad, minus the payments to foreign factors of production from domestic sources.

current account deficit: Situation in which the current account surplus is negative.

Questions for Review

1. What are the primary defining characteristics of macroeconomics?

2. What makes macroeconomics different from microeconomics? What do they have in common?

3. How much richer was the average Canadian in 2010 than in 1870?

4. What are two striking business cycle events in Canada during the past 80 years?

5. List six fundamental macroeconomic questions.

6. In a graph of the natural logarithm of an economic time series, what does the slope of the graph represent?

7. What is the difference between the trend and the business cycle component of an economic time series?

8. Explain why experimentation is difficult in macroeconomics.

9. Why should a macroeconomic model be simple?

10. Should a macroeconomic model be an exact description of the world? Explain why or why not.

11. What are the five elements that make up the basic structure of a macroeconomic model?

12. Why can macroeconomic models be useful? How do we determine whether or not they are useful?

13. Explain why a macroeconomic model should be built from microeconomic principles.

14. What are the four theories of the business cycle that we will study?

15. What are two possible causes of a productivity slowdown?

16. What is the principal effect of an increase in government spending?

17. Why might a decrease in taxes have no effect?

18. What is the cause of inflation in the long run?

19. How have unemployment rates behaved recently in Canada and the United States?

20. Explain the difference between the nominal interest rate and the real interest rate.

21. What has driven the increase in trade between Canada and the rest of the world?

22. How has the Canadian economy performed during the financial crisis and the recent global recession?

Problems

1. Consider the following data on real GDP per capita in Canada:

Year	Per Capita real GDP
1950	11 903.35
1960	14 403.56
1970	19 748.58
1980	25 510.79
1990	29 804.41
2000	35 864.06
2001	36 111.59
2002	36 770.99
2003	37 124.03
2004	37 921.52
2005	38 697.44
2006	39 385.75
2007	39 819.98
2008	39 625.65
2009	38 059.1
2010	38 826.27

a. Calculate the percentage growth rates in real GDP per capita in each of the years 2001 through 2010, from the previous year.

b. Now, instead of calculating the annual percentage growth rates in the years 2001 through 2010 directly, use as an approximation $100 \times (\log y_t - \log y_{t-1})$, where y_t is real per capita GDP in year t. How close does this approximation come to the actual growth rates you calculated in part (a)?

c. Repeat parts (a) and (b), but now calculate the percentage rates of growth in real per capita GDP from 1950 to 1960, from 1960 to 1970, from 1970 to 1980, from 1980 to 1990, 1990 to 2000, and 2000 to 2010. In this case, how large an error do you make by approximating the growth rate by the change in the log? Why is there a difference here relative to parts (a) and (b)?

d. During what decade from 1950 to 2010 was growth in real per capita GDP the highest? When was it the lowest?

2. Suppose that you had the special powers to travel in time and to carry out any experiment you wanted on the economy. If you could turn back the clock to the time of the Great Depression, what experiment would you like to run on the Canadian economy? Why?

3. Give an example of a model that is used in some area other than economics, other than the road-map example explained in this chapter. What is unrealistic about this model? How well does it perform its intended function?

4. Why do you think government outlays would increase during a recession, as happened in the early 1980s, the early 1990s, and the most recent recession? (See Figure 1.6.)

5. Explain why the total government deficit in Canada was eliminated in the late 1990s, in terms of the behaviour of government income and government outlays.

6. Does Figure 1.9 make you suspicious of the claim that a high rate of inflation is caused by a higher rate of money growth? Why or why not?

7. Why do you think the real interest rate was low during the recession in the mid-1970s and during the recent recession?

8. After 2000, the current account surplus increased. Relate this increase to what happened to exports and imports at the time.

2 *Measurement*

The two key elements in Economics are measurement and theory. Measurements of the performance of the economy motivate macroeconomists to build simple models that can organize our thinking about how the economy works. For example, surveys of consumer prices done every year can tell us something about how prices change over time and, coupled with observations on other economic variables, can help us to develop theories that explain *why* prices change over time. Meanwhile, economic theory can better inform us about the most efficient ways to carry out economic measurement. For example, theories of consumer behaviour can tell us something about the appropriate way to use the prices of consumer goods to derive a price index that is a good measure of the price level.

Our goal in this chapter is to understand the basic issues concerning how key macroeconomic variables are measured. These key macroeconomic variables will play the most important roles in the economic models that we will construct and study in the remainder of this book. In particular, in the rest of this chapter we will examine the measurement of GDP and its components, and the measurement of prices, savings, wealth, capital, and labour market variables.

Measuring GDP: The National Income and Expenditure Accounts

The chief aim of national income accounting is to obtain a measure of the total quantity of goods and services produced for the market in a given country over a given period of time. For many issues in macroeconomics (though by no means for all), the measure of aggregate economic activity we are interested in is **gross domestic product (GDP)**, which is the dollar value of final output produced during a given period of time within the borders of Canada. GDP is published on a quarterly basis by Statistics Canada as part of the **National Income and Expenditure Accounts (NIEA)**.

There are three approaches to measuring GDP, each of which is incorporated in some way in NIEA. All three approaches will give exactly the same measure of GDP, provided there are no errors of measurement in using any of these approaches. The three approaches are the **product approach**, the **expenditure approach**, and the **income approach**. We will discuss each in turn, using an example.

In our running example, we consider a simple fictional economy that captures the essentials of national income accounting. This is an island economy in which there is a coconut producer, a restaurant, consumers, and a government. The coconut producer owns all of the coconut trees on the island, harvests the coconuts that grow on the trees, and in the current year produces 10 million coconuts, which are sold for $2 each, yielding total revenue of $20 million. The coconut producer pays wages of $5 million to its workers (who are some of the consumers in this economy), $0.5 million in interest on a loan to some consumers, and $1.5 million in taxes to the government. The relevant data for the coconut producer are shown in Table 2.1.

TABLE 2.1 **Coconut Producer**	
Total revenue	$20 million
Wages	$ 5 million
Interest on loan	$ 0.5 million
Taxes	$ 1.5 million

Of the 10 million coconuts produced, 6 million go to the restaurant, which specializes in innovative ways of serving coconuts—for example "shredded coconut in its own milk," "coconut soup," and "coconut in the half-shell." Consumers buy the remaining 4 million coconuts. Again, all coconuts are $2 each. Coconuts serve two roles in this economy. First, a coconut is an **intermediate good**, a good that is produced and then used as an input to another production process—here, the production of restaurant food. Second, it is a final consumption good, in that consumers purchase coconuts. The restaurant sells $30 million in restaurant meals during the year (this is a rather large restaurant). The total cost of coconuts for the restaurant is $12 million, and the restaurant pays its workers $4 million in wages and the government $3 million in taxes. Data for the restaurant are provided in Table 2.2.

TABLE 2.2 **Restaurant**	
Total revenue	$30 million
Cost of coconuts	$12 million
Wages	$ 4 million
Taxes	$ 3 million

Next, we need to calculate after-tax profits for each of the producers. After-tax profits in this example are simply

After-tax profits = Total revenue − Wages − Interest − Cost of intermediate inputs − Taxes.

Therefore, from Tables 2.1 and 2.2 above, we calculate after-tax profits in Table 2.3.

TABLE 2.3	After-Tax Profits
Coconut producer	$13 million
Restaurant	$11 million

The government's role in this economy is to provide protection from attacks by people on other islands. In the past, foreign invaders have destroyed coconut trees and made off with coconuts. The government collects taxes to provide national defence. That is, it uses all of its tax revenue to pay wages to the army. Total taxes collected are $5.5 million ($4.5 million from producers and $1 million from consumers). The data for the government are shown in Table 2.4.

TABLE 2.4	Government
Tax revenue	$5.5 million
Wages	$5.5 million

Consumers work for the producers and for the government, earning total wages of $14.5 million. They receive $0.5 million in interest from the coconut producer, pay $1 million in taxes to the government, and they also receive after-tax profits of $24 million from the producers, since some of the consumers own all the production units. Data for the consumers are shown in Table 2.5.

TABLE 2.5	Consumers
Wage income	$14.5 million
Interest income	$ 0.5 million
Taxes	$ 1 million
Profits distributed by producers	$24 million

Now, given the above data for this simple economy, we will examine how GDP would be calculated by using the three different national income accounting approaches.

THE PRODUCT APPROACH TO MEASURING GDP

The product approach to NIEA is also called the **value-added** approach. This is because the main principle in the product approach is that GDP is calculated as *the sum of value added to goods and services in production across all productive units in the economy*. To calculate GDP by using the product approach, we want to add the value of all goods produced in the economy, and then subtract the value of all intermediate goods used in production to obtain total value added. If we did not subtract the value of intermediate goods used in production, we would be double-counting. In our example, we do not want to count the value of the coconuts used in the restaurant as part of GDP.

In the example, the coconut producer does not use any intermediate goods in production, so value added in producing coconuts, which is the coconut producer's total revenue, is $20 million. For the restaurant, however, valued added is total revenue minus the value of the coconuts used in production; thus, total value added for the restaurant is $18 million. For government production, we have a problem, because the national defence services were not sold at market prices. Standard practice here is to value the national defence services at the cost of the inputs to production. Here, the only input to production was labour, so the total value added for the government is $5.5 million. Therefore, total value added, or GDP, is $43.5 million. The GDP calculation using the product approach is summarized in Table 2.6.

TABLE 2.6   **GDP Using the Product Approach**

Value added—coconuts	$20 million
Value added—restaurant	$18 million
Value added—government	$ 5.5 million
GDP	$43.5 million

THE EXPENDITURE APPROACH

In the expenditure approach, we calculate GDP as *total spending on all final goods and services production in the economy*. Note again that we do not count spending on intermediate goods. In the NIEA, total expenditure is calculated as

$$\text{Total expenditure} = C + I + G + NX,$$

where C denotes expenditures on consumption, I is investment expenditure (i.e., expenditure on goods produced but not consumed during the period under consideration), G is government expenditure, and NX is net exports—that is, total exports of goods and services minus total imports. We add exports because this includes goods and services produced within the country. Imports are subtracted because, in general, each of C, I, and G includes some goods and services that were produced abroad, and we do not want to include these in GDP.

In our example, there is no investment, no exports, and no imports, so that $I = NX = 0$. Consumers spend $8 million on coconuts and $30 million on restaurant food, so that $C = \$38$ million. For government expenditures, again we count the $5.5 million in wages spent by the government as if national defence services were a final good at $5.5 million, and so $G = \$5.5$ million. Therefore, calculating GDP by using the expenditure approach, we get

$$GDP = C + I + G + NX = \$43.5 \text{ million.}$$

The GDP calculation using the expenditure approach is shown in Table 2.7. Note that we obtain the same answer calculating GDP this way as using the product approach.

TABLE 2.7   **GDP Using the Expenditure Approach**

Consumption	$38 million
Investment	0
Government expenditures	$ 5.5 million
Net exports	0
GDP	$43.5 million

THE INCOME APPROACH

To calculate GDP by using the income approach, we want to *add up all incomes received by economic agents contributing to production.* Incomes will include the profits made by firms. In the NIEA, incomes include compensation of employees (wages, salaries, and benefits), corporate profits, net interest, net income of farm operators and unincorporated businesses, taxes less subsidies on factors of production, taxes less subsidies on products, government business enterprise profits before taxes, inventory valuation adjustment, and depreciation. Depreciation represents the value of productive capital (plant and equipment) that wears out during the period we are considering. Depreciation is taken out when we calculate profits, and so it needs to be added in again when we compute GDP. The inventory valuation adjustment enters for a similar reason.

In the example, we need to include the wage income of consumers, $14.5 million, as a component of GDP. In addition, we need to count the profits of producers. If we do this on an after-tax basis, total profits for the two producers are $24 million. Next, we add the interest income of consumers (this is net interest), which is $0.5 million. Finally, we need to add the taxes paid by producers to the government, which are essentially government income. This amount is $4.5 million. Total GDP is then $43.5 million, which of course is the same answer that we obtained for the other two approaches. The calculation of GDP by using the income approach is summarized in Table 2.8.

TABLE 2.8 GDP Using the Income Approach	
Wage income	$14.5 million
After-tax profits	$24 million
Interest income	$ 0.5 million
Taxes	$ 4.5 million
GDP	$43.5 million

Why do the product approach, the expenditure approach, and the income approach yield the same GDP measure? This happens because the total quantity of output, or value added, in the economy is ultimately sold, thus showing up as expenditure, and what is spent on all output produced is income in some form or other for someone in the economy. If we let Y denote total GDP in the economy, then Y is total aggregate output, and it is also aggregate income. Further, it is also true as an identity that aggregate income equals aggregate expenditure, or

$$Y = C + I + G + NX.$$

This relationship is sometimes referred to as the **income–expenditure identity**, as the quantity on the left-hand side of the identity is aggregate income, and the right-hand side is the sum of the components of aggregate expenditure.

AN EXAMPLE WITH INVENTORY INVESTMENT

One component of investment expenditures is inventory investment, which consists of any goods that are produced but are not consumed during the current period. Stocks of inventories consist of inventories of finished goods (e.g., automobiles stored on the lot), goods in process (e.g., automobiles still on the assembly line), and raw materials.

Suppose in our running example that everything is identical to the above, except that the coconut producer produces 13 million coconuts instead of 10 million, and that the extra 3 million coconuts are not sold but are stored as inventory. In terms of the value-added approach, GDP is the total value of coconuts produced, which is now $26 million, plus the value of restaurant food produced, $30 million, minus the value of intermediate goods used up in the production of restaurant food, $12 million, plus value added by the government, $5.5 million, for total GDP of $49.5 million. Note that we value the coconut inventory at the market price of coconuts in the example. In practice, this need not be the case; sometimes the book value of inventories carried by firms is not the same as market value, though sound economics says it should be.

Now, for the expenditure approach, $C = \$38$ million, $NX = 0$, and $G = \$5.5$ million as before, but now $I = \$6$ million, so GDP $= C + I + G + NX = \$49.5$ million. It might seem odd that the inventory investment of $6 million is counted as expenditure, because this does not appear to be expenditure on a final good or service. The convention, however, is to treat the inventory investment here as if the coconut producer bought $6 million in coconuts from itself.

Finally, in terms of the income approach, wage income to consumers is $14.5 million, interest income to consumers is $0.5 million, taxes are $4.5 million, as before, and total profits after taxes for the two producers are now $30 million, for total GDP of $49.5 million. Here, we add the $6 million in inventories to the coconut producer's profits, because this is an addition to the firm's assets.

AN EXAMPLE WITH INTERNATIONAL TRADE

To show what can happen when international trade in goods comes into the picture, we take our original example and alter it slightly. Suppose that the restaurant imports 2 million coconuts from other islands at $2 each, in addition to the coconuts purchased from the domestic coconut producer, and that all of these coconuts are used in the restaurant. The restaurant still sells $30 million in restaurant food to domestic consumers.

Here, following the value-added approach, the value added by the domestic coconut producer is $20 million as before. For the restaurant, value added is the value of food produced, $30 million, minus the value of intermediate inputs, which is $16 million, including the cost of imported coconuts. As before, total value added for the government is $5.5 million. Therefore, GDP is total value added for the two producers and the government, or $39.5 million.

Next, using the expenditure approach, consumption of coconuts by consumers is $8 million and restaurant service consumption is $30 million, so that $C =$ $38 million. Government expenditures are the same as in the initial example, with $G =$ $5.5 million, and we have $I = 0$. Total exports are 0, while imports (of coconuts) are $4 million, so that net exports are $NX = -\$4$ million. We then have GDP $= C + I + G + NX =$ $39.5 million.

Finally, following the income approach, the wage income of consumers is $14.5 million, interest income of consumers is $0.5 million, and taxes are $4.5 million, as in the initial example. The after-tax profits of the coconut producer are $13 million, also as before. The change here is in the after-tax profits of the restaurant, which are reduced by $4 million, the value of the imported coconuts, so that after-tax restaurant profits are $7 million. Total GDP is then $39.5 million.

GROSS NATIONAL PRODUCT (GNP)

At one time, **gross national product (GNP)** was used in Canada as the official measure of aggregate production. In line with international practice, however, the official measure is now GDP. GNP measures the value of output produced by domestic factors of production, whether or not the production takes place (as is the case for GDP) inside Canadian borders. For example, if an oil well in South America is owned and managed by Canadian residents, then the incomes accruing to Canadian factors of production include the managerial income and profits of this oil well, and this is included in Canadian GNP, but not in Canadian GDP. Similarly, if a Walmart store in Saskatchewan has U.S. owners, the profits of the store would not be included in GNP, as these profits are not income for Canadian residents, but the profits would be included in GDP.

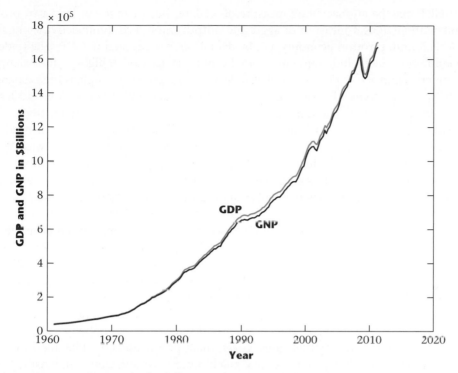

FIGURE 2.1

GDP and GNP for Canada, 1961–2011

GNP is GDP plus payments from abroad to Canadian factors of production, minus payments to foreign factors of production for output produced in Canada. The figure shows that there is a significant difference between GNP and GDP in Canada. This is because the net factor payments flowing out of Canada are relatively large.

Source: Adapted from the Statistics Canada CANSIM database, Series v498086, v499686.

In practice, there is little difference between GDP and GNP in some countries, such as the United States. However, for Canada the difference is significant. Figure 2.1 shows GNP (the black line) and GDP (the coloured line) for Canada during the period 1961–2011. Clearly, GNP is typically significantly smaller than GDP in Canada. For example, in the second quarter of 2011, GDP was 1.7% higher than GNP. The reason for this difference is that a significant fraction of productive plant and equipment in Canada is foreign-owned.

WHAT DOES GDP LEAVE OUT?

GDP is intended simply as a measure of the quantity of output produced and exchanged in the economy as a whole. However, sometimes GDP, or GDP per person, is used as a measure of aggregate economic welfare. There are at least two problems with this approach. The first is that aggregate GDP does not take into account how income is distributed across the individuals in the population. At the extreme, if one person in the economy has all the income and the rest of the people have no income, the average level of economic welfare in the economy would be very low. Second, GDP leaves out all nonmarket activity, such as work in the home. If people eat restaurant meals rather than eating at home, then GDP will rise, because there are now more services produced in the market than before. People should be better off as a result, since they had the option of eating at home but chose to go out. However, this increase in GDP exaggerates the increase in economic welfare, as GDP does not measure the value added when food is cooked at home.

GDP may be an inaccurate measure of welfare, but there are at least two problems with GDP as a measure of aggregate output. First, economic activities in the so-called **underground economy** are, by definition, not counted in GDP. The underground economy includes any unreported economic activity. A high-profile example of underground activity is trade in illegal drugs; a low-profile example is the exchange of babysitting services for cash. Economic activity goes underground to avoid legal penalties and taxation, and underground activity often involves cash transactions. The size of the underground economy may indeed be significant in Canada, as evidenced by the fact that the quantity of Canadian currency held per Canadian resident was about $1672 in August 2011.[1] Clearly, most individuals engaged only in standard market transactions do not hold this much currency. Further, this large quantity of Canadian currency in circulation does not reflect underground transactions that take place in Canada with the use of other currencies, particularly U.S. dollars.

A second problem in measuring GDP, which we encountered in our example, is how to count government expenditures. Most of what the government produces is not sold at market prices. For example, how are we to value roads, bridges, and national defence services? The solution in the NIEA, as in our example, is to value government expenditures at cost, that is, the payments to all of the factors of production that went into producing the good or service. In some cases, this could overvalue what is produced; for example, if the government produced something that nobody used, such as a highway to nowhere. In other cases, government production could be undervalued; for example, we might be willing to pay much more for health care than what it costs in terms of wages, salaries, materials, and so forth.

THE COMPONENTS OF AGGREGATE EXPENDITURE

Typically, particularly in constructing economic models to understand how the economy works, we are interested mainly in the expenditure side of the NIEA. Here, we will consider each of the expenditure components in more detail. Table 2.9 gives the GDP components for Canada for 2010.

Consumption Consumption expenditures are the largest expenditure component of Canadian GDP, accounting for 57.9% of GDP in 2010 (see Table 2.9). **Consumption** is expenditure on consumer goods and services during the current period, and the components of consumption are durable goods, semi-durable goods, nondurable goods, and services. Durable goods include household appliances, furniture, and video equipment; examples of semi-durables are clothing, window coverings, and footwear. Nondurable goods include food, electricity, and fuel, whereas services are intangible items, such as haircuts and hotel stays. Note that some items included in consumption are clearly not consumed within the period. For example, if the period is one year, an automobile may provide services to the buyer for ten years or more, and is therefore not a consumption good, but might economically be more appropriately considered investment expenditure rather than consumption expenditure when it is bought.

---

[1]*Bank of Canada Weekly Financial Statistics*, October 2011, and Statistics Canada CANSIM database, Series v1.

TABLE 2.9   **Gross Domestic Product for Canada for 2010**

Component of GDP	$ Billions	% of GDP*
GDP	1624.6	100
Consumption	940.6	57.9
Durables	112.7	6.9
Semi-durables	71.5	4.4
Nondurables	225.4	13.9
Services	531.1	32.7
Investment	293.5	18.1
Nonresidential	178.5	11.0
Residential	112.7	6.9
Change in inventories	2.3	0.1
Government expenditures	420.9	25.9
Government consumption	353.6	21.8
Government investment	67.3	4.1
Net exports	−30.6	−1.9
Exports	478.1	29.4
Imports	−508.7	−31.3

Source: Statistics Canada, CANSIM database, Table 380-0002.
*Percentages do not add up to 100 because of rounding.

Note that the purchase of a used car or other used durable good is not included in GDP, but the services provided (e.g., by a dealer) in selling a used car would be included.

Investment In Table 2.9, investment expenditures were 18.1% of GDP in 2010. **Investment** is expenditure on goods that are produced but not consumed during the current period. There are two types of investment. These are **fixed investment**, which is production of capital, such as plant, equipment, and housing, and **inventory investment**, which consists of goods that are essentially put into storage. The components of fixed investment are *nonresidential investment* and *residential investment*. Nonresidential investment adds to the plant, equipment, and software that make up the capital stock for producing goods and services. Residential investment—housing—is also productive, in that it produces housing services.

Though investment is a much smaller fraction of GDP than consumption is, investment plays a very important role in business cycles. Investment is much more variable than consumption or GDP, and some components of investment also tend to lead the business cycle. For example, an upward or downward blip in housing investment tends to precede an upward or downward blip in GDP. We will study this phenomenon further in Chapter 3.

Net Exports As exports were less than imports in 2010, Canada ran a trade deficit in goods and services with the rest of the world—that is, **net exports** were negative (see Table 2.9). Net exports, at −1.9% of GDP, contribute significantly (in this case negatively) to Canadian production, though the contribution of net exports to GDP is small relative to consumption and investment expenditure. Exports were 29.4% of GDP in 2010; imports were 31.3% of GDP. Thus, trade with the rest of the world in goods and services is very important to the Canadian economy, as we noted in Chapter 1.

Government Expenditures **Government expenditures**, which consist of expenditures by federal, provincial or territorial, and municipal governments on final goods and services, were 25.9% of GDP in 2010, as seen in Table 2.9. The main components of government expenditures are *government consumption* (21.8% of GDP in 2010) and *government investment* (4.1% of GDP in 2010). In the NIEA we make the important distinction between government consumption and government gross investment, just as we distinguish between private consumption and private investment. An important point is that the government spending included in the NIEA is only the expenditures on final goods and services. This does not include **transfers**, which are very important in the government budget. These outlays essentially transfer purchasing power from one group of economic agents to another, and they include such items as payments under Old Age Security and the Canada Pension Plan as well as benefits under the employment insurance system. Transfers are not included in GDP, as they are simply money transfers from one group of people to another—in other words, income redistribution rather than income creation.

Nominal and Real GDP and Price Indices

Although the components of GDP for any specific time period give us the total dollar value of goods and services produced in the economy during that period, for many purposes we would like to make comparisons of GDP in different time periods. Such comparisons can tell us something about growth in the productive capacity of the economy over time and about growth in our standard of living. However, one obstacle is that the average level of prices changes over time, so that part of the increase in GDP that we typically observe is due to inflation. In this section, we show how to adjust for this effect of inflation on the growth in GDP, and in so doing we arrive also at a measure of the price level and the inflation rate.

A **price index** is a weighted average of the prices of a set of the goods and services produced in the economy over a period of time. If the price index includes prices of all goods and services, then that price index is a measure of the general **price level**, or the average level of prices across all goods and services. We use price indices to measure the inflation rate, which is the rate of change in the price level from one period of time to another. If we can measure the **inflation rate**, we can also determine how much of a change in GDP from one period to another is purely *nominal* and how much is *real*.

A **nominal change** in GDP is a change in GDP that occurred only because the price level changed, whereas a **real change** in GDP is an increase in the physical quantity of output.

REAL GDP

To see how real GDP is calculated in the NIEA, it helps to consider an example. Imagine an economy in which the only goods produced are apples and oranges. In year 1, 50 apples and 100 oranges are produced, and the prices of apples and oranges are $1 and $0.80, respectively. In year 2, 80 apples and 120 oranges are produced, and the prices of apples and oranges are $1.25 and $1.60, respectively. These data are displayed in Table 2.10. For convenience in constructing the formulas for real GDP calculations, we let the quantities of apples and oranges, respectively, in year 1 be denoted by Q_1^a and Q_1^o with respective prices denoted by P_1^a and P_1^o. Quantities and prices in year 2 are represented similarly (see Table 2.10).

TABLE 2.10   **Data for Real GDP Example**

	Apples	Oranges
Quantity in year 1	50	100
Price in year 1	$1	$0.80
Quantity in year 2	80	120
Price in year 2	$1.25	$1.60

The calculation of nominal GDP in each year is straightforward here, as there are no intermediate goods. Year 1 nominal GDP is

$$GDP_1 = P_1^a Q_1^a + P_1^o Q_1^o = (\$1 \times 50) + (\$0.80 \times 100) = \$130.$$

Similarly, year 2 nominal GDP is

$$GDP_2 = P_2^a Q_2^a + P_2^o Q_2^o = (\$1.25 \times 80) + (\$1.60 \times 120) = \$292,$$

so the percentage increase in nominal GDP from year 1 to year 2 is equal to

$$\left(\frac{GDP_2}{GDP_1} - 1 \right) \times 100\% = \left(\frac{292}{130} - 1 \right) \times 100\% = 125\%.$$

That is, nominal GDP more than doubled from year 1 to year 2.

Now, the question is, how much of this increase in nominal GDP is accounted for by inflation, and how much by an increase in the real quantity of aggregate output produced? Until recently, the practice in Canadian NIEA was first to choose a base year and then to calculate real GDP using these base year prices. That is, rather than multiplying the quantities produced in a given year by current year prices (which is what we do when calculating nominal GDP), we multiply by base year prices to obtain real GDP. In the example, suppose that we use year 1 as the base year, and let $RGDP_1^1$ and $RGDP_2^1$ denote real GDP in years 1 and 2, respectively, calculated using year 1 as the base year. Then, real GDP in year 1 is the same as nominal GDP for that year, because year 1 is the base year, so we have

$$RGDP_1^1 = GDP_1 = \$130.$$

Now, for year 2 real GDP, we use year 2 quantities and year 1 prices to obtain

$$RGDP_2^1 = P_1^a Q_2^a + P_1^o Q_2^o = (\$1 \times 80) + (\$0.80 \times 120) = \$176.$$

Therefore, the ratio of real GDP in year 2 to real GDP in year 1, using year 1 as the base year, is

$$g_1 = \frac{RGDP_2^1}{RGDP_1^1} = \frac{176}{130} = 1.354,$$

so the percentage increase in real GDP using this approach is $(1.354 - 1) \times 100\%$ $= 35.4\%$. Alternatively, suppose that we use year 2 as the base year and let $RGDP_1^2$ and $RGDP_2^2$ denote real GDP in years 1 and 2, respectively, calculated by using this approach. Then year 2 real GDP is the same as year 2 nominal GDP, that is,

$$RGDP_2^2 = GDP_2 = \$292.$$

Year 1 GDP, using year 1 quantities and year 2 prices, is

$$RGDP_1^2 = P_2^a Q_1^a + P_2^o Q_1^o = (\$1.25 \times 50) + (\$1.60 \times 100) = 222.50.$$

Then the ratio of real GDP in year 2 to real GDP in year 1, using year 2 as the base year, is

$$g_2 = \frac{RGDP_2^2}{RGDP_1^2} = \frac{292}{222.5} = 1.312,$$

and the percentage increase in GDP from year 1 to year 2 is $(1.312 - 1) \times 100\% = 31.2\%$.

A key message from the example is that the choice of the base year matters for the calculation of GDP. If year 1 is used as the base year, then the increase in real GDP is 35.4%, and if year 2 is the base year, real GDP is calculated to increase by 31.2%. The reason the choice of the base year matters in the example, and in reality, is that the relative prices of goods change over time. That is, the relative price of apples to oranges is $\frac{\$1.00}{\$0.80} = 1.25$ in year 1, and this relative price is $\frac{\$1.25}{\$1.60} = 0.78$ in year 2. Therefore, apples became cheaper relative to oranges from year 1 to year 2. If relative prices had remained the same between year 1 and year 2, then the choice of the base year would not matter. In calculating real GDP, the problem of changing relative prices would not be too great in calculating GDP close to the base year (say 2004 or 2005 relative to a base year in 2003), because relative prices would typically not change much over a short period of time. Over many years, however, the problem could be severe, for example, in calculating real GDP in 2008 relative to a base year in 1982. The solution to this problem, adopted in the NIEA, is to use a **chain-weighting** scheme for calculating real GDP.

With the chain-weighting approach, a "Fisher index" is used, and the approach is essentially like using a rolling base period. The chain-weighted ratio of real GDP in year 2 to real GDP in year 1 is

$$g_c = \sqrt{g_1 \times g_2} = \sqrt{1.354 \times 1.312} = 1.333,$$

so that the chain-weighted ratio of real GDP in the two years is a geometric average of the ratios calculated by using each of years 1 and 2 as base years. In the example, we calculate the percentage growth rate in real GDP from year 1 to year 2 by using the chain-weighting method to be $(1.333 - 1) \times 100\% = 33.3\%$. The growth rate in this case falls between the growth rates we calculated using the other two approaches, which is of course what we should get given that chain-weighting effectively averages (geometrically) the growth rates found by using years 1 and 2 as base years.

Now, once we have the chain-weighted ratio of real GDP in one year relative to another (g_c in this case), we can calculate real GDP in terms of the dollars of any year we choose. In our example, if we want real GDP in year 1 dollars, then real GDP in year 1 is the same as nominal GDP or $GDP_1 = \$130$, and real GDP in year 2 is equal to $GDP_1 \times g_c = \$130 \times 1.333 = \$173.29$. Alternatively, if we want real GDP in year 2 dollars, then real GDP in year 2 is $GDP_2 = \$295$, and real GDP in year 1 is

$$\frac{GDP_2}{g_c} = \frac{\$292}{1.333} = \$219.05.$$

In practice, the growth rates in real GDP in adjacent years are calculated just as we have done here, and then real GDP is "chained" together from one year to the next. Chain-weighting should in principle give a more accurate measure of the year-to-year, or quarter-to-quarter, changes in real GDP. In Figure 2.2 we show nominal GDP and real GDP, calculated by using the chain-weighting approach, for Canada over the period 1961–2011. Real GDP is measured here in 2002 dollars, so that real GDP is equal to nominal GDP in 2002. Because the inflation rate was generally positive over the period 1961–2011, and was particularly high in the 1970s, real GDP grows in Figure 2.2 at a lower rate than does nominal GDP.

MEASURES OF THE PRICE LEVEL

There are two commonly used measures of the price level: the **implicit GDP price deflator** and the **consumer price index (CPI)**. The implicit GDP price deflator is measured as

$$\text{Implicit GDP price deflator} = \frac{\text{Nominal GDP}}{\text{Real GDP}} \times 100$$

Here, multiplying by 100 just normalizes the price deflator to 100 in the base year (if there is one). For the example above, the price deflator we calculate would depend on whether we use year 1 or year 2 as a base year, or compute chain-weighted GDP.

FIGURE 2.2

Nominal GDP (black line) and Chain-Weighted Real GDP (coloured line), 1961–2011

Note that the two time series cross in 2002 because real GDP is measured in 2002 dollars. The growth rate in real GDP is smaller than the growth rate for nominal GDP because of positive inflation over this period.

Source: Adapted from the Statistics Canada CANSIM database, Series v498086, v1992067.

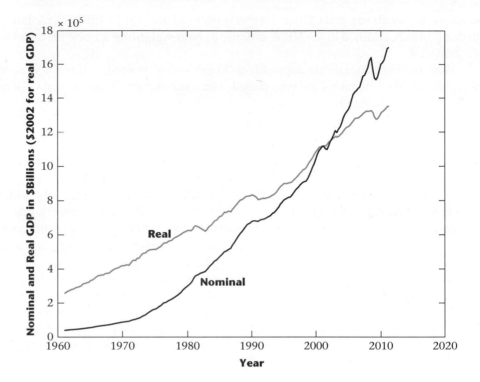

We give the results in Table 2.11. Note in Table 2.11 that the answers we get for the percentage rate of inflation between year 1 and year 2 depend critically on how we measure real GDP.

The alternative measure of the price level, the CPI, is not as broadly based as the implicit GDP price deflator, because it includes only goods and services that are purchased by consumers. Further, the CPI is a fixed-weight price index, which takes the quantities in some base year as being the typical goods bought by the average consumer during that base year, and then uses those quantities as weights to calculate the index in each year. Thus, the CPI in the current year would be

$$\text{Current year CPI} = \frac{\text{Cost of base year quantities at current prices}}{\text{Cost of base year quantities at base year prices}} \times 100.$$

TABLE 2.11 **Implicit GDP Price Deflators, Example**

	Year 1	Year 2	% Increase
Year 1 = base year	100	165.9	65.9
Year 2 = base year	58.4	100	71.2
Chain-weighting	100	168.5	68.5

In the example, if we take year 1 as the base year, then the year 1 (base year) CPI is 100 and the year 2 CPI is $\frac{222.5}{130} \times 100 = 171.2$, so that the percentage increase in the CPI from year 1 to year 2 is 71.2%.

In practice, there can be substantial differences between the inflation rates calculated by using the implicit GDP price deflator and those calculated by using the CPI. Figure 2.3 shows the GDP deflator inflation rate (the black line) and CPI inflation rate (the coloured line), calculated quarter by quarter, for Canada over the period 1962–2011. Note that the two measures of the inflation rate track each other broadly, but at times there can be substantial differences between the two measures. These differences in inflation rate measures could matter greatly for contracts that are geared to the inflation rate or for the formulation of monetary policy, where close attention is paid to inflation performance.

PROBLEMS WITH MEASURING REAL GDP AND THE PRICE LEVEL

As we saw above, particularly in how the implicit GDP price deflator is derived, the measurement of real GDP and the measurement of the price level are intimately related. If a particular measure of real GDP underestimates the growth in real GDP, the rate of inflation will be overestimated. In practice, there are three important problems with measuring real GDP and the price level.

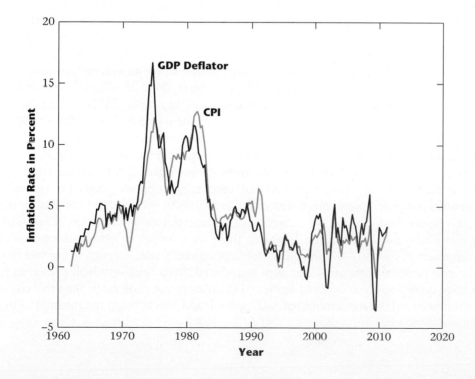

FIGURE 2.3

Quarterly Inflation Rate Calculated from the CPI (coloured line) and the Implicit GDP Price Deflator (black line), 1962–2011

These measures are broadly similar, but there can be substantial differences.

Source: Adapted from the Statistics Canada CANSIM database, Series v1997756, v735319.

The first problem was mentioned above, which is that relative prices change over time. We showed how chain-weighting corrects this problem in the measurement of real GDP, and therefore corrects for the bias that relative price changes would introduce in the measurement of inflation using the implicit GDP price deflator. Changes in relative prices can also introduce severe bias in how the CPI measures inflation. When there is a relative price change, consumers typically will purchase less of the goods that have become more expensive and more of those that have become relatively cheap. This is what is represented in the previous example, where apples became cheaper relative to oranges in year 2, and the ratio of apples consumed to oranges consumed increased. In computing the CPI, the implicit assumption that consumers do not change their buying habits when relative price changes occur is clearly false. As a result, goods that become relatively more expensive are given a higher weight than they should in the CPI, and therefore the CPI-based measure of the rate of inflation will be biased upward. This is, in fact, a serious policy issue (see the box Macroeconomics in Action 2.1). Since some federal transfer payments, including Canada Pension Plan and Old Age Security payments, are indexed to the CPI, an upward bias in CPI inflation would also commit the federal government to higher transfer payments. This would in turn increase the size of the federal government budget deficit. Also, federal income tax brackets are geared to CPI inflation. Upward bias in CPI inflation causes tax revenues to fall, increasing the government deficit. Rather than the rate of increase in the CPI, a more accurate measure of the rate of inflation in consumer goods is the implicit consumption price deflator, which is the price deflator associated with chain-weighted real consumption expenditures (see Macroeconomics in Action 2.1).

A second problem in measuring real GDP concerns the changes in the quality of goods over time. Consider the case of 2008 cars versus 1950 vintage cars. Clearly, the price of a new car in 2008 was much higher than the price of a new car in 1950, but the 2008 car is very different from the 1950 car. In 2008, most cars sold in Canada had computerized devices to monitor engine performance, automatic transmissions, power windows, air bags, seatbelts, and CD players, none of which were standard equipment (or in some cases even invented) in 1950. In a sense, the 2008 car is "more car," because its quality is higher, and so some of the increase in price from 1950 to 2008 simply represents the fact that the buyer is receiving more in exchange for his or her money. To the extent that NIEA does not compensate for changes in quality over time, growth in real GDP will be biased downward and inflation will be biased upward.

A third problem is how measured GDP takes account of new goods. For example, personal computers were introduced in the early 1980s, and they did not exist in the NIEA before then. Clearly, we cannot make a straightforward calculation of real GDP growth from the 1970s to the 1980s, as there were no prices existing for personal computers in the 1970s. If the NIEA does not correctly take account of the fact that the new personal computers that were introduced (initially at very high prices) were a huge quality advance over old-fashioned calculators and slide rules, then this could bias downward the measure of real GDP growth and bias upward the measure of the inflation rate.

In February 1991, the Bank of Canada adopted inflation targets as an explicit objective for monetary policy. Other central banks in the world, including the Bank of England, the Reserve Bank of New Zealand, the Swedish Riksbank, and the Reserve Bank of Australia, have similar targets.

If a central bank adopts inflation targeting as a goal, an important consideration is the choice of the measure of inflation to use in the targeting procedure. First, the measure of inflation used should be easily understood and observed by the public, so that the performance of the central bank in meeting its goals can be readily evaluated. Second, the measure should accurately reflect actual inflation in the economy. Third, the measure of inflation should be easily controlled by the central bank.

The inflation rate that was chosen for the Bank of Canada to target was the 12-month rate of increase in the consumer price index (CPI). The CPI certainly meets the criterion of being easily understood and observed by the public. Statistics Canada reports the CPI on a monthly basis, and these reports are typically widely reported in the news media. However, as pointed out in this chapter, the rate of change in the CPI is a biased measure of inflation. The Boskin Commission, which studied the CPI in the United States in the mid-1990s, found that the rate of change in the U.S. consumer price index tended to be about one percentage point higher than the actual inflation rate.[2] In Canada, the upward bias in inflation by using the CPI is thought to be about 0.5 percentage points.

There are many factors other than monetary policy that cause the CPI to change from month to month. For example, the CPI might spike upward because of a drought that results in a shortage of food and higher food prices, because the government increases sales taxes, or because of a temporary shortage of crude oil on world markets. The Bank of Canada may not want to respond to these temporary increases in the rate of inflation, as they are likely to be reversed before monetary policy could have any effect on the rate of inflation. As a result, in addition to targeting the CPI rate of inflation, the Bank of Canada monitors a "core" measure of the inflation rate, which is the CPI rate of inflation neglecting effects on inflation that are judged to be temporary. [3]

The current measure of the core price level used by the Bank of Canada is what was previously known as CPIX. This price index leaves out the eight components of expenditure in the CPI for which prices are most volatile. These components are fruit, vegetables, gasoline, fuel oil, natural gas, intercity transportation, tobacco, and mortgage interest costs. As well, CPIX adjusts the CPI for the effects of indirect taxes, such as sales and excise taxes. Although the use of this more narrow measure perhaps has merit, there are drawbacks. First, what is to stop the Bank of Canada from focusing the public's attention on particular measures of inflation that put the Bank's performance in a favourable light? We need to be aware of the natural tendency of central bankers to hide information. Second, the particular goods that have the most volatile prices during the current year may not be the same ones having volatile prices next year, or ten years from now, necessitating continual changes in the measure of core inflation. Note that the Bank of Canada changed its measure of the core price level to CPIX from CPIXFET in May 2001.

What other choices does the Bank of Canada have in trying to measure and target inflation? It might monitor the CPI rather than some core measure of the price level and, in light of the limitations of the CPI, widen its inflation targets. Alternatively, it might try a different measure of the price level. For example, one possibility is to use the implicit GDP price deflator, which has the advantage of not being biased to the degree that the CPI is, but the disadvantage of including some goods, such as government-provided goods and services, that do not have market prices that can be affected by monetary policy. In the United States, some proponents of inflation targeting argue that a good measure of the inflation rate is the rate of change in the implicit consumption deflator. The implicit consumption deflator is calculated similarly to the implicit GDP deflator but is measured as the ratio of nominal consumption expenditures to real consumption expenditures.

The reason the Bank of Canada gives for using the CPIX, rather than the CPI for example, as an "operational guide" to policy relies on some subtle arguments having to do with the fact that, in the data, CPIX inflation tends to provide a good forecast of future CPI inflation. Thus, if the Bank controls current CPIX inflation well, it may be doing a good job

of controlling future CPI inflation, which is what it really cares about. Where this argument falters is in terms of the "Lucas critique," which was discussed in Chapter 1. The Lucas critique comes into play in this context due to the fact that, if the Bank of Canada changes its behaviour, the relationships we observe among particular economic variables can change. For example, we might observe that CPIX inflation tends to predict future CPI inflation, but if the Bank of Canada targets CPIX inflation, the relationship between CPIX inflation and CPI inflation might go away.

_____

[2]See M. Boskin, E. Deulberger, R. Gordon, Z. Griliches, and D. Jorgensen, 1996, "Toward a More Accurate Measure of the Cost of Living," *Final Report of the Senate Finance Committee.*

[3]See T. Macklem, 2001, "A New Measure of Core Inflation," *Bank of Canada Review*, Autumn, 3–12.

Savings, Wealth, and Capital

Although the components of GDP in the NIEA measure aggregate activity that takes place within the current period, another key aspect of the economy that is of interest to macroeconomists is aggregate productive capacity and how aggregate savings adds to this productive capacity. In this section we will explore, by way of several accounting identities, the relationships among savings, wealth, and capital.

An important distinction in economics is between *flows* and *stocks*. A **flow** is a rate per unit time, whereas a **stock** is the quantity in existence of some object at a point in time. GDP, consumption, investment, government spending, and net exports are all flows in the NIEA. For example, GDP is measured in dollars spent per period. In contrast, the quantity of housing in existence in Canada at the end of a given year is a stock. In the following, we will see that national saving is a flow, while the nation's wealth is a stock. In particular, national saving is the flow that is added to the stock of the nation's wealth in each year. A classic analogy is the example of water flowing into a bathtub, in which the quantity of water coming out of the faucet per minute is a flow, whereas the quantity of water in the bathtub at any point in time is a stock.

Savings can mean very different things, depending on whether we are referring to the private (nongovernment) sector, the government, or the nation as a whole. For the private sector, to determine savings we first need to start with what the private sector has available to spend, which is **private disposable income**, denoted Y^d. We have

$$Y^d = Y + NFP + TR + INT - T,$$

Comparing Real GDP across Countries and the Penn Effect 2.2

Just as it is useful to obtain a measure of real GDP for a given country so that we can study the growth of output over time in that country, it is also important to be able to make comparisons between real GDPs, or GDPs per person, in different countries. For example, if we can compare real GDP across all countries in the world, we might learn the reasons for differences in the standard of living across countries. This is one of the issues that will concern us when we study economic growth, particularly in Chapter 8.

Coming up with comparable measures of GDP can be a daunting task. First, though international organizations have worked to standardize the national income and product accounts across countries, there can still be significant differences in how key data are collected in different countries. For example, poor countries might have limited resources available to devote to data collection. However, even if the prices and quantities of final goods and services were measured without error in all countries, there would still be a problem in making international real GDP comparisons. This is because the prices of identical goods sold in different countries are typically significantly different, even after we express prices in units of the same currency.

To understand the measurement problem, suppose that P denotes the price of goods and services in Canada (in Canadian dollars), and P^* is the price of goods and services in Mexico (in Mexican pesos). Also, suppose that e is the exchange rate of Canadian dollars for Mexican pesos, that is, e is the price of a peso in Canadian dollars. Then eP^* would be the cost of Mexican goods and services for a Canadian, or the price in Canadian dollars of Mexican goods and services. If we observed that $P = eP^*$, then we would say that we observed the law of one price or purchasing power parity, in that

prices of goods and services would be the same in Canada and Mexico, correcting for exchange rates. In fact, what we tend to observe is that $P > eP^*$ for Canada and Mexico; that is, goods and services priced in Canadian dollars tend to be higher in Canada than in Mexico. This difference is particularly large for services, such as auto repairs, which are difficult to trade across international borders.

The Penn effect refers to the regularity in data on prices and exchange rates across countries that shows that prices tend to be higher, correcting for currency exchange rates, in high-income countries than in low-income countries. The problem is that, if we made real GDP comparisons across countries by just expressing all prices in the same currencies, then we would exaggerate the differences in income between rich and poor countries. For example, for Canada and Mexico, if the same quantity of a given good were produced in each country, we would tend to measure this as a smaller contribution to real GDP in Mexico than in Canada if we expressed the quantity produced in terms of its value in Canadian dollars.

An approach to correcting for the Penn effect is to make international real GDP comparisons based on purchasing power parity. For example, for Canada and Mexico, if P is the Canadian price level (in Canadian dollars), and P^* is the Mexican price level (in Mexican pesos), then to compare GDP in Canada with GDP in Mexico, we would multiply nominal quantities for Mexico by P/P^* rather than by e. This is the approach taken in the Penn World Tables, a comprehensive set of international data developed by Alan Heston, Robert Summers, and Bettina Aten at the University of Pennsylvania.[4]

---

[4]Alan Heston, Robert Summers, and Bettina Aten, "Penn World Table Version 6.2," Center for International Comparisons of Production, Income, and Prices at the University of Pennsylvania, September 2006.

where Y is GDP, NFP is net factor payments from abroad to Canadian residents, TR is transfers from the government to the private sector, INT is interest on the government debt, and T is taxes. Recall that GNP is $Y + $ NFP. What the private sector saves is simply what it has available to spend minus what it consumes, and so letting S^p denote **private sector saving**, we have

$$S^p = Y^d - C = Y + NFP + TR + INT - T - C.$$

What the government has available to spend is its tax revenue, T, minus TR, minus INT, and what it consumes is government expenditures, G. Thus, **government saving** S^g is given by

$$S^g = T - TR - INT - G.$$

Government saving is the **government surplus**, and the government surplus is equal to the negative of the **government deficit**, denoted D, or

$$D = S^g = -T + TR + INT + G,$$

which is just government outlays minus government receipts.

If we add private saving and government saving, we obtain **national saving**,

$$S = S^p + S^g = Y + NFP - C - G,$$

which is GNP minus private consumption, minus government consumption. Since the income–expenditure identity gives $Y = C + I + G + NX$, we can substitute for Y in the above equation to obtain

$$\begin{aligned} S &= Y + NFP - C - G \\ &= C + I + G + NX + NFP - C - G \\ &= I + NX + NFP. \end{aligned}$$

Thus, national saving must equal investment plus net exports plus net factor payments from abroad. The quantity $NX + NFP$ is the current account surplus with the rest of the world, which we will denote CA; thus, we have

$$S = I + CA.$$

The **current account surplus** is a measure of the balance of trade in goods with the rest of the world. The above identity reflects the fact that any domestic savings not absorbed by domestic investment must be shipped outside the country in the form of goods and services.

As a flow, national saving represents additions to the **national wealth** (the stock of assets held by the country as a whole). Since $S = I + CA$, wealth is accumulated in two ways. First, wealth is accumulated through investment, I, which is the addition to the nation's **capital stock**. The capital stock is the quantity of plants, equipment, housing, and inventories in existence in an economy at a point in time. Second, wealth is accumulated through current account surpluses, *CA*, since a current account surplus implies that Canadian residents are accumulating claims on foreigners. The current account surplus, *CA*, represents increases in claims on foreigners. If goods are flowing from Canada to other countries, then these goods must be paid for with a transfer of wealth from outside Canada to Canadian residents. The current account surplus is then a flow, while the quantity of claims on foreigners in existence in Canada at a particular point in time is a stock.

Labour Market Measurement

The labour market variables we will focus on here are those measured in the monthly survey carried out by Statistics Canada. In this survey, the population aged 15 and older is divided into three groups: the **employed**—those who worked part-time or full-time during the past week; the **unemployed**—those who were not employed during the past week but actively searched for work at some time during the last four weeks; and **not in the labour force**—those who are neither employed or unemployed. Thus, the labour force is the employed plus the unemployed.

Of key interest in analyzing the results of the household survey is the **unemployment rate**, measured as

$$\text{Unemployment rate} = \frac{\text{Number unemployed}}{\text{Labour force}},$$

the **participation rate**, measured as

$$\text{Participation rate} = \frac{\text{Labour force}}{\text{Total working} - \text{age population}},$$

and the **employment/population ratio**, measured as

$$\text{Employment/population ratio} = \frac{\text{Employment}}{\text{Total working} - \text{age population}}.$$

The unemployment rate is potentially useful as a measure of **labour market tightness**, which is the degree of difficulty firms face in hiring workers. However, there are two ways in which the unemployment rate might mismeasure labour market tightness. First, some people, referred to as **discouraged workers**, are not counted in the labour force and have stopped searching for work but actually want to be employed. Thus, during a long recession, when the level of aggregate economic activity is depressed for an extended period of time, it is possible that the unemployment rate might fall only because some unemployed people have become discouraged and stopped looking for work. In this circumstance, labour market tightness would not really have increased with the decrease in the unemployment rate, but we might be fooled into thinking so.

Differences in Unemployment Rates in Canada and the United States

There is typically a substantial difference in the unemployment rates in Canada and the United States. There are many economic reasons for these differences. For example, government labour market policies are substantially different in the two countries, the sectoral composition of aggregate output is different, the structure of the population is different, and business cycle events can affect Canada and the United States in different ways. While these economic determinants of unemployment are important, and will be analyzed in Chapter 6, a significant contributor to the difference in observed unemployment rates in Canada and the United is measurement differences.

Figure 2.4 shows three unemployment rate measures: the first, labelled "Canada" is the offi-cial Canadian unemployment rate, as measured by Statistics Canada; the second, labelled "Canada (U.S.)," is the Canadian unemployment rate measured using the same approach as for the U.S. unemployment rate; the third, labelled "United States," is the U.S. official unemployment rate. Note first that, before 2008, the unemployment rate in Canada was typically higher than in the United States. The Canadian unemployment rate was as much as 4 percentage points higher than the U.S. rate in the mid-1990s, and from 2000 to 2007 the unemployment rate in Canada was about 2 percentage points higher than in the United States. However, this relationship changed during the recent worldwide recession. In 2010, the Canadian unemployment rate was 8.0%, while the U.S. rate was 9.4%.

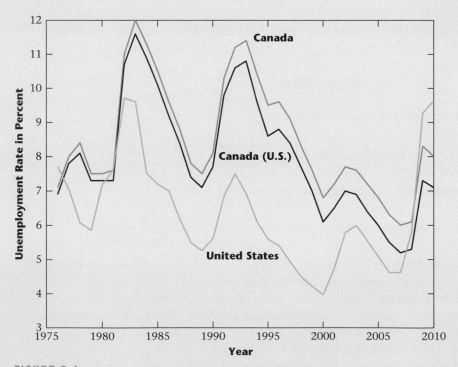

FIGURE 2.4

Unemployment Rates in Canada and the U.S.

Source: Adapted from the Statistics Canada CANSIM database, Series v2461224, v2170200.

Next, we can see in Figure 2.4 that the official unemployment rate in Canada is higher than the Canadian unemployment rate measured using the same methods as in the United States. Further, the difference due to these alternative approaches has grown over time, from about 0.2% in 1976 to 0.9% in 2010.

If one examines the definitions of employment, unemployment, and not-in-the-labour-force, applied by Statistics Canada, and by the Bureau of Labor Statistics in the United States, those definitions look essentially identical, so it seems hard to identify where the measurement differences are coming from. In Canada and the United States, employment is defined in the same fashion, and an unemployed person is someone who was not employed during the "reference week" particular to the monthly labour force survey, and has searched for work during the previous four weeks.

A published paper by Craig Riddell at the University of British Columbia[5] provides a detailed explanation of the underlying measurement differences between Canada and the United States. First, in the United States, a person is judged to be searching for work only if he or she were actively searching. For example, if a person were not employed and engaged only in "passive" search, such as looking at job advertisements, then he or she would be unemployed in Canada, but out-of-the-labour-force in the United States. As well, the Bureau of Labor Statistics in the U.S. does not count a person who has found a job but not yet started work as unemployed, but Statistics Canada does. Both of these factors act to increase the unemployment rate in Canada relative to that of the United States.

What is the correct way of measuring unemployment, the Statistics Canada approach or the approach of the U.S. Bureau of Labor Statistics? On the question of active and passive search and what constitutes unemployment, there is a whole spectrum of behaviour that we would characterize as job search. It is clear that we want to distinguish economically between the activity of searching for a job, employment, and activities that involve neither employment nor job search. Ideally, we would like to have some measure of the intensity of job search by all people. Some people who are not employed put little effort into looking for a job, while others put considerable time and other resources into it. As well, employed people also engage in job search, and as economists we should care about that. Unfortunately, the intensity of search is impossible to measure accurately, and we have to rely on survey responses to questions about search activity. Where we draw the line between search activity that constitutes or does not constitute "unemployment" is arbitrary. Thus, on this dimension, it is hard to express a preference for Canadian measurement over U.S. measurement.

On the question of how we should categorize individuals who have found work but have not yet started their new jobs, to be consistent these people should be counted as "not in the labour force." Some individuals "not in the labour force" transition directly from that state to employment, without a period of job search. Surely, those people look essentially the same as people who have found a job but have not started work. Thus, consistently with U.S. practice, the latter group should be counted as out of the labour force.

[5]Riddell, W.C. 2005. "Why Is Canada's Unemployment Rate Persistently Higher Than in the United States?" *Canadian Public Policy* 31, 93–100.

The second factor that could cause the unemployment rate to be a bad measure of labour market tightness is that the unemployment rate does not adjust for how intensively the unemployed are searching for work. Thus, it could be the case that when the unemployment rate is high, the unemployed do not search very hard for work, because they think their chances of success are low. For example, each worker might spend only one or two hours per day trying to find work. However, when the unemployment rate is low, the unemployed might be searching very hard, because their prospects for success seem good. For example, each worker might search eight or ten hours per day. If this were the case, we might actually think of a high unemployment rate as being associated with high labour market tightness and a low unemployment rate as being associated with low labour market tightness. For example, if a firm is looking to hire, it is more difficult to find workers if the unemployed are not looking hard for work.

Partly because of problems in interpreting what movements in the unemployment rate mean, macroeconomists often focus attention on the level and growth rate of employment when they analyze the implications of labour market activity. Empirically, sometimes we have a greater interest in the behaviour of the participation rate or the employment/population ratio than in the unemployment rate. Theoretically, in many of the models we will analyze in this book we do not explain the behaviour of unemployment. However, we will study some explanations for unemployment in Chapters 6 and 14.

So far, we have learned how aggregate economic activity is measured in the NIEA, how nominal GDP can be decomposed to obtain measures of real GDP and the price level, what the relationships are among savings, wealth, and capital, and what the key measurement issues in the labour market are. In the next chapter we will deal with business cycle measurement and derive a set of key business cycle facts that will help focus our study of macroeconomic theory beginning in Chapter 4.

Chapter Summary

- This chapter focused on the measurement of gross domestic product (GDP) and its components, and the measurement of the price level, savings, wealth, capital, and labour market variables.

- We first discussed how GDP is measured in the National Income and Expenditure Accounts (NIEA) of Canada. GDP can be measured by using the product approach, the expenditure approach, or the income approach, which will each yield the same quantity of GDP in a given period if there is no measurement error.

- GDP must be used carefully as a measure of aggregate welfare because it leaves out home production. Further, there are problems with GDP as a measure of aggregate output because of the existence of the underground economy and because government output is difficult to measure.

- It is useful to distinguish how much of nominal GDP growth is accounted for by inflation and how much is growth in real GDP. Two approaches to measuring real GDP are choosing a base year and chain-weighting. The latter is the current method used in the NIEA.

Chain-weighting corrects for the bias that arises in real GDP calculations when a base year is used and relative prices change over time.

■ Problems with real GDP measurement arise because it is difficult to account for changes in the quality of goods over time and because new goods are introduced and others become obsolete.

■ Private saving is private disposable income minus consumption, while government saving is government receipts minus government spending and transfers.

■ Government surplus is equal to government saving. National saving is the sum of private and government saving and is equal to investment expenditures plus the current account surplus. National saving is just the accumulation of national wealth, which comes in the form of additions to the capital stock (investment) and additions to domestic claims on foreigners (the current account surplus).

■ The labour market variables we focus on are those measured in the monthly survey by Statistics Canada. The working-age population consists of the employed, the unemployed (those searching for work), and those not in the labour force. Two key labour market variables are the unemployment rate and the participation rate. The unemployment rate is sometimes used as a measure of labour market tightness, but care needs to be taken in interpreting the unemployment rate in this way.

Key Terms

gross domestic product (GDP): The dollar value of final output produced during a given period of time within a country's borders.

National Income and Expenditure Accounts (NIEA): The official Canadian accounts of aggregate economic activity, which include GDP measurements conducted by Statistics Canada.

product approach: The approach to GDP measurement that determines GDP as the sum of value added to goods and services in production across all productive units in the economy.

expenditure approach: The approach to GDP measurement that determines GDP as total spending on all final goods and services production in the economy.

income approach: The approach to GDP measurement that determines GDP as the sum of all incomes received by economic agents contributing to production.

intermediate good: A good that is produced and then used as an input in another production process.

value added: The value of goods produced, minus the value of intermediate goods used in production.

income–expenditure identity: $Y = C + I + G + NX$, where Y is aggregate income (output), C is consumption expenditures, I is investment expenditures, G is government expenditures, and NX is net exports.

gross national product (GNP): GNP = GDP + Net factor payments to Canadian residents from abroad.

underground economy: All unreported economic activity.

consumption: Goods and services produced and consumed during the current period.

investment: Goods produced in the current period but not consumed in the current period.

fixed investment: Investment in plant, equipment, and housing.

inventory investment: Goods produced in the current period that are set aside for future periods.

net exports: Expenditures on domestically produced goods and services by foreigners (exports) minus expenditures on foreign-produced goods and services by domestic residents (imports).

government expenditures: Expenditures by the federal, provincial or territorial, and municipal governments on final goods and services.

transfers: Government outlays that are transfers of purchasing power from one group of private economic agents to another.

price index: A weighted average of prices of some set of goods produced in the economy during a particular period.

price level: The average level of prices across all goods and services in the economy.

inflation rate: The rate of change in the price level from one period to another.

nominal change: The change in the dollar value of a good, a service, or an asset.

real change: The change in the quantity of a good, a service, or an asset.

chain-weighting: An approach to calculating real GDP that uses a rolling base year.

implicit GDP price deflator: Nominal GDP divided by real GDP, all multiplied by 100.

consumer price index (CPI): Current-year total expenditures, divided by current-year total expenditures at base year prices, all multiplied by 100.

flow: A rate per unit time.

stock: Quantity in existence of some object at a point in time.

private disposable income: GDP plus net factor payments, plus transfers from the government, plus interest on the government debt, minus taxes.

private sector saving: Private disposable income minus consumption expenditures.

government saving: Taxes minus transfers, minus interest on the government debt, minus government expenditures.

government surplus: Identical to government saving.

government deficit: The negative of the government surplus.

national saving: Private sector saving plus government saving.

current account surplus: Net exports plus net factor payments from abroad.

national wealth: The stock of assets held by the country as a whole.

capital stock: The quantity of plant, equipment, housing, and inventories in existence in an economy at a point in time.

employed: In the Statistics Canada monthly household survey, those who worked part-time or full-time during the past week.

unemployed: In the Statistics Canada monthly household survey, those who were not employed during the past week but actively searched for work at some time during the last four weeks.

not in the labour force: In the Statistics Canada household survey, those who are neither employed or unemployed.

unemployment rate: The number of unemployed divided by the number in the labour force.

participation rate: The number in the labour force divided by the working-age population.

Employment/population ratio: The ratio of total employment to the total working-age population.

labour market tightness: The degree of difficulty firms face in hiring workers.

discouraged workers: Those who are not counted in the labour force and have stopped searching for work, but actually want to be employed.

Questions for Review

1. What three approaches are used to measure GDP?

2. Explain the concept of *value added*.

3. Why is the income–expenditure identity important?

4. What is the difference between GDP and GNP?

5. Is GDP a good measure of economic welfare? Why or why not?

6. What are two difficulties in the measurement of aggregate output using GDP?

7. What is the largest expenditure component of GDP?

8. What is investment?

9. What are government transfers? Explain why they are not included in GDP.

10. Why does the base year matter in calculating real GDP?

11. Explain what *chain-weighting* is.

12. Explain three problems in the measurement of real GDP.

13. What are the differences and similarities among private sector saving, government saving, and national saving?

14. What are the two ways in which national wealth is accumulated?

Problems

1. Assume an economy in which there are two producers: a wheat producer and a bread producer. In a given year, the wheat producer grows 3 million tonnes of wheat, of which 2.5 million tonnes are sold to the bread producer at $30 per tonne, and 0.5 million tonnes are stored by the wheat producer to use as seed for next year's crop. The bread producer produces and sells 100 million loaves of bread to consumers for $3.50 per loaf. Determine GDP in this economy during this year by using the product and expenditure approaches.

2. Assume an economy with a coal producer, a steel producer, and some consumers. (There is no government.) In a given year, the coal producer produces 15 million tonnes of coal and sells it for $5 per tonne. The coal producer pays $50 million in wages to consumers. The steel producer uses 25 million tonnes of coal as an input into steel production, all purchased at $5 per tonne. Of this, 15 million tonnes of coal comes from the domestic coal producer, and 10 million tonnes is imported. The steel producer produces 10 million tonnes of steel and sells it for $20 per tonne. Domestic consumers buy 8 million tonnes of steel, and 2 million tonnes are exported. The steel producer pays consumers $40 million in wages. All profits made by domestic producers are distributed to domestic consumers.
   a. Determine GDP using (i) the product approach, (ii) the expenditure approach, and (iii) the income approach.
   b. Determine the current account surplus.
   c. What is GNP in this economy? Determine GNP and GDP in the case where the coal producer is owned by foreigners, so that the profits of the domestic coal producer go to foreigners and are not distributed to domestic consumers.

3. Assume an economy with two firms. Firm A produces wheat and firm B produces bread. In a given year, firm A produces 5000 tonnes of wheat, sells 2000 tonnes of wheat to firm B at $30 per tonne, exports 2500 tonnes of wheat at $30 per tonne, and stores 500 tonnes as inventory. Firm A pays $50 000 in wages to consumers. Firm B produces 50 000 loaves of bread, and sells all of it to domestic consumers at $2 per loaf. Firm B pays consumers $20 000 in wages. In addition to the 50 000 loaves of bread consumers buy from firm B, consumers import and consume 15 000 loaves of bread, and they pay $1 per loaf for this imported bread. Calculate gross domestic product using (a) the product approach, (b) the expenditure approach, and (c) the income approach.

4. In year 1 and year 2, there are two products produced in a given economy: computers and bread. Suppose that there are no intermediate goods. In year 1, 20 computers are produced and sold at $1000 each, and in year 2, 25 computers are produced and sold at $1500 each. In year 1, 10 000 loaves of bread are sold for $1 each, and in year 2, 12 000 loaves of bread are sold for $1.10 each.
   a. Calculate nominal GDP in each year.
   b. Calculate real GDP in each year and the percentage increase in real GDP from year 1 to year 2 by using year 1 as the base year. Next, do the same calculations by using the chain-weighting method.
   c. Calculate the implicit GDP price deflator and the percentage inflation rate from year 1 to year 2 by using year 1 as the base year. Next, do the same calculations by using the chain-weighting method.
   d. Suppose that computers in year 2 are twice as productive as computers in year 1. How does this change your calculations in parts (a)–(c)? Explain any differences.

5. Assume an economy in which only broccoli and cauliflower are produced. In year 1, 500 million kilograms of broccoli are produced and consumed and its price is $0.50 per kilogram, while 300 million kilograms of cauliflower are produced and consumed and its price is $0.80 per kilogram. In year 2, 400 million kilograms of broccoli are produced and consumed and its price is $0.60 per kilogram, while 350 million kilograms of cauliflower are produced and its price is $0.85 per kilogram.
   a. Using year 1 as the base year, calculate the GDP price deflator in years 1 and 2, and calculate the rate of inflation between years 1 and 2 from the GDP price deflator.
   b. Using year 1 as the base year, calculate the CPI in years 1 and 2, and calculate the CPI rate of inflation. Explain any differences in your results between parts (a) and (b).

6. In some countries, price controls exist on some goods, which set maximum prices at which these goods can be sold. Indeed, Canada experienced a period of wage and price controls in the 1970s, under the Anti-Inflation Board. Sometimes the existence of price controls leads to the growth of black markets, in which goods are exchanged at prices above the legal maximums. Carefully explain how price controls present a problem for measuring GDP and for measuring the price level and inflation.

7. In this chapter, we learned that the quantity of Canadian currency outstanding per Canadian resident was $1672 in 2011. Suppose we were to try to use this number to estimate the amount of output produced in the underground economy in Canada during 2011. Discuss how we would use this information on the quantity of currency in circulation. What additional information would you want to have to come up with a good estimate? In your answer, you will need to consider how underground transactions might take place in Canada by other means than through the use of Canadian currency.

8. Consider an economy with a corn producer, some consumers, and a government. In a given year, the corn producer grows 3 million tonnes of corn, and the market price for corn is $50 per tonne. Of the 3 million tonnes produced, 2 million tonnes are sold to consumers, 0.5 million are stored in inventory, and 0.5 million are sold to the government to feed the army. The corn producer pays $60 million in wages to consumers and $20 million in taxes to the government. Consumers pay $10 million in taxes to the government, receive $10 million in interest on the government debt, and receive $5 million in Canada Pension Plan payments from the government. The profits of the corn producer are distributed to consumers.
   a. Calculate GDP using (i) the product approach, (ii) the expenditure approach, and (iii) the income approach.
   b. Calculate private disposable income, private sector saving, government saving, national saving, and the government deficit. Is the government budget in deficit or surplus?

9. Part of gross domestic product consists of production in the so called FIRE sector (finance, insurance, real estate, and rental and leasing). Value-added is notoriously difficult to measure in this sector, as it is hard to determine exactly what the inputs and outputs are. For example, banks are included in the FIRE sector, and we know that they contribute to our well-being by making borrowing and lending more efficient and by providing transactions services. However, as most of the inputs and outputs associated with a bank are not actual physical quantities, it is much more difficult to measure value-added in banking than in, say, the production of apples. During the global financial crisis, people began to question some types of financial activity and their value to society; in particular, they observed some financial firms and individuals earning large incomes and argued that these firms and individuals actually provide little or no financial services. Discuss the implications that questionable financial activity has for the measurement of GDP.

10. In Canada, transactions among banks and other financial institutions takes place through the Large Value Transfer System (LVTS) operated by the Bank of Canada. During 2009, on an average day, 22 250 payments were made through LVTS, with a total value of $153.5 billion. To put this in context, annual GDP in 2009 was $1.528 trillion, so average total daily transactions over Fedwire were about 10% of total annual GDP. Do these statistics indicate that there might be some large measurement error in the official national income and expenditure accounts, or is this entirely consistent with official GDP numbers being accurate measures of aggregate economic activity? Explain, and discuss your answer.

11. Let K_t denote the quantity of capital a country has at the beginning of period t. Also, suppose that capital depreciates at a constant rate d, so that dK_t of the capital stock wears out during period t. If investment during period t is denoted by I_t, and the country does not trade with the rest of the world (the current account surplus is always zero), then we can say that the quantity of capital at the beginning of period $t + 1$ is given by

$$K_{t-1} = (1-d)K_t + I_t.$$

   Suppose at the beginning of year 0 that this country has 80 units of capital. Investment expenditures are 10 units in each of years 0, 1, 2, 3, 4, ... 10. The capital stock depreciates by 10% per year.
   a. Calculate the quantity of capital at the beginning of years 0, 1, 2, 3, 4, ..., 10.
   b. Repeat part (a), except assume now that the country begins year 0 with 100 units of capital. Explain what happens now, and discuss your results in parts (a) and (b).

12. Consider the identity

$$S^P - I = CA + D,$$

where S^P is private sector saving, I is investment, CA is the current account surplus, and D is the government deficit.

a. Show that the above identity holds.

b. Explain what the above identity means.

13. Suppose that the government deficit is 10, interest on the government debt is 5, taxes are 40, government expenditures are 30, consumption expenditures are 80, net factor payments are 10, the current account surplus is −5, and national saving is 20. Calculate the following (not necessarily in the order given):

a. Private disposable income

b. Transfers from the government to the private sector

c. Gross national product

d. Gross domestic product

e. The government surplus

f. Net exports

g. Investment expenditures

14. Suppose that the unemployment rate is 5%, the total working-age population is 100 million, and the number of unemployed is 2.5 million. Determine (a) the participation rate; (b) the labour force; (c) the number of employed workers; (d) the employment/population ratio.

Business Cycle Measurement

Before we go on to build models of aggregate economic activity that can explain why business cycles exist and what, if anything, should be done about them, we must understand the key features that we observe in economic data that define a business cycle. In this chapter, we move beyond the study of the measurement of gross domestic product, the price level, savings, and wealth, which we covered in Chapter 2, to an examination of the regularities in the relationships among aggregate economic variables as they fluctuate over time.

We will show that business cycles are quite irregular, and therefore somewhat unpredictable; macroeconomic forecasters often have difficulty predicting the timing of a business cycle upturn or downturn. However, business cycles are quite regular in terms of comovements, which is to say that macroeconomic variables move together in highly predictable ways. We will focus separately on the components of real GDP, nominal variables, and labour market variables.

This chapter describes a set of key business cycle facts concerning comovements in Canadian macroeconomic data. In Chapters 4, 5, 6, 11, and 12, we will use these facts to show how our models can make sense of what we observe in the data. Then, in Chapters 13 and 14, we will use the key business cycle facts to help us evaluate alternative theories of the business cycle. These facts show how our models can make sense of what we observe in the data, and help us evaluate alternative theories of the business cycle.

Regularities in GDP Fluctuations

The primary defining feature of **business cycles** is that they are *fluctuations about trend in real gross domestic product*. Recall from Chapter 1 that we represent the trend in real GDP with a smooth curve that closely fits actual real GDP, with the trend representing that part of real GDP that can be explained by long-run growth factors. What is left over, the deviations from trend, we take to represent business cycle activity.

In Figure 3.1 we show idealized business cycle activity in real GDP, with fluctuations about a long-run trend. In the figure, real GDP is represented by the black line, while the trend is represented by the coloured line. There are **peaks** and **troughs** in real GDP, a peak being a relatively large positive deviation from trend, and a trough a relatively large negative deviation from trend. Peaks and troughs in the deviations from trend in real GDP are referred to as **turning points**. In a manner analogous to wave motion in the physical sciences, we can think of the maximum deviation from trend in Figure 3.1 as the **amplitude** of the business cycle, and the number of peaks in real GDP that occur per year as the **frequency** of the business cycle.

Next, in Figure 3.2 we show the actual percentage deviations from trend in real GDP for Canada over the period 1961–2011. A series of positive deviations from trend culminating in a peak represents a **boom**, whereas a series of negative deviations from trend culminating in a trough represents a **recession**. In Figure 3.2, we have marked four important recent recessions: the 1974–1975, 1981–1982, 1990–1992, and 2008–2009 recessions. The 1974–1975 recession was relatively mild, with a negative deviation from trend of less than 2%, while the 1981–1982 recession was relatively severe, with a negative deviation from trend of about 5%. In the 1990–1992 recession, the negative deviation from trend was fairly moderate, at about 2%, but that recession was fairly prolonged. Finally, with a negative percentage deviation from trend of about 3%, the most recent recession in 2008–2009 was more severe than all of the other three recessions, except the one in 1981–1982.

An examination of Figure 3.2 indicates a striking regularity, which is that the deviations from trend in real GDP are **persistent**. That is, when real GDP is above trend, it tends to stay above trend, and when it is below trend, it tends to stay below trend. This feature is quite important in terms of economic forecasting over the short run; persistence implies that we can fairly confidently predict that if real GDP is currently

FIGURE 3.1

Idealized Business Cycles

The black curve is an idealized path for real GDP over time, while the coloured line is the growth trend in real GDP. Note that real GDP cycles around the trend over time, with the maximum negative deviation from trend being a trough and the maximum positive deviation from trend being a peak. The amplitude is the size of the maximum deviation from trend, and the frequency is the number of peaks that occur within a year's time.

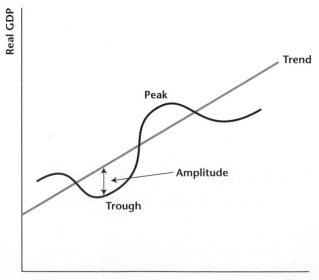

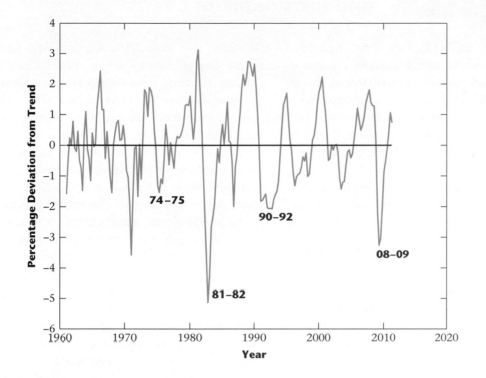

FIGURE 3.2
**Percentage Deviations
from Trend in Real GDP,
1961–2011**
Of particular note are the
four most recent recessions,
in 1974–1975, 1981–1982,
1990–1992, and 2008–2009.

Source: Adapted from the Statistics
Canada CANSIM database, Series
v1992067.

below (above) trend, it will be below (above) trend several months from now. Other than being persistent, however, the deviations from trend in real GDP are actually quite irregular. There are three other features to note from Figure 3.2:

1. The time series of deviations from trend in real GDP is quite choppy.

2. There is no regularity in the amplitude of fluctuations in real GDP about trend. Some of the peaks and troughs represent large deviations from trend, whereas other peaks and troughs represent small deviations from trend.

3. There is no regularity in the frequency of fluctuations in real GDP about trend. The length of time between peaks and troughs in real GDP varies considerably.

Though deviations from trend in real GDP are persistent, which makes short-term forecasting relatively easy, the above three features imply that longer-term forecasting is difficult. The choppiness of fluctuations in real GDP will make these fluctuations difficult to predict, while the lack of regularity in the amplitude and frequency of fluctuations implies that it is difficult to predict the severity and length of recessions and booms. Therefore, predicting future fluctuations in real GDP by looking only at past real GDP is much like attempting to forecast the weather by looking out the window. If it is sunny today, it is likely that it will be sunny tomorrow (weather is persistent), but the fact that it is sunny today may give us very little information on whether it will be sunny one week from today. (See Macroeconomics in Action 3.1 for a discussion of economic forecasting and the financial crisis.)

Economic Forecasting and the Financial Crisis

As was discussed in Chapter 1, a macroeconomic model is designed with a particular purpose in mind. First, we might want a model that will help us understand a particular economic phenomenon. For example, we may wish to understand why economics grow over time. Second, we might want to make predictions about the effects of economic policies, such as the effects on real GDP and employment of a particular government tax proposal. For these types of problems—understanding economic phenomena and predicting the effects of economic policy—it is important to work with structural models. By "structural," we mean models built from basic microeconomic principles, and for which private behavioural relationships do not change when policymakers change their behaviour. A structural model is said to be immune to the "Lucas critique."[2]

Predicting the effects of economic policies is quite different from macroeconomic forecasting, which involves predicting the course of future economic variables on the basis of what we are observing today. Some economists have argued that economic theory is not a necessary input in a forecasting exercise. Christopher Sims, winner (with Thomas Sargent) of the 2011 Nobel Prize in Economics, is famous in part for inventing vector autoregression methodology, an atheoretical statistical approach to capturing the dynamics in economic time series.[3] This approach was used in the Bayesian vector autoregression (BVAR) models developed at the Federal Reserve Bank of Minneapolis in the 1970s and 1980s. These BVAR models were used successfully in forecasting. Economic theory is not an input in setting up or running a BVAR model. All that is required is a knowledge of statistics and computation. A BVAR model captures the detail that we see in Figure 3.2 and more; part of what the BVAR will do is to forecast real GDP on the basis of the historical behaviour of real GDP—its persistence and variability for example. The BVAR will also take account of the historical relationships between real GDP and other economic variables in producing a forecast.

If we take the ideas of people like Christopher Sims seriously, the value of macroeconomic knowledge is not in producing forecasts, but in understanding macroeconomic phenomena and guiding macroeconomic policy. That is perhaps at odds with the views of lay people concerning what economists do. Just as meteorologists are expected to do a good job predicting the weather, macroeconomists are sometimes expected to do a good job predicting important macroeconomic events. Indeed, macroeconomists have suffered some criticism after the recent global financial crisis for not warning everyone about it. Is that criticism justified?

Comovement

Although real GDP fluctuates in irregular patterns, macroeconomic variables fluctuate together in patterns that exhibit strong regularities. We refer to these patterns in fluctuations as **comovement**. Robert Lucas once remarked that "with respect to qualitative behaviour of comovements among [economic time] series, business cycles are all alike."[1]

---

[1]See R. Lucas, 1980, "Understanding Business Cycles," in *Studies in Business Cycle Theory*, MIT Press, 218.

Sometimes economic theory tells us that fore-casting is in fact futile. For example, basic theory tells us that the changes in stock prices from one day to the next cannot be forecast. If we knew that the price of a stock would be higher tomorrow than today, we should buy that stock. As a result, today's market price for the stock would tend to rise (because of the increase in the demand for it), to the point where the price of the stock today is the same as the price tomorrow. Similarly, the widely held view that a stock's price will be lower tomor-row than today will tend to force today's stock price down. What we should observe is that, at any point in time, the price of a given stock is the best forecast available of its price tomorrow. Economic theory thus tells us that the changes in stock prices from day to day cannot be forecast. This is sometimes called the "efficient markets hypothesis."

A similar idea applies to financial crises. A financial crisis involves severe turmoil in credit mar-kets. Interest rates and stock prices can move by large amounts, and there is a dramatic reduction in credit market activity. If anyone could predict such an event he or she could profit handsomely from that information. Just as with the efficient markets hypothesis, a widely held belief that a financial crisis will happen tomorrow should make it happen today. For example, if people expect a financial crisis to

push down the price of stocks by 20%, the price of stocks should drop by 20% today.

In economic models of financial crises, the ficti-tious people living in the model know that a financial crisis can happen, but they cannot predict it. As well, it can be the case that the policymakers living in the model cannot predict the financial crisis, and are not able to prevent it.[4] Further, we can have an excellent model of a financial crisis, but an econo-mist equipped with that model will not be able to predict a financial crisis. The economist may, how-ever, be able to use the financial crisis model to design regulations that will prevent a financial crisis from happening, or perhaps mitigate its effects.

The conclusion is that the ability to forecast future events is not a litmus test for macroeconom-ics. Macroeconomics can be useful in many ways that have nothing to do with forecasting.

[2]See R. Lucas, 1976, "Econometric Policy Evaluation: A Critique," *Carnegie-Rochester Conference Volume on Public Policy* 1, 19–46.

[3]See C. Sims, 1980, "Macroeconomics and Reality," *Econometrica* 48, 1–48.

[4]See for example H. Ennis and T. Keister, 2010, "Banking Panics and Policy Responses," *Journal of Monetary Economics* 57, 404–419.

Macroeconomic variables are measured as **time series**; for example, real GDP is measured in a series of quarterly observations over time. When we examine comove-ments in macroeconomic time series, typically we look at these time series two at a time, and a good starting point is to plot the data. Suppose, for example, that we have two macroeconomic time series and we would like to study their comovement. We first transform these two time series by removing trends, and we will let x and y denote the percentage deviations from trend in the two time series. One way to plot x and y is in time series form, as in Figure 3.3. What we look for first in the time series plot is a pat-tern of **positive correlation** or **negative correlation** in x and y. In Figure 3.3(a), there is positive correlation between x and y: x is high when y is high, and x is low when y is low.

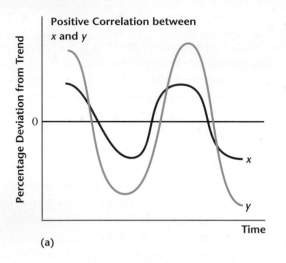
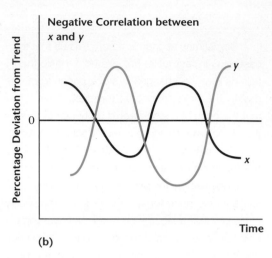

FIGURE 3.3 **Time Series Plots of *x* and *y***

(a) Two time series that are positively correlated: when *x* is high (low), *y* tends to be high (low). (b) Two time series that are negatively correlated: when *x* is high (low), *y* tends to be low (high).

That is, one economic time series tends to be above (below) trend when the other economic time series is above (below) trend. In Figure 3.3(b), *x* and *y* are negatively correlated: *x* is high (low) when *y* is low (high).

Another way to plot the data is as a **scatter plot**, with *x* on the horizontal axis and *y* on the vertical axis. In Figure 3.4, each point in the scatter plot is an observation on *x* and *y* for a particular time period. Here, whether *x* and *y* are positively or negatively correlated is determined by the slope of a straight line that best fits the points in the scatter plot. Part (a) of Figure 3.4 shows a positive correlation between *x* and *y*, part (b) shows a negative correlation, and part (c) shows a zero correlation. It should be emphasized that a first pass at data carried out in this fashion tells us nothing about why two variables might be correlated in the fashion that we observe in the time series and scatter plot. To organize our thinking about the data, we need other evidence and macroeconomic theory.

Macroeconomists are often primarily interested in how an individual macroeconomic variable comoves with real GDP. An economic variable is said to be **procyclical** if its deviations from trend are positively correlated with the deviations from trend in real GDP, **countercyclical** if its deviations from trend are negatively correlated with the deviations from trend in real GDP, and **acyclical** if it is neither procyclical nor countercyclical. As an example of comovement between two macroeconomic time series, we will consider real GDP and real imports for Canada over the period 1961–2011. In Figure 3.5 we plot the percentage deviations from trend in real GDP (the coloured line) and real imports (the black line) in time series form. There is a distinct pattern of positive correlation in Figure 3.5; when GDP is high (low) relative to trend, imports tend to be high (low) relative to trend. This positive correlation also shows up in the scatter plot in Figure 3.6, where we show a graph of observations of percentage devia-

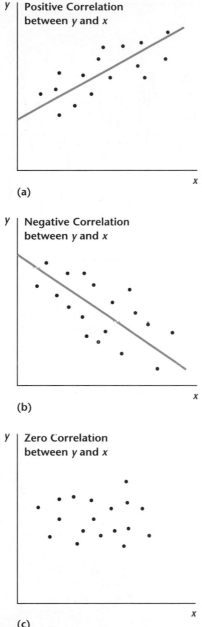

(a)

(b)

(c)

FIGURE 3.4

Scatter Plots of y and x
(a) *x* and *y* are positively correlated. (b) *x* and *y* are negatively correlated. (c) *x* and *y* are uncorrelated.

tions from trend in imports versus percentage deviations from trend in GDP. Note that a straight line fit to the points in Figure 3.6 would have a positive slope. In this example, we have established an important fact: deviations from trend in imports and GDP are positively correlated. Any theory that we develop that is intended to help us understand, for example, business cycle activity and how it is transmitted across countries should be consistent with this fact.

FIGURE 3.5

Imports and GDP for Canada, 1961–2011

This figure, as an example, shows the time series of percentage deviations from trend in real imports (the black line) and real GDP (the coloured line) for Canada for the period 1961–2011. Imports and GDP are clearly positively correlated, so imports are procyclical.

Source: Adapted from the Statistics Canada CANSIM database, Series v1992067, v1992063.

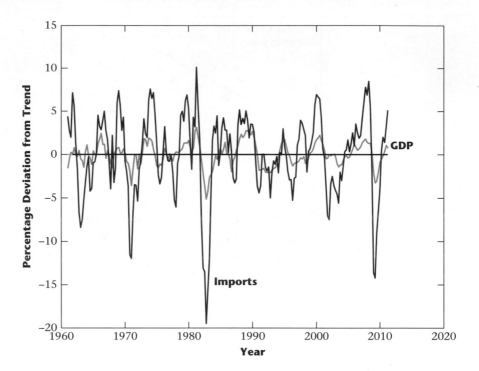

FIGURE 3.6

Scatter Plot of Imports and GDP for Canada, 1961–2011

This figure shows the same data as Figure 3.5 but in scatter plot rather than time series form. We again observe the positive correlation between imports and GDP, as a positively sloped straight line would best fit the scatter plot; and again, imports are procyclical.

Source: Adapted from the Statistics Canada CANSIM database, Series v1992067, v1992063.

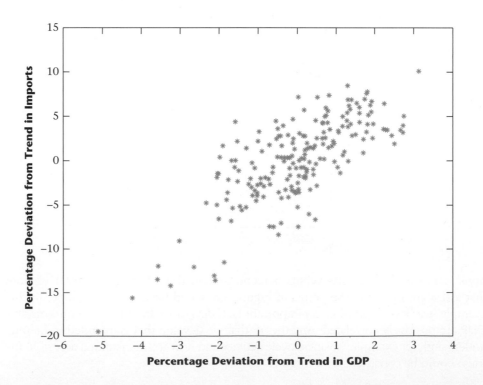

A measure of the degree of correlation between two variables is the **correlation coefficient**. The correlation coefficient between two variables, x and y, takes on values between −1 and 1. If the correlation coefficient is 1, x and y are **perfectly positively correlated**, and a scatter plot of observations on x and y will fall on a positively sloped straight line. If the correlation coefficient is −1, x and y are **perfectly negatively correlated**, and a scatter plot would consist of points on a negatively sloped straight line. If the correlation coefficient is 0, x and y are uncorrelated. In the example above, the percentage deviations from trend in real GDP and real imports have a correlation coefficient of 0.75, indicating positive correlation.

An important element of comovement is the leading and lagging relationships that exist in macroeconomic data. If a macroeconomic variable tends to aid in predicting the future path of real GDP, we say that it is a **leading variable**; whereas if real GDP helps to predict the future path of a particular macroeconomic variable, that variable is said to be a **lagging variable**. In Figure 3.7 we show idealized time series plots of the percentage deviations from trend in real GDP and two variables, x and y. In part (a) of the figure, variable x is a leading variable, whereas in (b) variable x is a lagging variable. A **coincident variable** is one that neither leads nor lags real GDP.

If it is known that some set of macroeconomic variables all tend to be leading variables, this information can be very useful in macroeconomic forecasting, as timely information on leading variables can then be used to forecast real GDP. One way to use this information is to construct a macroeconomic model, grounded in economic theory, that incorporates the relationships between leading variables and real GDP, which can then be used for forecasting. However, some economists argue that forecasting can be done simply by exploiting past statistical relationships among macroeconomic variables to project into the future. A very simple form of this approach is the construction

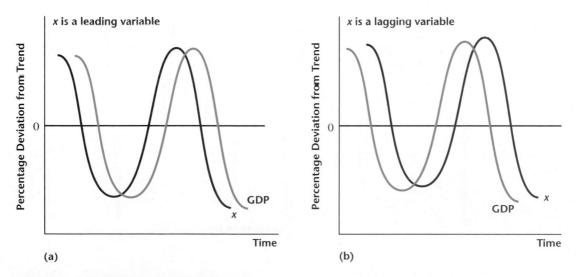

FIGURE 3.7 Leading and Lagging Variables

In (a), x is a leading variable, as its peaks and troughs tend to precede those of real GDP. In (b), x is a lagging variable, as the peaks and troughs in real GDP tend to lead those in x.

and use of the **composite index of business leading indicators** (or **index of leading indicators** for short). This index is a weighted average of macroeconomic variables that has been found to do a good job of predicting future real GDP. Watching the index of leading economic indicators can sometimes provide useful information for forecasters, particularly with respect to the turning points in aggregate economic activity. In Figure 3.8 we show a plot of the percentage deviations from trend in real GDP (the coloured line) and in the index of leading indicators (the black line). Note that the index of leading economic indicators tends to track real GDP fairly closely, but with a lead. In particular, turning points in the index of leading economic indicators in Figure 3.8 tend to fall before turning points in real GDP.

Finally, there are key regularities in terms of the variability of economic variables over the business cycle. As we will see, some macroeconomic variables are highly volatile, while others behave in a very smooth way relative to trend. These patterns in variability are an important part of business cycle behaviour that we would like to understand. A measure of cyclical variability is the **standard deviation** of the percentage deviations from trend. For example, in Figure 3.5, imports are much more variable than GDP. The standard deviation of the percentage deviations from trend in imports is more than twice that for GDP.

Next we will examine some key macroeconomic variables and will evaluate for each whether they are (i) procyclical or countercyclical; (ii) leading or lagging; and (iii) more or less variable relative to real GDP. These facts will then make up the set of important business cycle regularities that we would like to explain by using macroeconomic theory.

FIGURE 3.8

Percentage Deviations from Trend in Real GDP (coloured line) and the Composite Index of Business Leading Indicators (black line), 1961–2011

The index is a weighted average of leading variables and so, not surprisingly, it tends to lead real GDP.

Source: Adapted from the Statistics Canada CANSIM database, Series v1992067, v7687.

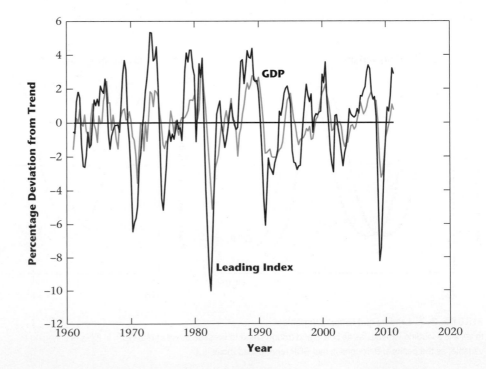

THE COMPONENTS OF GDP

In Figure 3.9 we show the percentage deviations from trend in real aggregate consumption (the black line) and real GDP (the coloured line). Clearly, the deviations from trend in consumption and in GDP are highly positively correlated, in that consumption tends to be above (below) trend when GDP is above (below) trend; these two time series move very closely together. The correlation coefficient between the percentage deviation from trend in real consumption and the percentage deviation from trend in real GDP is 0.80, which is greater than zero, so consumption is procyclical. There appears to be no discernible lead/lag relationship between real consumption and real GDP in Figure 3.9—the turning points in consumption do not appear to lead or lag the turning points in real GDP. Thus, consumption is a coincident variable.

From Figure 3.9, note that consumption is less variable than GDP, in that the deviations from trend in consumption tend to be smaller than those in GDP. In Chapter 9 we will study the theory of consumption decisions over time, and this theory will explain why consumption tends to be smoother than GDP. For the data displayed in Figure 3.9, the standard deviation of the percentage deviations in real consumption is 82.9% of that for real GDP. This is a more precise measure of what our eyes tell us about Figure 3.9, which is that consumption is smoother than GDP.

The percentage deviations from trend in real investment (the black line) and real GDP (the coloured line) are plotted in Figure 3.10. As with consumption, investment is procyclical, since it tends to be above (below) trend when GDP is above (below) trend. The correlation coefficient between the percentage deviations from trend in investment and those in GDP is 0.80. There is no tendency for investment to lead or lag GDP from

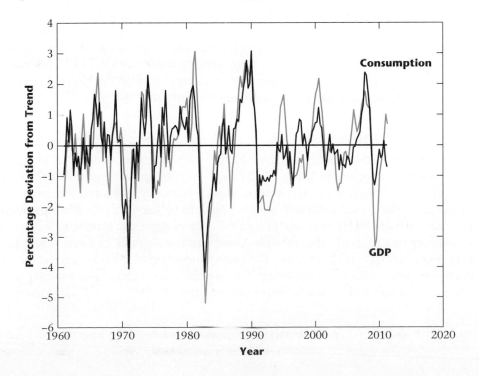

FIGURE 3.9
Percentage Deviations from Trend in Real Consumption (black line) and Real GDP (coloured line) for Canada, 1961–2011
From the figure, we can observe that consumption is procyclical, coincident, and less variable than GDP.

Source: Adapted from the Statistics Canada CANSIM database, Series v1992067, v1992044.

FIGURE 3.10

Percentage Deviations from Trend in Real Investment (black line) and Real GDP (coloured line) for Canada, 1961–2011

We can observe from the figure that investment is pro-cyclical, coincident, and more variable than GDP.

Source: Adapted from the Statistics Canada CANSIM database, Series v1992052, v1992057, v1992067.

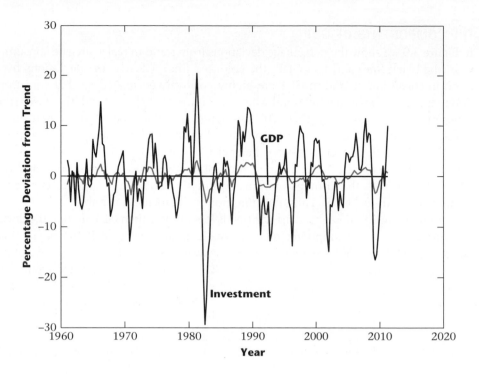

Figure 3.10, and so investment is a coincident variable. However, it is well known that some components of investment, in particular residential investment and inventory investment, tend to lead the business cycle. In contrast to consumption, investment is much more volatile than is GDP. This is indicated in Figure 3.10, where the deviations from trend in investment tend to be much larger than those for GDP. The standard deviation of the percentage deviations from trend in investment is 519.1% of what it is for GDP. Given that some components of investment lead GDP and that it is highly volatile, investment can play a very important role over the business cycle.

NOMINAL VARIABLES

The correlation between money prices and aggregate economic activity has long been of interest to macroeconomists. In the 1950s, A. W. Phillips[5] observed that there was a negative relationship between the rate of change in money wages and the unemployment rate in the United Kingdom, one that came to be known as the **Phillips curve**. If we take the unemployment rate to be a measure of aggregate economic activity (as we will see in Chapter 6, the unemployment rate is a strongly countercyclical variable; when real GDP is above trend, the unemployment rate is low), then the Phillips curve captures a positive relationship between the rate of change in a money price (the money wage) and the level of aggregate economic activity. Since Phillips made his

---

[5]See A. W. Phillips, 1958, "The Relationship between Unemployment and the Rate of Change in Money Wages in the United Kingdom, 1861–1957," *Economica* 25, 283–299.

initial observation, "Phillips curve" has come to be applied to any positive relationship between the rate of change in money prices or wages, or the deviation from trend in money prices or wages, and the deviation from trend in aggregate economic activity. As we will see in Chapter 18, observed Phillips curves are notoriously unstable—that is, they tend to shift over time—and there are sound theories to explain this instability. In the 1961–2011 period the deviations from trend in the price level and deviations from trend in GDP, are essentially uncorrelated. There is no discernible correlation in Figure 3.11, and the correlation coefficient for the two variables is –.05. Thus there is no evidence of a Phillips curve relation, and the price level is acyclical.

Note from Figure 3.12 that the price level (the black line) is about as variable as real GDP (the coloured line); the standard deviation of the percentage deviations from trend in the price level is 101.0% of that for GDP. Also, the price level tends to be much smoother than most asset prices. For example, the average price of shares traded on the Toronto Stock Exchange is highly variable relative to the money prices of goods and services. In Figure 3.12 there appears to be no tendency for the price level to lead or lag real GDP, so that the price level appears to be coincident.

Whether the price level is procyclical or countercyclical, and whether it is a leading or a lagging variable, can play an important role in resolving debates concerning the causes of business cycles, as we will see in Chapters 13 and 14. In contrast to the 1961–2011 Canadian data examined above, it appears that the price level was a procyclical variable over some periods of history in some countries (see Macroeconomics in Action 3.2), for example, in Canada during the period between the World Wars, and the price level is countercyclical in U.S. post-World War II data.

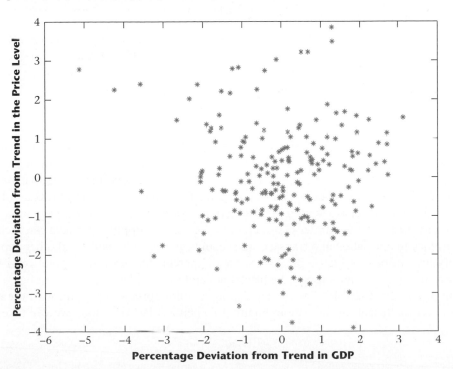

FIGURE 3.11

Scatter Plot for the Percentage Deviations from Trend in the Price Level (the Implicit GDP Price Deflator) and Real GDP for Canada, 1961–2011

The figure shows a correlation between the two variables which is essentially zero for 1961–2011. Therefore, the price level is acyclical for the period 1961–2011.

Source: Adapted from the Statistics Canada CANSIM database, Series v1992067, v1997756.

The Correlation between the Price Level and Aggregate Output across Countries and over Time

In Chapters 12 through 14 we will study how the comovements among macroeconomic variables can be affected by the types of shocks that are hitting the economy, the relative severity of those shocks, and the manner in which macroeconomic policy reacts to these shocks. One interesting way this is reflected in the data is in the correlation we see between the price level and aggregate output. For example, a decrease in aggregate productivity will tend to increase the price level and reduce aggregate output, producing a negative correlation between these two variables, or a countercyclical price level. However, an increase in the money supply, engineered by the Bank of Canada, will tend to increase the price level and increase aggregate output, producing a procyclical price level. If the Bank of Canada reacts to a negative shock to aggregate productivity by increasing the money supply, then the price level could be observed to be countercyclical or procyclical. Whether the price level is countercyclical or procyclical in the data might then be determined by whether shocks to aggregate productivity or money supply shocks

are more important, or by how monetary policy reacts to shocks to the economy.

David Backus and Patrick Kehoe have studied the properties of business cycles across countries and over long periods of time.[6] A finding of theirs is that the correlations among real aggregate variables are remarkably similar across countries and over time. However, the correlation between the price level and aggregate output is not. After World War II, the price level was countercyclical in most of the countries that Backus and Kehoe studied.[7] But before World War I and between the World Wars, the price level was procyclical in most of the countries in this set. This is an important piece of information that will be useful for us in evaluating theories of the business cycle in Chapters 13 and 14.

---

[6]See D. Backus and P. Kehoe, 1992, "International Evidence on the Historical Properties of Business Cycles," *American Economic Review* 82, 864–888.

[7]Australia, Canada, Denmark, Germany, Italy, Japan, Norway, Sweden, the United Kingdom, and the United States.

In addition to Phillips curve relationships and reverse Phillips curve relationships, a key element of the comovement between nominal variables and aggregate economic activity is the positive correlation between deviations from trend in the nominal money supply and deviations from trend in real GDP. The money supply is a measure of the nominal quantity of assets used in making transactions in the economy. Depending on the measure of money under consideration, the money supply in Canada can include currency in circulation and transactions accounts at chartered banks and other depository institutions. In Figure 3.13 we show the percentage deviations from trend in a measure of the money supply (the black line) and in real GDP (the coloured line) over the period 1961–2011.[8] The money supply is mildly procyclical here, with the correlation coefficient for the data in Figure 3.13 being 0.19. Therefore, we will take the

---

[8]The money supply measure used here is the *monetary base*, a narrow measure of money. In Chapters 12 and 17, we will discuss the measurement of the money supply in more detail.

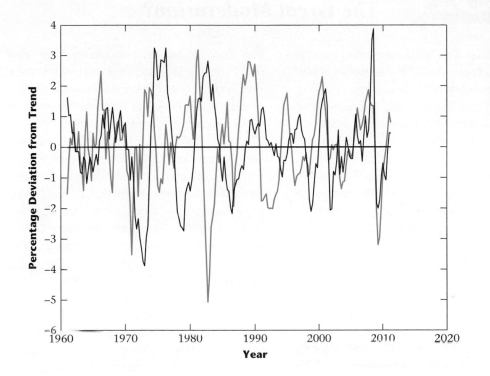

FIGURE 3.12

Price Level and GDP for Canada, 1961–2011

This figure shows the time series plot of the same data as in Figure 3.11. Here, we see that the price level (the black line) is countercyclical, coincident, and about as variable as real GDP (the coloured line).

Source: Adapted from the Statistics Canada CANSIM database, Series v1992067, v1997756.

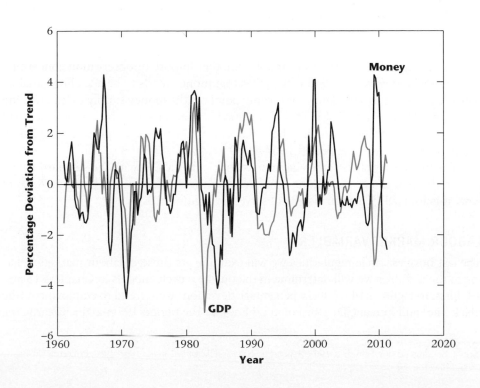

FIGURE 3.13

Percentage Deviations from Trend in the Money Supply (black line) and Real GDP (coloured line) for Canada, 1961–2011

Money is a procyclical and leading variable, and it is more variable than real GDP.

Source: Adapted from the Statistics Canada CANSIM database, Series v1192067, v37145.

The Great Moderation is a period running from the mid-1980s until about 2007 that featured relatively low variability in real GDP about trend, as well as low inflation and low variability in prices about trend. These features of the data are most pronounced for the United States, but some researchers have claimed that this pattern exists more widely. For example, Peter Summers[10] claims that a decline in the variability of real GDP occurred in Canada, France, Germany, Italy, Japan, the U.K., the U.S., and Australia after about 1985.

Consider the data displayed in Figure 3.12. If there were a Great Moderation in Canada, what we should observe is a decline in absolute percentage deviations from trend in the period 1986–2007, relative to 1961–1985. In fact, if we calculate the standard deviation of percentage deviations from trend in real GDP, this was 1.39 for 1961–1985, and 1.32 for 1986–2007. This might be characterized as a

Very Small Moderation, but certainly not a Great one. Further, if we include the most recent recession, and calculate the standard deviation for the period 1986–2011, we get 1.37, which is very close to the standard deviation for 1961–1985.

The United States certainly did experience a Great Moderation; the variability in real GDP about trend is much larger for 1961–1985 than for 1986–2007. The difference between the U.S. and Canada in this respect is explained primarily by two recessions: the 1973–1975 recession was mild in Canada and severe in the United States, while the recession in the early 1990s was mild in the United States and severe in Canada.

The picture is very different when we look at the behaviour of inflation and the price level in Canada, rather than GDP variability. If we measure the inflation rate as the percentage change in the implicit GDP price deflator from four quarters

money supply to be a procyclical variable. Another important observation concerning the nominal money supply and real GDP is that money tends to be a leading variable, which we observe as a tendency for turning points in the money supply to lead turning points in GDP in Figure 3.13. This observation was emphasized by Milton Friedman and Anna Schwartz,[9] who studied the behaviour of the money supply and real GDP in the United States over the period 1867–1960.

The money supply is somewhat more variable than GDP, with the standard deviation of the percentage deviations from trend in the money supply being 127.3% of what it is for GDP. This can also be observed in Figure 3.13.

LABOUR MARKET VARIABLES

The last business cycle regularities we will examine are those in labour markets, relating to the variables we will determine in the business cycle models in Chapters 13 and 14. First, in Figure 3.14 we show percentage deviations from trend in employment (the black line) and in real GDP (the coloured line) for the period 1976–2011. Clearly, the

---

[9]See M. Friedman and A. Schwartz, 1963, *A Monetary History of the United States: 1867–1960*, Princeton University Press, Princeton, NJ.

previously, then the average Canadian inflation rate was 6.4% for 1962–1985, 2.5% for 1986–2007, and 2.4% for 1986–2011. The standard deviation in percentage deviations from trend in the implicit GDP price deflator was 1.66 for 1961–1985, .91 for 1986–2007, and 1.08 for 1986–2011. Therefore, the inflation rate dropped, and prices became more stable in the period after 1985 than in the period before, so there was an unambiguous moderation in this respect.

The reduction in the inflation rate and lower price level variability after 1985 can be attributed mainly to the policies of the Bank of Canada, which has been committed to inflation control at least since the late 1970s, and adopted explicit inflation targets in 1991. In other countries, particularly the United States, researchers have attempted to disentangle the reasons for the moderation in real GDP variability after 1985. Generally, the Great

Moderation in the United States has been attributed in varying proportions to better macroeconomic policy, financial development, and good luck.[11] However, Canadian and U.S. monetary policies differ little in practice, and financial development in Canada and the United States has been similar. Therefore, if we are looking for an explanation of why the U.S. experienced a moderation in real GDP variability and Canada did not, the best one seems to be that Canadian luck was worse than the U.S.'s over this period.

---

[10]See P. Summers, 2005, "What Caused the Great Moderation? Some Cross-Country Evidence," *Federal Reserve Bank of Kansas City Economic Review*, Third Quarter, 5–32.

[11]See www.federalreserve.gov/boarddocs/speeches/2004/20040220/default.htm.

---

deviations from trend in employment closely track those in real GDP, and so employment is a procyclical variable. The correlation coefficient for the data in Figure 3.14 is 0.80. In terms of lead/lag relationships, we can observe a tendency in Figure 3.14 for turning points in employment to lag turning points in GDP, and so employment is a lagging variable. Employment is less variable than GDP, with the standard deviation of the percentage deviation from trend for employment being 83.4% of that for real GDP in Figure 3.14.

In the macroeconomic models we analyze, a key variable will be the market **real wage**, which is the purchasing power of the wage earned per hour worked for the average worker. This is measured from the data as the average money wage for all workers, divided by the price level. The cyclical behaviour of the real wage will prove to be crucial in helping us discriminate among different theories of the business cycle in Chapters 13 and 14. The weight of empirical evidence indicates that the real wage is procyclical.[12] We do not show data on the aggregate real wage, as it is difficult to measure the relationship between real wages and real GDP by examining aggregate data.

---

[12]For the evidence for the United States, see G. Solon, R. Barsky, and J. Parker, 1994, "Measuring the Cyclicality of Real Wages: How Important Is Composition Bias?" *Quarterly Journal of Economics*, February, 1–25.

FIGURE 3.14

Percentage Deviations from Trend in Employment (black line) and Real GDP (coloured line) for Canada, 1976–2011
Employment is procyclical; it is a lagging variable; and it is less variable than real GDP.

Source: Adapted from the Statistics Canada CANSIM database, Series v1992067, v2062811.

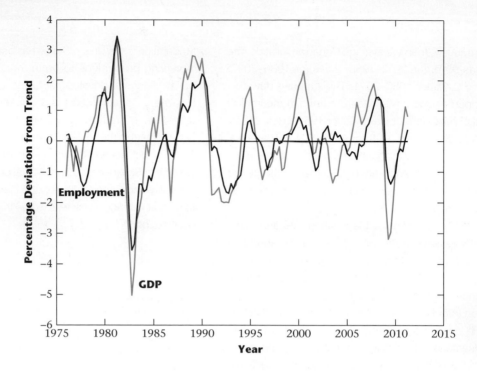

The key problem is that the composition of the labour force tends to change over the business cycle, which tends to bias the correlation between the real wage and real GDP. There is no strong evidence on whether the real wage is a leading or a lagging variable.

Productivity plays a key role in the economy, as was mentioned in Chapter 1, and in later chapters productivity will be an important element in our study of business cycles and economic growth. One measure of productivity is **average labour productivity**, Y/N, where Y is aggregate real output and N is total labour input. For our purposes Y is real GDP and N is total employment, so we are measuring average labour productivity as output per worker. In Figure 3.15 we show the percentage deviations from trend in real GDP (coloured line) and average labour productivity (black line). From the figure, average labour productivity is clearly a procyclical variable. The correlation coefficient for percentage deviations from trend in real GDP and average labour productivity is 0.63. Average labour productivity is less volatile than GDP; the standard deviation of the percentage deviations from trend in average labour productivity is 63.9% of that for real GDP. Further, there is no apparent tendency for average labour productivity to lead or lag real GDP in Figure 3.15, so average labour productivity is a coincident variable. In Chapters 13 and 14, the predictions of different business cycle theories for the comovements between average labour productivity and real GDP are important in helping us to evaluate and compare these theories.

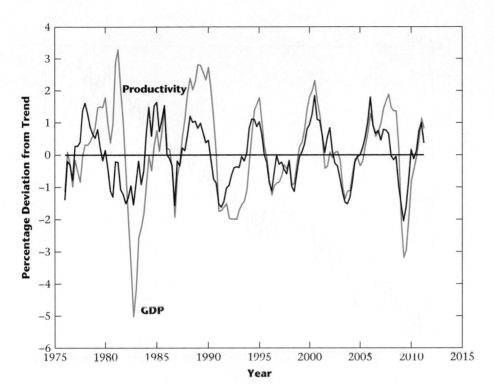

FIGURE 3.15

Percentage Deviations from Trend in Average Labour Productivity (black line) and Real GDP (coloured line)

Average labour productivity is procyclical and coincident, and it is less variable than real GDP.

Source: Adapted from the Statistics Canada CANSIM database, Series v1992067, v2062811.

SEASONAL ADJUSTMENT

The economic data we are studying in this chapter, and most data used in macroeconomic research and in formulating macroeconomic policy, is **seasonally adjusted**. That is, in most macroeconomic time series, there exists a predictable seasonal component. For example, GDP tends to be low during the summer months when workers are on vacation; investment expenditure tends to be low in the winter months when undertaking construction projects is more difficult; and the money supply tends to be high during the December holiday season, when the quantity of retail transactions is high.

There are various methods for seasonally adjusting data, but the basic idea is to observe historical seasonal patterns and then take out the extra amount that we tend to see on average during a particular week, month, or quarter, simply because of the time of year. For example, to seasonally adjust the money supply, in December we would want to subtract some quantity that is due only to the extra spending over the holiday season. To see what seasonal adjustment can do, in Figure 3.16 we show the seasonally adjusted quantity of employment and seasonally unadjusted employment for Canada from 1976–2011. In the figure, the smooth line is the seasonally adjusted time series, and the more variable line is unadjusted. As can be seen in the figure, there is a regular seasonal pattern that is repeated over time in the unadjusted time series, and seasonal adjustment tends to smooth out the time series. This is typical of the effect of seasonal adjustment on any time series.

FIGURE 3.16

Seasonally Adjusted (coloured line) and Unadjusted (black line) Employment, 1976–2011

Seasonal adjustment tends to smooth a time series with a seasonal component.

Source: Adapted from Statistics Canada CANSIM database, Series v2062811, v2064890.

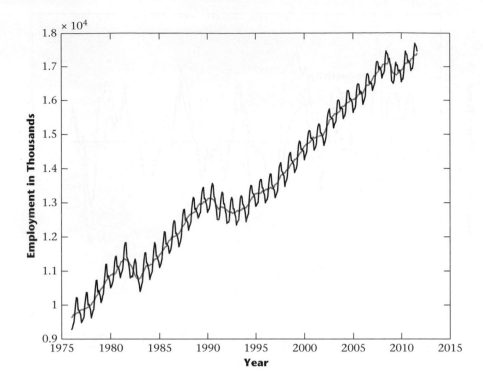

Working with seasonally adjusted data can often be the appropriate thing to do, but one has to be careful that the process of seasonal adjustment is not masking important phenomena that might interest us. For example, there may be economic factors that cause the nature of seasonality to change over time. For example, technological developments may make it less costly to build houses in the winter, and thus reduce the seasonal fluctuations we see in investment expenditure. If we confine our attention to only seasonally adjusted data, we might not be aware that this process is occurring.

COMOVEMENT SUMMARY

To summarize the business cycle facts discussed above, we present Table 3.1 and Table 3.2. These, particularly Table 3.2, will prove very useful, especially when we discuss the predictions of different theories of the business cycle in Chapters 13 and 14. A first test of the usefulness of macroeconomic theories is their ability to match what we see in macroeconomic data.

We have concluded our study of measurement issues, in that we now know the basics of national income accounting, basic macroeconomic accounting identities, price measurement, labour market facts, and business cycle facts. In the next chapters, we will proceed to build useful macroeconomic models, starting with some basic microeconomic principles concerning the behaviour of consumers and firms.

TABLE 3.1   Correlation Coefficients and Variability of Percentage Deviations from Trend

	Correlation Coefficient (GDP)	Std. Dev. (% of S.D. of GDP)
Consumption	0.80	82.9%
Investment	0.80	519.1
Price level	−0.05	101.0
Money supply	0.19	124.7
Employment	0.80	83.4
Average labour productivity	0.63	63.9

TABLE 3.2   Summary of Business Cycle Facts

	Cyclicality	Lead/Lag	Variability Relative to GDP
Consumption	Procyclical	Coincident	Smaller
Investment	Procyclical	Coincident	Larger
Price level	Acyclical	Coincident	Larger
Money supply	Procyclical	Leading	Larger
Employment	Procyclical	Lagging	Smaller
Real wage rate	Procyclical	?	?
Average labour productivity	Procyclical	Coincident	Smaller

Chapter Summary

- The key business cycle facts relate to the deviations of important macroeconomic variables from their trends and the comovements in these deviations from trend.

- The most important business cycle fact is that real GDP fluctuates about trend in an irregular fashion. Though deviations from trend in real GDP are persistent, there is no observed regularity in the amplitude or frequency of fluctuations in real GDP about trend.

- Business cycles are similar mainly in terms of the comovements among macroeconomic time series. Comovement can be discerned by plotting the percentage deviations from trend in two economic variables in a time series or in a scatter plot or by calculating the correlation coefficient between the percentage deviations from trend.

- We are interested principally in how a particular variable moves about trend relative to real GDP (be it procyclical, countercyclical, or acyclical); whether it is a leading, lagging, or coincident variable (relative to real GDP); and how variable it is relative to real GDP.

- Consumption is procyclical, coincident, and less variable than real GDP.

- Investment is procyclical, coincident, and more variable than real GDP.

- In the data set we examined here, the price level is acyclical, coincident, and less variable than GDP.

- The money supply is procyclical, leading, and about as variable as real GDP. The fact that the money supply tends to lead real GDP was assigned much importance by Milton Friedman.

- In the labour market, employment is procyclical, lagging, and less variable than real GDP. The real wage, too, is procyclical. There is, however, no consensus among macroeconomists on whether the real wage is a leading or a lagging variable. Average labour productivity is procyclical, coincident, and less variable than real GDP.

- Seasonal adjustment is a process that smooths out predictable fluctuations in an economic variable associated with the day of the week, or the month or quarter of the year. Macroeconomists typically study data that is seasonally adjusted.

Key Terms

business cycles: Fluctuations about trend in real GDP.

peak: A relatively large positive deviation from trend in real GDP.

trough: A relatively large negative deviation from trend in real GDP.

turning points: Peaks and troughs in real GDP.

amplitude: The maximum deviation from trend in an economic time series.

frequency: The number of peaks in an economic time series that occur per year.

boom: A series of positive deviations from trend in real GDP, culminating in a peak.

recession: A series of negative deviations from trend in real GDP, culminating in a trough.

persistent: Describes an economic time series that tends to stay above (below) trend when it has been above (below) trend during the recent past.

comovement: How aggregate economic variables move together over the business cycle.

time series: Sequential measurements of an economic variable over time.

positive correlation: Relationship between two economic time series when a straight line fit to a scatter plot of the two variables has a positive slope.

negative correlation: Relationship between two economic time series when a straight line fit to a scatter plot of the two variables has a negative slope.

scatter plot: A plot of two variables, x and y, with x measured on the horizontal axis, and y measured on the vertical axis.

procyclical: Describes an economic variable that tends to be above (below) trend when real GDP is above (below) trend.

countercyclical: Describes an economic variable that tends to be below (above) trend when real GDP is above (below) trend.

acyclical: Describes an economic variable that is neither procyclical nor countercyclical.

correlation coefficient: A measure of the degree of correlation between two variables.

perfectly positively correlated: Describes two variables that have a correlation coefficient of 1.

perfectly negatively correlated: Describes two variables that have a correlation coefficient of −1.

leading variable: An economic variable that helps to predict future real GDP.

lagging variable: An economic variable that past real GDP helps to predict.

coincident variable: An economic variable that neither leads nor lags real GDP.

composite index of business leading indicators or **index of leading indicators:** A weighted average of leading macroeconomic variables, which is sometimes used to forecast the deviations of real GDP from trend.

standard deviation: A measure of variability. The cyclical variability in an economic time series can be measured by the standard deviation of the percentage deviations from trend.

Phillips curve: A positive correlation between a money price or the rate of change in a money price, and a measure of aggregate economic activity.

real wage: The purchasing power of the wage earned per hour worked.
average labour productivity: Total output divided by labour input.
seasonal adjustment: the process of smoothing a time series by removing predictable fluctuations associated with the day of the week or the month or quarter of the year.

Questions for Review

1. What is the primary defining feature of business cycles?
2. Besides persistence, what are three important features of the deviations from trend in GDP?
3. Explain why forecasting GDP over the long term is difficult.
4. Why are the comovements in aggregate economic variables important?
5. What did Robert Lucas say about the comovements among economic variables?
6. How can we discern positive and negative correlation in a time series plot? In a scatter plot?
7. Why is the index of leading economic indicators useful for forecasting GDP?
8. What are the three features of comovement that macroeconomists are interested in?
9. Describe the key business cycle regularities in consumption and investment expenditures.
10. What are the key business cycle regularities with respect to the price level and the money supply?
11. Does a Phillips curve relationship exist in the data set that was studied in this chapter?
12. What are the key business cycle regularities in the labour market?
13. Why do macroeconomists work with seasonally adjusted data?

Problems

1. We have measured average labour productivity in this chapter as Y/N, where Y is real GDP and N is employment. The business cycle facts concerning employment relate to how the denominator N comoves with the numerator Y, and those concerning average labour productivity relate to how Y/N comoves with Y. Explain how the business cycle facts concerning employment and average labour productivity in Table 3.1 and Table 3.2 are consistent.

2. Consumption of durables is more variable relative to trend than consumption of semi-durables, and consumption of semi-durables is more variable relative to trend than consumption of nondurables and services. Speculate on why we observe these phenomena, and relate this to the key business cycle facts in Table 3.1 and Table 3.2.

3. In Figure 3.17 the percentage deviations from trend in GDP (Y) and government expenditures (G) for the period 1961–2011 are plotted. Figure 3.18 is a scatter plot of the same data.
   a. Which is more variable, Y or G?
   b. Is G procyclical, countercyclical, or acyclical, and how can you tell? What do you think explains this?
   c. Is there any tendency for G to lead or lag Y, or is G coincident?
   d. Do you find any of these characteristics of the relationship between real GDP and government spending surprising? Explain.

FIGURE 3.17
Percentage Deviations from Trend in Real GDP (coloured line) and Government Expenditures (black line)

Source: Adapted from Statistics Canada CANSIM database, Series v1992067, v1992049, v1992050, v1992051.

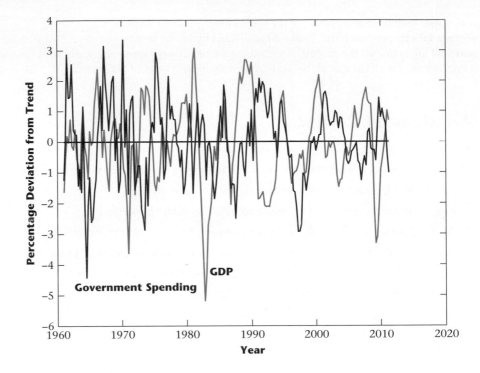

FIGURE 3.18
Scatter Plot of Government Expenditures against Real GDP

Source: Adapted from Statistics Canada CANSIM database, Series v1992067, v1992049, v1992050, v1992051. 4

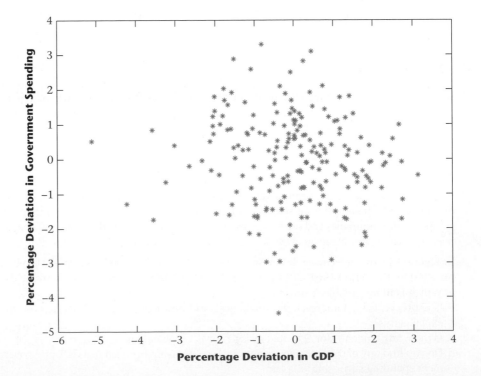

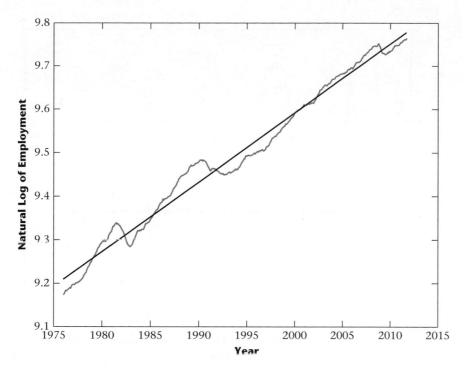

FIGURE 3.19

Natural Log of Employment and Linear Trend

Source: Adapted from Statistics Canada CANSIM database, Series v2062811.

4. In Figure 3.19, the natural logarithm of employment is displayed, along with a linear time trend fit to the data. The linear time trend, which is the best fit to actual employment, tells us that employment grew on average by 1.6% per year over the period 1976–2011. An interesting feature of Figure 3.19 is that it can sometimes take a very long time for employment to return to trend after a recession. After the 1981–1982 recession, it took only a couple of years for employment to return to trend, but this took about eight years after the 1990–1992 recession. To highlight this phenomenon, take note of Figure 3.20, which shows the percentage deviation of employment from the linear trend. Discuss why this phenomenon might be important, and comment on the behaviour of employment following the 2008–2009 recession.

5. Suppose I were to count the number of birds I see flying south, and also measure the temperature each day (averaged over 24 hours).

   a. If I plotted the two measured time series, and also constructed a scatter plot of number of birds flying south versus temperature, show what I would see.

   b. Considering the lead/lag relationships between birds flying south and temperature, what should I conclude about what is causing what?

   c. Explain the lesson here for how we should make inferences from lead/lag patterns in economic data.

   d. Milton Friedman liked to argue that, because money leads real GDP in the data, the fluctuations in money were causing the fluctuations in real GDP. Evaluate this argument.

6. Sometimes Phillips curve relationships are described in terms of inflation and unemployment. If a Phillips curve relationship of this type exists in the data, we should observe a negative correlation between the inflation rate and the unemployment rate. Figure 3.21 shows a scatter plot of annual inflation rates versus the unemployment rate for Canada over the period 1976–2010. Explain what you see, and discuss.

FIGURE 3.20
Percentage Deviation of Employment from a Linear Trend

Source: Adapted from Statistics Canada CANSIM database, Series v2062811.

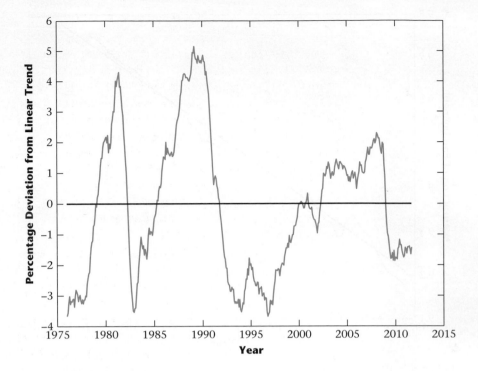

FIGURE 3.21
A Phillips Curve?

Source: Adapted from Statistics Canada CANSIM database, Series v2062815, v1997756.

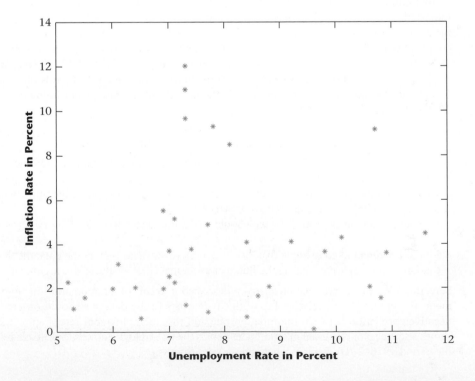

One-Period Models
of the Macroeconomy

In Part 2, two working models of the macroeconomy are constructed that can be used to analyze some key macroeconomic issues. The basic building blocks of both models will be the microeconomic behaviour of consumers and firms. We start in Chapter 4 by analyzing the behaviour of a representative consumer and a representative firm, with each making decisions over one period. The representative consumer's fundamental choice in this environment concerns how to allocate time between work and leisure, making himself or herself as well off as possible while obeying his or her budget constraint. The representative firm chooses how much labour it should hire so as to maximize profits. In Chapter 5, consumer behaviour and firm behaviour is built into a one-period macroeconomic model, in which there is a government that can spend and tax. This model is used to show that, under ideal conditions, free-market outcomes can be socially efficient, that government spending crowds out private consumption while increasing aggregate output, and that increases in productivity increase welfare, consumption, and aggregate output.

In Chapter 6, another one-period model is constructed that can deal with different issues, in particular the basic determinants of search behaviour in the labour market, and unemployment. This requires a somewhat different approach, but we will still be dealing with the behaviour of productive firms, and consumers who supply labour to those firms. We will explore the effects of unemployment insurance and productivity on unemployment, and take a first pass at Keynesian ideas, under which market outcomes may not be socially efficient.

4

Consumer and Firm Behaviour: The Work–Leisure Decision and Profit Maximization

Whereas Chapters 2 and 3 focused on how we measure variables of macroeconomic interest, we will now turn to the construction and analysis of a particular macroeconomic model. Recall that in Chapter 1, we saw how a macroeconomic model is built from a description of consumers and their preferences over goods, and of firms and the technology available to produce goods from available resources. In this chapter, we focus on the behaviour of consumers and firms in a simple model environment *with only one time period.* One-period decision making for consumers and firms will limit the kinds of macroeconomic issues we can address with the resulting model. However, this simplification will make it easier to understand the basic microeconomic principles of consumer and firm optimization on which we will build in the rest of this book. Given that there is only one time period, consumers and firms will make **static**, as opposed to **dynamic**, **decisions**. Dynamic decision making involves planning over more than one period, as, for example, when individuals make decisions concerning how much to spend today and how much to save for the future. Dynamic decisions will be analyzed in Part 3.

With regard to consumer behaviour, we will focus on how a consumer makes choices concerning the tradeoff between consuming and working. For the consumer, consuming more goods comes at a cost: the consumer must work harder and will enjoy less leisure time. Primarily, we are interested in how a consumer's work–leisure choice is affected by his or her preferences and by the constraints he or she faces. For example, we want to know how a change in the market wage rate and in the consumer's nonwage income affects his or her choices concerning how much to work, how much to consume, and how much leisure time to take. For the firm, we focus on how the available technology for producing goods and the market environment influence the firm's decision concerning how much labour to hire during the period.

As was discussed in Chapter 1, a fundamental principle that we adhere to here is that consumers and firms *optimize.* That is, a consumer wants to make himself or herself as well off as possible given the constraints he or she faces. Likewise, a firm acts to maximize profits given market prices and the available technology. The optimization principle is a very powerful and useful tool in economics, and it helps in sharpening the predictions of economic models. Given optimizing behaviour by consumers and firms, we can then analyze how these economic agents will respond to changes in the environment they live in. For example, we will show how consumers and firms change their labour supply and labour demand, respectively, in response to a change in the market wage rate, and how consumers respond to a change in taxes. The knowledge we build up in this chapter concerning these optimal responses will be critical in the next chapter, where we study what happens in the economy as a whole in the event of an important shock to the system, for example, a large increase in government spending or a major new invention.

The Representative Consumer

To begin, we will consider the behaviour of a single representative consumer, who will act as a stand-in for all of the consumers in the economy. We will show how to represent a consumer's preferences over the available goods in the economy, and how to represent the consumer's budget constraint, which tells us what goods it is feasible for the consumer to purchase given market prices. We then put preferences together with the budget constraint to determine how the consumer will behave given market prices, and how he or she responds to a change in nonwage income and to a change in the market wage rate.

THE REPRESENTATIVE CONSUMER'S PREFERENCES

It will prove simplest to analyze consumer choice, and it will be adequate for the issues we will want to address in this chapter and the next to suppose that there are two goods that consumers desire. The first is a physical good, which we can think of as an aggregation of all consumer goods in the economy, or measured aggregate consumption. We will call this the **consumption good**. The second good is **leisure**, which is any time spent not working in the market. Thus, in terms of our definition, leisure might include recreational activities, sleep, and work at home (cooking, yard work, housecleaning).

For macroeconomic purposes, it proves convenient to suppose that all consumers in the economy are identical. In reality, of course, consumers are not identical, but for many macroeconomic issues diversity among consumers is not essential to addressing the economics of the problem at hand, and considering it will only cloud our thinking. Identical consumers will in general behave in identical ways, so we need only analyze the behaviour of one consumer. Further, if all consumers are identical, the economy will behave *as if* there were only one, and it is therefore convenient to write down the model as having only a single, representative consumer. We must recognize, however, that the **representative consumer** in our model is a stand-in for all consumers in the economy.

A key step in determining how the representative consumer makes choices is to show how we can capture the preferences of the representative consumer over leisure and consumption goods by a **utility function**, written as

$$U(C, l),$$

where U is the utility function, C is the quantity of consumption, and l is the quantity of leisure. We will refer to a particular combination of consumption and leisure—for example, (C_1, l_1), where C_1 is a particular consumption quantity and l_1 is a particular quantity of leisure—as a **consumption bundle**. The utility function represents how the consumer ranks different consumption bundles. That is, suppose that there are two different consumption bundles, representing different quantities of consumption and leisure, denoted (C_1, l_1) and (C_2, l_2). We say that (C_1, l_1) is *strictly preferred* by the consumer to (C_2, l_2) if

$$U(C_1, l_1) > U(C_2, l_2);$$

(C_2, l_2) is strictly preferred to (C_1, l_1) if

$$U(C_1, l_1) < U(C_2, l_2);$$

and the consumer is indifferent between the two consumption bundles if

$$U(C_1, l_1) = U(C_2, l_2).$$

It is useful to think of $U(C, l)$ as giving the level of happiness, or utility, that the consumer receives from consuming the bundle (C, l). Note, however, that the actual level of utility is irrelevant; all that matters for the consumer is what the level of utility is from a given consumption bundle *relative* to another one.

To use our representation of the consumer's preferences for analyzing macroeconomic issues, we must make some assumptions concerning the form that preferences take. These assumptions are useful for making the analysis work, and they are also consistent with how consumers actually behave. We will assume that the representative consumer's preferences have three properties: more is preferred to less; the consumer likes diversity in his or her consumption bundle; and consumption and leisure are normal goods. We will discuss each of these in turn.

1. *More is always preferred to less.* A consumer always prefers a consumption bundle that contains more consumption, more leisure, or both. This may appear unnatural, since it seems that we can get too much of a good thing. For example, consuming too much of one good may sometimes make us worse off, as when we overeat. However, in terms of general consumption goods, the average consumer in Canada today consumes far more than the average consumer 200 years ago would have dreamed possible, and it certainly seems that the average consumer today in Canada would like to consume more if it were feasible. Indeed, even the extremely wealthy appear to desire more than they have.

2. *The consumer likes diversity in his or her consumption bundle.* To see that this is a natural property of consumer preferences, consider a consumer who, instead of consuming consumption goods and leisure, is making a decision about where to eat lunch during the week. Lynn can go to one of two restaurants to eat lunch, one of which serves only hamburgers, and the other serves only tuna sandwiches. One choice open to Lynn is to eat a hamburger for lunch on each day of the week, and another choice is to eat tuna sandwiches all week. Suppose that Lynn is indifferent between these two choices. However, if she has a preference for diversity, Lynn would prefer to alternate between restaurants during the week rather than eat at one place every day. In the case of our representative consumer, who is choosing among consumption bundles with different combinations of consumption goods and leisure, a preference for diversity means that, if the consumer is indifferent between two consumption bundles, then some mixture of the two consumption bundles will be preferable to either one. At the extreme, suppose that the consumer is indifferent between a consumption bundle that has 6 units of consumption and no leisure and another bundle that has no consumption goods and 8 units of leisure. Then, a preference for diversity implies that the consumer would prefer a third consumption bundle, consisting of half of each of the other bundles, to having either of the other consumption bundles. This preferable third consumption bundle would have 3 units of consumption goods and 4 units of leisure.

3. *Consumption and leisure are normal goods.* A good is normal for a consumer if the quantity of the good that he or she purchases increases when income increases. For example, meals at high-quality restaurants are a **normal good** for most people; if our income increases, we tend to eat out more in good places. In contrast, a good is inferior for a consumer if he or she purchases less of that good when income increases. An example of an **inferior good** is food from Harvey's; most people would tend to eat less at Harvey's as their income increases. In our model, then, given that consumption and leisure are normal goods, the representative consumer will purchase more consumption goods and increase his or her leisure time when income increases. This seems intuitively appealing; if, for example, you received a windfall increase in your income, perhaps through an inheritance, you would probably want to consume more goods as well as taking more vacation time (leisure). In practice, the behaviour of consumers is consistent with consumption and leisure being normal goods.

Although we will postpone discussion of property 3 of the representative consumer's preferences until we have more machinery to analyze how the consumer behaves, our next step will be to show how we represent properties 1 and 2 graphically. It is helpful to consider the representative consumer's preferences by using a graphical representation of the utility function, called the **indifference map**. The indifference map is a family of **indifference curves**.

DEFINITION

An **indifference curve** connects a set of points, with these points representing consumption bundles among which the consumer is indifferent.

FIGURE 4.1

Indifference Curves

The figure shows two indifference curves for the consumer. Each indifference curve represents a set of consumption bundles among which the consumer is indifferent. Higher indifference curves represent higher welfare for the consumer.

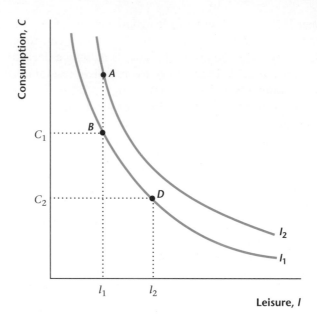

Figure 4.1 shows two indifference curves. In the figure, I_1 is an indifference curve, and two points on the indifference curve are (C_1, l_1) (point B) and (C_2, l_2) (point D). Since these two consumption bundles lie on the same indifference curve, we must have $U(C_1, l_1) = U(C_2, l_2)$. That is, being indifferent implies that the consumer obtains the same level of happiness from each consumption bundle. Another indifference curve is I_2. Since indifference curve I_2 lies above indifference curve I_1, and we know more is preferred to less, consumption bundles on I_2 are strictly preferred to consumption bundles on I_1. For example, consider point A, which represents a consumption bundle with the same quantity of leisure as at point B, but with a higher quantity of the consumption good. Since more is preferred to less, A is strictly preferred to B.

An indifference curve has two key properties:

1. An indifference curve slopes downward.

2. An indifference curve is convex, that is, bowed in toward the origin.

Since the indifference map is just the graphical representation of preferences, it should not be surprising that the properties of the indifference curve are related to the properties of preferences 1 and 2, described above. In fact, property 1 of an indifference curve follows from property 1 of preferences (more is always preferred to less), and property 2 of an indifference curve follows from property 2 of preferences (the consumer likes diversity in his or her consumption bundles).

To see why the fact that indifference curves slope downward follows from the fact that more is preferred to less, consider Figure 4.2. At point A, consumption is C_1 and leisure is l_1. Suppose that we now consider holding the quantity of leisure constant for the consumer at l_1 and reduce the consumer's quantity of consumption to C_2, so that the consumer now has the consumption bundle represented by point D. Since more is preferred to less, point D must be on a lower indifference curve (indifference curve I_2)

than is point A (on indifference curve I_1). Now we can ask how much leisure we would have to add to l_1, holding consumption constant at C_2, to obtain a consumption bundle B such that the consumer is indifferent between A and B. Point B must lie below and to the right of point A since, if we are taking consumption goods away from the consumer, we need to give him or her more leisure. Thus, the indifference curve I_1 is downward-sloping because more is preferred to less.

To understand why the convexity of the indifference curve follows from the preference of the representative consumer for diversity, it is useful to introduce the following concept.

DEFINITION

The **marginal rate of substitution** of leisure for consumption, denoted $MRS_{l,C}$, is the rate at which the consumer is just willing to substitute leisure for consumption goods.

We have

$$MRS_{l,C} = -[\text{The slope of the indifference curve passing through } (C, l)].$$

To see why the **marginal rate of substitution** is minus the slope of the indifference curve, consider consumption bundles A and B in Figure 4.2. There, the rate at which the consumer is willing to substitute leisure for consumption in moving from A to B is the ratio $\dfrac{C_1 - C_2}{l_2 - l_1}$, or minus the slope of the line segment AB. Minus the slope of AB tells us how much consumption we need to take away for each unit of leisure added as we move from A to B, with the consumer being just indifferent between A and B. If we imagine choosing a point like point B on the indifference curve I_1 below point

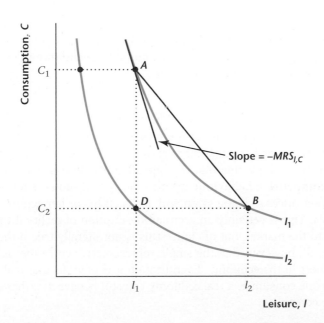

Consumption, C

C_1 ······ A

Slope $= -MRS_{l,C}$

C_2 ······ D ⋮ B

I_1

I_2

l_1 ⋮ l_2

Leisure, l

FIGURE 4.2

Properties of Indifference Curves

Indifference curves are downward-sloping because more is preferred to less. A preference for diversity implies that indifference curves are convex (bowed in toward the origin). The slope of an indifference curve is the negative of the marginal rate of substitution.

A but closer and closer to *A*, then as the distance between that point and *A* becomes small, the rate at which the consumer is willing to substitute leisure for consumption between *A* and the chosen point is the marginal rate of substitution, which is minus the slope of the indifference curve at point *A* (or minus the slope of a tangent to the indifference curve at *A*).

Suppose, for example, that Marla can choose how many weeks of vacation to take each year and that she currently works 50 weeks in the year and takes two weeks of vacation, so that her leisure time is two weeks. To keep things simple, suppose Marla consumes only coconuts, so that we can measure her consumption in coconuts. Currently, she eats 500 coconuts per year. If Marla were to take one more week of vacation per year, she would be just as happy as she is now if she were to give up 50 coconuts per year. This implies that Marla's marginal rate of substitution of leisure for consumption, given her current consumption bundle of 500 coconuts of consumption and two weeks of leisure, is 50 coconuts per week.

Stating that an indifference curve is convex (property 2 of the indifference curve) is identical to stating that the marginal rate of substitution is diminishing. That is, note that the indifference curve in Figure 4.2 becomes flatter as we move down the indifference curve from left to right, that is, as the consumer receives more leisure and less of the consumption good. Thus, minus the slope of the indifference curve becomes smaller as leisure increases and consumption decreases. In other words, the marginal rate of substitution is diminishing. As we increase the quantity of leisure and reduce the quantity of consumption, the consumer needs to be compensated more and more in terms of leisure time to give up another unit of consumption. The consumer requires this extra compensation because of a preference for diversity.

To give a concrete example of a preference for diversity in terms of a consumption–leisure choice, suppose that Allen sleeps 8 hours in every 24-hour period, and so has 112 hours per week to split between work and leisure. Consider two situations. In the first, Allen takes 10 hours of leisure per week and works 102 hours, and in the second he takes 102 hours of leisure per week and works 10 hours. In the first circumstance, Allen is willing to give up much more consumption expenditure in exchange for one extra hour of leisure than in the second case.

THE REPRESENTATIVE CONSUMER'S BUDGET CONSTRAINT

Now that we know something about the representative consumer's preferences, we must also specify his or her constraints and objectives in order to predict what he or she will do. We will assume that the representative consumer behaves competitively. Here, **competitive behaviour** means that the consumer is a *price-taker*; he or she treats market prices as being given and acts as if his or her actions have no effect on those prices. This is certainly an accurate description of reality if the consumer is small relative to the market, but of course this is not literally true if there is only one consumer. Recall, however, that the single representative consumer is a stand-in for all the consumers in the economy. Even though it is obvious that real economies do not have only one consumer, a real economy can still behave *as if* there were a single, representative consumer.

An important assumption that we make at this stage is that there is no money in this economy. That is, there is no government-supplied currency to be used in exchange and no banks through which people can conduct transactions—for example, through chequing accounts. For some macroeconomic issues, the complication of introducing money will not add anything to our analysis and is best left out. Later, however, in Chapters 12 to 14, we begin to analyze the role that money plays in the macroeconomy so that we can address issues such as the effects of inflation and the conduct of monetary policy.

An economy without monetary exchange is a **barter** economy. In a barter economy, all trade involves exchanges of goods for goods. There are only two goods here: consumption goods and time. When time is used at home, we call it leisure time, and when time is exchanged in the market, we call it work—more explicitly, labour time. Any trades in this economy must involve exchanges of labour time for consumption goods, or vice versa. The consumer is assumed to have h hours of time available, which can be allocated between leisure time, l, and time spent working (or labour supply), denoted by N^s. The **time constraint** for the consumer is then

$$l + N^s = h, \tag{4.1}$$

which states that leisure time plus time spent working must sum to total time available.

The Consumer's Real Disposable Income Having specified how the representative consumer allocates time between work and leisure, we can describe the consumer's real disposable income, which is wage income plus dividend income minus taxes.

Labour time is sold by the consumer in the labour market at a price w in terms of consumption goods. That is, one unit of labour time exchanges for w units of consumption goods. Therefore, w is the **real wage**, or the wage rate of the consumer in units of purchasing power. Throughout, the consumption good will play the role of **numeraire**, or the good in which all prices and quantities will be denominated. In actual economies, money is the numeraire, but in our barter economy model, the choice of numeraire is arbitrary. We choose the consumption good as numeraire, as this is a common convention.

If the consumer works N^s hours, then his or her real wage income will be wN^s, which is expressed in units of the consumption good. The second source of income for the consumer is profits distributed as dividends from firms. We will let π be the quantity of profits, in real terms, that the consumer receives. In our model, firms have to be owned by someone, and this someone must be the representative consumer. Therefore, any profits earned by firms must be distributed to the representative consumer as income, which we can think of as dividends. Thus, we will refer to π as real **dividend income**.

Finally, the consumer pays taxes to the government. We will assume that the real quantity of taxes is a lump-sum amount T. A **lump-sum tax** is a tax that does not depend in any way on the actions of the economic agent who is being taxed. In practice, no taxes are lump-sum; for example, the quantity of sales taxes we pay depends on the quantity of taxable goods that we buy, and our income taxes depend on how much we work. Taxes that are not lump-sum have important effects on the effective prices that consumers face in the market. For example, an increase in the sales tax on gasoline increases the effective price of gasoline for consumers relative to other goods. This change in the effective relative price of gasoline will in turn affect the demand for gasoline and for other goods. These distorting effects of taxation are important, but we will confine attention to lump-sum taxation for now, as this is simpler.

Real wage income plus real dividend income minus taxes is the consumer's real disposable income, and this is what the consumer has available to spend on consumption goods.

The Budget Constraint   Now that we know how the representative consumer can allocate time between work and leisure, and what his or her real disposable income is, we can derive the consumer's budget constraint algebraically and show it graphically.

We can view the representative consumer as receiving his or her real disposable income and spending it in the market for consumption goods. What actually happens, however, is that the consumer receives income and pays taxes in terms of consumption goods, and then he or she decides how much to consume out of this disposable income. Since this is a one-period economy, which implies that the consumer has no motive to save, and because the consumer prefers more to less, all disposable income is consumed, so that we have

$$C = wN^s + \pi - T, \tag{4.2}$$

or total real consumption equals real disposable income. Equation (4.2) is the consumer's **budget constraint**. Now, substituting for N^s in (4.2) by using (4.1), we get

$$C = w(h - l) + \pi - T \tag{4.3}$$

The interpretation of Equation (4.3) is that the right-hand side is real disposable income, while the left-hand side is expenditure on consumption goods, so that total market expenditure is equal to disposable income.

Alternatively if we add wl to both sides of (4.3), we get

$$C + wl = wh + \pi - T. \tag{4.4}$$

An interpretation of Equation (4.4) is that the right-hand side is the implicit quantity of real disposable income the consumer has, and the left-hand side is implicit expenditure on the two goods, consumption and leisure. On the right-hand side of (4.4), since the consumer has h units of time, with each unit of time valued in real terms according to the market real wage w, and $\pi - T$ is real dividend income minus taxes, the total quantity of implicit real disposable income is $wh + \pi - T$. On the left-hand side of (4.4), C is what is spent on consumption goods, while wl is what is implicitly "spent" on leisure. That is, w is the market price of leisure time, since each unit of leisure is forgone labour, and labour time is priced at the real wage w. Thus, $C + wl$ is implicit real expenditure on consumption goods and leisure.

To graph the consumer's budget constraint, it is convenient to write Equation (4.4) in slope–intercept form, with C as the dependent variable, to get

$$C = -wl + wh + \pi - T, \tag{4.5}$$

so that the slope of the budget constraint is $-w$, and the vertical intercept is $wh + \pi - T$. In Figure 4.3 we graph the budget constraint, Equation (4.5), as the line AB. Here, we have drawn the budget constraint for the case where $T > \pi$, so that dividend income minus taxes, $\pi - T$, is negative. Further, by setting $C = 0$ in Equation (4.5) and solving for l, we can get the horizontal intercept, $h + \dfrac{\pi - T}{w}$. The vertical intercept is the maximum quantity of consumption attainable for the consumer, which is what is achieved if the consumer works h hours and consumes no leisure. The horizontal intercept is the maximum number of hours of leisure that the consumer can take and still be able to pay the lump-sum tax.

Figure 4.4 shows what the consumer's budget constraint looks like in the case where $T < \pi$, in which case dividend income minus taxes, $\pi - T$, is positive. Here, the budget constraint is somewhat unusual, as it is kinked; the slope of the budget constraint is $-w$ over its upper portion, and the constraint is vertical over its lower portion. There is a kink in the budget constraint because the consumer cannot consume more than h hours of leisure. Thus, at point B we have $l = h$, which implies that the number of hours worked by the consumer is zero. Points along BD all involve the consumer working zero hours and consuming some amount $C \leq \pi - T$—that is, the consumer always has the option of throwing away some of his or her dividend income. Even though the consumer does not work at point B, we have $C = \pi - T > 0$, as dividend income exceeds taxes. In what follows, we will always consider the case where $\pi - T > 0$, as this is the more complicated case (because of the kink in the consumer's budget constraint) and because ultimately it will not make any difference for our analysis whether we look only at the case $\pi - T > 0$ or $\pi - T < 0$.

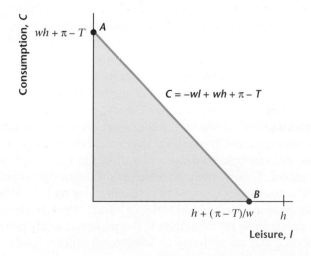

FIGURE 4.3

Representative Consumer's Budget Constraint (T > π)

The figure shows the consumer's budget constraint for the case where taxes are greater than the consumer's dividend income. The slope of the budget constraint is $-w$, and the constraint shifts with the quantity of nonwage real disposable income, $\pi - T$. All points in the shaded area and on the budget constraint can be purchased by the consumer.

FIGURE 4.4

Representative Consumer's Budget Constraint (T < π)
The figure shows the consumer's budget constraint when taxes are less than dividend income. This implies that the budget constraint is kinked. The examples we study will always deal with this case, rather than the one where taxes are greater than dividend income. Consumption bundles in the shaded region and on the budget constraint are feasible for the consumer; all other consumption bundles are not feasible.

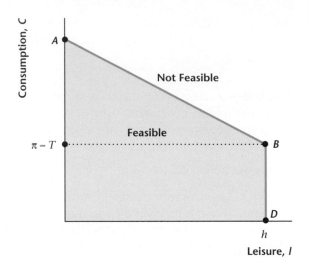

The representative consumer's budget constraint tells us what consumption bundles are feasible for him or her to consume given the market real wage, dividend income, and taxes. In Figure 4.4, consumption bundles in the shaded region inside and on the budget constraint are feasible; all other consumption bundles are infeasible.

CONSUMER OPTIMIZATION

We have now described the representative consumer's preferences over consumption and leisure, and have determined the budget constraint that tells us what combinations of consumption and leisure are feasible. Our next step is to put preferences together with the budget constraint so as to analyze how the representative consumer will behave.

To determine what choice of consumption and leisure the consumer will make, we will assume that the consumer is **rational**. Rationality in this context means that the representative consumer knows his or her own preferences and budget constraint and can evaluate which feasible consumption bundle is best for him or her. Basically, we are assuming that the consumer can make an informed optimization decision.

Consider Figure 4.5, and note that we are considering only the case where $T < \pi$ since ignoring the case where $T > \pi$ will not matter. We want to demonstrate why point H, where indifference curve I_1 is just tangent to the budget constraint ABD, is the **optimal consumption bundle** for the consumer. First, the consumer would never choose a consumption bundle inside the budget constraint because the consumer prefers more to less. For example, consider a point like J in Figure 4.5, which lies inside the budget constraint. Clearly, point F, which is on the budget constraint, is strictly preferred by the consumer to J, since the consumer gets more consumption at point F than at J while receiving the same quantity of leisure. Further, the consumer would not choose any points along BD other than B; B is preferred to any point on BD because more consumption goods are preferred to fewer consumption goods.

DEFINITION

*The **optimal consumption bundle** is the point representing a consumption–leisure pair that is on the highest possible indifference curve and is on or inside the consumer's budget constraint.*

In considering the consumer's optimization problem, given the above, we can restrict attention solely to points on the line segment *AB* in Figure 4.5. Which of these points will the consumer choose? Given the assumptions we have made about the representative consumer's preferences, we are guaranteed that there is a single consumption bundle on *AB* that is optimal for the consumer: the point at which an indifference curve is tangent to *AB*. Why is this the best the consumer can do? Again, consider Figure 4.5. At a point like *F*, minus the slope of the indifference curve passing through *F*, or $MRS_{l,C}$, is greater than minus the slope of the budget constraint at *F*, which is equal to *w*. Alternatively, at *F* the rate at which the consumer is willing to trade leisure for consumption is greater than the rate at which the consumer can trade leisure for consumption in the market, or $MRS_{l,C} > w$. Thus, the consumer would be better off if he or she sacrificed consumption for more leisure by moving from point *F* in the direction of *H*. Note that, in so doing, the consumer will move to successively higher indifference curves, which is another indication that he or she is becoming better off. Similarly, at point *E* in Figure 4.5, the indifference curve is flatter than the budget constraint, so that $MRS_{l,C} < w$. Thus, moving from point *E* toward point *H* implies that the consumer substitutes leisure for consumption and moves to higher indifference curves, becoming better off as a result. At point *H*, where an indifference curve is just tangent to the budget constraint, the rate at which the consumer is willing to trade leisure for consumption is equal to the rate at which leisure trades for consumption in

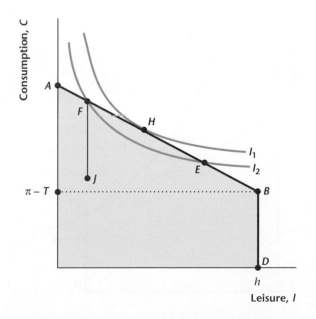

FIGURE 4.5

Consumer Optimization

The consumption bundle represented by point *H*, where an indifference curve is tangent to the budget constraint, is the optimal consumption bundle for the consumer. Points inside the budget constraint, such as *J*, cannot be optimal (more is preferred to less), and such points as *E* and *F*, where an indifference curve cuts the budget constraint, also cannot be optimal.

the market, and thus the consumer is at his or her optimum. In other words, when the representative consumer is optimizing, we have

$$MRS_{l,C} = w, \tag{4.6}$$

or the marginal rate of substitution of leisure for consumption is equal to the real wage. Note, in (4.6), that this optimizing, or marginal, condition, takes the following form: marginal rate of substitution of leisure for consumption equals the relative price of leisure in terms of consumption goods. In general, the **relative price** of a good x in terms of a good y is the number of units of y that trade for a unit of x. It is generally true that *consumer optimization in competitive markets will imply that the consumer sets the marginal rate of substitution of any good x for any other good y equal to the relative price of x in terms of y.* We will use this fact in later chapters.

Given the way we have drawn the budget constraint in Figure 4.5, there seems no obvious reason why the highest indifference curve could not be reached at point B, in which case the consumer would choose to consume all his or her time as leisure, as in Figure 4.6. However, this could not happen when we take account of the interaction of consumers and firms—it would imply that the representative consumer would not work, in which case nothing would be produced, and therefore the consumer would not have anything to consume. The assumption that the consumer always wants to consume some of both goods (the consumption good and leisure) will prevent the consumer from choosing either point A or point B in Figure 4.5.

The assumption that the representative consumer behaves optimally subject to his or her constraints will be very powerful in giving us predictions about what the consumer does when his or her budget constraint changes, or when his or her preferences change. Is it plausible to assume that a consumer makes optimizing decisions?

FIGURE 4.6

The Representative Consumer Chooses Not to Work

The consumer's optimal consumption bundle is at the kink in the budget constraint, at B, so that the consumer does not work ($l = h$). This is a situation that cannot happen, taking into account consistency between the actions of the consumer and of firms.

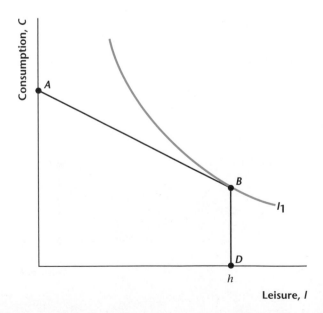

In our own lives, we can generally think of many occasions on which we did not make optimal decisions. For example, suppose Jennifer is self-employed and can choose how much vacation to take every year. Suppose that, for ten years, Jennifer takes two weeks of vacation every summer. One year, by chance, she takes three weeks of vacation, and finds that she is much happier than before. We might imagine this happening not because Jennifer's preferences or budget constraint changed, but because she does not really know her own preferences without experimenting with different consumption–leisure combinations. This would violate the assumption of rationality that we have made for the representative consumer, who always knows exactly what his or her preferences are. The defence for using optimizing behaviour for consumers as a fundamental principle in our models is that mistakes by the consumer are not likely to persist for a long time. Eventually, people learn how to behave optimally, and what is important, particularly in terms of macroeconomic models, is that people on average behave optimally, not that each individual in the economy always does so. Further, if we were to abandon optimization behaviour, there would be many possible alternatives, and it would be extremely difficult to get our models to make any predictions at all. Although there is typically only one way to behave optimally, there are many ways individuals can be stupid!

How Does the Representative Consumer Respond to a Change in Real Dividends or Taxes?

Recall from Chapter 1 that a macroeconomic model, once constructed, can be used to conduct "experiments," somewhat like the experiments conducted by a chemist or a physicist by using a laboratory apparatus. Now that we have shown how the representative consumer makes choices about consumption and leisure, we are interested as economists in how the consumer will respond to changes in the economic environment he or she faces. We will carry out two experiments on the representative consumer. The first will be to change his or her real dividend income minus taxes, $\pi - T$, and the second will be to change the market real wage w that he or she faces. In each case, we will be interested in how these experiments affect the quantities of consumption and leisure chosen by the representative consumer.

We will first look at a change in real dividend income minus taxes, or $\pi - T$, which is the component of real disposable income that does not depend on the real wage w. In changing $\pi - T$, we hold w constant. A change in $\pi - T$ could be caused by a change in either π or T, or in both. For example, an increase in π could be caused by an increase in the productivity of firms, which in turn results in an increase in the dividends that are paid to the consumer. Similarly, if T decreases, this represents a tax cut for the consumer, and disposable income increases. In any case, we will think of the increase in $\pi - T$ as producing a **pure income effect** on the consumer's choices, since prices remain the same (w remains constant) while disposable income increases.

For the case where $\pi > T$, we will consider an increase in $\pi - T$ (recall that the $\pi < T$ case will not be fundamentally different). In Figure 4.7 suppose that initially $\pi = \pi_1$ and $T = T_1$, and then there are changes in π and T so that $\pi = \pi_2$ and $T = T_2$ with $\pi_2 - T_2 > \pi_1 - T_1$. Recall that the vertical intercept of the budget constraint is $wh + \pi - T$, so that initially the budget constraint of the consumer is ABD, and with the increase in $\pi - T$, the constraint shifts out to FJD. Note that FJ is parallel to AB, since the real wage has not changed, leaving the slope of the budget constraint ($-w$) identical to what it was initially. Now suppose that initially the consumer chooses point H, where the highest indifference curve I_1 is reached on the initial budget constraint, and we have $l = l_1$ and $C = C_1$. When $\pi - T$ increases, which consumption bundle will the consumer choose? We have the consumer choosing point K, where the indifference curve I_2 is tangent to the new budget constraint. At point K, we have $l = l_2$ and $C = C_2$, so that consumption and leisure are both higher. Why would this necessarily be the case? Indeed, we could draw indifference curves that are consistent with more being preferred to less and a preference for diversity, and have consumption and leisure falling when income increases. Recall, however, our assumption earlier in this chapter that consumption and leisure are normal goods. This means that if we hold the real wage constant, an increase in income will imply that the representative consumer will choose more consumption and more leisure, as is the case in Figure 4.7.

To see why it is natural to assume that consumption and leisure are both normal goods, consider a consumer, Paula, who receives a windfall increase in her income from winning a lottery. It seems likely that, as a result, Paula will spend more on consumption goods and take more vacation time, thus working less and increasing leisure time. This would happen only if Paula's preferences have the property that consumption and leisure are normal goods.

The assumption that consumption and leisure are both normal implies that higher nonwage disposable income increases consumption and reduces labour supply. Thus, for example, given lower real taxes, consumers will spend more and work less. The increase in income is given in Figure 4.7 by the distance AF, but the increase

FIGURE 4.7

An Increase in the Consumer's Dividend Income
Initially the consumer chooses H, and when dividend income rises (or taxes fall) this shifts the budget constraint out in a parallel fashion (the real wage, which determines the slope of the budget constraint, stays constant). Consumption and leisure both increase, as both are normal goods.

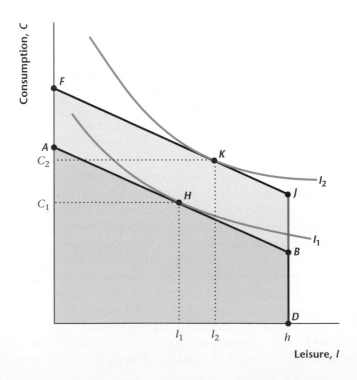

in consumption, $C_2 - C_1$, is less than AF. Though nonwage income increases, wage income falls since the consumer is working less. The reduction in income from the decrease in wage income will not completely offset the increase in nonwage income, as consumption has to increase because it is a normal good.

The Representative Consumer and Changes in the Real Wage: Income and Substitution Effects The second experiment we will examine is to change the real wage faced by the representative consumer, holding everything else constant. In studying how consumer behaviour changes when the market real wage changes, we have some interest in how the consumer's quantity of consumption is affected, but we are perhaps most concerned with what happens to leisure and labour supply. In elementary economics, we typically treat supply curves as being upward-sloping, in that the quantity of a good supplied increases with the market price of the good, holding everything else constant. Labour supply, however, is different. Although it is straightforward to show that the quantity of consumption goods chosen by the consumer increases when the real wage increases, labour supply, N^s, may rise *or* fall when the real wage rises. Part of this section will focus on why this is the case.

In considering how the behaviour of the consumer changes in response to a change in the real wage w, we hold constant real dividends π and real taxes T. We do the experiment in this way to remove the pure income effect on consumer behaviour that we studied in the previous subsection. Consider Figure 4.8, where initially the budget constraint is ABD, and an increase in the real wage w causes the budget constraint to shift out to EBD. Here, note that EB is steeper than AB, since the real wage

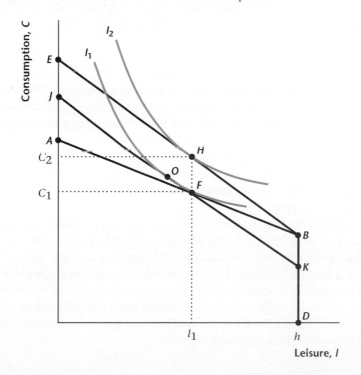

FIGURE 4.8
Increase in the Real Wage Rate—Income and Substitution Effects
An increase in the real wage shifts the budget constraint from *ABD* to *EBD*. The kink in the constraint remains fixed, and the budget constraint becomes steeper. Consumption must increase, but leisure may rise or fall because of opposing substitution and income effects. The substitution effect is the movement from *F* to *O*; the income effect is the movement from *O* to *H*.

has increased, but the kink in the budget constraint remains fixed at B, as nonwage disposable income, $\pi - T$, is unchanged. Initially, the consumer chooses point F, where indifference curve I_1 is tangent to the initial budget constraint. Here, $l = l_1$ and $C = C_1$. When the real wage increases, the consumer might choose a point like H, where indifference curve I_2 is tangent to the new budget constraint. As Figure 4.8 is drawn, leisure remains unchanged at l_1, and consumption increases from C_1 to C_2. What we want to show is that, given that consumption and leisure are normal goods, consumption must increase but leisure may increase or decrease in response to an increase in the real wage. To understand why this is the case, we need to introduce the concepts of **income effect** and **substitution effect**.

The effects of an increase in the real wage on the consumer's optimal choice of consumption and leisure can be broken down into an income effect and a substitution effect as follows. First, given the new higher real wage, suppose that we take away dividend income from the consumer or increase taxes until he or she chooses a consumption bundle O that is on the initial indifference curve I_1. Thus, given the increase in the real wage, we have taken real disposable income away from the consumer so that he or she is just indifferent between the consumption bundle chosen (point O) and the initial consumption bundle (F). It is as if the consumer now faces the budget constraint JKD. The movement from F to O is a pure substitution effect in that it just captures the movement along the indifference curve in response to the increase in the real wage. The real wage increases, so that leisure has become more expensive relative to consumption goods, and the consumer substitutes away from the good that has become more expensive (leisure) to the one that has become relatively cheaper (consumption). Therefore, the substitution effect of the real wage increase is for consumption to increase and for leisure to decrease, and so the substitution effect is for labour supply, $N^s = h - l$, to increase.

Now, the movement from O to H is then a pure income effect, as the real wage stays the same as the budget constraint shifts out from JKD to EBD, and nonwage income increases. Since both goods are normal, consumption increases and leisure increases in moving from O to H. Thus, when the real wage increases, the consumer can consume more consumption goods and more leisure, since the budget constraint has shifted out. On net, then, consumption must increase, since the substitution and income effects both act to increase consumption. However, there are opposing substitution and income effects on leisure, so that it is ultimately unclear whether leisure will rise or fall. Therefore, an increase in the real wage could lead to an increase or a decrease in labour supply N^s.

To understand the intuition behind this result, assume Alex is working 40 hours per week and earning $15 per hour, so that his weekly wage income is $600. Now suppose that Alex's wage rate increases to $20 per hour and that he is free to set his hours of work. On the one hand, because his wage rate is now higher, the cost of taking leisure has increased, and Alex may choose to work more (the substitution effect). On the other hand, he could now work 30 hours per week, still receive $600 in wage income per week, and enjoy 10 more hours of free time (the income effect), so that Alex may choose to reduce his hours of work.

It is straightforward to use the preceding analysis of income and substitution effects to capture the implications of changes in income tax rates for labour supply. See Macroeconomics in Action 4.1.

Although some of the analysis we will do, particularly in Chapter 5, will involve work with indifference curves, it is sometimes useful to summarize consumer behaviour with supply and demand relationships. In Chapter 11 and in later chapters, it will often prove useful to work at the level of supply and demand curves in different markets. Then, an important relationship will be the **labour supply curve**, which tells us how much labour the representative consumer wants to supply given any real wage. To construct the labour supply curve, one could imagine presenting the representative consumer with different real wage rates and asking what quantity of labour the consumer would choose to supply at each wage rate. That is, suppose $l(w)$ is a function that tells us how much leisure the consumer wants to consume, given the real wage w. Then, the labour supply curve is given by

$$N^s(w) = h - l(w).$$

Now, since the effect of a wage increase on the consumer's leisure choice is ambiguous, we do not know whether labour supply is increasing or decreasing in the real wage. Assuming that the substitution effect is larger than the income effect of a change in the real wage, labour supply will increase with an increase in the real wage, and the labour supply schedule will be upward-sloping, as in Figure 4.9. Furthermore, we know that, since the quantity of leisure increases when nonwage disposable income increases, an increase in nonwage disposable income will shift the labour supply curve to the left, that is, from N^s to N_1^s, as shown in Figure 4.10. In analysis where we work with supply and demand relationships, we will typically assume that the substitution effect of an increase in the real wage dominates the income effect, so that the labour supply curve is upward-sloping, as in Figure 4.9.

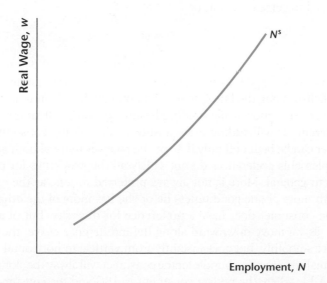

Employment, *N*

FIGURE 4.9

Labour Supply Curve

The labour supply curve tells us how much labour the consumer wants to supply for each possible value for the real wage. Here, the labour supply curve is upward-sloping, which implies that the substitution effect of an increase in the real wage is larger than the income effect for the consumer.

FIGURE 4.10

Effect of an Increase in Dividend Income or a Decrease in Taxes

The labour supply curve shifts to the left when dividend income increases or taxes fall, because of a positive income effect on leisure for the consumer.

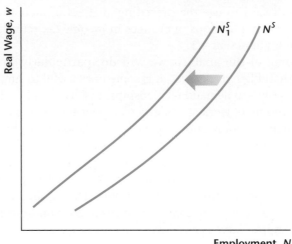

An Example: Consumption and Leisure Are Perfect Complements An example of consumer optimization that we can work out in a straightforward way, both algebraically and graphically, is the case in which the representative consumer's preferences have the perfect complements property. Goods are **perfect complements** for the consumer if he or she always wants to consume these goods in fixed proportions. In practice, there are many cases of goods that are perfect complements. For example, right shoes are almost always consumed one-to-one with left shoes, in that a right shoe is typically not much good without the left shoe. Also, cars and tires are usually consumed in fixed proportions of one to four (ignoring the spare tire, of course).

If consumption and leisure are perfect complements, the consumer always wants to have $\frac{C}{l}$ equal to some constant, or

$$C = al, \tag{4.7}$$

where $a > 0$ is a constant. With perfect complements, the indifference curves of the consumer will be L-shaped, as in Figure 4.11, with the right angles of the indifference curves falling along the line $C = al$. At a point such as E on indifference curve I_2, adding more consumption while holding leisure constant will simply make the consumer indifferent, as will adding more leisure while holding consumption constant. The consumer can be better off only if he or she receives more of both goods. Note that perfect complements preferences do not satisfy all the properties for preferences that we assumed in general. More is not always preferred to less, as the consumer is not better off with more of one good unless he or she has more of the other good as well. However, the consumer does have a preference for diversity, but of a very dramatic sort. That is, as we move downward along the indifference curve, the slope does not become flatter smoothly, but goes instantly from vertical to horizontal.

The optimal consumption bundle for the consumer will always be along the line $C = al$, as in Figure 4.11, where the budget constraint is *ABD* and the consumer optimizes by

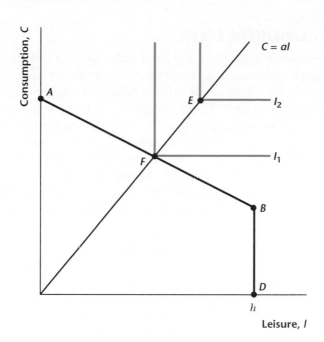

FIGURE 4.11

Perfect Complements
When consumption and leisure are perfect complements for the consumer, indifference curves are L-shaped with right angles along the line $C = al$, where a is a constant. The budget constraint is *ABD*, and the optimal consumption bundle will always be on the line $C = al$.

choosing a point on the budget constraint and on the highest indifference curve, which is point F. Algebraically, the quantities of consumption and leisure must solve (4.7) and must also satisfy the budget constraint

$$C = w(h - l) + \pi - T. \qquad (4.8)$$

Now, Equations (4.7) and (4.8) are in the unknowns C and l with a, w, h, π, and T given. We can solve them for both unknowns by substitution to get

$$l = \frac{wh + \pi - T}{a + w},$$

$$C = \frac{a(wh + \pi - T)}{a + w}.$$

Leisure and consumption therefore increase with nonwage disposable income, $\pi - T$, and we can also show that consumption and leisure both increase when the real wage, w, increases. Note that with perfect complements, there are no substitution effects. Further, if a increases, so that the consumer prefers more consumption relative to leisure, then it seems obvious the consumer will choose more of C and less of l at the optimum.

We will use perfect complements preferences in examples in Chapter 9. Another simple example dealt with in the problems at the end of this chapter is the case where preferences have the **perfect substitutes** property. In this case, the marginal rate of substitution is constant, and the indifference curves are downward-sloping straight lines.

The Representative Firm

In our model economy, consumers and firms come together to exchange labour for consumption goods. While the representative consumer supplies labour and demands consumption goods, we will turn now to the behaviour of firms, which demand labour and supply consumption goods. The choices of the firms are determined by the available technology and by profit maximization. As with consumer behaviour, we will ultimately focus here on the choices of a single, representative firm.

The firms in this economy own productive capital (plant and equipment), and they hire labour to produce consumption goods. We can describe the production technology available to each firm by a **production function**, which describes the technological possibilities for converting factor inputs into outputs. We can express this relationship in algebraic terms as

$$Y = zF(K, N^d),$$

where z is **total factor productivity**, Y is output of consumption goods, K is the quantity of capital input in the production process, N^d is the quantity of labour input measured as total hours worked by employees of the firm, and F is a function. Since this is a one-period or static (as opposed to dynamic) model, we treat K as being a fixed input to production, and N^d as a variable factor of production. That is, in the short run, firms cannot vary the quantity of plant and equipment (K) they have, but they have flexibility in hiring and laying off workers (N^d). Total factor productivity z captures the degree of sophistication of the production process. That is, an increase in z will make both factors of production, K and N^d, more productive, in that, given factor inputs, higher z implies that more output can be produced.

For example, suppose that the above production function represents the technology available to a bakery. The quantity of capital, K, includes the building in which the bakery operates, ovens for baking bread, a computer for doing the bakery accounts, and other miscellaneous equipment. The quantity of labour, N^d, is total hours worked by all the bakery employees, including the manager, the bakers who operate the ovens, and the employees who work selling the bakery's products to customers. The variable z, total factor productivity, can be affected by the techniques used for organizing production. For example, bread could be produced either by having each baker operate an individual oven, using this oven to produce different kinds of bread, or by having each baker specialize in making a particular kind of bread, using the oven that happens to be available when an oven is needed. If the latter production method produces more bread per day by using the same inputs of capital and labour, that method implies a higher value of z than the first method.

For our analysis, we need to discuss several important properties of the production function. Before doing this, we will need to understand **marginal product**.

DEFINITION

The **marginal product** *of a factor of production is the additional output that can be produced with one additional unit of that factor input, holding constant the quantities of the other factor inputs.*

It is tempting to view poverty as an easy problem to solve. If one assumed that real GDP was essentially fixed, then it might make sense to redistribute income from the lucky rich to the unlucky poor so that we could be collectively better off. Government income redistribution—through the tax system and the provision of goods and services such as parks and health care—might be seen as poverty insurance that for some reason is not provided by the private sector.

An important means for redistributing income in Canada and other countries is through the taxation of labour. In particular, federal and provincial income taxes in Canada are progressive, in that income taxes represent a smaller fraction of income for the typical poor person than for the typical rich person. This contrasts with the federal goods and services tax and provincial sales taxes, which tend to be slightly regressive—the typical poor person pays a larger fraction of their income to the government in the form of these taxes than does a typical rich person.

It is well-understood, though, that income taxation has incentive effects. In our simple model of consumer behaviour, an easy way to study the effects of income taxation on a consumer is to assume that the consumer's wage income is taxed at a constant rate, t. Then, supposing that the lump-sum tax is zero, or $T = 0$, the consumer would pay total taxes of $tw(h - l)$, and the consumer's budget constraint would be

$$C = w(1 - t)(h - l) + \pi$$

Then, if we wanted to analyze the effects of a change in the income tax rate t on labour supply, given the market real wage w, this would be the same as analyzing the effects of a change in the real wage, since now $w(1 - t)$ is the effective real wage for the consumer, and an increase in t is equivalent to a decrease in the consumer's effective real wage. From our analysis in this chapter, theory tells us that an increase in the income tax rate t may cause an increase or a decrease in the quantity of labour supplied, depending on the relative strengths of opposing income and substitution effects. For example, an increase in t will reduce labour supply only if the substitution effect is large relative to the income effect. That is, if the substitution effect is relatively large, then there can be a large disincentive effect on hours of work as the result of an income tax rate increase.

This disincentive effect might give us pause if we wanted to think of the income tax as a useful means for redistributing income. If the substitution effect is large, so that the elasticity of labour supply with respect to wages is large, then real GDP should not be considered a fixed pie that can be redistributed at will. An attempt to divide up the pie differently by increasing income tax rates for the rich and reducing them for the poor might actually reduce the pie substantially.

Whether the reduction in real GDP from a redistributive tax system is a serious problem turns on how large the elasticity of labour supply is. Typically, in studying how individuals adjust hours of work in response to changes in wages, labour economists find the effects to be small. Thus, according to microeconomic evidence, the elasticity of labour supply with respect to wages is small, therefore the disincentive effects from income taxation are small, and redistributing the pie will not reduce the size of the pie by very much.

However, for macroeconomists this is not the end of the story. In a recent working paper,[1] Michael Keane and Richard Rogerson review the evidence on labour supply elasticities. For macroeconomists, the key idea is that what matters for aggregate economic activity is total labour input, which is determined by three factors: (i) how many hours each individual works; (ii) how many individuals are working; and (iii) the quality of the labour hours supplied.

Microeconomic evidence on labour supply typically focuses on the labour hours supplied by individuals and how this responds to wages. This is the so-called intensive margin—how intensively an individual works. However, as Keane and Rogerson point out, changes in aggregate hours worked over both short and long periods of time are influenced in an important way by choices at the extensive margin, i.e. the choices of individuals about whether to work or not. While a higher market income tax rate might have little effect on any individual worker's hours of work, it might induce more people to leave the labour force. For example, some people might choose to care for their children at home rather than working in the market. In fact, if we take into account the extensive margin, the aggregate labour supply elasticity is much higher.

Thus, in our macroeconomic model, it is most useful to think of the representative consumer as a fictitious person who stands in for the average consumer in the economy. Hours of work for this fictitious person should be interpreted as average hours of work in the whole economy. Thus, when aggregate hours of work change in practice, because of changes along the intensive and extensive margins, we should think of this as changes in the representative consumer's hours of work in our model.

Another dimension on which labour supply can change, as mentioned above, is in terms of the quality of labour hours supplied. This is essentially a long-run effect that occurs through occupational choice. For example, if income tax rates are increased for the rich and reduced for the poor, this reduces the incentive of young people to obtain the education required to perform higher-paying jobs. Fewer people will choose to become engineers, and more will choose to become plumbers. The evidence in Keane and Rogerson's article suggests that this effect is large.

What would Canada look like if we chose to be a much more egalitarian society by using the income tax to redistribute income from rich to the poor? For a very rich person, the after-tax wage earned for on an extra hour of work would be much lower than it is now, and for a very poor person, the after tax wage at the margin would be much higher. Average hours worked among employed people in this egalitarian society would be somewhat lower than now, but there would be many more people who would choose not to participate in the labour force. As well, over the long run, the average level of skills acquired by the population would be much lower. Real GDP would fall.

There is some evidence that higher taxation of labour explains differences between the United States and Europe in labour supply and real GDP per capita.[2] Similarly, the Canadian income tax system is more progressive than the US system. Thus, a higher degree of income redistribution in Canada than in the United States could in part explain why US real GDP per capita is higher than in Canada.

[1]M. Keane and R. Rogerson, 2011. "Reconciling Micro and Macro Labor Supply Elasticities: A Structural Perspective," NBER working paper 17430.

[2]E. Prescott, 2004, "Why Do Americans Work More Than Europeans?" *Minneapolis Federal Reserve Bank Quarterly Review* 28, No. 1, 2–13.

In terms of the production function above, there are two factor inputs, labour and capital. Figure 4.12 shows a graph of the production function, fixing the quantity of capital at some arbitrary value, K^*, and allowing the labour input, N^d, to vary. Some of the properties of this graph require further explanation. In the figure, the marginal product of labour, given the quantity of labour N^*, is the slope of the production function at point A; this is because the slope of the production function is the additional

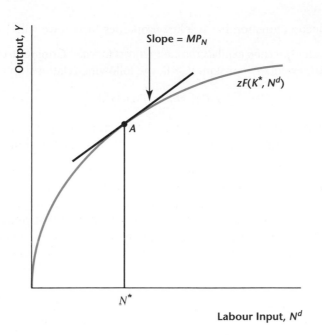

FIGURE 4.12

Production Function, Fixing the Quantity of Capital and Varying the Quantity of Labour

The marginal product of labour is the slope of the production function at a given point. Note that the marginal product of labour declines with the quantity of labour.

output produced from an additional unit of the labour input when the quantity of labour is N^* and the quantity of capital is K^*. We will let MP_N denote the marginal product of labour.

Next, in Figure 4.13 we graph the production function again, but this time we fix the quantity of labour at N^* and allow the quantity of capital to vary. In Figure 4.13, the marginal product of capital, denoted MP_K, given the quantity of capital K^*, is the slope of the production function at point A.

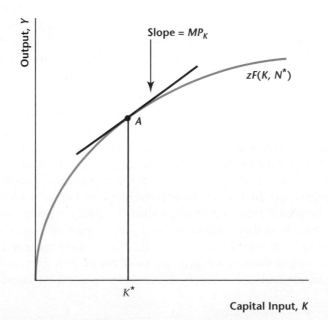

FIGURE 4.13

Production Function, Fixing the Quantity of Labour and Varying the Quantity of Capital

The slope of the production function is the marginal product of capital, and the marginal product of capital declines with the quantity of capital.

The production function has five key properties, which we will discuss in turn.

1. *The production function exhibits constant returns to scale.* **Constant returns to scale** means that, given any constant $x > 0$, the following relationship holds:

$$xzF(K, N^d) = zF(xK, xN^d).$$

That is, if all factor inputs are changed by a factor x, output changes by the same factor x. For example, if all factor inputs double ($x = 2$), then output also doubles.

The alternatives to constant returns to scale in production are **increasing returns to scale** and **decreasing returns to scale**. Increasing returns to scale implies that large firms (firms producing a large quantity of output) are more efficient than small firms, whereas decreasing returns to scale implies that small firms are more efficient than large firms. With constant returns to scale, a small firm is just as efficient as a large firm. Indeed, constant returns to scale means that a very large firm simply replicates, many times over, how a very small firm produces. Given a constant-returns-to-scale production function, the economy will behave in exactly the same way if there were many small firms producing consumption goods as it would if there were a few large firms, provided all firms behave competitively (they are price-takers in product and factor markets). Given this, it is most convenient to suppose that there is only one firm in the economy, the **representative firm**—which (as with the representative consumer) it is helpful to think of as a convenient stand-in for many firms, all with the same constant-returns-to-scale production function. In practice, it is clear that in some industries decreasing returns to scale are important. For example, high-quality restaurant food seems to be produced most efficiently on a small scale. Alternatively, increasing returns to scale are important in the automobile industry, where essentially all production occurs in large-scale firms, such as the Ford Motor Company of Canada. This does not mean, however, that it is harmful to assume there exists constant returns to scale in production at the aggregate level, as in our model. Even the largest firm in the Canadian economy produces a small amount of output relative to Canadian GDP. The aggregate economy can exhibit constant returns to scale in aggregate production, even if this is not literally true for each firm in the economy.

2. *The production function has the property that output increases when either the capital input or the labour input increases.* In other words, the marginal products of labour and capital are both positive: $MP_N > 0$ and $MP_K > 0$. In Figures 4.12 and 4.13, these properties of the production function are exhibited by the upward slope of the production function. Recall that the slope of the production function in Figure 4.12 is the marginal product of labour and the slope in Figure 4.13 is the marginal product of capital. Positive marginal product is a quite natural property of the production function, as this states simply that more inputs yield more output. In the bakery example discussed previously, if the bakery hires more workers given the same capital equipment, it will produce more bread, and if it installs more ovens given the same number of workers, it will also produce more bread.

3. *The marginal product of labour decreases as the quantity of labour increases.* In Figure 4.12 the declining marginal product of labour is reflected in the concavity of the production function. That is, the slope of the production function in Figure 4.12, which is equal to MP_N, decreases as N^d increases. The following example helps to illustrate why the marginal product of labour should fall as the quantity of labour input increases. Suppose accountants work in an office building that has one photocopy machine, and suppose they work with pencils and paper but at random intervals need to use the photocopy machine. The first accountant added to the production process, Sara, is very productive—that is, she has a high marginal product—as she can use the photocopy machine whenever she wants. However, when the second accountant, Paul, is added, on occasion when Sara wants to use the machine she gets up from her desk, walks to the machine, and finds that Paul is using it. Thus, some time is wasted. Paul and Sara produce more than Sara alone, but what Paul adds to production (his marginal product) is lower than the marginal product of Sara. Similarly, adding a third accountant, Julia, will make for even more congestion around the photocopy machine, and Julia's marginal product will be lower than Paul's marginal product, which is lower than Sara's. Figure 4.14 shows the representative firm's marginal product of labour schedule. This is a graph of the firm's marginal product, given a fixed quantity of capital, as a function of the labour input. That is, this is the graph of the slope of the production function in Figure 4.12. Note that the marginal product schedule is always positive and that it slopes downward.

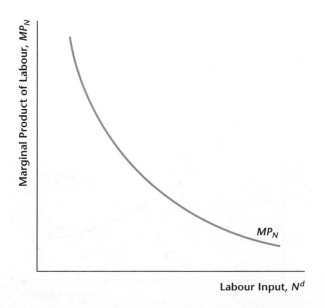

FIGURE 4.14

Marginal Product of Labour Schedule for the Representative Firm

The marginal product of labour declines as the quantity of labour used in the production process increases.

4. *The marginal product of capital decreases as the quantity of capital increases.* This property of the production function is very similar to the previous one, and it is illustrated in Figure 4.13 by the decreasing slope, or concavity, of the production function. In terms of the example above, if we suppose that Sara, Paul, and Julia are the accountants working in the office and imagine what happens as we add photocopy machines, we can gain some intuition as to why the decreasing-marginal-product-of-capital property is natural. Adding the first photocopy machine adds a great deal to total output, as Sara, Paul, and Julia now can duplicate documents that formerly had to be copied by hand. With three accountants in the office, however, there is congestion around the machine. This congestion is relieved with the addition of a second machine, so that the second machine increases output, but the marginal product of the second machine is smaller than the marginal product of the first machine, and so on.

5. *The marginal product of labour increases as the quantity of capital input increases.* To provide some intuition for this property of the production function, let's once again return to the example of the accounting firm. Suppose that Sara, Paul, and Julia initially have one photocopy machine to work with. Adding another photocopy machine amounts to adding capital equipment. This will relieve congestion around the copy machine and make each of Sara, Paul, and Julia more productive, including Julia, who was the last accountant added to the workforce at the firm. Therefore, adding more capital increases the marginal product of labour for each quantity of labour. In Figure 4.15 an increase in the quantity of capital from K_1 to K_2 shifts the marginal product of labour schedule to the right, from MP_N^1 to MP_N^2.

FIGURE 4.15

Adding Capital Increases the Marginal Product of Labour

For each quantity of the labour input, the marginal product of labour increases when the quantity of capital used in production increases.

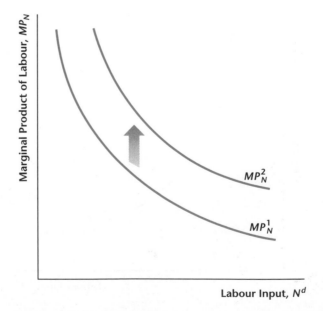

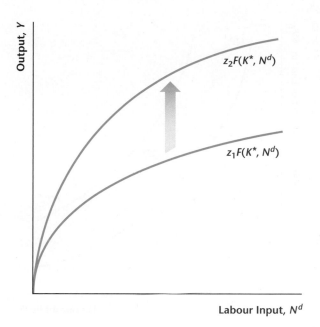

FIGURE 4.16
Total Factor Productivity Increases
An increase in total factor productivity has two effects: More output is produced given each quantity of the labour input, and the marginal product of labour increases for each quantity of the labour input.

THE EFFECT OF A CHANGE IN TOTAL FACTOR PRODUCTIVITY ON THE PRODUCTION FUNCTION

Changes in total factor productivity, z, will be critical to our understanding of the causes of economic growth and business cycles, and so we must understand how a change in z alters the production technology. An increase in total factor productivity, z, has two important effects. First, since more output can be produced given capital and labour inputs when z increases, this shifts the production function up. In Figure 4.16, with the quantity of capital fixed at K^*, there is an upward shift in the production function when z increases from z_1 to z_2. Second, the marginal product of labour increases when z increases. This is reflected in the fact that the slope of the production function when $z = z_2$ in Figure 4.16 is higher than the slope given $z = z_1$, for any given quantity of the labour input, N^d. In Figure 4.17 the marginal product of labour schedule shifts to the right from MP_N^1 to MP_N^2 when z increases. Note that an increase in z has a similar effect on the marginal product of labour schedule as an increase in the capital stock (see Figure 4.15).

What could cause a change in total factor productivity? In general, an increase in z arises from anything that permits more output to be produced for given inputs. In the macroeconomy, there are many factors that can cause z to increase. One of these factors is technological innovation. The best examples of technological innovations that increase total factor productivity are changes in the organization of production or in management techniques. For example, the assembly line, introduced to automobile manufacturing by Henry Ford (see Macroeconomics in Action 4.2) brought about a huge increase in the number of Model T Fords that could be produced by using the same quantity of capital equipment and number of workers. Some of the most

FIGURE 4.17

Effect of an Increase in Total Factor Productivity on the Marginal Product of Labour

When total factor productivity increases, the marginal product of labour schedule shifts to the right.

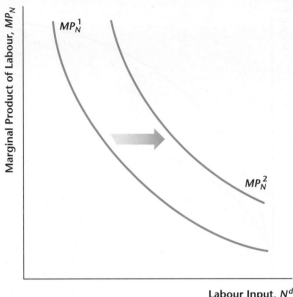

important inventions of the twentieth century—for example, the personal computer—might more appropriately be considered to involve increases in the capital stock rather than increases in z, since the new technology is embodied in capital equipment. A second factor that acts to increase z is good weather. Weather is especially important for production in the agricultural and construction sectors. For example, crop yields are higher, given factor inputs, if rainfall is higher (as long as it is not *too* high), and construction projects proceed more quickly if rainfall is lower. A third factor affecting z is government regulations. For example, if the government imposes regulations requiring that firms install pollution abatement equipment, this may be good for the welfare of the population, but it results in a decrease in z. This happens because pollution abatement equipment increases the quantity of the capital input in the production process, but contributes nothing to measured output. Finally, an increase in the relative price of energy is often interpreted as a decrease in z. When the relative price of energy increases, firms use less energy in production, and this reduces the productivity of both capital and labour, thus causing a decrease in z. Major increases in the price of energy occurred in Canada in the 1970s, early 1980s, and since 2000, with important macroeconomic consequences that we will study in Chapters 5, 11, and 13.

THE PROFIT MAXIMIZATION PROBLEM OF THE REPRESENTATIVE FIRM

Now that we have studied the properties of the representative firm's production technology, we can examine the determinants of the firm's demand for labour. Like the representative consumer, the representative firm behaves competitively, in that it takes as given the real wage, which is the price at which labour trades for consumption goods. The goal of the firm is to maximize its profits, given by $Y - wN^d$, where Y is the total revenue that the

The Ford Motor Company was founded in the United States in 1903 by Henry Ford and a financial backer, but Ford achieved only modest success until the introduction to the market of the Model T Ford in 1908. This car proved extremely popular, because it was light, strong, simple, and relatively easy to drive. Given the high demand for the Model T, Henry Ford decided to increase output, but he did not do this by simply replicating his existing production process through the construction of identical plants; rather, he increased total factor productivity while also augmenting the capital and labour inputs in production. A key element of the total factor productivity increase was the introduction of the assembly line to automobile manufacturing. Henry Ford borrowed this idea from assembly lines used in the Chicago meat-packing industry. However, the principle at work in the assembly line was known much earlier, for example by Adam Smith, the father of modern economics. In *The Wealth of Nations*, Smith discusses how production was organized in a pin factory, as an illustration of what he called the "division of labour":

> One man draws out the wire, another straightens it, a third cuts it ... the important business of making a pin is, in this manner, divided into about eighteen distinct operations....[3]

Smith was impressed by how the specialization of tasks led to increased productivity in the manufacture of pins. More than a century later, Henry Ford's assembly line replaced an arrangement in which automobiles were assembled by teams that each accumulated parts and completed a single automobile in a single location in the plant. Just as in the pin factory, Ford was able to exploit the gains from specialization that the assembly line permitted. Each worker performed only one specialized task, and therefore automobiles could be completed at a much higher rate.

The increase in total factor productivity at the Ford Motor Company was reflected in the fact that, in 1914, 13 000 workers produced 260 720 cars at Ford, while in the rest of the U.S. automobile industry 66 350 workers produced 286 770 cars. Thus, output per worker at Ford was almost five times that in the rest of the U.S. auto industry! We do not have measures of the size of the capital stock at Ford and elsewhere in the auto industry, so there is some small chance that the higher quantity of output per worker at Ford might have been due simply to higher capital per worker. However, it seems safe to say that total factor productivity at Ford Motor Company increased by a remarkable amount because of the innovations of Henry Ford, and these innovations were quickly imitated in the auto industry around the world.[4]

---

[3]See Adam Smith, reprinted 1981, *An Enquiry into the Nature and Causes of the Wealth of Nations*, Liberty Fund, Indianapolis, 15.

[4]See H. Ford, 1926, *My Life and Work*, Doubleday, Page and Co., New York; A. Nevins, 1954, *Ford: The Times, the Man, the Company*, Charles Scribner's and Sons, New York.

firm receives from selling its output, in units of the consumption good, and wN^d is the total real cost of the labour input, or total real variable costs. Then, substituting for Y by using the production function $Y = zF(K, N^d)$, the firm's problem is to choose N^d to maximize

$$\pi = zF(K, N^d) - wN^d,$$

So far we have assumed that the production function for the representative firm takes the form $Y = zF(K, N^d)$, where the function F has some very general properties (constant returns to scale, diminishing marginal products, etc.). When macroeconomists work with data to test theories, or when they want to simulate a macroeconomic model on the computer to study some quantitative aspects of a theory, they need to be much more specific about the form the production function takes. A very common production function used in theory and empirical work is the **Cobb-Douglas production function**. This function takes the form

$$Y = zK^a(N^d)^{1-a},$$

where a is a parameter, with $0 < a < 1$. The exponents on K and N^d in the function sum to 1 ($a + 1 - a = 1$), which reflects constant returns to scale. It will turn out that if there are profit-maximizing price-taking firms and constant returns to scale, then a Cobb-Douglas production function implies that a will be the share of national income that capital receives (in our model, the profits of firms), and $1 - a$ the share that labour receives (wage income before taxes) in equilibrium. What is remarkable is that, from the National Income and Expenditure Accounts of Canada, the capital and labour shares of national income have been roughly constant in Canada, which is consistent with the Cobb-Douglas production function. Given this, an empirical estimate of a is the average share of capital in national income, which from the data is about 0.3, or 30%, so a good approximation to the actual Canadian aggregate production function is

$$Y = zK^{0.3}(N^d)^{0.7} \tag{4.9}$$

In Equation (4.9), the quantities Y, K, and N^d can all be measured. For example, Y can be measured as real GDP from the NIEA, K can be measured as the total quantity of capital in existence, built up from investment expenditures in the NIEA, and N^d can be measured as total employment, in the survey done by Statistics Canada. But how is total factor productivity, z, measured? Total factor productivity cannot be measured directly, but it can be measured indirectly, as a residual. That is, from Equation (4.9), if we can measure Y, K, and N^d, then a measure of z is the **Solow residual** (named after Robert Solow),[5] which is calculated as

$$z = \frac{Y}{K^{0.3}(N^d)^{0.7}} \tag{4.10}$$

In Figure 4.18 we graph the Solow residual, calculated by using Equation (4.10) and measurements of Y, K, and N^d as described above. Note that measured total factor productivity grows over time, and that it fluctuates about trend. In Chapters 7, 8, and 13, we will see how growth and fluctuations in total factor productivity can cause growth and fluctuations in real GDP.

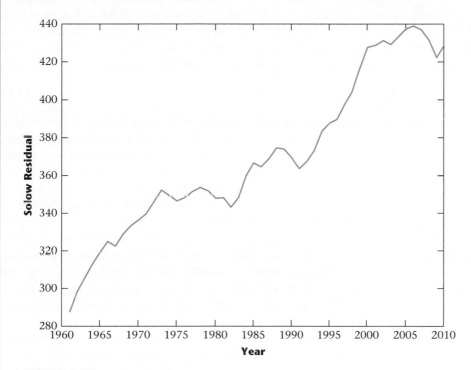

FIGURE 4.18

The Solow Residual for Canada, 1961–2010

The Solow residual is a measure of total factor productivity, and it is calculated here by using a Cobb-Douglas production function. Measured total factor productivity has increased over time, and it also fluctuates about trend, as shown.

Source: Adapted from the Statistics Canada CANSIM database, Series v3860085, v2461119, v3822183, v1078498, and from the Statistics Canada publication Historical Statistics of Canada, Catalogue 11-516, 1983, Series D175–189.

---

[5]See R. Solow, 1957, "Technical Change and the Aggregate Production Function," *Review of Economic Statistics* 39, 312–320.

where K is fixed. Here, π is real profit. In Figure 4.19 we graph the revenue function, $zF(K, N^d)$, and the variable cost function, wN^d. Profit is then the difference between total revenue and total variable cost. Here, to maximize profits, the firm will choose $N^d = N^*$ in Figure 4.19. The maximized quantity of profits, π^*, is the distance AB in Figure 4.19. For future reference, note also that π^* is the distance ED, where AE is a line drawn parallel to the variable cost function. Thus, AE has slope w. At the profit-maximizing quantity of labour, N^*, *the slope of the total revenue function is equal to the slope of the total variable cost function.* But the slope of the total revenue function is just the slope of the production function, or the marginal product of labour, and the slope of the total variable cost function is the real wage, w. Thus, the firm maximizes profits by setting

$$MP_N = w. \tag{4.11}$$

To understand the intuition behind Equation (4.11), note that the contribution to the firm's profits of having employees work an extra hour is the extra output produced minus what the extra input costs—that is, $MP_N - w$. Given a fixed quantity of capital, the marginal product of labour is very high for the first hour worked by employees, and the way we have drawn the production function in Figure 4.19, MP_N is very large for $N^d = 0$, so that $MP_N - w > 0$ for $N^d = 0$. Thus, it is worthwhile for the firm to hire the first unit of labour, as this implies positive profits. As the firm hires more labour, MP_N falls, and each additional unit of labour is contributing less to revenue, but contributing the same amount, w, to costs. Eventually, at $N^d = N^*$, the firm has hired enough labour so that hiring an additional unit will imply $MP_N - w < 0$, which in turn means that hiring an additional unit of labour will only cause profits to go down, and this cannot be optimal. Therefore, the profit-maximizing firm will choose its labour input according to Equation (4.11).

In our earlier example of the accounting firm, suppose that there is one photocopy machine at the firm, and output for the firm can be measured in terms of the clients

FIGURE 4.19

Revenue, Variable Costs, and Profit Maximization

$Y = zF(K, N^d)$ is the firm's revenue, while wN^d is the firm's variable cost. Profits are the difference between the former and the latter. The firm maximizes profits at the point where marginal revenue equals marginal cost, or $MPN = w$. Maximized profits are the distance AB, or the distance ED.

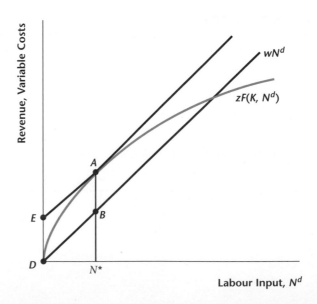

the firm has. Each client pays $20 000 per year to the firm, and the wage rate for an accountant is $50 000 per year. Therefore, the real wage is $\frac{50\ 000}{20\ 000} = 2.5$ clients. If the firm has one accountant, it can handle 5 clients per year, if it has two accountants it can handle 9 clients per year, and if it has three accountants it can handle 11 clients per year. What is the profit-maximizing number of accountants for the firm to hire? If the firm hires Sara, her marginal product is 5 clients per year. This exceeds the real wage of 2.5 clients, so it would be worthwhile for the firm to hire Sara. If the firm hires Sara and Paul, Paul's marginal product is 4 clients per year. This also exceeds the market real wage, and it would also be worthwhile to hire Paul. If the firm hires Sara, Paul, and Julia, Julia's marginal product is 2 clients per year, which is less than the market real wage of 2.5 clients. Therefore, it would be optimal to hire two accountants, Sara and Paul.

Our analysis tells us that the representative firm's marginal product of labour schedule, as shown in Figure 4.20, is the firm's demand curve for labour. This is because the firm maximizes profits for the quantity of labour input that implies $MP_N = w$. Therefore, given a real wage, w, the marginal product of labour schedule tells us how much labour the firm needs to hire such that $MP_N = w$ and so the marginal product of labour schedule and the firm's demand curve for labour are the same thing.

In this chapter, we have determined the important elements of the microeconomic behaviour of a representative consumer and a representative firm. In the next chapter, we will put this behaviour together in a macroeconomic model that can be used to address important macroeconomic issues. In this model, the consumer and the firm interact in markets, where the consumer supplies labour and demands consumption goods, and the firm demands labour and supplies consumption goods.

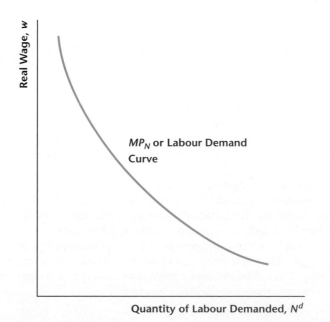

MP_N **or Labour Demand Curve**

Real Wage, w

Quantity of Labour Demanded, N^d

FIGURE 4.20

The Marginal Product of Labour Curve Is the Labour Demand Curve of the Profit-Maximizing Firm

This is true because the firm hires labour up to the point where $MP_N = w$.

Chapter Summary

- In this chapter, we studied the behaviour of the representative consumer and the representative firm in a one-period, or static, environment. This behaviour is the basis for constructing a macroeconomic model that we can work with in Chapter 5.
- The representative consumer stands in for the large number of consumers that exist in the economy as a whole, and the representative firm stands in for a large number of firms.
- The representative consumer's goal is to choose consumption and leisure to make himself or herself as well off as possible while respecting his or her budget constraint.
- The consumer's preferences have the properties that more is always preferred to less and that there is preference for diversity in consumption and leisure. The consumer is a price-taker in that he or she treats the market real wage as given, and his or her real disposable income is real wage income plus real dividend income, minus real taxes.
- Graphically, the representative consumer optimizes by choosing the consumption bundle where an indifference curve is tangent to the budget constraint, or what is the same thing, the marginal rate of substitution of leisure for consumption is equal to the real wage.
- Under the assumption that consumption and leisure are normal goods, an increase in the representative consumer's income leads to an increase in consumption and an increase in leisure, implying that labour supply goes down.
- An increase in the real wage leads to an increase in consumption, but it may cause leisure to rise or fall, because there are opposing income and substitution effects. The consumer's labour supply, therefore, may increase or decrease when the real wage increases.
- The representative firm chooses the quantity of labour to hire so as to maximize profits, with the quantity of capital fixed in this one-period environment.
- The firm's production technology is captured by the production function, which has constant returns to scale, a diminishing marginal product of labour, and a diminishing marginal product of capital. Further, the marginal products of labour and capital are positive, and the marginal product of labour increases with the quantity of capital.
- An increase in total factor productivity increases the quantity of output that can be produced with any quantities of labour and capital, and it increases the marginal product of labour.
- When the firm optimizes, it sets the marginal product of labour equal to the real wage. This implies that the firm's marginal product of labour schedule is its demand curve for labour.

Key Terms

static decision: A decision made by a consumer or firm for only one time period.

dynamic decision: A decision made by a consumer or firm for more than one time period.

consumption good: A single good that represents an aggregation of all consumer goods in the economy.

leisure: Time spent not working in the market.

representative consumer: A stand-in for all consumers in the economy.

utility function: A function that captures a consumer's preferences over goods.

consumption bundle: A given consumption–leisure combination.

normal good: A good for which consumption increases as income increases.

inferior good: A good for which consumption decreases as income increases.

indifference map: A set of indifference curves representing a consumer's preferences over goods; has the same information as the utility function.

indifference curve: A set of points that represent consumption bundles among which a consumer is indifferent.

marginal rate of substitution: Minus the slope of an indifference curve, or the rate at which the consumer is just willing to trade one good for another.

competitive behaviour: Actions taken by a consumer or firm if market prices are outside its control.

barter: An exchange of goods for goods.

time constraint: Condition that hours worked plus leisure time add up to the total time available to the consumer.

real wage: The wage rate in units of the consumption good.

numeraire: The good in which prices are denominated.

dividend income: Profits of firms that are distributed to the consumer, who owns the firms.

lump-sum tax: A tax that is unaffected by the actions of the consumer or firm being taxed.

budget constraint: Condition that consumption equals wage income plus nonwage income minus taxes.

rational: Describes a consumer who makes an informed optimizing decision.

optimal consumption bundle: The consumption bundle for which the consumer is as well off as possible while satisfying the budget constraint.

relative price: The price of a good in units of another good.

pure income effect: The effect on the consumer's optimal consumption bundle because of a change in real disposable income, holding prices constant.

income effect: The effect of a price change on the quantity consumed of a good, because of having effectively different income.

substitution effect: The effect of a price change on the quantity consumed of a good, holding the consumer's welfare constant.

labour supply curve: A relationship describing the quantity of labour supplied for each level of the real wage.

perfect complements: Two goods that are always consumed in fixed proportions.

perfect substitutes: Two goods with a constant marginal rate of substitution between them.

production function: A function describing the technological possibilities for converting factor inputs into output.

total factor productivity: A variable in the production function that makes all factors of production more productive if it increases.

marginal product: The additional output produced when another unit of a factor of production is added to the production process.

constant returns to scale: A property of the production technology whereby if the firm increases all inputs by a factor x, this increases output by the same factor x.

increasing returns to scale: A property of the production technology whereby if the firm increases all inputs by a factor x, this increases output by more than the factor x.

decreasing returns to scale: A property of the production technology whereby if the firm increases all inputs by a factor x, this increases output by less than the factor x.

representative firm: A stand-in for all firms in the economy.

Cobb-Douglas production function: A particular mathematical form for the production function that fits Canadian aggregate data well.

Solow residual: A measure of total factor productivity obtained as a residual from the production function, given measures of aggregate output, labour input, and capital input.

Questions for Review

All questions refer to the elements of the macroeconomic model developed in this chapter.

1. What goods do consumers consume in this model?

2. How are a consumer's preferences over goods represented?

3. What three properties do the preferences of the representative consumer have? Explain the importance of each.

4. What two properties do indifference curves have? How are these properties associated with the properties of the consumer's preferences?

5. What is the representative consumer's goal?

6. When the consumer chooses his or her optimal consumption bundle while respecting his or her budget constraint, what condition is satisfied?

7. How is the representative consumer's behaviour affected by an increase in real dividend income?

8. How is the representative consumer's behaviour affected by an increase in real taxes?

9. Why might hours worked by the representative consumer decrease when the real wage increases?

10. What is the representative firm's goal?

11. Why is the marginal product of labour diminishing?

12. What are the effects on the production function of an increase in total factor productivity?

13. Explain why the marginal product of labour curve is the firm's labour demand curve.

Problems

1. Use a diagram to show that if the consumer prefers more to less, then indifference curves cannot cross.

2. In this chapter, we showed an example in which the consumer has preferences for consumption with the perfect complements property. Suppose, alternatively, that leisure and consumption goods are *perfect substitutes*. In this case, an indifference curve is described by the equation

$$u = al + bC,$$

where a and b are positive constants, and u is the level of utility. That is, a given indifference curve has a particular value for u, with higher indifference curves having higher values for u.

a. Show what the consumer's indifference curves look like when consumption and leisure are perfect substitutes, and determine graphically and algebraically what consumption bundle the consumer will choose. Show that the consumption bundle the consumer chooses depends on the relationship between $\frac{a}{b}$ and w, and explain why.

b. Do you think it likely that any consumer would treat consumption goods and leisure as perfect substitutes?

c. Given perfect substitutes, is more preferred to less? Do preferences satisfy the diminishing-marginal-rate-of-substitution property?

3. Consider the consumer choice example in this chapter, where consumption and leisure are perfect complements. Assume that the consumer always desires a consumption bundle where the quantities of consumption and leisure are equal, that is $a = 1$.
   a. Suppose that $w = .75$, $\pi = .8$, and $T = 6$. Determine the consumer's optimal choice of consumption and leisure, and show this in a diagram.
   b. Now suppose that $w = 1.5$, $\pi = .8$, and $T = 6$. Again, determine the consumer's optimal choice of consumption and leisure, and show this in your diagram. Explain how and why the consumer's optimal consumption bundle changes, with reference to income and substitution effects.

4. Suppose that the government imposes a proportional income tax on the representative consumer's wage income. That is, the consumer's wage income is $w(1 - t)(h - l)$, where t is the tax rate. What effect does the income tax have on consumption and labour supply? Explain your results in terms of income and substitution effects.

5. Suppose, as in the federal income tax code for Canada, that the representative consumer faces a wage income tax with a standard deduction. That is, the representative consumer pays no tax on wage income for the first x units of real wage income, and then pays a proportional tax t on each unit of real wage income greater than x. Therefore, the consumer's budget constraint is given by $C = w(h - l) + \pi$ if $w(h - l) \le x$, or $C = w(1 - t)(h - l) + tx + \pi$ if $w(h - l) \ge x$. Now, suppose that the government reduces the tax deduction x. Using diagrams, determine the effects of this tax change on the consumer, and explain your results in terms of income and substitution effects. Make sure that you consider two cases. In the first case the consumer does not pay any tax before x is reduced, and in the second case the consumer pays a positive tax before x is reduced.

6. Show that the consumer is better off with a lump-sum tax rather than a proportional tax on wage income (as in question 3) given that either tax yields the same revenue for the government. You will need to use a diagram to show this. *Hint:* The consumption bundle the consumer chooses under the proportional tax must be just affordable given the lump-sum tax.

7. Suppose that the representative consumer's dividend income increases, and his or her wage rate falls at the same time. Determine the effects on consumption and labour supply, and explain your results in terms of income and substitution effects.

8. Suppose that a consumer can earn a higher wage rate for working "overtime." That is, for the first q hours the consumer works, he or she receives a real wage rate of w_1, and for hours worked more than q he or she receives w_2, where $w_2 > w_1$. Suppose that the consumer pays no taxes and receives no nonwage income, and he or she is free to choose hours of work.
   a. Draw the consumer's budget constraint, and show his or her optimal choice of consumption and leisure.
   b. Show that the consumer would never work q hours, or anything very close to q hours. Explain the intuition behind this.
   c. Determine what happens if the overtime wage rate, w_2, increases. Explain your results in terms of income and substitution effects. You will need to consider the cases of a worker who initially works overtime and a worker who initially does not work overtime.

9. Recall that leisure time in our model of the representative consumer is intended to capture any time spent not working in the market, including production at home, such as yard work and caring for children. Suppose that the government were to provide free day care for children and, for the purpose of analyzing the effects of this, assume that this has no effect on the market real wage w, taxes T, and dividend income π. Determine the effects of the daycare program on consumption, leisure, and hours worked for the consumer.

10. Suppose that a consumer cannot vary hours of work as he or she chooses. In particular, he or she must choose between working q hours and not working at all, where $q > 0$. Suppose that dividend income is zero, and that the consumer pays a tax T if he or she works, and receives a benefit b when not working, interpreted as an unemployment insurance payment.
    a. If the wage rate increases, how does this affect the consumer's hours of work? What does this have to say about what we would observe about the behaviour of actual consumers when wages change?
    b. Suppose that the unemployment insurance benefit increases. How will this affect hours of work? Explain the implications of this for unemployment insurance programs.

11. Suppose that the government imposes a producer tax. That is, the firm pays t units of consumption goods to the government for each unit of output it produces. Determine the effect of this tax on the firm's demand for labour.

12. Suppose that the government subsidizes employment. That is, the government pays the firm s units of consumption goods for each unit of labour that the firm hires. Determine the effect of the subsidy on the firm's demand for labour.

13. Suppose that the firm has a minimum quantity of employment, N^*; that is, the firm can produce no output unless the labour input is greater than or equal to N^*. Otherwise, the firm produces output according to the same production function as specified in this chapter. Given these circumstances, determine the effects of an increase in the real wage on the firm's choice of labour input. As well, construct the firm's demand curve for labour.

14. Supposing that a single consumer works for a firm, the quantity of labour input for the firm, N, is identical to the quantity of hours worked by the consumer, $h - l$. Graph the relationship between output produced, Y, on the vertical axis and leisure hours of the consumer, l, on the horizontal axis, which is implied by the production function of the firm. (In Chapter 5, we will refer to this relationship as the *production possibilities frontier*.) What is the slope of the curve you have graphed?

15. In the course of producing its output, a firm causes pollution. The government passes a law that requires the firm to stop polluting, and the firm discovers that it can prevent the pollution by hiring x workers for every worker that is producing output. That is, if the firm hires N workers, then xN workers are required to clean up the pollution caused by the N workers who are actually producing output. Determine the effects of the pollution regulation on the firm's profit-maximizing choice of labour input and on the firm's labour demand curve.

16. Suppose a firm has a production function given by $Y = zK^{0.3}N^{0.7}$.
    a. If $z = 1$ and $K = 1$, graph the production function. Is the marginal product of labour positive and diminishing?
    b. Now, graph the production function when $z = 2$ and $K = 1$. Explain how the production function changed from part (a).
    c. Next, graph the production function when $z = 1$ and $K = 2$. What happened now?
    d. Given this production function, the marginal product of labour is given by $MP_N = 0.7zK^{0.3}N^{-0.3}$. Graph the marginal product of labour for $(z, K) = (1, 1), (2, 1), (1, 2)$, and explain what you get.

17. Suppose that the production function $zF(K, N)$ exhibits increasing returns to scale, to the extent that the marginal product of labour increases when the quantity of labour input increases.
    a. Given this production function, what will be the representative firm's demand for labour?
    b. What problems do you see this presenting, for example if we try to build a competitive equilibrium model with increasing-returns-to-scale production?

A Closed-Economy One-Period Macroeconomic Model

5

In Chapter 4, we studied the microeconomic behaviour of a representative consumer and a representative firm. In this chapter, our first goal will be to take that microeconomic behaviour of a representative consumer and a representative firm and build it into a working model of the macroeconomy. Then, we will use this model to illustrate how unconstrained markets can produce economic outcomes that are socially efficient. This social efficiency will prove to be useful in how we use our model to analyze some important macroeconomic issues. We will show how increases in government spending increase aggregate output and crowd out private consumption expenditures, and how increases in productivity can lead to increases in aggregate output and the standard of living. Finally, we will consider a version of the model where the economic outcome is not socially efficient in an economy with unconstrained private markets, and we also consider a simple model of how the government should determine government spending. This result occurs because government tax collection distorts private decisions. In this context, we explore how the incentive effects of the income tax matter for aggregate economic activity.

We want to start our approach to macroeconomic modelling in this chapter by analyzing how consumers and firms interact in markets in a **closed economy**. This is a model of a single country that has no interaction with the rest of the world—it does not trade with other countries. It is easier to first understand how a closed economy works, and much of the economic intuition we will build up for the closed-economy case will carry over to an **open economy**, where international trade is allowed. Further, for many economic questions, particularly the ones addressed in this chapter, the answers will not be fundamentally different if we allow the economy to be open.

There are three different actors in this economy: the representative consumer who stands in for the many consumers in the economy who sell labour and buy goods, the representative firm that stands in for the many firms in the economy that buy labour and sell goods, and the government. We have already described the behaviour of the representative consumer and representative firm in detail in Chapter 4; it only remains to explain what the government does.

Government

The behaviour of the government here is quite simple. It wants to purchase a given quantity of consumption goods, G, and finances these purchases by taxing the representative consumer. In practice, governments provide many different goods and services, including roads and bridges, national defence, air traffic control, and education. Which goods and services the government should provide is subject to both political and economic debate, but economists generally agree that the government has a special role to play in providing **public goods**, such as national defence, that are difficult or impossible for the private sector to provide. National defence is a good example of a public good, since it is difficult to get an individual to pay for it in a private market according to how much of it he or she uses.

To keep things as simple as possible, for now we will not be specific about the public-goods nature of government expenditure, though that will be addressed later in this chapter. What we want to capture here is that government spending uses up resources, and we will model this by assuming that government spending simply involves taking goods from the private sector. Output is produced, and the government purchases an exogenous amount G of this output, with the remainder consumed by the representative consumer. An **exogenous variable** is determined outside the model, while an **endogenous variable** is determined by the model itself. Government spending is exogenous in our model, as we are assuming that government spending is independent of what happens in the rest of the economy. The government must abide by the **government budget constraint**, which we write as

$$G = T,$$

or government purchases are equal to taxes, in real terms.

Introducing the government in this way allows us to study some basic effects of **fiscal policy**. In general, fiscal policy refers to the government's choices over its expenditures, taxes, transfers, and borrowing. Recall from Chapter 2 that government expenditures are purchases of final goods and services, while transfers are simply reallocations of purchasing power from one set of individuals to another. Since this is a one-period economic environment, the government's choices are very limited, as described by the above government budget constraint. The government cannot borrow to finance government expenditures, since there is no future in which to repay its debt, and the government does not tax more than it spends, as this would imply that the government would foolishly throw goods away. The government budget deficit, which is $G - T$ here, is always zero. Thus, the only elements of fiscal policy we will study in this chapter are the setting of government purchases, G, and the macroeconomic effects of changing G. In Chapter 9, we will explore what happens when the government can run deficits and surpluses.

Competitive Equilibrium

Now that we have looked at the behaviour of the representative consumer, the representative firm, and the government, what remains in constructing our model is to show how consistency is obtained in the actions of all these economic agents. Once we have done this, we can use this model to make predictions about how the whole economy behaves in response to changes in the economic environment.

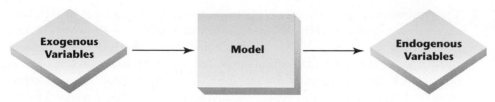

FIGURE 5.1
A Model Takes Exogenous Variables and Determines Endogenous Variables
Exogenous variables are determined outside a macroeconomic model. Given the exogenous variables, the model determines the endogenous variables. In experiments, we are interested in how the endogenous variables change when there are changes in exogenous variables.

Mathematically, a macroeconomic model takes the exogenous variables, which for the purposes of the problem at hand are determined outside the system we are modelling, and determines values for the endogenous variables, as outlined in Figure 5.1. In the model we are working with here, the exogenous variables are G, z, and K—that is, government spending, total factor productivity, and the economy's capital stock, respectively. The endogenous variables are C, N^s, N^d, T, Y, and w—that is, consumption, the quantity of labour supplied, the quantity of labour demanded, taxes, aggregate output, and the market real wage. Making use of the model is a process of running experiments in order to determine how changes in the exogenous variables will change the endogenous variables. By running these experiments, we hope to understand real-world macroeconomic events and to say something about macroeconomic policy. For example, one of the experiments we will run on our model in this chapter is to change exogenous government spending and then determine the effects on consumption, employment, aggregate output, and the real wage. An example of the phenomena that will help us to understand are the events that occurred in the economy during World War II, when there was a large increase in government spending.

By consistency we mean that, given market prices, demand is equal to supply in each market in the economy. Such a state of affairs is called a **competitive equilibrium**. Here, *competitive* refers to the fact that all consumers and firms are price-takers, and the economy is in *equilibrium* when the actions of all consumers and firms are consistent. When demand equals supply in all markets, we refer to that as **market clearing**. In our model economy, there is only one price, which is the real wage, w. We can also think of the economy as having only one market, on which labour time is exchanged for consumption goods. In this labour market, the representative consumer supplies labour and the representative firm demands labour. A competitive equilibrium is achieved when, given the exogenous variables G, z, and K, the real wage w is such that *the quantity of labour the consumer wants to supply is equal to the quantity of labour the firm wants to hire*. Also, note that the consumer's supply of labour is in part determined by taxes T and dividend income π. In a competitive equilibrium, T must satisfy the government budget constraint, and π must be equal to the profits generated by the firm.

A competitive equilibrium is a set of endogenous quantities, C (consumption), N^s (labour supply), N^d (labour demand), T (taxes), Y (aggregate output), and an endogenous real wage, w, such that, given the exogenous variables G (government spending), z (total factor productivity), and K (capital stock), the following are satisfied:

1. The representative consumer chooses C (consumption) and N^s (labour supply) to make himself or herself as well off as possible subject to his or her budget constraint, given w (the real wage), T (taxes), and π (dividend income). That is, the representative consumer optimizes given his or her budget constraint, which is determined by the real wage, taxes, and the profits the consumer receives from the firm as dividend income.

2. The representative firm chooses N^d (labour demand) to maximize profits, with maximized output $Y = zF(K, N^d)$ and maximized profits $\pi = Y - wN^d$. The firm treats z (total factor productivity), K (the capital stock), and w (the real wage) as given. That is, the representative firm optimizes given total factor productivity, its capital stock, and the market real wage. In equilibrium, the profits that the representative firm earns must be equal to the dividend income that is received by the consumer.

3. The market for labour clears, that is, $N^d = N^s$. The quantity of labour that the representative firm wants to hire is equal to the quantity of labour the representative consumer wants to supply.

4. The government budget constraint is satisfied—that is, $G = T$. The taxes paid by consumers are equal to the exogenous quantity of government spending.

An important property of a competitive equilibrium is that

$$Y = C + G, \tag{5.1}$$

which is the income–expenditure identity. Recall from Chapter 2 that we generally state the income–expenditure identity as $Y = C + I + G + NX$, where I is investment and NX is net exports. In this economy, there is no investment expenditure, as there is only one period, and net exports are zero, as the economy is closed, so that $I = 0$ and $NX = 0$.

To show why the income–expenditure identity holds in equilibrium, we start with the representative consumer's budget constraint,

$$C = wN^s + \pi - T, \tag{5.2}$$

or consumption expenditures equal real wage income plus real dividend income minus taxes. In equilibrium, dividend income is equal to the firm's maximized profits, or $\pi = Y - wN^d$, and the government budget constraint is satisfied, so that $T = G$. If we then substitute in Equation (5.2) for π and T, we get

$$C = wN^s + Y - wN^d - G. \tag{5.3}$$

In equilibrium, labour supply is equal to labour demand, or $N^s = N^d$, which then gives us, substituting for N^s in Equation (5.3) and rearranging, the identity in Equation (5.1).

There are many ways to work with macroeconomic models. Modern macroeconomic researchers sometimes work with an algebraic representation of a model, sometimes with a formulation of a model that can be put on a computer and simulated, and sometimes with a model in graphical form. We will use the latter approach most often in this book. In doing graphical analysis, sometimes the simplest approach will be to work with a model in the form of supply and demand curves, with one supply curve and one demand curve for each market under consideration. As the number of markets in the model increases, this approach will become most practical, and in Chapters 11 to 14 and some later chapters, we will work mainly with models in the form of supply and demand curves. These supply and demand curves will be derived from the microeconomic behaviour of consumers and firms, as was the case when we examined labour supply and labour demand curves in Chapter 4, but the underlying microeconomic behaviour will not be explicit. For our analysis here, however, where exchange takes place between the representative consumer and the representative firm in only one market, it is relatively straightforward to be entirely explicit about microeconomic principles. The approach we will follow in this chapter is to study competitive equilibrium in our model by examining the consumer's and the firm's decisions in the same diagram, so that we can determine how aggregate consistency is achieved in competitive equilibrium.

We want to start first with the production technology operated by the representative firm. In a competitive equilibrium, $N^d = N^s = N$—that is, labour demand equals labour supply—and we will refer to N as employment. Then, as in Chapter 4, from the production function, output is given by

$$Y = zF(K, N), \tag{5.4}$$

and we graph the production function in Figure 5.2(a), for a given capital stock K. Note that, since the representative consumer has a maximum of h hours to spend working, N can be no larger than h, which implies that the maximum output that could be produced in this economy is Y^* in Figure 5.2(a).

Another way to graph the production function, which will prove very useful for integrating the firm's production behaviour with the consumer's behaviour, is to use the fact that, in equilibrium, we have $N = h - l$. Substituting for N in the production function (5.4), we get

$$Y = zF(K, h - l), \tag{5.5}$$

which is a relationship between output Y and leisure l, given the exogenous variables z and K. If we graph this relationship, as in Figure 5.2(b), with leisure on the horizontal axis and Y on the vertical axis, then we get a mirror image of the production function in Figure 5.2(a). That is, the point $(l, Y) = (h, 0)$ in panel (b) of the figure corresponds to the point $(N, Y) = (0, 0)$ in panel (a). When the consumer takes all of his or her time as leisure, then employment is zero and nothing gets produced. As leisure falls in (b) from h, employment increases in (a) from zero, and output increases. In (b), when $l = 0$, the consumer is using all of his or her time for work and consuming no leisure, and the maximum quantity of output, Y^*, is produced. Note that since the slope of the production function in panel (a) of the figure is MP_N, the marginal product of labour, the slope of the relationship in panel (b) is $-MP_N$, since this relationship is just the mirror image of the production function.

Now, since in equilibrium $C = Y - G$, from the income–expenditure identity, from (5.5) we get

$$C = zF(K, h - l) - G,$$

which is a relationship between C and l, given the exogenous variables z, K, and G. This relationship, graphed in Figure 5.2(c), is just the relationship in (b) shifted down by the amount G, since consumption is output minus government spending in equilibrium.

FIGURE 5.2
**The Production Function
and the Production
Possibilities Frontier**
Panel (a) shows the
production function of
the representative firm,
while panel (b) shows the
equilibrium relationship
between the quantity of
leisure consumed by the
representative consumer
and aggregate output.
The relationship in (b) is
the mirror image of the
production function in (a). In
(c), we show the production
possibilities frontier (*PPF*),
which is the technological
relationship between *C* and
I, determined by shifting the
relationship in (b) down by
the amount *G*. The shaded
region in (c) represents
consumption bundles that
are technologically feasible to
produce in this economy.

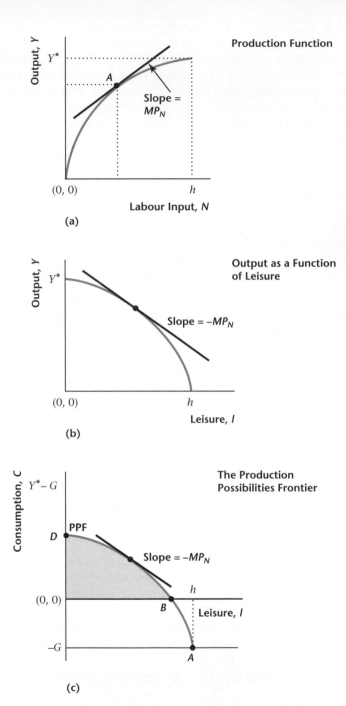

The relationship is called a **production possibilities frontier** (*PPF*), and it describes
what the technological possibilities are for the economy as a whole, in terms of the production of consumption goods and leisure. Though leisure is not literally produced,
all of the points in the shaded area inside the *PPF* and on the *PPF* in Figure 5.2(c)
are technologically possible in this economy. The *PPF* captures the tradeoff between

leisure and consumption that the available production technology makes available to the representative consumer in the economy. Note that the points on the *PPF* on line *AB* are not feasible for this economy, as consumption is negative. Only the points on the *PPF* on line *DB* are feasible, since here enough consumption goods are produced so that the government can take some of these goods and still leave something for private consumption.

As in Figure 5.2(b), the slope of the *PPF* in (c) is $-MP_N$. Another name for the negative of the slope of the *PPF* is the marginal rate of transformation. The **marginal rate of transformation** is the rate at which one good can be converted technologically into another; in this case, the marginal rate of transformation is the rate at which leisure can be converted in the economy into consumption goods through work. We will let $MRT_{l,C}$ denote the marginal rate of transformation of leisure into consumption. Then, we have

$$MRT_{l,C} = MP_N = -(\text{Slope of the } PPF).$$

Our next step will be to put the *PPF* together with the consumer's indifference curves and show how we can analyze a competitive equilibrium in a single diagram in Figure 5.3. In the figure, the *PPF* is given by the curve *HF*. From the relationship between the production function and the *PPF* in Figure 5.2, and given what we know about the profit-maximizing decision of the firm from Chapter 4, we can determine the production point on the *PPF* chosen by the firm, given the equilibrium real wage, w. Namely, the representative firm chooses the labour input to maximize profits in

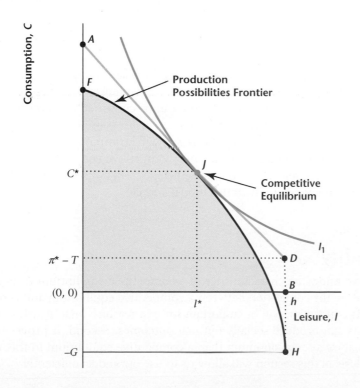

FIGURE 5.3
Competitive Equilibrium
This figure brings together the representative consumer's preferences and the representative firm's production technology to determine a competitive equilibrium. Point *J* represents the equilibrium consumption bundle. *ADB* is the budget constraint faced by the consumer in equilibrium, with the slope of *AD* equal to minus the real wage and the distance *DB* equal to dividend income minus taxes.

equilibrium by setting $MP_N = w$, and so in equilibrium minus the slope of the *PPF* must be equal to w, since $MRT_{l,C} = MP_N = w$ in equilibrium. Therefore, if w is an equilibrium real wage rate, we can draw a line *AD* in Figure 5.3 that has slope $-w$ and is tangent to the *PPF* at point *J*, where $MP_N = w$. Then, the firm chooses labour demand equal to $h - l^*$ and produces $Y^* = zF(K, h - l^*)$, from the production function. Maximized profits for the firm are $\pi^* = zF(K, h - l^*) - w(h - l^*)$ (total revenue minus the cost of hiring labour), or the distance *DH* in Figure 5.3. (Recall this from Chapter 4.) Now, *DB* in Figure 5.3 is equal to $\pi^* - G = \pi^* - T$, from the government budget constraint $G = T$.

It is important to recognize that *ADB* in the figure is the budget constraint that the consumer faces in equilibrium, since the slope of *AD* is $-w$ and the length of *DB* is the consumer's dividend income minus taxes, where dividend income is the profits that the firm earns and distributes to the consumer. Since *J* represents the competitive equilibrium production point, where C^* is the quantity of consumption goods produced by the firm, and $h - l^*$ is the quantity of labour hired by the firm, it must be the case (as is required for aggregate consistency) that C^* is also the quantity of consumption goods that the representative consumer desires, and l^* is the quantity of leisure the consumer desires. This implies that an indifference curve (curve I_1 in Figure 5.3) must be tangent to *AD* (the budget constraint) at point *J* in Figure 5.3. Given this, in equilibrium at point *J* we will have $MRS_{l,C} = w$—that is, the marginal rate of substitution of leisure for consumption for the consumer is equal to the real wage. Since $MRT_{l,C} = MP_N = w$ in equilibrium, we have, at point *J* in Figure 5.3,

$$MRS_{l,C} = MRT_{l,C} = MP_N. \qquad (5.6)$$

In other words, the marginal rate of substitution of leisure for consumption is equal to the marginal rate of transformation, which is equal to the marginal product of labour. That is, because the consumer and the firm face the same market real wage in equilibrium, the rate at which the consumer is just willing to trade leisure for consumption is the same as the rate at which leisure can be converted into consumption goods by using the production technology.

The condition expressed in Equation (5.6) will be important in the next subsection in establishing the economic efficiency of a competitive equilibrium. The connection between market outcomes and economic efficiency will be critical in making the analysis of macroeconomic issues with this model simple.

Optimality

Now that we know the characteristics of a competitive equilibrium from Figure 5.3, we can analyze the connection between a competitive equilibrium and economic efficiency. This connection will be important for two reasons. First, it will illustrate how free markets can produce socially optimal outcomes. Second, it proves to be much easier to analyze a social optimum than a competitive equilibrium in this model, and so our analysis in this section will allow us to use our model efficiently.

An important part of economics is analyzing how markets act to arrange production and consumption activities, and asking how this arrangement compares with some ideal or efficient arrangement. Typically, the efficiency criterion that economists use in evaluating market outcomes is **Pareto-optimality**. (Pareto, a nineteenth-century Italian economist, is famous for, among other things, his application of mathematics to economic analysis and the introduction of the concept of indifference curves.)

DEFINITION

*A competitive equilibrium is **Pareto-optimal** if there is no way to rearrange production or to reallocate goods so that someone is made better off without making someone else worse off.*

For this model, we would like to ask whether the competitive equilibrium is Pareto-optimal, but our job is relatively easy because there is only one representative consumer. We do not have to consider how goods are allocated across people. In our model, we can focus solely on how production is arranged to make the representative consumer as well off as possible. To construct the Pareto optimum here, we introduce the device of a fictitious social planner, a device commonly used to determine efficiency in economic models. The planner does not have to deal with markets, and he or she can simply order the representative firm to hire a given quantity of labour and produce a given quantity of consumption goods. The planner also has the power to coerce the consumer into supplying the required amount of labour. Produced consumption goods are taken by the planner, G is given to the government, and the remainder is allocated to the consumer. The planner is benevolent, and he or she chooses quantities so as to make the representative consumer as well off as possible. In this way, the planner's choices tell us what, in the best possible circumstances, could be achieved in our model economy.

The social planner's problem is to choose C and l, given the technology for converting l into C, to make the representative consumer as well off as possible. That is, the social planner chooses a consumption bundle that is on or within the production possibilities frontier (*PPF*) and that is on the highest possible indifference curve for the consumer. In Figure 5.4 the Pareto optimum is located at point B, where an indifference curve is just tangent to the *PPF*—curve AH. The social planner's problem is very similar to the representative consumer's problem of making himself or herself as well off as possible given his or her budget constraint. The only difference is that the budget constraint of the consumer is a straight line, while the *PPF* is concave (i.e., bowed out from the origin).

In Figure 5.4, since the slope of the indifference curve is minus the marginal rate of substitution, $-MRS_{l,C}$, and the slope of the *PPF* is minus the marginal rate of transformation, $-MRT_{l,C}$, or minus the marginal product of labour, $-MP_N$, the Pareto optimum has the property that

$$MRS_{l,C} = MRT_{l,C} = MP_N.$$

This is the same property that a competitive equilibrium has—or Equation (5.6). Comparing Figures 5.3 and 5.4, we easily see that the Pareto optimum and the competitive equilibrium are the same thing, since a competitive equilibrium is the point

FIGURE 5.4

Pareto-Optimality

The Pareto optimum is the point that a social planner would choose, where the representative consumer is as well off as possible given the technology for producing consumption goods by using labour as an input. Here, the Pareto optimum is *B*, where an indifference curve is tangent to the *PPF*.

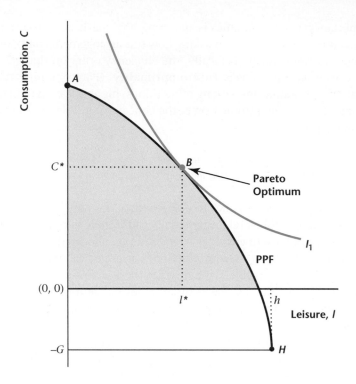

where an indifference curve is tangent to the *PPF* in Figure 5.3, and the same is true of the Pareto optimum in Figure 5.4. A key result of this chapter is that, for this model, the competitive equilibrium is identical to the Pareto optimum.

Two fundamental principles in economics apply here, the **first fundamental theorem of welfare economics** and the **second fundamental theorem of welfare economics**, which are defined as follows:

DEFINITION

The **first fundamental theorem of welfare economics** *states that, under certain conditions, a competitive equilibrium is* **Pareto-optimal***.*

DEFINITION

The **second fundamental theorem of welfare economics** *states that, under certain conditions, a Pareto optimum is a competitive equilibrium.*

The above two theorems are often referred to as the "first welfare theorem" and the "second welfare theorem." In our model, it is straightforward to see, from Figures 5.3 and 5.4, that the first and second welfare theorems hold, since there is one competitive equilibrium and one Pareto optimum, and they are clearly the same thing. In other kinds of economic models, however, showing whether the first and second welfare theorems hold can be hard work.

The idea behind the first welfare theorem goes back at least as far as Adam Smith's *The Wealth of Nations*. Smith argued that an unfettered market economy composed of self-interested consumers and firms could achieve an allocation of resources and goods that was socially efficient, as if an "invisible hand" were guiding the actions of individuals toward a state of affairs beneficial for all. The model we have constructed here has the property that a competitive equilibrium, or unfettered market outcome, is the same outcome that would be chosen by the invisible hand of the fictitious social planner.

The first welfare theorem is quite remarkable, since it appears to be inconsistent with the training we receive early in life, when we are typically encouraged to have empathy for others and to share our belongings. Most people value generosity and compassion, and so it certainly seems surprising that individuals motivated only by greed and profit maximization could achieve some kind of social utopia. Note, however, that if we consider economies with many consumers instead of a single representative consumer, a Pareto optimum might have the property that some people are very poor and some are very rich. That is, we may not be able to make the poor better off without making the rich worse off. At the extreme, a state of affairs in which one person has all of society's wealth may be Pareto-optimal, but few would argue that this is a sensible way to arrange an economy. Pareto-optimality is a very narrow concept of social optimality. In some instances, society is interested in equity as well as efficiency, and there may be a tradeoff between the two.

SOURCES OF SOCIAL INEFFICIENCIES

What could cause a competitive equilibrium to fail to be Pareto-optimal? In practice, many factors can result in inefficiency in a market economy.

First, a competitive equilibrium may not be Pareto-optimal because of externalities. An **externality** is any activity for which an individual firm or consumer does not take account of all associated costs and benefits; externalities can be positive or negative. For example, pollution is a common example of a negative externality. Suppose that Disgusting Chemical Corporation (DCC) produces and sells chemicals, and in the production process generates a byproduct released as a gas into the atmosphere. This byproduct smells and is hazardous, and there are people who live close to DCC who are worse off as a result of the air pollution it produces. However, the negative externality that is produced in the form of pollution costs to the neighbours of DCC is not reflected in any way in DCC's profits. Therefore, DCC does not take the pollution externality into account in deciding how much labour to hire and the quantity of chemicals to produce. As a result, DCC will tend to produce more of these pollution-causing chemicals than is socially optimal. The key problem is that there is not a market on which pollution (or the rights to pollute) is traded. If such a market existed, private markets would not fail to produce a socially optimal outcome. This is because the people who bear the costs of pollution could sell the rights to pollute to DCC, and there would then be a cost to DCC for polluting, which DCC would take into account in making production decisions. In practice, markets in pollution rights for all types of pollution do not exist, though there have been some experiments with such markets.

Typically, governments take other kinds of approaches, such as regulation and taxation, to try to correct the negative externalities generated by pollution.

A positive externality is a benefit other people receive for which no one is compensated. For example, suppose that DCC has an attractive head office designed by a high-profile architect in a major city. This building yields a benefit to people who can walk by the building on a public street and admire the fine architecture. These people do not compensate the firm for this positive externality, as it would be very costly or impossible to set up a fee structure for the public viewing of the building. As a result, DCC will tend to underinvest in its head office. Likely, the building that DCC would construct would be less attractive than if the firm took account of the positive externality. Therefore, positive externalities lead to social inefficiencies, just as negative externalities do, and the root cause of an externality is a market failure. It is too costly or impossible to set up a market to buy and sell the benefits or costs associated with the externality.

A second reason a competitive equilibrium may not be Pareto-optimal is that there are **distorting taxes**. In Chapter 4 we discussed the difference between a lump-sum tax, which does not depend on the actions of the person being taxed, and a distorting tax, which does. An example of a distorting tax in our model would be if government purchases were financed by a proportional wage income tax rather than by a lump-sum tax. That is, for each unit of real wage income earned, the representative consumer pays t units of consumption goods to the government, so that t is the tax rate. Then, wage income is $w(1 - t)(h - l)$, and the effective wage for the consumer is $w(1 - t)$. Then, when the consumer optimizes, he or she will set $MRS_{l,C} = w(1 - t)$, while the firm optimizes by setting $MP_N = w$. Therefore, in a competitive equilibrium

$$MRS_{l,C} < MP_N = MRT_{l,C},$$

so that the tax drives a "wedge" between the marginal rate of substitution and the marginal product of labour. Thus, Equation (5.6) does not hold, as required for a Pareto optimum, so that the first welfare theorem does not hold. In a competitive equilibrium, a proportional wage income tax will tend to discourage work (so long as the substitution effect of a change in the wage is larger than the income effect), and there will tend to be too much leisure consumed relative to consumption goods. We will explore the aggregate effects of distorting taxes on labour income later in this chapter.

In practice, all real-world taxes, including sales taxes, income tax, and property taxes, cause distortions; lump-sum taxes are, in fact, not feasible.[1] This does not mean, however, that having lump-sum taxes in our model is nonsense. The assumption of lump-sum taxation in our model is an appropriate simplification, because for most of the issues we will address, the effects of more realistic distorting taxation will be unimportant.

A third reason market economies do not achieve efficiency is that firms may not be price-takers. If a firm is large relative to the market, it can use its monopoly power

---

[1]This is because any lump-sum tax is large enough that someone cannot pay it. Therefore, some people must be exempted from the tax; but if this is so, people will alter their behaviour so as to be considered exempt. Thus, the tax will distort private decisions.

to restrict output, raise prices, and increase profits. Monopoly power tends to lead to underproduction relative to what is socially optimal. There are many examples of monopoly power in Canada. For example, Canadian telecommunications and automobile manufacturing are each dominated by a few producers.

Since there are good reasons to believe that the three inefficiencies discussed above—externalities, tax distortions, and monopoly power—are important in modern economies, two questions arise. First, why should we analyze an economy that is efficient in the sense that a competitive equilibrium for this economy is Pareto-optimal? The reason is that in studying most macroeconomic issues, an economic model with inefficiencies will behave much like an economic model without inefficiencies, so actually modelling all these inefficiencies would merely add clutter to our model. With the assumption of the equivalence of the competitive equilibrium and the Pareto optimum, determining the competitive equilibrium need only involve solving the social planner's problem and not the more complicated one of determining prices and quantities.

A second question that arises concerning real-world social inefficiencies is whether Adam Smith was completely off track in emphasizing the tendency of unrestricted markets to produce socially efficient outcomes. It might appear that the existence of externalities, tax distortions, and monopoly power should lead us to press for various government regulations to offset the negative effects of these inefficiencies. However, the tendency of unregulated markets to produce efficient outcomes is a powerful one, and sometimes the cost of government regulations, in terms of added waste, outweighs the gains, in terms of correcting private market failures. The cure can often be worse than the disease.

HOW TO USE THE MODEL

The key to using our model is the equivalence between the competitive equilibrium and the Pareto optimum. We need only draw a picture as in Figure 5.5, where we are essentially considering the solution to the social planner's problem. Here, the *PPF* is curve *AH*, and the competitive equilibrium (or Pareto optimum) is at point *B*, where an indifference curve, I_1, is tangent to the *PPF*. The equilibrium quantity of consumption is then C^*, and the equilibrium quantity of leisure is l^*. The quantity of employment is $N^* = h - l^*$, as shown in Figure 5.5, and the quantity of output is $Y^* = C^* + G$, as also shown in the figure. The real wage, w, is determined by minus the slope of the *PPF*, or minus the slope of the indifference curve, I_1, at point *B*. The real wage is determined in this way because we know that, in equilibrium, the firm optimizes by setting the marginal product of labour equal to the real wage, and the consumer optimizes by setting the marginal rate of substitution equal to the real wage.

What we are primarily interested in now is how a change in an exogenous variable will affect the key endogenous variables C, Y, N, and w. The exogenous variables G, z, and K, which are government spending, total factor productivity, and the capital stock, respectively, will all alter the endogenous variables by shifting the *PPF* in particular ways. We will examine these effects and their interpretation in the next sections.

Figure 5.5 illustrates a key concept of this chapter in the clearest possible way. What is produced and consumed in the economy is determined entirely by the

FIGURE 5.5

Using the Second Welfare Theorem to Determine a Competitive Equilibrium
Since the competitive equilibrium and the Pareto optimum are the same thing, we can analyze a competitive equilibrium by working out the Pareto optimum, which is point *B* in the figure. At the Pareto optimum, an indifference curve is tangent to the *PPF*, and the equilibrium real wage is equal to minus the slope of the *PPF* and minus the slope of the indifference curve at *B*.

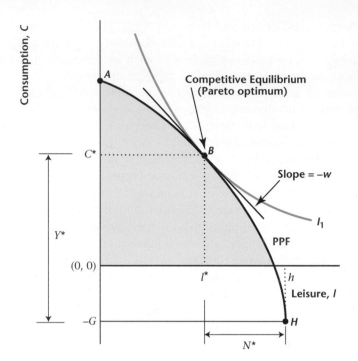

interaction of consumers' preferences with the technology available to firms. Though economic activity involves a complicated array of transactions among many economic actors, aggregate economic activity boils down to the preferences of consumers, as captured by the representative consumer's indifference curves, and the technology of firms, as captured by the *PPF*. Both consumer preferences and the firm's technology are important for determining aggregate output, aggregate consumption, employment, and the real wage. A change in either indifference curves or the *PPF* will affect what is produced and consumed.

Working with the Model: The Effects of a Change in Government Purchases

Recall from Chapter 1 that working with a macroeconomic model involves carrying out experiments. The first experiment we will conduct here is to change government spending, G, and ask what this does to aggregate output, consumption, employment, and the real wage. In Figure 5.6 an increase in G from G_1 to G_2 shifts the *PPF* from PPF_1 to PPF_2, where the shift down is by the same amount, $G_2 - G_1$, for each quantity of leisure, l. This shift leaves the slope of the *PPF* constant for each l. The effect of

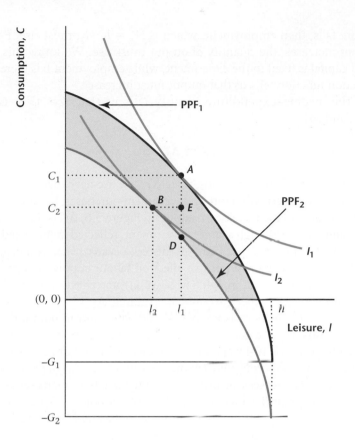

FIGURE 5.6
Equilibrium Effects of an Increase in Government Spending
An increase in government spending shifts the *PPF* down by the amount of the increase in *G*. There are negative income effects on consumption and leisure, so that both *C* and *I* fall, and employment rises, while output (equal to *C* + *G*) increases.

shifting the *PPF* downward by a constant amount is very similar to shifting the budget constraint for the consumer through a reduction in his or her nonwage disposable income, as we did in Chapter 4. Indeed, since $G = T$, an increase in government spending must necessarily increase taxes by the same amount, which will reduce the consumer's disposable income. It should not be surprising, then, that the effects of an increase in government spending essentially involve a negative income effect on consumption and leisure.

In Figure 5.6 the initial equilibrium is at point *A*, where indifference curve I_1 is tangent to PPF_1, the initial *PPF*. Here, equilibrium consumption is C_1, while the equilibrium quantity of leisure is l_1, and so equilibrium employment is $N_1 = h - l_1$. The initial equilibrium real wage is minus the slope of the indifference curve (or PPF_1) at point *A*. Now, when government spending increases, the *PPF* shifts to PPF_2, and the equilibrium point is at *B*, where consumption and leisure are both lower, at C_2 and l_2, respectively. Why do consumption and leisure decrease? This is because consumption and leisure are normal goods. Given the normal goods assumption, a negative income effect from the downward shift in the *PPF* must reduce consumption and leisure.

Since leisure falls, then employment, which is $N_2 = h - l_2$, must rise. Further, since employment increases, the quantity of output must rise. We know this because the quantity of capital is fixed in the experiment, while employment has increased, and so the production function tells us that output must increase.

Now, the income–expenditure identity tells us that $Y = C + G$; therefore, $C = Y - G$, and so

$$\Delta C = \Delta Y - \Delta G,$$

where Δ denotes "the change in." Thus, since $\Delta Y > 0$, we have that $\Delta C > -\Delta G$, so that private consumption is **crowded out** by government purchases, but it is not completely crowded out because of the increase in output. In Figure 5.6, ΔG is the distance AD, and ΔC is the distance AE. Although a larger government, reflected in increased government spending, results in more output being produced, because there is a negative income effect on leisure and therefore a positive effect on labour supply, a larger government reduces private consumption through a negative income effect produced by the higher taxes required to finance higher government spending. As the representative consumer pays higher taxes, his or her disposable income falls, and in equilibrium he or she spends less on consumption goods and works harder to support a larger government.

What happens to the real wage when G increases? In Figure 5.6 the slope of PPF_2 is identical to the slope of PPF_1 for each quantity of leisure, l. Therefore, since the PPF becomes steeper as l increases (the marginal product of labour increases as employment decreases), PPF_2 at point B is less steep than is PPF_1 at point A. Thus, since minus the slope of the PPF at the equilibrium point is equal to the equilibrium real wage, the real wage falls because of the increase in government spending. The real wage must fall, as we know that equilibrium employment rises, and the representative firm would hire more labour only in response to a reduction in the market real wage.

Now, a question we might like to ask is whether fluctuations in government spending are a likely cause of business cycles. To answer this, we must keep in mind a set of key business cycle facts. If fluctuations in government spending are important in causing business cycles, it should be the case that our model can replicate these key business cycle facts in response to a change in G. The model predicts that when government spending increases, aggregate output and employment increase, and consumption and the real wage decrease. One of our key business cycle facts is that employment is procyclical. This fact is consistent with government spending shocks causing business cycles, since employment will always move in the same direction as aggregate output in response to a change in G. Additional business cycle facts are that consumption and the real wage are procyclical, but the model predicts that consumption and the real wage are countercyclical in response to government spending shocks. This is because when G changes, consumption and the real wage always move in the direction opposite to the resulting change in Y. Therefore, government spending shocks do not appear to be a good candidate as a cause of business cycles. Whatever the primary cause of business cycles, it is unlikely to be the fact that governments change their spending plans from time to time. We will explore this idea further in Chapters 13 and 14.

Government Spending in World War II

Wars typically involve huge increases in government expenditure, and they therefore represent interesting "natural experiments" that we can examine as an informal empirical test of the predictions of our model. For example, a key economic effect on the Canadian economy of World War II, because it was so large, was an increase in the quantity of government purchases. During World War II, aggregate output was quickly channelled from private consumption to military uses. Figure 5.7 shows the natural logarithms of real GDP, real consumption expenditures, and real government expenditures for the period 1926–2010. Of particular note is the extremely large increase in government expenditures that occurred during World War II, which clearly swamps the small fluctuations in *G* about trend that happened before and after World War II. Clearly, GDP also increases above trend in the figure during World War II, and consumption dips somewhat below trend. Thus, these observations on the behaviour of consumption and output during World War II are consistent with our model, in that private consumption is crowded out somewhat and output increases.

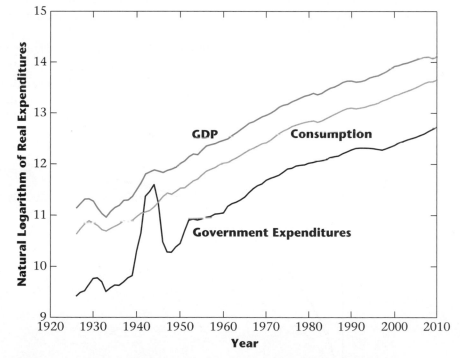

FIGURE 5.7 GDP, Consumption, and Government Expenditures for Canada, 1926–2010
During World War II, an increase in government spending is associated with an increase in aggregate output and a slight decrease in consumption from trend, as is consistent with our model.

Source: Adapted from the Statistics Canada CANSIM database, Series v3860085, v3860062, v3860067, v3860068, v3860069, and from the Statistics Canada publication *Historical Statistics of Canada*, Catalogue 11-516, 1983, Series F14–32.

Working with the Model: A Change in Total Factor Productivity

An increase in total factor productivity involves a better technology for converting factor inputs into aggregate output. As we will see in this section, increases in total factor productivity increase consumption and aggregate output, but there is an ambiguous effect on employment. This ambiguity is the result of opposing income and substitution effects on labour supply. Although an increase in government spending essentially produces only an income effect on consumer behaviour, an increase in total factor productivity generates both an income effect and a substitution effect.

Suppose that total factor productivity, z, increases. As mentioned previously, the interpretation of an increase in z is as a technological innovation (a new invention or an advance in management techniques), a spell of good weather, a relaxation in government regulations, or a decrease in the price of energy. The interpretation of the increase in z and the resulting effects depend on what we take one period in the model to represent relative to time in the real world. One period could be many years, in which case our model captures **long-run** effects; or one period could be just a month, a quarter, or a year, in which case it captures **short-run** effects. In macroeconomics the *short run* typically means a year or less, and the *long run* means more than a year. However, what is taken to be the boundary between the short run and the long run can vary considerably in different contexts.

The effect of an increase in z is to shift the production function up, as in Figure 5.8. Note that an increase in z not only permits more output to be produced given the quantity of labour input, but it also increases the marginal product of labour for each quantity of labour input. That is, the slope of the production function increases for each N. In Figure 5.8, z increases from z_1 to z_2. We can show exactly the same shift in the

FIGURE 5.8

Increase in Total Factor Productivity

An increase in total factor productivity shifts the production function up and increases the marginal product of labour for each quantity of the labour input.

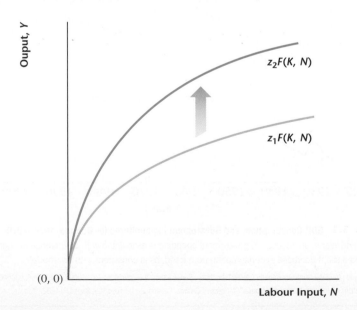

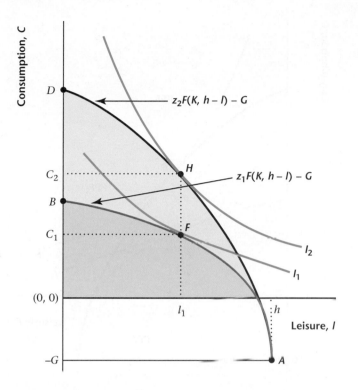

FIGURE 5.9

Competitive Equilibrium Effects of an Increase in Total Factor Productivity
An increase in total factor productivity shifts the *PPF* from *AB* to *AD*. The competitive equilibrium changes from *F* to *H* as a result. Output and consumption increase, the real wage increases, and leisure may rise or fall. Since employment is $N = h - l$, employment may rise or fall.

production function as a shift outward in the *PPF* in Figure 5.9 from *AB* to *AD*. Here, more consumption is attainable given the better technology, for any quantity of leisure consumed. Further, the tradeoff between consumption and leisure has improved, in that the new *PPF* is steeper for any given quantity of leisure. That is, since MP_N increases, and the slope of the *PPF* is $-MP_N$, the *PPF* will be steeper when z increases.

Figure 5.9 allows us to determine all the equilibrium effects of an increase in z. Here, indifference curve I_1 is tangent to the initial *PPF* at point *F*. After the shift in the *PPF*, the economy will be at a point, such as *H*, where there is a tangency between the new *PPF* and indifference curve I_2. What must be the case is that consumption increases in moving from *F* to *H*, in this case increasing from C_1 to C_2. However, leisure may increase or decrease, and here we have shown the case where it remains the same at l_1. Since $Y = C + G$ in equilibrium, and since G remains constant and C increases, there is an increase in aggregate output, and since $N = h - l$, employment is unchanged (but employment could have increased or decreased). The equilibrium real wage is minus the slope of the *PPF* at point *H* (i.e., $w = MP_N$). When we separate the income and substitution effects of the increase in z, we will show that the real wage must increase in equilibrium. In Figure 5.9 it is clear that the *PPF* is steeper at *H* than at *F*, so that the real wage is higher in equilibrium, but we will show how this must be true in general, even when the quantities of leisure and employment change.

To see why consumption has to increase, and why the change in leisure is ambiguous, we separate the shift in the *PPF* into an income effect and a substitution effect. In Figure 5.10, PPF_1 is the original *PPF*, and it shifts to PPF_2 when z increases from z_1 to z_2.

FIGURE 5.10

**Income and Substitution
Effects of an Increase in
Total Factor Productivity**
Here, the effects of an
increase in total factor
productivity are separated
into substitution and income
effects. The increase in total
factor productivity involves
a shift from PPF_1 to PPF_2.
The curve PPF_3 is an artificial
PPF, and it is PPF_2 with the
income effect of the increase
in z taken out. The substitution effect is the movement
from A to D, and the income
effect is the movement from
D to B.

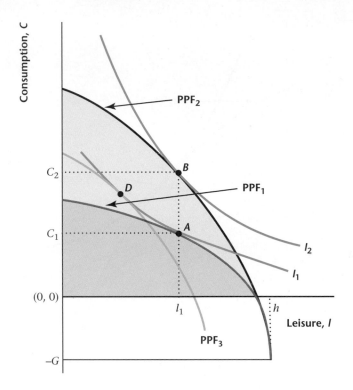

The initial equilibrium is at point A, and the final equilibrium is at point B after z increases. The equation for PPF_2 is given by

$$C = z_2 F(K, h - l) - G.$$

Now, consider constructing an artificial PPF, called PPF_3, which is obtained by shifting PPF_2 downward by a constant amount. That is, the equation for PPF_3 is given by

$$C = z_2 F(K, h - l) - G - C_0.$$

Here, C_0 is a constant large enough that PPF_3 is just tangent to the initial indifference curve I_1. What we are doing here is taking consumption (i.e., "income") away from the representative consumer to obtain the pure substitution effect of an increase in z. In Figure 5.10 the substitution effect is then the movement from A to D, and the income effect is the movement from D to B. Much the same as when we considered income and substitution effects for a consumer facing an increase in his or her wage rate, here the substitution effect is for consumption to increase and leisure to decrease, so that hours worked increase. Also, the income effect is for both consumption and leisure to increase. As before, consumption must increase as both goods are normal, but leisure may increase or decrease because of opposing income and substitution effects.

Now, why must the real wage increase in moving from A to B, even if the quantities of leisure and employment rise or fall? First, the substitution effect involves an increase in $MRS_{l,C}$ (the indifference curve gets steeper) in moving along the indifference curve from A to D. Second, since PPF_2 is just PPF_3 shifted up by a fixed amount, the slope of

PPF_2 is the same as the slope of PPF_3 for each quantity of leisure. As the quantity of leisure is higher at point B than at point D, the PPF is steeper at B than at D, and so $MRS_{l,C}$ also increases in moving from D to B. Thus, the real wage, which is equal to the marginal rate of substitution in equilibrium, must be higher in equilibrium when z is higher.

The increase in total factor productivity causes an increase in the marginal productivity of labour, which increases the demand for labour by firms, driving up the real wage. Workers now have more income given the number of hours worked, and they spend the increased income on consumption goods. Since there are offsetting income and substitution effects on labour supply, however, hours worked may increase or decrease. An important feature of the increase in total factor productivity is that the welfare of the representative consumer must increase. That is, the representative consumer must consume on a higher indifference curve when z increases. Therefore, increases in total factor productivity unambiguously increase the aggregate standard of living.

INTERPRETATION OF THE MODEL'S PREDICTIONS

Figure 5.9 tells a story about the long-term economic effects of long-run improvements in technology, such as those that have occurred since World War II in Canada. There have been many important technological innovations since World War II, particularly in electronics and information technology. Also, some key observations from post–World War II Canadian data are that aggregate output has increased steadily, consumption has increased, the real wage has increased, and hours worked per employed person have remained roughly constant. Figure 5.9 matches these observations in predicting that a technological advance leads to increased output, increased consumption, a higher real wage, and ambiguous effects on hours worked. Thus, if income and substitution effects roughly cancel each other out over the long run, the model is consistent with the fact that hours worked per person have remained roughly constant over the post–World War II period in Canada. There may have been many other factors in addition to technological change affecting output, consumption, the real wage, and hours worked over this period in Canadian history. However, our model tells us that empirical observations for this period are consistent with technological innovations having been an important contributing factor to changes in these key macroeconomic variables. Macroeconomics in Action 5.1 compares total productivity growth in Canada and the United States, to give some perspective on long-run relative trends in the two countries.

A second interpretation of Figure 5.9 is in terms of short-run aggregate fluctuations in macroeconomic variables. Could fluctuations in total factor productivity be an important cause of business cycles? Recall from Chapter 3 that three key business cycle facts are that consumption is procyclical, employment is procyclical, and the real wage is procyclical. From Figure 5.9, our model predicts that in response to an increase in z, aggregate output increases, consumption increases, employment may increase or decrease, and the real wage increases. Therefore, the model is consistent with procyclical consumption and real wages, as consumption and the real wage always move in the same direction as output when z changes. However, employment may be procyclical or countercyclical, depending on the strength of opposing income and substitution effects. For the model to be consistent with the data requires that the substitution effect dominate the income

The Short Run: Total Factor Productivity, GDP, and Energy Prices

The model constructed in this chapter predicts that an increase (decrease) in total factor productivity makes GDP increase (decrease). This suggests that fluctuations in total factor productivity are at least partly responsible for the fluctuations in GDP that we observe over time, and that they are a primary defining feature of business cycles.

To explore this idea, recall from Chapter 4 that a measure of total factor productivity for the Canadian economy is the Solow residual, and that movements in the Solow residual are the movements in GDP not accounted for by movements in capital and labour inputs to production. In Figure 5.11 we show percentage deviations from trend in the Solow residual and in real GDP for Canada for the years 1961–2010. These two time series track each other surprisingly closely, which is consistent with the view that fluctuations in total factor productivity are a primary explanation for business cycles in Canada over this time period.

However, the fact that the Solow residual and real GDP are highly correlated does not tell us much about what is causing business cycles, unless we know

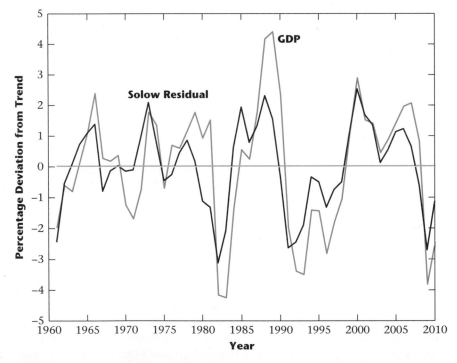

FIGURE 5.11 **Deviations from Trend in the Solow Residual and Real GDP, 1961–2010**

The figure shows the percentage deviations from trend in the Solow residual, a measure of total factor productivity, and in real GDP. The two time series track each other very closely, consistent with the view that total factor productivity fluctuations are an important cause of business cycles.

Source: Adapted from the Statistics Canada CANSIM database, Series v3860085, v2461119, v3822183, v1078498, and from the Statistics Canada publication *Historical Statistics of Canada*, Catalogue 11-516, 1983, Series D175–189.

something about why the Solow residual is fluctuating over time. In Chapter 4, we listed one of several factors that are important in determining total factor productivity, one of which is the relative price of energy. Recall that if the relative price of energy is high, then firms will tend to use less energy in production, and this will reduce the productivity of capital and labour. Therefore, we should tend to see a negative correlation between the relative price of energy and total factor productivity. The more important fluctuations in energy prices are in explaining fluctuations in total factor productivity, the higher the correlation will be between the relative price of energy and total factor productivity.

In Figure 5.12, we show the percentage deviations in the Solow residual and in the relative price of energy for the period 1961–2010. There is clearly a tendency for the Solow residual to be below (above) trend when the relative price of energy is above (below) trend, but this tendency is not strong. The correlation between the two time series is 0.16, which is negative, but relatively small in absolute value. This evidence is

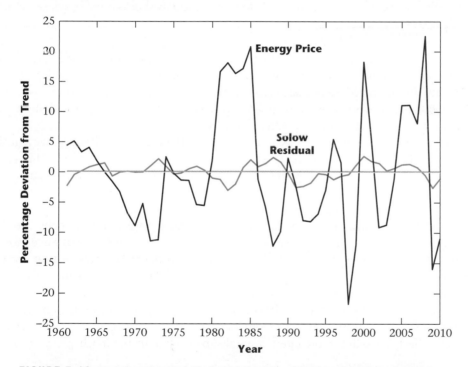

FIGURE 5.12 **Deviations from Trend in the Relative Price of Energy and the Solow Residual, 1961–2010**

The figure shows the percentage deviations from trend in the relative price of energy and the Solow residual. The relative price of energy tends to be above (below) trend when the Solow residual is below (above) trend. The two time series are negatively correlated, but the absolute value of the correlation is small. This is consistent with fluctuations in energy prices causing fluctuations in total factor productivity, but there appear to be important determinants of total factor productivity other than energy prices.

Source: Adapted from the Statistics Canada CANSIM database, Series v735319, v3822650, v83718, v3860085, v2461119, v3822183, v1078498, and from the Statistics Canada publication *Historical Statistics of Canada*, Catalogue 11-516, 1983, Series D175–189.

consistent with movements in energy prices being a contributing factor to fluctuations in total factor productivity and real GDP, but is also consistent with the existence of important additional factors explaining productivity and GDP fluctuations.

In Canada, increases in energy prices will tend to reduce productivity in most industries, particularly manufacturing and services. However, the energy industry, particularly oil and gas production, benefits from energy price increases, and this sector of the economy is important in Canada. This is consistent with the weak correlation between total factor productivity and energy prices in Canada. In the United States, total factor productivity is more closely tied to energy prices, and the United States is also much more dependent on imported energy than is Canada. Thus, the United States does not experience the same beneficial effect of an increase in energy prices that Canada does.

In conclusion, our evidence here indicates that although total factor productivity fluctuations seem to be important in explaining business cycles in Canada, energy prices do not play a large role in determining Canadian total factor productivity. In Chapter 14, we will examine in more detail how total factor productivity shocks cause business cycles.

effect, so that the consumer wants to increase the quantity of labour supplied in response to an increase in the market real wage. Thus, it is certainly possible that total factor productivity shocks could be a primary cause of business cycles, but to be consistent with the data requires that workers increase and decrease labour supply in response to increases and decreases in total factor productivity over the business cycle.

Some macroeconomists—advocates of **real business cycle theory**—view total factor productivity shocks as the most important cause of business cycles. This view may seem to be contradicted by the long-run evidence that the income and substitution effects on labour supply of real wage increases appear to roughly cancel each other out in the post–World War II period. However, real business cycle theorists argue that much of the short-run variation in labour supply is due to **intertemporal substitution of labour**, which is the substitution of labour over time in response to real wage movements. For example, a worker may choose to work harder in the present if he or she views his or her wage as being temporarily high, while planning to take more vacation in the future. The worker basically "makes hay while the sun shines." In this way, even though income and substitution effects may cancel each other out in the long run, in the short run the substitution effect of an increase in the real wage could outweigh the income effect. We will explore intertemporal substitution further in Chapters 11 to 14.

A Distorting Tax on Wage Income, Tax Rate Changes, and the Laffer Curve

We are now ready to consider a version of the model in which there is a distorting tax. As was discussed earlier in this chapter, distorting taxes imply in general that a competitive equilibrium is not Pareto-optimal, and so we will not be able to use the same approach to analyzing the model as previously. The distorting tax we will consider is a proportional tax on wage income. This will capture, in a simple way, some features of income taxation

Figure 5.13 shows total factor productivity, as measured by the Solow residual, for Canada and the United States over the period 1961–2010. For each country, total factor productivity has been normalized to 100 for the year 1961 so that we can observe the relative growth in total factor productivity in the two countries from 1961–2010. In the figure, note that total factor productivity in Canada roughly tracks that of the United States until the late 1970s, at which time a productivity gap opens up between the United States and Canada, with Canada falling behind. The gap increases sharply during the recession in the early 1990s (which was more severe in Canada than in the United States), and widens even further from the year 2000 on, and during the most recent recession. What could explain this poor productivity growth in Canada relative to the United States?

In Chapter 4, we explained that changes in total factor productivity could occur because of technological innovation, changes in the weather, changes in government regulations, and changes in the relative price of energy. We might think of these factors as affecting total productivity for individual firms. Another factor that may be relevant for explaining the difference in productivity between Canada and the United States is differences in the sectoral composition of output in the two countries. For example, firms producing computer software may be just as productive in Canada as in the United States, and firms extracting natural resources may have comparable total factor productivities in the two countries.

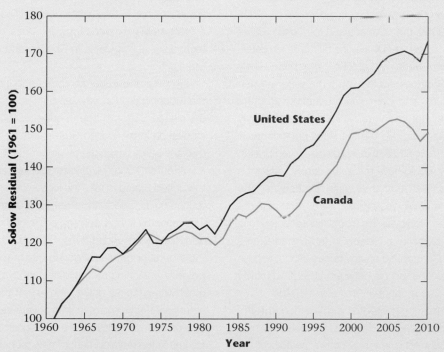

FIGURE 5.13 **Total Factor Productivity in Canada and the U.S.**

Productivity in Canada tracks that in the United States until the late 1970s, when a productivity gap opens up between the United States and Canada.

Source: Adapted from the Statistics Canada CANSIM database, Series v3860085, v2461119, v3822183, v1078498, and from the Statistics Canada publication *Historical Statistics of Canada*, Catalogue 11-516, 1983, Series D175–189. U.S. data: Bureau of Labor Statistics and Bureau of Economic Analysis.

However, if for example productivity is higher in the production of computer software than in the extraction of natural resources, and if Canada has relatively more production in natural resource extraction than in computer software than does the United States, then total factor productivity will tend to be higher in the United States than in Canada as a result.

In comparing Canada and the United States, it is unlikely that weather or government regulations can explain the increasing productivity gap we see in Figure 5.13. There have not been large adverse weather events in Canada relative to the United States over the period 1961–2010, and government regulations apparently have not changed adversely in Canada relative to the United States (if anything, the reverse is true).

With regard to energy prices, a key determinant of the price of energy is the price of crude oil. Since the mid-1980s, both Canada and the United States essentially faced the same price for crude oil, determined on the world market for oil. Thus, it is unlikely that energy prices could explain the widening gap between U.S. and Canadian productivity after the mid-1980s. Before the mid-1980s, federal energy policy in Canada held the domestic price of crude oil below the world price faced by the United States. This policy would have made the largest difference in Canada relative to the United States when the world price of oil was highest from 1973 until the early 1980s. However, this would have affected total factor productivity adversely in the United States relative to Canada, so energy prices cannot explain why a gap opened up between U.S. productivity and Canadian productivity in the mid-1970s.

A remaining potential explanation for the U.S.–Canada productivity gap is that relatively high growth occurred in low-productivity sectors of the Canadian economy compared with the United States. An article by Richard Dion in the *Bank of Canada Review*,[2] summarizing research on productivity in Canada, concludes that this factor indeed contributed to the increasing productivity gap between the United States and Canada, but that the contribution was small.

We have now eliminated all factors but one as potentially important determinants of the widening productivity gap between the U.S. and Canada. The remaining candidate is pure technological innovation. For this to explain the productivity gap, it would have to be the case that American firms in particular sectors of the economy have been superior to Canadian firms in the same sectors at adopting new production processes and management techniques. We do not know as much as we would like about technology adoption in Canada versus the United States. However, in his *Bank of Canada Review* article, Richard Dion points to evidence that spending on research and development is proportionally higher in the United States. Thus, there is a measurable difference in resources devoted to technological innovation in Canada and the United States.

Though the evidence appears to indicate that the widening productivity gap between Canada and the United States is due to superior technological innovation in the United States, it is far from clear that any policy response by government in Canada is warranted. It may be efficient for Canada to permit the United States to take the lead in developing new technologies, and then to reap the benefits of this innovation by simply copying advanced techniques adopted by American firms. Further, attempts by the federal or provincial governments to subsidize potentially winning technological innovation would meet with success only to the extent that governments are better informed than private-sector investors or that we believe there are significant market failures in the development of new technologies.

[2] R. Dion, 2007, "Interpreting Canada's Productivity Performance in the Past Decade: Lessons from Recent Research," *Bank of Canada Review*, Summer, 19–32.

in Canada and other countries, and will allow us to discuss some fiscal policy issues, including the incentive effects of income taxation. We will show that, surprisingly, it is possible for tax revenue collected by the government to increase when the income tax rate goes down, a feature illustrated in what has come to be known as the "Laffer curve." The form that the Laffer curve takes in the Canadian economy is of key importance for the effects of tax rate changes on labour supply and on tax revenue for the government.

A SIMPLIFIED ONE-PERIOD MODEL WITH PROPORTIONAL INCOME TAXATION

To keep the analysis simple and transparent for the purpose at hand, assume that output is produced only with labour as an input, with production by the representative firm according to the relationship

$$Y = zN^d, \tag{5.7}$$

with Y denoting aggregate output, N^d the firm's labour input, and z total factor productivity. Here, with only one factor of production, labour, we have continued to assume that there is constant returns to scale in production, that is increasing N^d by a factor x increases output Y by the same factor x.

Now, in a competitive equilibrium, since labour demand equals labour supply, or $N^d = h - l$, and consumption plus government spending equals output, or $C + G = Y$, from (5.7) we can write the production possibilities frontier (*PPF*) as

$$C = z(h - l) - G, \tag{5.8}$$

and we have graphed the *PPF* as *AB* in Figure 5.14. Note that the *PPF* is now linear. At point *A*, the representative consumer takes zero units of leisure and then consumes

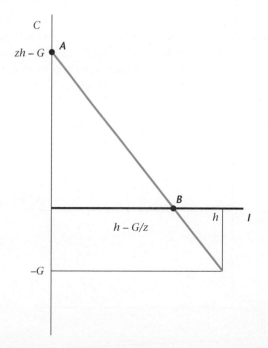

FIGURE 5.14

The Production Possibilities Frontier in the Simplified Model

The production possibilities frontier is linear. The maximum quantity of consumption (when the quantity of leisure is zero) is $zh - G$.

the maximum amount of consumption possible, $zh - G$, while at point B the consumer consumes zero and works G/z units of time (with $l = h - (G/z)$) so as to supply the government with G units of goods.

To purchase G units of goods, the government imposes a proportional tax on the consumer's wage income. Assume that this is the only tax in this economy. In particular, there are no lump-sum taxes, or $T = 0$. Letting t denote the tax rate, the consumer will pay $tw(h - l)$ in taxes to the government, so that we can write the consumer's budget constraint as

$$C = w(1 - t)(h - l) + \pi, \tag{5.9}$$

or consumption is equal to after-tax wage income plus dividend income. Note that $w(1 - t)$ is the effective wage rate for the consumer, or the after-tax real wage.

Next, consider the profit maximization problem for the representative firm. Profits for the firm are given by

$$\pi = Y - wN^d = (z - w)N^d \tag{5.10}$$

from (5.7). The firm chooses N^d to make π as large as possible, given z and w. Here, $z - w$ is the profit that the firm makes for each unit of labour input, and this is the same no matter how much labour the firm hires. Thus, if $z > w$, then the firm earns positive profits for each unit of labour hired, and it would want to hire an infinite quantity of labour. If $z - w$, then profits are negative for any quantity of labour hired, so the firm would hire no labour. However, if $z = w$, then profits are zero for the firm no matter what it does, that is, the firm is indifferent concerning how much labour to hire. As a result, the firm's demand curve for labour, denoted by $N^d(w)$ is infinitely elastic at the wage $w = z$, as shown in Figure 5.15.

Therefore, in equilibrium, no matter what the supply curve for labour $N^s(w)$ looks like (as determined by the representative consumer's behaviour), the equilibrium wage must be $w = z$. This simplifies our work dramatically. Further, since $w = z$ in equilibrium, therefore from (5.10) the firm must earn zero profits in equilibrium, or $\pi = 0$,

FIGURE 5.15

The Labour Demand Curve in the Simplified Model

Since productivity is constant at z, the representative firm's demand curve for labour is infinitely elastic at $w = z$.

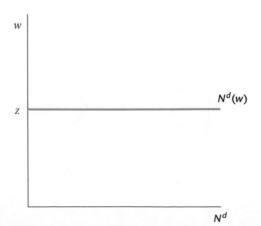

so dividend income for the representative consumer must also be zero in equilibrium. Therefore, setting $w = z$ and $\pi = 0$ in Equation (5.9), the consumer's budget constraint is

$$C = z(1-t)(h-l) \tag{5.11}$$

In equilibrium, the consumer chooses consumption C and leisure l to satisfy his or her budget constraint Equation (5.11), and markets clear, which is summarized by Equation (5.8). Note that Equations (5.8) and (5.11) in turn imply that the government's budget constraint is satisfied, since if we substitute for C in Equation (5.8) using Equation (5.11), we get $G = zt(h - l)$, or total government spending equals total tax revenue. We can depict a competitive equilibrium as in Figure 5.16. Here, AB is the PPF, or the combinations of C and l that satisfy Equation (5.8). As well, the budget constraint faced by the consumer in equilibrium is DF, or the combinations of C and l that satisfy Equation (5.11). In equilibrium the tax rate t adjusts so that the point on DF that the consumer chooses is at point H, where DF intersects AB, which is what is required for market clearing. Therefore, in equilibrium, an indifference curve is tangent to DF at point H. This indifference curve necessarily cuts the PPF as shown, since AB is steeper than DF ($z > z(1 - t)$).

One conclusion is that the Pareto optimum, at E, is different from the competitive equilibrium, at H. That is, because the income tax distorts private decisions, the competitive equilibrium is not socially efficient. The welfare loss due to the distorting tax can be measured by how much better off the consumer is at point E than at point H (note that H is on a lower indifference curve than E). A second conclusion is that consumption and output must be higher and leisure lower at point E than at point H.

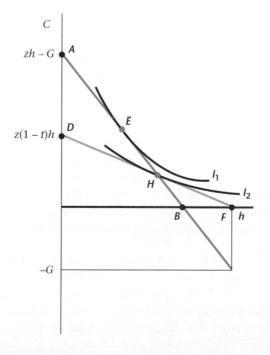

FIGURE 5.16

Competitive Equilibrium in the Simplified Model with a Proportional Tax on Labour Income
The competitive equilibrium is point H, and the Pareto optimum is point E.

This is due to the fact that indifference curves cannot cross, a property of indifference curves illustrated in a problem in Chapter 4. That is, the distorting income tax gives consumers a disincentive to work, and tends to lower aggregate consumption and aggregate output. Of course, if the government needs to collect taxes, and all taxes distort private decisions, it may be necessary to put up with these negative incentive effects of income taxation.

INCOME TAX REVENUE AND THE LAFFER CURVE

To get another perspective on a competitive equilibrium with an income tax, we will take the following approach. First, we can ask how much income tax revenue the government could generate for each tax rate t, taking into account the quantity of labour that the consumer will want to supply at each of those tax rates. Then, we can determine the equilibrium tax rate (or tax rates) that will finance government expenditures G. This approach will be informative about the potential effects of changing the tax rate.

To start, we know that in equilibrium the consumer faces his or her budget constraint (5.11) and chooses C and l to satisfy (5.11) given the tax rate t, and that the equilibrium real wage is $w = z$. If we ask what quantity of leisure the consumer would choose given each tax rate t, we can derive a function $l(t)$, which describes the quantity of leisure the consumer chooses if the after-tax real wage is $z(1 - t)$, taking z as given. This would then tell us that the tax revenue that the government can collect if the income tax rate is t is

$$\text{REV} = tz[h - l(t)] \tag{5.12}$$

where REV is total revenue from the income tax. In Equation (5.12), t is the tax rate, and $z[h - l(t)]$ is the **tax base**, which is the quantity traded in the market of the object being traded, which in this case is the quantity of labour, in units of consumption goods. It is important to recognize in Equation (5.12) that total tax revenue depends not only on the tax rate, but on the size of the tax base, which in turn depends on the tax rate. If the tax base does not change when t increases, then tax revenue will increase when the tax rate increases. However, it is possible for tax revenue to go down when t increases. This would occur if, when t increases, $l(t)$ increases sufficiently that a declining tax base offsets the effect of an increase in the tax rate on REV in Equation (5.12) so that REV falls when t increases. For this to occur, the substitution effect of a change in the after-tax real wage would have to be large relative to the income effect. That is, since an increase in t implies a decrease in the equilibrium real wage $z(1 - t)$, for REV to decline when t increases there would have to be a large decrease in the quantity of labour supplied, $h - l(t)$, in other words a large disincentive to work due to a higher income tax rate.

In Figure 5.17, we show a typical graph for Equation (5.12), where we plot total tax revenue against the tax rate, taking into account the effects of the consumer's choice concerning the quantity of labour supplied in response to the tax rate. The curve AB in the figure is called a **Laffer curve**. The Laffer curve gets its name from the economist Arthur Laffer, and it is any curve that shows the quantity of tax revenue generated by

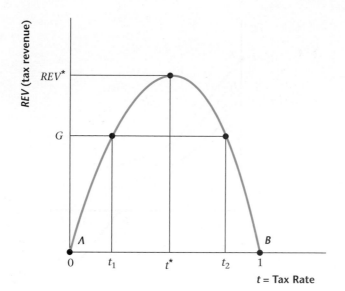

FIGURE 5.17
A Laffer Curve
The Laffer curve is the relationship between income tax revenue and the income tax rate. Tax revenue must be zero when $t = 0$ (the tax rate is zero) and $t = 1$ (because no one will work if all income is taxed away). The government can maximize tax revenue by setting $t = t^*$. If the government wishes to finance government spending equal to G, it can set a tax rate of t_1 (on the good side of the Laffer curve) or t_2 (on the bad side of the Laffer curve).

the government as a function of a tax rate. Theoretically, we cannot say much about the shape of the curve between the points A and B in Figure 5.17. In practice, how the curve looks between A and B depends on the details of labour supply behaviour for all possible after-tax real wage rates. However, points A and B will always be on the curve, since if the tax rate t is zero, then tax revenue must be zero ($t = 0$ implies REV $= 0$ in Equation (5.12)), which gives us point A, and the consumer will not work and the tax base is zero if $t = 1$ ($t = 1$ implies $l(1) = h$ and REV $= 0$ in Equation (5.12)), which gives us point B. In the figure, there is a maximum amount of tax revenue that the government can generate. That is, if the tax rate is t^*, then the maximum tax revenue REV* accrues to the government.

Now, given the quantity of government spending G, in our model the government will have to choose the tax rate t to generate enough revenue to finance this quantity of spending, or from (5.12), in equilibrium,

$$G = tz[h - l(t)],$$

which is another version of the government's budget constraint. In Figure 5.17, note first that if $G >$ REV* then it is impossible for the government to collect enough tax revenue to finance its spending. However, if $G <$ REV* (the case we want to consider) then given the quantity of government spending G, there are two possible equilibrium tax rates, shown here as t_1 and t_2, where $t_1 < t_2$.

Now, given that there are two equilibrium tax rates, t_1 and t_2, for any quantity of government expenditure G, consider what a competitive equilibrium will look like in the context of the diagram we used earlier in this section. In Figure 5.18, the competitive equilibrium with the low tax rate t_1 is given by point F, while the one with the high tax rate t_2 is given by point H. Recall that a competitive equilibrium will always lie

FIGURE 5.18

**Equilibria with High and
Low Tax Rates**

Given government spending
equal to *G*, as in Figure 5.17,
there are two equilibrium
tax rates. The low-tax-rate
(high-tax-rate) equilibrium is
at point *F* (*H*). In the low-tax-
rate equilibrium, consumption
and output are higher and
leisure is lower than in the
high-tax-rate equilibrium.

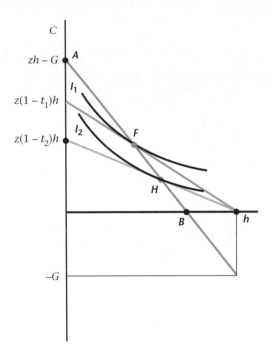

on the *PPF* given by curve *AB*, and on the budget constraint faced by the consumer in equilibrium. When the tax rate is t_2, the consumer's budget constraint is less steep and lies below the budget constraint in the equilibrium where the tax rate is t_1. Therefore, we can say that the quantity of consumption, *C*, is higher, the quantity of labour supplied, $h - l$, is higher, leisure *l* is lower, and aggregate output ($Y = C + G$) is higher in the low-tax-rate equilibrium than in the high-tax-rate equilibrium. Further, since point *F* must be on a higher indifference curve than point *H*, the consumer is better off in the equilibrium with a low tax rate than in the one with a higher tax rate.

A sensible government would never choose the high tax rate, t_2, since it could collect the same quantity of tax revenue with the low tax rate, t_1, and make the representative consumer better off. However, we might imagine that a less-than-sensible government could get stuck in a bad equilibrium with the high tax rate, t_2, and thus be on the wrong side of the Laffer curve in Figure 5.17; that is, it would be on the side of the Laffer curve at which an increase in the tax rate will reduce tax revenue, rather than on the side at which an increase in the tax rate will increase tax revenue. During the 1980 U.S. presidential election, Ronald Reagan, supported by the reasoning of so-called **supply-side economists**, put forward an economic program including reductions in income tax rates. Supply-side economists typically believe that there are large incentive effects of income taxes on labour supply, and that tax rate reductions will increase the quantity of labour supplied by a large amount. Reagan's arguments can be interpreted as being that the U.S. economy in 1980 was at a point corresponding to the equilibrium in Figures 5.17 and 5.18 with the high tax rate t_2. That is, Reagan argued that tax rates could be reduced without sacrificing any tax revenue, everyone would work harder as a result, GDP would be higher, and everyone would be better off. Reagan's views are consistent with theory, but the empirical question is whether the U.S. economy was operating in 1980 on the good side of the Laffer curve (the upward-sloping portion) or the bad side (the downward-sloping portion). Supply-side arguments surfaced again during the second Bush administration in the United States, though George W. Bush did not use supply-side arguments as the primary focus of his tax-rate reduction plan. The general consensus among economists concerning this debate is that the U.S. economy, and the Canadian economy, are typically on the good side rather than the bad side of the Laffer curve. We discuss this further in the following Theory Confronts the Data 5.3 box.

A Model of Public Goods: How Large Should the Government Be?

To this point in this chapter, we have considered only one type of government spending in our model. When the government purchases goods, G, consumers receive no benefit from these goods. We have assumed thus far that goods confiscated by the government through taxation are simply thrown away. While this approach allows us to focus on the resource costs of government activity, and may capture the essence of some types of government spending—defense expenditures for example—much of government spending has other effects that we should model.

It will help to simplify. Assume that there is no production, and that the economy consists only of a representative consumer and the government. The representative consumer has no choice about how to use his or her time, and simply receives an exogenous quantity of goods, Y. Thus GDP is fixed by assumption, so that we can focus on the problem of how resources should be allocated between the government and the private sector. As we assumed in our basic model, the government can tax the consumer lump-sum, with T denoting the total tax, so the consumer's budget constraint is

$$C + T = Y. \tag{5.13}$$

The government takes the goods it collects as taxes, and transforms those private consumption goods into public goods using its technology. Assume that one unit of consumption goods acquired through taxation can be transformed by the government into q units of public goods. These public goods represent public parks, public transportation, health services, and other goods and services that governments typically provide. We then have $G = qT$, so substituting for T in Equation (5.13) and rearranging, we get the production possibilities frontier (PPF) for this economy,

$$C = Y - G/q. \tag{5.14}$$

In Equation (5.14), q represents the efficiency of the government relative to the private sector. The larger is q, the smaller is the drain in resources, at the margin, from converting private goods into public goods. In Figure 5.19, we show the PPF for this economy along with indifference curves representing the preferences of the representative consumer over private and public goods—C and G, respectively.

FIGURE 5.19

**The Optimal Choice of
Government Spending**

At point *A* the equilibrium is
Pareto-optimal if the government chooses *G* = *G**.
Points *B* and *D* represent
suboptimal choices for the
government.

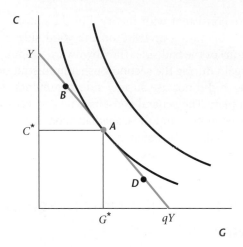

Preferences over private and public goods have the same properties as did the consumer's preferences over consumption and leisure in Chapter 4.

If the government were behaving optimally, it would choose the quantity of government spending to be G^*, as in Figure 5.19, which would imply taxes $T = G^*/q$ and
quantity of private consumption C^*. The competitive equilibrium for this economy would
then be at point A in Figure 5.19, where an indifference curve for the representative consumer is tangent to the PPF, which is Pareto-optimal. However, there is nothing to prevent
the government from choosing a quantity of government spending that is too small, for
example at point B in Figure 5.19, or a quantity that is too large, for example at point D.

Note that what is happening in Figure 5.3 is quite different from what is happening in Figure 5.19. In Figure 5.3, individual private-sector economic agents respond
optimally to market prices, markets clear, and the resulting equilibrium happens to
be Pareto-optimal. However, in Figure 5.19, for the government to arrive at a Pareto
optimum requires that it be able to figure out the representative consumer's preferences
and to understand its own technology for converting private goods into public goods.
The private sector is able to solve a very complicated resource allocation problem,
through the decisions of many economic agents responding to their own circumstances
and information. It is much more difficult for the government to solve its problem of
determining the optimal quantity of G, since it has to collect a lot of detailed information to make an informed decision.

In Figure 5.19, what are the factors determining G^*, the optimal quantity of government spending? Clearly, this decision depends on total GDP, Y, on q, the relative
efficiency of the government and the private sector, and on the consumer's preferences
over private and public goods. To gain some perspective on this, we will consider how
the government's decision is altered by changes in Y and in q, respectively.

First, in Figure 5.20, we consider what happens when GDP increases from Y_1 to
Y_2. The production possibilities frontier shifts out from PPF_1 to PPF_2 and the slope of
the PPF remains unchanged, since that is determined by q. Assuming, as we did in our
basic model in this chapter, that private goods and public goods are both normal, the
equilibrium point will shift from A to B, and the government will choose to increase

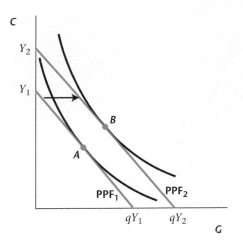

FIGURE 5.20
The Effects of an Increase in GDP.
Y increases, shifting out the PPF. Assuming normal goods, government spending increases.

spending. Thus, with a higher level of GDP, there is a positive income effect on both private and public goods, and the government will choose to spend more on public goods, as that is what the public wants. Whether public goods increase as a fraction of GDP depends on whether public goods are luxury goods or not. If public goods are luxury goods—for example, if private-sector economic agents wish to spend a larger fraction of their income supporting public parks as their income increases—the size of the government as a percentage of GDP will grow as GDP increases. It seems likely that public goods are luxury goods, as in fact government spending tends to account for a larger fraction of GDP as countries develop. However, there could be other factors that contribute to this. For example, as countries develop they acquire better technologies for collecting taxes, making it less costly to support government activity. This would be reflected in q rather than Y.

Second, Figure 5.21 shows the effects of an increase in q, the efficiency with which the government can convert private goods into public goods, from q_1 to q_2. In this case the PPF shifts to the right from PPF_1 to PPF_2 and the PPF becomes more flat. As we know from our analysis in this chapter and in Chapter 4, there will be income and substitution effects in the government's choice of the optimal quantity of spending. In the figure, the equilibrium point moves from A to B. In separating the income and substitution effects, the line tangent to indifference curve I_2 at point D has the same slope as PPF_1, the movement from A to D is the income effect, and the movement from D to B is the substitution effect. The income effect increases both C and G, and the substitution effect reduces C and increases G, since it is now cheaper for the government to produce G, in terms of private goods foregone. Thus, G increases but C may increase or decrease.

Thus, if the government becomes more efficient relative to the private sector, then the government should expand, but this need not imply that the private sector contracts. Note that the government might be quite inefficient—q could be quite small—but it might still be the case that the government would want to provide some public goods. This might occur, for example, if public goods and private goods are poor substitutes (there is much curvature in the indifference curves).

FIGURE 5.21

The Effects of an Increase in Government Efficiency.

q increases, shifting out the PPF, and making the slope of the PPF flatter. Government spending, if chosen optimally by the government, will increase, but private spending may increase (if the substitution effect is small) or decrease (if the substitution effect is large).

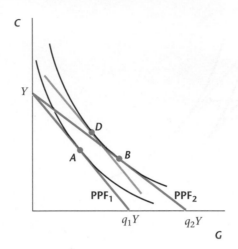

THEORY CONFRONTS THE DATA **5.3** *Canada's Economic Action Plan*

Canada's Economic Action Plan (CEAP) was introduced by the federal government in its January 2009 budget.[3] This fiscal program was a response to the global financial crisis and recession that began in 2008. The government's reasoning was that decreases in taxes, and increases in transfers and government spending on goods and services, were needed to counteract the shock that had produced the recession.

CEAP accounted for total changes of about $30 billion in items in the government budget. However, not all of those items would result directly in expenditures on final goods and services, the quantity denoted by G in the models we considered in this chapter. In fact, only about one-third, or approximately $10 billion, was accounted for by expenditure that we would include as G. Recall that transfers, such as employment insurance, are not included in the National Income and Expenditure Accounts as part of GDP. Further, while taxes enter the government budget, as we saw in Chapter 2, this quantity also is not part of the GDP calculation.

At $30 billion, the planned government expenditures on final goods and services in the CEAP were about 2% of GDP for 2009. This increase in government expenditure was therefore similar, as a fraction of GDP, to the amount included in the *American Recovery and Reinvestment Act*, passed by the U.S. government in February 2009.

In Figure 5.22, we show government expenditures on goods and services in Canada (for all levels of government), as a percentage of GDP, from 1961 to 2011. Before 1990, government expenditures fluctuated around an average of about 27% of GDP. Then, fiscal reforms in the 1990s reduced government expenditures dramatically, to a pre–financial crisis low of about 22% of GDP in 2007. By 2011 however, government spending had risen to about 25.5% of GDP. We can attribute about 2 percentage points of the 3.5 percentage point increase in the ratio of government expenditures to GDP to the direct effects of the CEAP, and the rest to the negative effects of the recession on GDP. As we see in Figure 5.22, it is typical for government expenditures as a percentage of GDP to rise during recessions (note the increases in 1974–75, 1981–82, and 1990–92), since government expenditures tend to be acyclical.

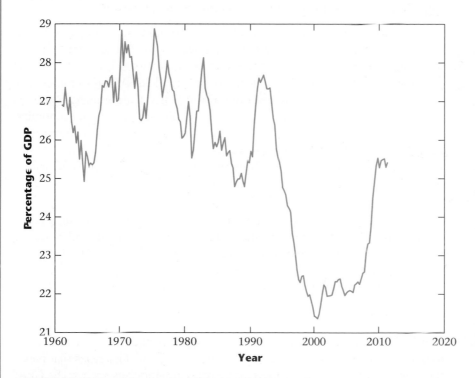

FIGURE 5.22 **Government Expenditures as a Percentage of GDP**

Government expenditures as a percentage of GDP rose during the last recession, in part because of the direct effects of Canada's Economic Action Plan.

Source: Adapted from the Statistics Canada CANSIM database, Series v1992067, v1992049, v1992050, v1992051.

Can the models we studied in this chapter provide a rationale for the CEAP? Certainly, if GDP falls, for whatever reason, our basic model tells us that the government can increase G and cause an increase in Y that will offset the initial GDP decrease. But should the government do this? In our basic model the equilibrium allocation of resources is Pareto-optimal, so government intervention, though it can increase GDP, cannot increase economic welfare. Further, our analysis of the optimal provision of public goods tells us that, when GDP falls, the provision of public goods should decrease, that is, G should fall, not rise.

We might say our model of the optimal provision of public goods applies to the long run, and does not take into account the fact that a recession is typically temporary. Thus, we would not want to adjust, for example, the provision of public parks whenever there is a short-lived recession. However, this still would not imply that we would want to increase government expenditures in a recession.

While the models in this chapter give some insight into the role of government expenditures in the macroeconomy, there might be important factors the model is missing that are relevant to evaluating the CEAP. Some of these are:

1. The primary motivation for the CEAP, and for stimulus spending in response to the recent recession in the United States, was Keynesian economics. In Keynesian theory, there exist inefficiencies in the economy due to the fact that prices and wages do not move quickly to clear markets. As a result, according to Keynesians, government intervention through fiscal and monetary policy can bring about Pareto improvements. We will discuss Keynesian economics in Chapters 12 and 13. There is plenty of debate among macroeconomists about the efficacy of Keynesian fiscal policy interventions such as the CEAP. Prices and wages may not in fact be very "sticky" in the short run and, even if they are, it may be very difficult to time fiscal policy interventions well, particularly given the potentially long and awkward legislative process.

2. During a recession, it is possible that the opportunity cost of investing in public capital falls. For example, the cost of constructing roads and bridges may be lower in a recession than in a boom. Thus, it may be cost-effective for the government to invest more in public infrastructure during a recession. Our models do not include such effects, but it is not difficult to extend these models so that they do.

3. Our models in this chapter do not account for financial factors, which were clearly important in the last recession. Taking account of these financial factors, their role in causing the recession, and possible inefficiencies that may have resulted, may be very important in evaluating policies such as the CEAP. However, the one-period models in this chapter give us a good start, and some useful insights. Financial factors will be addressed later in this book, particularly in Chapters 8 to 13.

---

[3]See www.budget.gc.ca/2009/pdf/budget-planbugetaire-eng.pdf.

Now that we have gained some knowledge The knowledge we have now gained from a one-period model concerning how the macroeconomy functions, we can move on in Chapter 7 will enable us to study economic growth.

Chapter Summary

- In this chapter, we took our knowledge of consumer behaviour and firm behaviour developed in Chapter 4, added government behaviour, and constructed a complete one-period macroeconomic model.

- In a competitive equilibrium, the actions of the representative consumer, the representative firm, and the government must be mutually consistent, which implies that the market on which labour is exchanged for goods must clear, and the government budget constraint must hold.

- In a competitive equilibrium, we determined aggregate output, consumption, employment, taxes, and the real wage (the endogenous variables) given the capital stock, total factor productivity, and government spending (the exogenous variables).

- A competitive equilibrium can be represented in a single diagram, and we used this diagram to illustrate the equivalence between the competitive equilibrium and the Pareto optimum, which is an economically efficient state of affairs.

- The model shows how an increase in government spending has a pure negative income effect on the representative consumer, so that employment increases and consumption decreases. Government spending thus crowds out private consumption, but not completely, as there is an increase in aggregate output.

- An increase in total factor productivity, which may arise from improved technology, leads to an increase in output, consumption, and the real wage, but employment may increase or decrease because of opposing income and substitution effects.

- A simplified version of the one-period model illustrates the incentive effects of proportional income taxes. The model exhibits a Laffer curve, a relationship between tax revenue and the tax rate.

- The one-period model was modified to include public goods, and to show how we might determine an optimal size for the government. The model shows that the size of the government increases with GDP, through a pure income effect on the demand for public goods. The size of the government also increases as public goods provision becomes more efficient.

Key Terms

closed economy: An economy that does not trade with the rest of the world.

open economy: An economy that trades with the rest of the world.

public goods: Goods that are difficult or impossible for the private sector to provide, for example, national defence.

exogenous variable: A variable determined outside the model.

endogenous variable: A variable that the model determines.

government budget constraint: An equation describing the sources and uses of government revenues.

fiscal policy: The government's choices over government expenditures, taxes, transfers, and government borrowing.

competitive equilibrium: A state of the economy in which prices and quantities are such that the behaviour of price-taking consumers and firms is consistent.

market clearing: When supply equals demand in a particular market or markets.

production possibilities frontier (PPF): The boundary of a set that describes what consumption bundles are technologically feasible to produce.

marginal rate of transformation: Minus the slope of the PPF, or the rate at which one good in the economy can be technologically exchanged for another.

Pareto-optimality: A state of the economy that cannot be improved on by making one consumer better off without making another worse off.

first fundamental theorem of welfare economics (or first welfare theorem): Result stating that, under certain conditions, a competitive equilibrium is Pareto-optimal.

second fundamental theorem of welfare economics (or second welfare theorem): Result stating that, under certain conditions, a Pareto optimum is a competitive equilibrium.

externality: The effect an action taken by an economic agent has on another economic agent or agents, where the agent performing the action does not take into account this effect on others.

distorting tax: A tax, such as an income tax, that creates a difference between the effective prices faced by buyers and sellers of some good.

crowded out: Decreased; the term is used in referring to what happens to private expenditures when there is an increase in government spending.

long run: Typically describes macroeconomic effects that occur beyond a year's time.

short run: Typically describes macroeconomic effects that occur within a year's time.

real business cycle theory: A theory postulating that the primary cause of aggregate fluctuations is fluctuations in total factor productivity.

intertemporal substitution of labour: The substitution of labour over time by a worker in response to movements in real wages.

tax base: The quantity that is subject to a particular tax. For example, the tax base for the tax on labour income is the quantity of labour supplied.

Laffer curve: The relationship between the tax revenue collected by the government and the tax rate.

supply-side economists: Economists who argue that there are large incentive effects from income taxation, so that a decrease in the income tax rate will cause a very large increase in the quantity of labour supplied.

Questions for Review

1. Why is it useful to study a closed-economy model?

2. What is the role of the government in the one-period closed-economy model?

3. Can the government run a deficit in the one-period model? Why or why not?

4. What are the endogenous variables in the model?

5. What are the exogenous variables in the model?

6. What are the four conditions that a competitive equilibrium must satisfy for this model?

7. What is the economic significance of the slope of the production possibilities frontier?

8. Why is the competitive equilibrium in this model Pareto-optimal?

9. Explain the difference between the first and second welfare theorems. Why is each useful?

10. Give three reasons why an equilibrium might not be Pareto-optimal.

11. What are the effects of an increase in government purchases?

12. Why does government spending crowd out private purchases?

13. What are the equilibrium effects of an increase in total factor productivity?

14. Explain why employment may rise or fall in response to an increase in total factor productivity.

15. Why does a distorting tax on labour income lead to an inefficient economic outcome?

16. How are the incentive effects of income taxation important for the Laffer curve?

17. Explain what happens when the economy is on the bad side of the Laffer curve and the tax rate falls.

18. What are the two determinants of the optimal quantity of public goods?

19. What happens to public goods provision and private consumption when GDP increases, and when the opportunity cost of public goods provision becomes larger?

Problems

1. Many negative externalities exist in cities. For example, a high concentration of automobile traffic in cities generates pollution and causes congestion, and both pollution and congestion are negative externalities When someone decides to drive a car in a city on a given day, he or she does not take into account the negative effects that driving a car has in terms of pollution and deterring other drivers from reaching their destinations (congestion). Although negative externalities (including pollution and congestion) appear to abound in cities, people still prefer to live there. (Otherwise, cities would not exist.) In economic terms, discuss the forces that cause people to prefer life in the city. How do these forces relate to whether market outcomes are economically efficient?

2. Suppose that the government decides to reduce taxes. In the model used in this chapter, determine the effects this will have on aggregate output, consumption, employment, and the real wage, and explain your results.

3. Suppose that there is a natural disaster that destroys part of the nation's capital stock.
   a. Determine the effects on aggregate output, consumption, employment, and the real wage, with reference to income and substitution effects, and explain your results.
   b. Do you think that changes in the capital stock are a likely cause of business cycles? Explain, with reference to your answer in part (a) and the key business cycle facts described in Chapter 3.

4. Suppose that total factor productivity, z, affects the productivity of government production just as it affects private production. That is, suppose that when the government collects taxes, it acquires goods that are then turned into government-produced goods according to $G = zT$, so that z units of government goods are produced for each unit of taxes collected. With the government setting G, an increase in z will imply that a smaller quantity of taxes are required to finance the given quantity of government purchases, G. Under these circumstances, use a diagram to determine the effects of an increase in z on output, consumption, employment, and the real wage, treating G as given. Explain your results.

5. Suppose that the representative consumer's preferences change, in that his or her marginal rate of substitution of leisure for consumption increases for any quantities of consumption and leisure.
   a. Explain what this change in preferences means in more intuitive language.
   b. What effects does this have on the equilibrium real wage, hours worked, output, and consumption?
   c. Do you think that preference shifts like this might explain why economies experience recessions (periods when output is low)? Explain why or why not, with reference to the key business cycle facts in Chapter 3.

6. Suppose that government spending makes private firms more productive; for example, government spending on roads and bridges lowers the cost of transportation. This means that there will now be two effects of government spending, the first being the effects discussed in this chapter of an increase in G, and the second being similar to the effects of an increase in the nation's capital stock, K.
   a. Show that an increase in government spending that is productive in this fashion could increase welfare for the representative consumer.
   b. Show that the equilibrium effects on consumption and hours worked of an increase in government spending of this type are ambiguous, but that output increases. You will need to consider income and substitution effects to show this.

7. In the one-period model, education can be represented as time spent by the representative consumer that is neither leisure nor time applied to producing output. What the economy gains in the future is that the representative consumer then has more time available, as measured in terms of effective units of labour time (adjusted for skill level, or what economists call human capital).
   a. Using the one-period model, show what effects additional education has in the present on consumption, leisure, employment, aggregate output, and the real wage.
   b. Similarly, show the effects the additional education that people acquire today will have in the future on consumption, leisure, employment, aggregate output, and the real wage.
   c. What does your analysis in parts (a) and (b) have to say about the tradeoffs society makes between the present and the future in investing in education?

8. In the simplified model with proportional taxation, there can be two equilibria, one with a high tax rate and one with a low tax rate. Now, suppose that government spending increases. Determine the effects of an increase in G on consumption, leisure, labour supply, real output, and the tax rate in a high-tax equilibrium and in a low-tax equilibrium. How do your results differ? Explain why.

9. Suppose that the substitution effect of an increase in the real wage is always larger than the income effect for the representative consumer. Also assume that the economy is always in the low-tax-rate equilibrium on the good side of the Laffer curve. Determine the effects of an increase in total factor productivity, z, on the Laffer curve, on the equilibrium tax rate, and on consumption, leisure, the quantity of labour supplied, and output. Explain your results and discuss.

10. Consider the model of public goods, in the last section of this chapter.
    a. Suppose that preferences over private consumption C and public goods G are such that these two goods are perfect substitutes, that is, the marginal rate of substitution of public goods for private goods is a constant $b > 0$. Now determine the optimal quantity of public goods that the government should provide, and interpret your results. Make sure you show all of the relevant cases. What happens when b changes, or when q changes?

    b. Repeat part (a), except with perfect complements preferences, that is, for the case in which the representative consumer always wishes to consume private consumption goods and public goods in fixed proportions, or $C = aG$, with $a > 0$.

11. Extend the model of public goods, in the last section of this chapter, as follows: Suppose that output is produced, as in the simplified model with proportional taxation, only with labour, and that $z = 1$. Here, however, there is lump-sum taxation, and the PPF is given by $Y = h - l - G$. Now the consumer has preferences over three goods: private goods C, public goods G, and leisure l. Assume that C and l are perfect complements for the consumer, that is, the consumer always wants to consume C and l in fixed proportions, with $C = dl$, and $d > 0$.

    a. Suppose, just as in part (a) of problem 10, that public goods and private goods are perfect substitutes. Now, determine the effects of an increase in G on consumption and labour supply, and explain your results.

    b. Alternatively, assume, just as in part (b) of problem 10, that public goods and private goods are perfect complements. Again, determine the effects of an increase in G on consumption and labour supply, and explain your results.

6

Search and Unemployment

In Chapters 4 and 5, we developed a one-period competitive equilibrium macroeconomic model to provide a basic understanding of the factors determining aggregate output and the allocation of time between leisure and market work. In this chapter, our goal is to build on those basic ideas, by taking account of labour market *frictions*. In macroeconomics there are several types of frictions that take us beyond basic competitive equilibrium models, and allow us to understand and explain more about how the macroeconomy works. One such friction is search. In general, it takes time for an individual who wants to work to find a suitable job with a firm that wishes to hire him or her. Similarly it takes time for a firm to fill a vacancy. Search is required on both sides of the labour market; there are always would-be workers searching for jobs, and firms searching for workers to fill vacancies.

Every month, Statistics Canada measures the number of unemployed—people of working age who are not employed, but are actively searching for work. It is important to understand what determines unemployment. In particular, we are interested in how government policy affects search behaviour, and whether the unemployment rate might be inefficiently high or low.

Our first goal in this chapter will be to examine the behaviour of the unemployment rate in Canada. As well, we will study the behaviour of two other key labour market variables, the participation rate and the employment/population ratio. We will show how the unemployment rate, the participation rate, and the employment/population ratio move over the business cycle, and discuss some of the determinants of these three variables.

Next, we will study a one-period search model of unemployment, based on the work of Peter Diamond, Dale Mortensen, and Christopher Pissarides, for which they received the Nobel Prize in Economics in 2010. This model will be quite different from our one-period model constructed in Chapters 4 and 5. Though the search model we will construct is built up from the optimizing behaviour of consumers and firms, search models require that we construct an equilibrium in a different way than in the competitive equilibrium model of Chapter 5. In a search process with labour market frictions we cannot think in terms of prices moving to clear markets in which there are many participants.

The search model will be used to show how productivity, unemployment insurance, and opportunities outside the market affect the unemployment rate and labour force participation. Then it will be used to take a first pass at Keynesian ideas, which will be revisited in Chapters 13 and 14.

The Behaviour of the Unemployment Rate, the Participation Rate, and the Employment/Population Ratio in Canada

Before studying a search model of unemployment, we will explore the empirical behaviour of the unemployment rate, the participation rate, and the employment/population ratio in Canada. Recall from Chapter 2 that if N is the working age population, Q is the labour force (employed plus unemployed), and U is the number of unemployed, then the unemployment rate and participation rate are defined by

$$\text{Unemployment rate} = \frac{U}{Q},$$

$$\text{Participation rate} = \frac{Q}{N}.$$

In addition, we will be interested in the behaviour of the employment/population ratio, defined as

$$\text{Employment/population ratio} = \frac{Q - U}{N}.$$

Figure 6.1 shows a plot of the annual unemployment rate for Canada for the years 1946–2010. The unemployment rate is a countercyclical variable: high during recessions and low during booms. In particular, note in the figure that the unemployment rate spiked during the recessions of 1973–1975, 1981–1982, 1990–1992, and 2008–2009, and decreased during the economic booms of the late 1970s, the late 1980s, and from the early 1990s to 2008, following the 1990–1992 recession. In addition to the cyclical behaviour of the unemployment rate, there also appear to be longer-run movements in the unemployment rate in the figure. For example, from the late 1960s until the mid-1980s there was a trend increase in the unemployment rate, and there was a slight trend decrease from the mid-1980s on. We would like to understand the reasons for both the cyclical behaviour and the long-run behaviour of the unemployment rate.

The key determinants of the unemployment rate are the following:

- *Aggregate economic activity.* When aggregate real GDP is high relative to trend, the unemployment rate tends to be low. As mentioned above, the unemployment rate is a countercyclical variable. In Figure 6.2, which shows the deviations from trend in the unemployment rate and in real GDP (percentages in this case), we see that the unemployment rate tends to be below (above) trend when real GDP is above (below) trend.

FIGURE 6.1

The Canadian Unemployment Rate, 1946–2010

The unemployment rate shows considerable cyclical volatility. In Canada, there was also a trend increase in the unemployment rate from the late 1960s until the mid-1980s, and a small trend decrease from the mid-1980s through the 1990s.

Source: Adapted from the Statistics Canada CANSIM database, Series v2461224, and from the Statistics Canada publication *Historical Statistics of Canada*, Catalogue 11-516, 1983, Series D491.

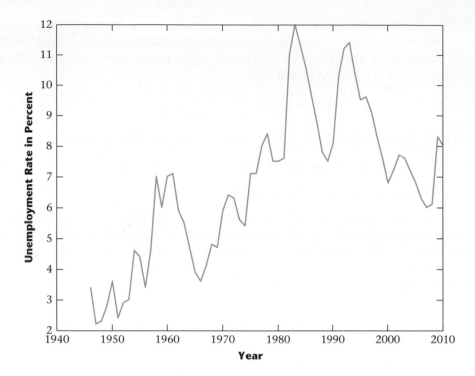

FIGURE 6.2

Deviations from Trend in the Unemployment Rate and Percentage Deviations from Trend in Real GDP for 1976–2011

The unemployment rate is countercyclical, as it tends to be above (below) trend when real GDP is below (above) trend.

Source: Adapted from the Statistics Canada CANSIM database, Series v2062815, v1992067.

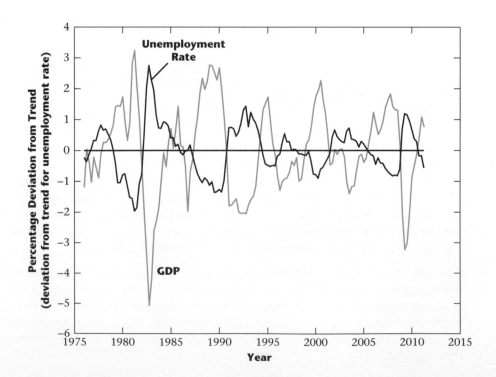

- *Demographics.* **Demography** is the study of population. The age structure of the population matters a great deal for the unemployment rate, as workers of different ages behave quite differently in the labour market. The unemployment rate for the young tends to be higher than that for the old, as younger workers have a weaker attachment to the labour force and switch jobs more frequently early in their careers, thus suffering more frequent spells of unemployment. In Figure 6.1, part of the cause of the increase in the average unemployment rate in the 1970s was that many members of the post–World War II baby boom generation entered the labour force at that time. Then, the average unemployment rate fell during the 1980s and 1990s as baby boomers aged.

- *Government intervention.* A key government program that affects the unemployment rate over the long run is government-provided employment insurance. Workers who suffer a spell of unemployment typically experience a drop in their consumption. Why shouldn't this loss be insurable, just as is the loss from an automobile accident, a fire, or ill health? The problem is that employment insurance is not supplied by private firms, and the government has taken on this role in most developed countries. Employment insurance was introduced in Canada in 1941 under the *Unemployment Insurance Act*. Its scope was widened and the level of benefits was increased significantly in 1971. Since then, there has been a tightening of the rules for eligibility for such insurance and a lowering of the level of benefits, culminating in the last major program changes in 1996, when the program was renamed Employment Insurance (EI).

  As with other types of insurance, there is moral hazard associated with EI. That is, the behaviour of an insured person changes in a way that makes a loss more likely, as we will discuss later in connection with deposit insurance in Chapter 16. In the case of EI programs, more generous EI benefits will tend to increase the unemployment rate through several mechanisms, one of which we explore in the search model in this chapter. Part of the increase in the unemployment rate from 1971 until the 1980s and part of the slight trend decrease in the unemployment rate from the early 1980s to the late 1990s in Figure 6.1 can be attributed to the increase in the generosity of the program in 1971 and the later tightening.

- *Mismatch.* Mismatch in the labour market can occur for two reasons, both of which act to increase the unemployment rate. First, there could be changes in the availability of information, which make it easier or more difficult to match firms who want to hire workers with the workers who have the requisite skills. Most changes in information technology have worked to reduce the degree of mismatch, for example growth in internet communication.

  Second, there could be a higher degree of mismatch in the labour market because of a **sectoral shift**, which is a change in the economy's aggregate structure of production. For example, recently in Canada there has been a shift away from manufacturing (the production of tangible goods) and toward services (intangible goods). As a result, workers in manufacturing industries have been displaced. Displacement can imply a long period of unemployment, particularly for older workers, as displaced workers may have obsolete skills and will need to acquire new ones, and finding work in a different sector of the economy will take time. Displacement can also be a regional phenomenon. For example, as manufacturing has declined in central Canada, and resource-extraction activities have grown in Alberta, the movement of labour across sectors of the economy also entails costly geographical migration. Given the level of aggregate economic activity, the greater the restructuring occurring among industries in the economy, the higher the unemployment rate will tend to be.

The search model of unemployment that we construct later in this chapter will capture the correlation between aggregate economic activity and the unemployment rate, along with some effects of government intervention (particularly EI), and mismatch. Modelling demographics, however, is too complicated for our purposes.

Let us now turn to another key labour market variable, the participation rate, depicted in Figure 6.3 for the years 1946–2010. Here, note that the fraction of the working-age population in the labour force increased substantially, from about 55% in 1946 to about 67% in 2010. In Figure 6.4 we show the participation rates of men and women, which show a decline for men and a huge increase for women. Therefore, the increase in the total participation rate in Figure 6.3 is accounted for solely by an increase in the labour force participation rate for women. Some point to sociological explanations for the increase in the participation rate of women, but economists do not find it surprising that more women would choose market work in the face of large increases in market real wages in the post–World War II period. The declining participation rate

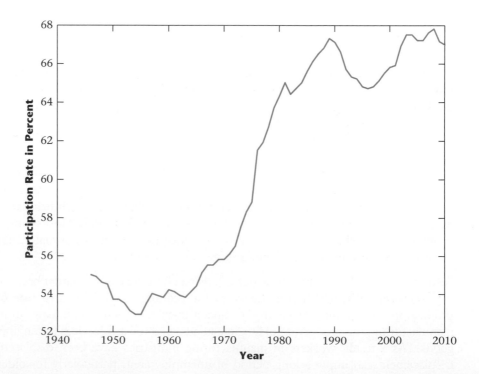

FIGURE 6.3

The Canadian Participation Rate, 1946–2010

The participation rate has increased in Canada from about 55% in 1946 to close to 68% in 2008.

Source: Adapted from the Statistics Canada CANSIM database, Series v2461245, and from the Statistics Canada publication *Historical Statistics of Canada*, Catalogue 11-516, 1983, Series D484.

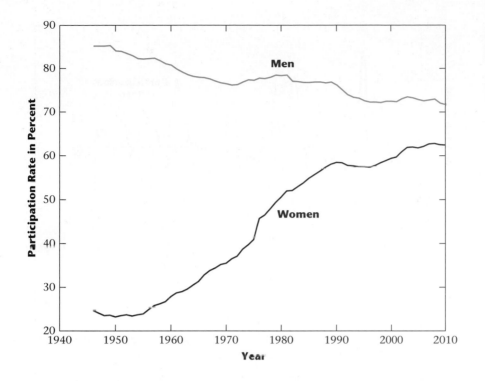

FIGURE 6.4
Labour Force Participation of Women and Men
Although the labour force participation rate of women has increased almost continuously since 1946, the participation rate of men has decreased.

Source: Adapted from the Statistics Canada CANSIM database, Series v2461455, v2461665, and from the Statistics Canada publication *Historical Statistics of Canada*, Catalogue 11-516, 1983, Series D221, D222.

of men is closely connected to the increasing participation rate of women, since family decisions concerning labour market participation are made jointly.

In Figure 6.5 we show the percentage deviations from trend in the participation rate and real GDP in Canada. The participation rate is a procyclical variable, in that it tends to be above trend when real GDP is above trend. The important point to note is that, as aggregate economic activity expands, employment expands not only because workers are drawn out of the unemployment pool, but because more working age people find it advantageous to enter the labour force. In our search model of unemployment, we will be able to capture this phenomenon.

The employment/population ratio, which is the fraction of people of working age who are employed full-time or part-time, is depicted in Figure 6.6 for the period 1976–2011, along with the participation rate. The employment/population ratio is one measure of the quantity of labour used as an input in aggregate production. Two interesting features can be observed in Figure 6.6. The first is that the trend increase in the participation rate in the figure is roughly similar to the trend increase in the employment/population ratio. That is, the factors determining the size of the labour force in the long run are similar to those determining the quantity of employment. The second is that the employment/population ratio exhibits more cyclical variation than does the participation rate in the figure. That is, when there is a cyclical downturn, in the short run the size of the labour force does not decrease much; the important change is in how many labour-force participants are employed and how many are unemployed.

FIGURE 6.5

Deviations from Trend in the Participation Rate and GDP

The participation rate is procyclical: an increase (decrease) in aggregate economic activity tends to cause an increase (decrease) in labour force participation.

Source: Adapted from the Statistics Canada CANSIM database, Series v2062810, v1992067.

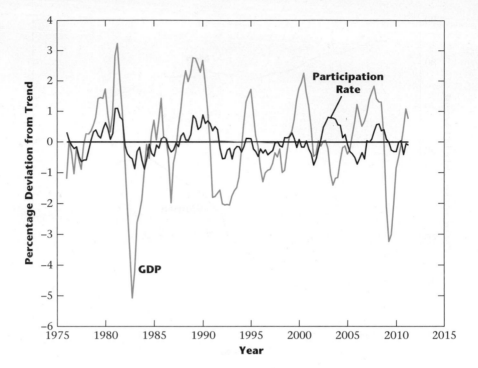

FIGURE 6.6

The Employment/Population Ratio and the Participation Rate, 1976–2011

Both series have increased on trend, but there is more cyclical variability in the employment/population ratio.

Source: Adapted from the Statistics Canada CANSIM database, Series v2062817, v2062834.

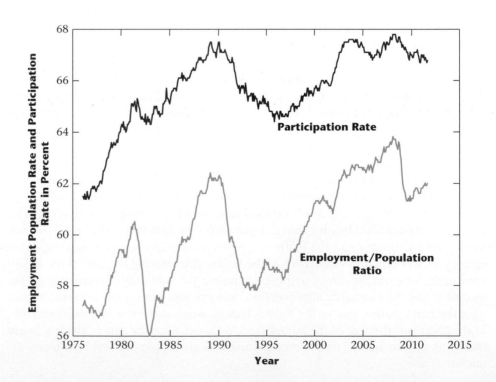

A Diamond-Mortensen-Pissarides Model of Search and Unemployment

The first search models were developed by economists in the late 1960s,[1] and they have since been refined and put into wide use in labour economics and macroeconomics. The model we will work with is a simplified version of a framework constructed by Dale Mortensen and Christopher Pissarides,[2] and we will refer to it as the "DMP model."

As in the model of Chapters 4 and 5, there is one period, but in this search model there are many consumers and firms rather than a single representative consumer and single representative firm. There are N consumers, who are all potential workers— think of N as the working-age population. The number of firms is a quantity to be determined by the model; that is, the number of firms is endogenous.

CONSUMERS

Each of the N consumers can choose to work outside the market or to search for market work. Think of work outside the market as home production, which might be child care, yard work, or household chores, for example. Let Q denote the quantity of consumers who decide to search for work, so that $N - Q$ is the number of consumers who choose home production. We will interpret Q as the labour force, and $N - Q$ as working-age people not in the labour force.

Let $v(Q)$ define a supply curve for workers who choose to search for market work. Thus, $v(Q)$ represents the expected payoff to searching for market work that would induce Q consumers to search. The supply curve $v(Q)$ is depicted in Figure 6.7. In the figure, the supply curve is upward-sloping because the value of home production is different for different consumers. Therefore, if the expected payoff from searching is higher, this induces more consumers to forego home production to search for market work.

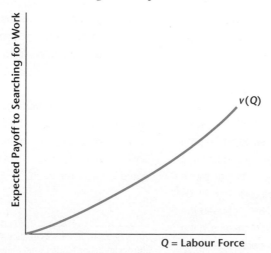

FIGURE 6.7

The Supply Curve of Consumers Searching for Work

The curve $v(Q)$ defines the expected payoff required to induce Q consumers to search for work. The supply curve is upward-sloping because different consumers have different payoffs to working in the home.

---

[1]See J. McCall, 1970, "Economics of Information and Job Search," *Quarterly Journal of Economics* 84, 113–126.

[2]D. Mortensen and C. Pissarides, 1994, "Job Creation and Job Destruction in the Theory of Unemployment," *Review of Economic Studies* 61, 397–416.

Unemployment and Employment in the United States and Europe

Economists who study labour markets have long been interested in the differences between North America and Europe in labour market outcomes. There has been much interest, for example, in explaining why, since the 1970s, unemployment rates have increased in European countries relative to North America. Most research has focused on how labour market rigidities in Europe, including generous unemployment insurance, high minimum wages, high taxes, and tough restrictions on the hiring and firing of employees, act to increase European unemployment. The United States and Canada are generally characterized as countries with a small amount of labour market rigidity, and so the question for many researchers has been only whether the greater rigidity in Europe can generate the observed quantitative difference in unemployment rates between Europe and the North America.

Richard Rogerson, in an article in the *Journal of the European Economic Association*,[3] comes up with a different characterization of European labour market problems that suggests new directions for economic research. Rogerson examines the behaviour of the employment/population ratios in Europe and the United States, as well as unemployment rates in the two places. For Europe, he focuses on three countries: France, Germany, and Italy. Rogerson documents an increase in the gap between the European unemployment rate and the unemployment rate in the United States of about 6% between the 1970s and 2000, just as other authors have found. However, regarding the employment/population ratio, Rogerson documents a relative deterioration in Europe that begins much earlier. He finds that a gap opened up in the 1950s whose size increased by about 18% between the 1950s and 2000. That is, the trend increases in the employment/population ratio that were observed in Canada and the United States during that period did not occur in Europe. This is perhaps a more startling finding than the relative deterioration in Europe in terms of unemployment rates, since it indicates a fundamental difference in growth in labour inputs in the United States and Europe.

What might explain this difference in labour market outcomes? Rogerson explores the labour market data further, but rather than seeking an explanation in terms of labour market rigidities, he studies the sectoral composition of output in Europe and the United States. Like the U.S., Europe has experienced a sectoral shift from manufacturing to services since the 1950s. However, the nature of the sectoral shift was different in Europe. In the United States there was much more growth in the service sector than was the case in Europe. Thus, one explanation for the difference in labour market outcomes is the following. In both Europe and the United States, unemployment increased because of a sectoral shift from manufacturing to services, as workers were displaced from manufacturing jobs and experienced a spell of unemployment in transitioning to employment in the service sector. However, in Europe this generated more long-term unemployment, because the service sector there was not growing as much as in the United States, so that service-sector growth could not absorb all the workers displaced from manufacturing jobs. Also, it is possible that labour market rigidities in Europe exacerbated the transition, as protections for unemployed workers discouraged displaced workers from acquiring the new skills required for service-sector employment. In any event, these are only conjectures, which need to be carefully investigated in future research.

---

[3]R. Rogerson, 2004, "Two Views on the Deterioration of European Labor Market Outcomes," *Journal of the European Economic Association* 2, 447–455.

FIRMS

In order to produce, a firm must post a vacancy and be matched with a worker. Recruiting workers is costly, so we assume that it costs the firm k to post a vacancy. Firms that do not post a vacancy are inactive and cannot produce. Let A denote the number of active firms, that is, the number of firms that choose to post vacancies.

MATCHING

At the beginning of the period, there will be Q consumers searching for work and A firms posting vacancies. We want to capture, in a simple way, the idea that matching workers with firms is a time-consuming and costly process. In general, firms are very different from each other in the kinds of jobs they offer, and workers have very different characteristics. This makes the process of matching firms with workers difficult. In standard models of labour search, difficulties in matching are captured by a **matching function**. Letting M denote the number of successful matches between workers and firms, M is determined by

$$M = em(Q, A) \tag{6.1}$$

In Equation (6.1), the matching function on the right-hand side of the equation is much like a production function that "produces" matches between workers and firms as "output" given "inputs" of searching consumers and firms. The variable e denotes matching efficiency, and plays much the same role as does total factor productivity in the production function we studied in Chapter 4. With higher e, more matches occur given the numbers of consumers and firms searching. Matching efficiency e can increase in practice due to better information, for example more efficient search technologies such as Internet advertising, or because the skills that consumers have are better-matched to the skills that firms want.

The function m has properties very similar to those of the function F described in Chapter 4 in the context of production. In particular,

1. The function m has constant returns to scale. Recall that this means that

$$m(xQ, xA) = xm(Q, A), \tag{6.2}$$

for any $x > 0$. For the matching function, constant returns to scale implies that a large economy is no more efficient at producing matches between workers and firms than a small economy, and vice versa.

2. If there are no consumers searching for work or no firms searching for workers, then there are no matches, that is, $m(0, A) = m(Q, 0) = 0$.

3. The number of matches M increases when either Q or A increases.

4. Marginal products are diminishing; that is, the increase in matches obtained for a one-unit increase in Q decreases as Q increases, and similarly for A.

OPTIMIZATION BY CONSUMERS

If a consumer chooses to search for work, he or she may find a job, in which case the consumer would be counted as employed by Statistics Canada. However, the consumer may not find work even if he or she chooses to search. In that instance, the consumer would be counted as unemployed, since he or she has been actively engaged in search, but is not employed. If the consumer finds work, he or she earns the real wage w, and we will assume that, if unemployed, the consumer receives an employment insurance benefit b. Thus, the consumer knows his or her value of home production, the wage if he or she finds work, and the unemployment benefit if he or she is unemployed. The consumer also knows the chances of finding work, given by the matching function. If there are Q consumers searching and M successful matches, then for an individual consumer, the probability of finding work is M/Q or from the matching function (6.1),

$$p_c = \frac{em(Q, A)}{Q}, \tag{6.3}$$

where p_c is the probability of finding work for a consumer. Then, given the constant-returns-to-scale property of the matching function, setting $x = 1/Q$ in (6.2), and defining $j = A/Q$, from (6.3) we get

$$p_c = em\left(1, \frac{A}{Q}\right) = em(1, j). \tag{6.4}$$

Therefore, from Equation (6.4), the probability of finding work for a consumer depends only on the ratio $j = A/Q$—that is, the ratio of firms searching for workers relative to consumers searching for work. This ratio is a measure of **labour market tightness**. Since Equation (6.4) gives the probability of finding work for a consumer, the probability of being unemployed if a consumer chooses to search is then

$$1 - p_c = 1 - em(1, j) \tag{6.5}$$

Recall that $v(Q)$ defines the supply curve for the number of consumers choosing to search for work, Q. In equilibrium, $v(Q)$ must be equal to the expected payoff a consumer receives from searching, so

$$v(Q) = p_c w + (1 - p_c)b = b + em(1, j)(w - b). \tag{6.6}$$

In Equation (6.6), the expression after the first equality is the expected payoff the consumer obtains from searching for work—the probability of finding a job multiplied by the market wage, plus the probability of being unemployed, multiplied by the employment insurance benefit—and the expression after the second equality is obtained by substituting using (6.4).

Figure 6.8 is an illustration of Equation (6.6). In the figure, the "market price" for searching workers, that is, the expected payoff to searching for work on the vertical axis, is determined by the market wage w, the employment insurance benefit b, and market tightness j. Then, given this market price, the supply curve for searching workers determines the quantity of searching workers Q.

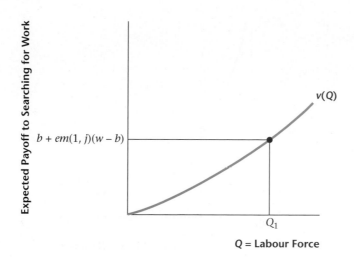

FIGURE 6.8

**Determination of
the Labour Force**

The market wage, the EI
benefit, and labour market
tightness determine the
expected payoff to searching
for work for a consumer.
Then, given this expected
payoff, the supply curve
for searching consumers
determines the labour force.

OPTIMIZATION BY FIRMS

Firms that choose to bear the cost k of posting a vacancy have a probability $p_f = M/A$ of finding a worker, since the ratio of total matches to the number of firms searching determines the chances of achieving a successful match. Then, from the matching function (6.1), we obtain

$$p_f = \frac{em(Q, A)}{A} = em\left(\frac{Q}{A}, 1\right) = em\left(\frac{1}{j}, 1\right), \qquad (6.7)$$

where the second equality follows from (6.2), that is, constant returns to scale in the matching function.

Given a successful match with a worker, the firm and worker produce output z, so the profit the firm receives from the match is $z - w$, or output minus the wage paid to the worker. Firms will enter the labour market, posting vacancies, until the expected net payoff from doing so is zero, or $p_f(z - w) - k = 0$. Given (6.7), we can write this equation as

$$em\left(\frac{1}{j}, 1\right) = \frac{k}{z - w}, \qquad (6.8)$$

which determines labour market tightness j given the wage w, productivity z, and the cost of posting a vacancy k. We depict this in Figure 6.9, where, given $k/(z - w)$, labour market tightness is j_1.

EQUILIBRIUM

When a firm is matched with a worker, together they can produce output z. In this model, z is both total factor productivity and average labour productivity, since we can think of this as a model with no capital in which one firm and one worker produce z units of output. The firm and worker need to come to an agreement concerning

FIGURE 6.9

Determination of Labour Market Tightness

Firms post vacancies up to the point where the probability for a firm of matching with a worker is equal to the ratio of the cost of posting a vacancy to the profit the firm receives from a successful match.

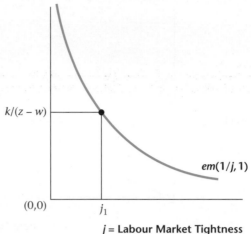

$k/(z - w)$

$em(1/j, 1)$

$(0,0)$

j_1

j = Labour Market Tightness

the wage w that the worker is to receive. In economic theory, a large body of work addresses how economic agents bargain, with one particularly famous contribution made by John Nash, who developed what is now known as Nash Bargaining Theory.[4]

In the Nash bargaining solution, two individuals strike a bargain that depends on what each person faces as an alternative if the two cannot agree, and on the relative bargaining power of the two people. Critical to the solution in the case of the firm and the worker in our setup is the notion of surplus: the surplus the worker receives as a result of the bargain; the surplus the firm receives; and the total surplus available to the firm and the worker, which is what they collectively stand to gain from coming to an agreement. In this case, the worker will receive a surplus of $w - b$, which is the wage the worker receives minus the employment insurance benefit, where b represents the alternative for the worker if he or she cannot come to an agreement with the firm. The firm's surplus is $z - w$, which is the profit the firm makes. Then, if we add the worker's surplus and the firm's surplus, we obtain total surplus, which is $z - b$.

Nash bargaining theory in this circumstance dictates that the firm and the worker will each receive a constant share of the total surplus. Let a denote the worker's share of total surplus, where $0 < a < 1$. Here a represents the bargaining power of the worker. Then, the worker and firm agree to a contract such that the worker's surplus is a fraction a of total surplus, or

$$w - b = a(z - b), \tag{6.9}$$

so if we solve Equation (6.9) for the wage, we obtain

$$w = az + (1 - a)b. \tag{6.10}$$

Then, the last step to determine an equilibrium solution is to substitute for w in Equations (6.6) and (6.8) using Equation (6.10), obtaining

$$v(Q) = b + em(1, j)a(z - b) \tag{6.11}$$

---

[4]J. Nash, 1950, "The Bargaining Problem," *Econometrica* 18, 155–162.

and

$$em\left(\frac{1}{j}, 1\right) = \frac{k}{(1-a)(z-b)},$$

(6.12)

and then Equations (6.11) and (6.12) solve for the endogenous variables j and Q. We depict the two Equations (6.11) and (6.12) in Figure 6.10. In panel (b) of the figure, we depict Equation (6.12), which determines labour market tightness j. The smaller the cost of posting a vacancy, k, relative to the firm's share of total surplus $(1-a)$ $(z-b)$, the more firms will post vacancies and enter the labour market, which will make j larger. In panel (a) of the figure, the upward-sloping relationship between Q and j is the relationship defined by Equation (6.11). If labour market tightness j is

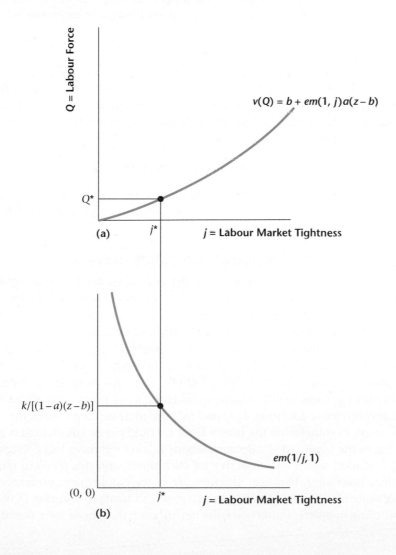

(a)

(b)

FIGURE 6.10

Equilibrium in the DMP Model

In panel (b), the ratio of the cost of posting a vacancy to the firm's surplus from a successful match determines labour market tightness. Then, in panel (a), labour market tightness determines the size of the labour force.

higher, then the chances of finding a job are greater for consumers, more of them will decide to search for work, and therefore Q is higher. For example, in Figure 6.8, higher j increases the expected payoff to searching for work, and then a higher supply of searching workers, Q, is forthcoming. In Figure 6.10, given labour market tightness j^* determined in panel (b), in panel (a) we determine the quantity of consumers who choose to search, Q^*.

Once we have determined j and Q, we can work back to determine all other variables of interest. First, the number of consumers who do not search for work is $N - Q$, and these are the people who would be counted as not in the labour force. Then, since Q is the number of people in the labour force, the unemployment rate is

$$u = \frac{Q(1 - p_c)}{Q} = 1 - em(1, j), \tag{6.13}$$

using (6.5). Similarly, the vacancy rate is the number of vacancies that go unfilled, relative to the number of jobs that were originally posted, so the vacancy rate is

$$v = \frac{A(1 - p_f)}{A} = 1 - em\left(\frac{1}{j^*}, 1\right). \tag{6.14}$$

Finally, the quantity of aggregate output in this economy is $Y = Mz$, that is, the number of matches multiplied by the output produced in each match. From Equation (6.1), and using the constant-returns-to-scale property of the matching function, we can express aggregate output as

$$Y = em(Q, A) = Qem(1, j). \tag{6.15}$$

In Equation (6.15), aggregate output is then increasing in Q and increasing in j. Thus, if there is a larger labour force or a tighter labour market, aggregate output will be higher.

AN INCREASE IN THE EMPLOYMENT INSURANCE BENEFIT

Now that we have worked through the model and understand how an equilibrium is constructed, we can use the model to study some macroeconomic issues. We will look at three different experiments, the first of which is an increase in the employment insurance benefit b. If b increases, this has the effect of reducing the total surplus from a match between a worker and a firm, $z - b$. In Figure 6.11, initial labour market tightness is j_1 and initially there are Q_1 consumers in the labour force. With the reduction in total surplus, in panel (b) of the figure, $k/[(1 - a)(z - b)]$ increases, and this causes labour market tightness to fall to j_2 in equilibrium, since posting vacancies has now become less attractive for firms. In panel (a), the increase in b causes the curve to shift up. Then, in equilibrium the labour force Q could rise or fall, though it is shown decreasing in the figure, to Q_2. Because labour market tightness has decreased, this makes job market search less attractive for consumers, and this tends to reduce the size of the labour force. However, the increase in the employment insurance benefit b acts to make labour search more attractive, which tends to increase Q. With two effects working in different directions, the net effect on the labour force is ambiguous.

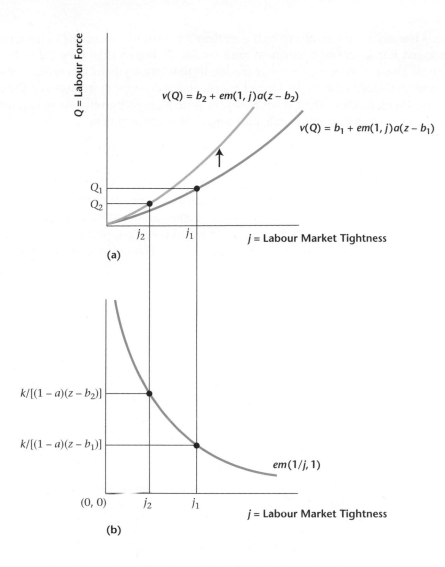

FIGURE 6.11

An Increase in the EI Benefit, *b*

An increase in *b* reduces the surplus the firm receives from a match, which reduces labour market tightness in panel (b). Then, in panel (a), the increase in *b* acts shifts the curve up. The labour force could increase or decrease.

However, from Equations (6.12) and (6.13), it is clear that the unemployment rate must rise and the vacancy rate must fall, because of the reduction in labour market tightness, which acts to reduce the probability of finding a job for a consumer, and increase the probability of a successful match for a firm posting a vacancy.

In terms of aggregate output, from Equation (6.15), the effect is ambiguous. Lower labour market tightness *j* acts to reduce output, but *Q* may rise or fall, so in principle there could be a decrease or an increase in aggregate output. Our intuition might tell us that better social insurance, provided through employment insurance, should reduce real GDP, since people will be less inclined to work. However, the model tells us that it is possible that more generous employment insurance could have the effect of drawing more people into the labour force and therefore increasing aggregate output.

These results in the model are broadly consistent with observations on average unemployment rates across different countries. In particular, the unemployment rate in

Canada has tended historically to be higher than the unemployment rate in the United States, and European unemployment rates tend to be higher than they are in North America. This is consistent with our model, in that employment insurance is more generous in Canada than in the United States, and is even more generous in Europe than in either Canada or the United States. In general, higher employment insurance benefits act to encourage job search and to increase unemployment.

AN INCREASE IN PRODUCTIVITY

Next, we consider what happens when productivity z increases. In Figure 6.12, panel (b), this acts to reduce $k/[(1-a)(z-b)]$ and so labour market tightness increases in equilibrium from j_1 to j_2. This occurs because higher productivity increases the total surplus available from a match between a firm and a worker, and firms then find it more attractive to post vacancies. Then, in panel (a) of Figure 6.12, higher z shifts up

FIGURE 6.12

An Increase in Productivity, z

An increase in productivity acts to increase the surplus from a match for both workers and firms. In panel (b), labour market tightness increases, and the curve shifts up in panel (a), so that the labour force must increase.

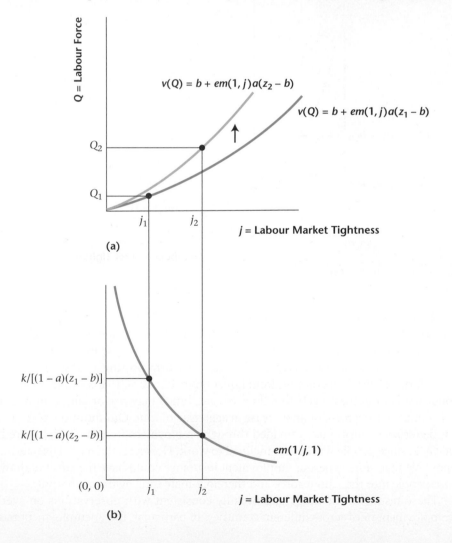

the curve, and so the labour force increases from Q_1 to Q_2, since consumers find it more attractive to enter the labour force, both because wages are higher and because the chances of finding a job are greater. From Equations (6.13) and (6.14), since labour market tightness has risen, the unemployment rate falls and the vacancy rate rises. Further, from Equation (6.15), since Q and j both increase, there is an increase in aggregate output.

These predictions are consistent with both long-run observations and with the comovements in labour market variables over the business cycle. First, in Figure 4.18, we observe an increase over time in productivity in Canada, and in Figure 6.3, we see that this coincides with an increase in the labour force participation rate. In the model, the participation rate is the ratio Q/N, which indeed increases in response to the increase in productivity in the model, just as we observe as a long-run feature of the data. Second, with regard to short-run phenomena, a key set of predictions of the model is that, when productivity increases, aggregate output increases, the unemployment rate falls, and the vacancy rate rises. Therefore, the model predicts that the unemployment rate should be countercyclical and the vacancy rate should be procyclical. While the unemployment rate is clearly countercyclical in the data, as we showed in Figure 6.2, the vacancy rate is not measured by Statistics Canada. However, in the United States, the measured vacancy rate is indeed procyclical,[5] just as our model predicts under productivity shocks.

This gives us some reasons to think that productivity may be an important driving force, both for long-run growth and for business cycles. We will study the role of productivity in economic growth in Chapters 7 and 8, and will examine some further implications of productivity shocks for business cycles in Chapters 13 and 14.

A DECREASE IN MATCHING EFFICIENCY

The factor e in the matching function represents matching efficiency, that is, the ease with which firms and workers can get together. Matching efficiency can increase through better information technologies that speed up the matching of jobs with particular skill requirements with workers who have particular skills. More importantly, particularly for short-run phenomena, matching efficiency can decrease when the degree of mismatch between the skills firms need and the skills consumers possess increases. This can occur, for example, when there is a sectoral shock to the economy, as we discussed earlier in this chapter.

In Figure 6.13, we show the effects of a decrease in matching efficiency. In panel (b) of the figure, the decrease in e acts to shift the curve to the left, so that labour market tightness falls from j_1 to j_2. Essentially, because firms find it more difficult to find the right workers, entry of firms into the labour market decreases, and the labour market becomes less tight. In panel (a) of Figure 6.13, the curve shifts to the right, and so Q must fall from Q_1 to Q_2. Thus, fewer consumers choose to search for work (the labour force contracts) because the chances of finding work are lower, and the chances

---

[5] See R. Shimer, 2005, "The Cyclical Behavior of Equilibrium Unemployment and Vacancies," *American Economic Review* 95, 25–49.

FIGURE 6.13

A Decrease in Matching Efficiency, *e*

This acts to shift the curves down in panels (a) and (b). Labour market tightness and the labour force must both decrease.

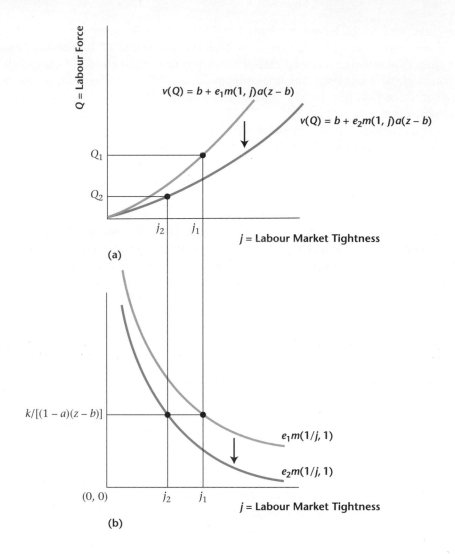

FIGURE 6.13

A Decrease in Matching Efficiency, *e*

This acts to shift the curves down in panels (a) and (b). Labour market tightness and the labour force must both decrease.

of finding work are lower for two reasons. First, lower matching efficiency reduces the probability of a match and, second, there are fewer firms searching.

Then, from Equation (6.13), the unemployment rate must rise, since j and e have fallen. With respect to vacancies there are two effects working in different directions. In Equation (6.14), the decrease in labour market tightness acts to increase vacancies, but the decrease in e decreases vacancies. However, from Equation (6.12), we know that the right-hand side does not change when e changes, so the left-hand side remains unchanged as well, and from Equation (6.14) the vacancy rate must remain constant. Therefore, since Q falls and $j = A/Q$ also falls, A must fall as well. As a result, from Equation (6.15) aggregate output must go down, since e, Q, and j have all fallen.

Thus, a decrease in the efficiency of matching, for example because of an increase in the mismatch of skills with jobs in the labour market, results in a smaller labour force, fewer job postings, a higher unemployment rate, and lower aggregate output.

This effect might be quite important, particularly in Canada, where there can be considerable variation in relative opportunities in different sectors of the economy. For example, the energy sector plays an important role in the Canadian economy, but the price of energy, driven particularly by the price of oil, is quite volatile. Therefore, when energy prices are high, profits are high in the energy sector, and labour should be moving from other sectors of the economy to the energy sector, and vice versa when energy prices are low. However, there may be considerable differences in the skills required in the energy sector relative to other sectors of the economy, for example manufacturing and services. Thus, there could be considerable mismatch that would impede the flows of labour in and out of the energy sector, and sectoral shocks could therefore have very important implications for fluctuations in aggregate output and unemployment.

THE BEVERIDGE CURVE

The **Beveridge curve**, which gets its name from William Beveridge, a twentieth-century British economist, is a negative relationship observed in the data between the unemployment rate and the vacancy rate. Since Statistics Canada does not collect data on job vacancies, we cannot show an empirical Beveridge curve for Canada, but it is possible to do so for the United States, where good-quality vacancy data has been collected since 2000. Figure 6.14 shows a scatter plot of the U.S. vacancy rate against the unemployment rate for the period 2000–2011. For later reference, the line in the figure

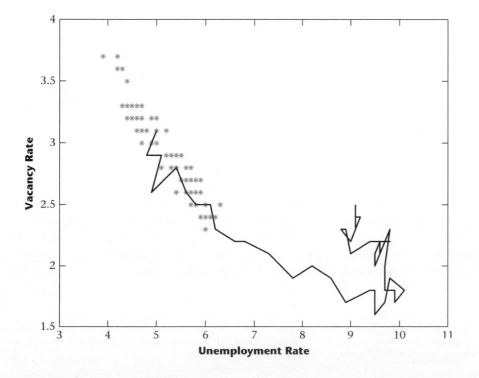

FIGURE 6.14

The Beveridge Curve for the United States

The scatter plot shows the vacancy rate against the unemployment rate for the United States for 2000–2011. The line in the figure connects data points from January 2008 through September 2011, in chronological order, beginning with January 2008 at the farthest point to the northwest.

Source: U.S. data source: Bureau of Labor Statistics.

connects the data points since the beginning of 2008, when the last recession began in the United States. The figure shows a clear negative correlation between the vacancy rate and the unemployment rate, which is the Beveridge relationship.

What causes the observed Beveridge relationship? We know from our analysis of the Diamond-Mortensen-Pissarides model that changes in the employment insurance benefit will cause the unemployment rate and the vacancy rate to move in different directions. Thus, fluctuations in employment insurance benefits could produce a Beveridge curve relationship. However, there would have to be large and frequent changes in employment insurance to generate what we observe in the data, and such large and frequent changes do not happen in practice. However, changes in productivity would also make the vacancy rate and unemployment rate move in opposite directions, and we know from Chapter 4 that in fact productivity does fluctuate significantly about trend. Thus, productivity fluctuations provide a candidate explanation for the Beveridge curve correlation. Indeed, work by Robert Shimer and by Marcus Hagedorn and Iourii Manovskii shows, using a DMP search model, that productivity shocks can replicate the observed cyclical variability in vacancies and unemployment in U.S. data.[6]

As shown in Figure 6.14, an interesting feature of the U.S. data is that there seems to have been a recent shift to the right in the Beveridge curve relationship. Recall that the line in the figure connects points observed from the beginning of 2008. As the unemployment rate climbed during the recession, the observed unemployment rate/vacancy rate combinations seemed to be on a stable downward-sloping Beveridge curve. But then, when the unemployment rate approached 10%, the vacancy rate began to increase, with essentially no change in the unemployment rate.

Though macroeconomists think that the key factors driving the recent recession were financial factors, we can represent this in our model as a negative shock to productivity, z. But there was also an important sectoral-shift aspect to the recession in the United States, in that construction sector activity—particularly residential investment—dropped dramatically, but some sectors—health care for example—continued to grow. Clearly, it is quite difficult to convert roofers into nurses, so we can think of this sectoral shift as a decrease in e.

Therefore, to explain the observations in Figure 6.14, with the initial decrease in z and in e, the unemployment rate rises and the vacancy rate falls initially in the recession, and there is movement down what appears to be a stable Beveridge curve. Then, once the unemployment rate reaches the vicinity of 10%, the recession bottoms out, z begins to increase and e continues to decrease. The result of this is that, on net, the unemployment rate does not change much (the increase in z causes the unemployment rate to fall, the decrease in e causes the unemployment rate to rise, and these effects roughly net out) and the vacancy rate rises (the increase in z causes the vacancy rate to rise, and the decrease in e has no effect on the vacancy rate).

---

[6]See S. Shimer, 2005, "The Cyclical Behavior of Equilibrium Unemployment and Vacancies," *American Economic Review* 95, 25–49; M. Hagedorn and I. Manovskii, 2008, "The Cyclical Behavior of Equilibrium Unemployment and Vacancies Revisited." *American Economic Review* 98, 1692–1706.

A KEYNESIAN DMP MODEL

We can use the DMP model to take a first pass at Keynesian ideas, though a broader treatment of Keynesian models and policy will have to wait until Chapters 13 and 14. A key element of Keynesian theory, one that goes back to Keynes's *General Theory*, is the idea that a certain type of market failure is associated with the setting of wages and prices. According to this view, there is a fundamental inability of private-sector economic agents to agree on wages and prices that are in the public interest. Sometimes this is described as an "inflexibility" or "stickiness" in wages and prices, in that prices and wages are somehow costly to change and therefore may not move quickly enough to clear markets or to transmit the right market signals to workers, firms, and consumers.

In the previous section, we assumed that a matched worker and producer get together and come to some agreement concerning how they should split the surplus from the match. The market real wage w was determined by the outside opportunities of firms and workers, and by relative bargaining power. However, Roger Farmer has argued, in the context of a search model of unemployment,[7] that it is useful to capture Keynesian market failure by thinking of the wage w as being determined by what Keynes called "animal spirits." In this context, we could take this to mean that the relative bargaining power of workers and firms is in some sense random. Firms may decide to drive a hard bargain with workers, and this is contagious, making the market wage relatively low, or firms in a similarly contagious manner decide to go easy on workers and pay them a high wage. Alternatively, we might think of the market wage as being sticky and determined from history.

To see how this idea works in our DMP model, think of Equations 6.6 and 6.8 as determining labour market tightness j and the labour force Q given the wage w, where w could in principle be anything. Then, in Figure 6.15, consider two alternative scenarios, one in which the wage is w_1 and one in which the wage is w_2, with $w_1 > w_2$. In panel (b) of the figure, with the high wage w_1 labour market tightness is j_1, and with the low wage w_2 labour market tightness is j_2, with $j_1 < j_2$. Thus, with a higher market wage, posting vacancies is less attractive for firms, and so labour market tightness falls. Then, in panel (a) of Figure 6.15, under a higher wage the curve shifts up, but labour market tightness is lower with a higher wage. Thus, a higher wage makes labour force participation more attractive, but lower labour market tightness makes it harder to find a job. These two effects work in opposite directions, which implies that Q_1 could be larger or smaller than Q_2, though in the figure we show the case where $Q_1 < Q_2$, in which case high wages are associated with low labour force participation.

Finally, Equations (6.13) to (6.15) allow us to say something about how unemployment rates, vacancy rates, and levels of aggregate output compare in the high-wage and low-wage equilibria. When the wage is high ($w = w_1$) labour market tightness j is low, and so from Equations (6.13) and (6.14), the unemployment rate is high and the vacancy rate is low. With respect to aggregate output, from Equation (6.15), we cannot say whether output is higher in the high-wage equilibrium than

[7]R. Farmer, 2011, "Animal Spirits, Rational Bubbles and Unemployment in an Old-Keynesian Model," working paper, UCLA.

FIGURE 6.15

The DMP Keynesian Model
A comparison of equilibria
with high and low wages,
with $w_1 > w_2$. In the high-
wage equilibrium, labour
market tightness is low,
and the labour force is low,
though it is possible for the
labour force to be high in the
high-wage equilibrium.

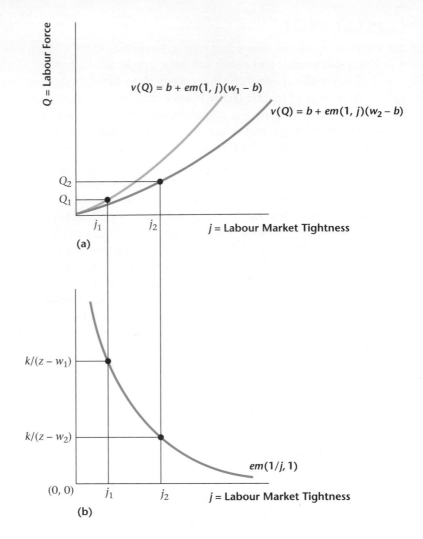

in the low-wage equilibrium. While we know that labour market tightness is low in
the high-wage equilibrium, which would tend to make output low, the labour force
might be low or high in the high-wage equilibrium, so this effect might either work
in the same direction on output as the effect coming from labour market tightness,
from Equation (6.15), or work in the opposite direction.

For the model to work for the most part consistently with Keynesian ideas, and
with the data, requires that $Q_1 < Q_2$, which is the case shown in Figure 6.15. Then,
the model implies that, when the wage is high, not only is the unemployment rate
high and the vacancy rate low (which is the case under any conditions), but the labour
force is low and output is low as well. Thus, we can think of the world being in a bad
state, with a real market wage that is in some sense "too high," and this bad state of the
world is associated with a high unemployment rate and low aggregate output—that is,
a recession. Everyone is optimizing in this world, but market forces somehow do not
yield the "right" market wage, an idea fundamental in Keynesian economics.

A large part of Keynesian economics is addressed to the question of how we "fix" bad states of the world, such as the one in Figure 6.15 where the wage is high. We have not set up the Keynesian search model in a way that addresses policy questions, but we will deal with these policy questions later, in Chapters 13 and 14.

The Keynesian search model gives us an alternative to productivity shocks as an explanation for the Beveridge curve relationship. If business cycles are driven by Keynesian "animal spirits," with fluctuating wages, as in Figure 6.15, then when wages are high the unemployment rate will be high and the vacancy rate low, and when wages are low the unemployment rate will be low and the vacancy rate will be high. Thus, we would observe a Beveridge relationship in the data. Therefore, at least in terms of some aspects of labour market activity, it can be difficult to distinguish between non-Keynesian and Keynesian explanations for what we are observing.

The key criticism of the Keynesian search model, relative to the basic Diamond-Mortensen-Pissarides model, is that it misses out on some basic economics. It indeed makes good sense to think of wages as being governed by market forces—the bargaining power of workers and firms, and their outside opportunities. Further, there are no good reasons to think that bargaining power shifts in dramatic ways over time, in a way unconnected to economic fundamentals, so as to produce the fluctuations we observe in aggregate output, employment, and unemployment. We will discuss this further, particularly in Chapters 13 and 14. Keynesian economics, while it may have something useful to tell us, has not as yet provided a sound underpinning for the stickiness of wages and prices that is at the core of Keynesian ideas.

THEORY CONFRONTS THE DATA	6.1	*Unemployment, Productivity, and Real GDP in Canada and the United States: The 2008–2009 Recession*

During the recent 2007–2009 recession, the Canadian and U.S. economies behaved quite differently, particularly with regard to labour market activity. Our goal in this feature is to use the DMP model constructed in this chapter to make sense of the data from this episode.

In Figures 6.16 through 6.18 we show, respectively, data on productivity, the unemployment rate, and real GDP in Canada and the United States, from the beginning of 2008 through mid-2011. In Figure 6.16, the measure of productivity we are using is average labour productivity (real GDP divided by total employment), which corresponds well to the concept of productivity in the DMP model. Productivity measures in the figure have been normalized to 100 in the first quarter of 2008. Figure 6.16 shows that, while productivity initially declined during the 2008–2009 recession in both countries, increases in productivity began as the two economies recovered. However, the recovery in productivity growth in Canada was much more sluggish than in the United States. Note that, while Canadian productivity was about 0.5% higher in mid-2011 than at the beginning of 2008, U.S. productivity grew by almost 5% over the same period.

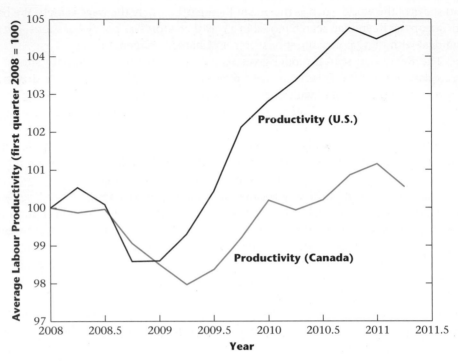

FIGURE 6.16 **Average Labour Productivity in Canada and the United States, 2008–2011**
Productivity grew much more during the recession in the United States than in Canada.

Source: Adapted from the Statistics Canada CANSIM database, Series v1992067, v2062811. U.S. data sources: Bureau of Labour Statistics and Bureau of Economic Analysis.

Next, in Figure 6.17, we show unemployment rates for Canada and the US for the same period of time. As was pointed out in Chapter 2, the unemployment rate in Canada has tended historically to be higher than in the United States. Indeed, at the beginning of 2008, the unemployment rate was about 6% in Canada and about 5% in the U.S. However, during the 2008–2009 recession the unemployment rate increased by a much larger amount in the U.S. than in Canada. By mid-2011, the unemployment rate was 7.4% in Canada and 9.2% in the U.S. Finally, in Figure 6.18, the paths for real GDP are depicted, again from the beginning of 2008 to mid-2011, with real GDP normalized to 100 at the beginning of 2008 for both countries. This last figure shows that the recent recession was both deeper and longer in the U.S. than in Canada, with a stronger recovery in Canada. While Canadian real GDP was about 2% higher in mid-2011 than at the beginning of 2008, real GDP in the U.S. was about the same.

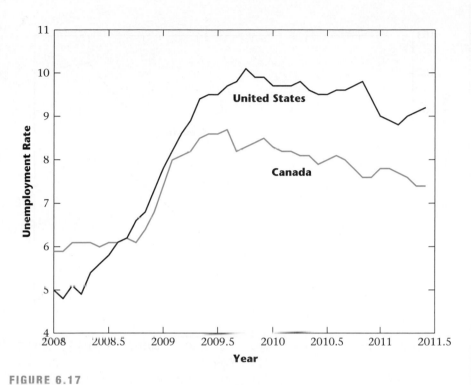

FIGURE 6.17

Unemployment Rates in Canada and the United States, 2008–2011

The unemployment rate rose much more during the recent recession in the United States than in Canada.

Source: Adapted from the Statistics Canada CANSIM database, Series v2062815. U.S. data source: Bureau of Labour Statistics.

What might explain these observations? Some aspects of the data are puzzling. For example, the DMP model tells us that an increase in productivity will increase aggregate output and reduce the unemployment rate. But this should tell us that, given the good productivity performance in the United States relative to Canada, that real GDP should have grown more, and the unemployment rate performed better, in the U.S. than in Canada. However, real GDP grew less in the U.S., and the unemployment rate increased more. What's going on?

One explanation might be that the degree of mismatch in the U.S. labour market increased much more in the U.S. than in Canada from the beginning of 2008 to mid-2011. This mismatch can be traced in the U.S. to the dramatic drop in construction, which was felt disproportionately in different geographical regions in the U.S. Thus, there was a key sectoral shift during the 2008–2009 recession from construction to other sectors, and the increases in unemployment were much higher

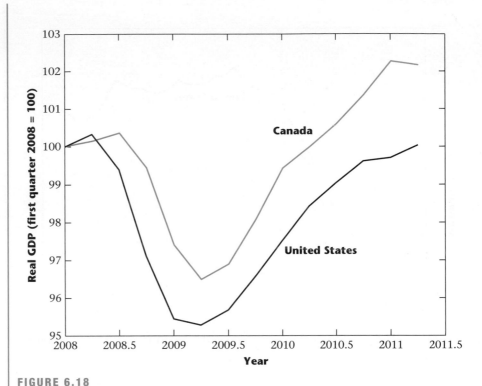

FIGURE 6.18

Real GDP in Canada and the United States, 2008–2011

The recession was shallower and shorter in Canada than in the United States, and percentage real GDP growth was higher in Canada than in the U.S. over the sample period.

Source: Adapted from the Statistics Canada CANSIM database, Series v1992067. U.S. data source: Bureau of Economic Analysis.

in some areas of the U.S. than in others. In contrast, Canada experienced only a moderate decline in construction during the 2008–2009 recession, and housing construction in particular recovered strongly relative to the United States.

Thus, the DMP model might explain the data in Figures 6.16 to 6.18, if we take account of the increase in labour market mismatch that occurred in the United States. In spite of the good performance in productivity in the U.S. relative to Canada, unemployment was relatively high and real GDP growth relatively low in the U.S. during the period in question, possibly because of labour market mismatch.

The DMP model illustrates one effect of EI, which is that higher EI benefits improve the bargaining position of workers relative to firms, which increases wages, discouraging firms from posting vacancies. As a result, the unemployment rate increases. However, there are other effects of EI, which we have not included in our simple DMP model.

A second effect of EI arises when we take account of the fact that wages are different for different jobs. Then, when a would-be worker receives a wage offer, he or she must make a decision on whether to accept the offer or continue to search. In this context, higher EI benefits will lower the cost of search and will therefore make the unemployed more picky concerning the types of jobs they will accept. This will tend to increase the unemployment rate.

A third effect of EI is its influence on on-the-job performance. For those employed, effort is required to retain a job. If an employer feels that a worker does not meet some threshold level of effort, the worker might be fired. Of course, it is difficult to observe a worker's effort level perfectly, so errors might be made: workers with good levels of effort might sometimes be fired and workers with poor levels of effort might be retained. However, in general, if a worker increases his or her effort, the chance of being fired is reduced. With higher EI benefits, though, the cost of being fired from a job is lower, and workers therefore exert less effort on the job and stand a greater chance of losing their jobs. Higher EI benefits thus act to increase the rate of transition from employment to unemployment through this effect, and this increases the unemployment rate.

A fourth effect of EI is its influence on the effort that the unemployed put into searching for work. Just as the unemployed become more choosy concerning the job offers they take with higher EI benefits, they also tend to search less intensively, because higher EI benefits decrease the cost of being unemployed.

A key feature of the latter three effects of EI on behaviour—the effect on job acceptances, the effect on on-the-job effort, and the effect on search effort—is that all of these effects are imperfectly observable. That is, there are moral hazard problems associated with EI, just as there are moral hazard problems for other forms of insurance (including deposit insurance, as we will discuss in Chapter 17). It is difficult for the provider of EI to observe whether the unemployed are turning down good job offers, whether workers are being fired because their effort is too low, or whether long spells of unemployment are the result of low search effort. Indeed, the fact that EI is provided by the government in Canada may indicate that the moral hazard problems associated with EI are so severe that EI would not be provided by a private insurer in the absence of government provision.

EI systems need to be designed with moral hazard problems in mind, and the system in Canada certainly has features that, at least partially, correct for moral hazard. For example, the level of benefits does not imply full insurance, in that the replacement rate (the ratio of benefits when unemployed to wages when employed) is less than one, and benefits are limited in duration for individuals, extending at most to 45 weeks. An optimal EI system achieves an optimal tradeoff between the benefits of insurance and the costs of moral hazard. If there is too much insurance (e.g., if the unemployed receive benefits equal to their wages on the job forever) workers and the unemployed have poor incentives; but if there is too little insurance, unemployment is too painful.

What would an optimal unemployment insurance system look like, and how close does Canada come to such a system? Several articles in the economics literature have attempted to address how close to optimal the U.S. unemployment insurance system is. An approach that is useful in this context is a dynamic contracting model, which allows us to think about economic problems in a dynamic framework in which information is not perfect, as is the case with unemployment insurance. An early article by S. Shavell and L. Weiss[8] shows that the optimal unemployment insurance benefit decreases over time. That is, in contrast to the Canadian EI system and the unemployment insurance system in the United States, in which benefits are constant for six months of unemployment and then go to zero, optimally benefits should decrease over time continuously and extend indefinitely. The optimal benefit schedule looks like this because the longer a person has been unemployed, the more likely it is that he or she is not looking very hard, and so a person should be penalized with lower benefits. However, a person may have been unemployed for a long time simply because he or she was unlucky, so it does not make sense to reduce benefits to zero for the long-term unemployed.

A more recent paper by Cheng Wang and Stephen Williamson[9] broadens the approach of Shavell and Weiss. Wang and Williamson show that an optimal unemployment insurance system should be more individual-specific while having the Shavell-Weiss feature that EI benefits decline with the duration of unemployment. That is, the level of benefits for an unemployed person should depend not only on the length of time since the person became unemployed and the wage when employed, but also on the whole history of employment and unemployment for that person. Such an optimal system would be implemented by having each Canadian citizen hold an account with the EI authority that would be credited during periods of employment and debited during periods of unemployment when the individual is drawing EI benefits. The level of the current EI benefit allowed would depend on the balance in the account at that time. Although such a system looks far different from the EI system currently in place in Canada or the United States, the discouraging news is that the welfare gain from moving to an optimal system would be small. Wang and Williamson estimate that switching from the current unemployment insurance system to an optimal system would result in a welfare increase for the United States equivalent to about 1% of GDP at most.

---

[8]S. Shavell and L. Weiss, 1979, "The Optimal Payment of Unemployment Insurance Benefits over Time," *Journal of Political Economy* 87, 1347–1362.

[9]C. Wang and S. Williamson, 2002, "Moral Hazard, Optimal Unemployment Insurance, and Experience Rating," *Journal of Monetary Economics* 49, 1337–1372.

Chapter Summary

- The key determinants of the unemployment rate are aggregate economic activity, demographics, government intervention, and sectoral shifts.

- The participation rate is affected by demographics and by the different labour market behaviour of men and women.

- The unemployment rate is a countercyclical variable, whereas the participation rate is procyclical.

- The employment/population ratio is more cyclically variable than is the participation rate.

- In the DMP search model, firms pay a cost to post a vacancy, and consumers must decide whether to work at home or to search for market work.

- In the DMP model, when a worker is matched with a firm, he or she bargains over the wage, which is determined by the outside opportunities of the worker and the firm, and by relative bargaining power.

- The DMP model determines labour market tightness (the ratio of firms searching to consumers searching for work), the labour force, the market wage, the vacancy rate, and the unemployment rate.

- An increase in the EI benefit acts to reduce the surplus of a firm in a match, which acts to reduce labour market tightness, increase the unemployment rate, and reduce the vacancy rate. The size of the labour force may rise or fall, as may aggregate output.

- In the DMP model, an increase in productivity acts to increase the surplus of both workers and firms in matches, and this increases labour market tightness and the size of the labour force. The unemployment rate falls, the vacancy rate rises, and aggregate output rises.

- A decrease in matching efficiency reduces labour market tightness and the size of the labour force. The unemployment rate increases, the vacancy rate does not change, and aggregate output falls. Changes in matching efficiency are a potential explanation for the recent behaviour of unemployment and vacancies in the United States.

- In the Keynesian DMP model, firms and workers have difficulty making agreements on wages that are in the interests of society. In a high-wage equilibrium, the unemployment rate is high, the vacancy rate is low, and aggregate output may be low.

Key Terms

demography: The study of population.
sectoral shift: A change in an economy's structure of production.
matching function: In the DMP model, a function that determines the number of successful matches between workers and firms, given the number of firms posting vacancies and the number of consumers searching for work.
labour market tightness: The ratio of firms posting vacancies to consumers searching for work.
Beveridge curve: A negative relationship observed between the vacancy rate and the unemployment rate.

Questions for Review

1. What are the four key determinants of the unemployment rate?

2. Is the unemployment rate procyclical or countercyclical?

3. How do demographic factors affect the participation rate?

4. Is the participation rate procyclical or countercyclical?

5. How does the employment/population ratio behave relative to the participation rate, and why?

6. In the DMP model, what determines a consumer's decision to search for work?

7. In the DMP model, what determines a firm's decision to post a vacancy?

8. What are total surplus, worker surplus, and firm surplus in the DMP model?

9. In the DMP model, when a worker and firm are matched, what determines the wage paid to the worker?

10. In the DMP model, what are the effects of an increase in the EI benefit?

11. In the DMP model, what are the effects of an increase in productivity?

12. In the DMP model, what are the effects of a decrease in matching efficiency?

13. What is the Beveridge curve, and why is it important?

14. What are three potential explanations for the Beveridge relation?

15. What is the basic market failure in Keynesian economics?

16. What explains aggregate fluctuations in the Keynesian DMP model?

Problems

1. What does the DMP model predict would be the effects of labour-saving devices in the home, for example dishwashers, washing machines, and vacuum cleaners? Use diagrams to show the effects on the unemployment rate, the vacancy rate, the labour force, the number of firms, aggregate output, and labour market tightness, and discuss your results.

2. Suppose the government's goal is to reduce the unemployment rate. Some legislators propose that the government should give a subsidy s to any firm that hires a worker. Others argue that it would be more effective to simply pay consumers to stay home rather than search for work; that is, anyone who chooses not to participate in the labour force should receive a payment q. Which policy is more effective in achieving the government's goal? Explain using the DMP model, with the aid of diagrams. (In your answer, do not concern yourself with how the subsidies from the government are financed.)

3. Suppose that there is technological change that reduces the costs of recruiting for firms. Using the DMP model, determine the effects on the unemployment rate, the vacancy rate, the labour force, the number of firms, aggregate output, and labour market tightness. Use diagrams, and explain your results.

4. Adapt the DMP model to include government activity as follows. Suppose that the government can operate firms, subject to the same constraints as private firms. In particular, the government must incur a cost k to post a vacancy. Supposing that the government operates G firms, then the number of matches in the economy as a whole is $M = em\,(Q, A + G)$, where A is the number of private firms that choose to post vacancies. Assume that the government pays the same wages as do private sector firms. Determine the effects of G on the unemployment rate, the vacancy rate, the labour force, the number of private firms, the total number of firms (private and government-run), aggregate output, and labour market tightness. Explain your results.

5. Show that, in the Keynesian DMP model, if the wage is judged to be inefficiently high, so that unemployment is inefficiently high, the government can pay a subsidy to firms that corrects the problem. Explain your results. Does it matter whether the government subsidizes firms that post vacancies or only successful matches? Discuss.

6. Suppose that all social programs simultaneously become more generous. In particular, suppose that there is an increase in EI benefits, and also an increase in welfare benefits, which are represented in the DMP model as payments to everyone who is not in the labour force. What will be the effects on the unemployment rate, the vacancy rate, the labour force, the number of firms, aggregate output, and labour market tightness? Explain your results.

Part 3

Economic Growth

In this Part, we study the primary facts of economic growth and the key macroeconomic models that economists have used to understand these facts. In Chapter 7, we first examine the Malthusian model of economic growth, in which population growth increases with the standard of living. Any improvements in the technology for producing goods lead to more population growth, and in the long run there is no improvement in the standard of living. The Malthusian model does a good job of explaining economic growth in the world prior to the Industrial Revolution in the nineteenth century, but it cannot explain growth experience after 1800. What Malthus did not envision was the role of capital accumulation in economic growth. Capital accumulation plays an important role in the Solow model of economic growth, which is the preeminent framework used in modern economic growth theory. The Solow growth model predicts that long-run improvements in the standard of living are generated by technological progress, that countries with high (low) savings rates tend to have high (low) level of per capita income, and that countries with high (low) rates of population growth tend to have low (high) levels of per capita income. The Solow growth model is much more optimistic than the Malthusian model about the prospects for improvements in the standard of living. Finally, in Chapter 7 we study growth accounting, an approach to attributing economic growth to growth in factors of production and in productivity.

In Chapter 8, we first study the predictions of the Solow growth model for convergence in standards of living across countries. In the data, there is a tendency for convergence in per capita incomes among the richest countries in the world, but apparently no tendency for convergence among all countries. The Solow model is consistent with this if we allow for differences in the adoption of technology across countries. Next in Chapter 8, we examine an endogenous growth model, which helps us analyze the determinants of the rate of economic growth. This endogenous growth model has the property that differences in standards of living persist across countries, and that education is an important factor in determining the rate of economic growth.

7

Economic Growth: Malthus and Solow

The two primary phenomena that macroeconomists study are business cycles and economic growth. Though much macroeconomic research focuses on business cycles, the study of economic growth has also received a good deal of attention, especially since the late 1980s. Robert Lucas[1] has argued that the potential social gains from a greater understanding of business cycles are dwarfed by the gains from understanding growth. This is because, even if (most optimistically) business cycles could be completely eliminated, the worst events we would be able to avoid would be reductions of real GDP below trend on the order of 5%, based on the last 50 years of Canadian data. However, if changes in economic policy could cause the growth rate of real GDP to increase by 1% per year for 100 years, then GDP would be 2.7 times higher after 100 years than it would otherwise have been.

The effects of economic growth have been phenomenal. Per capita Canadian income[2] in 2010 was $47 606, but before the Industrial Revolution in the early nineteenth century, per capita Canadian income was only several hundred 2010 dollars. In fact, before 1800 the standard of living differed little over time and across countries. Since the Industrial Revolution, however, economic growth has not been uniform across countries, and there are currently wide disparities in standards of living among the countries of the world. In 2000, income per capita in Mexico was 23.5% of what it was in the United States; in Egypt it was 13.2% of that in the U.S.; and in Burundi it was about 2.0% of the U.S. figure. Currently, there are also large differences in rates of growth across countries. Between 1960 and 2000, while income per capita was growing at an average rate of 2.31% in Canada and 2.48% in the United States, the comparable figure for Madagascar was −1.07%; for Nicaragua it was −0.03%; for Hong Kong it was 5.40%; and for Taiwan it was 6.68%.[3]

---

[1]See R. Lucas, 1987, *Models of Business Cycles*, Basil Blackwell, Oxford, UK.

[2]Source: Statistics Canada CANSIM database, Series v3860085, v1.

[3]The income-per-worker statistics come from A. Heston, R. Summers, and B. Aten, *Penn World Table Version 6.2*, Center for International Comparisons at the University of Pennsylvania (CICUP), available at pwt.econ.upenn.edu, accessed January 22, 2009.

In this chapter we first discuss some basic economic growth facts, and this provides a useful context in which to organize our thinking by using some standard models of growth. The first model we study formalizes the ideas of Thomas Malthus, who wrote in the late eighteenth century. This Malthusian model has the property that any improvement in the technology for producing goods leads to increased population growth, so that in the long run there is no improvement in the standard of living. The population is sufficiently higher so that there is no increase in per capita consumption and per capita output. Consistent with the conclusions of Malthus, the model predicts that population control is the only means for improving the standard of living.

The Malthusian model yields quite pessimistic predictions concerning the prospects for long-run growth in per capita incomes. Of course, the predictions of Malthus were wrong, as he did not foresee the Industrial Revolution. After the Industrial Revolution, economic growth was in part driven by growth in the stock of capital over time and was not limited by fixed factors of production (such as land), as in the Malthusian model. An approach to separating out the sources of growth is growth accounting. We use this approach in this chapter to determine how growth in capital, labour, and total factor productivity account for growth in output over particular periods of time.

Next, we study the Solow growth model, the most widely used model of economic growth, developed by Robert Solow in the 1950s.[4] This model makes important predictions concerning the effects of savings rates, population growth, and changes in total factor productivity on a nation's standard of living and growth rate of GDP. We show that these predictions match economic data quite well.

A key implication of the Solow growth model is that a country's standard of living cannot continue to improve in the long run in the absence of continuing increases in total factor productivity. In the short run, the standard of living can improve if a country's residents save and invest more, thus accumulating more capital. However, the Solow growth model tells us that building more productive capacity will not improve long-run living standards unless the production technology becomes more efficient. The model is thus more optimistic about the prospects for long-run improvement in the standard of living than the Malthusian model is, but only up to a point. It tells us that improvements in knowledge and technical ability are necessary to sustain growth.

The Solow growth model is an **exogenous growth model**, meaning that growth is caused in the model by forces that are not explained by the model itself. To gain a deeper understanding of economic growth, it is useful to examine the economic factors that cause growth, and this is done in **endogenous growth models**, in which growth is caused by forces determined by the model; we examine one such model in Chapter 8.

Finally, in this chapter we study growth accounting, which is an approach to attributing the growth in GDP to growth in factor inputs and in total factor productivity. Growth accounting can highlight interesting features of the data, such as medium-term swings in productivity growth in the economy.

---

[4]See R. Solow, 1956, "A Contribution to the Theory of Economic Growth," *Quarterly Journal of Economics* 70, 65–94.

Economic Growth Facts

Before proceeding to construct and analyze models of economic growth, we summarize the key empirical regularities relating to growth within and across countries. This gives us a framework for evaluating our models and helps organize our thinking about growth. The important growth facts are the following:

1. *Before the Industrial Revolution, in about 1800, standards of living differed little over time and across countries.* There appear to have been no improvements in standards of living for a long period of time prior to 1800. Though population and aggregate income grew, with growth sometimes interrupted by disease and wars, population growth kept up with growth in aggregate income, so that there was little change in per capita income. Living standards did not vary much across the countries of the world. In particular, Western Europe and Asia had similar standards of living.[5]

2. *Since the Industrial Revolution, per capita income growth has been sustained in the richest countries.* In Canada, average annual growth in per capita income has been about 2% since 1870. The Industrial Revolution began in about 1800 in the United Kingdom, and the United States eventually surpassed the United Kingdom as the world industrial leader. Canada is one of the richest countries in the world, with per capita income of about 88% of that in the United States in 2009.[6] Figure 7.1 shows the natural logarithm of per capita income in Canada for the years 1870–2010. Recall from Chapter 1 that the slope of the natural log of a time series is approximately equal to the growth rate. What is remarkable about the figure is that a straight line would be a fairly good fit to the natural log of per capita income in Canada over this period of 141 years. That is, average per capita income growth in Canada has not strayed far from an average growth rate of about 2% per year for the whole period, except for major interruptions, such as the Great Depression (1929–1939) and the minor variability introduced by business cycles.

3. *There is a positive correlation between the rate of investment and real income per capita across countries.* In Figure 7.2 we show a scatter plot of real income per capita (as a percentage of real income per capita in the United States) versus the rate of investment (as a percentage of aggregate output) in the countries of the world in 2000. Clearly, a straight line fit to these points would have a positive slope, so the two variables are positively correlated. Thus, countries in which a relatively large (small) fraction of output is channelled into investment tend to have a relatively high (low) standard of living. This fact is particularly important in checking the predictions of the Solow growth model against the data.

---

[5]See S. Parente and E. Prescott, 2000, *Barriers to Riches*, MIT Press, Cambridge, MA.

[6]A. Heston, R. Summers, and B. Aten, *Penn World Table Version 7.0*, Center for International Comparisons at the University of Pennsylvania (CICUP), available at pwt.econ.upenn.edu, accessed December 31, 2011.

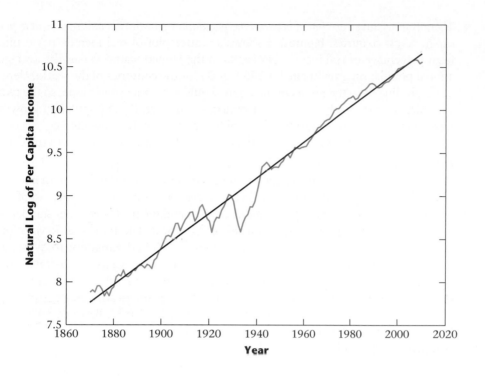

FIGURE 7.1

Natural Log of Real per Capita Income in Canada, 1870–2010

A straight line provides a good fit. Growth in per capita income in Canada has not strayed far from 2% per year for this period.

Source: Adapted from the Statistics Canada CANSIM database, Series v3860085, v1, and from the Statistics Canada publication *Historical Statistics of Canada*, Catalogue 11-516, 1983, Series 533–55, A1, and M. C. Urquart, "New Estimates of Gross National Product, Canada, 1870–1926: Some Implications for Canadian Development," in S. Engerman and R. Gallman, *Long-Term Factors in American Economic Growth*, University of Chicago Press, Chicago.

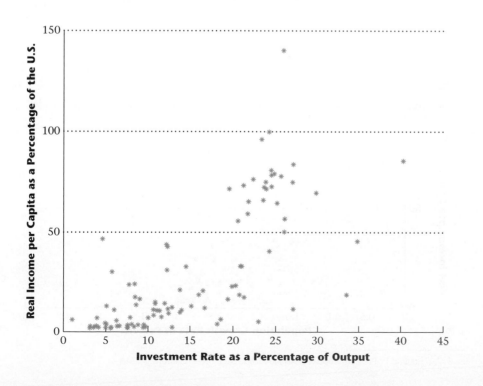

FIGURE 7.2

Real Income per Capita vs. Investment Rate

The figure shows a positive correlation across the countries of the world between real income per capita and the investment rate.

Source of Data: A. Heston, R. Summers, and B. Aten, *Penn World Table Version 6.2*, Center for International Comparisons at the University of Pennsylvania (CICUP).

4. *There is a negative correlation between the population growth rate and real income per capita across countries.* Figure 7.3 shows a scatter plot of real income per capita (as a percentage of real income per capita in the United States) versus the average annual population growth rate for 1960–2004 for the countries of the world. Here, a straight line fit to the points in the figure would have a negative slope, so the two variables are negatively correlated. Countries with high (low) population growth rates tend to have low (high) standards of living. As with the previous fact, this one is important in matching the predictions of the Solow growth model with the data.

5. *Differences in per capita incomes increased dramatically among countries of the world between 1800 and 1950, with the gap widening between the countries of Western Europe, the United States, Canada, Australia, and New Zealand, as a group, and the rest of the world.* A question that interests us in this chapter and the next is whether standards of living are converging across countries of the world. The Industrial Revolution spread in the early nineteenth century from the United Kingdom to Western Europe and the United States, then to the new countries of Canada, Australia, and New Zealand. The countries in Africa, Asia, and South America were mainly left behind, with some Asian (and to some extent South American) countries closing the gap with the rich countries later in the twentieth century. Between 1800 and 1950, there was a divergence between living standards in the richest and poorest countries of the world.[7]

FIGURE 7.3

Real Income per Capita vs. the Population Growth Rate
The figure shows a negative correlation across the countries of the world between output per worker and the population growth rate.

Source of Data: A. Heston, R. Summers, and B. Aten, *Penn World Table Version 6.2*, Center for International Comparisons at the University of Pennsylvania (CICUP).

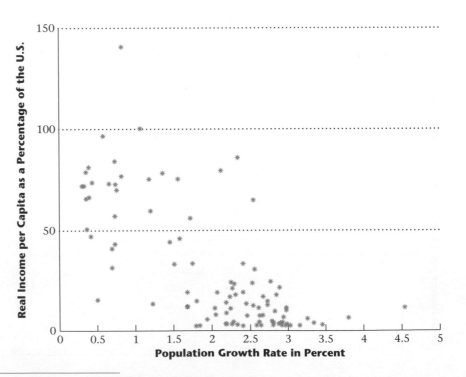

[7]See S. Parente and E. Prescott, 2000, *Barriers to Riches*, MIT Press, Cambridge, MA.

6. *There is essentially no correlation across countries between the level of output per capita in 1960 and the average rate of growth in output per capita for the years 1960–2000.* Standards of living would be converging across countries if income per capita were converging to a common value. For this to happen, it would have to be the case that poor countries (those with low levels of income per capita) are growing at a higher rate than are rich countries (those with high levels of income per capita). Thus, if convergence in incomes per capita is occurring, we should observe a negative correlation between the growth rate in income per capita and the level of income per capita across countries. Figure 7.4 shows data for 1960–2000, the period for which good data exists for most of the countries in the world. The figure shows the average rate of growth in real income per capita for the period 1960–2000 versus the level of real income per capita (as a percentage of real income per capita in the United States) in 1960 for a set of 99 countries. There is essentially no correlation shown in the figure, which indicates that for all countries of the world, convergence is not detectable for this period.

7. *Richer countries are much more alike in terms of rates of growth of real per capita income than are poor countries.* In Figure 7.4, we observe that there is a much wider vertical scatter in the points on the left-hand side of the scatter plot than on the right-hand side. That is, the variability in the real income growth rates is much smaller for rich countries than for poor countries.

In this chapter and Chapter 8, we use growth facts 1 to 7 to motivate the structure of our models and as checks on the predictions of those models.

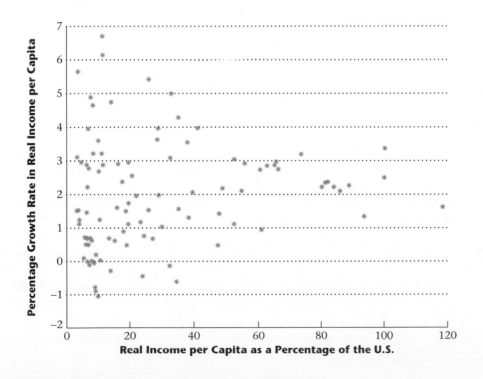

FIGURE 7.4

Growth Rate in per Capita Real Income vs. Real Income per Capita for the Countries of the World

There is no correlation between the growth rate of real income per capita and the level of real income per capita for the countries of the world. Rich countries are more alike in terms of their growth rates than are poor countries.

Source of Data: A. Heston, R. Summers, and B. Aten, *Penn World Table Version 6.2*, Center for International Comparisons at the University of Pennsylvania (CICUP).

The Malthusian Model of Economic Growth

In 1798, Thomas Malthus, a political economist in England, wrote the highly influential *An Essay on the Principle of Population*.[8] Malthus did not construct a formal economic model of the type that we would use in modern economic arguments, but his ideas are clearly stated and coherent and can be easily translated into a structure that is easy to understand.

Malthus argued that any advances in the technology for producing food would inevitably lead to further population growth, with the higher population ultimately reducing the average person to the subsistence level of consumption they had before the advance in technology. The population and level of aggregate consumption could grow over time, but in the long run there would be no increase in the standard of living unless there were some limits on population growth. Malthusian theory is, therefore, very pessimistic about the prospects for increases in the standard of living, with collective intervention in the form of forced family planning required to bring about gains in per capita income.

The following model formalizes Malthusian theory. The model is a dynamic one with many periods, though for most of the analysis we confine attention to what happens in the *current period* and the *future period* (the period following the current period). We start with an aggregate production function that specifies how current aggregate output, *Y*, is produced by using current inputs of land, *L*, and current labour, *N*, that is,

$$Y = zF(L, N), \tag{7.1}$$

where *z* is total factor productivity, and *F* is a function having the same properties, including constant returns to scale, that we specified in Chapter 4, except here land replaces capital in the production function. It helps to think of *Y* as being food, which is perishable from period to period. In this economy there is no investment (and, therefore, no saving—recall from Chapter 2 that savings equals investment in a closed economy) because we assume there is no way to store food from one period to the next and no technology for converting food into capital. For simplicity, there is assumed to be no government spending. Land, *L*, is in fixed supply. That is, as was the case in Western Europe in 1798, all of the land that might be used for agriculture is under cultivation. Assume that each person in this economy is willing to work at any wage and has one unit of labour to supply (a normalization), so that *N* in Equation (7.1) is both the population and the labour input.

Next, suppose that population growth depends on the quantity of consumption per worker, or

$$\frac{N'}{N} = g\left(\frac{C}{N}\right), \tag{7.2}$$

where *N'* denotes the population in the future (next) period, *g* is an increasing function, and *C* is aggregate consumption, so that *C/N* is current consumption per worker.

---

[8]See T. Malthus, 1798, "An Essay on the Principle of Population," St. Paul's Church-Yard, London, available at www.ac.wwu.edu/~stephan/malthus/malthus.0.html.

We show the relationship described by Equation (7.2) in Figure 7.5. In Equation (7.2), the ratio of future population to current population depends positively on consumption per worker mainly because of the fact that higher food consumption per worker reduces death rates through better nutrition. With poor nutrition, infants have a low probability of surviving childhood, and children and adults are highly susceptible to disease.

In equilibrium, all goods produced are consumed, so $C = Y$, which is the income–expenditure identity for this economy (because $I = G = NX = 0$ here; see Chapter 2). Therefore, substituting C for Y in Equation (7.2), in equilibrium we have

$$C = zF(L, N). \tag{7.3}$$

We can then use Equation (7.3) to substitute for C in Equation (7.2) to get

$$\frac{N'}{N} = g\left(\frac{zF(L, N)}{N}\right). \tag{7.4}$$

Now, recall from Chapter 4 that the constant-returns-to-scale property of the production function implies that

$$xzF(L, N) = zF(xL, xN)$$

for any $x > 0$, so if $x = 1/N$ in the above equation, then

$$\frac{zF(L, N)}{N} = zF\left(\frac{L}{N}, 1\right).$$

As a result, we can rewrite Equation (7.4), after multiplying each side by N, as

$$N' = g\left[zF\left(\frac{L}{N}, 1\right)\right]N. \tag{7.5}$$

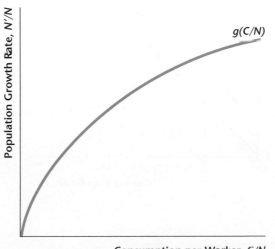

Consumption per Worker, C/N

(y-axis: Population Growth Rate, N'/N)

(curve label: g(C/N))

FIGURE 7.5

The Relationship Between Population Growth and Consumption Per Worker
Population growth depends on consumption per worker in the Malthusian model.

Here, Equation (7.5) tells us how the population evolves over time in equilibrium, as it gives the future population as a function of the current population. We assume that the relationship described in Equation (7.5) can be depicted as in Figure 7.6.[9] In the figure, N^* is a rest point or steady state for the population, determined by the point where the curve intersects the 45° line. If the current population is N^* then the future population is N^* and the population is N^* forever after. In the figure, if $N < N^*$ then $N' > N$ and the population increases, whereas if $N > N^*$ then $N' < N$ and the population decreases. Thus, whatever the population is currently, it eventually comes to rest at N^* in the long run. That is, the **steady state**, N^*, is the long-run equilibrium for the population. The reason that population converges to a steady state is the following. Suppose, on the one hand, that the population is currently below its steady state value. Then there will be a relatively large quantity of consumption per worker, and this will imply that the population growth rate is relatively large and positive, and the population will increase. On the other hand, suppose that the population is above its steady state value. Then there will be a small quantity of consumption per worker, and the population growth rate will be relatively low and negative, so that the population will decrease.

Because the quantity of land is fixed, when the population converges to the long-run equilibrium, N^*, aggregate consumption (equal to aggregate output here) converges, from Equation (7.3), to

$$C^* = zF(L, N^*).$$

FIGURE 7.6

Determination of the Population in the Steady State

In the figure, N^* is the steady state population, determined by the intersection of the curve and the 45° line. If $N > N^*$ then $N' < N$ and the population falls over time, and if $N < N^*$ then $N' > N$ and the population rises over time.

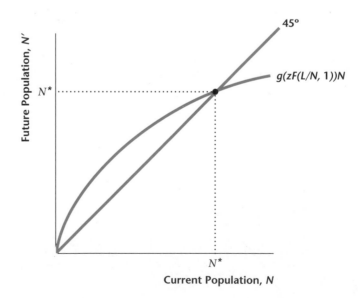

ANALYSIS OF THE STEADY STATE IN THE MALTHUSIAN MODEL

Because the Malthusian economy converges to a long-run steady state equilibrium with constant population and constant aggregate consumption, it is useful to analyze this steady state to determine what features of the environment affect steady state variables. In this subsection, we show how this type of analysis is done.

Given that the production function F has the constant-returns-to-scale property, if we divide the left-hand and right-hand sides of Equation (7.1) by N and rearrange, we get

$$\frac{Y}{N} = zF\left(\frac{L}{N}, 1\right).$$

Then, letting lowercase letters denote per-worker quantities, that is, $y = \frac{Y}{N}$ (output per worker), $l = \frac{L}{N}$ (land per worker), $c = \frac{C}{N}$ (consumption per worker), we have

$$y = zf(l), \tag{7.6}$$

where $zf(l)$ is the **per-worker production function**, which describes the quantity of output per worker, y, that can be produced for each quantity of land per worker, l, with the function f defined by $f(l) = F(l, 1)$. The per-worker production function is displayed in Figure 7.7. Then, as $c = y$ in equilibrium, from Equation (7.6) we have

$$c = zf(l). \tag{7.7}$$

We can also rewrite Equation (7.2) as

$$\frac{N'}{N} = g(c) \tag{7.8}$$

Now, we can display Equations (7.7) and (7.8) in Figure 7.8. In the steady state, $N = N' = N^*$, so $\frac{N'}{N} = 1$, and in panel (b) of the figure this determines c^*, the

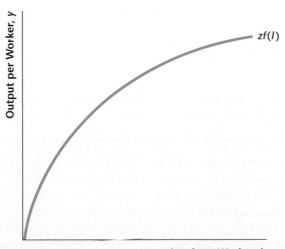

FIGURE 7.7

The Per-Worker Production Function
This describes the relationship between output per worker and land per worker in the Malthusian model, assuming constant returns to scale.

FIGURE 7.8

**Determination of the
Steady State in the
Malthusian Model**

In panel (b), steady state
consumption per worker, c^*,
is determined as the level of
consumption per worker that
implies no population growth.
Given c^*, the quantity of land
per worker in the steady
state, l^*, is determined from
the per-worker production
function in panel (a).

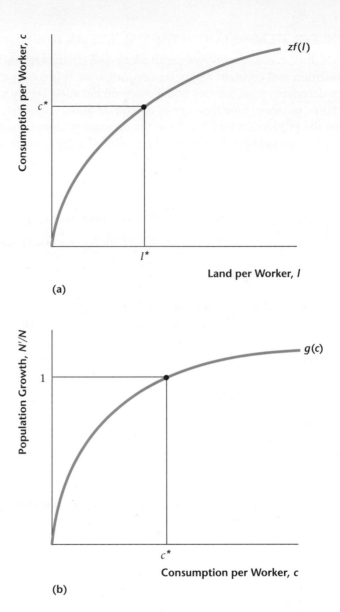

steady state quantity of consumption per worker. Then, in panel (a) of the figure, c^* determines the steady state quantity of land per worker, l^*. Because the quantity of land is fixed at L we can then determine the steady state population as $N^* = \dfrac{L}{l^*}$.

In the model, we can take the standard of living as being given by steady state consumption per worker, c^*. Therefore, the long-run standard of living is determined entirely by the function g, which captures the effect of the standard of living on population growth. The key property of the model is that nothing in panel (a) of Figure 7.8 affects c^*, so that improvements in the production technology or increases in the quantity of land have no effect on the long-run standard of living.

The Effects of an Increase in z on the Steady State We now consider an experiment in which total factor productivity increases, which we can interpret as an improvement in agricultural techniques. That is, suppose that the economy is initially in a steady state, with a given level of total factor productivity, z_1, which then increases once and for all time to z_2. The steady state effects are shown in Figure 7.9. In panel (a) of the figure, the per-worker production function shifts up from $z_1 f(l)$ to $z_2 f(l)$. This has no effect on steady state consumption per worker c^*, which is determined

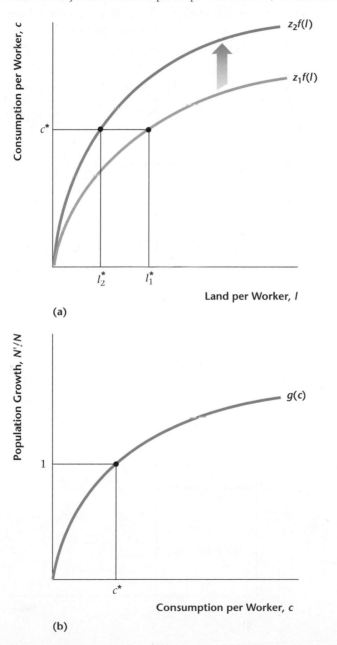

FIGURE 7.9

The Effect of an Increase in z in the Malthusian Model
When z increases, land per worker decreases in the steady state (so the population increases and consumption per worker remains the same).

(a)

(b)

in panel (b) of the figure. In the new steady state, in panel (a) the quantity of land per worker falls from l_1^* to l_2^*. This implies that the steady state population increases from $N_1^* = \dfrac{L}{l_1^*}$ to $N_2^* = \dfrac{L}{l_2^*}$.

The economy does not move to the new steady state instantaneously, as it takes time for the population and consumption to adjust. Figure 7.10 shows how the adjustment takes place in terms of the paths of consumption per worker and population. The economy is in a steady state before time T, at which time there is an increase in total factor productivity. Initially, the effect of this is to increase output, consumption, and consumption per worker, as there is no effect on the current population at time T.

FIGURE 7.10

Adjustment to the Steady State in the Malthusian Model When z Increases
In the figure, z increases at time T, which causes consumption per worker to increase and then decline to its steady state value over time, with the population increasing over time to its steady state value.

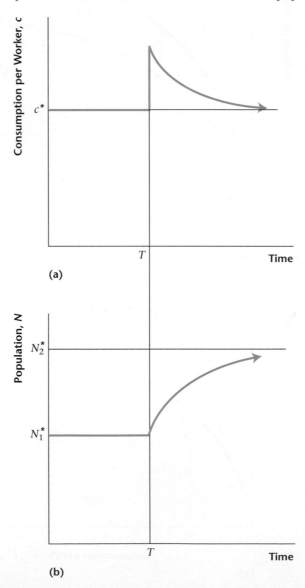

However, because consumption per worker has increased, there is an increase in population growth. As the population grows after period T, in panel (b) of the figure, consumption per worker falls (given the fixed quantity of land), until consumption per worker converges to c^*, its initial level, and the population converges to its new higher level N_2^*.

This, then, gives the pessimistic Malthusian result that improvements in the technology for producing food do not improve the standard of living in the long run. A better technology generates better nutrition and more population growth, and the extra population ultimately consumes all of the extra food produced, so that each person is no better off than before the technological improvement.

Population Control How can society be better off in a Malthusian world? The prescription Malthus proposed was state-mandated population control. If the government were to institute something like the one-child-only policy introduced in China, this would have the effect of reducing the rate of population growth for each level of consumption per worker. In panel (b) of Figure 7.11, the function $g_1(c)$ shifts down to $g_2(c)$ as the result of the population control policy. In the steady state, consumption per worker increases from c_1^* to c_2^* in panel (b) of the figure, and this implies that the quantity of land per worker rises in the steady state in panel (a) from l_1^* to l_2^*. Because the quantity of land is fixed, the population falls in the steady state from $N_1^* = \dfrac{L}{l_1^*}$ to $N_2^* = \dfrac{L}{l_2^*}$. Here, a reduction in the size of the population increases output per worker and consumption per worker, and everyone is better off in the long run.

HOW USEFUL IS THE MALTHUSIAN MODEL OF ECONOMIC GROWTH?

Given what was known in 1798, when Malthus wrote his essay, the Malthusian model could be judged to be quite successful. Our first economic growth fact, discussed at the beginning of this chapter, was that before the Industrial Revolution in about 1800, standards of living differed little over time and across countries. The Malthusian model predicts this, if population growth depends in the same way on consumption per worker across countries. Before the Industrial Revolution, production in the world was mainly agricultural; the population grew over time, as did aggregate production, but there appeared to have been no significant improvements in the average standard of living. This is all consistent with the Malthusian model.

As is well-known from the perspective of the early twenty-first century, however, Malthus was far too pessimistic. There was sustained growth in standards of living in the richest countries of the world after 1800 without any significant government population control in place in the countries with the strongest performance. As well, the richest countries of the world have experienced a large drop in birth rates. Currently, in spite of advances in health care that have increased life expectancy dramatically in the richer countries, population in most of these richer countries would be declining without immigration. Thus, Malthus was ultimately wrong, concerning both the ability of economies to produce long-run improvements in the standard of living and the effect of the standard of living on population growth.

FIGURE 7.11

Population Control in the Malthusian Model

In the figure, population control policy shifts the function $g_1(c)$ to $g_2(c)$. In the steady state, consumption per worker increases and land per worker decreases (the population falls).

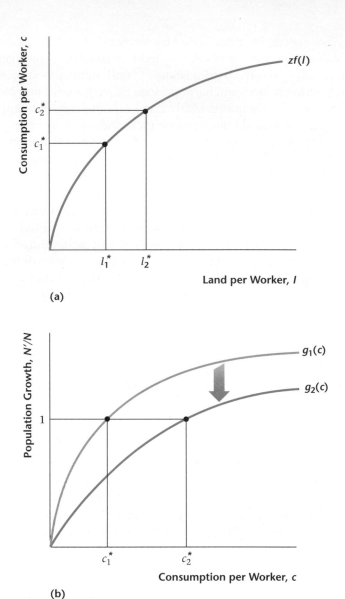

(a)

(b)

Why was Malthus wrong? First, he did not allow for the effect of increases in the capital stock on production. In contrast to land, which is limited in supply, there is no limit to the size of the capital stock, and having more capital implies that there is more productive capacity to produce additional capital. That is, capital can reproduce itself. The Solow growth model, which we develop later in this chapter, allows us to explore the role of capital accumulation in growth.

Second, Malthus did not account for all of the effects of economic forces on population growth. While it is clear that a higher standard of living reduces death rates through better nutrition and health care, there has also proved to be a reduction in birth rates.

As the economy develops, there are better opportunities for working outside the home. In terms of family decisions, the opportunity cost of raising a large family becomes large in the face of high market wages, and more time is spent working in the market rather than raising children at home.

The Solow Model: Exogenous Growth

The Solow growth model is very simple, yet it makes sharp predictions concerning the sources of economic growth, what causes living standards to increase over time, what happens to the level and growth rate of aggregate income when the savings rate or the population growth rate rises, and what we should observe happening to relative living standards across countries over time. This model is much more optimistic about the prospects for long-run improvements in the standard of living than is the Malthusian model. Sustained increases in the standard of living can occur in the model, but sustained technological advances are necessary for this. As well, the Solow model does a good job of explaining the economic growth facts discussed earlier in this chapter.

In constructing this model, we begin with a description of the consumers who live in this environment and of the production technology. As with the Malthusian model we treat dynamics seriously here. We study how this economy evolves over time in a competitive equilibrium, and a good part of our analysis concerns the steady state of the model, which, we know from our analysis of the Malthusian model, is the long-run equilibrium or rest point.

CONSUMERS

As in the Malthusian model, there are many periods, but we will analyze the economy in terms of the "current" and the "future" period. In contrast to the Malthusian model, we suppose that the population grows exogenously. That is, there is a growing population of consumers, with N denoting the population in the current period. As in the Malthusian model, N also is the labour force, or the quantity of employment. The population grows over time, with

$$N' = (1 + n)N \qquad (7.9)$$

where N' is the population in the future period and $n > -1$. Here, n is the rate of growth in the population, which is assumed to be constant over time. We are allowing for the possibility that $n < 0$, in which case the population would be shrinking over time. In each period, a given consumer has one unit of time available, and we assume that consumers do not value leisure, so that they supply their one unit of time as labour in each period. In this model, the population is identical to the labour force, because we have assumed that all members of the population work. We then refer to N as the number of workers or the labour force and to n as the growth rate in the labour force.

Consumers collectively receive all current real output, Y, as income (through wage income and dividend income from firms), because there is no government sector and no taxes. In contrast to all of the models we have considered to this point, consumers here face a decision concerning how much of their current income to consume and how much to save. For simplicity, we assume that consumers consume a constant fraction of income in each period; that is,

$$C = (1 - s)Y, \tag{7.10}$$

where C is current consumption. For consumers, $C + S = Y$ where S is aggregate savings, so from Equation (7.10) we have $S = sY$ and s is then the aggregate savings rate. In Chapter 9 we discuss in more depth how consumers make their consumption–savings decisions.

THE REPRESENTATIVE FIRM

Output is produced by a representative firm, according to the production function

$$Y = zF(K, N), \tag{7.11}$$

where Y is current output, z is current total factor productivity, K is the current capital stock, and N is the current labour input. The production function F has all of the properties that we studied in Chapter 4. As in the Malthusian model, constant returns to scale implies that, dividing both sides of Equation (7.11) by N and rearranging, we get

$$\frac{Y}{N} = zF\left(\frac{K}{N}, 1\right). \tag{7.12}$$

In Equation (7.12), $\frac{Y}{N}$ is output per worker, and $\frac{K}{N}$ is capital per worker, and so (7.12) tells us that if the production function has constant returns to scale, then output per worker on the left-hand side of (7.12) depends only on the quantity of capital per worker, on the right-hand side of (7.12). For simplicity, as in the Malthusian model, we can rewrite Equation (7.12) as

$$y = zf(k),$$

where y is output per worker, k is capital per worker, and $zf(k)$ is the per-worker production function, which is defined by $zf(k) = zF(k,1)$. We use lowercase letters in what follows to refer to per-worker quantities. The per-worker production function is graphed in Figure 7.12. A key property of the per-worker production function is that its slope is the marginal product of capital, MP_K. This is because adding one unit to k, the quantity of capital per worker, increases y, output per worker, by the marginal product of capital, because $zf(k) = zF(k,1)$. Since the slope of the per-worker production function is MP_K, and because MP_K is diminishing with K, the per-worker production function in the figure is concave—that is, its slope decreases as k increases.

We suppose that some of the capital stock wears out through use each period. That is, there is depreciation, and we assume that the depreciation rate is a constant d where $0 < d < 1$. Then, the capital stock changes over time according to

$$K' = (1 - d)K + I, \tag{7.13}$$

where K' is the future capital stock, K is the current capital stock, and I is investment.

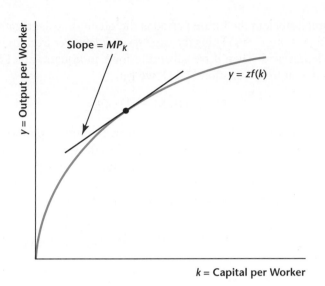

FIGURE 7.12
The Per-Worker
Production Function
This function is the
relationship between
aggregate output per
worker and capital per worker
determined by the constant-
returns-to-scale production
function. The slope of the
per-worker production
function is the marginal
product of capital, MP_K.

COMPETITIVE EQUILIBRIUM

Now that we have described the behaviour of consumers and firms in the Solow growth model, we can put this behaviour together and determine how consistency is achieved in a competitive equilibrium. In this economy, there are two markets in the current period. In the first market, current consumption goods are traded for current labour; in the second market, current consumption goods are traded for capital. That is, capital is the asset in this model, and consumers save by accumulating it. The labour market and the capital market must clear in each period. In the labour market, the quantity of labour is always determined by the inelastic supply of labour, which is N. That is, because the supply of labour is N no matter what the real wage, the real wage adjusts in the current period so that the representative firm wants to hire N workers. Letting S denote the aggregate quantity of saving in the current period, the capital market is in equilibrium in the current period if $S = I$, that is, if what consumers want to save equals the quantity of investment. However, because $S = Y - C$ in this economy—that is, national savings is aggregate income minus consumption as there is no government—we can write the equilibrium condition as

$$Y = C + I, \tag{7.14}$$

or current output is equal to aggregate consumption plus aggregate investment. From Equation (7.13) we have that $I = K' - (1 - d)K$, and so by using this and Equation (7.10) to substitute for C and I in Equation (7.14), we get

$$Y = (1 - s)Y + K' - (1 - d)K,$$

or, rearranging terms and simplifying,

$$K' = sY + (1 - d)K; \tag{7.15}$$

that is, the capital stock in the future period is the quantity of aggregate savings in the current period ($S = Y - C = sY$) plus the capital stock left over from the current period that has not depreciated. Then if we substitute for Y in Equation (7.15) by using the production function from Equation (7.11), we get

$$K' = szF(K,N) + (1 - d)K. \tag{7.16}$$

Equation (7.16) states that the stock of capital in the future period is equal to the quantity of savings in the current period (identical to the quantity of investment) plus the quantity of current capital that remains in the future after depreciation. Now, it is convenient to express Equation (7.16) in per-worker terms, by dividing each term on the right-hand and left-hand sides of (7.16) by N, the number of workers, to get

$$\frac{K'}{N} = sz\frac{F(K, N)}{N} + (1 - d)\frac{K}{N},$$

and then multiplying the left-hand side by $1 = \dfrac{N'}{N'}$, which gives $\dfrac{K'N'}{N N'} = sz\dfrac{F(K, N)}{N} + (1 - d)\dfrac{K}{N}$. Then we can write this as

$$k'(1 + n) = szf(k) + (1 - d)k \tag{7.17}$$

In Equation (7.17), $k' = \dfrac{K'}{N'}$ is the future quantity of capital per worker, $\dfrac{N'}{N} = 1 + n$ from Equation (7.9), and the first term on the right-hand side of (7.17) comes from the fact that $\dfrac{F(K, N)}{N} = F\left(\dfrac{K}{N}, 1\right)$, and because the production function has constant returns to scale, and $F\left(\dfrac{K}{N}, 1\right) = f(k)$ by definition. We can then divide the right-hand and left-hand sides of Equation (7.17) by $1 + n$ to obtain

$$k' = \frac{szf(k)}{1 + n} + \frac{(1 - d)k}{1 + n}. \tag{7.18}$$

Equation (7.18) is a key equation that summarizes most of what we need to know about competitive equilibrium in the Solow growth model, and we use this equation to derive the important implications of the model. This equation determines the future stock of capital per worker, k', on the left-hand side of the equation, as a function of the current stock of capital per worker, k, on the right-hand side.

In Figure 7.13 we graph the relationship given by Equation (7.18). In the figure, the curve has a decreasing slope because of the decreasing slope of the per-worker production function $zf(k)$ in Figure 7.12. In the figure, the 45° line is the line along which $k' = k$, and the point at which the 45° line intersects the curve given by Equation (7.18) is the steady state. Once the economy reaches the steady state, where current capital per worker $k = k^*$, then future capital per worker $k' = k^*$, and the

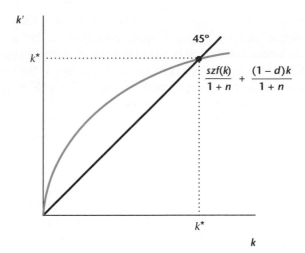

FIGURE 7.13

Determination of the Steady State Quantity of Capital per Worker

In the figure, the coloured curve is the relationship between current capital per worker, *k*, and future capital per worker, *k′*, determined in a competitive equilibrium in the Solow growth model. The steady state quantity of capital per worker is *k**, given by the intersection of the 45° line (the black line) with the coloured curve.

economy has k^* units of capital per worker forever after. If the current stock of capital per worker, k, is less than the steady state value, so $k < k^*$, then from the figure $k' > k$, and the capital stock per worker increases from the current period to the future period. In this situation, current investment is sufficiently large, relative to depreciation and growth in the labour force, that the per-worker quantity of capital increases. However, if $k > k^*$, then we have $k' < k$, and the capital stock per worker decreases from the current period to the future period. In this situation, investment is sufficiently small that it cannot keep up with depreciation and labour force growth, and the per-worker quantity of capital declines from the current period to the future period. Therefore, if the quantity of capital per worker is smaller than its steady state value, it increases until it reaches the steady state, and if the quantity of capital per worker is larger than its steady state value, it decreases until it reaches the steady state.

Because the Solow growth model predicts that the quantity of capital per worker converges to a constant, k^*, in the long run, it also predicts that the quantity of output per worker converges to a constant, which is $y^* = zf(k^*)$ from the per-worker production function. The Solow model then tells us that if the savings rate, s, the labour force growth rate, n, and total factor productivity, z, are constant, then real income per worker cannot grow in the long run. Thus, if we take real GDP per worker as a measure of the standard of living, then there can be no long-run betterment in living standards under these circumstances. Why does this happen? The reason is that the marginal product of capital is diminishing. Output per worker can grow only as long as capital per worker continues to grow. However, the marginal return to investment, which is determined by the marginal product of capital, declines as the per-worker capital stock grows. That is, as the capital stock per worker grows, it takes more and more investment per worker in the current period to produce one unit of additional capital per worker for the future period. Therefore, as the economy grows, new investment ultimately just keeps up with depreciation and the growth of the labour force, and growth in per-worker output ceases.

In the long run, when the economy converges to the steady state quantity of capital per worker, k^*, all real aggregate quantities grow at the rate n, which is the growth rate of the labour force. That is, the aggregate quantity of capital in the steady state is $K = k^*N$, and because k^* is a constant and N grows at the rate n, K must also grow at the rate n. Similarly, aggregate real output is $Y = y^*N = zf(k^*)N$, and so Y also grows at the rate n. Further, the quantity of investment is equal to savings, so that investment in the steady state is $I = sY = szf(k^*)N$, and because $szf(k^*)$ is a constant, I also grows at the rate n in the steady state. As well, aggregate consumption is $C = (1 - s)zf(k^*)N$, so that consumption also grows at the rate n in the steady state. In the long run, therefore, if the savings rate, the labour force growth rate, and total factor productivity are constant, then growth rates in aggregate quantities are determined by the growth rate in the labour force. This is one sense in which the Solow growth model is an exogenous growth model. In the long run, the Solow model tells us that growth in key macroeconomic aggregates is determined by exogenous labour force growth when the savings rate, the labour force growth rate, and total factor productivity are constant.

ANALYSIS OF THE STEADY STATE

In this section, we put the Solow growth model to work. We perform some experiments with the model, analyzing how the steady state or long-run equilibrium is affected by changes in the savings rate, the population growth rate, and total factor productivity. We then show how the response of the model to these experiments is consistent with what we see in the data.

To analyze the steady state, we start with Equation (7.18), which determines the future capital stock per worker, k', given the current capital stock per worker, k. In the steady state, we have, $k' = k = k^*$ and so substituting k^* in Equation (7.18) for k and k' we get

$$k^* = \frac{szf(k^*)}{1 + n} + \frac{(1 - d)k^*}{1 + n};$$

multiplying both sides of this equation by $1 + n$ and rearranging, we get

$$szf(k^*) = (n + d)k^*. \tag{7.19}$$

Equation (7.19) solves for the steady state capital stock per worker, k^*. It is this equation we want to analyze to determine the effects of changes in the savings rate, s, in the population growth rate, n, and in total factor productivity, z, on the steady state quantity of capital per worker, k^*.

We graph the left-hand and right-hand sides of Equation (7.19) in Figure 7.14, where the intersection of the two curves determines the steady state quantity of capital per worker, which we denote by k_1^* in the figure. The curve $szf(k^*)$ is the per-worker production function multiplied by the savings rate, s, and so this function inherits the properties of the per-worker production function in Figure 7.12. The curve $(n + d)k^*$ in Figure 7.14 is a straight line with slope $(n + d)$.

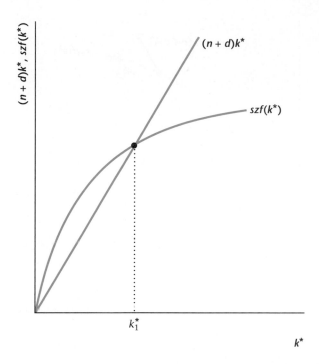

FIGURE 7.14

**Determination of the
Steady State Quantity of
Capital per Worker**

The steady state quantity of
capital, k_1^* is determined by
the intersection of the curve
$szf(k^*)$ with the line $(n + d)k^*$.

The Steady State Effects of an Increase in the Savings Rate A key experiment to consider in the Solow growth model is a change in the savings rate, s. We can interpret a change in s as occurring because of a change in the preferences of consumers. For example, if consumers care more about the future, they save more, and s increases. A change in s could also be brought about through government policy, for example, if the government were to subsidize savings (though in Chapter 9 we show that this has opposing income and substitution effects on savings). With regard to government policy, we need to be careful about interpreting our results, because to be completely rigorous we should build a description of government behaviour into the model.

In Figure 7.15 we show the effect of an increase in the savings rate, from s_1 to s_2, on the steady state quantity of capital per worker. The increase in s shifts the curve $szf(k^*)$ up, and k^* increases from k_1^* to k_2^*. Therefore, in the new steady state, the quantity of capital per worker is higher, which implies that output per worker is also higher, given the per-worker production function $y^* = zf(k^*)$. Though the levels of capital per worker and output per worker are higher in the new steady state, the increase in the savings rate has no effect on the growth rates of aggregate variables. Before and after the increase in the savings rate, the aggregate capital stock, K, aggregate output, Y, aggregate investment, I, and aggregate consumption, C, grow at the rate of growth in the labour force, n. This is perhaps surprising, as we might think that a country that invests and saves more, thus accumulating capital at a higher rate, would grow faster.

FIGURE 7.15

Effect of an Increase in the Savings Rate on the Steady State Quantity of Capital per Worker

An increase in the savings rate shifts the curve $szf(k^*)$ up, resulting in an increase in the quantity of capital per worker from k_1^* to k_2^*.

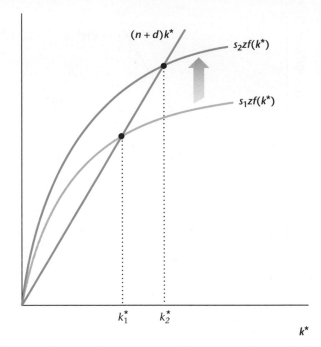

Though the growth rates of aggregate variables are unaffected by the increase in the savings rate in the steady state, it may take some time for the adjustment from one steady state to another to take place. In Figure 7.16 we show the path that the natural logarithm of output follows when there is an increase in the savings rate, with time measured along the horizontal axis. Before time T, aggregate output is growing at the constant rate, n (if the growth rate is constant, then the time path of the natural logarithm is essentially a straight line), and then the savings rate increases at time T. Aggregate output then adjusts to its higher growth path after period T, but in the transition to the new growth path, the rate of growth in Y is higher than n. The temporarily high growth rate in transition results from a higher rate of capital accumulation when the savings rate increases, which translates into a higher growth rate in aggregate output. As capital is accumulated

FIGURE 7.16

Effect of an Increase in the Savings Rate at Time *T*

The figure shows the natural logarithm of aggregate output. Before time *T*, the economy is in a steady state. At time *T*, the savings rate increases, and output then converges in the long run to a new higher steady state growth path.

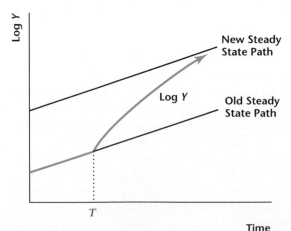

at a higher rate, however, the marginal product of capital diminishes, and growth slows down, ultimately converging to the steady state growth rate n.

Consumption per Worker and Golden Rule Capital Accumulation We know from Chapter 2 that GDP, or GDP per person, is often used as a measure of aggregate welfare. However, what consumers ultimately care about is their lifetime consumption. In this model, given our focus on steady states, an aggregate welfare measure we might want to consider is the steady state level of consumption per worker. In this subsection, we show how to determine steady state consumption per worker from a diagram similar to Figure 7.15. Then, we show that there is a given quantity of capital per worker that maximizes consumption per worker in the steady state. This implies that an increase in the savings rate could cause a decrease in steady state consumption per worker, even though an increase in the savings rate always increases output per worker.

Consumption per worker in the steady state is $c^* = (1 - s)zf(k^*)$, which is the difference between steady state income per worker, $y^* = zf(k^*)$, and steady state savings per worker, which is $szf(k^*)$. If we add the per-worker production function to Figure 7.15, as we have done in Figure 7.17, then the steady state quantity of capital per worker in the figure is k_1^*, and steady state consumption per worker is the distance AB, which is the difference between output per worker and savings per worker. Consumption per worker in the steady state is also the difference between output per worker, $y^* = zf(k^*)$, and $(n + d)k^*$.

Next, because consumption per worker in the steady state is

$$c^* = zf(k^*) - (n + d)k^*$$

in Figure 7.18(b) we have plotted c^* against the steady state quantity of capital per worker, k^*. There is a quantity of capital per worker for which consumption per worker is maximized, which we denote by k_{gr}^* in the figure. If the steady state quantity

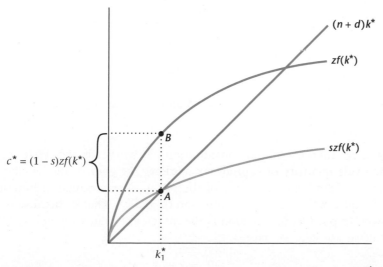

FIGURE 7.17
Steady State Consumption per Worker
Consumption per worker in the steady state is shown as the distance AB, given the steady state quantity of capital per worker, k_1^*.

FIGURE 7.18

The Golden Rule Quantity of Capital per Worker
This quantity, which maximizes consumption per worker in the steady state, is k_{gr}^*, and the maximized quantity of consumption per worker is c^{**}. The golden rule savings rate s_{gr} achieves the golden rule quantity of capital per worker in a competitive equilibrium steady state.

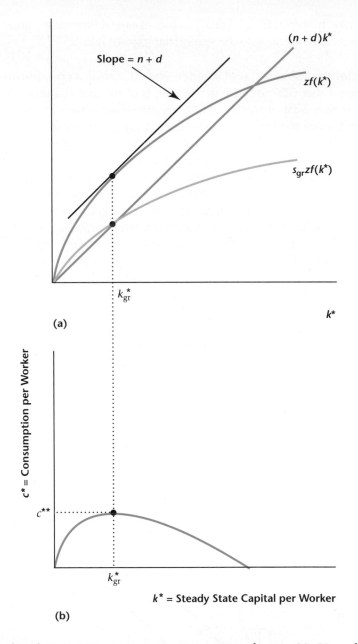

(a)

(b)

of capital is k_{gr}^*, then maximum consumption per worker is c^{**}. Here, k_{gr}^* is called the **golden rule quantity of capital per worker**. The golden rule has the property, from Figure 7.18(a), that the slope of the per-worker production function where $k^* = k_{gr}^*$ is equal to the slope of the function $(n + d)k^*$. That is, because the slope of the per-worker production function is the marginal product of capital, MP_K, at the golden rule steady state we have

$$MP_K = n + d.$$

Therefore, when capital is accumulated at a rate that maximizes consumption per worker in the steady state, the marginal product of capital equals the population growth rate plus the depreciation rate.

How can the golden rule be achieved in the steady state? In Figure 7.18(a), we show that if the savings rate is s_{gr}, then the curve $s_{gr}zf(k^*)$ intersects the line $(n + d)k^*$ where $k^* = k_{gr}^*$. Thus, s_{gr} is the **golden rule savings rate**. If savings takes place at the golden rule savings rate, then in the steady state the current population consumes and saves the appropriate amount so that in each succeeding period, the population can continue to consume this maximum amount per person. "Golden rule" is a biblical reference, which comes from the dictum that we should treat others as we would like to be treated. From Figure 7.18(b), if the steady state capital stock per worker is less than k_{gr}^*, then an increase in the savings rate, s, increases the steady state capital stock per worker and increases consumption per worker. However, if $k^* > k_{gr}^*$, then an increase in the savings rate increases k^* and causes a decrease in consumption per worker. Suppose that we calculated the golden rule savings rate for the United States and found that the actual U.S. savings rate was different from the golden rule rate. For example, suppose we found that the actual savings rate was lower than the golden rule savings rate. Would this necessarily imply that the government should implement a change in policy that would increase the savings rate? The answer is no, for two reasons. First, any increase in the savings rate would come at a cost in current consumption. It would take time to build up a higher stock of capital to support higher consumption per worker in the new steady state, and the current generation may be unwilling to bear this short-term cost. Second, in practice, savings behaviour is the result of optimizing decisions by individual consumers. In general, we should presume that private market outcomes achieve the correct tradeoff between current consumption and savings, unless we have good reason to believe that there exists some market failure the government can efficiently correct.

The Steady State Effects of an Increase in Labour Force Growth The next experiment we carry out with the Solow model is to ask what happens in the long run if the labour force growth rate increases. As labour is a factor of production, it is clear that higher labour force growth ultimately causes aggregate output to grow at a higher rate. But what is the effect on output per worker in the steady state? With aggregate output growing at a higher rate, there is a larger and larger "income pie" to split up, but with more and more workers to share this pie. As we show, the Solow growth model predicts that capital per worker and output per worker will decrease in the steady state when the labour force growth rate increases, but aggregate output will grow at a higher rate, which is the new rate of labour force growth.

In Figure 7.19 we show the steady state effects of an increase in the labour force growth rate, from n_1 to n_2. Initially, the quantity of capital per worker is k_1^*, determined by the intersection of the curves $szf(k^*)$ and $(n_1 + d)k^*$. When the population growth rate increases, this results in a decrease in the quantity of capital per worker to k_2^* in the figure. Because capital per worker falls, output per worker also falls, from the per-worker production function. That is, output per worker falls from $zf(k_1^*)$ to $zf(k_2^*)$.

FIGURE 7.19

Steady State Effects of an Increase in the Labour Force Growth Rate

An increase in the labour force growth rate from n_1 to n_2 causes a decrease in the steady state quantity of capital per worker.

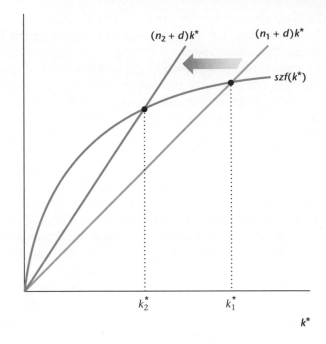

The reason for this result is that, when the labour force grows at a higher rate, the current labour force faces a tougher task in building capital for next period's consumers, who are a proportionately larger group. Thus, output per worker and capital per worker are ultimately lower in the steady state.

We have already determined that aggregate output, aggregate consumption, and aggregate investment grow at the labour force growth rate, n, in the steady state. Therefore, when the labour force growth rate increases, growth in all of these variables must also increase. This is an example that shows that higher growth in aggregate income need not be associated, in the long run, with higher income per worker.

The Steady State Effects of an Increase in Total Factor Productivity If we take real income per worker to be a measure of the standard of living in a country, what we have shown thus far is that in the Solow model, an increase in the savings rate or a decrease in the labour force growth rate can increase the standard of living in the long run. However, increases in the savings rate and reductions in the labour force growth rate cannot bring about an ever-increasing standard of living in a country. This is because the savings rate must always be below 1 (no country would have a savings rate equal to 1, as this would imply zero consumption), and the labour force growth rate cannot fall indefinitely. The Solow model predicts that a country's standard of living can continue to increase in the long run only if there are continuing increases in total factor productivity, as we show here.

In Figure 7.20 we show the effect of increases in total factor productivity. First, an increase in total factor productivity from z_1 to z_2 results in an increase in capital per worker from k_1^* to k_2^* and an increase in output per worker as a result. A further increase in total factor productivity to z_3 causes an additional increase in capital per worker to k_3^* and an additional increase in output per worker. These increases in capital per worker and output per worker can continue indefinitely, as long as the increases in total factor productivity continue.

This is a key insight that comes from the Solow growth model. An increase in a country's propensity to save or a decrease in the labour force growth rate imply one-time increases in a country's standard of living, but there can be unbounded growth in the standard of living only if total factor productivity continues to grow. The source of continual long-run betterment in a country's standard of living, therefore, can only be the process of devising better methods for putting factor inputs together to produce output, thereby generating increases in total factor productivity.

In contrast to the Malthusian model, where the gains from technological advances are dissipated by a higher population, the Solow model gives a more optimistic outlook for increases in the standard of living over time. If we accept the Solow model, it tells us that the steady increase in per capita income that occurred since 1870 in Canada (see Figure 7.1) was caused by sustained increases in total factor productivity over a period of 137 years. If technological advances can be sustained for such a long period, there appears to be no reason that these advances cannot occur indefinitely into the future.

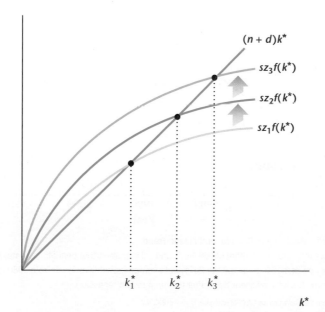

FIGURE 7.20

Increases in Total Factor Productivity in the Solow Growth Model

Increases in total factor productivity from z_1 to z_2, and from z_2 to z_3, cause increases in the quantity of capital per worker from k_1^* to k_2^*, and from k_2^* to k_3^*. Thus, increases in total factor productivity lead to increases in output per worker.

<table>
<tr><td>THEORY
CONFRONTS
THE DATA</td><td>7.1</td><td>*The Recent Trend in Economic*
Growth in Canada</td></tr>
</table>

Figure 7.1 showed sustained growth in real GDP per capita in Canada, extending back essentially to Confederation. The Solow growth model, if subjected to constant growth in total factor productivity (TFP), will indeed exhibit constant growth in real GDP per capita in the long run. Thus, Figure 7.1 seems consistent with the idea that the growth process in Canada is driven by TFP growth, just as it is in the Solow growth model.

But why should TFP grow at roughly a constant rate over the long run? TFP growth in the Solow growth model is exogenous. While exogenous TFP growth at a constant rate over a long period of time fits the Canadian per-capita real GDP reasonably well, the economic growth theory we have described thus far in this book will not tell us why TFP should grow at a constant rate. Thus, who is to say that the sustained growth we have seen in Canada in the past will continue into the future?

Figure 7.21 shows the natural logarithm of real GDP for Canada, over the period 1961–2011, along with a linear trend fit to the data. The trend, which is

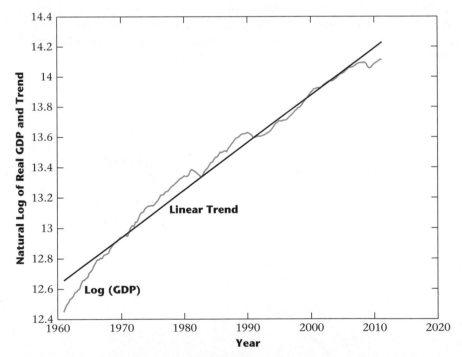

FIGURE 7.21 Real GDP in Canada, and Linear Trend

The figure shows the natural logarithm of real GDP, and a linear trend that best fits the data. Real GDP grew on average at a rate of 3.13% from 1961 to 2011, but average growth was lower from 1980 to 2011, and real GDP has not come back to the linear trend after the most recent recession.

Source: Adapted from Statistics Canada CANSIM database, Series v1992067.

the best fit to the real GDP time series, indicates that the average growth rate in real GDP over this period was 3.13%. As can be seen from Figure 7.21, and even more clearly in Figure 7.22, which shows the deviations of the log of real GDP from the linear trend, average growth was higher from 1961–1980 than it was over the period 1980–2011.

Further, even though the most recent recession is over, real GDP would have to be growing faster than 3.11% in order to return to the linear trend, and that is not happening. Indeed, real GDP is currently about 10% below trend, so there is much ground to "make up."

There are at least two possibilities here. One is that there are particular reasons why the recovery from the recent recession should be more prolonged than for a typical recession. For example, Carmen Reinhart and Kenneth Rogoff[10] examine evidence from eight centuries of financial crises and argue that they are typically followed by a long period of macroeconomic adjustment. That idea certainly deserves attention, though the economic mechanism behind the prolonged downturn a financial crisis might engender is not well understood.

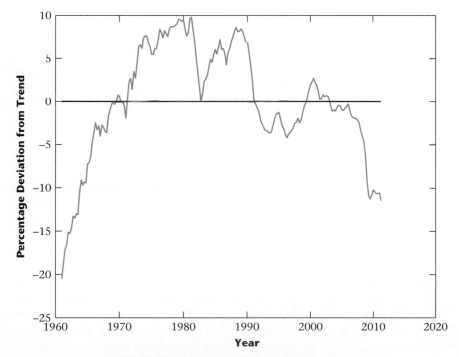

FIGURE 7.22 **Percentage Deviation of Real GDP in Canada from a Linear Trend**

This figure shows the percentage difference between actual real GDP in Canada and the linear trend in Figure 7.21. Note in particular that, in the second quarter of 2011, real GDP was still about 10% below the trend.

Source: Adapted from Statistics Canada CANSIM database, Series v1992067.

A second possibility is that what we see in Figures 7.21 and 7.22 is a downward adjustment after the recent recession to a lower growth path. For example, there may have been a level adjustment downward in aggregate real GDP in Canada, and henceforth real GDP will continue to grow at a 3% rate, on average. In this scenario, the Canadian economy never picks up the ground lost during the financial crisis and recession. If the future unfolds in this way, it might be the result of basic structural changes occurring in the Canadian economy. The sectoral shift from manufacturing to services in the Canadian economy might have led to a level adjustment in Canadian aggregate productivity. Or Canada might have lost its edge as a world technological leader. Untangling these issues will most certainly be an active topic of macroeconomic research.

---

[10]C. Reinhart and K. Rogoff, 2009, *This Time Is Different: Eight Centuries of Financial Folly*, Princeton University Press, Princeton NJ.

Growth Accounting

If aggregate real output is to grow over time, it is necessary for a factor or factors of production to increase over time, or for there to be increases in total factor productivity. Typically, growing economies are experiencing growth in factors of production *and* in total factor productivity. A useful exercise is to measure how much of the growth in aggregate output over a given period of time is accounted for by growth in each of the inputs to production and by increases in total factor productivity. This exercise is called **growth accounting**, and it can be helpful in developing theories of economic growth and for discriminating among different theories. Growth accounting was introduced in the 1950s by Robert Solow.[11]

Growth accounting starts by considering the aggregate production function from the Solow growth model,

$$Y = zF(K, N),$$

where Y is aggregate output, z is total factor productivity, F is a function, K is the capital input, and N is the labour input. To use the aggregate production function to organize our thinking about measured output and factor inputs, we need a specific form for the function F. The widely used Cobb-Douglas production function, as discussed in Chapter 4, provides a good fit to aggregate data and is also a good analytical tool for growth accounting. For the production function to be Cobb-Douglas, the function F takes the form

$$F(K, N) = K^a N^{1-a}, \tag{7.20}$$

---

[11]See R. Solow, 1957, "Technical Change and the Aggregate Production Function," *Review of Economic Statistics* 39, 312–320.

where a is a number between 0 and 1. Recall from Chapter 4 that, in a competitive equilibrium, a is the fraction of national income that goes to the capital input, and $1 - a$ is the fraction that goes to the labour input. In recent Canadian data, the labour share in national income has been roughly constant at 70%, so we can set $a = 0.3$, and our production function is then

$$Y = zK^{0.3}N^{0.7}. \tag{7.21}$$

If we have measures of aggregate output, the capital input, and the labour input, denoted $\hat{Y}, \hat{K}$, and $\hat{N}$, respectively, then total factor productivity, z, can be measured as a residual, as discussed in Chapter 4. The Solow residual, denoted by $\hat{z}$, is measured from the production function, Equation (7.21), as

$$\hat{z} = \frac{\hat{Y}}{\hat{K}^{0.3}\hat{N}^{0.7}}. \tag{7.22}$$

This measure of total factor productivity is a residual, since it is the output that remains to be accounted for after we measure the direct contribution of the capital and labour inputs to output. Total factor productivity has many interpretations, as we studied in Chapters 4 and 5, and hence so does the Solow residual. Increases in measured total factor productivity could be the result of new inventions, good weather, new management techniques, favourable changes in government regulations, decreases in the relative price of energy, or any other factor that causes more aggregate output to be produced given the same quantities of aggregate factor inputs. Macroeconomics in Action 7.1 contains a discussion of how the misallocation of resources across firms in the economy can affect total factor productivity.

| THEORY CONFRONTS THE DATA | 7.2 | *The Solow Growth Model, Investment Rates, and Population Growth* |

Now that we know something about the predictions that the Solow growth model makes, we can evaluate the model by matching its predictions with the data. It is only relatively recently that economists have had access to comprehensive national income accounts data for essentially all countries in the world. The Penn World Tables, which are the work of Alan Heston, Robert Summers, and Bettina Aten at the University of Pennsylvania,[12] allow for comparisons of GDP, among other macroeconomic variables, across countries. Making these comparisons is a complicated measurement exercise, as GDP in different countries at a given point in time is measured in different currencies, and simply making adjustments by using foreign exchange rates does not give the right answers. A limitation of the Penn World Tables is that they extend back only to 1950. A few decades of data may not tell us all we need to know in terms of matching the long-run predictions of the Solow growth model. Can the steady state be achieved within a few decades? As we will see, however, two of the predictions of the Solow model appear to match the data in the Penn World Tables quite well.

Two key predictions of the Solow growth model are that in the long run, an increase in the savings rate causes an increase in the quantity of income per worker, and an increase in the labour force growth rate causes a decrease in the quantity of income per worker. We examine, in turn, the fit of each of these predictions with the data.

The savings rate in the Solow growth model is the ratio of investment expenditures to GDP. The Solow model thus predicts that if we look at data from a set of countries in the world, we should see a positive correlation between GDP per worker and the ratio of investment to GDP. This is the correlation that we discussed in the "Economic Growth Facts" section earlier in this chapter. In Figure 7.2, we observed that a positively sloped line would provide the best fit for the points in the figure, so that the investment rate and income per worker are positively correlated across the countries of the world. Clearly, as the Solow model predicts, countries with high (low) ratios of investment to GDP also have high (low) quantities of income per worker.

Next, the Solow model predicts that in data for a set of countries, we should observe the labour force growth rate to be negatively correlated with output per worker. If we use population growth as a proxy for labour force growth, this is the fourth economic growth fact we discussed earlier in this chapter. In Figure 7.3, we observed a negative correlation between the population growth rate and income per worker across countries, as the Solow model predicts.

---

[12]The income-per-worker statistics come from A. Heston, R. Summers, and B. Aten, *Penn World Table Version 6.2*, Center for International Comparisons at the University of Pennsylvania (CICUP), available at pwt.econ.upenn.edu, accessed January 22, 2009.

SOLOW RESIDUALS AND PRODUCTIVITY SLOWDOWNS

A first exercise we will work through is to calculate and graph Solow residuals from Canadian data for 1961–2010, and then explain what is interesting in the resulting figure. Using GDP for $\hat{Y}$, measured aggregate output, total employment for $\hat{N}$, and a measure of the capital stock for $\hat{K}$, we calculated the Solow residual, $\hat{z}$, by using Equation (7.22), and plotted its natural logarithm in Figure 7.23, for the period 1961–2010. We can see that growth in total factor productivity was very high from 1961 until the early 1970s, as evidenced by the steep slope in the graph during that period. However, there was a dramatic decrease in total factor productivity growth beginning about 1973 and continuing until the early 1990s, which is referred to as the **productivity slowdown**.[13] Productivity then grows at a high rate from the early 1990s until about 2000, when there is a second productivity slowdown.

---

[13]There was a similar productivity slowdown in the United States, but it continued only until the early 1980s.

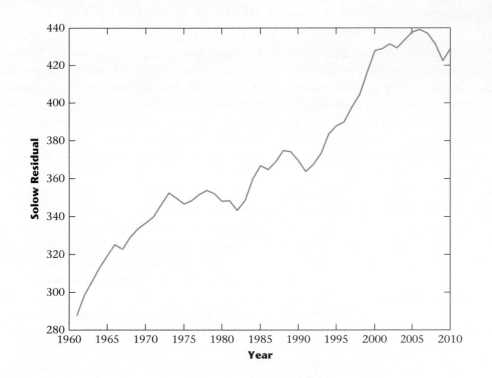

FIGURE 7.23

Natural Log of the Solow Residual, 1961–2010

The Solow residual is a measure of total factor productivity. Growth in total factor productivity slows from the early 1970s to the early 1990s, and from 2000–2010.

Source: Adapted from the Statistics Canada CANSIM database, Series v3860085, v2461119, v3822183, v1078498, and from the Statistics Canada publication *Historical Statistics of Canada*, Catalogue 11-516, 1983, Series D175–189.

The two slowdowns are also seen in Table 7.1, where we show the average percentage growth in the Solow residual during the periods 1961–1971, 1971–1981, 1981–1991, 1991–2001, and 2001–2010. Note in the table that total factor productivity growth, as measured by growth in the Solow residual, was low during the periods 1971–1981, 1981–1991, and 2001–2010 and high from 1961–1971 and from 1991–2001.

What could account for the two productivity slowdowns in Canada, the first occurring from the early 1970s to the early 1980s and the second after 2000? Such slowdowns could be a concern, if they represent lower rates of increase in the acquisition of new technologies and in the development of new production techniques.

TABLE 7.1   **Average Annual Growth Rates in the Solow Residual**

Period	Average Annual Growth Rate
1961–1971	1.68%
1971–1981	0.25%
1981–1991	0.43%
1991–2001	1.66%
2001–2010	0.00%

Much macroeconomic research on the sources of total factor productivity growth and on explanations for the differences in total factor productivity across countries focuses on the determinants of productivity for an individual firm. This is the approach we take in using the Solow growth model to help us understand economic growth, in that output in the Solow growth model is produced by a representative firm, and aggregate total factor productivity is the same as total factor productivity for the representative firm.

While there is much we can learn about the relationship between productivity and economic growth by studying how an individual firm behaves, macroeconomists have recently begun to recognize the important role that the allocation of capital and labour across different firms in an economy plays in determining aggregate productivity. To understand how the allocation of factors of production across firms can affect aggregate total factor productivity, first consider how factors of production would be allocated in a perfect world with no inefficiencies. In such a world, we know that market forces will tend to reallocate labour and capital from less productive firms to more productive firms. In a particular industry, for example the automobile industry, manufacturers with

low total factor productivity will earn lower profits than those manufacturers with high productivity, and the low-productivity firms will tend to go out of business while the high-productivity firms grow. Across industries, labour and capital will tend to flow to those industries where productivity is highest, because in those industries the wages and the returns to capital will tend to be higher. This is the process that led to the growth of the information technology sector in the United States while the manufacturing sector was shrinking.

Now, in the imperfect world we live in, an economy may have distortions that prevent market forces from efficiently allocating capital and labour. First, government taxes and subsidies can distort the returns to capital and labour across firms. For example, U.S. lumber producers have long complained that the "stumpage rates" charged to Canadian lumber producers for cutting lumber on public land in Canada are too low, implying a government subsidy for Canadian lumber producers. If the complaints are justified, these subsidies act to make Canadian lumber production more profitable than it would otherwise be, which attracts labour and capital away from other uses in Canada to lumber production.

In that case, the Solow growth model tells us that growth in the Canadian standard of living might stagnate. However, there are at least three reasons why the productivity slowdowns we have seen may not be a concern:

1. *Measurement problems.* There are two reasons why we might mismeasure total factor productivity (TFP) and TFP growth. First, we might be measuring output incorrectly. In Chapter 2, we discussed the problems associated with measuring real growth in GDP because of changes in the quality of goods and services over time. Measuring the quality of goods becomes increasingly difficult as the economy shifts production to services from manufactured goods, and toward information-intensive goods and services. There is a tendency for downward bias in accounting for increases in the quality of what is produced over time, which will bias downward our measure of the growth rates in real GDP and TFP.

Second, labour and capital could be misallocated across firms because of political corruption. For example, if a government contract is allocated to the firm that will give government officials the largest bribe rather than to the firm that is most efficient, this can cause a misallocation of factors of production across firms.

Third, there can be inefficiencies in the allocation of credit across firms in an industry or across industries. We can think of these inefficiencies as altering the returns to capital in different firms or industries. For example, it is sometimes argued that monopoly power in the Japanese banking industry leads to inefficiencies in credit allocation, in that lending decisions by banks can be determined more by personal relationships between a borrower and a banker than by profitability.

If distortions in an economy act to allocate labour and capital away from firms where total factor productivity is highest, then this will reduce aggregate productivity below what it would be in a world without distortions. Recent research indicates that these distortions might be very important in practice, and that differences in distortions might be a key determinant of differences in productivity and per capita income across countries. Research

by Diego Restuccia and Richard Rogerson[14] considers hypothetical tax and subsidy distortions and shows that the resulting misallocation in factors of production across firms could reduce aggregate productivity by 30–50%. Related work by Chang-Tai Hsieh and Peter Klenow[15] takes a very different approach but arrives at similar conclusions. Hsieh and Klenow analyze microeconomic data on manufacturing in China and India and determine that if distortions were reduced to the level that exists in the United States, then total factor productivity in manufacturing would rise by 30–50% in China and 40–60% in India. These magnitudes are substantial and indicate that efforts in developing countries (and in rich countries as well) to root out inefficient taxes and subsidies, corruption, and monopoly power could have very large effects on standards of living.

---

[14]D. Restuccia and R. Rogerson, 2008, "Policy Distortions and Aggregate Productivity with Heterogeneous Establishments," *Review of Economic Dynamics* 11, 707–720.

[15]C. Hsieh, and P. Klenow, 2009, "Misallocation and Manufacturing TFP in China and India," *Quarterly Journal of Economics* 124, 1403–1448.

Second, TFP measurement could be biased because we are not measuring the inputs to production properly. For example, during the first productivity slowdown in the 1970s, there was a large increase in the relative price of energy, which made some types of energy-inefficient capital obsolete. This would then create an upward bias in the measure of the capital stock, since some of what was measured as productive capital was in fact not being used. This would bias downward our measure of TFP.

2. *Sectoral shifts.* Over time, changes in the relative demands for different goods and services, changes in technology, and changes in the relative prices of raw materials, bring about changes in the sectoral composition of production. In Canada, two key sectoral shifts that have occurred over several decades are the increase in production of services relative to manufactured goods, and the increase in the share of the

energy sector in production. The sectoral shift from manufacturing to services was driven by both demand and technology, and this shift contributed to the measurement problems discussed in (1) above, since it is harder to measure output in the service industry. A sectoral shift toward the energy sector from other sectors in the Canadian economy was caused mainly by an increase in the worldwide demand for energy, which in turn drove increases in the relative price of oil and natural gas in particular. With increases in the relative price of energy, new energy deposits, for example the Alberta oil sands, become profitable to exploit, and it also becomes profitable to develop new energy-extraction technologies. But, in spite of the fact that new oil and gas deposits are being tapped with increasingly sophisticated technologies, we might measure productivity in the energy sector and find it to be low, simply because the new deposits that are being exploited require more inputs to extract a given amount of physical output.

3. *Learning to use new technologies.* When a new technology is introduced—for example the personal computer or the Internet—it takes time for individuals to learn how to use it and to integrate it into how production is organized. The learning period required for the adoption of a new technology might be long. Also, productivity might actually go down initially when the new technology is introduced, as workers are spending a significant fraction of their time learning rather than producing anything measurable. For example, Jeremy Greenwood and Mehmet Yorukoglu[16] mark the early 1970s as the beginning of the information revolution, when computer and other information technology began to be widely adopted in developed countries, and they argue that learning was a key factor that explains the earlier productivity slowdown. However, learning associated with new technologies is likely not an important contributing factor to the post-2000 productivity slowdown in Canada, as the United States did not have a similar productivity slowdown (see Macroeconomics in Action 5.1 in Chapter 5), and the U.S. and Canada share essentially the same technology.

THE CYCLICAL PROPERTIES OF SOLOW RESIDUALS

From Figure 7.23, it is clear that there are cyclical fluctuations in Solow residuals about trend growth. In Figure 7.24 we plot percentage deviations from trend in Solow residuals for the years 1961–2010, along with percentage deviations from trend in real GDP. Note that the fluctuations in Solow residuals about trend are highly positively correlated with the fluctuations in real GDP about trend (recall our discussion of correlations and comovements from Chapter 3). In fact, the Solow residual moves very closely with GDP, so that fluctuations in total factor productivity could be an important explanation for why GDP fluctuates. This is the key idea in real business cycle theory, which we will study in Chapter 13.

---

[16]See J. Greenwood and M. Yorukoglu, 1997, "1974," *Carnegie-Rochester Conference Series on Public Policy* 46, 49–95.

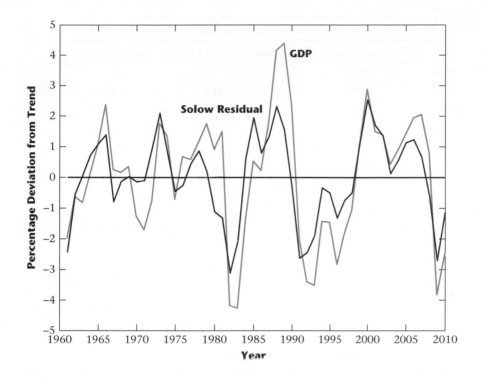

FIGURE 7.24
Percentage Deviations from Trend in Real GDP (coloured line) and the Solow Residual (black line), 1961–2010
Note that the Solow residual tracks GDP quite closely.

Source: Adapted from the Statistics Canada CANSIM database, Series v3860085, v2461119, v3822183, v1078498, and from the Statistics Canada publication *Historical Statistics of Canada*, Catalogue 11-516, 1983, Series D175–189.

A GROWTH ACCOUNTING EXERCISE

Now that we know how the Solow residual is constructed and its empirical properties, we can do a full growth accounting exercise. By way of example, we will show here how we can use the Cobb-Douglas production function (Equation 7.21) and observations on GDP, the capital stock, and employment to obtain measures of the contributions to growth in real output of growth in the capital stock, in employment, and in total factor productivity.

In Table 7.2 we show data on real GDP, the capital stock, and employment for 1961, 1971, 1981, 1991, 2001, and 2010. These are the data we use to carry out our growth accounting exercise. To do growth accounting, we use Equation (7.22) to calculate the Solow residual $\hat{z}$. Now, taking the data from Table 7.2, we calculate the average annual growth rates for measured output, capital, employment, and the Solow residual for the periods 1961–1971, 1971–1981, 1981–1991, 1991–2001, and 2001–2010. If X_n is the value of a variable in year n, and X_m is the value of that variable in year m, where $n > m$, then the average annual growth in X between year m and year n, denoted by g_{mn}, is given by

$$g_{mn} = \left(\frac{X_n}{X_m}\right)^{\frac{1}{n-m}} - 1.$$

For example, in Table 7.2, GDP in 1961 is 264.5 billion 2002 dollars, or $Y_{1961} = 264.5$. Further, $Y_{1971} = 437.7$ from Table 7.2. Then, we have $n - m = 10$, and the

TABLE 7.2   Measured GDP, Capital Stock, and Employment

Year	$\hat{Y}$ (billions of 2002 dollars)	$\hat{K}$ (billions of 2002 dollars)	$\hat{N}$ (millions)	$\hat{z}$
1961	264.5	525.6	6.06	11.45
1971	437.7	824.7	8.08	13.53
1981	647.3	1277.4	11.31	13.87
1991	808.1	1715.1	12.86	14.48
2001	1120.1	2071.1	14.94	17.07
2010	1325.0	2668.7	17.04	17.07

average annual growth rate in GDP from 1961 to 1971, shown in Table 7.3, is

$$\left(\frac{437.7}{264.5}\right)^{\frac{1}{10}} - 1 = 0.0517 \text{ or } 5.17\%.$$

Table 7.3 shows that average annual growth in real GDP was very high during 1961–1971, somewhat lower during 1971–1981, lowest during 1981–1991, relatively high over the period 1991–2001, and relatively low over the period 2001–2010. The very high growth during 1961–1971 came from all sources, as growth in capital was very high, growth in employment somewhat high, and growth in total factor productivity (as measured by growth in $\hat{z}$) high. Note that in spite of the productivity slowdown during 1971–1981, output still grew at a reasonably high rate because of high growth in factors of production. During the 1970s, capital was accumulated at a high rate. Further, employment growth was unusually high, in part because of rapid increases in the female labour force participation rate. Although growth in capital and employment declined during 1981–1991 and 1991–2001, there was a pickup in total factor productivity growth during 1991–2001. This increase in total factor productivity growth was the driving force behind the high growth rate in aggregate output during 1991–2001. During the period 2001–2010, measured total factor productivity growth was nil. Thus, growth in real GDP over the period 2001–2010 was lower than during 1991–2001, in spite of the fact that growth in capital and labour inputs was higher.

It is possible to take a broader approach to accounting for the determinants of economic growth. A discussion of such an approach is in Macroeconomics in Action 7.2.

TABLE 7.3   Average Annual Growth Rates,
in Percentage Terms

Year	$\hat{Y}$	$\hat{K}$	$\hat{N}$	$\hat{z}$
1961–1971	5.17	4.61	2.92	1.68
1971–1981	3.99	4.47	3.42	0.25
1981–1991	2.24	2.99	1.30	0.43
1991–2001	3.32	1.90	1.90	1.66
2001–2010	1.99	2.86	2.86	0.00

Development Accounting 72

The growth accounting approach taken in this section of the chapter is framed in terms of the structure of the Solow growth model. Aggregate output is produced using inputs of labour and capital, and we can then proceed to use aggregate data to disentangle the contributions of labour, capital, and TFP to economic growth.

Once we go deeper into studying the economic growth process, we need to take a broader view of the determinants of economic growth, as is done to some extent in Chapter 8. One useful approach is to specify the aggregate production function as

$$Y = zF(hN, K),$$

where h is the quantity of human capital per worker and N is the number of workers. Human capital is a measure of the stock of skills and education a person possesses, and so hN is the total labour input to aggregate production, which increases with the skills and education that have been acquired by the average person.

Thus, we can attribute growth in real GDP in a particular country to growth in aggregate human capital, growth in physical capital, K, and growth in TFP. As well, we could consider making comparisons across countries, where we explain how much of the differences in incomes across countries can be explained by three factors: differences in human capital, differences in physical capital, and differences in TFP.

Work by Chang-Tai Hsieh and Peter Klenow[17] provides a nice summary of published economic research on development accounting. Hsieh and Klenow frame the question by discussing how, in terms of economic theory and empirical evidence, economists have attributed differences in incomes across countries to fundamental differences in geography, climate, luck, institutions, culture, government policies, rule of law, and corruption. These fundamentals in turn feed into differences in human capital, physical capital, and TFP, which in turn determine differences in incomes across countries.

Hsieh and Klenow tell us that the conclusions of economic research in development are that differences in incomes across countries can be attributed as follows: 10–30% to differences in human capital; about 20% to differences in physical capital, and 50–70% to differences in TFP. This is consistent with our results from analyzing the Solow growth model, which predicts that sustained growth in per capita incomes is driven by sustained growth in TFP. If we look at a set of countries, the Solow model tells us that differences in TFP should explain much of the differences in per capita incomes across countries, which is what we actually see.

Human capital differences across countries, though less important than TFP differences, are still an important contributor to differences in incomes across countries. As well, it is possible that human capital differences also contribute to differences in incomes by affecting differences in TFP. High-human-capital countries with highly educated work forces may be very good at research and development, which drives TFP growth. This process is not captured in the Solow growth model, but is the subject of much ongoing macroeconomic research.

What determines human capital accumulation in a particular country? Government policy may be important, for example the funding of public education, the tax treatment of private education, and subsidies for on-the-job training. As well, how efficiently a society uses the innate abilities of a population can be important. Some work by Chang-Tai Hsieh, Erik Hurst, Charles Jones, and Peter Klenow[18] sheds some light on this topic.

Think of an economy as solving a large problem of allocating people with different kinds of innate ability to different occupations. Some people have a comparative advantage in medicine, and those people should be doctors; some have a comparative advantage in accounting, and those people should be accountants. But society may not be very good at solving that problem. There may be inequality in educational opportunities or discrimination that prevents visible minorities from gaining entry to high-skilled occupations. The treatment of women in the workplace may distort female occupational choices.

Hsieh, Hurst, Jones, and Klenow observe that, in the United States in 1960 the fraction of doctors, lawyers, and managers, respectively, who were white men was 94%, 96%, and 86%. By 2008, those numbers had changed to 63%, 61%, and 57%, respectively. To these authors, those observations suggest that it is possible that society might have come up with a better allocation of talent in 2008 than what it had in 1960, and they set out to measure the economic consequences. In their paper, Hsieh, Hurst, Jones, and Klenow argue that

17% to 20% of growth in real GDP over the period 1960–2008 can be attributed to a better allocation of raw talent among occupations in the United States. They do not attempt to explain exactly which factors explain this, for example they cannot tell us whether affirmative action programs were an important contributor to this better allocation. However, these numbers are striking, and indicate that removing barriers to efficient occupational choice can improve society's average economic well-being substantially.

[17]C. Hsieh, and P. Klenow, 2010, "Development Accounting," *American Economic Journal: Macroeconomics* 2, 207–223.

[18]C. Hsieh, E. Hurst, C. Jones, and P. Klenow, 2011, "The Allocation of Talent and U.S. Economic Growth," working paper, Stanford University, klenow.com/HHJK.pdf.

Chapter Summary

- We discussed seven economic growth facts. These are:

  1. Before the Industrial Revolution in about 1800, standards of living differed little over time and across countries.

  2. Since the Industrial Revolution, per capita income growth has been sustained in the richest countries. In Canada, average annual growth in per capita income has been about 2% since 1870.

  3. There is a positive correlation between the rate of investment and output per worker across countries.

  4. There is a negative correlation between the population growth rate and output per worker across countries.

  5. Differences in per capita incomes increased dramatically among countries of the world between 1800 and 1950, with the gap widening between the countries of Western Europe, the United States, Canada, Australia, and New Zealand, as a group, and the rest of the world.

  6. There is essentially no correlation across countries between the level of output per worker in 1960 and the average rate of growth in output per worker for the years 1960–2000.

  7. Richer countries are much more alike in terms of rates of growth of real per capita income than are poor countries.

- The first model was the Malthusian growth model, in which population growth depends positively on consumption per worker, and output is produced from the labour input and a fixed quantity of land.

- The Malthusian model predicts that an increase in total factor productivity has no effect on consumption per worker in the long run, but the population increases. The standard of living can increase in the long run only if population growth is reduced, perhaps by governmental population control.

- The Solow growth model is a model of exogenous growth that maintains that in the long-run steady state of this model, growth in aggregate output, aggregate consumption, and aggregate investment is explained by exogenous growth in the labour force.

- In the Solow growth model, output per worker converges in the long run to a steady state level, in the absence of a change in total factor productivity. The model predicts that output per worker increases in the long run when the savings rate increases or when the population growth rate decreases. Both of these predictions are consistent with the data.

- An increase in the savings rate could cause consumption per worker to increase or decrease in the Solow growth model. The golden rule savings rate maximizes consumption per worker in the steady state. The Solow growth model also predicts that a country's standard of living, as measured by income per worker, cannot increase in the long run unless there is ever-increasing total factor productivity.

- Growth accounting is an approach to measuring the contributions to growth in aggregate output from growth in the capital stock, in employment, and in total factor productivity. The latter is measured by the Solow residual.

- Measured Solow residuals for Canada using a Cobb-Douglas production function show productivity slowdowns running from the early 1970s to the early 1980s, and after 2000.

- The Canadian productivity slowdowns may not be a problem as: (i) productivity may not be measured well; (ii) there have been sectoral shifts in the Canadian economy; (iii) there is learning associated with technology adoption.

- Cyclically, deviations from trend in the Solow residual track closely the deviations from trend in aggregate output. This empirical observation is important for real business cycle theory, discussed in Chapter 13.

Key Terms

exogenous growth model: A model in which growth is not caused by forces determined by the model.

endogenous growth model: A model in which growth is caused by forces determined by the model.

steady state: A long-run equilibrium or rest point. The Malthusian model and Solow model both have the property that the economy converges to a single steady state.

per-worker production function: In the Malthusian model, $y = zf(1)$, where y is output per worker, z is total factor productivity, l is the quantity of land per worker, and f is a function. This describes the relationship between output per worker and land per worker, given constant returns to scale. In the Solow growth model, the per-worker production function is $y = zf(k)$, where y is output per worker, z is total factor productivity, k is the quantity of capital per worker, and f is a function. The per-worker production function in this case describes the relationship between output per worker and capital per worker, given constant returns to scale.

golden rule quantity of capital per worker: The quantity of capital per worker that maximizes consumption per worker in the steady state.

golden rule savings rate: The savings rate that implies consumption per worker is maximized in the steady state of a competitive equilibrium.

growth accounting: Uses the production function and data on aggregate output, the capital input, and the labour input to measure the contributions of growth in capital, the labour force, and total factor productivity to growth in aggregate output.

productivity slowdowns: Decreases in the rate of measured total factor productivity growth occurring in Canada from the early 1970s to the early 1980s and beginning in 2000.

Questions for Review

1. What is the difference between exogenous growth and endogenous growth?

2. What are the seven economic growth facts?

3. What is the effect of an increase in total factor productivity on steady state population and consumption per worker in the Malthusian model?

4. What can increase the standard of living in the Malthusian model?

5. Was Malthus right? Why or why not?

6. What are the characteristics of a steady state in the Solow growth model?

7. In the Solow growth model, what are the steady state effects of an increase in the savings rate, an increase in the population growth rate, and an increase in total factor productivity?

8. Explain what determines the golden rule quantity of capital per worker and the golden rule savings rate.

9. In what sense does the Solow growth model give optimistic conclusions about the prospects for improvement in the standard of living, relative to the Malthusian model?

10. Why is a Cobb-Douglas production function useful for analyzing economic growth?

11. What is the parameter in the production function in Equation (7.20)?

12. What does the Solow residual measure, and what are its empirical properties?

13. What are three possible causes for productivity slowdowns?

14. What are the three factors that account for growth in GDP?

Problems

1. In the Malthusian model, suppose that the quantity of land increases. Using diagrams, determine what effects this has in the long-run steady state and explain your results.

2. In the Malthusian model, suppose that there is a technological advance that reduces death rates. Using diagrams, determine the effects of this in the long-run steady state and explain your results.

3. In the Solow growth model, suppose that the marginal product of capital increases for each quantity of the capital input, given the labour input.
   a. Show the effects of this on the aggregate production function.
   b. Using a diagram, determine the effects on the quantity of capital per worker and on output per worker in the steady state.
   c. Explain your results.

4. Suppose that the depreciation rate increases. In the Solow growth model, determine the effects of this on the quantity of capital per worker and on output per worker in the steady state. Explain the economic intuition behind your results.

5. Suppose that the economy is initially in a steady state and that some of the nation's capital stock is destroyed because of a natural disaster or a war.
   a. Determine the long-run effects of this on the quantity of capital per worker and on output per worker.
   b. In the short run, does aggregate output grow at a rate higher or lower than the growth rate of the labour force?
   c. After World War II, growth in real GDP in Germany and Japan was very high. How do your results in parts (a) and (b) shed light on this historical experience?

6. If total factor productivity decreases, determine by using diagrams how this affects the golden rule quantity of capital per worker and the golden rule savings rate. Explain your results.

7. Consider a numerical example using the Solow growth model. Suppose that $F(K,N) = K^{0.5} N^{0.5}$, with $d = 0.1$, $s = 0.2$, $n = 0.01$, and $z = 1$, and take a period to be a year.
   a. Determine capital per worker, income per capita, and consumption per capita in the steady state.
   b. Now, suppose that the economy is initially in the steady state that you calculated in part (a). Then, s increases to 0.4. (i) Determine capital per worker, income per capita, and consumption per capita in each of the 10 years following the increase in the savings rate. (ii) Determine capital per worker, income per capita, and consumption per capita in the new steady state. (iii) Discuss your results; in particular comment on the speed of adjustment to the new steady state after the change in the savings rate, and the paths followed by capital per worker, income per capita, and consumption per capita.

8. Modify the Solow growth model by including government spending, as follows. The government purchases G units of consumption goods in the current period, where $G = gN$ and g is a positive constant. The government finances its purchases through lump-sum taxes on consumers, where T denotes total taxes, and the government budget is balanced each period, so that $G = T$. Consumers consume a constant fraction of disposable income—that is, $C = (1 - s)(Y - T)$, where s is the savings rate, with $0 < s < 1$.
   a. Derive equations similar to Equations (7.17), (7.18), and (7.19), and show in a diagram how the quantity of capital per worker, k^*, is determined.
   b. Show that there can be two steady states, one with high k^* and one with low k^*.
   c. Ignore the steady state with low k^*. (It can be shown that this steady state is "unstable.") Determine the effects of an increase in g on capital per worker and on output per worker in the steady state. What are the effects on the growth rates of aggregate output, aggregate consumption, and aggregate investment?
   d. Explain your results.

9. Determine the effects of a decrease in the population growth rate on the golden rule quantity of capital per worker and on the golden rule savings rate. Explain your results.

10. Suppose that we modify the Solow growth model by allowing long-run technological progress. That is, suppose that $z = 1$ for convenience, and that there is labour-augmenting technological progress, with a production function

$$Y = F(K, bN),$$

where b denotes the number of units of "human capital" per worker, and bN is "efficiency units" of labour. Letting b' denote future human capital per worker, assume that $b' = (1 + f)b$, where f is the growth rate in human capital.

   a. Show that the long run equilibrium has the property that $k^{**} = \dfrac{K}{bN}$ is a constant. At

   what rate does aggregate output, aggregate consumption, aggregate investment, and per capita income grow in this steady state? Explain.
   b. What is the effect of an increase in f on the growth in per capita income? Discuss how this model behaves relative to the standard Solow growth model.

11. Alter the Solow growth model so that the production technology is given by $Y = zK$, where Y is output, K is capital, and z is total factor productivity. Thus, output is produced only with capital.
   a. Show that it is possible for income per person to grow indefinitely.
   b. Also show that an increase in the savings rate increases the growth rate in per capita income.
   c. From parts (a) and (b), what are the differences between this model and the basic Solow growth model? Account for these differences and discuss.

12. Consider a numerical example. In the Solow model, assume that $n = 0, s = 0.2, d = 0.1$, $F(K, N) = K^{0.3} N^{0.7}$. Suppose that initially, in period $t = 0$, that $z = 1$ and the economy is in a steady state.
   a. Determine consumption, investment, savings, and aggregate output in the initial steady state.
   b. Suppose that at $t = 1$, total factor productivity falls to $z = 0.9$ and then returns to $z = 1$ for periods $t = 2, 3, 4, \ldots$. Calculate consumption, investment, savings, and aggregate output for each period $t = 1, 2, 3, 4, \ldots$.
   c. Repeat part (b) for the case where, at $t = 1$, total factor productivity falls to $z = 0.9$ and stays there forever.
   d. Comment on what your results in parts (a)–(c).

13. Consider the data on the following page:
   a. Calculate the Solow residual for each year from 2000 to 2010.
   b. Calculate percentage rates of growth in output, capital, employment, and total factor productivity for the years 2000 to 2010. In each year, what contributes the most to growth in aggregate output? What contributes the least? Are there any surprises here? If so, explain.

Year	$\hat{Y}$ (*billions of* 2000 *dollars*)	$\hat{K}$ (*billions of* 2000 *dollars*)	$\hat{N}$ (*millions*)
2000	1100.5	2026.1	14.76
2001	1120.1	2071.1	14.95
2002	1152.9	2113.6	15.31
2003	1174.6	2165.2	15.67
2004	1211.2	2229.7	15.95
2005	1247.8	2308.0	16.17
2006	1283.0	2394.8	16.48
2007	1311.3	2479.5	16.87
2008	1320.3	2565.9	17.09
2009	1283.7	2607.6	16.81
2010	1325.0	2668.7	17.04

8

Income Disparity among Countries and Endogenous Growth

This chapter extends the material in Chapter 7 to additional issues related to the predictions of the Solow growth model and to the study of endogenous growth theory. Here, we are particularly interested in learning more about the reasons for the large income disparities that continue to exist among the countries of the world.

The Solow growth model makes strong predictions concerning the ability of poor countries to catch up with rich countries. That is, in this model, income per capita converges among countries that are initially rich and poor but otherwise identical. The model tells us that countries that are initially poor in terms of income per capita grow at a higher rate than countries that are initially rich. In the context of the Solow growth model, the richest countries of the world look roughly as if they have converged. That is, among the countries that were relatively rich in 1960, subsequent average annual growth rates of per capita income did not differ that much. However, among the poorer countries of the world, income per capita does not appear to be converging, and the poorest countries of the world seem to be falling behind the richest ones rather than catching up. Therefore, if we suppose that all countries are identical, particularly with regard to the technology that they have access to, then the Solow model is not entirely consistent with the way in which the distribution of income is evolving in the world.

However, what if different countries do not have access to the same technology? This can arise if groups of people in particular countries who might lose from technological change have the power to prevent new technologies from being adopted. For example, if the legal structure in a country gives power to labour unions, then these unions might prevent firms from introducing technologies that make the skills of union members obsolete. As well, political barriers to international trade (tariffs, import quotas, and subsidies) shield firms from international competition and block incentives to develop new technologies. Then, if different countries have different barriers to technology adoption, this can explain the differences in standards of living across countries, in a manner consistent with the Solow growth model.

An alternative set of models that can explain persistent differences in standards of living across countries is the set of endogenous growth models. In this chapter, we consider a simple model of endogenous growth, and we show how some of the predictions of this model differ from those of the Solow growth model. The endogenous growth model we study shows how the accumulation of skills and education is important to economic growth. We use the model to evaluate how economic policy might affect the quantity of resources allocated to skills and education and how this affects growth.

In contrast to the Solow growth model, the endogenous growth model we study does not predict convergence in levels of per capita income across countries when countries are identical except for being initially rich and initially poor. In fact, the endogenous growth model predicts that differences in per capita income persist forever. The model indicates some of the factors that can be important in explaining the continuing disparities in living standards between the richest and poorest countries of the world.

Convergence

In Chapter 7, we discussed large disparities that exist in levels of per capita income and in growth rates of per capita income across the countries of the world. While these statistics tell us something about the wide variation in standards of living and in growth experience in the world, we would also like to know whether these disparities are increasing or decreasing over time and why. Is there a tendency for poor countries to catch up with rich countries with respect to standards of living? If the poor countries are not catching up, why is this so, and what could the poor countries do about it?

The Solow growth model makes strong predictions about the ability of poor countries to catch up with rich ones. For example, suppose two countries are identical with respect to total factor productivities (i.e., they share the same technology), labour force growth rates, and savings rates. However, the rich country initially has a higher level of capital per worker than does the poor country. Given the per-worker production function, the rich country also has a higher quantity of output per worker than the poor country. The Solow growth model predicts that both countries will converge to the same level of capital per worker and output per worker. Ultimately, the poor country will catch up to the rich country with regard to living standards.

In Figure 8.1, we show the relationship between current capital per worker, k, and future capital per worker, k', from the Solow growth model. The poor country initially has quantity k_p of capital per worker, while the rich country initially has quantity k_r of capital per worker. Capital per worker and output per worker grow in both countries, but in the long run, both countries have k^* units of capital per worker and the same quantity of output per worker. In Figure 8.2 we show the paths followed over time by real income per worker in both the rich country and the poor country. The initial gap between the rich and poor countries narrows over time and disappears in the long run.

The rich country and poor country in the example above also have identical growth rates of aggregate output (equal to their identical labour force growth rates) in the long run. Recall that the Solow growth model predicts that aggregate output will grow at the rate of labour force growth in the long run, and so if the rich and poor countries have the same labour force growth rate, their long-run growth rates in aggregate output

FIGURE 8.1

Rich and Poor Countries and the Steady State

Two otherwise identical countries have initial capital stocks per worker of k_p (the poor country) and k_r (the rich country). The two countries will converge in the long-run steady state to the quantity k^* of capital per worker.

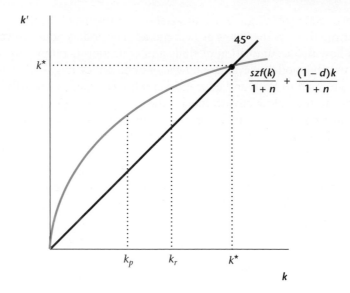

will be identical. Supposing that the rich and poor countries also have the same initial labour force levels, the growth paths of aggregate output, as predicted by the Solow growth model, will be the same in the long run. In Figure 8.3 the black line denotes the long-run growth path of the natural logarithm of aggregate output in the rich and poor countries. As predicted by the Solow growth model, if aggregate output is initially lower in the poor country, its growth rate in aggregate output will be larger than that for the rich country, and this will cause the level of aggregate output in the poor country to catch up to the level in the rich country. In the long run, the growth rates in aggregate output in the rich and poor countries converge.

FIGURE 8.2

Convergence in Income per Worker across Countries in the Solow Growth Model

Two otherwise identical countries, one with lower income per worker (the poor country) than the other (the rich country), converge in the long-run steady state to the same level of income per worker, y^*_1.

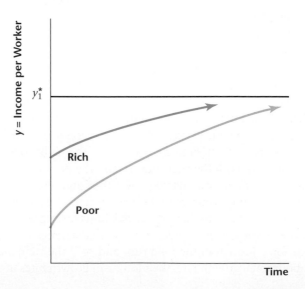

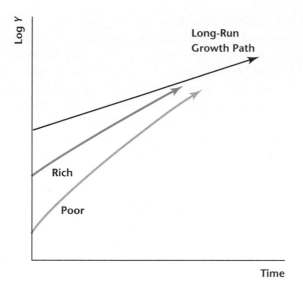

FIGURE 8.3

Convergence in Aggregate Output across Countries in the Solow Growth Model
The initially rich country and the initially poor country converge in the long run to the same long-run growth path, where aggregate output grows at a constant rate.

Therefore, given no differences among countries in terms of access to technology, the Solow model is quite optimistic about the prospects for countries of the world that are currently poor. Under these conditions the model predicts that, left alone, the countries of the world will converge to similar standards of living, with some differences across countries explained by differences in savings rates and population growth rates.

However, suppose that countries do not have access to the same technology. There are good reasons that significant barriers to the adoption of new technology exist, and these barriers can differ across countries.[1] Barriers to technology adoption arise for at least two reasons. First, if the government introduces laws that make it easy for labour unions to organize and gives them greater power in bargaining with firms, then unions will find it easier to block the introduction of new technologies. Powerful unions are able to negotiate high wages and benefits for their members, and they also try to prevent their members from being displaced from their jobs by new technologies that make union members' skills obsolete. For example, automobile industry unions would typically resist the use of robots that would displace labour in auto assembly plants.

Second, governments can introduce trade restrictions that shield domestic industries from foreign competition. This can have the effect of taking away the incentives for firms in those industries to develop more efficient technologies. Most rich countries in the world, including Canada, restrict imports of agricultural goods by imposing tariffs and quotas and by subsidizing domestic producers. These government interventions act to reduce technological innovation in the agricultural sectors of rich countries, and this has a negative effect on total factor productivity. To the extent that barriers to the adoption of new technology differ across countries, this causes total factor productivity to differ, and convergence in standards of living does not occur. To see how this works,

---

[1]See S. Parente and E. Prescott, 2000, *Barriers to Riches*, MIT Press, Cambridge, MA.

consider Figure 8.4. Suppose that there are three different countries, which we call poor, middle income, and rich, and that these countries have levels of total factor productivity, z_p, z_m, and, z_r, respectively, where $z_p < z_m < z_r$. We also suppose that these countries have identical population growth rates and identical savings rates. Then in Figure 8.4, in the steady state the poor, middle income, and rich countries have levels of capital per worker of k_p^*, k_m^*, and k_r^*, respectively, so that output per worker in the steady state is ranked according to poor, middle income, and rich, in ascending order. In the steady state, standards of living are permanently different in the three countries, but aggregate output grows at the same rate in these countries. Thus, the Solow model can explain disparities across countries in income per worker, if there are differences in barriers to technology adoption across countries.

If the large disparity in incomes per worker across countries of the world is in part caused by technology adoption barriers, what can poor countries do to catch up to the rich countries?[2] First, governments can promote greater competition among firms. If monopoly power is not protected by governments, then firms have to develop and implement new technologies to remain competitive, so that productivity will be higher. Second, governments can promote free trade. Just as with greater domestic competition, greater competition between countries promotes innovation and the adoption of the best technologies. Third, governments should privatize production where there is no good economic case for government ownership. Government ownership where it is unnecessary often leads to protection of employment at the expense of efficiency, and this tends to lower total factor productivity.

FIGURE 8.4

Differences in Total Factor Productivity Can Explain Disparity in Income per Worker across Countries
If countries have different levels of total factor productivity because of differing barriers to technology adoption, then capital per worker and income per worker differ across countries in the steady state.

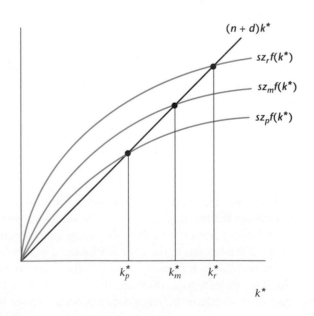

[2]For an elaboration on these arguments, see S. Parente and E. Prescott, 2000, *Barriers to Riches*, MIT Press, Cambridge, MA.

Our discussion and analysis thus far has focused on the differences across countries in GDP per capita, and how these differences might be explained. As is well known, GDP per capita is a measure only of the value of final output exchanged on organized markets, per person, and thus an imperfect measure of the economic welfare of the average person in the economy. Macroeconomics in Action 8.1 contains a discussion of broader measures of national economic welfare, and how use of those measures might change how we look at cross-country differences in standards of living.

THEORY CONFRONTS THE DATA **8.1** *Is Income per Worker Converging in the World?*

If income per worker were converging among countries of the world, we would observe over time that the dispersion in income per worker was falling. As well, if we were to observe the countries of the world at a given point in time, we would see that income per worker was growing at a higher rate in poor countries than in rich countries. That is, we would see a negative correlation between the rate of growth in income per worker and the level of income per worker across countries.

In this section we look at the evidence for convergence in the world economy. From fact (6) in the "Economic Growth Facts" section in Chapter 7, recall that, when we look at all countries in the world, we see essentially no correlation between the level of output per worker in 1960 and the average growth rate of output per worker between 1960 and 2000. Fact (7) is that richer countries are much more alike in terms of rates of growth of real per capita income than are poor countries. Therefore, between 1960 and 2000 there appeared to be no convergence among all the countries in the world. However, there is evidence for convergence among the richest countries of the world for the same period, since these countries behave roughly like a group of countries that has achieved convergence, with their growth rates in per capita income not differing much (at least relative to what we see for poor countries).

The following story makes these observations on convergence from the data consistent with the predictions of the Solow growth model. First, we can think of the richest countries of the world in 1960 (i.e., the Western European countries, the United States, Canada, Australia, and New Zealand) as having access to roughly the same technology. The Solow growth model then tells us that we should expect convergence in standards of living among these countries, with some minor differences accounted for by differences in population growth and savings rates. Second, the tendency for differences in standards of living to persist among the poor countries of the world can be explained in the Solow model by different levels of total factor productivity in those countries brought about by differing barriers to technology adoption.

To support the idea that persistent disparity in incomes per worker across countries could be caused by barriers to technology adoption, we need additional evidence for the existence of such barriers and evidence that the barriers differ significantly among countries. In their book *Barriers to Riches*, Stephen Parente and Edward Prescott provide considerable evidence of both in examining experience in particular industries and countries.[3] They argue that evidence of resistance to the adoption of new technology can be found in the textiles industry and in the mining industry in the United States. Further, if we look at particular industries and measure productivities in those industries across countries, the evidence supports the idea that barriers to technology adoption are important for explaining the productivity differences.

A key feature of the data that supports the idea of barriers preventing poor countries from adopting the technologies used by the richest countries of the world is that growth miracles have not occurred for the very rich. In Canada, as we observed in Chapter 7, the growth rate of income per capita has not strayed far from 2% per annum since 1870, and the same is true for the United States. The important growth miracles after World War II occurred in Japan, South Korea, Taiwan, Singapore, and Hong Kong. At the time when growth took off in these countries, they were all well behind the standard of living in the leading industrial countries. The growth miracles in these countries are consistent with barriers to technology adoption being removed, which then allowed incomes per worker to quickly approach that of the United States.

An idea related to, but somewhat different from, the role played by barriers to technology adoption in explaining cross-country differences in aggregate total factor productivity is the idea that such differences are in part due to the misallocation of labour and capital across firms in the economy. This idea was discussed in Macroeconomics in Action 7.1 in Chapter 7. Aggregate productivity might differ across countries because different countries have different degrees of market distortions, rather than different barriers to technology adoption. That is, if government taxes and subsidies, political corruption, or the concentration of market power among a few firms in an industry act to direct capital and labour toward inefficient low-productivity firms, this will tend to lower aggregate productivity. The problem of misallocation of resources is similar to the problem of barriers to technology adoption in that the remedy for the problem lies in changes in government behaviour. If the misallocation of resources is an important contributor to the gap in per capita incomes between rich and poor countries, as evidence indicates, then poor countries can close the gap with rich countries through the elimination of taxes and subsidies, corruption, and monopoly power.

---

[3]See S. Parente and E. Prescott, 2000, Barriers to Riches, MIT Press, Cambridge, MA.

Measuring Economic Welfare: Per Capita Income, Income Distribution, Leisure, and Longevity

8.1

In this chapter, we have focused attention on a particular measure of a nation's economic well-being, per capita real GDP. As was discussed in Chapter 2, per capita GDP is a good measure of market economic activity, which is indeed highly positively correlated with aggregate economic welfare. However, per capita real GDP misses several dimensions of economic activity and economic welfare that are important for assessing a country's economic health, and for making comparisons across countries.

What does per capita real GDP miss, as a measure of aggregate economic welfare? First, this measure takes no account of how income is distributed across the population. At the extreme, society is not well off if one person has all the income and the rest of the population has nothing. Everything else held constant, as a society we might prefer a more egalitarian distribution of income. The issue of income and wealth distribution has become more

pressing in recent years. For reasons having to do with the demand for high-skilled workers, changes in technology, and import competition from less-developed countries, the wage gap between high-skilled and low-skilled workers has grown in developed countries, particularly the United States. This has tended to increase the dispersion in income across households in developed countries. As well, there has been a growing public concern, particularly following the financial crisis, that people working in the upper echelons of the financial industry and receiving top incomes were somehow undeserving of their rewards. Such concerns are legitimate, as some of those high financial incomes were the result of government bailouts (redistribution of income by the government from the poor to the rich), corruption, and possibly fraud, particularly in the United States.

A second drawback to real GDP per capita as a measure of economic welfare is that it does not

(Continued)

Endogenous Growth: A Model of Human Capital Accumulation

Perhaps the primary deficiency of the Solow growth model is that it does not explain a key observation, which is growth itself. The Solow model relies on increases in total factor productivity coming from outside the model to generate long-run increases in per capita output, and this seems unsatisfactory, as we would like to understand the economic forces behind increases in total factor productivity. Total factor productivity growth involves research and development by firms, education, and training on the job, and all of these activities are responsive to the economic environment. We might like an economic growth model to answer the following questions: How does total factor productivity growth respond to the quantity of public funds spent on public education? How is total factor productivity growth affected by subsidies to research and development? Does it make sense to have the government intervene to promote economic growth? Although the Solow growth model cannot answer these questions, a model of endogenous growth, in which growth rates are explained by the model, might do so.

account for leisure. A country may be well off in part because its inhabitants spend all of their time working, and little time enjoying the fruits of their labour. Third, the health of the population matters, something that we can measure by longevity. Finally, a country may have high income but low consumption, if it invests a lot, or is indebted to the residents of other countries. We would rather account for economic welfare by measuring consumption instead of income.

Research by Charles Jones and Peter Klenow[4] is aimed at deriving a single number for a given country that can capture all of the above factors, and represent a measure of economic welfare that can be compared across countries. The welfare measure is derived from a choice-theoretic framework, and yields a number in units of consumption for the average person.

The Jones-Klenow results are very interesting. In one sense, their research is assuring, in that it shows that real GDP per capita is useful as a rough guide in making welfare comparisons across countries. Jones and Klenow find that the correlation between their welfare measure and real

GDP per capita across countries is 0.95. However, the Jones-Klenow measure shrinks the difference between western European countries and the United States. For example, in 2000, France had per capita real income that was 70% of what it was in the United States, but by the Jones-Klenow welfare measure, residents of France were 94% as well off as residents of the U.S. in 2000. This shrinkage is due to the fact that the French are more egalitarian, they take more leisure, and they live longer than Americans. Jones and Klenow do not report results for Canada, but they would likely show results similar to those for France. Indeed, because the income distribution is less dispersed in Canada than in the U.S., as Canadians live longer than Americans, and because the Canadian economy performed better than the U.S. economy coming out of the recent recession, Canadians are probably better off currently than Americans, by the Jones-Klenow welfare measure.

---

[4]C. Jones, and P. Klenow, 2011, "Beyond GDP? Welfare across Countries and Time," working paper, Stanford University, http://klenow.com/Jones_Klenow.pdf.

The endogenous growth model we will work with here is a simplification of one developed by Robert Lucas.[5] Another important earlier contributor to research on endogenous growth was Paul Romer.[6] In our model, the representative consumer allocates his or her time between supplying labour to produce output and accumulating **human capital**, where human capital is the accumulated stock of skills and education that a worker has at a point in time. The higher the human capital that workers have, the more they can produce and the more new human capital they can produce. Thus, a higher level of human capital means that the economy can grow at a faster rate.

If we think in terms of real-world economies, at any given time some of the working-age population will be employed, thus producing goods and services, some will be in school, and some will be unemployed or not in the labour force. There is an opportunity cost associated with people of working age who are in school, as these

---

[5]R. Lucas, 1988, "On the Mechanics of Economic Development," *Journal of Monetary Economics* 22, July, 3–42.

[6]See P. Romer, 1986, "Increasing Returns and Long-Run Growth," *Journal of Political Economy* 94, 500–521.

people could otherwise be producing goods and services. By acquiring schooling, however, people accumulate skills (human capital), and a more highly skilled labour force in the future permits more future output to be produced. Also, a more highly skilled population can better pass skills on to others, and so human capital accumulation is more efficient if the level of human capital is higher.

Human capital accumulation is therefore an investment, just like investment in plant and equipment, as there are associated current costs and future benefits. However, there are good reasons to think that physical investment is fundamentally different from human capital investment, in addition to the obvious difference that physical investment is embodied in machines and buildings and human capital investment is embodied in people. Recall that we have assumed in all our models that there are diminishing marginal returns to the accumulation of physical capital, since adding more plant and equipment to a fixed labour force should eventually yield lower increases in output at the margin. Human capital accumulation differs in that there appears to be no limit to human knowledge or to how productive individuals can become given increases in knowledge and skills. Paul Romer has argued that a key feature of knowledge is **nonrivalry**.[7] That is, a given person's acquisition of knowledge does not reduce the ability of someone else to acquire the same knowledge. Most goods are rivalrous; for example, my consumption of hotel services will limit the ability of others to benefit from hotel services, as only a fixed number of hotel rooms is available in a given city at a given time. Physical capital accumulation also involves rivalry, as the acquisition of plant and equipment by a firm uses up resources that could be used by other firms to acquire plant and equipment. Thus, diminishing marginal returns to human capital investment seem unnatural. It is the lack of diminishing returns to human capital investment that will lead to unbounded growth in the model we study here, even though there are no exogenous forces propelling economic growth.

THE REPRESENTATIVE CONSUMER

Our endogenous growth model has a representative consumer, who starts the current period with H^s units of human capital. In each period, the consumer has one unit of time (as in the Solow model, the fact that there is one unit of time is simply a normalization), which can be allocated between work and accumulating human capital. For simplicity, we assume the consumer does not use time for leisure. Let u denote the fraction of time devoted to working in each period, so that the number of **efficiency units of labour** devoted to work is uH^s. That is, the number of units of labour that the consumer effectively supplies is the number of units of time spent working multiplied by the consumer's quantity of human capital. The consumer's quantity of human capital is the measure of the productivity of the consumer's time when he or she is working. For each efficiency unit of labour supplied, the consumer receives the current real wage w. For simplicity, we assume the consumer cannot save, and so the consumer's budget constraint in the current period is

$$C = wuH^s. \tag{8.1}$$

[7]See P. Romer, 1990, "Endogenous Technological Change," *Journal of Political Economy* 98, S71–S102.

Though the consumer cannot save, he or she can trade off current consumption for future consumption by accumulating human capital. Since u units of time are used for work, the remainder, $1 - u$, is used for human capital accumulation. The technology for accumulating human capital is given by

$$H^{s'} = b(1-u)H^s;$$ (8.2)

that is, the stock of human capital in the future period, denoted by $H^{s'}$ varies in proportion to the number of current efficiency units of labour devoted to human capital accumulation, which is $(1 - u)H^s$. Here, b is a parameter that captures the efficiency of the human capital accumulation technology, with $b > 0$. Thus, Equation (8.2) represents the idea that the easier it is to accumulate skills and education, the more skills and education an individual (or society) has.

THE REPRESENTATIVE FIRM

The representative firm produces output by using only efficiency units of labour, since for simplicity there is no physical capital in this model. The production function is given by

$$Y = zuH^d,$$ (8.3)

where Y is current output, $z > 0$ is the marginal product of efficiency units of labour, and uH^d is the current input of efficiency units of labour into production. That is, uH^d is the demand for efficiency units of labour by the representative firm. The production function in Equation (8.3) has constant returns to scale, since there is only one input into production, efficiency units of labour, and increasing the quantity of efficiency units of labour increases output in the same proportion. For example, increasing efficiency units of labour uH^d by 1% will increase current output by 1%.

The representative firm hires the quantity of efficiency units of labour, uH^d, that maximizes current profits, where profits are

$$\pi = Y - wuH^d,$$

which is the quantity of output produced minus the wages paid to workers. Substituting for Y from Equation (8.3), we get

$$\pi = zuH^d - wuH^d = (z - w)uH^d.$$ (8.4)

Now, if $z - w < 0$, then in Equation (8.4) profits are negative if the firm hires a positive quantity of efficiency units of labour, so that the firm will maximize profits by setting $uH^d = 0$. If $z - w > 0$, then profits are $z - w > 0$ for each efficiency unit hired, so that the firm will want to hire an infinite number of workers to maximize profits. If $z = w$, then the firm's profits are zero for any number of workers hired, so that the firm will be indifferent about the number of efficiency units of labour hired. We conclude that the firm's demand curve for efficiency units of labour is infinitely elastic at $w = z$.

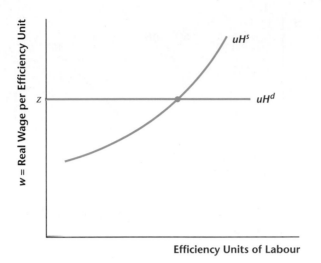

FIGURE 8.5

Determination of the Equilibrium Real Wage in the Endogenous Growth Model

The figure shows the demand and supply of efficiency units of labour in the endogenous growth model. The equilibrium wage will be z, the constant marginal product of efficiency units of labour.

In Figure 8.5 we show the firm's demand curve for efficiency units of labour, which is just a special case of the demand curve being identical to the marginal product schedule for efficiency units of labour. Here, the marginal product of efficiency units of labour is a constant, z. What this implies is that no matter what the supply curve for efficiency units of labour, the intersection between demand and supply will always occur, as in Figure 8.5, at a real wage of $w = z$. That is, the equilibrium real wage per efficiency unit of labour will always be $w = z$. This then implies that the real wage per hour of work is $wH^d = zH^d$, and so the real wage as we would measure it empirically will change in proportion to the quantity of human capital of the representative consumer.

COMPETITIVE EQUILIBRIUM

Working out the competitive equilibrium here is quite straightforward. There is only one market each period, on which consumption goods are traded for efficiency units of labour. We know already that this market always clears at a real wage of $w = z$. Market clearing gives $uH^s = uH^d$ (the supply of efficiency units of labour is equal to the demand), and so $H^s = H^d = H$. Therefore, substituting in Equations (8.1) and (8.2) for w and H^s, we get

$$C = zuH, \qquad (8.5)$$

and

$$H' = b(1 - u)H. \qquad (8.6)$$

Therefore, Equation (8.6) determines future human capital H' given current human capital H, and we show this relationship in Figure 8.6. The slope of the coloured line in the figure is $b(1 - u)$, and if $b(1 - u) > 1$, then we will have $H' > H$, so that future human capital is always greater than current human capital, and therefore

FIGURE 8.6

**Human Capital
Accumulation in the
Endogenous Growth Model**
The coloured line shows the
quantity of future human
capital *H* as a function of
current human capital *H'*.
As drawn *H' > H* for any *H*,
and so human capital will
continue to increase forever.

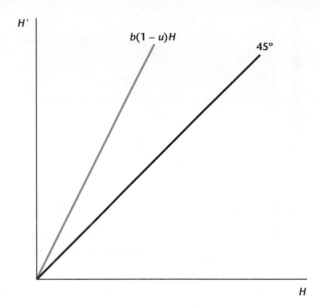

human capital will grow over time without bound. From Equation (8.6), the growth rate of human capital is

$$\frac{H'}{H} - 1 = b(1 - u) - 1, \tag{8.7}$$

which is a constant. What is important here is that the growth rate of human capital will increase if b increases or if u decreases. Recall that b determines the efficiency of the human capital accumulation technology, which could be interpreted as the efficiency of the educational sector. Thus, the model predicts that countries with more efficient education systems should experience higher rates of growth in human capital. If u decreases, more time is devoted to human capital accumulation and less to producing output in each period. As seems natural, this causes the growth rate in human capital to increase.

Now, Equation (8.5) will also hold in the future period, so that $C' = zuH'$, where C' is future consumption, and therefore from Equation (8.5) we can determine the growth rate of consumption, which is

$$\frac{C'}{C} - 1 = \frac{zuH'}{zuH} - 1 = \frac{H'}{H} - 1 = b(1 - u) - 1.$$

That is, the growth rate of consumption is identical to the growth rate of human capital. Further, note from Equations (8.3) and (8.5), that $C = Y$, which we also know must hold in equilibrium, given the income–expenditure identity from Chapter 2 (our model has no investment, no government, and no net exports). Therefore, human capital, consumption, and output all grow at the same rate, $b(1 - u) - 1$, in equilibrium.

Note that this model economy does not grow because of any exogenous force. There is no population growth (there is a single representative consumer), and the production technology does not change over time (b and z remain fixed). Thus, growth occurs because of endogenous forces, with the growth rate determined by b and u. The key element in the model that leads to unbounded growth is the fact that the production function, given by Equation (8.3), does not exhibit decreasing returns to scale in human capital. That is, the production function has constant returns to scale in human capital, since output will increase in proportion to human capital, given u. For example, if human capital increases by 10%, then, holding u constant, output will increase by 10%. In the Solow growth model, growth is limited because of the decreasing marginal product of physical capital, but here the marginal product of human capital does not decrease as the quantity of human capital used in production increases. The marginal product of human capital does not fall as human capital increases, because knowledge and skills are nonrivalrous; additional education and skills do not reduce the extra output that can be achieved through the acquisition of more education and skills.

ECONOMIC POLICY AND GROWTH

Our endogenous growth model suggests that government policies can affect the growth rates of aggregate output and consumption. Since the common growth rate of human capital, consumption, and output depends on b and u, it is useful to think about how government policy might affect b and u. As b represents the efficiency of the human capital accumulation technology, b could be affected by government policies that make the educational system more efficient. For example, this might be accomplished through the implementation of better incentives for performance in the school system, or possibly by changing the mix of public and private education. Exactly what policies the government would have to pursue to increase b we cannot say here without being much more specific in modelling the education system. However, it certainly seems feasible for governments to affect the efficiency of education, and politicians seem to believe this too.

Government policy could also change the rate of economic growth by changing u. For example, this could be done through taxes or subsidies to education. If the government subsidizes education, such a policy would make human capital accumulation more desirable relative to current production, and so u would decrease and the growth rate of output and consumption would increase. Macroeconomics in Action 8.2 contains a discussion of some research on the role of education in economic growth.

Now, suppose that the government had the power to decrease u or to increase b, increasing the growth rate of consumption and output. Would this be a good idea or not? To answer this question, we would have to ask how the representative consumer's welfare would change as a result. Now, clearly a decrease in u will increase the growth rate of consumption, which is $b(1-u)-1$, but there is also a second effect in that the level of consumption goes down. That is, current consumption is $C = zuH$, and so in the very first period if u decreases, then C must also fall, since initial human capital H is given. Recall from Chapter 1 that if we graph the natural logarithm of a variable against time, then the slope of the graph is approximately the growth rate. Since consumption grows at the constant rate $b(1-u)-1$ in equilibrium, if we graph the natural log of consumption against time, this will be a straight line. The slope of the graph of consumption will increase as u decreases and the growth rate of consumption increases, and the vertical intercept of the graph will decrease as u decreases, as this reduces consumption in the very first period. There is, therefore, a tradeoff for the representative consumer when u decreases: consumption is sacrificed early on, but consumption will grow at a higher rate, so that consumption will ultimately be higher than it was with a higher level of u. Thus, the path for consumption shifts as in Figure 8.7. In the figure, consumption will be lower after the change in u until period T, at which time consumption with a lower value of u overtakes consumption with a higher value of u.

It is not clear that the consumer would prefer the new consumption path with the higher growth rate of consumption, even though consumption will be higher in the long run. There is a cost to higher growth: consumption in the near future must be forgone. Which consumption path the consumer prefers will depend on how patient he or she is. Preferences could be such that the consumer is very impatient, in which case he or she would tend to prefer the initial consumption path with a low growth rate of consumption. Alternatively, the consumer might be very patient, tending to prefer the new consumption path with a high growth rate of consumption. The conclusion is that, even if the government could engineer a higher rate of growth by causing u to fall—say through education subsidies—this may not be desirable because of the near-term costs involved.

We could do a similar analysis for the case in which the government causes the growth rate of consumption to increase because of an increase in b, the parameter governing the efficiency of human capital accumulation. In this case, the model is not explicit about the near-term costs of increasing the growth rate of consumption by increasing b. That is, current consumption is given by $C = zuH$, and so consumption in the very first period does not depend on b. However, if the government were to

FIGURE 8.7

Effect of a Decrease in *u* on the Consumption Path in the Endogenous Growth Model
The figure shows the effect of a decrease in u, which increases the fraction of time spent accumulating human capital each period. The growth path for consumption (note that consumption is equal to income) pivots; thus, there is a short-run decrease in consumption, but consumption will be higher in the long run.

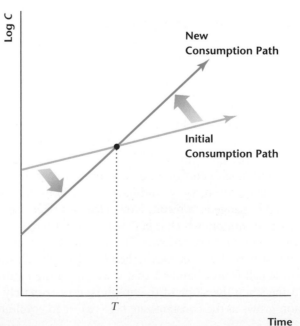

increase b through education policy, for example, this would entail some real resource costs. Suppose that the government chose to make public education more efficient by increasing monitoring of teacher and student performance. Clearly, there would be a cost attached to this monitoring in terms of labour time. We might represent this cost in our model as a reduction in the level of consumption, as labour is diverted from goods production to government monitoring activities. Therefore, b would increase, which would increase the growth rate of consumption, but, as in the case in which we examined the effects of a decrease in u, there would be a decrease in consumption in the very first period. Thus, the relationship between the new consumption path after the increase in b and the initial consumption path would be just as in Figure 8.7. As in the case where u falls, it is not clear whether the representative consumer is better off when the growth rate of consumption is higher, because there are short-term costs in terms of lost consumption.

CONVERGENCE IN THE ENDOGENOUS GROWTH MODEL

In the Solow growth model, with exogenous growth, countries that are in all respects identical, except for their initial quantities of capital per worker, will in the long run have the same level and growth rate of income per capita. We showed in the previous section that this prediction of the Solow growth model is consistent with data on the evolution of incomes per capita in the richest countries of the world, but not with data for poorer countries. That is, there appears to be no tendency for the poorest countries to catch up with the richest, and the Solow growth model fails to predict this.

In the endogenous growth model we have constructed here, convergence does not occur. To see this, note first that in the endogenous growth model, consumption is equal to income, and there is only one consumer, so that per capita income is identical to aggregate income. From above, current consumption is given by $C = zuH$, and consumption grows at a constant rate $b(1 - u) - 1$, so that the natural log of consumption graphed against time is a straight line, as we showed in Figure 8.7. Now, suppose we consider two countries that have the same technology and allocate labour in the same way between goods production and human capital accumulation. That is, b, z, and u are the same in the two countries. However, suppose also that these countries differ according to their initial human capital levels. The rich country has a high level of initial human capital, denoted H_r, and the poor country has a low level of human capital, denoted H_p. This implies that consumption in the rich country is initially $C = zuH_r$, which is greater than initial consumption in the poor country, $C = zuH_p$. Now, since b and u are identical in the two countries, $b(1 - u) - 1$, the growth rate of consumption is also identical for the rich and poor countries. Therefore, the growth paths of consumption for the rich country and the poor country are as in Figure 8.8. That is, initial differences in income and consumption across rich and poor countries will persist forever, and there is no convergence.

How do we reconcile the predictions of the endogenous growth model concerning convergence with the facts? The model appears consistent with the fact that there are persistent differences in income per worker among poorer countries, and persistent differences in income per worker between the poorer countries of the world and the richer countries. However, the model appears inconsistent with the fact that incomes

FIGURE 8.8

No Convergence in the Endogenous Growth Model
In the endogenous growth model, two identical countries that differ only in their initial incomes will never converge.

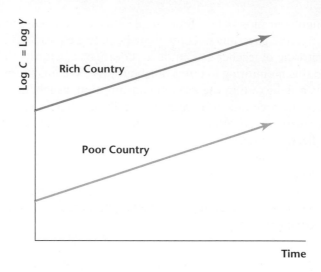

per worker seem to be converging among the richer nations of the world. Perhaps an explanation for this is that in regions of the world where labour and capital are mobile and where skills are more easily transferred, there are important **human capital externalities**, as discussed by Robert Lucas.[8] A human capital externality exists when contact with others with high levels of human capital increases our human capital or makes us more productive. Human capital externalities can explain the existence of cities and the specialized activities that take place there. Why, for example, would people specializing in financial activities want to bear the congestion and pollution of New York City unless there were significant positive externalities involved in working there? In highly developed regions of the world where there are greater opportunities for taking advantage of human capital externalities, through business contacts and education in other countries and regions, large differences in the levels of human capital across regions cannot persist. There will be convergence in income per worker. However, less developed countries interact to a low degree with highly developed countries, and people with high levels of human capital tend to move to the highly developed countries from the less developed countries (the "brain drain"). Thus, differences in human capital can persist across very rich and very poor countries.

We have now completed our study of economic growth in this part. In Part 4, we move on to a detailed examination of savings behaviour and government deficits, and we begin building a model that is the basis for our study of business cycles.

---

[8]R. Lucas, 1988, "On the Mechanics of Economic Development," *Journal of Monetary Economics* 22, July, 3–42.

In cross-country economic data, economists have observed that there is a positive correlation between the level of education of a country's population (as measured, for example, by average years of schooling across the population) and the rate of growth in real GDP.[9] Mark Bils and Peter Klenow estimate that, in terms of average educational attainment of a country in 1960, one more year of schooling on average is associated with 0.30 more percentage points in average annual growth in GDP per capita from 1960 to 1990.[10] One might be tempted to conclude, given this observation, that a more highly educated population causes the economic growth rate to rise. Then, some might argue that since economic growth is a good thing, it would be a good idea for the government to take steps to increase schooling and boost growth. However, this argument would be sloppy economics.

A correlation observed in economic data need not reflect causation, just as correlations observed in other kinds of scientific data need not tell us what causes what. For example, one could conclude from observing a positive correlation between the incidence of lung cancer and smoking across the population that lung cancer causes people to smoke. There are at least two other possible explanations for the lung cancer–smoking correlation. One is that there is some third factor that is correlated with both the incidence of lung cancer and with smoking, and that is actually the root explanation for the correlation. For example, it might be that poor people tend to have lung cancer, and poor people tend to smoke, and that there is something about being poor (bad living conditions, for example) that causes lung cancer. A second alternative explanation—the one backed by a large body of scientific evidence—is that smoking causes lung cancer.

Now, in terms of the correlation between average educational attainment and economic growth, we have an analogous empirical problem to the one of interpreting the correlation between lung cancer and smoking. That is, the correlation between education and growth might mean that (i) higher education causes the growth rate of GDP to be higher; (ii) some third factor causes educational attainment and the growth rate of GDP to be positively correlated; or (iii) higher economic growth causes more education. In fact, all of (i)–(iii) might be at work, and as economists we are interested in how each of (i)–(iii) contributes to the correlation, in part because this will be informative about the potential effects of government policies toward education. This is the type of exercise carried out by Mark Bils and Peter Klenow in an article in the *American Economic Review*.[11]

What particular economic mechanisms are at work in cases (i)–(iii) above? For (i), the model of endogenous growth we studied in the previous section of this chapter provides some insight into how more education can cause the economic growth rate to be higher. In the model, if the average individual in society devotes more time to accumulating human capital, which we can interpret as education, then aggregate output will grow at a higher rate. With regard to (ii) above, how might factors other than education and economic growth cause educational attainment and the economic growth rate to move together? As Bils and Klenow argue, in countries with sound legal systems that adequately enforce property rights, educational attainment is high because people know that investing in education will have large future payoffs. In such societies, the growth rate of GDP is also high, in part because the enforcement of property rights leads to greater innovation, research, and development. Thus, we will see a positive correlation across countries between education and growth, but not because of a direct causal relationship between the two. Finally, for (iii) above, educational attainment could be high because people anticipate high future economic growth. A high rate of future economic growth will imply a high rate of return to education, since a high rate of growth should increase the gap between the wages of high-skill and low-skill workers.

Bils and Klenow essentially find that causation running from education to growth accounts for only about 30% of the relationship between education and growth. This suggests that, if we are interested in government policies that promote growth, then perhaps improvements in patent policy or in the role of government in research and development are more important than improvements in education policy.

_____

[9]See, for example, R. Barro, 1990, "Economic Growth in a Cross Section of Countries," *Quarterly Journal of Economics* 106, 407–443.

[10]M. Bils and P. Klenow, 2000, "Does Schooling Cause Growth?" *American Economic Review* 90, 1160–1183.

[11]Ibid.

Chapter Summary

- If all countries are identical, except for initial differences in capital per worker, the Solow growth model predicts that there will be convergence among countries. That is, in the long run, all countries will have the same level of income per worker, and aggregate income will be growing at the same rate in all countries.

- In the data, there is evidence for convergence among the richest countries of the world, but convergence does not appear to be occurring among all countries or among the poorest countries.

- The Solow growth model is consistent with the data if there are significant barriers to technology adoption, and these barriers differ among countries. This implies long-run differences in the level of total factor productivity and standards of living across countries.

- We constructed an endogenous growth model with human capital accumulation. This model has the property that, even with no increases in total factor productivity and no population growth, there can be unlimited growth in aggregate output and aggregate consumption, fuelled by growth in the stock of human capital (i.e., skills and education).

- In the endogenous growth model, the rate of growth of output and consumption is determined by the efficiency of human capital accumulation and the allocation of labour time between goods production and human capital accumulation.

- If the government could introduce policies that altered the efficiency of human capital accumulation or the allocation of labour time, it could alter the rate of economic growth in the endogenous growth model.

- Increasing the rate of economic growth may or may not improve economic welfare, because an increase in the growth rate of aggregate consumption is always associated with lower consumption in the short run.

- In the endogenous growth model, per capita incomes do not converge across rich and poor countries, even if countries are identical except for initial levels of human capital.

Key Terms

human capital: The accumulated stock of skills and education that a worker has at a point in time.

nonrivalry: A feature of knowledge, in that acquisition of knowledge does not reduce the ability of others to acquire it.

efficiency units of labour: The effective number of units of labour input after adjusting for the quantity of human capital possessed by workers.
human capital externalities: Effects that exist if the human capital of others affects one's productivity.

Questions for Review

1. If countries are initially identical, except with respect to levels of capital per worker, what does the Solow model predict will happen to these countries in the long run? Is this consistent with the data?

2. How is the Solow model consistent with evidence on convergence across countries?

3. What can cause barriers to the adoption of technology?

4. How can a country overcome barriers to technology adoption?

5. What causes economic growth in the endogenous growth model?

6. Why is knowledge nonrivalrous?

7. What two factors affect the growth rate of income and consumption in the endogenous growth model?

8. If the government could increase the rate of growth of consumption, should it? Why or why not?

9. Is there convergence in the levels and rates of growth of per capita income in the endogenous growth model? Why or why not?

Problems

1. Might differences across countries in population growth account for the persistence in income disparity across countries? Use the Solow growth model to address this question and discuss.

2. In the Solow growth model, suppose that the per-worker production function is given by $y = zk^{.3}$ with $s = 0.25$, $d = 0.1$, and $n = 0.02$.
   a. Suppose in country A that $z = 1$. Calculate income per capita and capital per worker in country A.
   b. Suppose in country B that $z = 2$. Now calculate income per capita and capital per worker in country B.
   c. As measured by GDP per capita, how much richer is country B than country A? What does this tell us about the potential differences in total factor productivity to explain differences in standards of living across countries?

3. Suppose that z, the marginal product of efficiency units of labour, increases in the endogenous growth model. What effects does this have on the rates of growth and the levels of human capital, consumption, and output? Explain your results.

4. Introduce government activity in the endogenous growth model as follows. In addition to working u units of time in producing goods, the representative consumer works v units of time for the government and produces gvH goods for government use in the current period, where $g > 0$. The consumer now spends $1 - u - v$ units of time each period accumulating human capital.
   a. Suppose that v increases with u decreasing by an equal amount. Determine the effects on the level and the rate of growth of consumption. Draw a diagram showing the initial path followed by the natural logarithm of consumption and the corresponding path after v increases.

b. Suppose that v increases with u held constant. Determine the effects on the level and the rate of growth of consumption. Draw a diagram showing the initial path followed by the natural logarithm of consumption and the corresponding path after v increases.

c. Explain your results and any differences between parts (a) and (b).

5. Suppose that the government makes a one-time investment in new public school buildings, which results in a one-time reduction in consumption. The new public school buildings increase the efficiency with which human capital is accumulated. Determine the effects of this on the paths of aggregate consumption and aggregate output over time. Is it clear that this investment in new schools is a good idea? Explain.

6. Reinterpret the endogenous growth model in this chapter as follows. Suppose that there are two groups of people in a country, the low-skilled and the high-skilled. The low-skilled have less human capital per person initially than do the high-skilled. In the economy as a whole, output is produced using efficiency units of labour, and total factor productivity is z, just as in the endogenous growth model in this chapter. Each individual in this economy accumulates human capital on his or her own, and each has one unit of time to split between human capital accumulation and work. However, now $b = b_h$ for the high-skilled, $b = b_l$ for the low-skilled, $u = u_h$ for the high-skilled, and $u = u_l$ for the low-skilled. Particularly in the United States over the last 30 years or so, there has been an increase in the gap between the wages of high-skilled workers and low-skilled workers. Determine how this model can explain this observation, and discuss.

7. Suppose there are two countries. In the rich country the representative consumer has H_r units of human capital, and total factor productivity is z_r. In the poor country, the representative consumer has H_p units of human capital, and total factor productivity is z_p. Assume that b and u are the same in the rich and poor countries, that $H_r > H_p$ and $z_r > z_p$.

a. How do the levels of income per capita, the growth rates of income per capita, and real wages compare between the rich and poor countries?

b. If consumers could choose their country of residence, where would they want to live?

c. If each country could determine immigration policy, what should they do to maximize the welfare of the current residents?

d. What is the immigration policy that maximizes the welfare of the citizens of both countries?

e. Explain your results. Do you think this is a good model for analyzing the effects of immigration? Why or why not?

8. In the endogenous growth model, suppose that there are now three possible uses of time. Let u denote the fraction of time spent working, s the fraction of time spent neither working nor accumulating human capital (call this unemployment), with $1 - u - s$ the fraction of time spent accumulating human capital. Assume that $z = 1$ and $b = 4.2$. Assume that the economy begins period 1 with 100 units of human capital.

a. Suppose that for periods 1, 2, 3, ..., 10, that $u = 0.7$ and $s = 0.05$. Calculate aggregate consumption, output, and the quantity of human capital in each of these periods.

b. Suppose that, in period 11, $u = 0.6$ and $s = 0.15$. Then in periods 12, 13, 14, ..., $u = 0.7$ and $s = 0.05$. Calculate aggregate consumption, output, and the quantity of human capital in periods 11, 12, 13, ..., 20.

c. Suppose alternatively that, in period 11, $u = 0.6$ and $s = 0.05$. Again, calculate aggregate consumption, output, and the quantity of human capital in periods 11, 12, 13, ..., 20.

d. Now, suppose that, in period 11, $u = 0.6$ and $s = 0.10$. Again, calculate aggregate consumption, output, and the quantity of human capital in periods 11, 12, 13, ..., 20.

e. What do you conclude from your results in (a)–(d)? Discuss.

Savings, Investment, and Government Deficits

In this Part, we explore further the macroeconomics of intertemporal decisions and dynamic issues. We start in Chapter 9 by considering the consumption–savings decisions of consumers, building on our knowledge of consumer behaviour from Chapter 4. We then study the Ricardian equivalence theorem, which states that, under certain conditions, a change in the timing of taxes by the government has no effects on real macroeconomic variables or on the welfare of consumers. A key implication of the Ricardian equivalence theorem is that a cut in taxes by the government is not a free lunch.

The Ricardian equivalence theorem provides a foundation on which to build our understanding of some key credit market "frictions," which matter a great deal for macroeconomic policy. We explore the issues related to these key frictions in Chapter 10. The first frictions relate to credit market imperfections—asymmetric information and limited commitment—that cause the interest rates at which credit market participants borrow to exceed the rates at which they lend, and result in situations where borrowers are required to post collateral to get loans. Credit market imperfections played an important role in the recent financial crisis, and we will explore this in Chapter 10. Another credit market friction relates to the fact that people only live for finite periods of time, which can provide a role for social security programs. Pay-as-you-go and fully funded social security systems are studied in the latter sections of Chapter 10.

In Chapter 11, we use what was learned about the microeconomics of consumption–savings behaviour in Chapters 9 and 10, along with an analysis of the intertemporal labour supply behaviour of consumers and the investment decisions of firms, to construct a complete intertemporal macroeconomic model. This model is the basis for much of what we do in Parts 5 and 6. The model is used in Chapter 11 to show the effects of macroeconomic shocks on output, employment, consumption, investment, the real wage, and the real interest rate. As well, we focus on the effects of expectations about the future on current events.

9

A Two-Period Model: The Consumption–Savings Decision and Credit Markets

This chapter focuses on **intertemporal decisions** and the implications of intertemporal decision making for how government deficits affect macroeconomic activity. Intertemporal decisions involve economic tradeoffs across periods of time. We will first analyze the microeconomic behaviour of a consumer who must make a dynamic **consumption–savings decision**. In doing so, we will apply what was learned in Chapter 4 concerning how a consumer optimizes subject to his or her budget constraint. We will then study a model with many consumers and with a government that need not balance its budget and can issue debt to finance a government budget deficit. An important implication of this model is that the **Ricardian equivalence theorem** holds. This theorem states that there are conditions under which the size of the government's deficit is irrelevant, in that it does not affect any macroeconomic variables of importance or the economic welfare of any individual.

The consumption–savings decision involves intertemporal choice, as this is fundamentally a decision involving a tradeoff between current and future consumption. Similarly, the government's decision concerning the financing of government expenditures is an intertemporal choice, involving a tradeoff between current and future taxes. If the government decreases taxes in the present, it must borrow from the private sector to do so, which implies that future taxes must increase to pay off the higher government debt. Essentially, the government's financing decision is a decision about the quantity of government saving, or the size of the government deficit, making it closely related to the consumption–savings decisions of private consumers.

To study the consumption–savings decisions of consumers and the government's intertemporal choices, we will work in this chapter with a **two-period model**, which is the simplest framework for understanding intertemporal choice and dynamic issues. We will treat the first period in the model as the current period and the second period as the future period. In intertemporal choice, a key variable of interest is the **real interest rate**, which in the model is the interest rate at which consumers and the government can borrow and lend. The real interest rate determines the relative price of consumption in the future in terms of consumption in the present. With respect to consumer choice, we are interested in how savings and consumption in the present and in the future are affected by changes in the real interest rate and in current and future incomes. With respect to the effects of real interest rate changes, income and substitution effects will be important, and we can apply here what was learned in Chapters 4 and 5 about how to isolate income and substitution effects in a consumer's choice problem.

An important principle in the response of consumption to changes in income is **consumption smoothing**. That is, there are natural forces that cause consumers to want to have a smooth consumption path over time, as opposed to a choppy one. Consumption-smoothing behaviour is implied by particular properties of indifference curves that we have already studied in Chapter 4. As well, consumption-smoothing behaviour has important implications for how consumers will respond in the aggregate to changes in government policies or other features of their external environment that affect their income streams.

While it remains true here, as in the one-period model studied in Chapter 5, that an increase in government spending has real effects on macroeconomic activity, the Ricardian equivalence theorem establishes conditions under which the timing of taxation does not matter for aggregate economic activity. David Ricardo, for whom the Ricardian equivalence theorem is named, is best known for his work in the early nineteenth century on the theory of comparative advantage and international trade. Ricardian equivalence runs counter to much of public debate, which attaches importance to the size of the government deficit. We explain why Ricardian equivalence is important in economic analysis and why the Ricardian equivalence theorem is a useful starting point for thinking about how the burden of the government debt is shared. A key implication of the Ricardian equivalence theorem is that a tax cut is not a free lunch. A tax cut may not matter at all, or it may involve a redistribution of wealth within the current population or across generations.

Some interesting issues arise due to "frictions" in credit markets that cause departures from Ricardian equivalence. These frictions are important in analyzing the current financial crisis, and in understanding how social security systems work. These issues will be addressed in Chapter 10.

To maintain simplicity and to retain focus on the important ideas in this chapter, our two-period model leaves out production and investment. In Chapter 11, we reintroduce production and add investment decisions by firms so that we can understand more completely the aggregate determination of output, employment, consumption, investment, the real wage rate, and the interest rate.

A Two-Period Model of the Economy

A consumer's consumption–savings decision is fundamentally a decision involving a tradeoff between current and future consumption. By saving, a consumer gives up consumption in exchange for assets in the present, in order to consume more in the future. Alternatively, a consumer can dissave by borrowing in the present to gain more current consumption, thereby sacrificing future consumption when the loan is repaid. Borrowing (or dissaving) is thus negative savings.

A consumer's consumption–savings decision is a dynamic decision, in that it has implications over more than one period of time, as opposed to the consumer's static work–leisure decision considered in Chapters 4 and 5. We will model the consumer's dynamic problem here in the simplest possible way, namely, in a two-period model. In this model, we will denote the first period as the *current period*, and the second period as the *future period*. For some economic problems, assuming that decision making by consumers takes place over two periods is obviously unrealistic. For example, if a period is a quarter, and since the working life of a typical individual is about 200 quarters, then a 200-period model might seem more appropriate. However, the results we consider in this chapter all generalize to more elaborate models with many periods or an infinite number of periods. The reason for studying models with two periods is that they are simple to analyze while capturing the essentials of dynamic decision making by consumers and firms.

CONSUMERS

It will not cause any difficulties, in terms of what we want to accomplish with this model, to suppose that there are many different consumers rather than a single representative consumer. Therefore, we will assume that there are m consumers, where we can think of m as being a large number. We will assume that each consumer lives for two periods, the current period and the future period. We will further suppose that consumers do not make a work–leisure decision in either period, but simply receive exogenous income. Assuming that incomes are exogenous allows us to focus attention on what we are interested in here: the consumer's consumption–savings decision. Let y be a consumer's real income in the current period, and y' be real income in the future period. Throughout, we will use lowercase letters to refer to variables at the individual level, and uppercase letters for aggregate variables. Primes will denote variables in the future period (e.g., y' denotes the consumer's future income). Each consumer pays lump-sum taxes, t, in the current period and t' in the future period. Suppose that incomes can be different for different consumers, but that all consumers pay the same taxes. If we let a consumer's savings in the current period be s, then the consumer's budget constraint in the current period is

$$c + s = y - t, \tag{9.1}$$

where c is current period consumption. Equation (9.1) states that consumption plus savings in the current period must equal disposable income in the current period. Note that we assume that the consumer starts the current period with no assets. This will not matter in any important way for our analysis.

In Equation (9.1), if $s > 0$ then the consumer will be a lender on the credit market, and if $s < 0$ the consumer will be a borrower. We will suppose that the financial asset that is traded in the credit market is a bond. In the model, bonds can be issued by consumers as well as by the government. If a consumer lends, he or she buys bonds; if he or she borrows, there is a sale of bonds. There are two important assumptions here. The first is that all bonds are indistinguishable, because consumers never default on their debts, so there is no risk associated with holding a bond. In practice, different credit instruments are associated with different levels of risk. Interest-bearing securities issued by the government are essentially risk-less, while corporate bonds may be risky if default by corporate debt issuers is a possibility, and a loan made by a bank to a consumer may also be quite risky. The second important assumption is that bonds are traded directly in the credit market. In practice, much of the economy's credit activity is channelled through financial intermediaries, such as chartered banks. For example, when a consumer borrows to purchase a car, the loan is usually taken out at a chartered bank or other depository institution; a consumer typically does not borrow directly from the ultimate lender. (In the case of a chartered bank, the ultimate lenders include the depositors at the bank.) For the problems we will address with this model, it will simplify matters considerably, without any key loss in the insights we will get, to assume away credit risk and financial institutions like chartered banks. We will discuss some issues related to credit risk later in this chapter. Credit risk and financial intermediation will be discussed in detail in Chapter 17.

In our model, one bond issued in the current period is a promise to pay $1 + r$ units of the consumption good in the future period, so that the real interest rate on each bond is r. Since this implies that one unit of current consumption can be exchanged in the credit market for $1 + r$ units of the future consumption good, the relative price of future consumption in terms of current consumption is $\dfrac{1}{1 + r}$. Recall from Chapter 1 that in practice the real interest rate is approximately the nominal interest rate (the interest rate in money terms) minus the inflation rate. We will study the relationship between real and nominal interest rates in Chapter 12.

A key assumption here is that the real rate of interest at which a consumer can lend is the same as the real rate of interest at which a consumer can borrow. In practice, con-sumers typically borrow at higher rates of interest than they can lend at. For example, the interest rates on consumer loans are usually several percentage points higher than the interest rates on bank deposits, reflecting the costs for the bank of taking deposits and making loans. The assumption that borrowing and lending rates of interest are the same will matter for some of what we do here, and we will ultimately show what dif-ference this makes to our analysis.

In the future period, the consumer has disposable income $y' - t'$ and receives the interest and principal on his or her savings, which totals $(1 + r)s$. Since the future period is the final period, the consumer will choose to finish this period with no assets, consuming all disposable income and the interest and principal on savings (we assume there are no bequests to descendants). We then have

$$c' = y' - t' + (1 + r)s, \qquad (9.2)$$

where c' is consumption in the future period. Note in Equation (9.2) that if $s < 0$, the consumer pays the interest and principal on his or her loan (retires the bonds he or she issued in the current period) and then consumes what remains of his or her future period disposable income.

The consumer chooses current consumption and future consumption, c and c', respectively, and savings, s, to make himself or herself as well off as possible while satisfying the budget constraints in Equations (9.1) and (9.2).

The Consumer's Lifetime Budget Constraint We can work with diagrams similar to those used in Chapter 4 to analyze the consumer's work–leisure decision, if we take the two budget constraints expressed in Equations (9.1) and (9.2) and write them as a single lifetime constraint. To do this, we first use Equation (9.2) to solve for s to get

$$s = \frac{c' - y' + t'}{1 + r}.$$ (9.3)

Then, substitute for s from (9.3) in (9.1) to get

$$c + \frac{c' - y' + t'}{1 + r} = y - t,$$

or rearranging,

$$c + \frac{c'}{1 + r} = y + \frac{y'}{1 + r} - t - \frac{t'}{1 + r}.$$ (9.4)

Equation (9.4) is the consumer's **lifetime budget constraint**, and it states that the **present value** of lifetime consumption $\left(c + \dfrac{c'}{1 + r} \right)$ equals the present value of lifetime income $\left(y + \dfrac{y'}{1 + r} \right)$ minus the present value of lifetime taxes $\left(t + \dfrac{t'}{1 + r} \right)$. The present value here is the value in terms of period 1 consumption goods. That is, $\dfrac{1}{1 + r}$ is the relative price of period 2 consumption goods in terms of period 1 consumption goods, since a consumer can give up 1 unit of period 1 consumption goods and obtain $1 + r$ units of period 2 consumption goods by saving for one period. The problem of the consumer is now simplified, in that he or she chooses c and c' to make himself or herself as well off as possible, while satisfying the budget constraint in Equation (9.4) and given r, y, y', t, and t'. Note that once we have determined what the consumer's optimal consumption is in the current and future periods, we can determine savings, s, from the current-period budget constraint in Equation (9.1).

For a numerical example to illustrate present values, suppose that current income is $y = 110$ and future income is $y' = 120$. Taxes in the current period are $t = 20$, and taxes in the future period are $t' = 10$. Also suppose that the real interest rate is 10%, so that $r = 0.1$. In this example, the relative price of future consumption goods in terms of current consumption goods is $\dfrac{1}{1 + r} = 0.909$. Here, when we discount future income and future taxes to obtain these quantities in units of current consumption goods, we will multiply by the discount factor 0.909. The fact that the discount factor is less than 1 indicates that having a given amount of income in the future is worth less to the consumer than having the same amount of income in the current period. The present discounted value of lifetime income is

$$y + y' \times \frac{1}{1 + r} = 110 + 120 \times 0.909 = 219.1,$$

and the present value of lifetime taxes is

$$t + t' \times \frac{1}{1 + r} = 20 + 10 \times 0.909 = 29.1.$$

Then, in this example, we can write the consumer's lifetime budget constraint from Equation (9.4) as

$$c + 0.909c' = 190.$$

We will label the present value of lifetime disposable income, the quantity on the right-hand side of Equation (9.4), as **lifetime wealth**, *we*, since this is the quantity of resources that the consumer has available to spend on consumption, in present-value terms, over his or her lifetime. We then have

$$we = y + \frac{y'}{1 + r} - t - \frac{t'}{1 + r} \qquad (9.5)$$

and we can rewrite (9.4) as

$$c + \frac{c'}{1 + r} = we. \qquad (9.6)$$

In Figure 9.1 we graph the consumer's lifetime budget constraint as expressed in Equation (9.6). Writing this equation in slope–intercept form, we have

$$c' = -(1 + r)c + we(1 + r). \qquad (9.7)$$

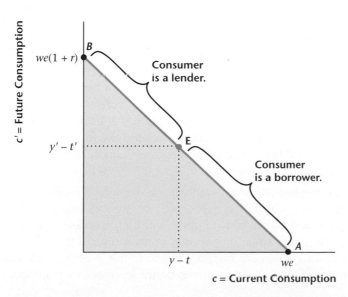

c = Current Consumption

FIGURE 9.1
Consumer's Lifetime Budget Constraint
The lifetime budget constraint defines the quantities of current and future consumption the consumer can acquire, given current and future income and taxes, through borrowing and lending on the credit market. To the northwest of the endowment point *E*, the consumer is a lender with positive savings; to the southeast of *E*, he or she is a borrower with negative savings.

Therefore, in Equation (9.7) and in Figure 9.1, the vertical intercept, $we(1 + r)$, is what could be consumed in the future period if the consumer saved all of his or her current-period disposable income and consumed lifetime wealth (after earning the real interest rate, r, on savings) in the future period. The horizontal intercept in Equation (9.7) and Figure 9.1, we, is what could be consumed if the consumer borrowed the maximum amount possible against future period disposable income and consumed all of lifetime wealth in period 1. The slope of the lifetime budget constraint is $-(1 + r)$, which is determined by the real interest rate. Point E in Figure 9.1 is the **endowment point**, which is the consumption bundle the consumer gets if he or she simply consumes disposable income in the current period and in the future period—that is, $c = y - t$ and $c' = y' - t'$—with zero savings in the current period. You can verify by substituting $c = y - t$ and $c' = y' - t'$ in Equation (9.4) that the endowment point satisfies the lifetime budget constraint. Now, note that any point along BE in Figure 9.1 implies that $s \geq 0$, so that the consumer is a lender, since $c \leq y - t$. Also, a consumption bundle along AE in Figure 9.1 implies that the consumer is a borrower with $s \leq 0$.

Any point on or inside AB in the shaded area in Figure 9.1 represents a feasible consumption bundle, that is, a combination of current-period and future-period consumptions that satisfies the consumer's lifetime budget constraint. As may be clear by now, the way we will approach the consumer's problem here will be very similar to our analysis of the consumer's work–leisure decision in Chapter 4. Once we describe the consumer's preferences, and add indifference curves to the budget constraint as depicted in Figure 9.1, we can determine the consumer's optimal consumption bundle.

The Consumer's Preferences As with the consumer's work–leisure decision in Chapter 4, the consumption bundle chosen by the consumer, here a combination of current-period and future-period consumptions, is determined jointly by the consumer's budget constraint and his or her preferences. Just as in Chapter 4, we will assume that preferences have three properties:

1. *More is always preferred to less.* Here, this means that more current consumption or more future consumption always makes the consumer better off.

2. *The consumer likes diversity in his or her consumption bundle.* Here, a preference for diversity has a specific meaning in terms of the consumer's desire to smooth consumption over time. Namely, the consumer has a dislike for consumption that is far from equal between the current period and the future period. Note that this does not mean that the consumer would always choose to have equal consumption in the current and future periods.

3. *Current consumption and future consumption are normal goods.* This implies that if there is a parallel shift to the right in the consumer's budget constraint, current consumption and future consumption will both increase. This is related to the consumer's desire to smooth consumption over time. If there is a parallel shift to the right in the consumer's budget constraint, this is because lifetime wealth, we, has increased. Given the consumer's desire to smooth consumption over time,

any increase in lifetime wealth will imply that the consumer will choose more consumption in the present *and* in the future.

As in Chapter 4, we represent preferences with an indifference map, which is a family of indifference curves. A typical indifference map is shown in Figure 9.2, where the marginal rate of substitution of consumption in the current period for consumption in the future period, or $MRS_{c,\,c'}$, is minus the slope of an indifference curve. For example, $MRS_{c,c'}$ at point A in Figure 9.2 is minus the slope of a tangent to the indifference curve at point A. Recall that a preference for diversity, or diminishing marginal rate of substitution, is captured by the convexity in an indifference curve, which here also represents a consumer's desire to smooth consumption over time. On indifference curve I_1, at point A the consumer has a large quantity of current consumption and a small quantity of future consumption. He or she needs to be given a large quantity of current consumption to willingly give up a small quantity of future consumption (minus the slope of the indifference curve at A is small). Conversely, at point B the consumer has a small quantity of current consumption and a large quantity of future consumption. He or she needs to be given a large quantity of future consumption to give up a small quantity of current consumption (minus the slope of the indifference curve is large). Thus, the consumer does not like large differences in consumption between the two periods.

As an example to show why consumption smoothing is a natural property for preferences to have, suppose that Sara is a consumer living on a desert island and that she eats only coconuts. Suppose that coconuts can be stored for two weeks without spoiling, and that Sara has 20 coconuts to last for this week (the current period) and

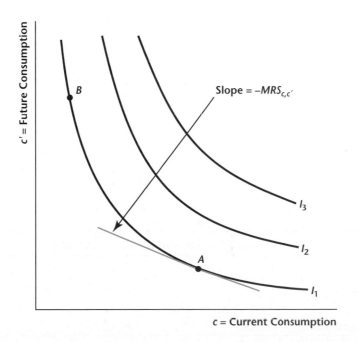

FIGURE 9.2
A Consumer's
Indifference Curves
The figure shows the indifference map of a consumer. Indifference curves are convex and downward-sloping. Minus the slope of an indifference curve is the marginal rate of substitution of current consumption for future consumption.

Slope = $-MRS_{c,c'}$

c' = Future Consumption

c = Current Consumption

I_3

I_2

I_1

B

A

next week (the future period). One option that Sara has is to eat 5 coconuts this week and 15 coconuts next week. Suppose that Sara is just indifferent between this first consumption bundle and a second bundle that involves eating 17 coconuts this week and 3 coconuts next week. However, eating only 5 coconuts in the first week or only 3 coconuts in the second week leaves Sara rather hungry. She would, in fact, prefer to eat 11 coconuts in the first week and 9 coconuts in the second week, rather than either of the other two consumption bundles. Note that this third consumption bundle combines half of the first consumption bundle with half of the second consumption bundle.

That is, $\dfrac{5 + 17}{2} = 11$ and $\dfrac{15 + 3}{2} = 9$. Sara's preferences reflect a desire for consumption smoothing, or a preference for diversity in her consumption bundle, that seems natural. In Table 9.1 we show the consumption bundles that Sara chooses among.

Consumer Optimization As with the work–leisure decision we considered in Chapter 4, the consumer's optimal consumption bundle here will be determined by where an indifference curve is tangent to the budget constraint. In Figure 9.3 we show the optimal consumption choice for a consumer who decides to be a lender. The endowment point is at E, while the consumer chooses the consumption bundle at point A, where $(c, c') = (c^*, c'^*)$. At point A, it is then the case that

$$MRS_{c, c'} = 1 + r; \qquad (9.8)$$

that is, the marginal rate of substitution of current consumption for future consumption (minus the slope of the indifference curve) is equal to the relative price of current consumption in terms of future consumption ($1 + r$, which is minus the slope of the consumer's lifetime budget constraint). Recall from Chapter 4 that Equation (9.8) is a particular case of a standard marginal condition that is implied by consumer optimization (at the optimum, the marginal rate of substitution of good 1 for good 2 is equal to the relative price of good 1 in terms of good 2). Here, the consumer optimizes by choosing the consumption bundle on his or her lifetime budget constraint where the rate at which he or she is willing to trade off current consumption for future consumption is the same as the rate at which he or she can trade current consumption for future consumption in the market (by saving). At point A in Figure 9.3, the quantity of savings is $s = y - t - c^*$, or the distance BD. Similarly, Figure 9.4 shows the case of a consumer who chooses to be a borrower. That is, the endowment point is E and the

TABLE 9.1   Sara's Desire for Consumption Smoothing

	Week 1 Coconuts	*Week 2 Coconuts*	*Total Consumption*
Bundle 1	5	15	20
Bundle 2	17	3	20
Preferred bundle	11	9	20

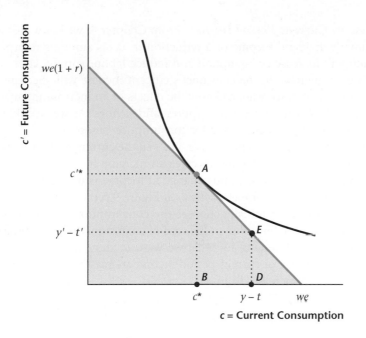

FIGURE 9.3
A Consumer Who Is a Lender

The optimal consumption bundle for the consumer is at point *A*, where the marginal rate of substitution (minus the slope of an indifference curve) is equal to $1 + r$ (minus the slope of the lifetime budget constraint). The consumer is a lender, as the consumption bundle chosen implies positive savings, with *E* being the endowment point.

consumer chooses point *A*, where $(c, c') = (c^*, c'^*)$. Here, the quantity the consumer borrows in the first period is $-s = c^* - y + t$, or the distance *DB*.

In the next stage in our analysis, we consider some experiments that will tell us how the consumer responds to changes in current income, future income, and interest rates.

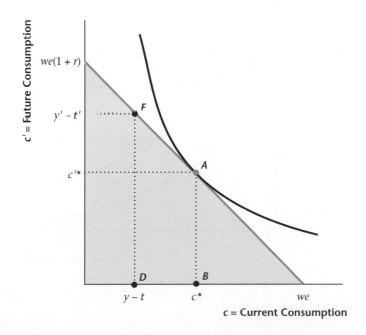

FIGURE 9.4
A Consumer Who Is a Borrower

The optimal consumption bundle is at point *A*. Since current consumption exceeds current disposable income, saving is negative, and so the consumer is a borrower.

An Increase in Current-Period Income   From Chapter 4, we know that an increase in a consumer's dividend income or a reduction in taxes amounts to a pure income effect, which will increase consumption and reduce labour supply. Here, we want to focus on how an increase in the consumer's current income will affect intertemporal decisions. In particular, we want to know the effects of an increase in current income on current consumption, future consumption, and savings. As we will show, these effects will reflect the consumer's desire for consumption smoothing.

Suppose that, holding the interest rate, taxes in the current and future periods, and future income constant, a consumer receives an increase in period 1 income. Asking about the consumer's response to this change in income is much like asking how an individual would react to winning a lottery. In Figure 9.5 the initial endowment point is at E_1, and the consumer initially chooses the consumption bundle represented by point A. In this figure we have shown the case of a consumer who is initially a lender, but it will not make a difference for what we want to show if the consumer is a borrower. We will suppose that current-period income increases from y_1 to y_2. The result is that lifetime wealth increases from

$$we_1 = y_1 + \frac{y'}{1 + r} - t - \frac{t'}{1 + r}$$

to

$$we_2 = y_2 + \frac{y'}{1 + r} - t - \frac{t'}{1 + r},$$

FIGURE 9.5

The Effects of an Increase in Current Income for a Lender

When current income increases, lifetime wealth increases from we_1 to we_2. The lifetime budget constraint shifts out, and the slope of the constraint remains unchanged, since the real interest rate does not change. Initially, the consumer chooses A, and he or she chooses B after current income increases. Current and future consumption both increase (both goods are normal), and current consumption increases by less than the increase in current income.

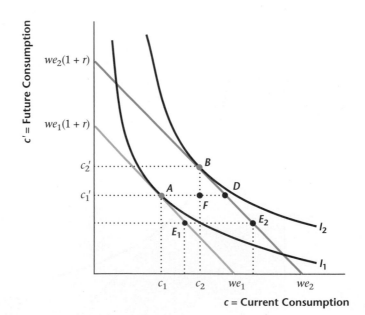

and the change in lifetime wealth is

$$\Delta we = we_2 - we_1 = y_2 - y_1.$$

The effect is that the budget constraint shifts to the right by the amount $y_2 - y_1$, which is the distance $E_1 E_2$, where E_2 is the new endowment point. Note that the slope of the budget constraint remains unchanged, as the real interest rate is the same.

Since current-period consumption and future consumption are normal goods, the consumer will now choose a consumption bundle represented by a point like B, where consumption in both periods has risen from the previous values. Current consumption increases from c_1 to c_2, and future consumption increases from c_1' to c_2'. Thus, if current income increases, the consumer wants to spread this additional income over both periods and not consume it all in the current period. In Figure 8.5 the increase in current income is the distance AD, while the increase in current consumption is the distance AF, which is less than the distance AD. The change in the consumer's savings is given by

$$\Delta s = \Delta y - \Delta t - \Delta c, \tag{9.9}$$

and since $\Delta t = 0$, and $\Delta y > \Delta c > 0$, we have $\Delta s > 0$. Thus, an increase in current income causes an increase in consumption in both periods and an increase in savings.

Our analysis tells us that any one consumer who receives an increase in his or her current income will consume more during the current period, but will also save some of the increase in income so as to consume more in the future as well. This behaviour, which arises because of the consumer's desire to smooth consumption over time, is certainly reasonable. For example, consider a consumer, Paul, who is currently 25 years of age and wins $1 million in a lottery. Paul could certainly spend all his winnings on consumption goods within the current year and save nothing, but it would seem more sensible if he consumed a small part of his winnings in the current year and saved a substantial fraction in order to consume more for the rest of his life.

If all consumers act to smooth their consumption relative to their income, aggregate consumption should likewise be smooth relative to aggregate income. Indeed, this prediction of our theory is consistent with what we see in the data. Recall from Chapter 3 that real aggregate consumption is less variable than real GDP. The difference in variability between aggregate consumption and GDP is even larger if we take account of the fact that some of what is included in aggregate consumption is not consumption in the economic sense. For example, purchases of new automobiles are included in the NIEA as consumption of durables, but the purchase of a car might more appropriately be included in investment, since the car will yield a flow of consumption services over its lifetime. In the data, expenditures on consumer durables are much more variable than actual consumption, measured as the flow of consumption services that consumers receive from goods. In Figure 9.6 we show the percentage deviations from trend in the consumption of durables, in the consumption of nondurables and services, and in GDP for the period 1961–2011. Clearly, the consumption of durables is much more variable than aggregate income, while the consumption of nondurables and services is much less variable than income. Since the consumption of nondurables and services

FIGURE 9.6

Percentage Deviations from Trend in GDP and Consumption, 1961–2011

Consumption of durables and semi-durables is much more variable than GDP, which is much more variable than consumption of nondurables and services. The consumption-smoothing behaviour of consumers is clearly reflected in the behaviour of nondurables and services.

Source: Adapted from the Statistics Canada CANSIM database, Series v1992069, v1992045, v1992046, v1992047, v1992048.

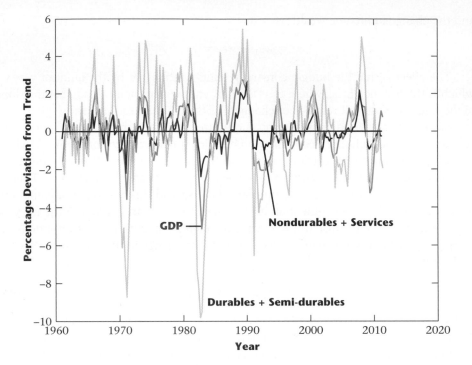

comes fairly close to measuring a flow of consumption services, the variability in this component of consumption reflects more accurately the tendency of consumers to smooth consumption.

Though aggregate data on consumption and income is clearly qualitatively consistent with consumption-smoothing behaviour on the part of consumers, macroeconomists have been interested in the quantitative match between consumption theory and the data. The question is whether measured consumption is smooth *enough* relative to measured income to be consistent with theory. Generally, the conclusion from empirical work is that, although the theory points in the right direction, there is some **excess variability** of aggregate consumption relative to aggregate income. That is, although consumption is smoother than income, as the theory predicts, consumption is not quite smooth enough to tightly match the theory.[1]

Thus, the theory needs some more work if it is to fit the facts. Two possible explanations for the excess variability in consumption are the following:

1. *There are imperfections in the credit market.* Our theory assumes that a consumer can smooth consumption by borrowing or lending at the market real interest rate *r*. In reality, consumers cannot borrow all they would like at the market interest rate, and market loan interest rates are typically higher than the interest rates at which consumers lend. As a result, in reality consumers may have less ability to

---

[1]See, for example, Orazio P. Attanasio, 1999, "Consumption," in J. B. Taylor and M. Woodford (eds.), *Handbook of Macroeconomics*, Elsevier, 741–812.

smooth consumption than they do in the theory. We could refine the model by introducing credit market imperfections, but this would make the model considerably more complicated. We will further discuss credit market imperfections later in this chapter.

2. *When all consumers are trying to smooth consumption in the same way simultaneously, this will change market prices.* The consumption-smoothing theory we have studied thus far does not take into account the interaction of consumers with each other and with other sectors of the economy. All consumers may want to smooth consumption over time, but aggregate consumption must fall during a recession because aggregate income is lower then, and, similarly, aggregate consumption must rise in a boom. The way that consumers are reconciled to having high consumption when output is high, and low consumption when output is low, is through movements in market prices, including the market interest rate. Shortly, we will study how individual consumers react to changes in the real interest rate.

An Increase in Future Income   Although a consumer's response to a change in his or her current income is informative about consumption smoothing behaviour, we are also interested in the effects on consumer behaviour of a change in income that is expected to occur in the future. Suppose, for example, that Jennifer is about to finish her university degree in four months, and she lines up a job that will start as soon as she graduates. On landing the job, Jennifer's future income has increased considerably. How would she react to this future increase in income? Clearly, this would imply that she would plan to increase her future consumption, but Jennifer also likes to smooth consumption, so she should want to have higher current consumption as well. She can consume more currently by borrowing against her future income and repaying the loan when she starts working.

In Figure 9.7 we show the effects of an increase for the consumer in future income, from y_1' to y_2'. This has an effect similar to the increase in current income on lifetime wealth, with lifetime wealth increasing from we_1 to we_2, and shifting the budget constraint up by the amount $y_2' - y_1'$. Initially, the consumer chooses consumption bundle A, and he or she chooses B after the increase in future income. Note again that both current and future consumption increase; current consumption increases from c_1 to c_2, and future consumption increases from c_1' to c_2'. The increase in future consumption, which is the distance AF in Figure 9.7, is less than the increase in future income, which is the distance AD. This occurs because, as with the increase in current income, the consumer wants to smooth consumption over time. Rather than spend all the increase in income in the future, the consumer saves less in the current period so that current consumption can increase. The change in saving is given by Equation (9.9), where $\Delta t = \Delta y = 0$, and since $\Delta c > 0$, we must have $\Delta s < 0$—that is, savings decreases.

In the case of an expected increase in future income, the consumer acts to smooth consumption over time, just as when he or she receives an increase in current income. The difference is that an increase in future income leads to smoothing backward, with the consumer saving less in the current period so that current consumption can increase, whereas an increase in current income leads to smoothing forward, with the consumer saving more in the current period so that future consumption can increase.

FIGURE 9.7

An Increase in Future Income

An increase in future income increases lifetime wealth from we_1 to we_2, shifting the lifetime budget constraint up and leaving its slope unchanged. The consumer initially chooses point A, and he or she chooses B after the budget constraint shifts. Future consumption increases by less than the increase in future income, saving decreases, and current consumption increases.

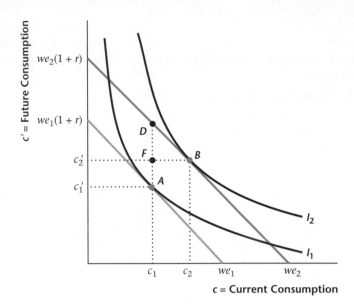

Temporary and Permanent Changes in Income When a consumer receives a change in his or her current income, it matters a great deal for his or her current consumption–savings choice whether this change in income is temporary or permanent. For example, Allen would respond quite differently to receiving a windfall increase in his income of $1000, say by winning a lottery, as opposed to receiving a $1000 yearly salary increase that he expects to continue indefinitely. In the case of the lottery winnings, we might expect that Allen would increase current consumption by only a small amount, saving most of the lottery winnings to increase consumption in the future. If Allen received a permanent increase in his income, as in the second case, we would expect his increase in current consumption to be much larger.

The difference between the effects of temporary and permanent changes in income on consumption was articulated by Milton Friedman in his **permanent income hypothesis**.[2] Friedman argued that a primary determinant of a consumer's current consumption is his or her permanent income, which is closely related to the concept of lifetime wealth in our model. Changes in income that are temporary yield small changes in permanent income (lifetime wealth), which have small effects on current consumption, whereas changes in income that are permanent have large effects on permanent income (lifetime wealth) and current consumption.

In our model, we can show the effects of temporary versus permanent changes in income by examining an increase in income that occurs only in the current period versus an increase in income occurring in the current period *and* the future period. In Figure 9.8 the budget constraint of the consumer is initially AB, and he or she chooses the consumption bundle represented by point H on indifference curve I_1. Then, the consumer experiences a temporary increase in income, with current income increasing from y_1 to y_2, so that the budget constraint shifts out to DE. The real interest rate does

---

[2]See M. Friedman, 1957, *A Theory of the Consumption Function*, Princeton University Press, Princeton, NJ.

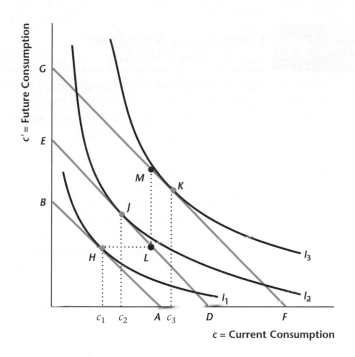

FIGURE 9.8
Temporary versus Permanent Increases in Income
A temporary increase in income is an increase in current income, with the budget constraint shifting from *AB* to *DE*, and the optimal consumption bundle changing from *H* to *J*. When there is a permanent increase in income, current and future income both increase, and the budget constraint shifts from *AB* to *FG*, with the optimal consumption bundle changing from *H* to *K*.

not change, so the slope of the budget constraint remains constant. The distance HL is equal to the change in current income, $y_2 - y_1$. Now, the consumer chooses point J on indifference curve I_2, and we know from our previous discussion that the increase in current consumption, $c_2 - c_1$, is less than the increase in current income, $y_2 - y_1$, as saving increases because of consumption-smoothing behaviour.

Now, suppose that the increase in income is permanent. We interpret this as an equal increase of $y_2 - y_1$ in both current and future income. That is, initially future income is y_1' and it increases to y_2' with $y_2' - y_1' = y_2 - y_1$. Now, the budget constraint is given by FG in Figure 9.8, where the upward shift in the budget constraint from DE is the distance LM, which is $y_2' - y_1' = y_2 - y_1$. The consumer now chooses point K on indifference curve I_3. At point K, current consumption is c_3. Given that current and future consumption are normal goods, current consumption increases from point H to point J and from point J to point K. Therefore, if income increases permanently, this has a larger effect on current consumption than if income increases only temporarily. Note that if income increases only temporarily, there is an increase in saving, so that consumption does not increase as much as income. However, if there is a permanent increase in income, there need not be an increase in saving, and current consumption could increase as much as or more than income.

Why is it important that consumers will respond differently to temporary and permanent changes in their income? Suppose that the government is considering cutting taxes, and this tax cut could be temporary or permanent. For now, ignore how the government will go about financing this tax cut (we will consider this later in the chapter). If consumers receive a tax cut that increases lifetime wealth, then this will increase aggregate consumption. However, if consumers expect the tax cut to be temporary, the increase in consumption will be much smaller than if they expect the tax cut to be permanent.

| THEORY CONFRONTS THE DATA | 9.1 | *Consumption Smoothing and the Stock Market* |

Thus far, our theory tells us that in response to increases in their lifetime wealth, consumers will increase consumption, but in such a way that their consumption path is smoothed over time. One way in which consumers' wealth changes is through variation in the prices of stocks traded on organized stock exchanges, such as the Toronto Stock Exchange.

How should we expect aggregate consumption to respond to a change in stock prices? On the one hand, publicly traded stock is not a large fraction of national wealth. That is, a large fraction of national wealth includes the housing stock and the capital of privately held companies, which are not traded on the stock market. Therefore, even if there is a large change in stock prices, this need not represent a large change in national wealth. On the other hand, financial theory tells us that when the price of a stock changes, we should expect this price change to be permanent.

Financial theory tells us (with some qualifications) that stock prices are martingales. A **martingale** has the property that the best prediction of its value tomorrow is its value today. In the case of a stock price, the best prediction of tomorrow's stock price is today's stock price. The reason that stock prices follow martingales is that if they did not, then there would be opportunities for investors to make profits. That is, suppose that a stock price does not follow a martingale, and suppose first that the best forecast is that tomorrow's stock price will be higher than today's stock price. Then, investors would want to buy the stock today so as to make a profit by selling it tomorrow. Ultimately, this would force up the market price of the stock today, to the point where the price today is what it is expected to be tomorrow. Similarly, if the price of the stock today were greater than what the stock's price was expected to be tomorrow, investors would want to sell the stock today so they could buy it at a cheaper price tomorrow. In this case, investors' actions would force the current stock price down to the point where it was equal to its expected price tomorrow. Since the current price of a stock is the best forecast of its future price, any change in prices is a surprise, and this change in prices is expected to be permanent.

A change in the overall value of the stock market does not represent a change in a large fraction of national wealth, and this would tend to dampen the effect of price movements in the stock market on aggregate consumption. However, the fact that any change in stock prices is expected to be permanent will tend to amplify the effects of changes in stock prices, as we know that permanent changes in wealth have larger effects on consumption than do temporary changes in wealth. What do the data tell us? In Figure 9.9 we show a time-series plot of the percentage deviations from trend in the Toronto Stock Exchange composite price index (relative to the GDP price deflator) and percentage deviations from trend in real consumption of nondurables and services. The data plotted are quarterly data for the period 1961–2011. Here, note in particular that the stock price index is highly volatile relative to consumption. On the one hand, deviations from trend in the stock price

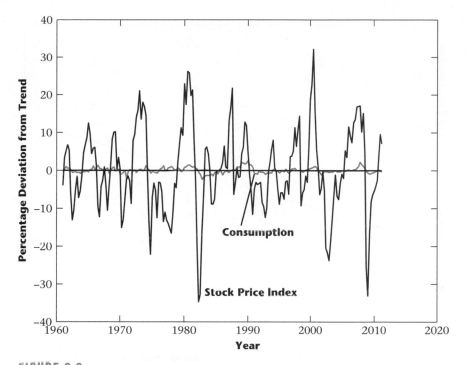

FIGURE 9.9

Stock Prices and Consumption of Nondurables and Services, 1961–2011

The graph shows that deviations from trend in stock prices (the black line) and in consumption of nondurables and services (the coloured line) are positively correlated. When there is a positive (negative) deviation from trend in stock prices, there tends to be a positive (negative) deviation from trend in consumption.

Source: Adapted from the Statistics Canada CANSIM database, Series v1992047, v1997756, v1992048, v122620.

index of 10% to 20% are not uncommon, and the stock price index dipped more than 30% below trend in the 1980s. However, a close examination of Figure 9.9 will indicate that deviations from trend in the stock price index are positively correlated with deviations from trend in consumption. Figure 9.10 shows this more clearly, where we show the same data as in Figure 9.9, except in a scatter plot. The positively sloped line in Figure 9.10 is the best fit to the data in the scatter plot, indicating that the stock price and consumption are positively correlated. The data indicate that the stock market is potentially an important channel for the effects of changes in wealth on aggregate consumption behaviour. The fact that consumption and stock prices move together is consistent with the notion that shocks to the financial system that are reflected in the prices of publicly traded stocks can cause significant movements in aggregate consumption. Though the value of publicly traded stock is not a large part of national wealth, the fact that stock price changes are expected to be permanent potentially contributes to the influence of the stock market on consumption behaviour.

FIGURE 9.10

Scatter Plot of Percentage Deviations from Trend in Consumption of Nondurables and Services versus Percentage Deviations from Trend in a Stock Price Index

The black line represents the best statistical fit to the scatter plot. Since this line is positively sloped, the two variables are positively correlated.

Source: Adapted from the Statistics Canada CANSIM database, Series v1992047, v1997756, v1992048, v122620.

An Increase in the Real Interest Rate To this point, we have examined how changes in a consumer's current income and future income affect his or her choices of consumption in the current and future periods. These are changes that shift the consumer's budget constraint but do not change its slope. In this subsection, we will study how the consumer responds to a change in the real interest rate, which will change the slope of the budget constraint. Changes in the market real interest rate will ultimately be an important part of the mechanism by which shocks to the economy, fiscal policy, and monetary policy affect real activity, as we will show in Chapters 12 to 14. A key channel for interest rate effects on real activity will be through aggregate consumption.

Since $\dfrac{1}{1 + r}$ is the relative price of future consumption goods in terms of current consumption goods, a change in the real interest rate effectively changes this intertemporal relative price. In Chapter 4, in the consumer's work–leisure choice problem, a change in the real wage was effectively a change in the relative price of leisure and consumption, and a change in the real wage had income and substitution effects. Here, in our two-period framework, a change in the real interest rate will also have income and sub-stitution effects in its influence on consumption in the present and the future.

Suppose the consumer faces an increase in the real interest rate, with taxes and income held constant in both periods. Note first that this will make the budget con-straint steeper, since the slope of the budget constraint is $-(1 + r)$. Further, under the assumption that the consumer never has to pay a tax larger than his or her income, so that $y' - t' > 0$, an increase in r will decrease lifetime wealth, we, as shown in Equation (9.5). Also from Equation (9.5), we have

$$we(1 + r) = (y - t)(1 + r) + y' - t',$$

and since $y > t$, there will be an increase in $we(1 + r)$ when r increases. Therefore, we know that an increase in r will cause the budget constraint to pivot, as in Figure 9.11, where r increases from r_1 to r_2, resulting in a decrease in we from we_1 to we_2. We also know that the budget constraint must pivot around the endowment point E, since it must always be possible for the consumer to consume his or her disposable income in each period, no matter what the real interest rate is.

A change in r results in a change in the relative price of consumption in the cur-rent and future periods; that is, an increase in r causes future consumption to become cheaper relative to current consumption. A higher interest rate implies that the return on savings is higher, so that more future consumption goods can be obtained for a given sacrifice of current consumption goods. As well, for a given loan in the first period, the consumer will have to forgo more future consumption goods when the loan is repaid. We can use what we learned about income and substitution effects in Chapter 4 to understand how an increase in the real interest rate will affect the con-sumer's behaviour. However, it turns out that the income effects of an increase in the real interest rate work in different directions for lenders and borrowers, which is what we want to show next.

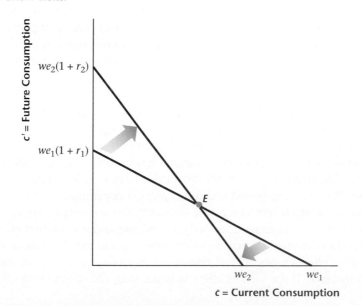

FIGURE 9.11

An Increase in the Real Interest Rate

An increase in the real interest rate causes the lifetime budget constraint of the consumer to become steeper and to pivot around the endowment point E.

FIGURE 9.12

An Increase in the Real Interest Rate for a Lender
When the real interest rate increases for a lender, the substitution effect is the movement from A to D, and the income effect is the movement from D to B. Current consumption and saving may rise or fall, while future consumption increases.

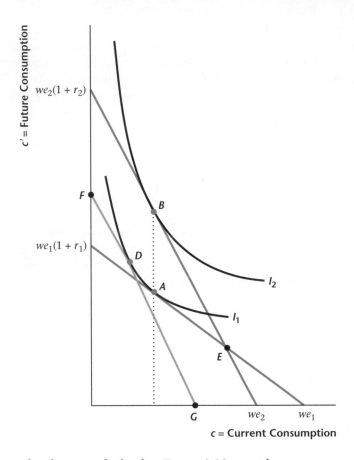

First, consider the case of a lender. Figure 9.12 considers a consumer who is initially a lender and faces an increase in the market real interest rate from r_1 to r_2. Initially, lifetime wealth is we_1, and this changes to we_2. The budget constraint pivots around the endowment point E. Initially, the consumer chose the consumption bundle A, and we suppose that the consumer chooses B after the increase in the real interest rate. To find the substitution effect of the real interest rate increase, we draw an artificial budget constraint FG, which has the same slope as the new budget constraint and is just tangent to the initial indifference curve I_1. Thus, we are taking wealth away from the consumer until he or she is as well off as before the increase in r. Then, the movement from A to D is a pure substitution effect, and in moving from A to D future consumption increases and current consumption decreases, as future consumption has become cheaper relative to current consumption. The remaining effect, the movement from D to B, is a pure income effect, which causes both current-period and future-period consumption to increase. (Recall that we assumed that current and future consumption are normal goods.) Therefore, future consumption must increase, as both the income and substitution effects work in the same direction. However, current-period consumption may increase or decrease, as the substitution effect causes current consumption to decrease, and the income effect causes it to increase. If the income effect is larger than the substitution effect, current consumption increases. Note that the effect on savings depends on the change in current consumption, as we are holding constant current disposable income. Thus, saving may increase or decrease. Saving increases if the substitution effect is larger than the income effect, and saving decreases otherwise. An increase in the real interest rate makes saving more attractive, since the relative price of future consumption is lower (the substitution effect), but it makes saving less attractive, since there is a positive income effect on period 1 consumption that will tend to reduce saving.

Consider the following example, which shows the intuition behind the income and substitution effects of a change in the real interest rate. Suppose Christine is currently a lender whose disposable income in the current year is $40 000. She currently saves 30% of her current income, and she faces a real interest rate of 5%. Her income next year will also be $40 000 (in current-year dollars), and so initially she consumes $0.7 \times \$40\ 000 = \$28\ 000$ this year, and she consumes $\$40\ 000 + (1 + 0.05) \times \$12\ 000 = \$52\ 600$ next year. Now, suppose that the real interest rate rises to 10%. How should Christine respond? If she continues to consume $28 000 in the current year and saves $12 000, she will have future consumption of $53 200, an increase over initial future consumption, reflecting the substitution effect. However, if she consumes the same amount next year, she can now save less in the current year to achieve the same result. That is, she could save $11 454 in the current year, which would imply that she could consume $52 600 next year. Then, she consumes $\$40\ 000 - \$11\ 454 = \$28\ 546$, which is more than before, reflecting the income effect. What Christine will do depends on her own preferences and how strong the relative income and substitution effects are for her as an individual.

Now consider the effects of an increase in r for a borrower. In Figure 9.13, r increases from r_1 to r_2, and lifetime wealth changes from we_1 to we_2. The endowment point is at E, and the consumer initially chooses consumption bundle A; then, he or she chooses B after r increases. Again, we can separate the movement from A to B into substitution and income effects by drawing an artificial budget constraint FG, which is parallel to the new budget constraint and tangent to the initial indifference curve I_1. Therefore, we are essentially compensating the consumer with extra wealth to make him or her as well off as initially when facing the higher interest rate. Then, the substitution effect is the movement from A to D, and the income effect is the movement from D to B. Here, the substitution effect is for future consumption to rise and current consumption to fall, just as was the case for a lender. However, the income effect in this case is negative for both current consumption and future consumption. As a result, current consumption falls for the borrower, but future consumption may rise or fall, depending on how strong the opposing substitution and income effects are. Savings must rise as current consumption falls and current disposable income is held constant.

As an example, suppose that Christopher is initially a borrower whose income in the current year and next year is $40 000 (in current-year dollars). Initially, Christopher takes out a loan of $20 000 in the current year, so that he can consume $60 000 in the current year. The real interest rate is 5%, so that the principal and interest on his loan is $21 000, and he consumes $19 000 next year. Now, suppose alternatively that the real interest rate is 10%. If Christopher holds constant his consumption in the future, this must imply that

FIGURE 9.13

**An Increase in the Real
Interest Rate for a Borrower**
When the real interest rate
increases for a borrower,
the substitution effect is
the movement from *A* to
D, and the income effect
is the movement from *D*
to *B*. Current consumption
decreases, saving increases,
and future consumption may
rise or fall.

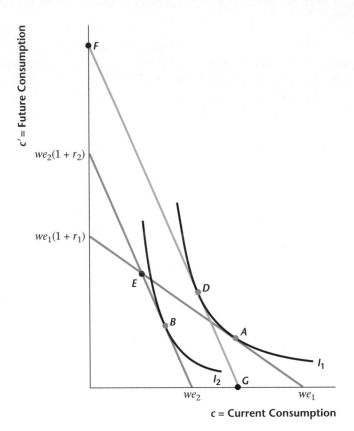

his current consumption will go down, reflecting the negative income effect. That is, if he continues to consume $19 000 next year, given a real interest rate of 10%, he can borrow only $19 091 this year, which implies that his current-year consumption is $59 091.

For both lenders and borrowers, there is an **intertemporal substitution effect** of an increase in the real interest rate. That is, a higher real interest rate lowers the relative price of future consumption in terms of current consumption, and this leads to a substitution of future consumption for current consumption and therefore to an increase in savings. In much of macroeconomics, we are interested in aggregate effects, but the above analysis tells us that there are potentially confounding income effects in determining the effect of an increase in the real interest rate on aggregate consumption. The population consists of many consumers, some of whom are lenders and some borrowers. Though consumption will decrease for each borrower when the real interest rate goes up, what happens to the consumption of lenders depends on the strength of opposing income and substitution effects. There is a tendency for the negative income effects on the consumption of borrowers to offset the positive income effects on the consumption of lenders, leaving us with only the substitution effects. However, there is no theoretical guarantee that aggregate consumption will fall when the real interest rate rises.

Tables 9.2 and 9.3 summarize the above discussion of the effects of an increase in the real interest rate.

TABLE 9.2   Effects of an Increase in the Real Interest Rate for a Lender

Current consumption	?
Future consumption	Increases
Current savings	?

TABLE 9.3   Effects of an Increase in the Real Interest Rate for a Borrower

Current consumption	Decreases
Future consumption	?
Current savings	Increases

An Example: Perfect Complements   A convenient example to work with is the case where a consumer has preferences with the perfect complements property. Recall from Chapter 4 that if two goods are perfect complements, they are always consumed in fixed proportions. In the case of current consumption and future consumption, the perfect complements property implies that the consumer will always choose c and c' such that

$$c' = ac, \qquad (9.10)$$

where a is a positive constant. In Figure 9.14 the consumer's indifference curves, for example I_1 and I_2, are L-shaped with the right angles on the line $c' = ac$. Perfect complementarity is an extreme case of a desire for consumption smoothing. The consumer will never want to deviate from having current and future consumption in fixed proportions, and the parameter a is a measure of the consumer's patience. A patient

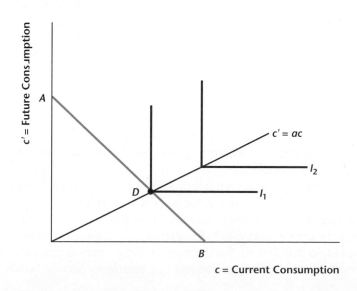

FIGURE 9.14

Example with Perfect Complements Preferences

The consumer desires current and future consumption in fixed proportions, with $c' = ac$. With indifference curves representing perfect complementarity between current and future consumption, the optimal consumption bundle is at point D on the lifetime budget constraint AB.

consumer has a high value of a, and an impatient consumer has a low value of a. The consumer's budget constraint is AB in the figure, which is described by the equation

$$c + \frac{c'}{1 + r} = we, \qquad (9.11)$$

where

$$we = y - t + \frac{y' - t'}{1 + r}. \qquad (9.12)$$

In Figure 9.14 the optimal consumption bundle will be at such a point as D, which is on the consumer's budget constraint, and also on the line $c' = ac$. Therefore, we can solve algebraically for current and future consumption c and c', respectively, by solving the two Equations (9.10) and (9.11) for the two variables c and c', given r and we. Using substitution, we get

$$c = \frac{we(1 + r)}{1 + r + a}, \qquad (9.13)$$

$$c' = \frac{awe(1 + r)}{1 + r + a}, \qquad (9.14)$$

substituting for we in (9.13) and (9.14) by using (9.12), we obtain

$$c = \frac{(y - t)(1 + r) + y' - t'}{1 + r + a}, \qquad (9.15)$$

$$c' = a\left[\frac{(y - t)(1 + r) + y' - t'}{1 + r + a}\right]. \qquad (9.16)$$

Note in particular from Equations (9.15) and (9.16) that current and future consumption increase with current income, y, and with future income, y'. The effects of a change in the interest rate, r, are more complicated, but essentially the effect of an increase in r on c and c' depends only on whether the consumer is a lender or a borrower. This is because there are no substitution effects when preferences have the perfect complements property. We will explore this further in the problems at the end of this chapter.

GOVERNMENT

Now that we have studied how consumers behave, to complete our description of the model we need only describe what the government does. We can then explore the equilibrium effects of tax policy.

We will suppose that the government wants to purchase G consumption goods in the current period and G' units in the future period, with these quantities of government purchases given exogenously. The aggregate quantity of taxes collected by the government in the current period is T. Recall that there are m consumers who each pay a current tax of t, so that $T = mt$. Similarly, in the future period total taxes are equal to T', and we have $T' = mt'$. The government can borrow by issuing bonds. Recall that government bonds and private bonds are indistinguishable, with these bonds all bearing the same real interest rate, r. Letting B denote the quantity of government bonds issued in the current period, the government's current-period budget constraint is

$$G = T + B; \tag{9.17}$$

that is, government spending is financed through taxes and the issue of bonds. Put another way, the current-period government deficit, $G - T$, is financed by issuing bonds. In the future period, the government's budget constraint is

$$G' + (1 + r)B = T'. \tag{9.18}$$

The left-hand side of Equation (9.18) is total government outlays in the future, consisting of future government purchases and the principal and interest on the government bonds issued in the current period. These government outlays are financed through future taxes, the quantity on the right-hand side of Equation (9.18). Note that the government's budget constraints allow for the possibility that $B < 0$. If $B < 0$, this would imply that the government was a lender to the private sector, rather than a borrower from it. Note that in practice the government engages in direct lending to the private sector, and it also issues debt to private economic agents, so that it is a lender *and* a borrower.

Recall that when we analyzed a consumer's budget constraint, we took the budget constraints for the current and future periods and collapsed them into a single lifetime budget constraint. Here, we can accomplish something similar, in taking the government's budget constraints expressed in Equations (9.17) and (9.18) and collapsing them into a single **government present-value budget constraint**. We obtain this constraint by first solving Equation (9.18) for B to get

$$B = \frac{T' - G'}{1 + r},$$

and then substituting in Equation (9.17) for B to get

$$G + \frac{G'}{1 + r} = T + \frac{T'}{1 + r}. \tag{9.19}$$

Equation (9.19) is the government present-value budget constraint, and it states that the present value of government purchases must equal the present value of taxes. This is similar to the consumer's lifetime budget constraint, which states that the present value of consumption is equal to the present value of lifetime disposable income. An interpretation of the government present-value budget constraint is that the government must eventually pay off all of its debt by taxing its citizens.

COMPETITIVE EQUILIBRIUM

Now that we have described the behaviour of the consumers and the government in our model, we can proceed with the final step in putting the model into working order, which is to specify how a competitive equilibrium is achieved.

The market in which the m consumers in this economy and the government interact is the credit market, a market in which consumers and the government can borrow and lend. In trading in the credit market, consumers and the government are effectively trading future consumption goods for current consumption goods. Recall that the relative price at which future consumption goods trade for current consumption goods is $\frac{1}{1+r}$, which is determined by the real interest rate, r.

In a competitive equilibrium for this two-period economy, three conditions must hold:

1. Each consumer chooses first- and second-period consumption and savings optimally given the real interest rate, r.
2. The government present-value budget constraint, Equation (9.19), holds.
3. The credit market clears.

The credit market clears when the net quantity that consumers want to lend in the current period is equal to the quantity that the government wants to borrow. Letting S^p denote the aggregate quantity of private savings—that is, the savings of consumers—the credit market equilibrium condition is

$$S^p = B, \tag{9.20}$$

or the aggregate quantity of private savings is equal to the quantity of debt issued by the government in the current period. Equation (9.20) also states that national saving, which is equal to aggregate private saving minus B, is equal to zero in equilibrium. Recall from Chapter 2 that a national income accounts identity states that $S^p + S^g = I + CA$, where S^g is government savings, I is investment, and CA is the current account surplus. Here, $S^g = -B$, $I = 0$ since there is no capital accumulation in this model, and $CA = 0$ since this is a closed economy model. Also recall that $S = S^p + S^g$, where S is national saving.

The equilibrium condition, Equation (9.20), implies that

$$Y = C + G, \tag{9.21}$$

where Y is aggregate income in the current period (the sum of incomes across all m consumers) and C is aggregate consumption in the current period (the sum of consumptions across all m consumers). Recall from Chapter 2 that Equation (9.21) is the income–expenditure identity for this economy, since there is no investment and no interaction with the rest of the world (net exports equal zero). To see why Equation (9.21) follows from Equation (9.20), note that

$$S^p = Y - C - T; \tag{9.22}$$

that is, aggregate private saving is equal to current-period income minus aggregate current consumption, minus aggregate current taxes. Also, from the government's current-period budget constraint, Equation (9.17), we have

$$B = G - T. \tag{9.23}$$

Then, substituting in Equation (9.20) for S^p from Equation (9.22) and for B from Equation (9.23), we get

$$Y - C - T = G - T,$$

or, rearranging,

$$Y = C + G.$$

This result will prove to be useful in the next section, as the economy can be shown to be in a competitive equilibrium if *either* Equation (9.20) or Equation (9.21) holds.

The Ricardian Equivalence Theorem

From Chapter 5, recall that an increase in government spending comes at a cost, in that it crowds out private consumption expenditures. However, in Chapter 5, we could not disentangle the effects of taxation from the effects of government spending, since the government was unable to borrow in the model considered there. That is certainly not true here, where we can independently evaluate the effects of changes in government spending and in taxes.

What we want to show is a key result in macroeconomics, called the Ricardian equivalence theorem. This theorem states that a change in the timing of taxes by the government is neutral. By neutral, we mean that in equilibrium a change in current taxes, exactly offset in present-value terms by an equal and opposite change in future taxes, has no effect on the real interest rate or on the consumption of individual consumers. This is a very strong result, as it says that there is a sense in which government deficits do not matter, which seems to run counter to standard intuition. As we will see, however, this is an important starting point for thinking about why government deficits *do* matter, and a key message that comes from the logic of the Ricardian equivalence theorem is that *a tax cut is not a free lunch.*

DEFINITION

The Ricardian Equivalence Theorem states that if current and future government spending are held constant, a change in current taxes with an equal and opposite change in the present value of future taxes leaves the equilibrium real interest rate and the consumptions of individuals unchanged.

To show why the Ricardian equivalence theorem holds in this model, we need only make some straightforward observations about the lifetime budget constraints of consumers and the government's present-value budget constraint. First, because each of the m consumers shares an equal amount of the total tax burden in the current and future periods, with $T = mt$ and $T' = mt'$, substituting in the government's present-value budget constraint, Equation (9.19), gives

$$G + \frac{G'}{1 + r} = mt + \frac{mt'}{1 + r}, \tag{9.24}$$

and then rearranging we get

$$t + \frac{t'}{1 + r} = \frac{1}{m}\left(G + \frac{G'}{1 + r}\right),$$
(9.25)

which states that the present value of taxes for a single consumer is identical to the consumer's share of the present value of government spending. Next, substitute for the present value of taxes from Equation (9.25) in a consumer's lifetime budget constraint, Equation (9.4), to get

$$c + \frac{c'}{1 + r} = y + \frac{y'}{1 + r} - \frac{1}{m}\left(G + \frac{G'}{1 + r}\right).$$
(9.26)

Now, suppose that the economy is in equilibrium for a given real interest rate, r. Each consumer chooses current consumption and future consumption, c and c', respectively, to make himself or herself as well off as possible subject to the lifetime budget constraint, Equation (9.26), given that the present-value government budget constraint, Equation (9.19), holds, and the credit market clears, so current aggregate income is equal to current aggregate consumption plus current government spending, $Y = C + G$.

Next, consider an experiment in which the timing of taxes changes in such a way that the government budget constraint continues to hold at the interest rate r. That is, current taxes change by Δt for each consumer, with future taxes changing by $-\Delta t(1 + r)$ so that the government budget constraint continues to hold, from Equation (9.24). Then, from Equation (9.26), there is no change in the consumer's lifetime wealth, the right-hand side of Equation (9.26), given r, because y, y', m, G, and G' remain unaffected. Because the consumer's lifetime wealth is unaffected, then given r the consumer makes the same decisions, choosing the same quantities of current and future consumption. This is true for every consumer, so given r, aggregate consumption, C, is the same. Thus, it is still the case that $Y = C + G$, so the credit market clears. Therefore, with the new timing of taxes and the same real interest rate, each consumer is optimizing, the government's present-value budget constraint holds, and the credit market clears, so r is still the equilibrium real interest rate.

Therefore, we have shown that a change in the timing of taxes has no effect on equilibrium consumption or the real interest rate. Because each consumer faces the same budget constraint before and after the change in the timing of taxes, all consumers are no better or worse off with the change in taxes. We have, thus, demonstrated that the Ricardian equivalence theorem holds in this model.

Though the timing of taxes has no effect on consumption, welfare, or the market real interest rate, there are effects on private saving and government saving. That is, because aggregate private saving is $S^p = Y - T - C$ and government saving is $S^g = T - G$, any change in the timing of taxes that increases current taxes, T, reduces current private saving and increases government saving by equal amounts. To give a more concrete example, suppose that there is a cut in current taxes, so that $\Delta t < 0$. Then, the government must issue more debt today to finance the tax cut, and it will have to increase taxes in the future to pay off this higher debt. Consumers anticipate this, and they increase their savings by the amount of the tax cut, because this is how much extra they have to save to pay the higher taxes they will face in the future. In the credit market, there is an increase in savings by consumers, which just matches the increase in borrowing by the government, so there is no effect on borrowing and lending among consumers and, therefore, no effect on the market real interest rate.

RICARDIAN EQUIVALENCE: A NUMERICAL EXAMPLE

To give a numerical example, assume an economy with 500 consumers who are all identical. Initially, the equilibrium real interest rate is 5%, and each consumer receives income of 10 units in the current period and income of 12 units in the future period. In the current and future periods, each consumer initially pays taxes of 3 and 4 units, respectively. Lifetime wealth for each consumer is then

$$we = 10 - 3 + \frac{12 - 4}{1.05} = 14.61.$$

Suppose that each consumer initially finds it optimal to consume 6 units in the current period and 9.04 units in the future period. We can verify that this consumption bundle satisfies the consumer's lifetime budget constraint. That is,

$$6 + \frac{9.04}{1.05} = 14.61.$$

Then, each consumer saves $10 - 6 - 3 = 1$ in the current period, so that aggregate private saving is initially 500 units.

The government purchases 2000 units in the current period and 1475 units in the second period. Since aggregate taxes are 1500 in the current period and 2000 in the second period, the government borrows $B = 500$ in the current period. Thus, note that national saving is private saving plus government saving, or $500 - 500 = 0$. The government's present-value budget constraint holds as

$$2000 + \frac{1475}{1.05} = 1500 + \frac{2000}{1.05}.$$

Further, aggregate current income is 5000, while aggregate current consumption is 3000. This implies that $Y = C + G$, and so the credit market is in equilibrium.

Now, suppose that the government reduces taxes for each consumer in the current period to 2 units and increases taxes for each consumer in the future period to 5.05 units. Suppose for now that the equilibrium real interest rate is unchanged at 5%. Then, the government's present-value budget constraint still holds, as

$$2000 + \frac{1475}{1.05} = 1000 + \frac{2525}{1.05}.$$

Further, lifetime wealth for each consumer is now

$$we = 10 - 2 + \frac{12 - 5.05}{1.05} = 14.61,$$

which is identical to lifetime wealth before the current tax cut, and so each consumer will still want to consume 6 units in the current period and 9.04 units in the future period.

As a result, it must still be the case that $Y = C + G$—that is, the credit market clears. Therefore, 5% is still the equilibrium real interest rate, and each consumer's consumption decisions are unchanged.

Aggregate private saving has now increased by the amount of the tax cut, to 1000, and government saving has decreased by the amount of the tax cut, to -1000, with equilibrium national saving unchanged at 0.

RICARDIAN EQUIVALENCE: A GRAPH

We can show more generally how the Ricardian equivalence theorem works by considering the effects of a current tax cut on an individual consumer. Here, the consumer also faces an increase in taxes in the future, since the government must pay off the current debt issued to finance the tax cut. Suppose that a consumer initially faces taxes t^* and $t^{*\prime}$ in the current period and future period, respectively. In Figure 9.15 he or she has an endowment point E_1 and chooses consumption bundle A. Now, suppose there is a tax cut in the current period, so that $\Delta t < 0$. Therefore, the government must borrow Δt more in period 1 to finance the larger current government deficit, and taxes must rise for each consumer by $-\Delta t(1 + r)$ in the future period to pay off the increased government debt. The effect of this on the consumer is that lifetime wealth, *we*, remains unchanged, as the present value of taxes has not changed. The budget constraint is unaffected, and the consumer will still choose point A in Figure 9.15. What will change is that the endowment point moves to E_2; that is, the consumer has more disposable income in the current period and less disposable income in the future period because of the tax cut in the current period. Since the consumer buys the same consumption bundle, what he or she does is to save *all* of the tax cut in the current period in order to pay the higher taxes that he or she will face in the future period.

FIGURE 9.15

Ricardian Equivalence with a Cut in Current Taxes for a Lender

A current tax cut with a future increase in taxes leaves the consumer's lifetime budget constraint unchanged, and so the consumer's optimal consumption bundle remains at A. The endowment point shifts from E_1 to E_2, so that there is an increase in saving by the amount of the current tax cut.

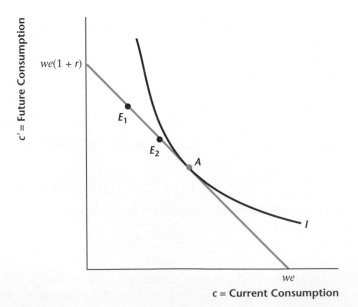

$c' = $ Future Consumption

$we(1 + r)$

E_1

E_2

A

I

we

$c = $ Current Consumption

RICARDIAN EQUIVALENCE AND CREDIT MARKET EQUILIBRIUM

Finally, we will consider a graph that shows the workings of the credit market under Ricardian equivalence. In Figure 9.16, the curve $S_1^p(r)$ denotes the private supply of credit, which is the total desired saving of private consumers given the market real interest rate r, drawn given a particular timing of taxes between the current and future periods. We have drawn $S_1^p(r)$ as being upward-sloping, under the assumption that substitution effects outweigh the income effects of changes in interest rates when we add these effects across all consumers. The government demand for credit is B_1, the exogenous supply of bonds issued by the government in the current period. The equilibrium real interest rate that clears the credit market is r_1.

Now, if the government reduces current taxes by the same amount for each individual, this results in an increase in government bonds issued from B_1 to B_2. This is not the end of the story, as savings behaviour changes for each consumer. In fact, total savings, or the supply of credit, increases for each consumer by an amount such that the credit supply curve shifts to the right by an amount $B_2 - B_1$ for each r, to $S_2^p(r)$. Therefore, the equilibrium real interest rate remains unchanged at r_1, and private savings increases by the same amount by which government savings falls.

Previously, when we looked at the effects of an increase in a consumer's current disposable income on current consumption, we determined that, because of the consumer's consumption-smoothing motive, some of the increase in disposable income would be saved. Thus, a temporary increase in disposable income would lead to a less than one-for-one increase in current consumption. In the real world, where individual consumption decisions are made over long horizons, any temporary increase in a consumer's disposable income should lead to a relatively small increase in his or her permanent income, in line with Friedman's permanent income hypothesis. Thus, Friedman's permanent income hypothesis would appear to imply that a temporary change in taxes leads to a very small change in current consumption. The Ricardian equivalence theorem carries this logic one step further by taking into account the implications of a current change in taxes for future taxes. For example, because any current tax cut must be paid for with government borrowing, this government borrowing implies higher future taxes

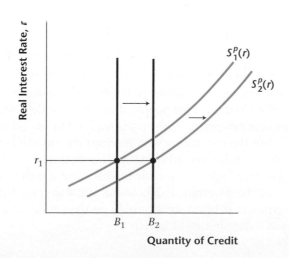

FIGURE 9.16

Ricardian Equivalance and Credit Market Equilibrium

With a decrease in current taxes, government debt increases from B_1 to B_2, and the credit supply curve shifts to the right by the same amount. The equilibrium real interest rate is unchanged, and private saving increases by an amount equal to the reduction in government saving.

to pay off the government debt. In making their lifetime wealth calculations, consumers recognize that the current tax cut is exactly offset by higher taxes in the future, and they save all of the current tax cut to pay the higher future taxes.

A key message from the Ricardian equivalence theorem is that a tax cut is not a free lunch. While a current tax cut can give all consumers higher current disposable incomes, and this seems like a good thing, consumers must pay for the current tax cut by bearing higher taxes in the future. Under the conditions studied in our model, the costs of a tax cut exactly offset the benefits, and consumers are no better off with the tax cut than without it.

RICARDIAN EQUIVALENCE AND THE BURDEN OF THE GOVERNMENT DEBT

At the individual level, debt represents a liability that reduces an individual's lifetime wealth. The Ricardian equivalence theorem implies that the same logic holds for the government debt, which the theorem tells us represents our future tax liabilities as a nation. The government debt is a burden in that it is something we owe to ourselves; the government must pay off its debt by taxing us in the future. In the model in which we explained the Ricardian equivalence theorem above, the burden of the debt is shared equally among consumers. In practice, however, many issues in fiscal policy revolve around how the burden of the government debt is shared, among the current population and between generations. To discuss these issues, we need to address the role played by four key assumptions in the above analysis of the Ricardian equivalence theorem.

1. The first key assumption is that when taxes change in the experiment we considered above, they change by the same amount for all consumers, both in the present and in the future. For example, when a particular consumer received a tax cut in the current period, this was offset by an equal and opposite (in present-value terms) increase in taxes in the future. The present-value tax burden for each individual was unchanged. Now, if some consumers received higher tax cuts than others, lifetime wealth could change for some consumers, and this would necessarily change their consumption choices and could change the equilibrium real interest rate. In the future, when the higher debt is paid off through higher future taxes, consumers might share unequally in this taxation, so that the burden of the debt might not be distributed equally. The government can redistribute wealth in society through tax policy, and the public debate concerning changes in taxes often focuses on how these tax changes affect consumers at different income levels.

2. A second key assumption in the model is that any debt issued by the government is paid off during the lifetimes of the people alive when the debt was issued. In practice, the government can postpone the taxes required to pay off the debt until long in the future, when the consumers who received the current benefits of a higher government debt are either retired or dead. That is, if the government cuts taxes, the current old receive higher disposable incomes, but it is the current young who will have to pay off the government debt in the future through higher taxes. In this sense, the government debt can be a burden on the young, and it can involve an intergenerational redistribution of wealth.

3. A third assumption made above was that taxes are lump-sum. In practice, as mentioned in Chapter 4, all taxes cause distortions, in that they change the effective relative prices of goods faced by consumers in the market. In Chapter 5, we analyzed the distortionary effects of a proportional tax on labour income. Distortions represent welfare losses from taxation. That is, if the government collects $1 million in taxes, the welfare cost to the economy will be something greater than $1 million, because of the distortions caused by taxation. The study of optimal taxation in public finance involves examining how large these welfare costs are for different kinds of taxes. For example, it could be that the welfare cost of income taxation at the margin is higher than the welfare cost of sales taxes at the margin. If the government taxes optimally, it minimizes the welfare cost of taxation, given the quantity of tax revenue it needs to generate. One of the tradeoffs made by the government in setting taxes optimally is that between current taxation and future taxation. The government debt represents a burden in part because the future taxes required to pay off the debt will cause distortions. Some work on optimal taxation by Robert Barro,[3] among others, shows that the government should act to smooth tax rates over time, so as to achieve the optimal tradeoff between current and future taxation.

4. A fourth key assumption made above is that there are **perfect credit markets**, in the sense that consumers can borrow and lend as much as they please, subject to their lifetime budget constraints, and they can borrow and lend at the same interest rate. In practice, consumers face constraints on how much they can borrow; for example, credit cards have borrowing limits, and sometimes consumers cannot borrow without collateral (as with mortgages and auto loans).[4] Consumers also typically borrow at higher interest rates than they can lend at. For example, the gap between the interest rate on a typical bank loan and the interest rate on a typical bank deposit can be 6 percentage points per annum or more. Further, the government borrows at lower interest rates than does the typical consumer. While all consumers need not be affected by **credit market imperfections**, to the extent that some consumers are credit-constrained, these consumers could be affected beneficially by a tax cut, even if there is an offsetting tax liability for these consumers in the future. In this sense, the government debt may not be a burden for some segments of the population; it may in fact increase welfare for these groups. We will explore this idea further in the next section.

The Ricardian equivalence theorem captures a key reality: current changes in taxes have consequences for future taxes. However, there are many complications associated with real-world tax policy that essentially involve shifts in the distribution of taxation across the population and in the distribution of the burden of the government debt. These complications are left out of our analysis of the Ricardian equivalence theorem.

---

[3]See R. Barro, 1979, "On the Determination of the Public Debt," *Journal of Political Economy* 87, 940–971.

[4]Collateral is the security a borrower puts up when the loan is made. If the borrower defaults on the loan, the collateral is seized by the lender. For a mortgage loan, the collateral is the house purchased with it, and for an auto loan, the collateral is the car purchased.

For some macroeconomic issues, the distributional effects of tax policy are irrelevant, but for other issues they matter a great deal. For example, if you were a macroeconomist working for a political party, how a particular tax policy affected the wealth of different consumers might be the key to your party's success. You would want to pay close attention to this detail.

THEORY CONFRONTS THE DATA	9.2	*Ricardian Equivalence, Consumption, and Taxes*

If the Ricardian equivalence theorem is a good description of reality, we might expect that fluctuations in taxes over time would have no effect on consumption. However, if credit market imperfections are important in practice, we would anticipate that taxes and consumption would be negatively correlated; increases (decreases) in taxes would tend to cause decreases (increases) in consumption.

Figure 9.17 is a time-series plot of the percentage deviations from trend in the consumption of nondurables and services and in taxes for Canada over the period 1961−2011. Here, taxes are measured as total government income minus transfers, which corresponds closely to what taxes represent in the two-period model in this chapter. As is clearly discernible in Figure 9.17, taxes and consumption are in fact positively correlated, which appears to be consistent with neither the Ricardian equivalence theorem nor the existence of significant credit market imperfections. What is going on here?

To find a natural experiment in the data that would be useful as a test of the Ricardian equivalence theorem, we would need to find a historical example of an exogenous increase in taxes. Typically, most changes in taxes in the data are not exogenous. That is, there are usually factors simultaneously affecting both consumption and taxes, and the principal factor that does so is income. When aggregate income rises (falls), consumption tends to rise (fall), and taxes tend to rise (fall) as well. We already know from our study of consumption/savings behaviour in this chapter the reasons consumption rises with income. Why do taxes rise with income? First, as income increases, governments collect more revenue from the income tax, the goods and services tax, and provincial sales taxes, among other taxes. Second, transfers will tend to decrease as income rises, for example, because employment insurance benefits fall. Transfers are simply a negative tax in the government budget.

As a result, the data in Figure 9.17 need not be interpreted as inconsistent with the Ricardian equivalence theorem. There is considerable debate in the literature about how good an approximation the theorem is to reality. In other countries there are historical events that appear to be consistent with Ricardian equivalence. For example, in 1992 there was a reduction in personal income tax withholding in the United States with no change in personal income tax liabilities. This was effectively a natural Ricardian experiment, and it seems to have led to no discernible change in aggregate consumption spending.

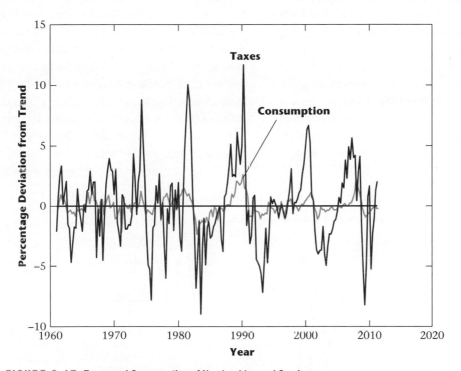

FIGURE 9.17 **Taxes and Consumption of Nondurables and Services**

The figure shows that detrended taxes (black line) and detrended consumption of nondurables and services (coloured line) are positively correlated, which appears to be inconsistent with Ricardian equivalence and with significant credit market imperfections.

Source: Adapted from the Statistics Canada CANSIM database, Series v498316, v498328, v1992047, v1992048, v498328.

9.1

Are Government Budget Deficits Sustainable?

In the model we worked with in this chapter, the government always pays off its debts. If the government chooses, it can run a deficit in the current period, but in the future it must collect enough taxes to pay off the debt. In practice, essentially all world governments are in debt, and we anticipate that this debt will never be paid off, in the sense that governments in all countries continuously issue new debt to pay off the old debt.

The level of government indebtedness varies substantially across countries. A typical measure of indebtedness is the level of government debt outstanding relative to GDP, that is, the debt/GDP ratio. In Australia, the debt/GDP ratio was 21% in 2010, and the comparable numbers for the United Kingdom, Germany, the United States, Italy, Greece, and Japan were 76%, 84%, 94%, 119%, 143%, and 220%, respectively.

Government debt rises when the government runs a deficit, and it falls when the government runs a surplus. Figure 9.18 shows the surplus for all levels of government in Canada (municipal, provincial, federal), while Figure 9.19 shows the level of government debt, indicating total government debt (all levels of government) and federal government debt. In Figure 9.18, the government surplus fell from a high of more than 4% of GDP in the early 1970s to a low of less than −8% in the early 1990s, at

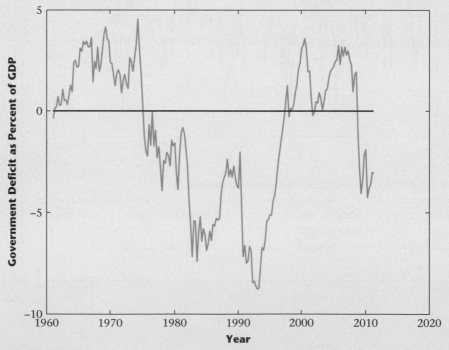

FIGURE 9.18

Total Government Surplus for Canada, 1961–2011

The figure shows the total government surplus (for all levels of government—federal, provincial, and municipal) as a percentage of GDP. Federal government fiscal reform in the 1990s increased the surplus substantially.

Source: Adapted from the Statistics Canada CANSIM database, Series v1992067, v498315.

which time the federal government instituted a fiscal reform. The surplus then increased to positive territory in the late 1990s, and the government again ran a deficit beginning in the recent recession. The pattern of deficits is reflected in government debt in Figure 9.19. When the government surplus is positive debt is falling, and while it is negative debt is rising. The 1990s federal government fiscal reforms reduced debt substantially, to a low of less than 100% of GDP, but this ratio was up to about 115% by mid-2011.

Note in Figure 9.19 that a substantial quantity of government debt outstanding is municipal and provincial government debt, which comprised less than half of total government debt in 1970, but more than half in 2011. Federal government debt in mid-2011 was about 47% of GDP. In spite of the important contributions of municipal and federal governments to total government debt in Canada, increases and decreases in total government debt in Figure 9.19 are explained mostly by increases and decreases in federal government debt.

Recall from Chapter 2 that the government surplus or, synonymously, government saving, is defined by

$$S^g = T - TR - INT - G, \qquad (9.27)$$

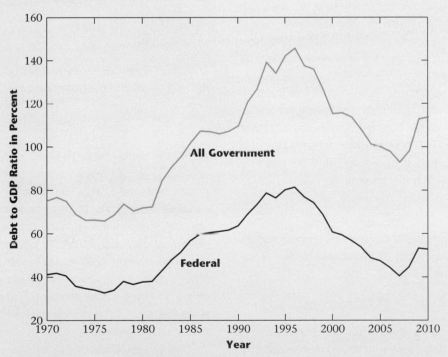

FIGURE 9.19

Total Government Debt (federal plus provincial plus municipal) and Federal Government Debt
Government debt increases when the surplus (see Figure 9.18) is negative, and decreases when the surplus is positive.

Source: Adapted from Statistics Canada CANSIM database, Series v52230574, v52230585.

where T denotes taxes, TR transfers, INT interest on the government debt, and G government expenditures on goods and services. In Equation (9.27), the quantity $T - TR - G$ is the **primary surplus**, that is, the government surplus neglecting interest payments on the government debt. The **primary deficit** is the negative of the primary surplus.

Recently some countries in southern Europe have had difficulty meeting their debt obligations. In particular, Greece would have defaulted on its debt in 2011 were it not for the intervention of European Union countries and the International Monetary Fund. Greece has a very high level of government debt—about 143% of GDP in 2010—but Japan's level of indebtedness is even higher, at 220% of GDP in 2010. Yet those who hold the Japanese debt seem confident that the Japanese government will be able to pay its debt obligations. How can such a large quantity of government debt be sustainable?

To help answer this question, it is useful to do some basic government budgeting arithmetic. Suppose that real GDP grows at a constant rate of g per year. Time begins in year zero, and t denotes the time period. If Y_0 denotes real GDP in year 0, then real GDP in year t is given by

$$Y_t = Y_0(1 + g)^t. \qquad (9.28)$$

Suppose that the primary government surplus in year t, denoted by S_t^{pr} is a constant fraction of real GDP, that is,

$$S_t^{pr} = aY_0(1 + g)^t, \qquad (9.29)$$

where a is a constant, which could be positive (if the government runs a surplus forever) or negative (if the government runs a deficit forever). Then, let B_t denote the government debt at the end of year t. Assume that the government debt is all one-year debt that has to be paid off in year $t + 1$ if it is issued in year t, and suppose that the real interest rate is a constant r forever. Then, using (9.27) and (9.29),

$$B_t = (1 + r)B_{t-1} - aY_0(1 + g)^t, \qquad (9.30)$$

that is, the new debt issued in period t, on the left-hand side of the equation, must finance the payments of principal and interest on the government debt issued in the previous period, minus the primary surplus in period t, respectively, on the right-hand side of the equation.

Next, suppose that the government runs a primary deficit forever, so that $a < 0$. Then, we can show that, in the long run, Equation (9.30) implies that the quantity of government debt in year t will converge to

$$B_t = \frac{-aY_0(1 + g)^t}{g - r}. \qquad (9.31)$$

Therefore, Equations (9.28) and (9.31) tell us that the long-run ratio of government debt to GDP is

$$\frac{B_t}{Y_t} = \frac{-a}{g - r}, \qquad (9.32)$$

so that, in the long run, this ratio depends only on the size of the primary surplus (given by a), the growth rate of real GDP, g, and the real interest rate, r. In order that the quantity of government debt not ultimately explode, it is necessary that $g > r$. Real GDP must grow faster than the real interest rate for the government to be able to sustain a primary deficit indefinitely, otherwise the interest payments on the government debt will continue to grow over time relative to GDP until those interest payments become too large to sustain.

We can use Equation (9.32) to get some idea of the quantitative implications for a country's long-run indebtedness of alternative scenarios for the economy's growth rate, the real interest rate, and the government deficit. For example, suppose the government runs a primary deficit of 5% of GDP, the growth rate of real GDP is 3% per year, and the real interest rate is 2%, so that $a = -0.05$, $g = 0.03$, and $r = 0.02$. Then, Equation (9.32) tells us that the long run ratio of government debt to GDP will be 5, or 500%. In this case, interest payments on the government debt in the long run will absorb 10% of GDP. Holding all other parameters constant, if the primary deficit falls to 1% of GDP, this would imply a long-run ratio of government debt to GDP of 100%, with interest payments on the government debt of 2% of GDP.

There are two important lessons here:

1. A government deficit can be sustained forever, in principle. A government can potentially remain solvent without ultimately reducing its deficit to zero, or running a surplus. If Canada were to choose to run a government deficit indefinitely, this need not imply a growing ratio of government debt to GDP.

2. The ratio of debt to GDP is not all that matters for a government's solvency. A government's fiscal position may be unsustainable because real GDP is growing too slowly relative to the real interest rate. For example, Japan is not currently seen as having a solvency problem, but Greece is. However, the ratio of government debt to GDP in Japan is 220%, and that ratio is 143% in Greece. One key difference between Japan and Greece is that the prospects for economic growth are much better in Japan than in Greece, that is, we can think of y being much higher in the future for Japan than Greece.

Chapter Summary

- A two-period macroeconomic model was constructed to understand the intertemporal consumption–savings decisions of consumers and the effects of fiscal policy choices concerning the timing of taxes and the quantity of government debt.

- In the model, there are many consumers, and each makes decisions over a two-period horizon where a consumer's incomes in the two periods are given, and the consumer pays lump-sum taxes in each period to the government.

- The lifetime budget constraint of the consumer states that the present value of consumption over the consumer's two-period time horizon is equal to the present value of disposable income.

- A consumer's lifetime wealth is his or her present value of disposable income.

- A consumer's preferences have the property that more is preferred to less with regard to current and future consumption, there is a preference for diversity in current and future consumption, and current and future consumption are normal goods. A preference for diversity implies that consumers wish to smooth consumption relative to income over the present and the future.

- Consumption smoothing yields the result that, if income increases in the current period for a consumer, then current consumption increases, future consumption increases, and current saving increases. If future income increases, then consumption increases in both periods and current saving decreases. A permanent increase in income (when current and future income increase) has a larger impact on current consumption than does a temporary increase in income (only current income increases).

- If there is an increase in the real interest rate that a consumer faces, then there are income and substitution effects on consumption. Because an increase in the real interest rate causes a reduction in the price of future consumption in terms of current consumption, the substitution effect is for current consumption to fall, future consumption to rise, and current saving to rise when the real interest rate rises. For a lender (borrower), the income effect of an increase in the real interest rate is positive (negative) for both current and future consumption.

- The Ricardian equivalence theorem states that changes in current taxes by the government that leave the present value of taxes constant have no effect on consumers' consumption choices or on the equilibrium real interest rate. This is because consumers change savings by an amount equal and opposite to the change in current taxes to compensate for the change in future taxes.

- Ricardian equivalence depends critically on the notion that the burden of the government debt is shared equally among the people alive when the debt is issued. The burden of the debt is not shared equally when (1) there are current distributional effects of changes in taxes; (2) there are intergenerational distribution effects; (3) taxes cause distortions; or (4) there are credit market imperfections.

Key Terms

intertemporal decisions: Decisions involving economic tradeoffs across periods of time.

consumption–savings decision: The decision by a consumer about how to split current income between current consumption and savings.

Ricardian equivalence theorem: This theorem, named for David Ricardo, states that changes in the stream of taxes faced by consumers that leave the present value of taxes unchanged have no effect on consumption, interest rates, or welfare.

two-period model: An economic model in which all decision makers (consumers and firms) have two-period planning horizons, with the two periods typically representing the present and the future.

real interest rate: The rate of return on savings in units of consumption goods.

consumption smoothing: The tendency of consumers to seek a consumption path over time that is smoother than income.

lifetime budget constraint: Condition that the present value of a consumer's lifetime disposable income equals the present value of his or her lifetime consumption.

present value: The value, in terms of money today or current goods, of a future stream of money or goods.

lifetime wealth: The present value of lifetime disposable income for a consumer.

endowment point: The point on a consumer's budget constraint where consumption is equal to disposable income in each period.

excess variability: The observed fact that measured consumption is more variable than theory appears to predict.

permanent income hypothesis: A theory developed by Milton Friedman that implies a consumer's current consumption depends on his or her permanent income. Permanent income is closely related to lifetime wealth in our model.

martingale: An economic variable with the property that the best forecast of its value tomorrow is its value today. Finance theory implies that stock prices are martingales.

intertemporal substitution effect: Substitution by a consumer of a good in one time period for a good in another time period, in response to a change in the relative price of the two goods. The intertemporal substitution effect of an increase in the real interest rate is for current consumption to fall and future consumption to rise.

government present-value budget constraint: Condition in which the present value of government purchases is equal to the present value of tax revenues.

perfect credit market: An idealized credit market in which consumers can borrow and lend all they want at the market interest rate, and the interest rate at which consumers lend is equal to the interest rate at which they borrow.

credit market imperfections: Constraints on borrowing or differences between borrowing and lending rates of interest.

primary surplus: The government surplus plus interest payments on the government debt.

primary deficit: The government deficit minus interest payments on the government debt

Questions for Review

All questions refer to the macroeconomic model developed in this chapter.

1. Why do consumers save?

2. How do consumers save in the two-period model?

3. What factors are important to a consumer in making his or her consumption–savings decision?

4. What is the price of future consumption in terms of current consumption?

5. Show how to derive the consumer's lifetime budget constraint from the consumer's current-period and future-period budget constraints.

6. What is the slope of a consumer's lifetime budget constraint?

7. What are the horizontal and vertical intercepts of a consumer's lifetime budget constraint?

8. If a consumer chooses the endowment point, how much does he or she consume in each period, and how much does he or she save?

9. What are the three properties of a consumer's preferences?

10. How is the consumer's motive to smooth consumption captured by the shape of an indifference curve?

11. What are the effects of an increase in current income on consumption in each period and on savings?

12. Give two reasons why consumption is more variable in the data than theory seems to predict.

13. What are the effects of an increase in future income on consumption in each period and on savings?

14. What produces a larger increase in a consumer's current consumption: a permanent increase in the consumer's income or a temporary increase?

15. What does theory tell us about how the value of stocks held by consumers should be related to consumption behaviour? Do the data support this?

16. What are the effects of an increase in the real interest rate on consumption in each period, and on savings? How does this depend on income and substitution effects and whether the consumer is a borrower or lender?

17. How does the government finance its purchases in the two-period model?

18. State the Ricardian equivalence theorem.

19. Give four reasons why the burden of the government debt is not shared equally in practice.

Problems

1. A consumer's income in the current period is $y = 100$, and income in the future period is $y' = 120$. He or she pays lump-sum taxes $t = 20$ in the current period and $t' = 10$ in the future period. The real interest rate is 0.1, or 10%, per period.

   a. Determine the consumer's lifetime wealth.

   b. Suppose that current and future consumption are perfect complements for the consumer and that he or she always wants to have equal consumption in the current and future periods. Draw the consumer's indifference curves.

   c. Determine what the consumer's optimal current-period and future-period consumption are and what optimal saving is, and show this in a diagram with the consumer's budget constraint and indifference curves. Is the consumer a lender or a borrower?

   d. Now suppose that instead of $y = 100$ the consumer has $y = 140$. Again, determine optimal consumption in the current and future periods and optimal saving, and show this in a diagram. Is the consumer a lender or a borrower?

   e. Explain the differences in your results between parts (c) and (d).

2. Suppose that a consumer's future income increases and the real interest rate increases as well. In a diagram, determine how the consumer's optimal choice of current consumption and future consumption changes and how saving changes. Show how your results depend on income and substitution effects, and consider the case where the consumer is initially a lender and where he or she is initially a borrower.

3. An employer offers an employee the option of shifting x units of income from next year to this year. That is, the option is to reduce income next year by x units and increase income this year by x units.

   a. Would the employee take this option? (Use a diagram.)

   b. Determine, using a diagram, how this shift in income will affect consumption this year and next year and saving this year. Explain your results.

4. Consider the following effects of an increase in taxes for a consumer:

   a. The consumer's taxes increase by Δt in the current period. How does this affect current consumption, future consumption, and current saving?

   b. The consumer's taxes increase permanently, increasing by Δt in the current period *and* future period. Using a diagram, determine how this affects current consumption, future consumption, and current saving. Explain the differences between your results here and in part (a).

5. Suppose that the government introduces a tax on interest earnings. That is, borrowers face a real interest rate of r before and after the tax is introduced, but lenders receive an interest rate of $(1 - x)r$ on their savings, where x is the tax rate. Therefore, we are looking at the

effects of having x increase from zero to some value greater than zero, with r assumed to remain constant.

    a. Show the effects of the increase in the tax rate on a consumer's lifetime budget constraint.

    b. How does the increase in the tax rate affect the optimal choice of consumption (in the current and future periods) and saving for the consumer? Show how income and substitution effects matter for your answer, and show how it matters whether the consumer is initially a borrower or a lender.

6. A consumer receives income y in the current period and income y' in the future period, and pays taxes of t and t' in the current and future periods, respectively. The consumer can borrow and lend at the real interest rate r. This consumer faces a constraint on how much he or she can borrow, much like the credit limit typically placed on a credit card account. That is, the consumer cannot borrow more than x, where $x < we - y + t$, with we denoting lifetime wealth. Use diagrams to determine the effects on the consumer's current consumption, future consumption, and saving of a change in x, and explain your results.

7. A consumer receives income y in the current period and income y in the future period, and pays taxes of t and t' in the current and future periods, respectively. The consumer can lend at the real interest rate r_1. The consumer is given two options. First, he or she can borrow at the interest rate r_1 but can borrow only an amount x or less, where $x < we - y + t$. Second, he or she can borrow an unlimited amount at the interest rate r_2, where $r_2 > r_1$. Use a diagram to determine which option the consumer chooses, and explain your results.

8. Assume a consumer has current-period income $y = 200$, future-period income $y' = 150$, current and future taxes $t = 40$ and $t' = 50$, respectively, and faces a market real interest rate of $r = 0.05$, or 5% per period. The consumer would like to consume equal amounts in both periods; that is, he or she would like to set $c = c'$, if possible. However, this consumer is faced with a credit market imperfection in that he or she cannot borrow at all; that is, $s \geq 0$

    a. Show the consumer's lifetime budget constraint and indifference curves in a diagram.

    b. Calculate his or her optimal current-period and future-period consumption and optimal saving, and show this in your diagram.

    c. Suppose that everything remains unchanged, except that now $t = 20$ and $t' = 71$. Calculate the effects on current and future consumption and optimal saving, and show this in your diagram.

    d. Now, suppose alternatively that $y = 100$. Repeat parts (a) to (c), and explain any differences.

9. Assume an economy with 1000 consumers. Each consumer has income in the current period of 50 units and future income of 60 units, and pays a lump-sum tax of 10 in the current period and 20 in the future period. The market real interest rate is 8%. Of the 1000 consumers, 500 consume 60 units in the future, while 500 consume 20 units in the future.

    a. Determine each consumer's current consumption and current saving.

    b. Determine aggregate private saving, aggregate consumption in each period, government spending in the current and future periods, the current-period government deficit, and the quantity of debt issued by the government in the current period.

    c. Suppose that current taxes increase to 15 for each consumer. Repeat parts (a) and (b) and explain your results.

10. Suppose that a consumer has income y in the current period, income y' in the future period, and faces proportional taxes on consumption in the current and future periods. There are no lump-sum taxes. That is, if consumption is c in the current period and c' in the future

period, the consumer pays a tax sc in the current period, and $s'c'$ in the future period, where s is the current-period tax rate on consumption, and s' is the future-period tax rate on consumption. The government wishes to collect total tax revenue in the current and future periods which has a present value of R. Suppose that the government reduces s and increases s' in such a way that it continues to collect the same present value of tax revenue R from the consumer, given the consumer's optimal choices of current-period and future-period consumptions.

a. Write down the consumer's lifetime budget constraint.

b. Show that lifetime wealth is the same for the consumer, before and after the tax change.

c. What effect, if any, does the change in tax rates have on the consumer's choice of current and future consumption, and on savings? Does Ricardian equivalence hold here? Explain why or why not.

11. Suppose in our two-period model of the economy that the government, instead of borrowing in the current period, runs a government loan program. That is, loans are made to consumers at the market real interest rate r, with the aggregate quantity of loans made in the current period denoted by L. Government loans are financed by lump-sum taxes on consumers in the current period, and we assume that government spending is zero in the current and future periods. In the future period, when consumers repay the government loans, the government rebates this amount as lump-sum transfers (negative taxes) to consumers.

a. Write down the government's current-period budget constraint and its future-period budget constraint.

b. Determine the present-value budget constraint of the government.

c. Write down the lifetime budget constraint of a consumer.

d. Show that the size of the government loan program (i.e., the quantity L) has no effect on current consumption or future consumption for each individual consumer and that there is no effect on the equilibrium real interest rate. Explain this result.

Credit Market Imperfections: Credit Frictions, Financial Crises, and Social Security

In Chapter 9, we explored the basic elements of consumer behaviour in credit markets—how consumers act to smooth consumption over time in response to changes in their incomes and in market interest rates. As well, we studied the aggregate effects of changes in government tax policy. A key theoretical result from Chapter 9 is the Ricardian equivalence theorem, which states that a change in the timing of taxes can have no effects on consumer behaviour or interest rates, provided that some special conditions hold. It provides us with a firm foundation for understanding the circumstances under which government tax policy will matter. In particular, as discussed in Chapter 9, the Ricardian equivalence theorem would not hold if the tax burden is shared unequally among consumers, if there is intergenerational redistribution resulting from a change in taxes, if there are tax distortions, or if there are credit market imperfections.

The cases under which Ricardian equivalence does not hold have practical importance in at least two respects. First, credit market imperfections—"frictions" that cause Ricardian equivalence to fail—are key to understanding some important features of how credit markets work. For example, in practice the interest rates at which consumers and firms can lend are lower than the interest rates at which they can borrow, consumers and firms cannot always borrow up to the quantity they would like at market interest rates, and borrowers are sometimes required to post collateral against a loan. All of these features of actual loan contracts can be understood as arising because of credit market frictions.

In this chapter, we will study two types of credit market frictions: **asymmetric information** and **limited commitment**. Asymmetric information refers to a situation in which, in a particular market, some market participant knows more about his or her own characteristics than do other market participants. In the credit market context we examine, asymmetric information exists in that a particular borrower knows more about his or her own creditworthiness than do potential lenders. This credit market friction then leads to differences between the interest rates at which consumers can lend and borrow. The loan interest rate reflects a **default premium** which acts to compensate lenders for the fact that some borrowers will default on their loans. Even good borrowers who will not default must pay the default premium, as lenders are unable to distinguish between good and bad borrowers. Asymmetric information is an important element that we can use to help understand the 2008–2009 financial crisis, which was characterized by dramatic increases in some **interest rate spreads**. These interest rate spreads are gaps between the interest rates on risky loans and safer loans, or between the rates of interest at which some class of borrowers can lend and borrow. As well, during the financial crisis there was a dramatic decrease in the quantity of lending in some segments of the credit market, which asymmetric information can help explain.

A second credit market friction, limited commitment, refers to situations in which it is impossible for a market participant to commit in advance to some future action. In credit markets, there can be lack of commitment in the sense that a borrower cannot commit to repaying a loan. Given the choice, a rational borrower would choose to default on a loan if there were no penalty to doing so. A typical incentive device used by lenders to prevent this type of strategic default is the posting of collateral. Indeed, most lending in credit markets is collateralized. For example, in consumer credit markets, an individual who takes out a mortgage loan is required to post his or her house as collateral, and when a consumer buys a car with a car loan, the car serves as collateral against the loan. When collateral is posted as part of a credit contract, the borrower gives the lender the right to seize the collateral in the event that the borrower defaults on the loan.

Limited commitment can lead to situations where consumers are constrained in their borrowing by how much wealth they have that can serve as collateral—their **collateralizable wealth**. For a typical consumer, collateralizable wealth is restricted to houses and cars, but could potentially include other assets. If a consumer is collateral-constrained, then a change in the value of collateral will matter for how much they can consume in the present. This effect mattered a great deal during the financial crisis, particularly in the United States, due to a large decrease in the price of housing, which acted to reduce consumer expenditure. From the late 1990s until the peak in housing prices in the United States in 2006, a significant fraction of consumer expenditure in the United States was financed by borrowing, through mortgages and home equity loans, using housing as collateral. With the decrease in housing prices in the United States that began in 2006, the value of collateralizable wealth in the U.S. economy fell, and consumer spending also decreased by a large amount, fueling the 2008–2009 recession. Canada did not experience this problem to the same degree, but the impact of what happened in the U.S. housing and mortgage markets was very important, though indirectly, for the recent recession in Canada. We will explore these ideas in depth in this chapter.

A second aspect in which the failure of Ricardian equivalence has practical significance, relates to the market failure that creates a role for social security programs. Government social security programs typically mandate some level of saving by the working age population in order to provide for benefits to retirees. It might seem that such programs can only make us worse off, since rational consumers know best how to save for their own retirement. However, government-provided social security can be rationalized by appealing to a credit market failure—the fact that those currently alive cannot write financial contracts with those as yet unborn. In the absence of such contracts, economic outcomes are not efficient. The first welfare theorem (see Chapter 5) does not hold, and there is a role for government in transferring resources across generations—taxing the working-age population to pay benefits to retirees through social security. We explore how social security works, and the effects of alternative types of social security programs, in this chapter. A key policy issue with respect to social security is the "privatization" of social security, that is, the replacement of "pay-as-you-go" systems with "fully funded" programs, as has partially occurred in Canada.

Credit Market Imperfections and Consumption

Our first step in the analysis of credit market imperfections is to show how Ricardian equivalence fails with a standard type of credit market friction—a gap between the interest rates at which a consumer can lend and borrow. Here, we will start with the basic credit market model from Chapter 9, in which an individual consumer lives for two periods, the current and future period. The consumer receives income y in the current period, receives income y' in the future period, and consumes c and c' in the current and future periods, respectively. The consumer's savings in the current period is denoted by s.

We want to show how a consumer who is credit-constrained can be affected by a change in taxes that would not have any effect on the consumer's choices if there were perfect credit markets. Consider a consumer who lends at a real interest rate r_1 and borrows at a real interest rate r_2, where $r_2 > r_1$. This difference in borrowing and lending rates of interest arises in practice, for example, when borrowing and lending is carried out through banks, and it is costly for banks to sort credit risks. If the bank borrows from lenders (depositors in the bank) at the real interest rate r_1, and it makes loans at the real interest rate r_2, the difference $r_2 - r_1 > 0$ could arise in equilibrium to compensate the bank for the costs of making loans. The difference between borrowing and lending rates of interest will lead to a more complicated lifetime budget constraint. As before, the current-period budget constraint of the consumer is given by the following equation:

$$c + s = y - t$$

but the future-period budget constraint is

$$c' = y' - t' + s(1 + r_1),$$

if $s \geq 0$ (the consumer is a lender), and

$$c' = y' - t' + s(1 + r_2),$$

if $s \leq 0$ (the consumer is a borrower). Going through the same mechanics as in Chapter 9 to derive the consumer's lifetime budget constraint, we obtain

$$c + \frac{c'}{1 + r_1} = y + \frac{y'}{1 + r_1} - t - \frac{t'}{1 + r_1} = we_1, \qquad (10.1)$$

if $c \leq y - t$ (the consumer is a lender), and

$$c + \frac{c'}{1 + r_2} = y + \frac{y'}{1 + r_2} - t - \frac{t'}{1 + r_2} = we_2, \qquad (10.2)$$

if $c \geq y - t$ (the consumer is a borrower).

We graph the consumer's budget constraint in Figure 10.1, where AB is given by Equation (10.1) and has slope $-(1 + r_1)$, and DF is given by Equation (10.2) and has slope $-(1 + r_2)$. The budget constraint is AEF, where E is the endowment point. Thus, the budget constraint has a kink at the endowment point, because the consumer lends at a lower interest rate than he or she can borrow at.

In a world where there are many different consumers, all having different indifference curves and different incomes, and where each consumer has a kinked budget constraint as in Figure 10.1, there will be a significant number of consumers whose optimal consumption bundle is the endowment point. For example, in Figure 10.2 the consumer faces budget constraint AE_1B, and the highest indifference curve on the budget constraint is reached at E_1, the endowment point. For this consumer, at the endowment point, the lending rate is too low to make lending worthwhile, and the borrowing rate is too high to make borrowing worthwhile.

Suppose in Figure 10.2 that the consumer receives a tax cut in the current period—that is, period 1 taxes change by $\Delta t < 0$—with a corresponding change of $-\Delta t(1 + r_1)$ in future taxes. This is the consumer's future tax liability implied by the tax cut, assuming that the interest rate that the government pays on its debt is r_1, the lending rate of interest. Assume that interest rates do not change as the result of the change in the government's tax policy. The effect of the change in current and future taxes is to shift

FIGURE 10.1

A Consumer Facing Different Lending and Borrowing Rates

When the borrowing rate of interest is higher than the lending rate, there is a kinked budget constraint, *AEF*, with the kink at the endowment point *E*.

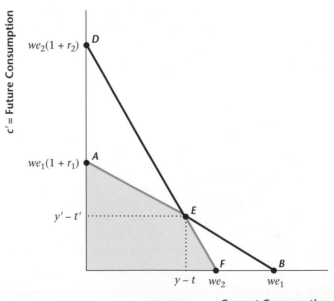

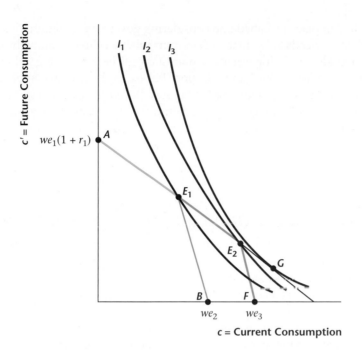

FIGURE 10.2

Effects of a Tax Cut for a Consumer with Different Borrowing and Lending Rates

The consumer receives a current tax cut, with a future increase in taxes, and this shifts the budget constraint from AE_1B to AE_2F. The consumer's optimal consumption bundle shifts from E_1 to E_2, and the consumer will consume the entire tax cut.

the endowment point to E_2, and given the way we have drawn the consumer's indifference curves, the consumer now chooses E_2 as his or her optimal consumption bundle on indifference curve I_2. Since he or she chooses the endowment point before and after the tax cut, period 1 consumption increases by the amount of the tax cut, –the quantity Δt. Contrast this with the Ricardian equivalence result in Chapter 9 where the consumer would save the entire tax cut and consumption would be unaffected.

The reason that the consumer's consumption increases is that the government is effectively making a low-interest loan available to him or her through the tax-cut scheme. In Figure 10.2, the consumer would like to consume at point G if he or she could borrow at the interest rate r_1. Giving the consumer a tax cut of Δt with a corresponding future tax liability of $\Delta t(1 + r_1)$ is just like having the government lend the consumer Δt at the interest rate r_1. Since the consumer would take such a loan willingly if it was offered, this tax cut makes the consumer better off.

Therefore, to the extent that credit market imperfections are important in practice, there can be beneficial effects of positive government debt. The government effectively acts like a bank that makes loans at below-market rates. If credit market imperfections matter significantly, then the people who are helped by current tax cuts are those who are affected most by credit market imperfections.

This might suggest to us that tax policy could be used in this way to increase general economic welfare. However, tax policy is quite a blunt instrument for relieving perceived problems arising from credit market imperfections. A preferable policy might be to target particular groups of people—for example, small businesses, farmers, or homeowners—with direct government credit programs. In fact, there are many such programs in place in Canada. In considering government credit policies, though, careful evaluation needs to be done to determine whether direct lending by the government is a good idea in each particular circumstance. There may be good reasons for a particular private market credit imperfection. For example, real loan interest rates may be high in a segment of the credit market because the costs of screening and evaluating loans are very high, and the government would face the same high costs. This would then imply that the government has no special advantage in offering credit to these borrowers, and it would be inefficient for the government to get into the business of lending to them.

Asymmetric Information and the Financial Crisis

A key feature of credit markets that can give rise to a budget constraint for a consumer like the one depicted in Figure 10.1 is asymmetric information. For our purposes, asymmetric information is particularly interesting because of the role it appears to have played in the recent financial crisis. In particular, the quality of information in credit markets declined significantly during 2008, with important implications for market interest rates, the quantity of lending, and aggregate economic activity.

Our first goal is to model asymmetric information in a simple and transparent way, using the tools we have already built up. It will be useful to consider an economy that has banks, in addition to the consumers and the government that were in the Chapter 9 two-period credit model. In our model, as in the real world, a bank is a **financial intermediary** that borrows from one set of individuals and lends to another set. We will study financial intermediaries in more depth in Chapter 17. In the model, a bank borrows from its depositors in the current period, and each depositor is an ultimate lender in the economy, with a depositor receiving a real interest rate r_1 on his or her deposits, which are held with the bank until the future period. The bank takes all of its deposits in the current period (which in the model are consumption goods), and makes loans to borrowers.

The problem for the bank is that some of the borrowers will default on their loans in the future period. To make things simple, suppose that a fraction a of the borrowers in the economy are good borrowers who have positive income in the future period, while a fraction $1 - a$ of borrowers are bad, in that they receive zero income in the future period, and therefore will default on any loan that is extended to them. However, there is asymmetric information in the credit market. Each borrower knows whether he or she is good or bad, but the bank cannot distinguish bad borrowers from the good borrowers who will pay off their loans with certainty. Assume that the bank can observe a consumer's income at the time it is received, so it knows which are good and bad borrowers once the future period arrives.

Now assume, again for simplicity, that all good borrowers are identical. Then, if the bank charges each borrower a real interest rate r_2 on loans, each good borrower chooses the same loan quantity, which we will denote by L. Bad borrowers do not want to reveal that they are bad to the bank, otherwise they will not receive a loan, so each bad borrower mimics the behaviour of good borrowers by also choosing the loan quantity L. Now, one of the reasons that banks exist is that large lending institutions are able to minimize risk by diversifying. In this case, the bank diversifies by lending to a large number of borrowers. This assures that, as the number of loans gets very large, that the fraction of the bank's borrowers defaulting will be a, the fraction of bad borrowers in the population. For example, if I flip a coin n times, the fraction of flips that turn up heads will get very close to $1/2$ as n gets large, just as the fraction of good borrowers the bank faces gets very close to a as the number of borrowers gets large.

For each L units of deposits acquired by the bank, the bank will have to pay out $L(1 + r_1)$ to depositors in the future period, the average payoff to the bank will be $aL(1 + r_2)$ in the future period, since fraction a of the bank's loans will be made to good borrowers, who will repay the bank $L(1 + r_2)$, and fraction $1 - a$ of the bank loans will be made to bad borrowers, who will repay zero. Thus, the average profit the bank makes on each loan in the future period is

$$\pi = aL(1 + r_2) - L(1 + r_1) = L[a(1 + r_2) - (1 + r_1)]. \qquad (10.3)$$

In equilibrium, each bank must earn zero profits, since negative profits would imply that banks would want to shut down, and positive profits would imply that banks would want to expand indefinitely. Therefore, $\pi = 0$ in equilibrium, which from Equation (10.3) implies that

$$r_2 = \frac{1 + r_1}{a} - 1. \qquad (10.4)$$

From Equation (10.4), note that when $a = 1$ and there are no bad borrowers, that $r_1 = r_2$, and there is no credit market imperfection. Therefore, when $a = 1$, the model is then just the standard credit model that we studied in Chapter 9. Note also from Equation (10.4) that r_2 increases as a decreases, given r_1, so that the credit market imperfection becomes more severe as the fraction of good borrowers in the population decreases and the fraction of bad borrowers increases. Each good borrower must pay a default premium on a loan from the bank, which is equal to the difference $r_2 - r_1$. This difference grows as the fraction of good borrowers in the population decreases.

Now, in Figure 10.3, consider what happens to a typical consumer's budget constraint as a decreases, given r_1. Before a decrease in a the budget constraint is AED, where E is the endowment point. When a falls, the budget constraint shifts to AEF. From our previous analysis in Chapter 9, we know that, for a consumer who is a borrower, that is, who chooses a consumption bundle on ED before the decline in a, consumption in the current period and borrowing must decrease when a falls. That is, with asymmetric information in the credit market and an increase in the incidence of default among borrowers, good borrowers face higher loan interest rates and reduce their borrowing and consumption as a result.

A feature of the recent financial crisis was that lending became very risky for banks and other financial institutions. Lending institutions perceived that the average borrower was much more likely to default, and these same institutions were finding it more difficult to screen borrowers. Thus, the asymmetric information problem became more severe during the crisis, in that it was harder to tell a good borrower from a bad one.

FIGURE 10.3

Asymmetric Information in the Credit Market and the Effect of a Decrease in Creditworthy Borrowers

Asymmetric information creates a kinked budget constraint *AED*, with the kink at the endowment point *E*. A decrease in the fraction of creditworthy borrowers in the population shifts the budget constraint to *AEF*.

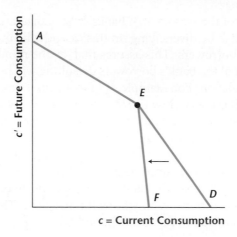

These effects are captured in our model by a decrease in *a*, and the model's predictions are consistent with what we observed during the financial crisis. In particular, lending by financial institutions dropped precipitously, interest rate "spreads" increased (in our model the interest rate differential $r_2 - r_1$ is the spread), and current consumption expenditures fell.

Limited Commitment and the Financial Crisis

Limited commitment is another type of credit market imperfection that is important to how real-world credit markets function, and this financial friction played an important role in the financial crisis. Any loan contract represents an intertemporal exchange—the borrower receives goods and services in the present in exchange for a promise to give the lender claims to goods and services in the future. However, when the future arrives, the borrower may find it disadvantageous to keep his or her promise.

Lenders are not stupid, of course, and will therefore set up a loan contract in a way that gives the borrower the incentive to pay off the loan as promised. One incentive device used widely by lenders is the requirement that a borrower post **collateral**. In general, collateral is an asset owned by the borrower that the lender has a right to seize if the borrower defaults on the loan (does not meet the promised payment). Most people are familiar with the role played by collateral in automobile loans and mortgage loans. For a typical auto loan, the auto itself serves as collateral, while an individual's house is the collateral for his or her mortgage loan. Collateral is also used in short-term lending among large financial institutions. For example, a **repurchase agreement** is a short-term loan under which a safe asset, such as government-issued debt, serves as collateral.

For macroeconomic activity, the use of collateral in loan contracts can potentially be very important. For example, mortgages are used by homeowners not only to finance the purchase of homes, but also to finance consumption. If the extent to which homeowners can borrow is constrained by the value of houses, and the price of houses

10.1 *Asymmetric Information
and Interest Rate Spreads*

Our analysis of asymmetric information in the credit market predicts that, in segments of the credit market where default is possible and lenders have difficulty sorting would-be borrowers, increases in the perceived probability of default will cause increases in interest rates, even for borrowers who are objectively creditworthy. In Figure (10.4), we show the difference in the interest rate on prime commercial paper (short-term corporate debt), and the interest rate on Government of Canada Treasury bills (essentially safe government short-term debt). This gives a measure of the interest rate spread between safe, short-term default-free debt, and high-quality short-term corporate debt. While our analysis deals with consumers, the interest rate spread in Figure (10.4) represents a good general measure of credit market default risk.

In Figure (10.4), note that the interest rate spread is unusually high, not only in the recent 2008–2009 recession, but in previous recessions as well, particularly the 1974–1975 recession and the 1981–1982 recession. Since we associate a high interest rate spread with financial stress, this suggests that the 1990–1992 recession—a significant event in Canada—would appear not to be associated with financial factors, since there is no spike in the interest rate spread at that time in Figure 10.4. However, the financial factors driving the recent 2008–2009 recession are clearly reflected in the high interest rate spread in the figure.

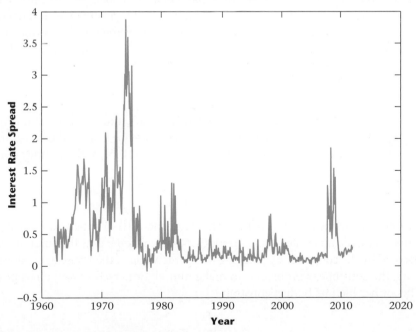

FIGURE 10.4 Interest Rate Spread

The figure depicts the difference between the interest rates on prime short-term corporate paper and short-term Government of Canada debt. This spread was high during the 1974–1975, 1981–1982, and 2008–2009 recessions, but not during the 1990–1992 recession.

Source: Adapted from the Statistics Canada CANSIM database, Series v122531, v122491.

falls, this will cause a decline in the quantity of lending in the economy as a whole, and a drop in current aggregate consumption.

To see how this works, consider an individual consumer exactly like the one we studied in Chapter 9, who also owns some quantity of an asset, denoted by H, which can be sold in the future period at the price p per unit, so that the value of the asset in the future is pH. To make this example concrete, think of H as the size of the consumer's house, and p as the price of housing per unit. Assume that the house is illiquid, which means that it is difficult to sell quickly. We will represent this by supposing that the consumer cannot sell the house in the current period. The consumer's lifetime wealth is then

$$we = y - t + \frac{y' - t' + pH}{1 + r},\tag{10.5}$$

which is the same expression as the one for lifetime wealth of a consumer in Chapter 9, except that we add the quantity $(pH)/(1 + r)$ to lifetime wealth. This quantity is the future value of the house, discounted to give its value in units of current consumption.

Now, in our model the lenders in the credit market know that there is a limited commitment problem. For simplicity, assume that a borrower will find it advantageous to default on any loan, if he or she can get away with it. However, if the consumer wishes to borrow, he or she can post his or her house as collateral. Lenders will then be willing to lend an amount to the consumer that will imply a loan payment in the future no larger than the value of the collateral, as otherwise the consumer would default on the loan. That is, given that s is that consumer's saving in the current period, with $-s$ the quantity of borrowing in the current period, then the amount borrowed by the consumer must satisfy the collateral constraint

$$-s(1 + r) \leq pH,\tag{10.6}$$

as $-s(1 + r)$ is the loan payment for the consumer in the future period, and pH is the value of the collateral in the future period. Then, since $s = y - t - c$ for the consumer, we can substitute for s in the collateral constraint, Equation (10.6), and rearrange to obtain

$$c \leq y - t + \frac{pH}{1 + r}.\tag{10.7}$$

The collateral constraint, rewritten in the form of Equation (10.7) states that current period consumption can be no greater than current disposable income plus the amount that can be borrowed by the consumer by pledging the future value of the house as collateral.

Now, the consumer's problem is to make himself or herself as well off as possible, given his or her lifetime budget constraint

$$c + \frac{c'}{1 + r} = we,\tag{10.8}$$

and also given the collateral constraint (10.7), where lifetime wealth we is given by Equation (10.5). As long as the value of collateral in the future, pH, is small enough, the collateral constraint implies that the budget constraint is kinked, as in Figure 10.5,

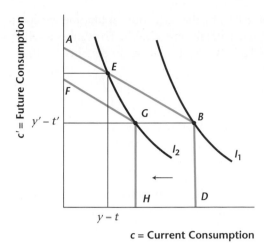

FIGURE 10.5

Limited Commitment with a Collateral Constraint

The consumer can borrow only with collateralizable wealth as security against the loan. As a result, the budget constraint is kinked. Initially the budget constraint is *ABD* and it shifts to *FGH* with a decrease in the price of collateral. For a constrained borrower, this causes no change in future consumption, but current consumption drops by the same amount as the decrease in the value of collateral.

where the budget constraint is initially *ABD*. In the figure, the endowment point is *E*, and if the consumer chose point *B*, at the kink in the budget constraint, then he or she would have a binding collateral constraint, borrowing up to the full amount that lenders will permit, and consuming future disposable income in the future period, with $c' = y' - t'$.

Next, suppose that the price of houses, *p*, declines, with everything else held constant. This reduces the quantity of the consumer's collateralizable wealth, that is, the quantity of wealth that the consumer can borrow against. As a result, in Figure 10.5, the budget constraint shifts from *ABD* to *FGH*. Note that the slope of *AB* is the same as the slope of *FG*, since the interest rate *r* has not changed, and that the point *G* is directly to the left of point *B*, since future disposable income $y' - t'$ is also unchanged.

If the collateral constraint of Equation 10.7 does not bind for the consumer, either before or after the decrease in *p*, then the consumer is affected in exactly the same way as in our analysis of the effects of a change in future income in Chapter 9. An unconstrained consumer will initially choose a point somewhere between *A* and *B* (but not including *B*) before the decrease in *p*, and will choose a point between *F* and *G* (but not including *G*) after the decrease in *p*. The unconstrained consumer can smooth the effects of the decrease in wealth resulting from the fall in *p* by reducing consumption in both the current and future periods.

However, suppose that the consumer's collateral constraint binds, both before and after the decrease in *p*. Then, as in Figure 10.5, the consumer chooses to consume at point *B* initially, on indifference curve I_1. When *p* falls, the budget constraint shifts to *FGH*, and the consumer chooses point *G*, on indifference curve I_2. A constrained consumer cannot smooth the effects of the decrease in his or her wealth. For any consumer, for example as in Chapter 9, a decrease in wealth must be absorbed in a reduction in consumption, either in the present or in the future. However, in this case, since the collateral constraint binds, all of the reduction of consumption occurs in the current period. In the figure, future consumption at points *B* and *G* is the same, but current consumption c falls by the reduction in lifetime wealth, that is, by the change in the present value of collateralizable wealth. To see this another way, if the collateral constraint, Equation 10.7, binds, it holds as an equality, so that

$$c = y - t + \frac{pH}{1 + r},$$

and if $y - t$ remains unchanged, then any reduction in the present value of collateralizable wealth, $(pH)/(1 + r)$, is reflected in a one-for-one reduction in current consumption, c.

The permanent income hypothesis tells us that, in a world with perfect credit markets, the motive of consumers to smooth consumption over time acts to lessen the impact of changes in wealth on consumer expenditure in the aggregate. Here, our analysis tells us that, if credit market imperfections arising from limited commitment matter in an important way for a significant fraction of the population, then changes in the value of collateralizable wealth (principally housing, for the consumer sector) can matter a great deal for aggregate consumption.

What does this have to do with the financial crisis? A key component of the crisis was that it was set off in the United States by a large drop in the price of housing, beginning in mid-2006. The price of housing in the United States declined about 33% from its peak in April 2006 to November 2011, when house prices in the U.S. were still falling.[1] Aside from the effects of mortgage loan defaults on the health of financial institutions, a 33% drop in the value of collateralizable wealth can have large effects on consumer expenditure in the United States, particularly as a large fraction of consumer expenditure in the U.S. has been financed by mortgage debt since the late 1990s. There was some reduction in housing prices in Canada during the financial crisis and the recent recession, but not to the extent seen in the U.S.. Thus, the direct effect of changes in collateralizable wealth is not as important a factor in the financial crisis in Canada as it was in the United States.

RICARDIAN EQUIVALENCE, INTERGENERATIONAL REDISTRIBUTION, AND SOCIAL SECURITY

As discussed above, Ricardian equivalence fails to hold if a change in taxation has consequences for the intergenerational distribution of wealth. This raises important public policy issues related to social security programs and how they should be designed.

Social security programs are government-provided means for saving for retirement. There are essentially two types of programs: **pay-as-you-go** and **fully funded social security**, though in practice social security can be some mix of the two, as is the case in Canada. With pay-as-you-go social security, the program simply involves transfers between the young and the old, while fully funded social security is a government-sponsored savings program in which the savings of the young are used to purchase assets, and the old receive the payoffs on the assets that were acquired when they were young. We discuss the two types of social security programs in turn.

---

[1]This is as measured by the Case-Shiller index of home prices (20-city composite).

Pay-as-You-Go Social Security In Canada, the Canada Pension Plan was a pure pay-as-you-go system until 1997, when federal legislation was enacted to move the Canadian system toward a hybrid of pay-as-you-go and fully funded public pension plans. In the United States, social security operates as a pay-as-you-go system, in that taxes on the young are used to finance social security transfers to the old.

To see the implications of pay-as-you-go social security for the distribution of wealth over time and across consumers, we assume for simplicity that social security has no effect on the market real interest rate, r, which we suppose is constant for all time. Each consumer lives for two periods, youth and old age, and so in any period there is a young generation and an old generation alive. Let N denote the number of old consumers currently alive, and N' the number of young consumers currently alive. Assume that

$$N' = (1 + n)N, \qquad (10.9)$$

so that the population is growing at the rate n, just as in the Solow growth model used in Chapters 7 and 8, though here people are explicitly finite lived. A given consumer receives income y when young and income y' when old, and we allow (as we have throughout this chapter) for the fact that incomes can differ across consumers. For simplicity, assume that government spending is zero in all periods.

Suppose that no social security program exists before some date, T, and that before date T the taxes on the young and old are zero in each period. Then, pay-as-you-go social security is established at date T and continues forever after. For simplicity, we suppose that the social security program guarantees each old-age consumer in periods T and later a benefit of b units of goods. This tax is represented in our model as a tax for each old consumer in periods T and after of $t' = -b$. The benefits for old consumers must be financed by taxes on the young, and we assume that each young consumer is taxed the same amount, t. Then, because total social security benefits equal total taxes on the young, we have

$$Nb = N't, \qquad (10.10)$$

and so, using Equation (10.9) to substitute for N in Equation (10.10), we can solve for t, obtaining

$$t = \frac{b}{1 + n}. \qquad (10.11)$$

How do consumers benefit from social security? Clearly, the consumers who are old when the program is introduced in period T gain, as these consumers receive the social security benefit but do not have to suffer any increase in taxes when they are young. In Figure 10.6, the lifetime budget constraint of a consumer who is old in period T is AB if there is no social security program, where the slope of AB is $-(1 + r)$ and the endowment point with no social security is E_1, determined by disposable income of y when young and y' when old. With the social security program, this consumer receives disposable income y when young and $y' + b$ when old and has an endowment point given by E_2 on the budget constraint DF (with slope $-(1 + r)$) in the figure.

FIGURE 10.6

Pay-as-You-Go Social Security for Consumers Who Are Old in Period *T*

In the period when social security is introduced, the old receive a social security benefit. The budget constraint of an old consumer shifts from *AB* to *DF*, and he or she is clearly better off.

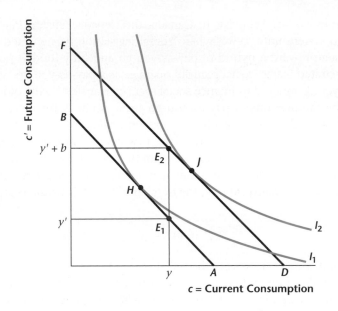

The optimal consumption bundle shifts from *H* to *J* and the consumer is clearly better off because his or her budget constraint has shifted out and he or she is able to choose a consumption bundle on a higher indifference curve.

What happens to consumers born in periods *T* and later? For these consumers, in Figure 10.7, the budget constraint would be *AB* without social security, with an endowment point at E_1 and the budget constraint having slope $-(1 + r)$. With social security, disposable income when young is $y - t = y - \dfrac{b}{1 + n}$ from Equation (10.11)

FIGURE 10.7

Pay-as-You-Go Social Security for Consumers Born in Period *T* and Later

If $n > r$, the budget constraint shifts out from *AB* to *DF*, and the consumer is better off.

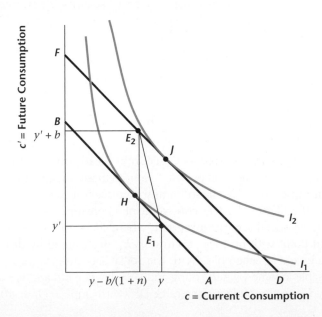

and disposable income when old is $y' + b$. The endowment point shifts to E_2 in the figure on the budget constraint DF. Because the market real interest rate has not changed, the slope of DF is $-(1 + r)$. The slope of $E_1 E_2$ is $-(1 + n)$, so in the figure we have shown the case where $n > r$. In this case, the budget constraint shifts out for this consumer, with the optimal consumption bundle shifting from H to J, and the consumer is better off. However, if $n < r$, the budget constraint would shift in, and the consumer would be worse off.

Therefore, social security makes everyone better off only if the population growth rate is greater than the real interest rate. Otherwise, the old in the initial period are made better off at the expense of the current young and each future generation. The reason that social security can potentially improve welfare is that there is a kind of private market failure in the model that the government can exploit. That is, there is no way for people to trade with those who are unborn, and the young and old alive in a given period cannot trade, as the young would like to exchange current consumption goods for future consumption goods, and the old would like to exchange current consumption goods for past consumption goods. The government is able to use its power to tax to bring about intergenerational transfers that may yield a Pareto improvement, whereby welfare increases for all consumers in the present and the future.

For pay-as-you-go social security to improve welfare for the consumers currently alive and those in future generations requires that the "rate of return" of the social security system be sufficiently high. This rate of return increases with the population growth rate, n, as the population growth rate determines the size of the tax burden for the young generation in paying social security benefits to the old. The smaller this tax burden for each young person, the higher the ratio of the social security benefit in old age to the tax paid to support social security when young, and this ratio is effectively the rate of return of the social security system. If n is larger than r, then the rate of return of the social security system is higher than the rate of return in the private credit market, and this is why social security increases welfare for everyone in this circumstance.

The issue of whether social security can bring about a Pareto improvement for consumers in all generations relates directly to contemporary issues facing the Canada Pension Plan. Recent changes in the plan were brought about because the Canada Pension Plan would not have been sustainable given current contribution rates (captured by the tax, t, in our model). This is because of the large cohort of baby boomers who are retiring and about to retire and because Canadians are living longer than they used to (both effects are captured by a large N' in our model). Thus, benefit levels have been maintained in Canada for retirees but at the expense of a heavier tax burden for the working-age population. This increased burden for the young is mitigated somewhat by the addition of a funded component to the Canada Pension Plan.

Fully Funded Social Security   To analyze fully funded social security, we can use the same apparatus as for the pay-as-you-go case. Again, suppose that government spending is zero forever, but now assume for simplicity that taxes are zero as well.

In the absence of social security, a consumer's lifetime budget constraint is given by AB in Figure 10.8, where the slope of AB is $-(1 + r)$. The consumer's endowment is given by point E, and we suppose that this consumer optimizes by choosing point D, where saving is positive. Fully funded social security is a program whereby the government invests the proceeds from social security taxes in the private credit market, with social security benefits determined by the payoff the government receives in the private credit market. Alternatively, the government could allow the consumer to choose in which assets to invest his or her social security savings. This would make no difference, as there is a single real rate of return, r, available on the credit market.

In any event, fully funded social security is effectively a forced savings program, and it matters only if the amount of social security saving is a binding constraint on consumers. That is, fully funded social security makes a difference only if the social security system mandates a higher level of saving than the consumer would choose in the absence of the program. Such a case is illustrated in Figure 10.8, where the amount of social security saving required by the government is $y - c_1$ so that the consumer receives the consumption bundle F. Clearly, the consumer is worse off than he or she was at point D in the absence of the program. At best, fully funded social security is ineffective, if the amount of social security saving is not binding, or if consumers can undo forced savings by borrowing against their future social security benefits when young. If fully funded social security is a binding constraint on at least some people in the population, then it can only make things worse for optimizing consumers. In spite of this, the changes in the Canada Pension Plan that make it a hybrid of pay-as-you-go and funded systems may in fact be welfare improving for everyone involved, relative to continuing with a pure pay-as-you-go system. For related issues in a European context, see Macroeconomics in Action 10.1.

FIGURE 10.8

Fully Funded Social Security When Mandated Retirement Saving Is Binding

With binding mandated retirement saving, the consumer must choose point F rather than D and is, therefore, worse off.

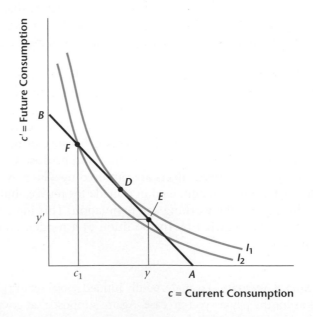

What if the population growth rate is sufficiently low that pay-as-you-go social security is dominated by saving in the private market? Is there any rationale for establishing a social security system so as to force consumers to save for their retirement? The answer is yes, as social security may be a device that solves a commitment problem for the government. This commitment problem takes the following form. In a perfect world, the government could announce to the public that no one will receive assistance from the government in retirement. In such a world, the public believes this announcement, all individuals save for their retirement, and consumption is optimally smoothed for each person over his or her lifetime. The problem is that the public understands that the government cannot commit to such a policy. If people are old and destitute, the government will feel obliged to provide for them. Since people then anticipate that they will receive some minimal standard of living on government assistance in retirement in any event, they may not save for retirement, particularly if they are poor. It may be preferable, given the government's commitment problem, to establish a government-mandated universal social security program, thus inducing something closer to an optimal amount of saving for retirement.

Now, suppose that we accept the argument that a social security system is a convenient device to get around the government's inability to commit. Which system is best, pay-as-you-go or fully funded? An argument in favour of a pure pay-as-you-go system (such as in the United States) is the following. Fully funded programs encounter two problems. First, they potentially allow public pension funds to be run inefficiently because of political interference. This problem occurs if the government manages the public pension fund rather than letting retirees manage their own retirement accounts. The existence of such a large quantity of assets in a public pension fund, seemingly at public disposal, often provides a tempting target for lawmakers and lobbyists. For example, in Canada, the Canada Pension Plan is a mixed fully funded and pay-as-you-go system, and has been the target of groups which advocate socially responsible investing. The theory behind socially responsible investing is that it is possible to change the behaviour of firms or to reduce their activities by directing investments away from them. For example, tobacco companies are a typical target of socially responsible investing, for obvious reasons. While socially responsible investing may be well intentioned, it may at best be ineffective, and at worst have the effect of constraining the management of public pension funds in ways that reduce benefits to retirees. A pay-as-you-go system avoids the issue entirely. With pay-as-you-go, the government is not put in the position of deciding which investments are morally appropriate and which are not, and political activity can be focused in ways that are potentially much more productive.

A second problem with fully funded social security programs is that they may be subject to a **moral hazard** problem. Moral hazard is a well-known feature of insurance, and refers to the fact that, if an individual is insured against a particular loss, he or she will then take less care to prevent the loss from happening. For example, if a person were fully insured against damages to his or her automobile, he or she will take less care in driving in parking lots. In the case of a fully funded social security program,

The viability of North American pay-as-you-go social security systems is being tested as the baby boom generation begins to retire, but European countries have already been forced to deal with the consequences for social security of an aging population. In some European countries (e.g., Germany and Italy) a transition from pay-as-you-go social security to some form of fully funded or partially funded social security is being considered. Research by Assaf Razin and Efraim Sadka analyzes some of the issues associated with such a transition.[2]

In our analysis of pay-as-you-go social security, we showed that the current young, the current old, and all future generations can benefit from such a social security program if the population growth rate exceeds the market real interest rate. However, in circumstances where there exists a very high ratio of current old to young, the current young would benefit from an immediate switch from pay-as-you-go to fully funded social security. The switch implies that the current young do not have to bear a high current tax in exchange for a standard-sized future retirement benefit. However, the transition from pay-as-you-go to fully funded systems would not be a Pareto improvement if the current old lost their retirement benefits (which they were expecting under the pay-as-you-go system in place when they were young).

An alternative approach to a transition from pay-as-you-go to fully funded social security that could yield a Pareto improvement is to have the government issue debt to finance the payment of social security benefits to the current old. If the government issues debt in the present, this of course implies higher future taxes to pay off this debt. However, these higher future taxes will be paid by those who will benefit from the transition to a fully funded system. If the net benefits of the transition are positive, then the current young and future generations can be made better off as a result, and the current old are no worse off. Any Pareto-improving economic policy is something that the population as a whole will clearly vote for, so political economy arguments tell us that governments with a very old population should choose to abandon pay-as-you-go social security and run temporary deficits to finance benefits for the current old.

A problem with this scenario in Europe is that member countries of the European Monetary Union (EMU) have made commitments to keep their budget deficits within certain bounds. Under the Stability and Growth Pact, which came into effect in 1999 for all EMU countries, the government deficit of an EMU member cannot exceed 3% of GDP without penalties being imposed. Thus, in the case of a transition from pay-as-you-go to fully funded social security, the Stability and Growth Pact could block an economic policy that is Pareto improving. The framers of the Pact clearly thought that the commitment it outlined was a good idea, as this would prevent some of the negative effects of large budget deficits. However, the Pact clearly did not account for the role of budget deficits in financing social security. As Razin and Sadka show, there are circumstances when a budget deficit can be a useful device in producing an intergenerational redistribution of wealth that makes an economic policy change (in this case a transition from pay-as-you-go to fully funded social security) produce positive benefits for everyone.

---

[2]A. Razin and E. Sadka, 2002, "The Stability and Growth Pact as an Impediment to Privatizing Social Security," NBER working paper.

suppose that the program allows people to choose how they save for retirement, constraining them only in how much they save. What would happen if an individual chose to invest in a very risky asset, was unlucky, and became destitute in retirement? Given the government's lack of ability to commit, this individual would likely be bailed out by the government. In effect, the government would be called upon to insure retirement accounts, much as it insures the deposits in banks. The moral hazard problem associated with the provision of deposit insurance by the government is well known, and we will study it in Chapter 17. Just as with banks, if retirement accounts were insured, the managers of retirement accounts would tend to take on too much risk. They would know that, if their highly risky investments pay off, so much the better; but if these assets do not pay off, they will be bailed out by the government. The moral hazard problem implies that another level of regulation would be needed to make sure that retirement account managers do not take on too much risk. The provision of government insurance for retirement accounts, and the necessary regulation required to solve the moral hazard problem, might create enough costs that a pay-as-you-go system would be preferable.

Chapter Summary

- With a credit market imperfection, modelled as a situation where the lending interest rate is less than the borrowing interest rate, Ricardian equivalence does not hold. A current tax cut that just changes the timing of taxes, with no effect on lifetime wealth, will increase current consumption and have no effect on savings.

- One credit market imperfection is asymmetric information, under which lenders cannot perfectly observe the creditworthiness of would-be borrowers. In a credit market with good and bad borrowers, the lending interest rate is less than the borrowing interest rate, reflecting a default premium on the loan interest rate. An increase in the fraction of bad borrowers in the market increases the default premium and reduces the quantity of lending.

- A second credit market imperfection is limited commitment—borrowers have an incentive to default on their debts. Lenders give borrowers the incentive to repay by requiring that borrowers post collateral. However, when borrowers are collateral-constrained, a decrease in the price of collateralizable wealth reduces lending and consumption.

- Social security programs can be rationalized by a credit market failure—the inability of the unborn to trade with those currently alive. There are two types of government provided social security programs—pay-as-you-go programs and fully funded programs.

- Pay-as-you-go social security, which funds retirement benefits from taxes on the working age population, increases welfare for everyone if the real interest rate is less than the rate of growth in the population.

- Fully funded social security at best has no effect, and at worst constrains retirement savings in ways that make consumers worse off.

- Even if the population growth rate is low, social security can be justified if we think that the government is unable to commit to providing social assistance to destitute senior citizens. In that event, pay-as-you-go systems may in fact be less costly than fully funded systems.

Key Terms

asymmetric information: Refers to a situation in which, in a particular market, some market participant knows more about his or her own characteristics than do other market participants.

limited commitment: Refers to situations in which it is impossible for a market participant to commit in advance to some future action.

default premium: The portion of a loan interest rate that compensates the lender for the possibility that the borrower may default on the loan.

interest rate spread: The gap between interest rates on risky loans and safer loans, or the difference between interest rates at which some class of individuals can lend and borrow.

collateralizable wealth: Assets that can serve as collateral.

financial intermediary: A financial institution that borrows from a large set of ultimate lenders and lends to a large set of ultimate borrowers. Examples are banks, insurance companies, and mutual funds.

collateral: An asset owned by the borrower that the lender has the right to seize if the borrower defaults on the loan.

repurchase agreement: A short-term loan under which a government security serves as collateral.

pay-as-you-go social security: A social security system in which benefits to the old are financed by taxes on the working population.

fully funded social security: A social security system in which the social security payments of the working population are invested in assets, and the payoffs on these assets finance the social security benefits of those people in old age.

moral hazard: A situation in which insurance against a potential loss reduces the effort taken by the insured to prevent the loss.

Questions for Review

1. What effects do credit market imperfections have on the interest rates faced by lenders and borrowers?

2. What are the effects of a tax cut on consumption and savings in the presence of a credit market imperfections? Does Ricardian equivalence hold?

3. Does the existence of credit market imperfections imply that there is a useful role for government tax policy?

4. What are two sources of credit market imperfections?

5. Explain how a default premium can arise, and what would cause it to increase.

6. If the default premium increases, what is the effect on the consumption and savings of an individual consumer?

7. For a borrower who is collateral-constrained, what happens when the value of collateralizable wealth falls? How does this matter for the financial crisis?

8. Under what conditions will a pay-as-you-go social security system improve welfare for those currently alive and for all future generations?

9. What are the effects of a fully funded social security system?

10. How does the government's ability to commit matter for social security programs?

Problems

1. Suppose that there is a credit market imperfection due to asymmetric information. In the economy, a fraction b of consumers consists of lenders, who each receive an endowment of y units of the consumption good in the current period, and 0 units in the future period. A fraction $(1-b)a$ consumers are good borrowers who each receive an endowment of 0 units in the current period and y units in the future period. Finally, a fraction $(1-b)(1-a)$ of consumers are bad borrowers who receive 0 units of endowment in the current and future periods. Banks cannot distinguish between good and bad borrowers. The government sets $G = G' = 0$, and each consumer is asked to pay a lump-sum tax of t in the current period and t' in the future period. The government also cannot distinguish between good and bad borrowers, but can observe endowments.

   a. Write down the government's budget constraint, making sure to take account of who is able to pay their taxes and who does not.

   b. Suppose that the government decreases t and increases t' in such a way that the government budget constraint holds. Does this have any effect on each consumer's decision about how much to consume in each period and how much to save? Show, with the aid of diagrams.

   c. Does Ricardian equivalence hold in this economy? Explain why or why not.

2. Suppose there is a credit market imperfection due to limited commitment. As in the setup with collateralizable wealth we examined in this chapter, each consumer has a component of wealth which has value pH in the future period, cannot be sold in the current period, and can be pledged as collateral against loans. Suppose also that the government requires each consumer to pay a lump-sum tax t in the current period, and a tax t' in the future period. Also suppose that there is limited commitment with respect to taxation. That is, if a consumer refuses to pay his or her taxes, the government can seize the consumer's collateralizable wealth, but cannot confiscate income (the consumer's endowment). Assume that, if a consumer fails to pay off their debts to private lenders, and also fails to pay their taxes, the government has to be paid first from the consumer's collateralizable wealth.

   a. Show how the limited commitment problem puts a limit on how much the government can spend in the current and future periods.

   b. Write down the consumer's collateral constraint, taking into account the limited commitment problem with respect to taxes.

   c. Now, suppose that the government reduces t and increases t' so that the government budget constraint continues to hold. What will be the effects on an individual consumer's consumption in the present and the future? Does Ricardian equivalence hold in this economy? Explain why or why not.

3. Suppose that there is limited commitment in the credit market, but lenders are uncertain about the value of collateral. Each consumer has a quantity of collateral H, but from the point of view of lender, there is a probability a that the collateral will be worth p in the future period, and probability $1-a$ that the collateral will be worthless in the future period. Suppose that all consumers are identical.

   a. Determine the collateral constraint for the consumer, and show the consumer's lifetime budget constraint in a diagram.

   b. How will a decrease in a affect the consumer's consumption and savings in the current period, and consumption in the future period? Explain your results.

4. Use the social security model developed in this chapter to answer this question. Suppose that the government establishes a social security program in period T which provides a social security benefit of b (in terms of consumption goods) for each old person forever. In period T the government finances the benefits to the current old by issuing debt. This debt is then paid off in period $T + 1$ through lump-sum taxes on the young. In periods $T + 1$ and later, lump-sum taxes on the young finance social security payments to the old.

   a. Show using diagrams that the young and old alive at time T all benefit from the social security program under any circumstances.

   b. What is the effect of the social security program on consumers born in periods $T + 1$ and later? How does this depend on the real interest rate and the population growth rate?

5. Suppose a pay-as-you-go social security system where social security is funded by a proportional tax on the consumption of the young. That is, the tax collected by the government is sc, where s is the tax rate and c is consumption of the young. Retirement benefits are given out as a fixed amount b to each old consumer. Can social security work to improve welfare for everyone under these conditions? Use diagrams to answer this question.

6. Use the social security model developed in this chapter to answer this question. Suppose that a government pay-as-you-go social security system has been in place for a long time, providing a social security payment to each old person of b units of consumption. Now, in period T, suppose that the government notices that $r > n$, and decides to eliminate this system. During period T, the government reduces the tax of each young person to zero, but still pays a social security benefit of b to each old person alive in period T. The government issues enough one-period government bonds, D_T, to finance the social security payments in period T. Then, in period $T + 1$, to pay off the principal and interest on the bonds issued in period T, the government taxes the old currently alive, and issues new one-period bonds D_{T+1}. The taxes on the old in period $T + 1$ are just large enough that the quantity of debt per old person stays constant, that is $D_{T+1} = (1 + n)D_T$. Then, the same thing is done in periods $T + 2$, $T + 3$, ..., so that the government debt per old person stays constant forever.

   a. Are the consumers born in periods T, $T + 1$, $T + 2$, ... better or worse off than they would have been if the pay-as-you-go social security program had stayed in place? Explain, using diagrams.

   b. Suppose that the government follows the same financing scheme as above, but replaces the pay-as-you-go system with a fully funded system in period T. Are consumers better off or worse off than they would have been with pay-as-you-go? Explain, using diagrams.

A Real Intertemporal Model with Investment

This chapter brings together the microeconomic behaviour we have studied in previous chapters to build a model that can serve as a basis for analyzing how macroeconomic shocks affect the economy and that can be used for evaluating the role of macroeconomic policy. With regard to consumer behaviour, we examined work–leisure choices in Chapter 4 and intertemporal consumption–savings choices in Chapters 9 and 10. From the production side, in Chapter 4 we studied a firm's production technology and its labour demand decision, and then in Chapter 5 we showed how changes in total factor productivity affect consumption, employment, and output in the economy as a whole. In Chapters 9 and 10, respectively, we looked at the effects of choices by the government concerning the financing of government expenditure and the timing of taxes, and the implications of credit market frictions. Although the Solow growth model studied in Chapters 7 and 8 included savings and investment, in this chapter we examine in detail how investment decisions are made at the level of the firm. This detail is important for our understanding of how interest rates and credit market conditions affect firms' investment decisions.

In this chapter we complete a model of the real side of the economy. That is, the real intertemporal model we construct here shows how real aggregate output, real consumption, real investment, employment, the real wage, and the real interest rate are determined in the macroeconomy. To predict nominal variables, we need to add money to the real intertemporal model, which is done in Chapter 12. The intertemporal aspect of the model refers to the fact that both consumers and firms make intertemporal decisions, reflecting tradeoffs between the present and the future.

Recall from Chapter 2 that the defining characteristic of investment—expenditure on plant, equipment, and housing—is that it consists of the goods that are produced currently for future use in the production of goods and services. For the economy as a whole, investment represents a tradeoff between present and future consumption. Productive capacity that is used for producing investment goods could otherwise be used for producing current consumption goods, but today's investment increases future productive capacity, which means that more consumption goods can be produced in the future. To understand the determinants of investment, we must study the micro-economic investment behaviour of a firm, which makes an intertemporal decision regarding investment in the current period. When a firm invests, it forgoes current profits so as to have a higher capital stock in the future, which allows it to earn higher future profits. As we show, a firm will invest more, everything else held constant, the lower its current capital stock, the higher its expected future total factor productivity, and the lower the real interest rate.

A key determinant of investment is the real interest rate, which represents the opportunity cost of investment. A higher real interest rate implies that the opportunity cost of investment is larger, at the margin, and so investment falls. Movements in the real interest rate are an important channel by which shocks to the economy affect investment, as we show in this chapter. Further, monetary policy may affect investment through its influence on the real interest rate, as we show in Chapters 12 to 14.

In addition to the effect of the market interest rates, the investment decisions of firms depend on credit market risk as perceived by lenders. That is, firms may find it more difficult to borrow to finance investment projects if lenders, including banks and other financial institutions, perceive lending in general to be more risky. Perceptions of an increase in the degree of riskiness in lending were an important factor in the global financial crisis that began in 2008. In this chapter, we will show how credit market risk can play a role in investment behaviour by incorporating asymmetric information, a credit market imperfection studied in Chapter 10, into our model. The role of asymmetric information in a firm's investment decision will be similar to its role in a consumer's consumption–savings decision, as studied in Chapter 10.

A good part of this chapter involves model building, and there are several important steps we must take before we can use this model to address some important economic issues. This requires some patience and work, but the payoff arrives in the last part of this chapter and continues through the remainder of this book, where the real intertemporal model is the basis for our analysis of monetary factors in Chapter 12, business cycles in Chapters 13 and 14, and other issues in later chapters.

This chapter focuses on the macroeconomic effects on aggregate output, investment, consumption, the real interest rate, labour market variables of aggregate shocks to government spending, total factor productivity, the nation's capital stock, and credit market risk. Although we studied elements of some of these effects in Chapters 5 and 9, this chapter provides new insights involving the effects on the interest rate and investment of these shocks, and the effects of the anticipation of future shocks on current economic activity. For example, including intertemporal factors shows how credit markets play a role in the effects of government spending on the economy. As well, we will be able to use the real intertemporal model to analyze aspects of the impact of the recent financial crisis on aggregate economic activity.

As in Chapters 4 and 5, we work with a model that has a representative consumer, a representative firm, and a government, and, for simplicity, we will boil down the model to the level of supply and demand curves. We are able to capture essential behaviour in this model economy by examining the participation of the representative consumer, the representative firm, and the government in two markets: the market for labour in the current period and the market for goods in the current period. The representative consumer supplies labour in the current labour market and purchases consumption goods in the current goods market, while the representative firm demands labour in the current labour market, supplies goods in the current goods market, and demands investment goods in the current goods market. The government demands goods in the current goods market in terms of government purchases.

The Representative Consumer

The behaviour of the representative consumer in this model will bring together the work–leisure choice from Chapter 4 with the intertemporal consumption behaviour from Chapter 9. That is, the consumer will make a work–leisure decision in each of the current and future periods, and he or she will make a consumption–savings decision in the current period.

The representative consumer works and consumes in the current period and the future period. He or she has h units of time in each period and divides this time between work and leisure in each period. Let w denote the real wage in the current period, w' the real wage in the future period, and r the real interest rate. The consumer pays lump-sum taxes to the government of T in the current period and T' in the future period. His or her goal is to choose current consumption, C, future consumption, C', leisure time in the current and future periods, l and l', respectively, and savings in the current period, S^p, to make himself or herself as well off as possible, given his or her budget constraints in the current and future periods. The representative consumer is a price-taker who takes w, w', and r as given. Taxes are also given from the consumer's point of view.

In the current period, the representative consumer earns real wage income, $w(h-l)$, receives dividend income, π, from the representative firm, and pays taxes, T, so that his or her current-period disposable income is $w(h-l) + \pi - T$, just as in Chapter 4. As in Chapter 9, disposable income in the current period is then split between consumption and savings, and savings takes the form of bonds that earn the one-period real interest rate, r. Just as in Chapter 9, savings can be negative, in which case the consumer borrows by issuing bonds. The consumer's current budget constraint is then

$$C + S^p = w(h-l) + \pi - T. \tag{11.1}$$

In the future period, the representative consumer receives real wage income, $w'(h-l')$, receives real dividend income, π', from the representative firm, pays taxes, T', to the government, and receives the principal and interest on savings from the current period, $(1 + r)S^p$. Because the future period is the last period and since the consumer is assumed to make no bequests, all wealth available to the consumer in the future is consumed, so that the consumer's future budget constraint is

$$C' = w'(h - l') + \pi' - T' + (1 + r)S^p \tag{11.2}$$

Just as in Chapter 9, we can substitute for savings, S^p, in Equation (11.1) by using Equation (11.2) to obtain a lifetime budget constraint for the representative consumer:

$$C + \frac{C'}{1 + r} = w(h - l) + \pi - T + \frac{w'(h - l') + \pi' - T'}{1 + r}. \tag{11.3}$$

This constraint states that the present value of lifetime consumption (on the left-hand side of the equation) equals the present value of lifetime disposable income (on the right-hand side of the equation). Note that a difference from the consumer's lifetime budget constraint in Chapter 9 is that the consumer in this model has some choice, through his or her current and future choices of leisure, l and l', over his or her lifetime wealth.

The representative consumer's problem is to choose C, C', l, and l' to make himself or herself as well off as possible while respecting his or her lifetime budget constraint, as given by Equation (11.3). We cannot depict this choice for the consumer conveniently in a graph, as the problem is four-dimensional (choosing current and future consumption and current and future leisure), while a graph is two-dimensional. It is straightforward, however, to describe the consumer's optimizing decision in terms of three marginal conditions we studied in Chapters 4 and 9. These are as follows:

1. The consumer makes a work–leisure decision in the current period, so that when he or she optimizes, we will have

$$MRS_{l,C} = w; \tag{11.4}$$

   that is, the consumer optimizes by choosing current leisure and consumption so that the marginal rate of substitution of leisure for consumption is equal to the real wage in the current period. This is the same marginal condition as in the work–leisure problem for a consumer that we considered in Chapter 4. Recall that, in general, a consumer optimizes by setting the marginal rate of substitution of one good for another equal to the relative price of the two goods. In Equation (11.4), the current real wage, w, is the relative price of leisure in terms of consumption goods.

2. Similarly, in the future the consumer makes another work–leisure decision, and he or she optimizes by setting

$$MRS_{l',C'} = w'; \tag{11.5}$$

   that is, at the optimum, the marginal rate of substitution of future leisure for future consumption must be equal to the future real wage.

3. With respect to his or her consumption–savings decision in the current period, as in Chapter 9, the consumer optimizes by setting

$$MRS_{C,C'} = 1 + r; \tag{11.6}$$

that is, when the consumer is optimizing the marginal rate of substitution of current consumption for future consumption equals the relative price of current consumption in terms of future consumption.

CURRENT LABOUR SUPPLY

Our ultimate focus will be on the interaction between the representative consumer and the representative firm in the markets for current labour and current consumption goods. Therefore, we will be interested in the determinants of the representative consumer's supply of labour and his or her demand for current consumption goods.

First, we will consider the representative consumer's current supply of labour, which is determined by three factors—the current real wage, the real interest rate, and lifetime wealth. These three factors affect current labour supply as described below.

1. *The quantity of current labour supplied increases when the current real wage increases.* The consumer's marginal condition, Equation (11.4), captures the idea that substitution between current leisure and current consumption is governed by the current real wage rate, w. Recall from Chapter 4 that a change in the real wage has opposing income and substitution effects on the quantity of leisure, so that an increase in the real wage could lead to an increase or a decrease in the quantity of leisure, depending on the size of the income effect. Here, we will assume that the substitution effect of a change in the real wage is always larger than the income effect, implying that leisure decreases and hours worked increases in response to an increase in the real wage. This might seem inconsistent with the fact, pointed out in Chapter 4, that income and substitution effects on labour supply appear to cancel over the long run. However, the model we are building here is intended mainly for analyzing short-run phenomena. As we argued in Chapter 4, the cancelling of income and substitution effects in the long run is consistent with the substitution effect dominating in the short run, as we assume here.

2. *Current labour supply increases when the real interest rate increases.* The consumer can substitute intertemporally not only by substituting current consumption for future consumption, as we studied in Chapter 9, but also by substituting current leisure for future leisure. In substituting leisure between the two periods, the representative consumer responds to the current price of leisure relative to the future price of leisure, which is $\frac{w(1 + r)}{w'}$. Here, w is the price of current leisure (labour) in terms of current consumption, w' is the price of future leisure in terms of future consumption, and $1 + r$ is the price of current consumption in terms of future consumption. Therefore, an increase in the real interest rate, r, given w and w', results in an increase in the price of current leisure relative to future leisure. Assuming again that the substitution effect is larger than the income effect, the consumer will want to consume less current leisure and more future leisure. An example of how this **intertemporal substitution of leisure** effect works is as follows. Suppose that Paul is self-employed and that the market interest rate rises. Then Paul faces a higher return on his savings, so that if he works more in the

current period and saves the proceeds, in the future he can both consume more and work less. It may be helpful to consider that leisure, like consumption, is a good. When the real interest rate increases, and if substitution effects dominate income effects for lenders, current consumption will fall (from Chapter 9), just as current leisure will decrease when the real interest rate increases and substitution effects dominate.

3. *Current labour supply decreases when lifetime wealth increases.* From Chapter 4, we know that an increase in current nonwage disposable income results in an increase in the quantity of leisure and a decrease in labour supply for the consumer, as leisure is a normal good. Further, in Chapter 9, we showed how income effects generalize to the intertemporal case in which the consumer chooses current and future consumption. That is, an increase in lifetime wealth will increase the quantities of current and future consumption chosen by the consumer. Here, when there is an increase in lifetime wealth, there will be an increase in current leisure and thus a decrease in current labour supply, since current leisure is assumed to be normal. The key wealth effect for our analysis in this chapter is the effect of a change in the present value of taxes for the consumer. Any increase in the present value of taxes implies a decrease in lifetime wealth and an increase in current labour supply.

Given these three factors, we can construct an upward-sloping current labour supply curve as in Figure 11.1. Here, the current real wage, w, is measured along the vertical axis, and current labour supply, N, is on the horizontal axis. The current labour supply curve is labelled $N^s(r)$ to indicate that labour supply depends on the current real interest rate. If the real interest rate rises, say from r_1 to r_2, the labour supply curve will shift to the right, as in Figure 11.2, since labour supply will increase for any current real wage, w. In Figure 11.3, an increase in lifetime wealth shifts the labour supply curve

FIGURE 11.1

The Representative Consumer's Current Labour Supply Curve

The current labour supply curve slopes upward, under the assumption that the substitution effect of an increase in the real wage outweighs the income effect.

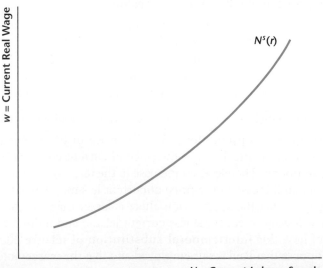

N = Current Labour Supply

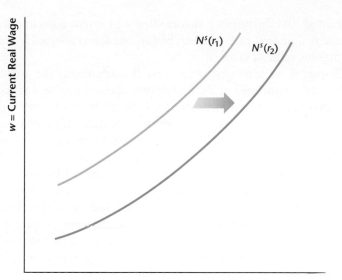

FIGURE 11.2

An Increase in the Real Interest Rate Shifts the Current Labour Supply Curve to the Right
The representative consumer will consume less leisure in the current period and more leisure in the future when r increases.

to the left from $N_1^s(r)$ to $N_2^s(r)$. Such an increase in lifetime wealth could be caused by a decrease in the present value of taxes for the consumer. Note in Figure 11.3 that the real interest rate is held constant as we shift the current labour supply curve to the left.

THE CURRENT DEMAND FOR CONSUMPTION GOODS

Now that we have dealt with the determinants of the representative consumer's current labour supply, we can turn to his or her demand for current consumption goods. The determinants of the demand for current consumption goods were studied in Chapter 9,

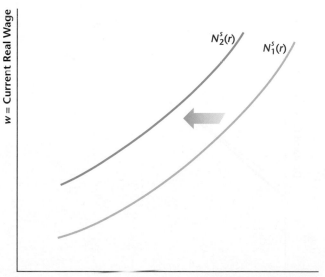

FIGURE 11.3

Effects of an Increase in Lifetime Wealth
More leisure is consumed in the present, because of the income effect, and the current labour supply curve shifts to the left.

where we showed that the primary factors affecting current consumption are lifetime wealth and the real interest rate. Further, lifetime wealth is affected by current income and by the present value of taxes.

As in Chapter 9, we can construct a curve that represents the quantity of current consumption goods demanded by the representative consumer, as a function of current aggregate income, Y, as shown in Figure 11.4. Recall from Chapter 9 that if the real interest rate is held constant and current income increases for the consumer, current consumption will increase. In Figure 11.4, we graph the quantity of current consumption chosen by the representative consumer, for each level of real income Y, holding constant the real interest rate r. In the figure, the demand for consumption goods is on the vertical axis, and aggregate income is on the horizontal axis. We let $C^d(r)$ denote the demand for current consumption goods, indicating the dependence of the demand for consumption on the real interest rate. Recall from Chapter 9 that if current income increases for the consumer, then consumption and savings both increase, so that the quantity of consumption increases by less than one unit for each unit increase in income. In Figure 11.4, the slope of the curve $C^d(r)$ is the *MPC*, or **marginal propensity to consume**, which is the amount that current consumption increases when there is a unit increase in aggregate real income Y.

When there is an increase in the real interest rate, assuming again that the substitution effect of this increase dominates the income effect, there will be a decrease in the demand for current consumption goods because of the intertemporal substitution of consumption (recall our analysis from Chapter 9). In Figure 11.5, if the real interest rate increases from r_1 to r_2, the demand curve for current consumption shifts

FIGURE 11.4

The Representative Consumer's Current Demand for Consumption Goods Increases with Income

The slope of the curve is the marginal propensity to consume, *MPC*. We have *MPC* < 1, since part of an increase in current income is saved.

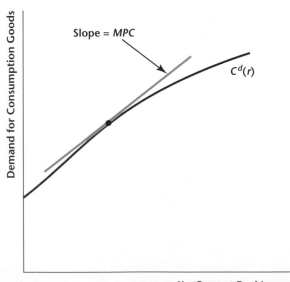

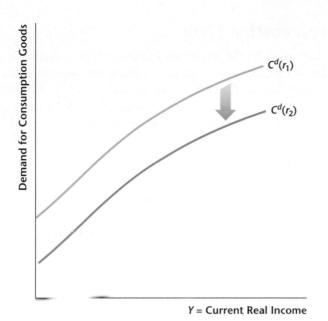

down from $C^d(r_1)$ to $C^d(r_2)$. Also, holding constant r and Y, if there is an increase in lifetime wealth, then, as in Figure 11.6, the demand curve for current consumption shifts up from $C_1^d(r)$ to $C_2^d(r)$. Such an increase in lifetime wealth could be caused by a decrease in the present value of taxes for the consumer or by an increase in future income.

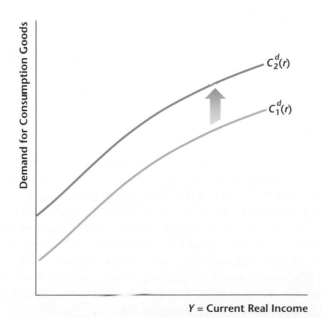

The Representative Firm

Now that we have covered the important features of the consumer's current labour supply and current consumption demand decisions, we can turn to the key decisions of the representative firm for the current labour market and the current goods market.

The representative firm, as in Chapter 4, produces goods by using inputs of labour and capital. The key differences here are that output is produced in both the current and future periods, and that the firm can invest in the current period by accumulating capital so as to expand the capacity to produce future output. In the current period, the representative firm produces output according to the production function

$$Y = zF(K, N), \tag{11.7}$$

where Y is current output, z is total factor productivity, F is the production function, K is current capital, and N is current labour input. Here, K is the capital with which the firm starts the current period, and this quantity is given. The production function, F, is identical in all respects to the production function we studied in Chapter 4.

Similarly, in the future period, output is produced according to

$$Y' = z'F(K', N'), \tag{11.8}$$

where Y' is future output, z' is future total factor productivity, K' is the future capital stock, and N' is the future labour input.

Recall from Chapter 2 that investment, as measured in the NIEA, is expenditure on plant, equipment, housing, and inventory accumulation. Here, we will model investment goods as being produced from output. That is, for simplicity we assume that it requires one unit of consumption goods in the current period to produce one unit of capital. The representative firm invests by acquiring capital in the current period, and the essence of investment is that something must be forgone in the current period in order to gain something in the future. What is forgone by the firm when it invests is current profits; that is, the firm uses some of the current output it produces to invest in capital, which becomes productive in the future. As in the Solow growth model in Chapter 7, capital depreciates at the rate d when used. Then, letting I denote the quantity of current investment, the future capital stock is given by

$$K' = (1 - d)K + I; \tag{11.9}$$

that is, the future capital stock is the current capital stock net of depreciation, plus the quantity of current investment that has been added to the capital stock. Further, the quantity of capital left at the end of the future period is $(1 - d)K'$. Since the future period is the last period, it would not be useful for the representative firm to retain this quantity of capital, and so the firm will liquidate it. We will suppose that the firm can take the quantity $(1 - d)K'$, the capital left at the end of the future period, and convert it one-for-one back into consumption goods, which it can then sell. This is a simple way to model a firm's ability to sell off capital for what it can fetch on the second-hand market. For example, a restaurant that goes out of business can sell its used tables, chairs, and kitchen equipment in a liquidation sale.

PROFITS AND CURRENT LABOUR DEMAND

Now that we know how the firm produces output in the present and the future, and how investment can take place, we are ready to determine present and future profits for the firm. The goal of the firm will be to maximize the present value of profits over the current and future periods, and this will allow us to determine the firm's demand for current labour. For the representative firm, current profits in units of the current consumption good are

$$\pi = Y - wN - I, \tag{11.10}$$

which is current output (or revenue), Y, minus wages paid to workers in the current period, minus current investment. Note again that the firm can produce one unit of capital by using one unit of output, so that each unit of investment decreases current profits by one unit. Future profits for the firm are

$$\pi' = Y' - w'N' + (1 - d)K', \tag{11.11}$$

which is future output minus wages paid to workers in the future, plus the value of the capital stock net of depreciation at the end of the future period.

Profits earned by the firm in the current and future periods are paid out to the shareholders of the firm as dividend income in each period. There is one shareholder in this economy, the representative consumer, and the firm acts in the interests of this shareholder. That implies that the firm will maximize the present value of the consumer's dividend income, which serves to maximize the lifetime wealth of the consumer. Letting V denote the present value of profits for the firm, the firm will then maximize

$$V = \pi + \frac{\pi'}{1 + r} \tag{11.12}$$

by choosing current labour demand N, future labour demand N', and current investment I.

The firm's choice of current labour demand N affects only current profits, π, in Equation (11.10). As in Chapter 4, the firm will hire current labour until the current marginal product of labour equals the current real wage, that is, $MP_N = w$. Also as in Chapter 4, the demand curve for labour in the current period is identical to the marginal product of labour schedule, as the MP_N schedule tells us how much labour the firm needs to hire so that $MP_N = w$. In Figure 11.7 we show the representative firm's demand curve for labour, N^d, with the current real wage, w, on the vertical axis and the current quantity of labour, N, on the horizontal axis. Recall from Chapter 4 that the labour demand curve is downward-sloping because the marginal product of labour declines with the quantity of labour employed.

As in Chapter 4, the labour demand curve shifts with changes in total factor productivity, z, or with changes in the initial capital stock, K. A higher current level of z or a higher level of K will shift the labour demand curve to the right, for example, from N_1^d to N_2^d in Figure 11.8.

The firm chooses labour demand in the future period in a similar way to its choice of current-period labour demand. However, we will ignore the firm's choice of N' in

FIGURE 11.7

The Demand Curve for Current Labour Is the Representative Firm's Marginal Product of Labour Schedule

The curve slopes downward because the marginal product of labour declines as the labour input increases.

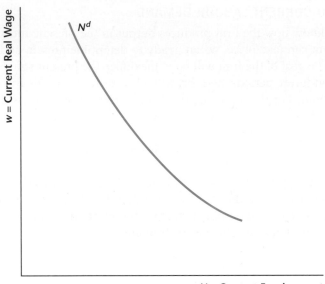

our analysis, as this will simplify our model in a way that makes the model's predictions clearer while doing no harm.

THE REPRESENTATIVE FIRM'S INVESTMENT DECISION

Having dealt with the representative firm's labour demand decision, and given the firm's goal of maximizing the present value of its profits, we can proceed to a central aspect of this chapter, which is analyzing the investment choice of the firm.

FIGURE 11.8

The Current Demand Curve for Labour Shifts Because of Changes in Current Total Factor Productivity, *z*, and in the Current Capital Stock, *K*

Here, an increase in *z* or in *K* shifts the curve to the right, reflecting the increase in the marginal product of labour for each quantity of labour input.

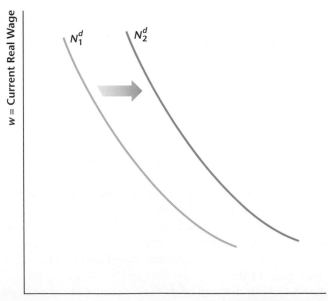

A key principle in economic decision making is that the optimal level of an economic activity is chosen so that the marginal benefit of the activity is equal to its marginal cost. In this respect, there is nothing different about the choice of investment by the representative firm, which will involve equating the marginal cost of investment with the marginal benefit of investment. We will let $MC(I)$ denote the **marginal cost of investment** for the firm, where

$$MC(I) = 1. \tag{11.13}$$

That is, the marginal cost of investment for the firm is what it gives up, in terms of the present value of profits, V, by investing in one unit of capital in the current period. This marginal cost is 1, as from Equations (11.12) and (11.10); an additional unit of current investment, I, reduces current profits, π, by one unit, which reduces the present value of profits, V, by one unit.

The **marginal benefit from investment**, denoted by $MB(I)$, is what one extra unit of investment in the current period adds to the present value of profits, V. In Equation (11.11), all the benefits from investment come in terms of future profits, π', and there are two components to the marginal benefit. First, an additional unit of current investment adds one unit to the future capital stock, K'. This implies that the firm will produce more output in the future, and the additional output produced is equal to the firm's future marginal product of capital, MP'_K. Second, each unit of current investment implies that there will be an additional $1 - d$ units of capital remaining at the end of the future period (after depreciation in the future period), which can be liquidated. Thus, one unit of additional investment in the current period implies an additional $MP'_K + 1 - d$ units of future profits, π'. In calculating the marginal benefit of investment, we have to discount these future profits, so we then have

$$MB(I) = \frac{MP'_K + 1 - d}{1 + r}. \tag{11.14}$$

The firm will invest until the marginal benefit from investment is equal to the marginal cost—that is, $MB(I) = MC(I)$—or from Equations (11.13) and (11.14),

$$\frac{MP'_K + 1 - d}{1 + r} = 1. \tag{11.15}$$

We can rewrite (11.15) as

$$MP'_K = r + d,$$

or

$$MP'_K - d = r. \tag{11.16}$$

Equation (11.16) states that the firm invests until the **net marginal product of capital**, $MP'_K - d$, is equal to the real interest rate. The net marginal product of capital, $MP'_K - d$, is the marginal product of capital after taking account of the depreciation of the capital stock. The intuition behind the **optimal investment rule**, (11.16), is that the opportunity cost of investing in more capital is the real rate of interest, which is the rate of return on the alternative asset in this economy. That is, in the model there are two assets: bonds traded on the credit market and capital held by the representative firm. If the firm invests in capital, it is forgoing lending in the credit market, where it could earn a real rate of return of r.

Effectively, the representative consumer holds the capital of the firm indirectly, since the consumer owns the firm and receives its profits as dividend income. From the consumer's point of view, the rate of return he or she receives between the current and future periods when the firm engages in investment is the net marginal product of capital. As the firm acts in the interests of the consumer, it would not be optimal for the firm to invest beyond the point where the net marginal product is equal to the real interest rate, as in Equation (11.16). This would imply that the consumer was receiving a lower rate of return on his or her savings than could be obtained by lending in the credit market at the real interest rate, r. Thus, the real interest rate represents the opportunity cost of investing for the representative firm.

Another aspect of the firm's investment decision can help clarify the role of the market real interest rate in the firm's optimal choice. Suppose, given the optimal choice of investment for the firm, that $\pi = Y - wN - I < 0$. How is this possible? Such a situation is much like what occurs when a consumer chooses to consume more than his or her income during the current period. That is, the firm borrows the amount $I + wN - Y$ so as to help finance current investment and must repay the quantity $(1 + r)(I + wN - Y)$ in the future period. It will be optimal for the firm to borrow only up to the point where the net rate of return on investment is equal to the market real interest rate, as borrowing any more would be unprofitable. This is just another sense in which the market real interest rate is the opportunity cost of investment for the firm.

In Figure 11.9 we graph the firm's **optimal investment schedule**, with the real interest rate on the vertical axis and the demand for investment goods, I^d, on the horizontal axis. Given Equation (11.16), the optimal investment schedule is the firm's net marginal product of capital for each level of investment in the current period. In the figure, if the real interest rate is r_1, the firm wants to invest I_1, and if the real interest rate falls to r_2, investment will increase to I_2. Note the similarity here to the firm's current labour demand decision, as represented, for example, in Figure 11.7. When making its current labour demand decision, the relevant price to consider is the current real wage, and the firm hires labour until the marginal product of labour is equal to the real wage. In making its investment decision, the relevant price is the real interest rate, and the firm acquires capital (invests) until the net marginal product of capital is equal to the real interest rate.

Optimal investment, I^d, is determined in part by the market real interest rate, r, as reflected in the negative slope of the optimal investment schedule in Figure 11.9. Also, the optimal investment schedule will shift because of any factor that changes the future net marginal product of capital. Primarily, we will be interested in the following two types of shifts in the optimal investment schedule:

1. *The optimal investment schedule shifts to the right if future total factor productivity, z', increases.* From Chapter 4, recall that an increase in total factor productivity will increase the marginal product of capital for each level of the capital stock.

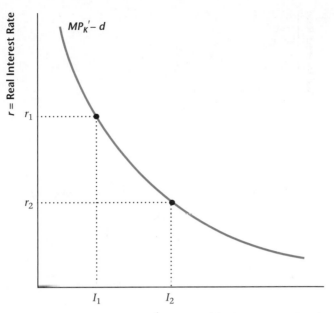

FIGURE 11.9
**Optimal Investment
Schedule for the
Representative Firm**
The optimal investment rule
states that the firm invests
until $MP'_K - d = r$. The
future net marginal product
schedule, $MP'_K - d$, is the
representative firm's optimal
investment schedule, since
this describes how much
investment is required for
the net marginal product of
future capital to equal the real
interest rate.

Therefore, if total factor productivity is expected to be higher in the future, so that z' increases, this increases the future marginal product of capital, and the firm will be more willing to invest during the current period. Higher investment in the current period leads to higher future productive capacity so that the firm can take advantage of high future total factor productivity.

2. *The optimal investment schedule shifts to the left if the current capital stock, K, is higher.* A higher capital stock at the beginning of the current period implies, from Equation (11.9), that for a given level of current investment, I, the future capital stock, K', will be larger. That is, if K is larger, there is more of this initial capital left after depreciation in the current period to use in future production. Therefore, higher K implies that the future marginal product of capital, MP'_K, will decrease for each level of investment, and the optimal investment schedule will then shift to the left.

In Figure 11.10 we show a shift to the right in the optimal investment schedule, which could be caused either by an increase in future total factor productivity, z', or by a lower current quantity of capital, K. Note that the optimal investment schedule will also shift if the depreciation rate, d, changes, but it will be left to the reader to determine the resulting shift in the curve as a problem at the end of this chapter.

This theory of investment helps explain why aggregate investment expenditure tends to be more variable over the business cycle than aggregate output or aggregate consumption. A key implication of consumer behaviour is smoothing; consumers want to smooth consumption over time relative to their income, and this explains why consumption tends to be less variable than income. However, investment behaviour is not about smoothing but about the response of the firm's investment behaviour to changes

FIGURE 11.10

The Optimal Investment Schedule Shifts to the Right If Current Capital Decreases or Future Total Factor Productivity Is Expected to Increase

Either of these changes causes the future marginal product of capital to increase. The figure shows the effect of a decrease in current capital from K_1 to K_2.

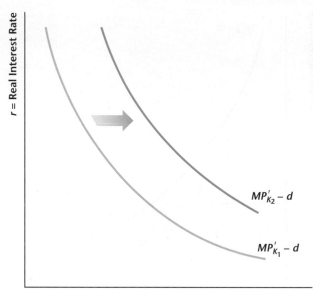

I^d = **Demand for Investment Goods**

in the firm's perceived marginal rate of return to investment. Provided the real interest rate and future total factor productivity vary sufficiently over the business cycle, our theory of the business cycle can explain the variability in observed investment expenditures. That is, investment will be variable if the real interest rate is variable, causing movements along the optimal investment schedule in Figure 11.9, or if there is variability in anticipated future total factor productivity, causing the optimal investment schedule to shift over time.

Optimal Investment: A Numerical Example To make the firm's optimal investment decision more concrete, consider the following numerical example. Paula, a small-scale farmer, has an apple orchard, which has 10 trees in the current period—that is, $K = 10$. For simplicity, suppose that the quantity of labour required to operate the orchard does not depend on the number of trees Paula has, at least for the number of trees that Paula can plant on her land. In the current period, the 10 trees produce 100 kilograms of apples; that is, $Y = 100$. Paula can invest in more trees by taking some of the apples, extracting the seeds (which we assume makes the apples useless), and planting them. Very few of the seeds grow, and it takes 1 kilogram of apples to yield 1 tree that will be productive in the future period. The first extra tree that Paula grows will be on her best land, and therefore it will have a high marginal product, bearing a relatively large amount of fruit. The second tree will be planted on slightly worse land, and so will have a smaller marginal product, and so on. Every period, some trees die. In fact, at the end of each period, Paula loses 20% of her trees, and so the depreciation rate is $d = 0.2$. At the end of the future period, Paula can liquidate her trees. Since each kilogram of apples can produce a tree, it is possible to exchange 1 tree for 1 kilogram

TABLE 11.1 **Data for Paula's Orchard**

K' = Trees in Future	I	Y'	V	$MP'_K - d$
8	0	95	196.57	—
9	1	98	199.19	2.8
10	2	100	200.86	1.8
11	3	101	201.57	0.8
12	4	101.5	201.81	0.3
13	5	101.65	201.71	−0.05
14	6	101.75	201.57	−0.1
15	7	101.77	201.35	−0.18

of apples on the open market, so that the liquidation value of a tree remaining in the future period, after depreciation, is 1 kilogram of apples. The real interest rate is 5%, or $r = 0.05$ in units of apples. Table 11.1 shows the quantity of future output that will be produced when the number of trees Paula has in the future is 8, 9, 10,..., 15, as well as the associated level of investment, the present discounted value of profits (in units of apples), and the net marginal product of capital (trees) in the future.

From Table 11.1, note that the present value of profits is maximized when the number of trees in the future is 12 and the quantity of investment is 4 kilograms of apples. Also note that for each unit of investment from 1 to 4, the net marginal product of capital in the future is greater than the real interest rate, which is 0.05, but that the net marginal product of capital is equal to or less than 0.05 for each unit of investment above 4. Therefore, it is optimal to invest as long as the net marginal product of future capital is greater than the real interest rate.

INVESTMENT WITH ASYMMETRIC INFORMATION: THE FINANCIAL CRISIS

In Chapter 10, we discussed and analyzed the importance of credit market imperfections in consumer credit markets, and some of the implications for the recent global financial crisis. One feature of credit markets that can give rise to credit market imperfections is asymmetric information—a situation where would-be borrowers in the credit market know more about their creditworthiness than do would-be lenders. The purpose of this section is to show how asymmetric information matters for the investment choices of firms, just as it matters for a consumer's saving behaviour, and to explore the importance of this for the current financial crisis.

As in Chapter 10, it will help to model borrowing and lending in the credit market as occurring only through banks. Anyone who wishes to lend holds a deposit with a bank that bears the market real interest rate r. Assume that these deposits are completely safe—a bank that takes deposits in the current period is always able to pay the rate of return r to each depositor in the future period. Also suppose that, instead of a single representative firm, there are many firms in the economy. Some of these firms will choose to lend in the current period, and these firms will have positive profits in the current period, with $\pi = Y - wN - I > 0$. There will also be some firms that choose to borrow. Among these borrowing firms, there are *good* firms, which have negative current profits, or $\pi = Y - wN - I < 0$. There are also *bad* firms that borrow in the credit market, but have no intention of producing anything in the future. The managers of a bad firm simply take the amount borrowed in the credit market and consume it as executive compensation rather than investing in new capital. This model captures, in a simple and realistic way, a key feature of information problems in credit markets.

Unfortunately, a bank is not able to distinguish between a good firm and a bad one, and therefore treats all firms wishing to borrow in the same way. This is the asymmetric information problem—each borrowing firm knows whether it is good or bad, but the bank cannot tell the difference. So that the bank can make good on its promise to pay each depositor a rate of return of r on his or her deposits, the bank must charge each borrower a real interest rate on loans that is greater than r. That is, if we let r^l denote the loan interest rate, we will have $r < r^l$, and the difference $r^l - r$ is a default premium, similar to the default premium we analyzed in Chapter 10. By lending to a large number of borrowers, the bank is able to accurately predict the chances of lending to a bad borrower. Then, the default premium charged to good borrowers will compensate the bank for loans made to bad borrowers, which will yield nothing for the bank.

For a firm that is a lender, investment is financed out of retained earnings. Such a firm has revenue remaining after paying its wage bill in the current period (the quantity $Y - wN$), uses some of this revenue to finance investment, and lends the remainder $(Y - wN - I)$ to the bank at the real interest rate r. For such a lending firm, the analysis of the firm's investment decision is identical to that in the previous subsection, and the firm's optimal investment rule is given by Equation (11.16), with the optimal investment schedule depicted in Figure 11.9.

A good firm that borrows will borrow at the real interest rate

$$r^l = r + x$$

where x is the default premium, and so the opportunity cost of investment for a good borrowing firm is $r + x$, and the optimal investment schedule for this firm is

$$MP'_K - d = r + x$$

or

$$MP'_K - d - x = r. \tag{11.17}$$

In Equation (11.17), note that the default premium acts to reduce the net marginal product of capital, given the safe credit market interest rate r. In Figure 11.11, we show the effect on the optimal investment schedule of a good borrowing firm when there is an increase in the default premium. Such an increase in the default premium could occur if banks perceive that bad borrowing firms have become more prevalent. In the figure, the default premium increases from x_1 to x_2. As a result, the optimal investment schedule for the firm shifts down (or to the left), and the firm will choose to invest less at each level of the safe market real interest rate, r.

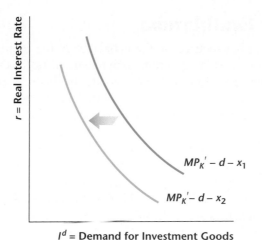

FIGURE 11.11

The Effect of an Increased Default Premium on a Firm's Optimal Investment Schedule

An increase in the default premium, from x_1 to x_2, shifts the optimal investment schedule down, so that the firm will invest less given any safe real interest rate, r.

How does this matter for the recent financial market crisis? A feature of the crisis was an increase in financial market uncertainty. Financial institutions, including banks, became increasingly unsure about which firms were likely to default on loans. This uncertainty is reflected in an increased "spread"—the difference between the interest rates on risky assets and the interest rates on safe assets. As a result, even healthy firms could suffer. In our model, a firm may know that it will be able to repay a loan in the future, but in spite of this it will face a higher default premium in the face of increased credit market uncertainty. For a given safe market interest rate (the interest rate r faced by bank depositors), the firm will choose to invest and borrow less.

Government

We have now shown how the representative consumer and the representative firm behave in the markets for current goods and current labour. It remains only to consider government behaviour before we show how all these economic agents interact in a competitive equilibrium. Government behaviour is identical to what it was in Chapter 10. The government sets government purchases of consumption goods exogenously in each period. The quantity of government purchases in the current period is G, and government purchases in the future are G'. The government finances government purchases in the current period through taxation and by issuing government bonds in the current period. Then, in the future, the government pays off the interest and principal on its bonds and finances future government spending through future lump-sum taxation. As in Chapter 10, the government must satisfy its present-value budget constraint,

$$G + \frac{G'}{1 + r} = T + \frac{T'}{1 + r}.$$ (11.18)

Competitive Equilibrium

Our analysis thus far has focused on the behaviour of the representative consumer, the representative firm, and the government in two markets, the current-period labour market and the current-period market for goods. In this real intertemporal model, the representative consumer supplies labour in the current-period labour market and demands consumption goods in the current-period goods market. The representative firm demands labour in the current period, supplies goods in the current period, and demands investment goods in the current period. Finally, the government demands goods in the current period, in terms of government purchases.

Perceptive readers might wonder why we have neglected the future markets for labour and goods and the market for credit. Markets in the future are disregarded to make our model simple to work with, and this simplification will be essentially harmless at this level of analysis. As for the credit market, later in this chapter we will show that we have not actually neglected it, as equilibrium in the current-period goods market will imply that the credit market clears, just as we showed in the two-period model in Chapter 10.

This section will show how a competitive equilibrium for our model, where supply equals demand in the current-period labour and goods markets, can be expressed in terms of diagrams. We will put together the labour supply and labour demand curves to capture how the labour market functions; then, we will derive an output supply curve that describes how the supply of goods is related to the real interest rate. Finally, we will derive an output demand curve, which describes how the sum of the demand for goods from the representative consumer (consumption goods), the representative firm (investment goods), and the government (government purchases) is related to the real interest rate. Putting the output demand and supply curves together in a diagram with the labour market will give us a working model, which will be used to address some key issues in macroeconomics in the following sections and in later chapters.

THE CURRENT LABOUR MARKET AND THE OUTPUT SUPPLY CURVE

First, we will consider how the market for labour in the current period works. In Figure 11.12(a), we show the labour demand curve for the representative firm, and the labour supply curve for the representative consumer, as derived in the previous sections, with the current real wage, w, on the vertical axis and the current quantity of labour, N, on the horizontal axis. Recall from earlier sections in this chapter that the labour supply curve slopes upward, as we are assuming that the substitution effect of an increase in the real wage dominates the income effect, and recall that the position of the labour supply curve depends on the real interest rate, r. Also, we determined that an increase (decrease) in the real interest rate will cause an increase (decrease) in labour supply for each real wage w, and the labour supply curve will shift to the right (left). Given the real interest rate, r, the equilibrium real wage in Figure 11.12(a) is w^* and the equilibrium quantity of employment is N^*, and from the production function in Figure 11.12(b), we determine the quantity of aggregate output supplied (given the real interest rate), which is Y^*. Recall from Chapter 4 that the position of the

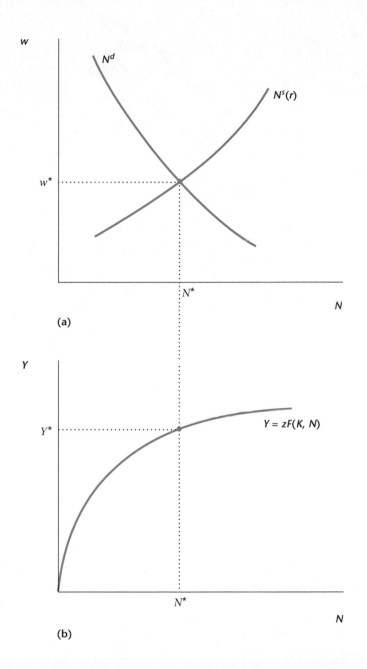

FIGURE 11.12

**Determination of
Equilibrium in the Labour
Market Given the Real
Interest Rate, *r***

In (a), the intersection of the
current labour supply and
demand curves determines
the current real wage and
current employment, and
the production function
in (b) then determines
aggregate output.

production function is determined by current total factor productivity, z, and by the current capital stock, K. An increase in z or K would shift the production function up.

Our next step will be to use the diagrams in Figure 11.12 to derive an output supply curve, which describes how much output will be supplied by firms for each possible level of the real interest rate. In Figure 11.13(a), the labour supply curves for two different interest rates, r_1 and r_2, are shown, where $r_1 < r_2$. Thus, with the increase in the real interest rate, the current labour supply curve shifts to the right, the current

FIGURE 11.13

Construction of the Output Supply Curve

The output supply curve, Y^s, is an upward-sloping curve in panel (c) of the figure, consisting of real current output and real interest rate pairs for which the labour market is in equilibrium.

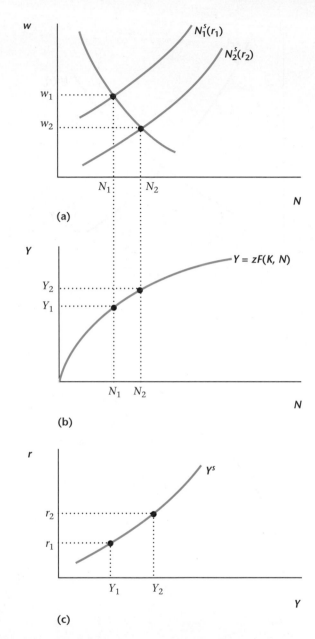

(a)

(b)

(c)

equilibrium real wage falls from w_1 to w_2, and current employment increases from N_1 to N_2. Further, current output increases from Y_1 to Y_2, in Figure 11.13(b), from the production function. We can then construct a curve called the **output supply curve**, which is an upward-sloping curve consisting of all combinations of current output and real interest rates, (Y, r), for which the current labour market is in equilibrium. This curve is denoted Y^s in Figure 11.13(c). Note that two points on the Y^s curve are (Y_1, r_1) and (Y_2, r_2), since at real interest rate r_1 the labour market is in equilibrium when the representative firm produces current output Y_1, and at real interest rate r_2 the labour market is in equilibrium when the representative firm produces current output Y_2. Thus, the output supply curve slopes upward because of the intertemporal substitution effect on labour supply. If the real interest rate is higher, the representative consumer will choose to supply more labour, resulting in an increase in employment and output.

Shifts in the Output Supply Curve When we work with our real intertemporal model, it will be critical to know how changes in particular exogenous variables shift supply and demand curves. In this subsection, we will show how three factors— lifetime wealth, current total factor productivity, and the current capital stock—can shift the output supply curve. It turns out that the latter two factors have much the same effect, and so we will deal with these together.

The output supply curve will shift because of a shift in the current labour sup- ply curve (not arising because of a change in the real interest rate; the output supply curve already takes this into account), because of a shift in the current labour demand curve, or because of a shift in the production function. From our analysis of consumer behaviour, we know that a change in lifetime wealth will shift the labour supply curve, whereas a change in either current total factor productivity or the current capital stock will shift the labour demand curve and the production function. We will deal with each of these shifts in turn.

Recall, from our discussion of the representative consumer's behaviour earlier in this chapter, that a decrease in lifetime wealth will reduce the consumer's demand for current leisure because of an income effect. Therefore, the consumer will supply more labour for any current real wage, and the labour supply curve will shift to the right. What would cause a reduction in lifetime wealth for the representative consumer? The key factor, from our point of view, will be an increase in government spending, either in the present or in the future. From the present-value government budget constraint (11.18), any increase in government spending, either in the present or the future (that is, an increase in G or G') must be reflected in an increase in the present value of taxes for the consumer, $T + \dfrac{T'}{1 + r}$. Therefore, an increase in G, in G', or in both, will result in an increase in the lifetime tax burden for the representative consumer. In Figure 11.14(a), this causes a shift to the right in the labour supply curve from $N_1^S(r_1)$ to $N_2^S(r_1)$, as there is a negative income effect on current leisure.

The shift to the right in the labour supply curve in Figure 11.14(a) implies that for a given real interest rate, the equilibrium quantity of employment in the labour market is higher; that is, employment rises from N_1 to N_2 in Figure 11.14(a), given a particular real interest rate, r_1. From the production function in Figure 11.14(b), output will rise from Y_1 to Y_2 given the real interest rate r_1. This will then imply that the output supply function shifts to the right, from Y_1^S to Y_2^S in 11.14(c). That is, output will be higher for each possible value for the real interest rate. The conclusion is that *an increase in G or G' shifts the labour supply curve to the right and shifts the output supply curve to the right because of the income effect on labour supply*.

From Chapter 4, recall that an increase in total factor productivity or in the capital stock will shift the production function up, since more output can be produced for any level of the labour input, and the labour demand curve shifts to the right, since

FIGURE 11.14

An Increase in Current or Future Government Spending Shifts the Y^s Curve

The increase in government spending increases the present value of taxes for the representative consumer, and current leisure falls, shifting the labour supply curve to the right in (a) and shifting the output supply curve to the right in (c).

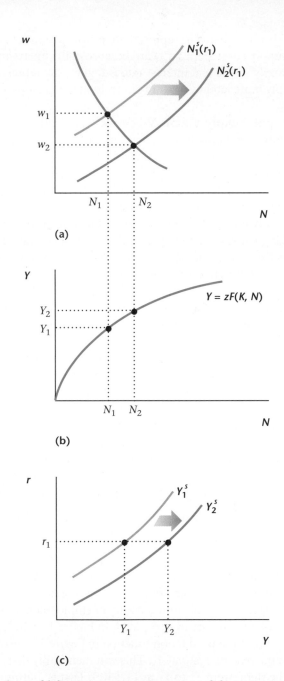

the marginal product of labour increases. In our model, an increase in current total factor productivity, z, or in the current capital stock, K, causes the production function to shift up. In Figure 11.15(b) we show the results of an increase in z from z_1 to z_2, but the effect of an increase in K would be identical. The labour demand curve shifts to the right in Figure 11.15(a), from N_1^d to N_2^d. As a result, given the real interest rate r_1, the equilibrium quantity of employment rises from N_1 to N_2. Therefore, from the production function in Figure 11.15(b), as employment is higher and z is higher,

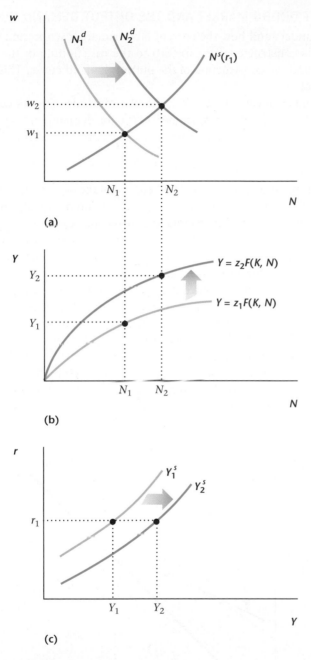

FIGURE 11.15

An Increase in Current Total Factor Productivity Shifts the Y^s Curve
An increase in z increases the marginal product of current labour, shifting the labour demand curve to the right in (a). As well, the production function shifts up, so the Y^s output supply curve shifts to the right in (c).

output increases from Y_1 to Y_2. The same effects (an increase in employment and output) would happen for any level of the real interest rate, which implies that the output supply curve in Figure 11.15(c) must shift to the right. The results would be identical if there had been an increase in the current capital stock. The conclusion is that *an increase in z or K will cause the production function to shift up, the labour demand curve to shift to the right, and the output supply curve to shift to the right.*

THE CURRENT GOODS MARKET AND THE OUTPUT DEMAND CURVE

Now that we understand how the current labour market works and how the output supply curve is constructed, we can turn to the functioning of the current-period goods market and the construction of the output demand curve. This will then complete our model.

Total current aggregate income, Y, is the sum of the demand for current consumption goods by the representative consumer, $C^d(r)$, the demand for investment goods by the representative firm, $I^d(r)$, and government purchases of current goods, G:

$$Y = C^d(r) + I^d(r) + G. \qquad (11.19)$$

Here, we use the notation $C^d(r)$ and $I^d(r)$ to reflect that the demand for current consumption goods and the demand for investment goods depend negatively on the real interest rate, r. Recall from our treatment of consumer behaviour earlier in this chapter that the demand for current consumption goods also depends on the lifetime wealth of the representative consumer, one component of which is current income. In Figure 11.16 we show the total demand for goods, the right-hand side of Equation (11.19), as a function of current aggregate income, Y. Since the demands for investment goods and government purchases do not depend on aggregate income, the slope of the curve $C^d(r) + I^d(r) + G$ in the figure is the marginal propensity to consume, MPC. What will be the equilibrium demand for current goods in the market, given the real interest rate, r? This will be determined by the point at which the curve $C^d(r) + I^d(r) + G$ intersects the $45°$ line, that is, where the demand for goods induced by the quantity of income, Y (through the dependence of the demand for consumption goods on income), is just equal to Y. Therefore, in Figure 11.16 the demand for current goods is Y_1, which is the

FIGURE 11.16

The Demand for Current Goods

This is an upward-sloping curve, as the demand for consumption goods increases with current income. The slope of the demand curve for current goods is the marginal propensity to consume (*MPC*).

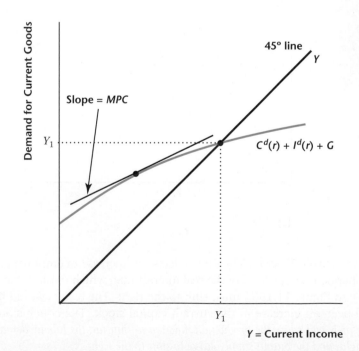

quantity of aggregate income that generates a total demand for goods just equal to that quantity of aggregate income.

The next step is to construct the **output demand curve**, which is a negative relationship between current aggregate output and the real interest rate. In Figure 11.17(a), if the real interest rate is r_1, the current demand for goods is $C^d(r_1) + I^d(r_1) + G$. If the real interest rate is r_2 with $r_2 > r_1$, the current demand for goods will fall for each level of aggregate current income Y, as the demand for current consumption goods and for current investment goods will be lower. Thus, the demand for goods will shift down to $C^d(r_2) + I^d(r_2) + G$. As a result, the equilibrium quantity of goods demanded will fall from Y_1 to Y_2. Now, in Figure 11.17(b), we can construct a downward-sloping curve in a diagram with the real interest rate, r, on the vertical axis, and current aggregate income, Y, on the horizontal axis. This curve, Y^d, is the output demand curve, and a point on the curve, (Y, r), represents the level of demand for goods (output), Y, given the real interest rate r. Note that two points on the output demand curve are (Y_1, r_1) and (Y_2, r_2), corresponding to Figure 11.17(a).

Shifts in the Output Demand Curve Before we put all the elements of our real intertemporal model together—the output demand curve, the output supply curve, the production function, and the current labour supply and demand curves—we need to understand the important factors that will shift the output demand curve. The output demand curve will shift as the result of a shift in the demand for current consumption goods, $C^d(r)$, a shift in the demand for investment goods, $I^d(r)$, or a change in the current quantity of government purchases, G. In Figure 11.18 we show the effects of an increase in the demand for goods of Δ, which could come from any of these sources. In Figure 11.18(a), the demand for current goods shifts up when goods

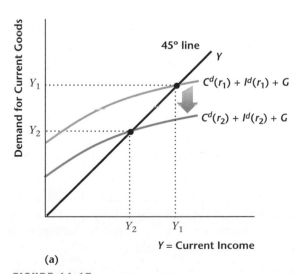
(a)

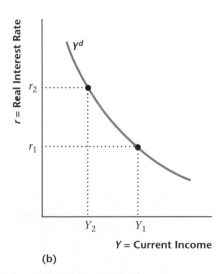
(b)

FIGURE 11.17

Construction of the Output Demand Curve

The output demand curve Y^d in (b) is a downward-sloping one describing the combinations of real output and the real interest rate for which the current goods market is in equilibrium.

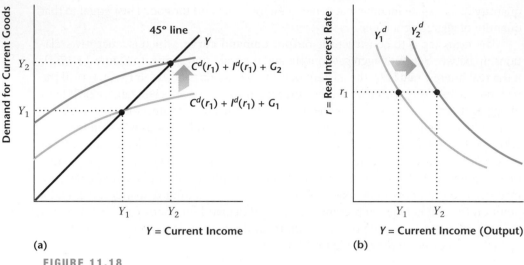

FIGURE 11.18

The Output Demand Curve Shifts to the Right if There Is a Shift in Demand Coming from any Component of Expenditure

The figure shows the effects on total demand of an increase of in exogenous spending.

demand increases by Δ. Then, given the real interest rate r_1, the quantity of current goods demanded will increase from Y_1 to Y_2. As a result, in Figure 11.18(b), the output demand curve shifts to the right from Y_1^d to Y_2^d; that is, the quantity of current goods demanded is higher for any real interest rate, including r_1. Other important factors that will shift the Y^d curve to the right, in a manner identical to the results for an increase in G in Figure 11.17, are the following:

- *A decrease in the present value of taxes shifts the Y^d curve to the right.* A decrease in the present value of taxes is caused by a reduction in current taxes, future taxes, or both. When this happens, the lifetime wealth of the representative consumer rises, and therefore the demand for consumption goods, $C^d(r)$, increases, which causes a shift to the right in the output demand curve.

- *An increase in future income, Y', shifts the Y^d curve to the right.* If the representative consumer anticipates that his or her future income will be higher, then this is an increase in lifetime wealth, which causes $C^d(r)$ to increase and brings about a shift to the right in the output demand curve.

- *An increase in future total factor productivity, z', causes the Y^d curve to shift to the right.* If the representative firm expects total factor productivity to be higher in the future, this increases the firm's demand for investment goods, so that $I^d(r)$ increases. The output demand curve then shifts to the right.

- *A decrease in the current capital stock, K, causes the Y^d curve to shift to the right.* When there is a lower current capital stock, perhaps because of destruction, the demand for investment goods, $I^d(r)$, will increase for each r. As a result, the output demand curve will shift to the right.

THE COMPLETE REAL INTERTEMPORAL MODEL

We now have all the building blocks for our real intertemporal model, and so we can put them together and use the model to address some interesting economic issues. Our model is presented in Figure 11.19, where a competitive equilibrium consists of a state of affairs where supply equals demand in the current labour market in panel (a), and in the current goods market in panel (b). In Figure 11.19(a), N^d is the current labour demand curve, while $N^s(r)$ is the current labour supply curve, which shifts with the real interest rate, r. The equilibrium real wage is given by w^*, and the equilibrium quantity of employment is N^*, where w^* and N^* are determined by the intersection of the demand and supply curves for current labour. Equilibrium output and the equilibrium real interest rate are Y^* and r^*, respectively, in Figure 11.19(b), and they are determined by the intersection of the output demand curve, Y^d, with the output supply curve, Y^s.

To use the model to help us understand how the macroeconomy works, we will perform some experiments that involve changing the value of some exogenous variable or variables and asking how the solution of the model will change as a result. We will then show how we interpret the results in terms of real-world macroeconomic events. Our experiments will answer the following questions:

1. How does an increase in current government purchases, anticipated to be temporary, affect current macroeconomic variables?

2. What are the effects on current macroeconomic variables of a decrease in the current capital stock, brought about by a natural disaster or a war?

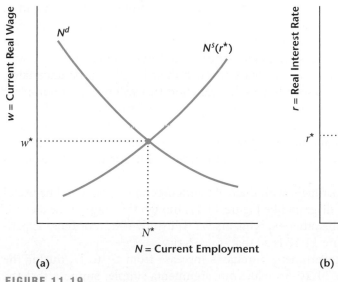
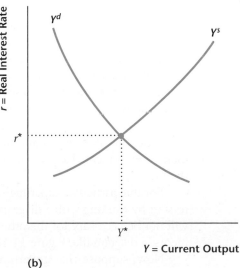

(a)   **(b)**

FIGURE 11.19

The Complete Real Intertemporal Model

(a) The current real wage and current employment are determined by the intersection of the current labour supply and demand curves, given the real interest rate. (b) Current aggregate output and the real interest rate are determined by the intersection of the output supply and demand curves.

3. How does a temporary increase in total factor productivity affect macroeconomic variables, and how does this fit the key business cycle facts?

4. If total factor productivity is expected to increase in the future, how does this affect current macroeconomic variables?

5. How does increased uncertainty in credit markets affect macroeconomic activity?

The Equilibrium Effects of a Temporary Increase in G: Stimulus, the Multiplier, and Crowding Out

This may seem like ground we have covered already, as we analyzed the effects of a change in government purchases in the one-period model in Chapter 5. There, we learned that there is an income effect of government spending that acts to increase labour supply and output and that government spending acts to crowd out private consumption. What we will learn using the real intertemporal model is, first, how the intertemporal choices of consumers affect the economy's response to a change in government spending. An increase in G will act to increase the real interest rate, and this will introduce additional crowding-out effects on private spending, working through both investment and consumption. Further, there will be an intertemporal substitution effect on labour supply as a result of the interest rate increase. Second, we will be able to study in detail the workings of the "Keynesian multiplier," familiar from most introductory macroeconomics courses, and show how the typical approach to the multiplier mechanism can be misleading.

We will model a temporary increase in government spending as an increase in G, the quantity of government purchases in the current period, leaving future government purchases, G', unchanged. When would the government choose to increase its expenditures on goods and services temporarily? An important example is a war. Typically, wars are known to be temporary (though their length can be uncertain), and the government commits spending to the war effort that will not remain in place when the war is over. Sometimes, however, a change in government spending can be essentially permanent. For example, when the Canadian government established medicare, this involved a commitment of resources that was as permanent as government commitments can be—no one expects universal health care to be abolished in the future.

For this particular experiment with the real intertemporal model, it will be useful to start by working with a diagram like Figure 11.17, though this stage of the analysis will not be necessary for the other experiments we will study next. For those experiments, a diagram like Figure 11.17 is all that is necessary.

Now, suppose that government purchases increase from G_1 to G_2 during the current period. In Figure 11.20, to make our arguments simple, suppose that the marginal propensity to consume, *MPC*, is a constant that does not depend on income or the real interest rate, so that the curve describing the demand for goods is a straight line with slope *MPC*. In the figure, the initial demand for goods is given by the line $C_1^d(r) + I^d(r) + G_1$.

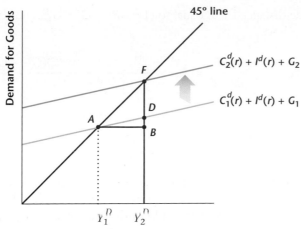

Total Demand for Goods

FIGURE 11.20

The Effect of an Increase in G on the Total Demand for Goods

The demand for goods as a function of current income Y shifts up by the amount $(1 - MPC)(G_2 - G_1)$. The increase in total demand for goods is $Y_2^D - Y_1^D$, and the expenditure multiplier is the ratio of the distance AB to the distance DF, which is 1.

When current government spending increases, there will be a direct effect on the total demand for goods, equal to the increase in government spending, $G_2 - G_1$. In addition, we have to take account of the effect that government spending has on consumption, as taxes must increase, either in the present or the future, to finance government spending. This will then reduce the lifetime wealth of the consumer. From the government's present-value budget constraint, Equation (11.18), an increase in G on the left-hand side of the equation must be matched by an equal increase in the present value of taxes on the right-hand side of the equation, so that lifetime wealth for the consumer must fall by $G_2 - G_1$. Note here that it is irrelevant whether the increase in government spending is financed by an increase in current taxes or by the issue of government bonds (which results in an increase in future taxes), as we know from the Ricardian equivalence theorem discussed in Chapter 9.

How will the decrease in lifetime wealth affect the demand for consumption goods? This is determined by the marginal propensity to consume. That is, the change in the demand for consumption goods is $- MPC(G_2 - G_1)$, minus the marginal propensity to consume multiplied by the decrease in lifetime wealth. Thus, the total change in the demand for goods is the direct effect on government spending plus the indirect effect on consumption, or $(1 - MPC)(G_2 - G_1)$.

Now, given the direct effect on government spending and the indirect effect on the demand for consumption goods, in Figure 11.20, the demand for goods shifts up to $C_2^d(r) + I^d(r) + G_2$, which is a shift up by $(1 - MPC)(G_2 - G_1)$. That is, the change $C_2^d(r) - C_1^d(r) = -MPC(G_2 - G_1)$ is the indirect effect on consumption of the decrease in lifetime wealth. The net effect on the total demand for goods is then determined by the intersection of the demand relationship with the 45° line in Figure 11.20, so that the total demand for output increases from Y_1^D to Y_2^D. From the figure, it is possible to determine exactly the difference $Y_2^D - Y_1^D$. The distance AB is equal to $Y_2^D - Y_1^D$, and since A and F are both on the 45° line, the distance AB is equal to the distance BF.

Further, since the distance *DF* is equal to $(1 - MPC)(G_2 - G_1)$, and the slope of *AD* is equal to *MPC*, we have

$$MPC = \frac{length(BF)}{length(AB)} = \frac{(Y_2^D - Y_1^D) - (1 - MPC)(G_2 - G_1)}{Y_2^D - Y_1^D} \tag{11.20}$$

Then, solving Equation (11.20) for $Y_2^D - Y_1^D$, we obtain

$$Y_2^D - Y_1^D = G_2 - G_1,$$

so that the total increase in the demand for goods generated by the increase in government spending is equal to the increase in government spending. That is, the **partial expenditure multiplier**, which is the ratio of the total increase in demand for goods to the increase in government spending, is

$$\frac{Y_2^D - Y_1^D}{G_2 - G_1} = 1.$$

Figure 11.20 looks much like the Keynesian cross-analysis that many students are exposed to in introductory macroeconomics courses. Keynesians typically argue that the expenditure multiplier for government spending is greater than 1, because they ignore the negative effect of the increase in taxes (present or future) on the demand for consumption goods. Basic Keynesian analysis also ignores production and intertemporal substitution, which will be key elements in the analysis that follows. What we have done so far is only an analysis of the effects of the increase in *G* on the demand side of the goods market. What remains is to work out the supply-side effects.

Before the increase in current government purchases, *G*, in Figure 11.21, the economy is in equilibrium with a current real wage, w_1, current employment, N_1, current output, Y_1, and real interest rate, r_1. When *G* increases, this will have two effects, one on output supply and one on output demand. We have determined the effect on output demand, which is a shift to the right in the output demand curve, from Y_1^d to Y_2^d, where the horizontal shift is equal to the increase in *G*. Since lifetime wealth decreases due to the increase in the present value of taxes, leisure will decrease (leisure is a normal good) for the representative consumer, given the current real wage, and so the labour supply curve in Figure 11.21(a) shifts to the right from $N_1^s(r_1)$ to $N_2^s(r_1)$, and the output supply curve in Figure 11.21(b) shifts to the right from Y_1^s to Y_2^s.

To determine all the equilibrium effects by using the model, we start first with Figure 11.21(b). It is clear that current aggregate output must increase, as both the output demand and output supply curves shift to the right, and so *Y* increases from Y_1 to Y_2. It may appear that the real interest rate may rise or fall; however, there is strong theoretical support for an increase in the real interest rate. This is because the temporary increase in government spending should lead to only a small decrease in lifetime wealth for the consumer, which will produce a small effect on labour supply. Therefore, there should be only a small shift to the right in the Y^s curve, and the real interest rate will rise, as in Figure 11.21(b).

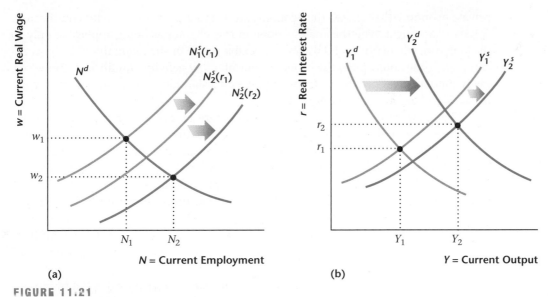

FIGURE 11.21

A Temporary Increase in Government Purchases

The increase in *G* shifts the labour supply curve to the right, the output supply curve to the right, and the output demand curve to the right. The real interest rate rises, and aggregate output increases in equilibrium. There is an additional shift to the right in the labour supply curve because of the increase in *r*, and so employment rises and the real wage falls in equilibrium.

What is the **total government expenditure multiplier** here, by which we mean the ratio of the equilibrium increase in real output to the increase in government spending? Since the output demand curve in Figure 11.21(b) shifted to the right by the increase in government spending, the equilibrium increase in current output (the difference $Y_2 - Y_1$) must be less than the increase in government spending. The multiplier is less than 1, and it will become smaller as the size of the wealth effect on labour supply falls (which makes the rightward shift in the output supply curve smaller) and as the intertemporal substitution effect of the real interest rate on labour supply falls (which makes the output supply curve steeper).

As mentioned previously, many Keynesians argue that the government expenditure multiplier is larger than one, which makes it appear that society can get something for nothing. In basic Keynesian analysis, each dollar spent by the government increases GDP by more than one dollar. If we followed this idea to its logical conclusion, we would let the government grow infinitely large, which would make everyone infinitely wealthy. Our analysis makes clear that the multiplier must be smaller than one, that government spending comes at a cost, and that the capacity of the government to increase real GDP is limited.

Keynesian ideas are explored in detail in Chapters 13 and 14. These ideas are based on the notion that price and wage inflexibility causes the economy to behave differently in the short run than it does in the long run, or that there is some imperfection in the private economy that causes the economy to be stuck in a low-activity equilibrium. A Keynesian might view the analysis done in this chapter as being applicable only to the long run, where prices and wages, are flexible, or he or she might think that government spending could push the economy out of a low-activity equilibrium. However, many modern macroeconomists argue that Keynesian ideas are unimportant for the behaviour of the macroeconomy.

What happens to current consumption in Figure 11.21? If the real interest rate did not change in equilibrium (e.g., if the output supply curve were horizontal), we know from the figure that real income would increase by an amount equal to the increase in government spending. If this occurred, then the change in the consumer's lifetime wealth would be zero, since the increase in the present value of taxes is equal to the increase in current income. As a result, current consumption would be unchanged. However, in Figure 11.21(b), the real interest rate rises in equilibrium, so the representative consumer will substitute future consumption for current consumption, and therefore current consumption declines. As well, investment expenditures must decrease because of the increase in the real interest rate. Thus, both components of private expenditure (current consumption and investment) are crowded out by current government expenditure. Recall from Chapter 5 that when we analyzed the effects of an increase in government spending in a one-period model, without taking intertemporal substitution and investment into account, government spending crowded out only consumption expenditure. Since government spending is shown here to crowd out private investment expenditure, a further cost of government is that it reduces the economy's future productive capacity, as the future capital stock will be lower (than it would otherwise have been).

On the demand side of the goods market, it is the crowding out of private consumption and investment expenditure that causes the government expenditure multiplier to be less than one. On the supply side, output increases because of two effects on labour supply. First, just as in our Chapter 5 analysis, there is a negative wealth effect on leisure from the increase in lifetime tax liabilities. Second, the increase in the real interest rate makes future leisure cheaper relative to current leisure, and there is a further increase in labour supply. Basic Keynesian analysis, as represented in typical Keynesian cross diagrams, neglects both the crowding-out effects and the effects on the supply side of the goods market.

The next step is to work through the effects of the increase in the real interest rate for the labour market. In Figure 11.21(a), given the initial interest rate r_1, the labour supply curve shifts from $N_1^s(r_1)$ to $N_2^s(r_1)$ because of the negative wealth effect arising from the increase in the present value of taxes. With an increase in the equilibrium real interest rate to r_2, the labour supply curve shifts further to the right, to $N_2^s(r_2)$. Therefore, the equilibrium real wage falls from w_1 to w_2.

What this analysis tells us is that increased temporary government spending, although it leads to higher aggregate output, comes at a cost. With higher current government spending, the representative consumer consumes less and takes less leisure, and he or she also faces a lower real wage rate. Further, current investment spending is lower, which implies that the capital stock will be lower in the future, and the future capacity of the economy for producing goods will be lower.

Our analysis in this subsection can help us understand the potential effects of the federal government budget tabled on January 27, 2009,[1] in the midst of the most recent recession. Much of the budget dealt with taxes and transfers, for example, subsidies for housing, education, and agriculture, and changes to employment insurance. These items are not part of government spending on goods and services and therefore not part of *G*. However, key parts of the budget included expenditures for federal construction projects and transfers to municipalities for infrastructure projects. All of these components of spending are part of *G*, and in the federal budget they were explicitly temporary, making our analysis here quite relevant.

The federal budget in January 2009 represented a large increase in government spending on goods and services, explicitly intended as a response to a decrease in aggregate economic activity in Canada, and a forecast that this decrease would continue, possibly for the next year or longer. Thus, it seems clear that the federal government would not be increasing its spending if there had not been a drop in aggregate economic activity. The federal government clearly held the view that, given the state of the economy, economic welfare for Canadians would be higher with a higher level of government spending than without it.

Our analysis here of the effects of an increase in government spending should make us skeptical of the federal government's view that increased spending is necessarily a good thing. Our analysis shows that increased government spending is costly—it crowds out private spending and reduces leisure. While there is more employment with higher government spending, people are working harder to support a larger public sector. However, to be fair to the federal government, there may be elements missing in our analysis that are important for the problem at hand. First, Keynesians argue that inefficiencies in the private economy can create situations where government spending can utilize resources that would otherwise be unemployed. We will study and evaluate Keynesian ideas in Chapters 13 and 14, and Macroeconomics in Action 11.1 contains a discussion of a recent policy debate related to the issues at hand. Second, a time of low aggregate economic activity may be an opportune time to invest in infrastructure, which is essentially publicly owned capital. In our model, public spending is not productive (it is just government consumption), and we do not model the tradeoff between the opportunity cost of government spending and the benefits from having more productive government capital. However, our model here can serve as a basis for a more complicated model including these features while still retaining what we have learned from this basic structure.

The Equilibrium Effects of a Decrease in the Current Capital Stock, K : Capital Destruction from Wars and Natural Disasters

Over time, through investment, a nation adds to its capital stock, and this generally occurs slowly, as investment expenditure is typically quite small relative to the total capital stock. Thus, increases in capital do not contribute much to short-run fluctuations

---

[1]See www.budget.gc.ca/2009/index.html, accessed February 10, 2009, for a summary of the federal budget.

The Total Government Spending Multiplier: Barro vs. Romer

The value of the total government spending multiplier was a key issue in the U.S. federal government's analysis of the effects of the *American Recovery and Reinvestment Act* (ARRA) of 2009, and the public debate about these effects. The issues in the debate over the effects of the U.S. "stimulus package" in February 2009, are essentially identical to the issues related to the effects of the Canadian federal government budget of January 2009.

On one side of the U.S. debate were economists such as Robert Barro, who argued in a *Wall Street Journal* article on January 22, 2009,[2] essentially along the same lines as what we have laid out in our model in this section. In particular, he stated that "government spending is no free lunch," and that theory tells us that the total government spending multiplier can be at most 1, and will be reduced to the extent that government spending crowds out private expenditures on consumption, investment, and net exports (net exports were of course omitted from our analysis here). Barro also cites his own empirical work on government spending in wartime, suggesting an estimate for the multiplier of 0.8.

Barro's arguments are countered in a speech made by Christina Romer, the Chair of the Council of Economic Advisers, on February 27, 2009.[3] Romer does not lay out much of a theoretical argument, but relies mainly on empirical work. At the centre of her argument is this statement: "In estimating the effects of the recovery package, Jared Bernstein [Chief Economist and Economic Policy Adviser to Vice President Joseph Biden] and I used tax and spending multipliers from very conventional macroeconomic models.... In these models, [the] spending ... multiplier [is] ... about 1.6."

What Romer means by "very conventional models" are large-scale Keynesian models fit to data. Such models are by no means conventional in the sense of being widely accepted. Indeed, a large group of professional economists thinks of these models as essentially useless, mainly because they do not satisfy the Lucas critique, discussed briefly in Chapter 1. The principle behind the Lucas critique is that, to be useful for evaluating policy, macroeconomic models need to incorporate the basic building blocks of preferences, endowments, and

in aggregate output and employment. However, sometimes major reductions in the aggregate capital stock occur over a short period of time. For example, a war can leave a country with a much lower capital stock, as happened because of bombing in Germany, Great Britain, and Japan during World War II, in Vietnam during the Vietnam War, and more recently in Iraq. The capital stock can also be reduced because of natural disasters, such as ice storms or hurricanes.

In this subsection, we examine the effects of an experiment in our model where the current capital stock, K, is reduced. Although this experiment can be interpreted as capturing the effects of wars and natural disasters on the capital stock, there is an alternative interpretation in terms of "rich" and "poor" countries. That is, this experiment allows us to explore the differences between two economies: a rich economy, with a high capital stock, and a poor economy, with a low capital stock.

Now, suppose that the representative firm begins the current period with a lower capital stock, K. This will affect both the supply and the demand for output. First, a decrease in K from K_1 to K_2 decreases the current marginal product of labour, which shifts the current demand for labour curve to the left from N_1^d to N_2^d in Figure 11.22(a).

technology, which are invariant to changes in economic policy. "Conventional" Keynesian macroeconomic models do not satisfy the Lucas critique and therefore give incorrect answers to such questions as "How large is the multiplier?"

Romer not only feels confident about making policy recommendations based on a total government spending multiplier of 1.6; she goes even further, stating: "... I feel quite confident that conventional multipliers are far more likely to be too small than too large."

In our real intertemporal model, one would have to work quite hard to obtain a multiplier of 1.6. We could obtain a multiplier of 1 if the output supply curve were horizontal, which would require an infinitely large elasticity of labor supply with respect to the interest rate—consumers would have to be highly willing to substitute leisure intertemporally in response to interest rate changes. To get a multiplier larger than 1 would require that government spending be financed by borrowing and that Ricardian equivalence not hold. The former is certainly true for the ARRA, which was in fact combined with cuts

in taxes. Thus, all the spending increases in the ARRA represented deferred taxation. For Ricardian equivalence not to hold, however, requires that a large fraction of consumers be credit-constrained, and therefore willing to spend each extra dollar of current disposable income on consumption. In fact, Romer argues that the financial crisis likely has made credit constraints matter more for consumers, which is certainly true. However, according to her reasoning, this is an argument for a multiplier larger than 1.6, since the 1.6 estimate comes from "normal" times.

In conclusion, Romer's case looks dubious in light of our analysis here and the arguments in Barro's *Wall Street Journal* article. However, to be fair to Romer, we will need to go into more depth on how Keynesian economics works, as this is at the heart of her argument. This analysis will have to wait until Chapters 13 and 14.

---

[2]See online.wsj.com/article/SB123258618204604599.html.
[3]See news.uchicago.edu/files/newsrelease_20090227.pdf.

The output supply curve will then shift to the left, from Y_1^s to Y_2^s in Figure 11.22(b). Second, a decrease in K will increase investment by the firm, since the future marginal product of capital will be higher. This shifts the output demand curve to the right in Figure 11.22(b), from Y_1^d to Y_2^d. The result is that, in equilibrium, in Figure 11.22(b), the real interest rate must rise from r_1 to r_2, but the effect on current aggregate output is ambiguous, depending on whether the output supply effect is larger or smaller than the output demand effect. In the figure, we have drawn the case where the output supply effect dominates, so that current real output falls. Empirically, there may be circumstances, such as with natural disasters, where aggregate output may not fall. It may be that the negative effect of the reduction in capital—less productive capacity implying lower output—is outweighed by the positive effect, in that less capital implies that investment spending is higher, which increases output.

In Figure 11.22 current consumption must fall, since the real interest rate has increased and current real income has decreased. The effects on investment appear to be ambiguous, since the decrease in K causes investment to increase, while the increase in the equilibrium real interest rate causes investment to fall. However, investment

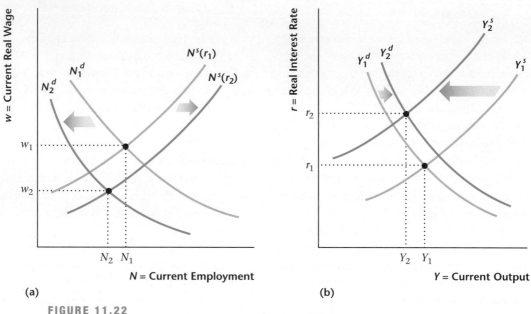

FIGURE 11.22

The Equilibrium Effects of a Decrease in the Current Capital Stock

If the current capital stock falls—for example, because of a natural disaster—the output demand curve shifts to the right and the output supply curve shifts to the left. The real interest rate rises, but current output may rise or fall.

must rise, because less capital would otherwise cause ever-decreasing investment, which would be inconsistent with the fact that the marginal product of capital rises as the quantity of capital falls. That is, as the quantity of capital falls, the marginal product of capital rises, making the return on investment very high, so that ultimately investment must increase if the capital stock decreases.

Because of the increase in the real interest rate, there will be intertemporal substitution of leisure, with the representative consumer working harder in the current period for each current real wage, w. Therefore, the labour supply curve shifts to the right in Figure 11.22(a), from $N^s(r_1)$ to $N^s(r_2)$. This reinforces the effect of the decrease in labour demand on the real wage, and so the real wage must fall, from w_1 to w_2. The equilibrium effect on the quantity of labour is ambiguous, since the effect on labour demand and on labour supply work in opposite directions on the quantity of employment. In Figure 11.22(a), we show employment falling from N_1 to N_2.

Now, suppose we interpret these results in terms of the macroeconomic effects of a natural disaster or a war that destroys part of the nation's capital stock. The model shows that there are two effects on the quantity of output. The lower quantity of capital implies that less output can be produced for a given quantity of labour input, which tends to reduce output. However, the lower quantity of capital acts to increase investment to replace the destroyed capital, which will tend to increase output. Theoretically, it is not clear whether output increases or decreases, and there appear to be empirical cases in which the output supply and output demand effects roughly cancel.

If we view the above results as predictions about how rich countries having high capital stocks should compare with poor countries having low capital stocks, the model fits some facts but not others. If the output demand effect is small and the effect of the real interest rate on labour supply is small, as in Figure 11.22, the model predicts that capital-rich countries should have relatively high output, relatively low real interest rates, relatively high employment, and relatively high real wages. Most of these predictions seem consistent with what we observe, except that rich countries typically do not have low real interest rates. Also, in U.S. post–World War II data, we see trend growth in real output, consumption, and the real wage. However, we do not see a trend decrease in the real interest rate, nor a decrease in investment. The Solow growth model, studied in Chapters 7 and 8, shows that differences across countries and over time in total factor productivity help explain the key facts about cross-country relationships and economic growth.

The Equilibrium Effects of an Increase in Current Total Factor Productivity, z

Temporary changes in total factor productivity are an important cause of business cycles. Recall from Chapter 4 that an increase in total factor productivity could be caused by good weather, a favourable change in government regulations, a new invention, a decrease in the relative price of energy, or any other factor that results in more aggregate output being produced with the same factor inputs.

The experiment we examine here in our real intertemporal model is to increase current total factor productivity, z, and then determine the effects of this change on current aggregate output, the real interest rate, current employment, the current real wage, current consumption, and investment. If current total factor productivity increases, the marginal product of labour goes up for each quantity of labour input, and so in Figure 11.23(a) the demand for labour curve shifts to the right, from N_1^d to N_2^d. Therefore, in Figure 11.23(b), the output supply curve shifts to the right, from Y_1^s to Y_2^s, and in equilibrium the quantity of output rises and the real interest rate must fall, from r_1 to r_2. The decrease in the real interest rate leads to increases in both consumption and investment and the increase in real income contributes to the increase in consumption.

In the labour market, the decrease in the real interest rate causes intertemporal substitution of leisure between the current and future periods, with current leisure increasing, and so the labour supply curve shifts to the left in Figure 11.23(a), from $N^s(r_1)$ to $N^s(r_2)$. In equilibrium, the real wage must increase from w_1 to w_2, but the net effect on the equilibrium quantity of employment is ambiguous. Empirically, however, the effect of the real interest rate on labour supply is relatively small and, as in Figure 11.23(a), employment rises from N_1 to N_2.

When total factor productivity increases, this increases the current demand for labour, which raises the market real wage. With this increase, workers are willing to supply more labour, employment increases, and output increases. In the goods market, the increased supply of goods decreases the market real interest rate, which results in an increased demand for investment goods and consumption goods, so that the demand for goods rises to meet the increased supply of goods on the market.

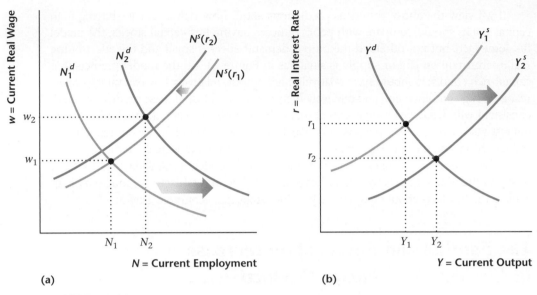

FIGURE 11.23

The Equilibrium Effects of an Increase in Current Total Factor Productivity

When total factor productivity increases temporarily, the output supply curve shifts to the right in (b), with the real interest rate falling and aggregate output rising. Investment and consumption rise, and employment and the real wage increase in (a).

From Chapter 3, recall that consumption, investment, employment, and the real wage are procyclical. Note that our real intertemporal model will predict these comovements in the data if the economy receives temporary shocks to total factor productivity. That is, since Figure 11.23 predicts that a temporary increase in total factor productivity increases aggregate output, consumption, investment, employment, and the real wage, the model predicts that consumption, investment, employment, and the real wage are procyclical, just as in the data. Thus, temporary shocks to total factor productivity are a candidate as a cause of business cycles. Indeed, the proponents of real business cycle theory, which we will study in detail in Chapter 13, argue that total factor productivity shocks are the most important cause of business cycles.

The Equilibrium Effects of an Increase in Future Total Factor Productivity, z': News about the Future and Aggregate Economic Activity

The anticipation of future events can have important macroeconomic consequences in the present, as when an increase in total factor productivity is expected to happen in the future. For example, firms might learn of a new invention, such as a new production process, which is not available currently but will come on line in the future. We will see that this shock will increase current investment, current output, and current employment, and reduce the real wage.

News about future events and the influence of this news has played an important role in macroeconomic theory. For example, Keynes had an interest in the "animal spirits" of financial market investors and the influence of swings in investor sentiment on economic activity. As the stock market represents a forum in which people take bets on the future health of firms in the economy, news that is informative about future productivity will tend to be reflected first in stock prices. In financial market theory, stock prices are typically the reflection of the average stock market participant's views on firms' future dividends, which are in good part determined by the future total factor productivity of firms. Empirical research in macroeconomics supports the view that news about future events is a key determinant of aggregate economic activity in the present.[4]

To capture the effect of news about future total factor productivity, suppose in our model that everyone learns in the current period that z' will increase in the future. This implies that the future marginal product of capital increases for the representative firm, and so the firm will want to invest more in the current period, which increases the demand for current goods, shifting the output demand curve to the right in Figure 11.24(b). In equilibrium, this implies that aggregate output increases from Y_1 to Y_2, and the real interest rate increases from r_1 to r_2. The increase in the real interest rate will then cause current consumption to fall, though the increase in real income

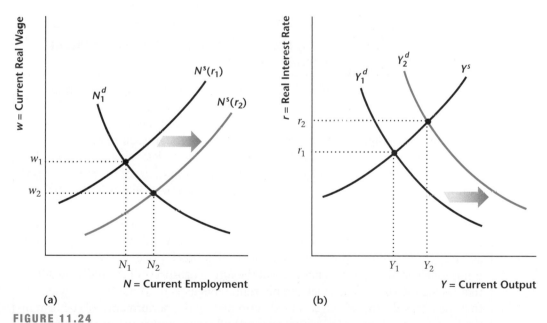

(a)

(b)

FIGURE 11.24

The Equilibrium Effects of an Increase in Future Total Factor Productivity

An anticipated increase in future total factor productivity shifts the output demand curve to the right, with current output and the real interest rate increasing in equilibrium. The real wage falls, and employment rises.

---

[4]P. Beaudry and F. Portier, 2006, "Stock Prices, News, and Economic Fluctuations," *American Economic Review* 96, 1293–1307; and M. Uribe and S. Schmitt-Grohe, 2008, "What's News in Business Cycles," NBER working paper 14215.

will tend to increase consumption. Since higher future total factor productivity will increase real income in the future, there will be a further positive effect on current consumption. As a result, consumption could rise or fall. In equilibrium, there are two effects on investment: the increase in z' causes investment to rise, and the increase in r causes it to fall. Therefore, investment may rise or fall, but the presumption here is that investment rises, as this was the initial source of the increase in the demand for current goods.

What are the effects in the labour market? The increase in the real interest rate leads to a rightward shift of the labour supply curve, from $N^s(r_1)$ to $N^s(r_2)$ in Figure 11.24(a). Therefore, in equilibrium, the quantity of employment increases from N_1 to N_2, and the real wage falls from w_1 to w_2.

In anticipation of a future increase in total factor productivity, firms increase investment expenditure, as the marginal payoff to having a higher future capital stock has increased. The increase in the demand for investment goods raises the market real interest rate, which increases labour supply and employment and generates an increase in aggregate output. The increase in labour supply causes the real wage to fall.

THEORY CONFRONTS THE DATA **11.1**   *News, the Stock Market, and Investment Expenditures*

The real intertemporal model tells us that news about future total factor productivity could potentially be an important factor affecting investment spending. If there are significant fluctuations in financial market views about the future (i.e., waves of optimism and pessimism), then these fluctuations, through their effects on investment spending, could be very important for business cycles. We have shown that good news about future total factor productivity acts to increase investment, consumption, aggregate output, and employment, and bad news works in the opposite direction.

If news about future productivity is important for investment, then we should see this in economic data. In particular, financial theory tells us that stock prices act to aggregate information. That is, an individual stock price moves in a way that immediately incorporates all news about the future prospects of the individual firm that issued the stock. The stock simply represents a claim to the future dividends that the firm will pay, which will be determined by the performance of the firm in the future. A stock price index that averages all stock market prices then captures all of the news about the future prospects of all firms in the economy and should include information about what is collectively known about what will happen to aggregate productivity in the future.

Therefore, if news about the future is an important determinant of aggregate investment, stock prices and investment expenditures should be highly positively correlated. In Figure 11.25, we show percentage deviations from trend in aggregate real investment spending and in a relative stock price index for Canada, for the period 1961–2011. The relative stock price is determined by dividing the stock price index by the consumer price index, so as to adjust for inflation. What we observe in the figure is a remarkably high degree of correlation between the two time series; that is, investment spending tracks the stock price index remarkably closely. Further, stock prices tend to lead investment in the figure, which is consistent with our theory. News about the future can affect stock prices and investment plans simultaneously, but it takes time to build capital equipment, plant, and housing. Therefore, stock prices should lead investment, just as we observe.

Figure 11.25 is consistent with the view that news about the future is a key determinant of investment spending. Therefore, since investment is a highly volatile component of GDP (e.g., much more volatile than consumption or government spending), fluctuations in sentiment about the future are likely a key source of business cycles.

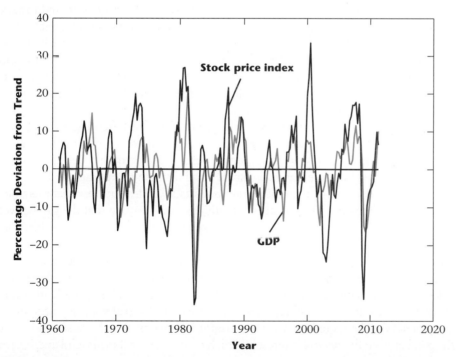

FIGURE 11.25

Percentage Deviations from Trend in Real GDP and a Relative Stock Price Index for Canada, 1961–2011

GDP and the stock price index are highly positively correlated, with stock prices leading GDP. This is consistent with the view that fluctuations in news about the future is an important source of business cycles.

Source: Adapted from the Statistics Canada CANSIM database, Series v1992057, v1992052, v122620.

An Increase in Credit Market Uncertainty: Asymmetric Information and the Financial Crisis

In Chapter 10, we analyzed the effects of asymmetric information in consumer credit markets, and early in this chapter we similarly studied how asymmetric information affects a firm's investment decision. In general, some firms or consumers in the economy might default on their debts, and financial institutions that lend to these firms may have difficulty distinguishing creditworthy borrowers from bad credit risks. This situation makes lending more costly, even for good borrowers. All borrowers will face loan interest rates that are higher than the safe rates of interest at which financial institutions borrow, as those institutions need to be compensated for the perceived default risk associated with lending. Thus, asymmetric information in credit markets creates a gap between the interest rates faced by borrowers and lenders, and this gap increases with the degree of uncertainty in credit markets.

The asymmetric information problem was an important factor in the recent financial crisis. A key feature of the crisis, particularly in the United States, was that financial market participants received critical news about a decrease in the value of assets held by financial institutions, firms, and consumers. However, the degree of credit market uncertainty increased, as there was not good information on which financial institutions, firms, and consumers were holding these bad assets, how bad the bad assets were, and how this would affect the credit worthiness of individual financial institutions, firms, and consumers. We want to use our model to understand the macroeconomic effects of an increase in credit market uncertainty, and this analysis will help us organize our thinking about recent events.

In the real intertemporal model, think of the model as representing a world where there are many different consumers and many different firms, some of whom borrow and some of whom lend, but with aggregate behaviour accurately described by the behaviour of a single representative consumer and a single representative firm. Now, suppose there is an increase in credit market uncertainty. Also suppose that this uncertainty affects consumers and firms in essentially the same way, in that the gap between borrowing and lending rates of interest increases by the same amount for firms and consumers.

In our model, the real interest rate r will denote the safe real rate of interest at which consumers and firms lend. However, the decisions of borrowers are determined by a loan rate that is higher than r. In Figure 11.26, the economy is initially in equilibrium with the real interest rate, r_1, level of real income, Y_1, real wage w_1, and level of employment N_1. Then, credit market uncertainty increases, which causes an increase in the gap between the rates of interest at which consumers and firms lend and borrow. The effect of this shock to the economy, which we will assume is temporary and does not continue to the future period, is to shift the output demand curve to the left from Y_1^d to Y_2^d. That is, any borrower now faces a higher real interest rate for any level of the safe lending r. Therefore, given r, a consumer who borrows faces a higher interest rate and will borrow and consume less, as we showed in Chapter 10. As well, a borrowing

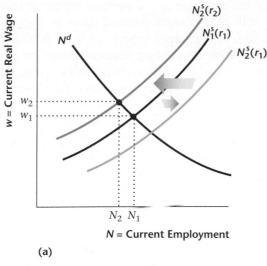

(a)

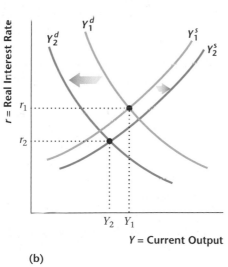

(b)

FIGURE 11.26

The Effect of an Increase in Credit Market Risk
The output demand curve shifts to the left, and the output supply curve shifts to the right, as the spread between loan interest rates and safe interest rates faced by lenders increases. Output, consumption, investment, and employment decrease. The safe real rate of interest falls, and the real wage rises.

firm will face a higher real interest rate and will choose to invest less. The vertical shift in the output demand curve in Figure 11.26(b) represents the increase in the effective gap between lending and borrowing rates of interest, for the representative stand-in consumer and firm.

In the labour market, consumers who are borrowers will face a higher interest rate, given the initial real interest rate r_1, and therefore borrowers will substitute leisure intertemporally by supplying more labour in the present, given the safe lending rate of interest r and the real wage. As a result, the labour supply curve shifts to the right from $N_1^S(r_1)$ to $N_2^S(r_1)$ in Figure 11.26(a). This shift in the labour supply curve leads to a shift to the right in the output supply curve in Figure 11.26(b) from Y_1^s to Y_2^s.

A key feature of the response to the increase in credit market uncertainty is that the downward shift of the output demand curve in Figure 11.26(b) is greater than the downward shift in the output supply curve. This is necessarily the case, as the increase in credit market uncertainty restricts the ability of consumers to substitute both consumption and leisure intertemporally. Thus, the result is that the real interest rate falls from r_1 to r_2, and real output falls from Y_1 to Y_2. Note that, though the interest rate faced by lenders falls from r_1 to r_2, the interest rate faced by borrowers rises, since r falls by less than the vertical shift in the output demand curve. The representative stand-in consumer and firm will face a higher real interest rate in equilibrium (the real interest rate drops by less than the downward shift in the output demand curve), in spite of the fact that the safe lending rate of interest falls. Therefore, investment and consumption will both decrease. There will be an additional negative effect on consumption because of the decline in equilibrium real income in the current period.

In the labour market in Figure 11.26(a), the decrease in the safe lending rate of interest r causes a shift to the left in the labour supply curve from $N_1^S(r_2)$ to $N_2^S(r_2)$. From Figure 11.26(a), we know that aggregate output must fall in equilibrium, and so what occurs in the labour market must be consistent with that. If output is to fall, and since total factor productivity and the capital stock have not changed, employment must fall. This requires that the net shift in the labour supply curve must be to the left, from its original position, with employment falling from N_1 to N_2 and the real wage rising from w_1 to w_2.

In our model, increased credit market uncertainty leads to a contraction in consumption, output, investment, and employment, much like what occurred in Canada, the United States, and the rest of the world during the recent global financial crisis. As well, the model is consistent with the observed recent decline in interest rates on essentially safe assets, and the increase in interest rates on risky assets, with a widening in the spread between interest rates at which consumers and firms lend and borrow.

Does our model tell us that there is some appropriate policy response to this shock to credit market uncertainty? The revelation of hidden information would certainly cure the problem—if consumers, firms, and financial institutions were all fully aware of who was holding bad assets and how bad those assets were, then much of the problem could be solved. Borrowers in credit markets would then face interest rates that were appropriate, given their true creditworthiness. However, the revelation of hidden information is something that would have been achieved had there been better financial disclosure and adequate regulatory supervision of credit markets in the United States so that shocks to credit market uncertainty would not occur, or would be dampened. Once the shock has hit the economy, it is not obvious that any type of government intervention will help. The government could attempt to use fiscal policy to extend credit to consumers and firms, sidestepping private financial institutions, but why should the government know any more than private lenders about evaluating creditworthiness? There may be a role for monetary policy in this context, but that is a topic for later in this book, when we study monetary economics, monetary policy, and banking.

11.2 *Interest Rate Spreads and Aggregate Economic Activity*

The predictions of the real intertemporal model in this section help explain features of the global financial market crisis and its implications for the recent recession in Canada and the rest of the world. However, we would like more evidence from the historical record that credit market risk has played an important role in generating aggregate economic fluctuations. The model suggests we should observe that the difference between the interest rates at which consumers and firms lend and borrow (the interest rate spread) should be negatively correlated with aggregate economic activity.

One measure of the interest rate spread, plotted in Figure 11.27 for the period January 1962 to June 2011, is the difference between the short-term interest rate faced by corporate borrowers (the loan rate faced by the most creditworthy firms) and the three-month Treasury bill rate (the safe interest rate at which the public lends to the government of Canada). If we compare Figure 11.27 to Figure 3.2 in Chapter 3, the key noteworthy feature of Figure 11.27 is that there are spikes in

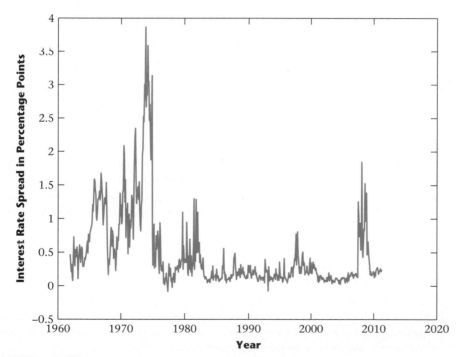

FIGURE 11.27

The Interest Rate Spread

The figure shows the gap between the interest rates on short-term prime corporate debt and Canadian government short-term debt. There are spikes during the 1974–1975 and 1981–1982 recessions, and in the financial crisis beginning in late 2008, but not during the 1990–1992 recession.

Source: Statistics Canada CANSIM database, Series v122531, v122491.

the interest rate spread, not only beginning in late 2008 during the recent financial crisis, but also during the recessions of 1974–1975 and 1981–1982. Note too that these spikes are of very different magnitudes, and there is no spike in the interest rate spread during the 1990–1992 recession. Thus, though increases in the interest rate spread are clearly associated with economic downturns, shocks to credit market risk may play a minor role or no role in some recessions.

Chapter Summary

- We developed a real intertemporal macroeconomic model that is useful for evaluating the macroeconomic effects of shocks to the economy and that we can build on in later chapters. This model allows us to study the determinants of investment, consumption, aggregate output, the real interest rate, and employment in an intertemporal setting.

- The real intertemporal model has two periods, the present and the future, and the representative consumer makes a work–leisure decision in each period and a consumption–savings decision in the current period. As the real interest rate increases, the consumer's demand for current consumption goods decreases, and his or her current labour supply increases. These effects are due to the intertemporal substitution of consumption and leisure between the present and the future in response to changes in the real interest rate.

- The representative firm produces output by using labour and capital in each period. The firm's current demand for labour is determined by the usual marginal productivity condition (the marginal product of labour equals the real wage in the current period when the firm optimizes), and the firm invests in new capital in the current period until the net marginal product of capital in the future is equal to the real interest rate.

- An increase in the real interest rate leads to a decrease in the firm's optimal quantity of investment, and investment increases if the firm's initial quantity of capital decreases or there is an anticipated increase in future total factor productivity.

- Asymmetric information in the credit market in which firms borrow affects a firm's investment decision. An increase in credit market risk that increases the default premium will cause the firm to reduce investment spending.

- In equilibrium in the real intertemporal model, the current goods market and the current labour market clear, and this implies that the credit market clears as well. For simplicity, we ignore markets in the future period.

- In the graphical representation of the model, there are two key elements: (1) output demand and supply, determining current aggregate output and the real interest rate; (2) current labour supply and current labour demand, determining current employment and the current real wage given the real interest rate.

- We conducted five experiments using the model:

  1. If current government purchases increase (a temporary increase in government spending), this increases the present value of taxes for the consumer, reducing lifetime wealth. As a result, the demand for current consumption goods falls, with the demand for current goods rising on net, and labour supply rises given the real interest rate. In equilibrium, current output rises, current employment rises, the current real wage

falls, and the real interest rate increases given that a temporary increase in government purchases implies that the output supply effect is small. Consumption and investment are crowded out. The government expenditure multiplier is less than one.

2. If the current capital stock decreases—for example, because of a natural disaster—then the optimal quantity of investment increases for the firm, given the real interest rate, so that output demand increases. Current output supply decreases, because the representative firm can produce less current output with a given input of labour. The real interest rate increases in equilibrium, but current aggregate output may rise or fall. If the output demand effect is small, then output falls.

3. If current total factor productivity increases (a temporary increase in total factor productivity), then output supply increases, the real interest rate falls, and consumption and investment increase in the current period. Current employment may rise or fall, but it rises provided the interest rate effect on labour supply is small. The current real wage rises. These predictions of the model replicate some of the key business cycle facts from Chapter 3.

4. An anticipated increase in future total factor productivity implies that the representative firm demands more investment goods, because the future marginal product of capital is expected to be higher. The demand for goods increases, causing the real interest rate and current aggregate output to rise. In the labour market, the real wage falls and employment rises, as the representative consumer substitutes leisure intertemporally in response to the real interest rate increase.

5. An increase in perceived credit market risk reduces the demand for consumption and investment goods, the safe real interest rate falls, employment falls, and real output decreases. This experiment is relevant for analyzing the effects of the current financial crisis on aggregate economic activity.

Key Terms

intertemporal substitution of leisure: The substitution of leisure between the current and the future period in response to the market real interest rate.

marginal propensity to consume: The amount that consumption increases for a consumer, if he or she experiences a one-unit increase in real income, holding everything else constant.

marginal cost of investment: The profit forgone by the firm in the current period from investing in an additional unit of capital.

marginal benefit from investment: The future marginal product of capital plus $1 - d$, where d is the depreciation rate.

net marginal product of capital: The marginal product of capital minus the depreciation rate.

optimal investment rule: Rule stating that the firm invests until the future net marginal product of capital is equal to the real interest rate.

optimal investment schedule: A negative relationship between the firm's optimal quantity of investment and the market real interest rate.

output supply curve: A positive relationship between the quantity of output supplied by firms and the real interest rate.

output demand curve: A negative relationship between the quantity of output demanded (in the form of consumption expenditures, investment expenditures, and government expenditures) and the real interest rate.

partial expenditure multiplier: The ratio of the total increase in aggregate expenditure to the exogenous increase in expenditure that generated it.

total government expenditure multiplier: The ratio of the equilibrium increase in current output to the increase in government expenditure.

Questions for Review

All questions refer to the macroeconomic model developed in this chapter.

1. Explain how intertemporal substitution is important for current labour supply and for the current demand for consumption goods.

2. What are three factors that determine current labour supply?

3. What determines the current demand for labour?

4. What is the goal of the representative firm in the real intertemporal model?

5. What rule does the representative firm follow in determining its optimal level of investment?

6. How does asymmetric information affect the default premium and the firm's investment choice?

7. How is optimal investment for the firm affected by an increase in the current capital stock?

8. How is optimal investment affected by an increase in future total factor productivity?

9. What is the government's budget constraint in the real intertemporal model? Can the government run a deficit or run a surplus in the current period?

10. What are the factors that shift the output supply curve?

11. What are the factors that shift the output demand curve?

12. How are aggregate output and the real interest rate determined in competitive equilibrium?

13. What are the effects of a temporary increase in government purchases on the real interest rate, aggregate output, employment, the real wage, consumption, and investment?

14. Why is typical analysis of the Keynesian multiplier misleading?

15. What are the effects of a decrease in the current capital stock on the real interest rate, aggregate output, employment, the real wage, consumption, and investment?

16. What are the effects of an increase in current total factor productivity on the real interest rate, aggregate output, employment, the real wage, consumption, and investment? Explain how these results relate to key business cycle facts and the causes of business cycles.

17. Determine the equilibrium effects of an anticipated increase in future total factor productivity in the real intertemporal model. Explain why these effects are different from the effects of an increase in current total factor productivity.

18. Explain what a sectoral shock is. What are the macroeconomic effects of a sectoral shock and what are empirical examples of sectoral shocks?

19. What are the effects of an increase in credit market risk on aggregate economic activity? How does this matter for the current financial crisis?

Problems

1. What is the effect of an increase in d, the depreciation rate, on the representative firm's investment decision and on its optimal investment schedule? Explain your results carefully.

2. Tom lives on an island and has 20 coconut trees in the current period, which currently produce 180 coconuts. Tom detests coconuts, but he can trade them with people on neighbouring islands for things that he wants. Further, Tom can borrow and lend coconuts with neighbouring islands. In the coconut credit market, a loan of 1 coconut in the current period is repaid with 2 coconuts in the future period. In each period, Tom's trees produce, and then 10% of them die. If Tom plants a coconut in the current period, it will grow into a productive coconut tree in the future period. At the end of the future period, Tom can sell any remaining coconut trees for 1 coconut each. When Tom plants coconuts in the current period, he plants them in successively less fertile ground, and the less fertile the ground, the less productive the coconut tree. For convenience, we will assume here that fractions of coconuts can be produced by trees. Output in the future period, for given numbers of trees in production in the future period, is given in the following table:

Trees in Production in the Future	Future Output of Coconuts
15	155
16	162
17	168
18	173
19	177
20	180
21	182
22	183.8
23	184.8
24	185.2
25	185.4

  a. Plot the level of output against the quantity of capital for the future period.
  b. Plot the marginal product of capital against the quantity of capital for the future period.
  c. Calculate Tom's present value of profits given each quantity of future trees.
  d. Calculate the net marginal product of capital for each quantity of future trees.
  e. Determine Tom's optimal quantity of investment, and explain your results.

3. The government wants to bring about an increase in investment expenditures and is considering two tax policies that policymakers think could bring this about. Under the first tax policy, firms would receive a subsidy in the current period of t per unit of current output produced. Policymakers reason that firms will use this subsidy for investment. The second policy under consideration is an investment tax credit, by which firms would receive a subsidy of s per unit of investment in the current period. Determine which tax policy would be more effective in accomplishing the government's goal of increasing current investment expenditures, and carefully explain your results.

4. Suppose that we modify the model of the firm's investment behaviour by supposing that any capital the firm has remaining at the end of the future period can be sold at the price p'_K (in our model, we had assumed that capital could be sold at the end of the future period at a price of one, in terms of consumption goods).
   a. Determine how this change affects the optimal investment rule of the firm.
   b. Suppose that we interpret p'_K as the firm's stock price. If p'_K rises, what effect does this have on the firm's investment schedule? What does this imply about the relationship between investment expenditures and stock prices?

5. Determine how the following will affect the slope of the output demand curve, and explain your results:
   a. The marginal propensity to consume increases.
   b. The intertemporal substitution effect of the real interest rate on current consumption increases.
   c. The demand for investment goods becomes less responsive to the real interest rate.

6. Determine how the following will affect the slope of the output supply curve, and explain your results:
   a. The marginal product of labour decreases at a faster rate as the quantity of labour used in production increases.
   b. The intertemporal substitution effect of the real interest rate on current leisure decreases.

7. The government decreases current taxes while holding government spending in the present and the future constant.
   a. Using diagrams, determine the equilibrium effects on consumption, investment, the real interest rate, aggregate output, employment, and the real wage. What is the multiplier, and how does it differ from the government expenditure multiplier?
   b. Now suppose that there are credit market imperfections in the market for consumer credit, for example, due to asymmetric information in the credit market. Repeat part (a), and explain any differences in your answers in parts (a) and (b).

8. Suppose there is a shift in the representative consumer's preferences: namely, the consumer prefers, given the market real interest rate, to consume less current leisure and more current consumption goods.
   a. Determine the effects of this on current aggregate output, current employment, the current real wage, current consumption, and current investment.
   b. Explain your results. What might cause such a change in the preferences of consumers?

9. Suppose there is a permanent increase in total factor productivity. Determine the implications of this for current macroeconomic variables, and show how the impact differs from the case in which total factor productivity is expected to increase only temporarily. Explain your results.

10. Suppose z' and K increase at the same time. Show that it is possible for the real interest rate to remain constant as a result. What does this say about the model's ability to explain the differences between poor and rich countries and to explain what happens as a country's economy grows?

11. There is a temporary increase in the relative price of energy. Determine how the response of current aggregate output to this shock depends on the marginal propensity to consume, and explain carefully why you get this result.

12. A war breaks out that is widely expected to last only one year. Show how the effect of this shock on aggregate output depends on the size of the intertemporal substitution effect of the real interest rate on current leisure, and carefully explain your results.

13. The nation experiences a major hurricane that destroys significant capital stock. Policymakers in the federal government reason that the destruction caused by the hurricane will reduce national income, and that this should be counteracted through an increase in government expenditures.

    a. Is the action suggested by these policymakers necessary, given what their goals appear to be?

    b. What would be the net effects on the economy if government expenditures were temporarily increased after the hurricane?

    c. Are there any circumstances when this course of action would make sense? Explain.

14. There is an increase in aggregate credit market risk, and the government responds to this aggregate shock by increasing government spending so that aggregate income remains unchanged. Using diagrams, determine the aggregate economic effects of the combination of the shock to the economy and the government's response to it. Is the government policy response to the aggregate shock a good idea or not? Explain why or why not.

Part 5

Money and Business Cycles

In this Part, our first task is to integrate monetary factors into the real intertemporal model that was developed in Chapter 11. The resulting model, a monetary intertemporal model, is used in Chapter 12 to study the role of currency and alternative means of payment in transactions, the effects of changes in the quantity of money, the interaction between real and nominal phenomena, and monetary policy. In Chapters 13 and 14, we then use the monetary intertemporal model to study the causes of business cycles and the role of fiscal and monetary policy over the business cycle. In Chapter 13, we examine three models of the business cycle with flexible wages and prices, and show how these models fit the key business cycle facts from Chapter 3, as well as features of the recent financial crisis and recession. The implications of these models arc also examined. Chapter 14 is devoted to the study of a new Keynesian sticky price model, which justifies a role for government intervention to smooth business cycles. The alternative business cycle models we study highlight the many possible causes of business cycles which are important in practice.

12

A Monetary Intertemporal Model: Money, Banking, Prices, and Monetary Policy

Money is important for two reasons. First, the economy functions better with money than without it, because carrying out transactions by trading one kind of good for another is difficult and because using credit in some transactions is costly or impossible. Second, changes in the quantity of money in existence matter for nominal quantities—for example, the price level and the inflation rate—and can also affect real economic activity. The quantity of money in circulation is governed in most countries by a central bank, and the primary monetary policy decisions of the central bank concern how to set the level and growth rate of the money supply.

In this chapter, we will construct a monetary intertemporal model, which builds on the real intertemporal model in Chapter 11. In the monetary intertemporal model, consumers and firms choose among means of payment to carry out transactions. That is, they use government-supplied currency for some transactions, and they also use the transactions services supplied by banks. In practice, these transactions services include the use of debit cards, credit cards, and cheques, but for simplicity we represent these services with one type of payments instrument, a credit card. A key part of the model is that consumers and firms make choices about their use of credit cards versus cash, and this is important for determining the demand for money. Building up a knowledge of the role of banks in the monetary system and in credit markets will add to our understanding of the role of financial factors in macroeconomics—a key contemporary issue. The monetary intertemporal model resulting from our work in this chapter will also serve as the basis for our study of business cycles in Chapters 13 and 14.

The first result we will derive using the monetary intertemporal model is the **neutrality of money**, under which a one-time change in the money supply has no real consequences for the economy. Consumption, investment, output, employment, the real interest rate, and economic welfare remain unaffected. The neutrality of money is a good starting point for examining the role of money in the economy, but most macroeconomists agree that money is neutral only in the long run and that, for various reasons, changes in the money supply will have real effects on the economy in the short run.

We then go on to show how one particular type of short-run nonneutrality of money works, by introducing the Friedman-Lucas money surprise model. This model allows us to introduce some basic ideas about how monetary policy is conducted. In particular, we will evaluate monetary policy rules, including money growth rate targeting, interest rate targeting, Taylor rules, and nominal GDP targeting. As well, we will explore the existence of liquidity traps—which occur when monetary policy hits the zero lower bound on the nominal interest rate—and quantitative easing.

What Is Money?

A traditional view of money is that it has three important functions. Money is a **medium of exchange**; it is a **store of value**; and it is a **unit of account**. Money is a medium of exchange in that it is accepted in exchange for goods for the sole reason that it can in turn be exchanged for other goods, not because it is wanted for consumption purposes. Money is a store of value, like other assets, such as stocks, bonds, housing, and so on. It allows consumers to trade current goods for future goods. Finally, money is a unit of account because essentially all contracts are denominated in terms of money. For example, in Canada, a typical labour contract is a promise to pay a specified number of Canadian dollars in exchange for a specified quantity of labour, and a typical loan contract is a promise to pay a specified number of Canadian dollars in the future in exchange for a specified quantity of Canadian dollars in the present. As well, Canadian firms keep their books in terms of Canadian dollars.

The distinguishing economic feature of money is its medium-of-exchange role. As mentioned above, there are other assets, such as stocks, bonds, and housing, that serve the store-of-value role played by money. However, there are difficulties in using these other assets in exchange. First, there can be imperfect information concerning the quality of assets. For example, it may be difficult to get the clerk in a convenience store to accept a stock certificate in exchange for a newspaper, as the clerk will likely not know the market value of the stock certificate, and it would be costly for him or her to sell the stock certificate. Second, some assets come in large denominations and are therefore difficult to use for small purchases. For example, even if the clerk in the convenience store knows the market value of a Treasury bill (a short-term debt instrument issued by the government), Treasury bills do not come in denominations of less than $1000, and so the clerk likely cannot make change for the purchase of a newspaper. Third, some assets take time to sell at their market value. For example, if I attempted to sell my house to the convenience store clerk, he or she would likely offer me much less for the house than I would receive if I searched the market for a buyer whose preferences best matched my house.

MEASURING THE MONEY SUPPLY

As we will discuss in more detail in Chapter 17, money has taken many forms historically. Money has circulated as commodity money (primarily silver and gold), circulating private bank notes (as was the case prior to 1935 in Canada), commodity-backed paper currency (e.g., under the gold standard), fiat money (e.g., Canadian currency in Canada), and transactions deposits at private financial institutions. In Canada today, money consists mainly of objects that take the latter two forms, fiat money and transactions deposits at financial institutions.

In modern developed economies, there are potentially many ways to measure the supply of money, depending on where we want to draw the line defining which assets satisfy the medium-of-exchange property and which do not. What is defined as money is somewhat arbitrary, and it is possible that we may want to use different definitions of money for different purposes. Table 12.1 shows measures of the standard **monetary aggregates** for September 2011, taken from the *Bank of Canada Weekly Financial Statistics*. A given monetary aggregate is simply the sum of a number of different assets for the Canadian economy.

TABLE 12.1   Monetary Aggregates

	September 2011 ($ millions)
Currency outside banks	58 085
M2	1 061 835
M3	1 502 624
M1+	632 678
M1++	863 789
M2+	1 393 795
M2++	2 044 471

Source: Bank of Canada, 2011, *Bank of Canada Weekly Financial Statistics*, October 17.

The first entry in Table 12.1 is currency outside banks, the narrowest definition of the money stock available to the nonbank private sector for making transactions. Currency outside banks is part of **outside money**. In addition to currency outside banks, outside money in Canada consists of currency held by banks (about $4337 million in September 2011) and deposits of financial institutions with the **Bank of Canada** (a relatively small number). We call the narrowest monetary aggregate "outside money" because it is the quantity of money *outside* of the financial system. The monetary aggregate M2 is obtained by adding currency outside banks plus personal chequing accounts in chartered banks, plus current accounts in chartered banks, plus nonpersonal notice deposits and personal savings deposits in chartered banks. The quantity of M3 is obtained by adding M2 plus chartered bank nonpersonal term deposits plus foreign currency deposits of residents of Canada. Finally, there are four modified monetary aggregates. The aggregates M1+, M1++, M2+, and M2++ are measures of M1 (a narrower definition of money than M2 that does not include notice deposits and savings deposits) and M2 that account for transactions deposits and other deposits in financial institutions other than chartered banks, as well as for some kinds of deposits at chartered banks that could be used for transactions but are not included in M1. The last two aggregates in Table 12.1, M1++ and M2++, are ones the Bank of Canada focuses on primarily in formulating monetary policy, to the extent that it regards any monetary aggregates as being important in the policymaking process.

The monetary aggregates are important, as they can be useful indirect measures of aggregate economic activity that are available on a more timely basis than GDP. Further, there are key regularities in the relationship between monetary aggregates and other aggregate variables, which make them useful in economic forecasting and in policy analysis. Finally, the paths followed by monetary aggregates over time can be useful in evaluating the performance of the Bank of Canada, though in this respect monetary aggregates are far less important than they were in the late 1970s. We will discuss this later in this chapter.

A Monetary Intertemporal Model

Why do we use money in exchange? A useful analogy is that money is to economic exchange as oil is to an engine; money overcomes "frictions." Two important economic frictions that make money useful are the following. First, in modern economies, barter exchange—the exchange of goods for goods—is difficult. As Adam Smith recognized in his *Wealth of Nations*, specialization is key to the efficiency gains that come from economic development. Once economic agents become specialized in what they produce and what they consume, it becomes very time-consuming to trade what one has for what one wants through barter exchange. For example, if Sara specializes in giving economics lectures and wants to buy car repairs, to make a barter exchange she must not only find someone willing to repair her car—a **single coincidence of wants**—but the car repair person must also want to receive a lecture in economics—a **double coincidence of wants**. Clearly, Sara may have to spend a great deal of time and energy searching for a trading partner! The double-coincidence problem was first studied by William Stanley Jevons in the nineteenth century.[1] Money solves the double-coincidence problem since, if everyone accepts money in exchange, then would-be buyers need only satisfy a single-coincidence problem to buy a good, which is much easier. Sara can sell economics lectures for money and then exchange this money for car repairs.

A second reason money is useful in exchange is that there are circumstances in which credit transactions may be difficult or impossible to make. For example, it would be unlikely that a street vendor in Toronto would accept my personal IOU in exchange for a hot dog. Since the vendor does not know me or my credit history, he or she cannot evaluate whether my IOU is good or not, and it would be costly for him or her to take legal action should I not be willing to honour it. Although modern credit card and debit card systems solve some of the information problems connected with the use of

---

[1]See S. Jevons, 1910, *Money and the Mechanism of Exchange*, 23rd ed., Kegan Paul, London.

personal credit in transactions, these systems are costly to operate, and there are sellers of goods who will not accept credit under any circumstances. Since money is easily recognizable, there are essentially no information problems associated with the use of money in exchange, other than the problems that arise from counterfeiting.

We will not include explicitly in our model the frictions that make money useful, as this would make things far too complicated for this level of analysis. It is important to keep these frictions in mind, however, and in Chapter 17 we will study a model that takes explicit account of the double-coincidence-of-wants problem in barter exchange. We will use that model to gain some insight into the fundamentals of the role of money in the economy, but to study the issues in this chapter—the key determinants of the demand for money, monetary neutrality, and the basics of monetary policy—we will do pretty well without being explicit about monetary frictions.

REAL AND NOMINAL INTEREST RATES AND THE FISHER RELATION

In the monetary intertemporal model that we construct, there are many periods, but our analysis will be mainly in terms of an arbitrary *current period* and the following period, which we refer to as the *future period*. There are two primary assets in the model, money and nominal bonds. We will use money as the numeraire here (recall that the *numeraire* is the object in which all prices are denominated in an economic model) with P denoting the current price level, or the current price of goods in terms of money. Similarly, P' denotes the price level in the future period. A **nominal bond** is an asset that sells for one unit of money (e.g., one dollar in Canada) in the current period and pays off $1 + R$ units of money in the future period. Therefore, R is the rate of return on a bond in units of money, or the **nominal interest rate**. Nominal bonds can be issued by the government, by consumers, or by firms.

As in Chapters 9, 10, and 11, the real rate of interest, r, is the rate of interest in terms of goods. The real interest rate is the real rate of return that someone receives when holding a nominal bond from the current period to the future period. The real interest rate can be determined from the nominal interest rate and the **inflation rate**, i, which is defined by

$$i = \frac{P' - P}{P}.$$ (12.1)

That is, the inflation rate is the rate of increase in the price level from the current period to the future period. Then, the real interest rate is determined by the **Fisher relation**, named after Irving Fisher, which is

$$1 + r = \frac{1 + R}{1 + i}.$$ (12.2)

To derive the Fisher relation, recall that $1 + R$ is the return in terms of money in the future period from giving up one unit of money in the current period to buy a *nominal* bond. In real terms, someone acquiring a nominal bond will give up $\frac{1}{P}$ goods in the current period and receive a payoff of $\dfrac{1 + R}{P'}$ goods in the future period. Therefore, from Equation (12.1), the gross rate of return on the nominal bond, in real terms, is

$$1 + r = \frac{\dfrac{(1 + R)}{P'}}{\dfrac{1}{P}} = \frac{1 + R}{1 + i},$$

which gives us the Fisher relation, Equation (12.2).

Given a positive nominal interest rate on nominal bonds—that is, $R > 0$—the rate of return on nominal bonds exceeds the rate of return on money. The nominal interest rate on money is zero, and the real interest rate on money can be determined just as we determined the real interest rate associated with the nominal bond above. That is, if r^m is the real rate of interest on money, then as in Equation (12.2) we have

$$1 + r^m = \frac{1 + 0}{1 + i} = \frac{1}{1 + i},$$

and so if $R > 0$ then $r^m < r$, or the real interest rate on money is less than the real interest rate on the nominal bond. In our monetary intertemporal model, we will need to explain why people are willing to hold money if they can receive a higher rate of return on the alternative asset, nominal bonds, when the nominal interest rate is positive.

Now, the Fisher relation can be rewritten by multiplying each side of Equation (12.2) by $1 + i$ and rearranging to get

$$r = R - i - ir.$$

Then, if the nominal interest rate and the inflation rate are small, ir will be negligible, for example, if the inflation rate is 10% and the real interest rate is 2%, then $i = 0.1$, $r = 0.02$, and $ir = 0.002$. As a result, we can say that, for small inflation rates and interest rates,

$$r \approx R - i; \tag{12.3}$$

that is, the real interest rate is approximately equal to the nominal interest rate minus the inflation rate. For example, if the nominal interest rate is 5%, or 0.05, and the inflation rate is 3%, or 0.03, then the real interest rate is approximately 2%, or 0.02.

Empirically, there is a problem in measuring the real interest rate. Nominal interest rates on many different assets can be observed, but economic agents do not know the inflation rate that will be realized over the time they hold a particular asset. The correct inflation rate to use might be the one that an economic agent expects, but expectations cannot be observed. However, one approach to measuring the real rate of interest is to calculate it on the basis of Equation (12.3), by using the realized inflation rate for i. In Figure 12.1 we show data on the nominal interest rate, measured as the interest rate on a three-month federal government Treasury bill over the period 1962–2011, and the corresponding real rate, calculated as the nominal interest rate minus the inflation

FIGURE 12.1

Real and Nominal Interest Rates, 1962–2011

The figure shows the nominal interest rate on three-month Canadian Treasury bills and the corresponding real interest rate, calculated as the nominal interest rate minus the rate of change in the implicit GDP deflator.

Source: Adapted from the Statistics Canada CANSIM database, Series v122531, v1997756.

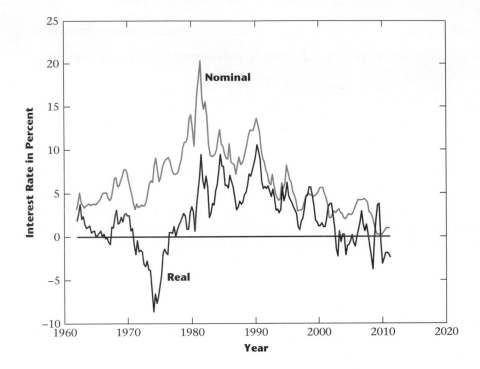

rate. Note that the measured real interest rate has varied considerably over time, and that it has sometimes been quite low, dipping below 0% several times over this sample period, particularly during the 1970s.

BANKS AND ALTERNATIVE MEANS OF PAYMENT

In constructing the monetary intertemporal model, we need to modify the real intertemporal model of Chapter 11 to account for how transactions are carried out using currency supplied by the central bank and transactions services supplied by private banks. For the analysis in this chapter and in Chapters 13 and 14, we do not have to alter how we model demand and supply in the labour market and goods market. However, we need to introduce a new market, the market for money. But we know that there are different definitions of "money," and that we might think of money in different ways depending on the task at hand. For this task—building our monetary intertemporal model—the money stock corresponds to the most narrow definition of money, outside money. The demand for money in the model will be determined, as we will show, by the behaviour of the representative consumer and the representative firm, and the supply of money is determined by the central bank. As we will see, the demand for money is a quite different concept from the demand for a good or service. In contrast to goods and services, we want money not because it contributes directly to our happiness, but because it allows us to acquire the goods and services that ultimately make us happy. To understand the determinants of the demand for money, we need to be specific about how consumers and firms make choices between using currency and the services of banks in making transactions.

Banks have two roles in practice. First, they serve to facilitate transactions among consumers, firms, and the government. Second, banks serve as financial intermediaries that manage the savings of their depositors in a more efficient way than could be accomplished by each depositor on their own. For our purposes here, it is simplest to deal only with the transactions-facilitating role of banks, and the second role of banks will be explored in some detail in Chapter 17.

The two primary alternatives to government-supplied currency that are in wide use in retail transactions are debit cards and credit cards. From a recent survey conducted by the Bank of Canada, currency accounted for 29%, debit cards for 26%, and credit cards for 31% of the total value of transactions in Canada.[2] It will be useful to start our analysis by thinking of credit cards as the only alternative to currency in transactions, and then show how we can generalize our thinking to include debit cards.

Though currency, credit cards, and debit cards all look essentially identical to a consumer—they all can be used in purchases of goods and services—there are important economic differences among them. The first key difference relates to whose liability the payments instrument represents. Currency is technically a liability of the central bank—all outstanding currency and coins in Canada show up as liabilities on the Bank of Canada's balance sheet. However, when I use my debit card, I am transferring a private bank liability (part of my account balance with the bank) to someone else. When I use a credit card to make a transaction, then there is a somewhat complicated transfer of liabilities. At the time of the transaction, I have issued a liability—my IOU—in exchange for some goods and services provided by a retailer. The retailer then takes my IOU and exchanges it with a financial intermediary, Visa for example. Visa now has my IOU, and I eventually pay Visa to extinguish the IOU.

A second key difference among means of payment relates to the payment of interest on the liabilities in question. Currency is a liability which pays no interest, because this is impractical. However, until the time I make a debit card transaction I can earn interest on the bank deposit liability that I am going to transfer through use of the debit card.[3] With credit card balances, the typical practice is for no interest to be paid on credit card debt extended during a monthly billing cycle, but interest is paid if the balance is carried over into the next month.

A third difference among means of payment is in the transactions costs involved. Government-supplied currency is a very low-tech means of payment, and exchange using currency is very low cost. Counterfeit currency may be a concern, but not if the government has done a good job of designing the currency to thwart counterfeiters and establishing serious legal penalties for counterfeiting. Accepting payment using credit cards or debit cards is a more costly matter, as a retailer needs to have an electronic

---

[2]See C. Arango and V. Taylor, 2008, "Merchant Acceptance, Costs, and Perceptions of Retail Payments: A Canadian Survey," Bank of Canada discussion paper 2008-12, www.bankofcanada.ca/wp-content/uploads/2010/01/dp08-12.pdf.

[3]In practice the interest rates on transactions deposits at banks can sometimes be very low—indeed close to zero—when short-term market interest rates are low.

terminal to communicate with the credit card issuer, and must have contractual arrangements with credit card issuers.

In our monetary intertemporal model, we will start by considering how payments by credit card would work as an alternative to currency in transactions. Suppose that goods can be purchased by consumers (who buy consumption goods C), firms (who purchase investment goods I) and the government (which purchases G) using currency or credit cards, and that firms sell goods at the same price P in terms of money, whether they are offered payment with currency or a credit card. Why do firms only accept currency and credit cards and not personal IOUs? This is because the information costs of checking an individual's credit history are too great. Monetary theorists would say that there is a lack of memory or recordkeeping on individuals in the credit system. Everyone recognizes government-supplied currency and Visa but few people know me or my creditworthiness.

Operating a credit card system is costly. The credit card issuer must set up a communication network, and must check the credit histories of individuals to whom it issues cards. Credit card holders must be billed every month, and debts collected. We will represent these costs by assuming that banks sell credit services for a price q, in units of goods, for each unit of real goods transacted using the credit card during the current period. As well, there exists a supply curve for credit card services $X^s(q)$ that denotes the quantity of credit card services (units of goods purchased with a credit card during the period) supplied given each price q. In Figure 12.2, the supply curve for credit card services is increasing because of the increasing marginal cost of supplying credit card services.

We will assume that when an economic agent buys some goods with a credit card, the economic agent acquires a debt with the bank that is paid off, at zero interest, at the end of the current period. If consumers, firms, or the government want to borrow (or lend) from one period to the next, they do so on the credit market at the market nominal interest rate R, with the borrowing and lending taking place at the beginning of the period.

FIGURE 12.2

The Supply Curve for Credit Card Services

The supply curve is upward-sloping as the profitability of extending credit balances increases as q increases, so banks increase quantity supplied.

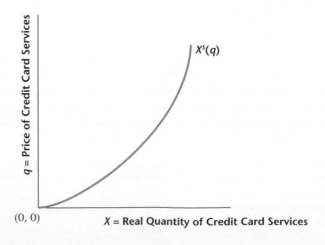

EQUILIBRIUM IN THE MARKET FOR CREDIT CARD SERVICES AND THE DEMAND FOR MONEY

To determine the demand for credit card services, we need to consider the behaviour of consumers, firms, and government purchasing agents who are on the demand side of the goods market. Given that all of these economic agents want to collectively purchase Y units of goods, their decision relates to the quantity of goods they wish to purchase with credit cards, denoted by $X^d(q)$ (or the demand for credit card services) relative to the remainder, $Y - X^d(q)$, which is the quantity of goods purchased with currency. We need to determine what $X^d(q)$ looks like and then, given the supply curve for credit card services in Figure 12.2, we can in turn determine the equilibrium quantity and price of credit card services.

Suppose that an economic agent considers buying one more unit of goods with credit, and one less unit of goods with currency. What are the costs and benefits, at the margin? The economic agent would then need to hold P fewer units of currency to make transactions during the current period, and this quantity could then be lent on the credit market, yielding $P(1 + R)$ units of money at the beginning of the future period. Thus, the marginal benefit is $P(1 + R)$ units of money at the beginning of the future period. However, the consumer must give up $P(1 + q)$ units of money at the end of the period in order to pay off the credit card debt and to pay the bank for its credit card services. Assume that any money available at the end of the period must be held as currency until the beginning of the next period. Thus, the marginal cost of buying one more unit of goods with a credit card is $P(1 + q)$, in units of money at the beginning of next period.

What does the economic agent want to do? This depends on the comparison between marginal benefit and marginal cost. If

$$P(1 + R) > P(1 + q), \tag{12.4}$$

or $R > q$, then marginal benefit is greater than marginal cost, and the economic agent will purchase all goods with a credit card. However, if

$$P(1 + R) < P(1 + q) \tag{12.5}$$

or $R < q$, then marginal benefit is less than marginal cost, and the economic agent will purchase all goods with currency. If $R = q$ then the agent is indifferent between using currency and a credit card. This implies that the demand curve for credit card services is as depicted in Figure 12.3, that is, it is perfectly elastic at $q = R$. The equilibrium price for credit card services is therefore R, and the equilibrium quantity of credit card services is X^* in the figure.

Then, in Figure 12.4, consider what happens if the nominal interest rate rises from R_1 to R_2. In equilibrium the price of credit card services rises, and the quantity of credit card services rises from X_1^* to X_2^*. We can then write the equilibrium quantity of credit card services as $X^*(R)$, which is a decreasing function of the nominal interest rate R, to capture the idea in Figure 12.4 that the equilibrium quantity of credit card services rises when the nominal interest rate rises. Effectively, this occurs because the opportunity cost of making a transaction with currency is higher the larger is the nominal interest rate. This implies that the quantity of goods purchased with currency

FIGURE 12.3

Equilibrium in the Market for Credit Card Services

The demand curve for credit balances is horizontal at the price $q = R$, the equilibrium price of credit card services is $q = R$ and the quantity is X^*.

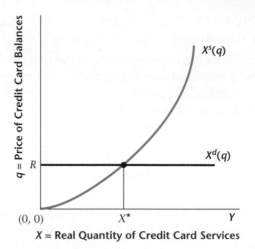

is $Y - X^*(R)$ when the market for credit card services is in equilibrium, which means that the nominal quantity of currency that consumers, firms, and the government want to hold to make transactions is

$$M^d = P[Y - X^*(R)], \qquad (12.5)$$

but since the function on the right-hand side of Equation (12.5) is increasing in Y and decreasing in R, it is simpler to write Equation (12.5) as

$$M^d = PL(Y, R), \qquad (12.6)$$

where the function L is increasing in real income, Y, and decreasing in the nominal interest rate, R. Note that, if we include an analysis of the use of debit cards as well, that the demand for currency will take the same form as in Equation (12.6). The use of a debit card in transactions involves the transfer of ownership of an interest-bearing bank liability. Thus, the use of debit cards must rise with the nominal interest rate, as a higher nominal interest rate implies a lower cost of using a debit card relative to currency.

FIGURE 12.4

The Effect of an Increase in the Nominal Interest Rate on the Market for Credit Card Services

An increase in the nominal interest rate from R_1 to R_2 shifts the demand curve for credit balances up from X_1^d to X_2^d. The equilibrium price of credit card balances increases from R_1 to R_2 and the equilibrium quantity increases from X_1^* to X_2^*.

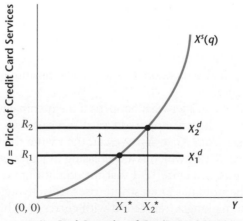

The function $PL(Y, R)$ in Equation (12.6) is a nominal money demand function, though it would be quite misleading to think of the money demand function as being much like the demand function for a good or service. In our model, the money demand function is derived as an equilibrium relationship given the choices of banks concerning the supply of credit card services, and the choices of consumers, firms, and the government concerning how they will use cash and credit cards in making transactions.

The nominal demand for money is proportional to the price level, as the quantity that matters to consumers and firms in their choice of means of payment is the real quantity of money, M^d/P. Money demand increases with real income as consumers and firms wish to engage in a larger real volume of transactions as real income rises, and the capacity of the banking system to supply alternative means of payment is limited. Finally, money demand falls as the nominal interest rate rises, because a higher nominal interest rate increases the opportunity cost of holding cash, and so consumers and firms are more inclined to use alternative means of payment such as credit cards and debit cards.

Now, taking the approximate Fisher relation, Equation (12.3), as an equality (that is, assuming the real interest rate and the inflation rate are small) implies that we can substitute $r + i$ for R in Equation (12.6) to get

$$M^d = PL(Y, r + i). \tag{12.7}$$

For most of the analysis that we do in this chapter and in Chapters 13 and 14, we look at economic experiments that do not deal with the effects of changes in long-run inflation. That is, most of the experiments we consider in these chapters leave i unaffected. When i is constant in Equation (12.7), it is harmless to set it to zero for convenience, which implies that Equation (12.7) becomes

$$M^d = PL(Y, r). \tag{12.8}$$

With Y and r given, the function on the right-hand side of Equation (12.8) is linear in P with slope $L(Y, r)$, and we depict this function in Figure 12.5. If real income increases, for example from Y_1 to Y_2, then in Figure 12.6 the money demand curve shifts to the

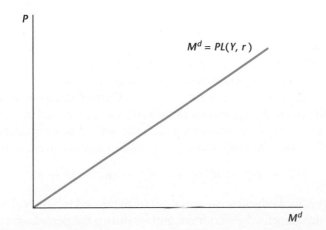

FIGURE 12.5

The Nominal Money Demand Curve in the Monetary Intertemporal Model

Current nominal money demand is a straight line, and it will shift with changes in real income, Y, or the real interest rate, r.

FIGURE 12.6

**The Effect of an Increase in
Current Real Income on the
Nominal Money Demand
Curve**
The current nominal money
demand curve shifts to the
right with an increase in
current real income, Y.

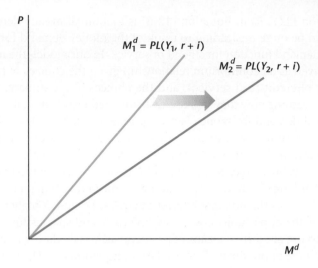

right from $PL(Y_1, r)$ to $PL(Y_2, r)$. We would obtain the same type of rightward shift in the money demand curve if the real interest rate, r, were to decrease.

GOVERNMENT

Including the ability of the government to issue money implies that we need to expand on our treatment of government from Chapter 11. For our purposes, it will be convenient to assume that there is a single institution in our model called the "government," which is responsible for both fiscal and monetary policy. Therefore, the government entity in this model is essentially what we would get if we merged the federal government with the Bank of Canada and placed them both under the control of Parliament. In Canada, the Bank of Canada, which is the monetary authority, has some independence from the Department of Finance, which is the federal fiscal authority controlled by the Canadian government. The arrangement between the central bank and the federal government varies considerably across countries. For example, the central bank in the United States, the Federal Reserve System, has somewhat more independence than the Bank of Canada. However, the central banks in some countries have little independence.

In the current period, the government purchases G consumption goods and pays the nominal interest and principal on the government debt outstanding from the last period, $(1 + R^-)B^-$, where B^- is the quantity of one-period nominal bonds issued by the government in the previous period, which come due in the current period, with each of these bonds bearing a nominal interest rate of R^-. Current government purchases and the interest and principal on government debt, which sum to total current government outlays, are financed through taxation, through the issue of new bonds, and by printing money. Therefore, the government budget constraint in the current period is given by

$$PG + (1 + R^-)B^- = PT + B + M - M^-. \qquad (12.9)$$

The government budget constraint (12.9) is expressed in nominal terms, with the left-hand side denoting total government outlays during the period, and the right-hand side denoting total government receipts. On the right-hand side, PT denotes nominal taxes; B denotes government bonds issued in the current period, which come due in the future period; and the final term, $M - M^-$, is the change in the nominal money supply, where M is the total quantity of money outstanding in the current period, and M^- is the previous period's money supply.

Adding money creation, $M - M^-$, to the government budget constraint is an important step here over the kinds of models we considered in Chapters 5, 9, 10, and 11, where we did not take account of the transactions using money and other means of payment that take place in the economy. We will now be able to consider the effects of monetary policy and how monetary and fiscal policy interact.

Competitive Equilibrium—The Complete Intertemporal Monetary Model

In the monetary intertemporal model, there are three markets to consider—the market for current goods, the market for current labour, and the money market. The markets for current goods and current labour operate exactly as in the real intertemporal model, so the only important difference here from the model of Chapter 11 is the addition of the money market. The nominal demand for money, M^d, is given by Equation (12.8), while the nominal money supply, M^s, is determined exogenously by the government, with $M^s = M$. When the money market is in equilibrium, the quantity of money supplied equals the quantity demanded, or $M^s = M^d$, so that from Equation (12.8),

$$M = PL(Y, r). \tag{12.10}$$

In Figure 12.7 we illustrate the workings of the money market, with the nominal money demand curve M^d being upward-sloping and linear in P, as we saw previously. Here, we have added the money supply curve, which is a vertical line at the quantity

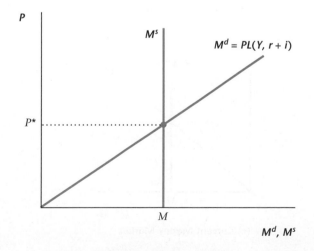

FIGURE 12.7
The Current Money Market in the Monetary Intertemporal Model
The figure shows the current nominal demand for money curve, M^d, and the money supply curve, M^s. The intersection of these two curves determines the equilibrium price level, which is P^* in the figure.

M, because the money supply is exogenous. The intersection of the nominal money demand and nominal money supply curves determines the price level P. In the figure, the equilibrium price level is P^*.

Next, integrating the money market into the real intertemporal model of Chapter 11, we show in Figure 12.8 how the endogenous variables in the monetary intertemporal

FIGURE 12.8

The Complete Monetary Intertemporal Model

In the model, the equilibrium real interest rate, r^*, and equilibrium current aggregate output, Y^*, are determined in panel (b). The real interest rate determines the position of the labour supply curve in panel (a), where the equilibrium real wage, w^*, and equilibrium employment, N^*, are determined. Finally, the equilibrium price level, P^*, is determined in the money market in panel (c), given the equilibrium real interest rate, r^*, and equilibrium output, Y^*.

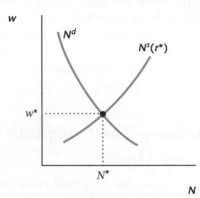

(a) Current Labour Market

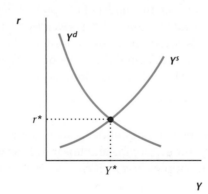

(b) Current Goods Market

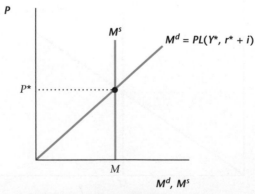

(c) Current Money Market

model are determined. In Figure 12.8(b), we depict equilibrium in the current goods market, where the output demand curve Y^d and the output supply curve Y^s jointly determine the equilibrium real interest rate r^* and the equilibrium quantity of aggregate output, Y^*. Then, in Figure 12.8(a), given the equilibrium real interest rate r^*, which determines the position of the labour supply curve $N^s(r^*)$, the labour demand curve N^d and the labour supply curve $N^s(r^*)$ jointly determine the equilibrium real wage w^* and the equilibrium quantity of employment, N^*. Then, in Figure 12.8(c), the equilibrium quantity of output, Y^*, and the equilibrium real interest rate r^* determine the position of the money demand curve M^d. Then, the money demand curve and the money supply curve in Figure 12.8(c) determine the equilibrium price level P^*.

A LEVEL INCREASE IN THE MONEY SUPPLY AND MONETARY NEUTRALITY

A government, through its central bank, has the power to increase the money supply by several different means. Historically, the power of a government to print money has been important, in that this can finance transfers to the private sector, it can involve changing the quantity of interest-bearing assets held by the private sector, and it can finance government expenditures. In this section, we would like to determine the effects on current macroeconomic variables of a one-time increase in the money supply. As we will see, a change in the level of the money supply of this sort will be **neutral**, in that no real variables will change, but all nominal quantities will change in proportion to the change in the money supply. The *neutrality of money* is an important concept in monetary economics, and we want to understand the theory behind it and what it means in practice.

In the experiment we will perform in the model, we will suppose that the money supply is fixed at the quantity $M = M_1$ until the current period, as in Figure 12.9. Until the current period, everyone anticipates that the money supply will remain fixed at the quantity M_1 forever. During the current period, however, the money supply increases from M_1 to M_2 and then remains at that level forever. What could cause such an increase in the money supply? From the government budget constraint, Equation (12.9), the change in the money supply in the current period, $M - M^- = M_2 - M_1$, is positive, and so this positive change in the money supply in the current period needs to be offset by some other term in Equation (12.9). Since the nominal interest rate from the previous period, R^-, and the quantity of bonds issued by the government in the previous period, B^-, were determined last period based on the expectation that the quantity of money in circulation would be M_1 forever, only the other terms in Equation (12.9) could be affected. There are three possibilities:

1. The government could reduce current taxes, T. Therefore, the money supply increase is reflected in a decrease in taxes on the household, which is the same as an increase in transfers. Milton Friedman referred to this method of increasing the money stock as a **helicopter drop**, since it is much like having a government helicopter fly over the countryside spewing money.

2. The government could reduce the quantity of bonds, B, that it issues during the current period. This is an **open market operation**, which in practice is carried out when the fiscal authority issues interest-bearing government debt, and then the

FIGURE 12.9

**A Level Increase in the
Money Supply in the
Current Period**

The figure shows a one-time
increase in the money supply,
from M_1 to M_2.

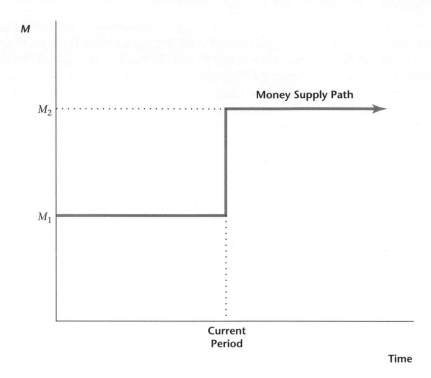

monetary authority—the central bank—purchases some of this debt by issuing
new money. An **open market purchase** is an exchange of money for interest-
bearing debt by the monetary authority, and an **open market sale** is the sale
of interest-bearing debt initially held by the monetary authority in exchange for
money. In the case we examine here, where the money supply increases, there is
an open market purchase. The day-to-day control of the money supply is accomplished in Canada mainly through open market operations by the Bank of Canada.

3. The government could temporarily increase the quantity of government spending,
   G, in the current period. Thus, the government would be printing money in order
   to finance government spending. When the government does this, it collects seigniorage. **Seigniorage** originally referred to the profit made by a *seigneur*, or ruler,
   from issuing coinage, but it has come to take on a broader meaning as the revenue
   earned by the government from issuing money. Seigniorage is also referred to as
   the revenue from the **inflation tax**, since the extra money that the government
   prints will in general increase prices. Historically, seigniorage has been an important revenue-generating device and has been a key source of revenue for governments during times of war.

For our purposes here, it will prove most convenient for now to suppose that the
money supply increase occurs through the first method above—a lump-sum transfer
of money to the representative consumer. What happens in equilibrium when the
money supply increases in the current period from M_1 to M_2? Here, since the level of

the money supply does not matter for labour supply, labour demand, and the demand and supply of goods, the equilibrium determination of N, Y, r, and w in Figure 12.10 is unaffected by the current money supply, M. That is, there is a **classical dichotomy**: the model solves for all the real variables (output, employment, the real interest rate,

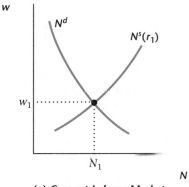

(a) **Current Labour Market**

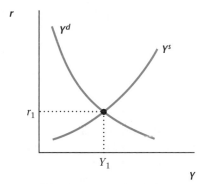

(b) **Current Goods Market**

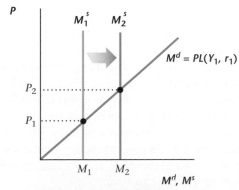

(c) **Current Money Market**

FIGURE 12.10

The Effects of a Level Increase in *M*—The Neutrality of Money

A level increase in the money supply in the monetary intertemporal model from M_1 to M_2 has no effects on any real variables, but the price level increases in proportion to the increase in the money supply. Money is neutral.

and the real wage) in the labour market and the goods market in Figure 12.10, and the price level is then determined, given real output, in the money market. Real activity is completely separated from nominal variables (the money supply, the price level). In Figure 12.10(b), the real interest rate and current real output are given by r_1 and Y_1, respectively, and in Figure 12.10(a), the equilibrium real wage and level of employment are w_1 and N_1, respectively.

In the model, we want to investigate the effects of having a money supply of M_2 from the current period on, rather than a money supply of M_1. In Figure 12.10 there is no effect on real activity, since the labour market and goods market are unaffected by the level of the money supply. However, there will be an effect on the price level. In Figure 12.10(c), the money supply curve shifts to the right because of the increase in the money supply from M_1 to M_2. The money demand curve is unaffected, since Y does not change, r does not change, and the current inflation rate, 0, will be unaffected because the money supply will not change after the current period. As a result, the price level increases in equilibrium from P_1 to P_2. Further, we can say something about how much the price level increases. Because $M = PL(Y, r)$ in equilibrium (money supply equals money demand) and because Y and r are unaffected by the increase in M, P must increase in proportion to M, so that $\dfrac{M}{P}$ remains unchanged. That is, if M increases by 10%, then P increases by 10%, so that the real money supply, $\dfrac{M}{P}$, is unaffected.

Note that the level increase in the money supply causes a level increase in the price level. There is only a one-time increase in the inflation rate (the rate of change in the price level), from the previous period to the current period, and no long-run increase in the inflation rate.

In this model, then, money is neutral. Money neutrality is said to hold if a change in the level of the money supply results only in a proportionate increase in prices, with no effects on any real variables. Thus, a change in the level of the money supply does not matter here. This does not mean, however, that money does not matter. In this model, if there were no money, then all transactions would have to take place through the banking system, and this would be much more costly. In the real world, even if money were neutral, we know that if we eliminated it, then in many circumstances people would have to use more cumbersome means to make transactions, such as barter. This would be much less efficient, and in general people would be worse off.

Is monetary neutrality a feature of the real world? In one sense, it almost obviously is. Suppose that the government could magically add a zero to the denominations of all currency. That is, suppose that overnight all $1 bills became $10 bills, $5 bills became $50 bills, and so on. Suppose further that this change were announced several months in advance. It seems clear that, on the morning when everyone wakes up with their currency holdings increased tenfold, all sellers of goods would have anticipated this change and would have increased their prices by a factor of ten as well, and that there would be no real change in aggregate economic activity. Though this thought experiment helps us understand the logic behind monetary neutrality, real-world increases in the money supply do not occur in this way, and there is, in fact, much debate about the extent of money neutrality in the short run.

There is broad agreement, however, that money is neutral in the long run. If the central bank engineers an increase in the money supply, after a long period of time it will make no difference to anyone whether the money supply increase ever occurred. Economists have different views, however, about what the long run means in practice. Do the effects of central bank actions on real economic variables essentially disappear after three months, six months, two years, or ten years? Later in this chapter, we will explore the implications of a particular model of the short-run nonneutrality of money. In that model, the difference between short run and long run has a very specific meaning.

Shifts in Money Demand

In the monetary intertemporal model, the demand for money is determined by the choices of consumers and firms concerning the means of payment to be used in transactions, and the choices of banks concerning the supply of credit card services. Any factor that affects either the demand or supply of credit card services will bring about a shift in the demand for money.

Here, we will focus on the effects of a shift in the supply of credit card services. In Figure 12.11, suppose that the supply curve for credit card services shifts to the left from $X_1^s(q)$ to $X_2^s(q)$. Such a shift could be caused, for example, by a widespread power failure that shuts down communications between some retailers and credit card issuers. As a result, while the price of credit card balances remains constant at $q = R$, the market quantity of credit balances falls from X_1^* to X_2^*. Therefore the equilibrium quantity of credit card services, $X^*(R)$, decreases for each R. Recall that the nominal demand for money is given by

$$M^d = PL(Y, R) = P[Y - X^*(R)],$$

so the demand for money is now higher for each P, Y, and R.

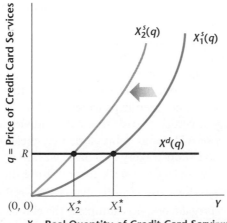

FIGURE 12.11
A Shift in the Supply of Credit Card Services
A decrease in the supply of credit card services does not change the equilibrium price, but equilibrium quantity falls.

FIGURE 12.12

**A Shift in the Demand for
Money**

The money demand curve
shifts to the right, causing a
decrease in the equilibrium
price level P, from P_1 to P_2.

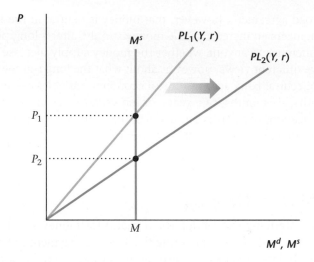

We will again set $i = 0$, so the nominal interest rate equals the real interest rate, or $R = r$. Then, in Figure 12.12, the demand for money increases and the money demand curve shifts to the right, from $PL_1(Y, r)$ to $PL_2(Y, r)$. Now, Y and r are determined in the goods market and labour market, and they are unaffected by what happens to the supply and demand for money. Thus, the price level falls from P_1 to P_2. That is, because the real demand for money has risen, the real money supply (M/P) must rise to meet the increased demand, and this can only happen if P falls.

What would cause shifts in the supply and demand curves for credit card services, other than our power failure example, leading to shifts in the money demand function?

1. *New information technologies that lower the cost for consumers of accessing bank accounts.* In 1970, banks did not provide ATM machines or debit cards. A typical transactions account could be accessed only by going to the bank or by making a transaction with a cheque. ATM machines dramatically reduced the cost of communicating with banks. As well, a typical debit card transaction, handled electronically, can be done at much lower cost than a transaction involving a cheque, which requires depositing the cheque in the bank and routing it through the cheque-clearing system. Thus, replacing the use of cheques with debit cards has reduced the cost of banking. Online banking is another technological development that has lowered the cost of banking transactions and reduced the demand for money. In the context of our model, we can think of these advances as reducing the average length of time between trips to replenish cash balances, which tends to reduce the average quantity of cash that each individual holds. For example, the wider availability of ATMs and debit cards may mean that an individual will switch to visiting the ATM once every two days, withdrawing $40 each time, and holding an average cash balance of $20, from visiting the ATM once per week, withdrawing $140 each time, and holding an average cash balance of $70.

2. *A change in government regulations.* An example is the elimination of reserve requirements in Canada in 1992. Reserve requirements are regulations that mandate that

banks hold a specified fraction of particular classes of bank deposits as outside money. Reserve requirements lower the rate of return that a bank can obtain on its investments and therefore increase the cost of banking to depositors. Therefore, the elimination of reserve requirements not only lowered the direct demand for outside money but also lowered the cost of providing transactions services for banks.

3. *A change in the perceived riskiness of banks.* If consumers and firms perceive that holding a banking deposit is a more risky proposition (e.g., if they think that banks could fail and they might lose their deposits), then consumers and firms may forgo dealing with the banking system and simply conduct transactions using currency. During the Great Depression in the United States, and around the world during the recent financial crisis, the perceived instability of banks made households more uncertain about the value of their bank deposits, and there was an increase in the demand for currency. This therefore increased the demand for money. Bank riskiness is currently not an issue for small depositors in banks, because of government-provided deposit insurance, but it potentially matters for large depositors. We will discuss this further in Chapter 16.

4. *Changes in hour-to-hour, day-to-day, or week-to-week circumstances in the banking system.* There are times of the day, times of the week, or times of the month when the volume of financial transactions is particularly high or particularly low. For example, the volume of transactions among banks and other financial institutions tends to increase as financial traders get close to the end of the financial trading day. As the volume of transactions rises, the marginal cost of making financial transactions rises, due to congestion. In our model, this works as a shift to the left in the supply curve for credit card balances. Many such effects are predictable, but there are sometimes unpredictable shocks to the financial system, such as the failure of a large financial institution or a breakdown in the financial network because of a power failure or terrorist attack. Such failures and breakdowns tend to increase the demand for money.

THEORY CONFRONTS THE DATA 12.1 *Instability in the Money Demand Function in Canada*

Are shifts in the money demand function a big deal in practice? To answer this question, we will look at the demand for outside money (currency plus reserves at financial institutions) in Canada for the period 1962–2011. In order to get started, we have to choose a specific function for $L(Y, R)$ that we can use to try to fit the data. We will assume that

$$L(Y, R) = Ye^{aR},$$

where e is approximately equal to 2.72, and is the base for the natural logarithm. The parameter a satisfies $a < 0$, and is what we want to choose so that this money demand function fits the data as closely as possible. This form for the money demand function implies that money demand is proportional to real income, so that the size of the economy is irrelevant to the real quantity of money that each person wishes to hold.

From Equation (12.12), the equilibrium condition for the money market, we then obtain

$$M = PYe^{aR},$$

or, if we rewrite the above equation and take natural logarithms on both sides of the equation,

$$\log\left(\frac{M}{PY}\right) = aR.$$

Suppose that our theory of money demand is a good one, that we have chosen a good functional form for the money demand function, and that there are only random shifts in the money demand function. Then a negatively sloped straight line should do a good job of fitting the data on the log of the ratio of money to nominal GDP and the nominal interest rate.

If we take M to be the measured quantity of money over the period 1962–2011, PY to be measured nominal GDP, and R to be the short-term Treasury bill rate for Canada, then we obtain the scatter plot in Figure 12.13. In the figure, we measure the nominal interest rate in percentage terms on the vertical axis, and the natural log of the ratio of money to nominal GDP on the horizontal axis. The points in the figure are identified separately as those for the period 1962–1980 (with a "*") and those for the period 1981–2011 (with a "+").

The money demand function fits quite well in Figure 12.13 for the period 1962–1980. A straight line fits the points for 1962–1980 closely, and there is a small amount of variability around that line. However, after 1980, what had seemed to be a stable money demand function began to shift dramatically. Indeed, if we mechanically fit a straight line to the points for 1981–2011, or fit the straight line to the points for the whole period 1962–2011, that straight line would be upward-sloping, which would make no sense in terms of our theory of money demand.

Of course we know a lot about factors that could have affected money demand in dramatic ways since 1980. There has been growth in the use of ATMs, debit cards, and credit cards, for example, and an elimination of reserve requirements, all of which acted to reduce the demand for outside money. Indeed, the 1981–2011 points in the figure would be best-fit by a positively sloped line because the nominal interest rate fell during this period during times when other factors were causing money demand to fall. Thus falling money demand coincided with falling nominal interest rates, in spite of the fact that the falling nominal interest rate was causing the quantity of money demanded to increase.

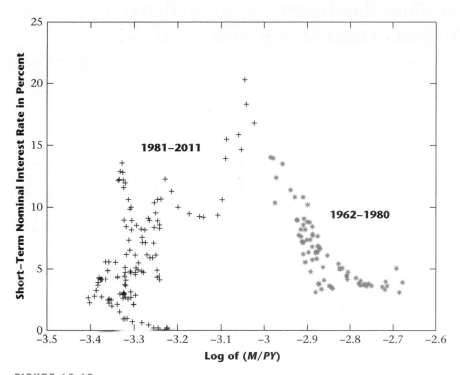

FIGURE 12.13

Shifts in the Demand for Money

A downward-sloping curve would fit the data for 1962–1980 quite well, consistent with a stable money demand function, but the data for 1981–2011 is not predicted well by the money demand function fit to the 1962–1980 data.

Source: Adapted from the Statistics Canada CANSIM database, Series v37145, v498086.

Money demand instability was a critical problem that led to central banks abandoning some monetarist ideas that were popular in the 1970s and 1980s. The instability we can see in Figure 12.13 was a problem not only in Canada, but also in other countries, the United States included. Monetarism, best represented by the ideas of Milton Friedman, took as a cornerstone the notion that the demand for money was stable and could be captured by a simple function of a few variables. Given the stable money demand function, monetarists recommended that central banks conduct and evaluate policy according to the observed behaviour of the money stock. The fact that money demand is unstable, and became increasingly so after 1980, caused a drift away from monetarist ideas, as we will discuss later in this chapter.

The Short Run Nonneutrality of Money: Friedman-Lucas Money Surprise Model

Macroeconomists have come up with many different ideas concerning how monetary policy matters in the short run for real aggregate economic variables. There are alternative macroeconomic models of nonneutralities of money which can have very different implications for how a central bank should conduct itself, so it is important that we sort out these potentially competing ideas.

In this section, we will study a particular model of monetary nonneutrality—the Friedman-Lucas money surprise model—which was developed in the late 1960s and early 1970s. We will also relate the money surprise model to the segmented markets model, which was a product of macroeconomic research in the 1980s and 1990s. In Chapters 13 and 14, we will further explore short-run monetary nonneutralities in the context of a New Monetarist model (in Chapter 13), and a New Keynesian sticky price model (in Chapter 14).

The theory behind the money surprise model was sketched out by Milton Friedman in 1968,[4] and formalized by Robert Lucas in 1972.[5] Lucas's work marked the start of the rational expectations revolution, and he was awarded the Nobel Prize in economics in 1995 for this work.

In the 1960s, macroeconomists had regarded any short-run nonneutralities of money as being the result of out-of-equilibrium behaviour of the economy arising from sticky wages or prices. The Friedman-Lucas model was the first attempt to construct a theory where changes in the level of the money supply could have real effects, with all markets clearing all the time.

The key element of the theory is that workers have imperfect information, in the short run, about aggregate variables that are important to their decision making. In the theory, a worker, who we will call Bob, has complete information about things that directly concern him, for example, the current nominal wage. However, because Bob is not buying all goods all the time, he has imperfect information about the price level. Further, Bob cannot immediately observe aggregate shocks, like changes in total factor productivity and changes in the money supply, that hit the economy. Under these circumstances, Bob might misperceive an increase in his nominal wage as an increase in his real wage, when it is really not, and be fooled into working harder. Money "surprises" can then cause output to fluctuate, but this can be a bad thing. The role for the central bank in this model is to try to prevent confusion, and this may mean making the money supply predictable.

The Friedman-Lucas money surprise model will be a modification of the monetary intertemporal model, with changes that account for the imperfect information problem. During the current period, Bob observes his current nominal wage W, where $W = wP$,

---

[4]See M. Friedman, 1968, "The Role of Monetary Policy," *American Economic Review* 58, 1–17.

[5]See R. Lucas, 1972, "Expectations and the Neutrality of Money," *Journal of Economic Theory* 4, 103–124.

with w the current real wage and P the price level. In terms of making his current labour supply decision, Bob cares about his real wage, not the nominal wage, but there would be no problem determining the real wage if Bob knew the current price level. Then, he could calculate the real wage as $w = W/P$. The problem is that Bob buys many goods, and he does not purchase all of these goods in any one period. For example, consumers in practice typically buy groceries and restaurant food every week, clothing perhaps monthly or seasonally, and a new car every two years or more. Suppose, for simplicity, that Bob simply does not know the current price level P during the current period. This implies that he also does not observe his current real wage w.

We will suppose that there are two shocks that may hit the macroeconomy. The first is a temporary change in z, total factor productivity, and the second is a permanent increase in M, the money supply. We will assume that Bob cannot observe either z or M during the current period. However, he does know that either temporary z-shocks or permanent M-shocks can hit the economy. Though Bob cannot observe the price level or the real wage directly, he can make inferences about the chances of a particular shock having hit the economy, based on how his nominal wage moves in the current period.

Given the environment that Bob lives in, how will he make decisions? Suppose that in the current period Bob sees an increase in his nominal wage W. Given what he knows about how the world works, Bob knows that W may have increased because the money supply went up permanently, or because there was a temporary increase in total factor productivity. If Bob knows how frequently total factor productivity shocks and money supply shocks hit the economy, he then knows the chances that W increased in the current period as the result of either shock. We know from our monetary neutrality result in Figure 12.10 that if there is perfect information (Bob can observe all variables in the economy), then a permanent increase in the level of the money supply would cause a proportionate increase in the price level and there would be no real effects, so that the current real wage w would remain unchanged. Therefore, Bob would not change labour supply. Also, if there were a temporary increase in z under perfect information, then the real wage w would increase and the current price level P would fall, because of an increase in the real demand for money $L(Y, r)$ (Y increases and r falls because of the increase in z). Assume that, with perfect information, wP increases. Thus, in this case, Bob would want to increase labour supply in response to the increase in the real wage, and an increase in the nominal wage effectively signals an increase in the real wage.

The problem is that Bob does not know whether the current nominal wage increased because the money supply increased permanently, or because total factor productivity increased temporarily. This implies that if the money supply actually went up, causing the nominal wage to increase, then Bob infers that there is some chance that the nominal wage increased because of a temporary productivity shock, and therefore he will increase labour supply. Higher labour supply will then cause output to go up.

To show how this works in the monetary intertemporal model, consider Figure 12.14. Initially, the economy is in equilibrium with current real output Y_1, real interest rate r_1, current price level P_1, current employment N_1, and current real wage w_1. Now, suppose that the money supply increases from M_1 to M_2 in Figure 12.14(c). However, Bob

FIGURE 12.14

The Effects of an Unanticipated Increase in the Money Supply in the Money Surprise Model

An unanticipated increase in the money supply shifts the labour supply curve to the right, as the actual real wage is lower than the real wage that the worker perceives. The output supply curve shifts to the right, output rises, and the real interest rate falls, increasing the demand for money, and causing the price level to rise. Money is not neutral.

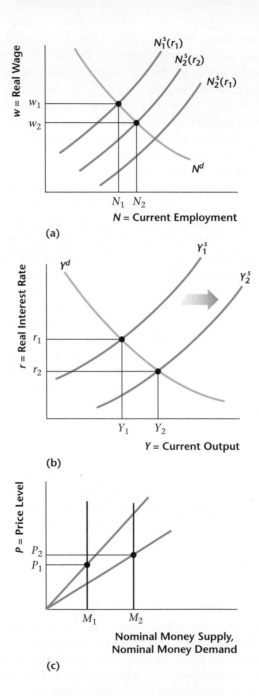

(a)

(b)

(c)

infers that z may have increased temporarily when he sees the increase in his nominal wage W. In terms of the actual real wage, which is the variable on the vertical axis in Figure 12.14(a), Bob then perceives the real wage to be higher than it actually is, and this implies that the labour supply curve shifts rightward, from $N_1^s(r_1)$ to $N_2^s(r_1)$. That is, a money supply increase does not increase the real wage, a total factor productivity increase causes the real wage to increase, and the consumer thinks there is some chance that either event happened, so that the consumer's estimate is that the real wage increased. Thus, when it was really the money supply that increased, Bob's estimate of the real wage is higher than the actual real wage. We know that when the labour supply curve shifts to the right, the output supply curve also shifts to the right, so there is a shift in the output supply curve from Y_1^s to Y_2^s in Figure 12.14(b). In equilibrium, the level of output increases to Y_2, and the real interest rate falls to r_2. Consumption increases as real income has increased and the real interest rate has fallen, and investment increases because of the decrease in the real interest rate. In Figure 12.14(c), the nominal money demand curve shifts rightward from $PL(Y_1,r_1)$ to $PL(Y_2,r_2)$, because real income has increased and the real interest rate has gone down. The money supply curve has also shifted to the right, with the increase in the money supply from M_1 to M_2, but on net the price level will have to increase, from P_1 to P_2.

In Figure 12.14(a), the labour supply curve shifts leftward from $N_2^s(r_1)$ to $N_2^s(r_2)$ when the real interest rate falls, but the shift to the left in the labour supply curve cannot be greater than the initial rightward shift, since we know that output must increase, and output could not increase unless employment increased. Therefore, employment goes up to N_2 and the actual real wage falls to w_2, though the perceived real wage of the consumer has risen. The perceived real wage of the consumer must have increased, as this is why the consumer is supplying more labour in equilibrium.

The key feature of the money surprise model is that money is not neutral. An increase in the nominal money supply in the short run will cause the real interest rate and the real wage to fall, and real output and employment to rise. Further, since $M/P = L(Y, r)$ in equilibrium, and because real output has increased and the real interest rate has decreased, causing real money demand $L(Y, r)$ to rise, M/P (the real money supply) rises. That is, the price level rises less than proportionally to the increase in the money supply.

IMPLICATIONS OF THE MONEY SURPRISE MODEL FOR MONETARY POLICY: MONEY SUPPLY TARGETING AND INTEREST RATE TARGETING

In the Friedman-Lucas money surprise model, an unanticipated increase in the money supply causes employment and output to increase, and it might seem that this is a good thing. In Keynesian models, like the New Keynesian sticky price model that we will study in Chapter 14, it is economically efficient in some circumstances for the central bank to increase the money supply so as to increase output and employment. In the money surprise model, however, an engineered money surprise by the central bank can be a bad thing.

In the money surprise model, given the assumptions we have made thus far, output increases with a money supply increase only because people are fooled. An optimal state of affairs in this model is when consumers and firms are perfectly informed about what is happening to the economy. Under perfect information, all markets clear, the optimal quantity of labour is bought and sold in the labour market, and the optimal quantity of goods is bought and sold in the goods market. That is, if there were perfect information in the money surprise model, then the equilibrium allocation of resources would be Pareto-optimal (recall our discussion from Chapter 5).

Market prices carry important signals about shocks that are hitting the economy. If those signals are transmitted clearly to market participants, then this aids in the appropriate allocation of resources in the economy. For example, an increase in the relative price of peaches signals a scarcity in the quantity of peaches. People who buy peaches respond by buying fewer peaches and substituting other goods, and people who sell peaches respond by trying to bring more peaches to market. Variability in the money supply can simply add noise to price signals, and this can mean that market participants receive the wrong messages. For example, in Figure 12.14, an increase in the nominal wage that is a purely nominal increase can be misinterpreted as an increase in the real wage.

The appropriate policy for the monetary authority to adopt in an environment like this, as emphasized by Friedman and Lucas, is to make the money supply as predictable as possible. Friedman's recommendation[6] was that the monetary authority should follow a constant money growth rule, according to which some monetary aggregate (and Friedman argued that it did not matter which one) should grow at a constant rate over time.

Money growth rate targeting was adopted by many central banks in the world in the 1970s and 1980s, in part due to the influence of **monetarist** macroeconomists like Friedman and Lucas. Monetarists argued that monetary factors are of primary importance for business cycles, and that economic performance would be enhanced if central banks controlled the growth in the money stock.

The Bank of Canada adopted explicit targets for the growth in M1 in 1975, and later abandoned those targets in 1982. Other central banks also judged money growth rate targeting a failure, and it is hard to find a central bank in the world that currently pays much attention to the behaviour of any monetary aggregate. What did the Friedman-Lucas money surprise model get wrong?

We can use the money surprise model to rationalize some features of observed central bank behaviour in Canada and other countries. Suppose we modify the model to include shifts in the money demand function. These shifts occur as shocks to the demand for money which are unobservable to both the central bank and private-sector economic agents. As well, suppose that the central bank, like workers and firms, cannot observe total factor productivity directly, and that the central bank cannot observe current prices and wages.

If a money demand shock occurs in the money surprise model, then the economy responds much as it does to a surprise change in the money supply. In Figure 12.15, suppose that there is an increase in the demand for money, with the money demand curve in Figure 12.15(c) shifting to the right from $PL_1(Y_1, r_1)$ to $PL_2(Y_1, r_1)$. The price level will tend to decrease, as will the nominal wage, so workers will think that their real wage could have decreased because of a decline in total factor productivity. In Figure 12.15(a) the labour supply curve shifts to the left (lower labour supply for

---

[6]See M. Friedman, 1968, "The Role of Monetary Policy," *American Economic Review* 58, 1–17.

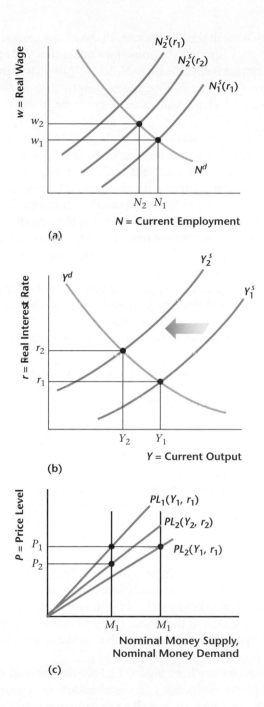

FIGURE 12.15
A Surprise Increase in Money Demand in the Money Surprise Model
If money demand increases and this is not directly observed, then output and employment fall because workers mistakenly think their real wage has gone down.

each level for the actual real wage w), from $N_1^s(r_1)$ to $N_2^s(r_1)$. Given this shift in labour supply, the output supply curve in Figure 12.15(b) shifts to the left from Y_1^s to Y_2^s.

Therefore, in Figure 12.15, in equilibrium the real interest rate rises from r_1 to r_2, aggregate real output falls from Y_1 to Y_2, and the labour supply curve ultimately shifts to $N_2^s(r_2)$ given the increase in the interest rate. In the labour market in Figure 12.15(a), the actual real wage rises (though the consumer infers that the real wage has fallen) from w_1 to w_2, and employment falls from N_1 to N_2. Just as was the case for a change in the money supply, the decline in aggregate output that occurs here is economically inefficient, relative to what would occur if everyone in this economy had perfect information.

A potential solution to the inefficiency problem is for the central bank to accommodate the increase in the demand for money by increasing the money supply. In Figure 12.15, if the central bank increases the money supply from M_1 to M_2 when money demand increases, then there is no change in the price level, and therefore no change in any real variables either. But how can the central bank accomplish this if it cannot observe the money demand shock? Note that the central bank can observe the market interest rate, so it can see the interest rate rising when the money demand shock occurs, and can then counteract the interest rate increase by easing monetary policy through an increase in the money supply.

Therefore, if the central bank engages in **interest rate targeting**, then it can prevent shocks to money demand from sending confusing signals to workers. If the central bank sees upward pressure on the market interest rate, it should ease by increasing the money supply, and if it sees downward pressure it should tighten by reducing the money supply.

However, there is a problem with interest rate targeting if there is a change in total factor productivity. If the change in total factor productivity is not directly observed by the central bank, the central bank will, for example, see the real interest rate start to fall when total factor productivity increases. In Figure 12.16, total factor productivity increases, which shifts the labour demand curve to the right in Figure 12.16(a), from N_1^d to N_2^d. The output supply curve in Figure 12.16(b) also shifts to the right from Y_1^s to Y_2^s. Since the central bank is targeting the interest rate, in order to hold the real interest rate constant at r_1 the central bank must tighten monetary policy by reducing the money supply from M_1 to M_2. This will act to reduce the price level. In the labour market, the increase in labour demand will act to increase the real wage, but what workers see is the nominal wage $W = wP$. An intervention by the central bank that holds the interest rate constant will act to reduce the price level sufficiently that the labour supply curve shifts to the left from $N_1^s(r_1)$ to $N_2^s(r_1)$. In equilibrium, the nominal wage that workers see is the same as it was before the productivity shock occurred, and so employment is the same as before the shock, at N_1. The output supply curve shifts back to Y_1^s because of the shift in the labour demand curve, and there is no change in aggregate output or in the real interest rate, that is, the central bank hits its interest rate target.

The key point to take away from Figure 12.16 is that interest rate targeting by the central bank will imply an inefficiency in the allocation of resources when total factor productivity changes. However, interest rate targeting could on average improve the efficiency of the economy if money demand shocks are more important than total factor productivity shocks in the short run. Indeed, over the course of a day, a week, a month, or even a quarter, financial market shocks that change the demand for money are a much more important source of volatility in the economy than are total

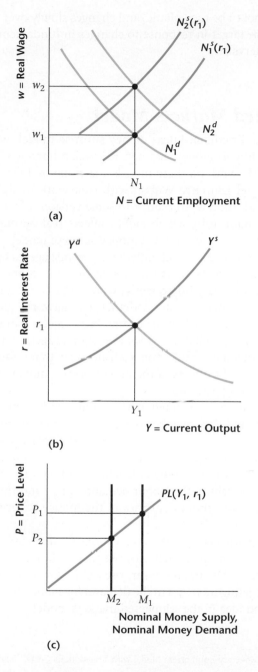

FIGURE 12.16
A Total Factor Productivity Increase When There Is Interest Rate Targeting by the Central Bank
The money supply adjusts so that the real interest rate is constant, and employment does not change.

factor productivity shocks. Typical central banking practice, which is what the Bank of Canada conforms to, is to fix a nominal interest rate target—the target for the overnight **bank rate**—about every six weeks. The theory tells us that changes in total factor productivity imply that this target rate should change. For example, if total factor productivity rises then the real interest rate should fall. But since total factor productivity tends not to be too volatile, and changes slowly over time, this allows for a readjustment of the target in response to changes in fundamental economic conditions at irregular intervals.

The Segmented Markets Model

An alternative to the Friedman-Lucas money surprise model, which also features a short-run nonneutrality of money in a non-Keynesian framework, is the **segmented markets model**. Early work on these models was done by Julio Rotemberg,[7] and by Sanford Grossman and Laurence Weiss,[8] with later work by Robert Lucas,[9] and by Fernando Alvarez and Andrew Atkeson.[10] In some versions of the segmented markets framework, the mechanism by which money affects real output in the short run is closely related to what is captured in the money surprise model.

In the segmented markets model, different economic agents have different degrees of access to financial markets, as is the case in practice. Some consumers transact with financial institutions very infrequently, while some firms, and particularly financial industry firms and financial intermediaries, can have minute-by-minute contact with financial markets. Thus, when the central bank injects money into the economy through an open market purchase, only some economic agents will immediately be on the receiving end of that money injection. Consumers with infrequent financial market contact will experience the effects of the central bank's money supply increase only indirectly and over a long period of time.

In some versions of the segmented markets framework, firms need liquid assets in order to hire labour, and they may be constrained by how much liquidity they have. However, if the central bank engineers an unanticipated increase in the money supply, these firms, because they have close contact with financial markets, will receive the extra liquidity injected by the central bank, and will hire more labour as a result. This produces a shift to the right in the labour demand curve, and this will work in much the same way as a positive money surprise in the money surprise model to increase output and employment in the short run.

The segmented markets model has implications for monetary policy that are much like those that come out of the money surprise model. In particular, money surprises may increase aggregate GDP, but these surprises add to uncertainty and are a bad idea. However, accommodating increases in the demand for money by increasing the money supply will be a good idea in the segmented markets model.

---

[7]J. Rotemberg, 1984, "A Monetary Equilibrium Model with Transactions Costs," *Journal of Political Economy* 92, 40–58.

[8]S. Grossman and L. Weiss, 1983, "A Transactions-Based Model of the Monetary Transmission Mechanism," *American Economic Review* 73, 871–880.

[9]R. Lucas, 1990, "Liquidity and Interest Rates," *Journal of Economic Theory* 50, 237–264.

[10]F. Alvarez and A. Atkeson, 1997, "Money and Exchange Rates in the Grossman–Weiss–Rotemberg Model," *Journal of Monetary Economics* 40, 619–640.

Alternative Monetary Policy Rules

Central bankers have learned that nominal interest rate targeting tends to perform well as a **monetary policy rule**. Further, justifying the use of nominal interest rate targeting does not particularly depend on our accepting the Friedman-Lucas money surprise model (or the segmented markets model, for that matter) as the only way to think about nonneutralities of money. There could be other channels by which monetary policy has real effects. As long as those real effects are related in some way to market interest rates, a policy of accommodating positive money demand shocks with money supply increases will typically insulate the real economy from the negative effects of money demand shocks.

Monetary policy rules—for example money growth rate targeting or interest rate targeting—are simple, easily-understood descriptions of the relationship between economic variables and central bank policy actions. The Friedman-Lucas money surprise model tells us something about why simplicity in a monetary policy rule is a good thing. The simpler the policy rule, the easier it is for the private sector to understand it and be able to predict the behaviour of the central bank. Uncertainty about what the central bank is up to is a bad thing, as it can confuse the signals that prices send to producers and consumers.

But there are other monetary policy rules than money growth targeting and interest rate targeting that are taken seriously by serious macroeconomists. Some central banks in the world, including the Reserve Bank of New Zealand, the Reserve Bank of Australia, the Bank of England, the European Central Bank, and the Bank of Canada, engage in **inflation targeting**. In particular, the Bank of Canada currently targets the annual rate of increase in the consumer price index at 2%, and then tries to keep that measure of the inflation rate within a range of 1% to 3%. If the inflation rate is too low (high), the Bank eases (tightens) by lowering (raising) the bank rate target. Thus, the inflation rate target is a kind of medium-run target, and the Bank of Canada engages in interest rate targeting over the very short run as a means of achieving its medium-term inflation target. In the models we have studied so far, we have not captured the long-run costs of inflation, but those costs are the primary concern that motivates inflation control as the goal of a central bank. We will study the costs of inflation in Chapters 17 and 18.

Another type of monetary policy rule that has been proposed is a **Taylor rule**. This rule, like an inflation target, is a rule that guides the choice of the short-run target for the central bank's policy interest rate. The Taylor rule dictates that the central bank's target interest rate should increase (decrease) if the inflation rate is above (below) its target, and should increase (decrease) if real economic activity is above (below) its target for real economic activity. The Taylor rule recognizes that there are nonneutralities of money that imply a stabilization role for monetary policy. The principal modern theory of inefficiencies that gives rise to a role for monetary policy in affecting real variables is New Keynesian economics, which we will study in Chapter 14.

Finally, a monetary policy rule that has received some recent attention is **nominal GDP (NGDP) targeting**. This is closely related to the Taylor rule, in that it recognizes a role for monetary policy in stabilizing real quantities, and to money growth rate targeting, in that it specifies the target in terms of one easily-measured economic variable.

Under NGDP targeting, the central would choose a future path for nominal GDP, and then do whatever it takes to make actual nominal GDP come as close as possible to that path. Advocates of NGDP targeting are not always so explicit about what the central bank should do to hit the NGDP target, but what they seem to have in mind is short-run interest rate targeting. If NGDP is above (below) target, the central bank should tighten (ease) by increasing (decreasing) its interest rate target.

The Zero Lower Bound and Quantitative Easing

The nominal interest rate cannot fall below zero. To see this, suppose that the nominal interest rate were negative. For example, the nominal interest rate would be negative if I could borrow $10 today and pay back $9 a year from now. But this would allow me to make a profit. I could borrow $10 today, hold that as cash until a year from now, pay back the $9, and make a profit of $1. Then, I could make an enormous profit by taking out an enormous loan. This is an **arbitrage opportunity** —an opportunity to make infinite profits that cannot exist in equilibrium. This tells us that the nominal interest cannot be less than zero because equilibrium in financial markets implies a lack of arbitrage opportunities.

In conducting monetary policy, the central bank cannot make the nominal interest rate fall below zero—there is a zero lower bound on the nominal interest rate that constrains monetary policy. In our discussion on nominal interest rate targeting, we saw that there were instances where monetary easing through a reduction in the interest rate would be appropriate. But easing is impossible if the nominal interest rate is at zero. In our model, since our analysis is conducted under the assumption that the inflation rate is zero, the central bank in our model hits the zero lower bound when the real interest rate $r = 0$.

Another way to think of this is that, when $r = 0$, the economy is in a **liquidity trap**. When there is a liquidity trap, think of the demand for money in Figure 12.17

FIGURE 12.17

A Liquidity Trap

The money demand curve is infinitely elastic at the price level P_1. An increase in the money supply has no effect.

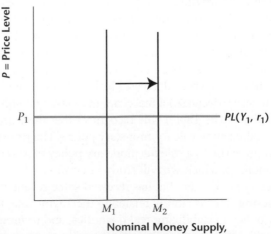

Nominal Money Supply, Nominal Money Demand

being infinitely elastic at the price level P_1. Then, if the money supply increases from M_1 to M_2 because of an open market purchase of government bonds by the central bank, this has no effect on anything, not even the price level. This is because, in a liquidity trap, government bonds and money are essentially identical—both bear no interest—so if the central bank swaps money for government bonds, this cannot make any difference.

During the recent financial crisis, and after, some central banks in the world were essentially in a liquidity trap state. For example, in Canada and the United States, central banks did not take their interest rate targets all the way to zero, but came very close, not going to zero only for technical reasons. In Canada, the bank rate was targeted at 0.25% from April 2009 until May 2010, and in the United States, the Federal Reserve System's target for the overnight federal funds rate was set to 0.0–0.25% from late 2008 until the present time, with a promise to maintain that target until mid-2013.

Once the central bank's nominal interest rate target goes to zero, can it still resort to policy easing? Some central bankers think so. Normally, a central bank attempts to control market interest rates through open market sales and purchases of short-term government debt. The traditional view is that an open market purchase of short-term government debt primarily reduces short-term interest rates, with little effect on long-term interest rates. But, if the central bank purchased long-term government debt, perhaps it could reduce long-term interest rates. Purchases of long-term government debt by the central bank are one type of **quantitative easing (QE)**. QE generally refers to long-term asset purchases by the central bank when there is a liquidity trap.

Figure 12.18 depicts a hypothetical **yield curve**, which is a plot of the yield to maturity (or average annual interest rate) on government bonds against time to maturity. Typically, but not always, the yield curve is upward-sloping, that is, interest rates on long-maturity government bonds tend to be higher than short-term interest rates. When the central bank conducts a conventional open market purchase of short-term government debt, typically what happens in the short run is that short-term interest rates fall, and long-term interest rates change little, so that the yield curve becomes steeper.

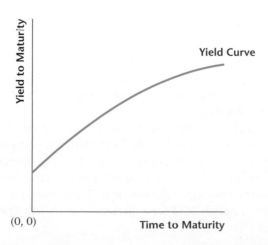

FIGURE 12.18

A Typical Yield Curve

The yield curve is a plot of the yield to maturity (interest rate) on government debt against time to maturity. The yield curve is typically, though not always, upward-sloping.

Advocates of QE think that if the short-term interest rate is zero and there is a liquidity trap, and the central bank purchases long-term government debt, then this will reduce long-term interest rates. They argue that this will occur because the central bank has reduced the supply of long-term government debt in the market, and so market participants will demand a smaller rate of return to induce them to hold this smaller quantity. The problem with this argument is that there is little in the way of theory or empirical evidence to support it. In fact, theory might tell us that QE is irrelevant.

In Chapter 9, we studied the Ricardian equivalence theorem, which gives us conditions under which changes in the timing of taxes by the government are irrelevant. This is a policy neutrality theorem, and there are other types of policy neutrality theorems that tell us something about when government policies do and do not work. The general idea behind these neutrality theorems is that government policy can affect real outcomes in the economy for the better only if the government has some advantage over the private sector in the activity in question. In the case of the Ricardian equivalence theorem, if the government has no advantage in the credit market over private lenders and borrowers, then the government's borrowing cannot improve matters.

Conventional open market operations matter because the government is engaged in a kind of banking activity which the private sector is effectively barred from. When the Bank of Canada issues outside money to purchase short-term government debt, it is issuing liabilities—currency and reserves—that private banks cannot issue. The Bank of Canada, as a financial intermediary, effectively turns short-term government debt into reserves that are used in intraday financial payments and into currency that is used in retail payments. That is an activity the private sector cannot replicate. So conventional monetary policy matters.

When the short-term nominal interest rate is zero, and there is a liquidity trap, then effectively all short-term assets—currency, reserves, short-term government debt, etc.—become identical. Then, if the Bank of Canada were to issue outside money for long-term government debt, this is essentially just swapping short-term debt for long-term debt. As a result, the private sector will be holding less long-term debt and more short-term debt. But the financial intermediation being done by the Bank of Canada is now just a conversion of long-term debt into short-term debt, and this is something that the private sector can do readily. For example, the Bank of Montreal can issue short-term debt and buy long-term government debt. What happens as a result of QE by the Bank of Canada? The private sector will just offset what the Bank of Canada does. If the Bank of Canada purchases more long-term debt, this will tend to lower long-term interest rates, make it less attractive for private banks to buy long-term debt, and those private banks will buy less. The result is that QE will do nothing—ultimately interest rates will be unchanged.

QE was attempted by the Bank of England in the United Kingdom during the financial crisis, and on a much larger scale in the United States from late 2008 until the present time, with the most recent quantitative easing operation by the Federal Reserve System to end in mid-2012. Obviously some central bankers think that QE matters, otherwise central banks would not do it. This remains a controversial matter. See Macroeconomics in Action 12.1 for a discussion of the empirical evidence on QE.

Evaluating the effects of macroeconomic policies is very difficult. Suppose, for example, that a change in fiscal policy is implemented. This will amount to an increase in real government spending of 2%, over what spending would otherwise be. How, as economists, should we attempt to understand the qualitative and quantitative effects of such a policy, after it has happened, so that we can make better policy choices in the future?

Suppose, to make the problem simple, that we are interested only in the effects of the government spending policy on real GDP. Ideally, we would have a time machine that could take us back to the time the policy was implemented, so that we could re-run history without the policy, see what happens, and then compare that with what happened the first time. If it were actually feasible to do this, the approach would be much like what experimental natural scientists do in the lab. While it is possible for economists to use experimental evidence, and experimental economics is a growing field of study, experiments are simply impractical for most macroeconomic issues, as was discussed in Chapter 1.

One feasible approach to evaluating government spending policy would be to simply look at the data, and search for evidence that real GDP behaved differently after the change in policy from what we might have expected. There are two problems with that approach, however. First, how are we supposed to know what would have happened in the absence of the policy? Again, to determine that we would have to re-run history without the policy. Second, even if we think we know what the world would have looked like without the policy change, just knowing that the policy had these particular effects in this instance may tell us little about closely related policy changes in other contexts. Perhaps the policy worked only because of the state of the economy—because the aggregate economy was

in a boom or recession. Perhaps there was some subtle aspect of the increase in government spending that made a critical difference to its effects, for example the types of goods and services the government was purchasing.

The bottom line relates to our discussion of the Lucas Critique in Chapter 1. In order to evaluate the effects of macroeconomic policies we need models that we trust, in the sense that we are confident that the economic behaviour we are capturing in these models will not change when the policies we want to evaluate change. We say that an economic model with these properties is "structurally invariant" with respect to the policy change in question. For example, our analysis of tax policy and Ricardian equivalence in Chapter 9 tells us that private savings behaviour can change in response to a tax cut, because consumers take account of the implications of the current tax cut for their future taxes. If we fail to take this effect into account in evaluating tax policy, we will get the wrong answers.

All of these issues come into play in evaluating the effects of QE. The most dramatic QE policy experiments occurred in the United States following the recent financial crisis. The first such QE intervention, typically called "QE1," involved the purchase by "the Fed" (Federal Reserve System—the U.S. central bank) of close to $1.3 trillion in long-maturity mortgage-related assets, principally mortgage-backed securities, from late 2008 until mid-2010. QE1 was notable, first because of its size, which more than doubled the quantity of outside money outstanding in the United States. Second, these were purchases of essentially private assets by the central bank, rather than standard purchases of government debt. Given the unprecedented nature of QE1, the Fed had little to go on in predicting its effects.

The second key quantitative easing experiment in the United States was "QE2," which was the purchase by the Fed of $600 billion in long-maturity government bonds between November 2010 and June 2011. QE2 was also unprecedented, both because of the enormous size of the open market purchase relative to typical Fed open market operations, and because the purchases were of long-term rather than short-term government debt.

Finally, in September 2011, the Fed embarked on a program to swap $400 billion in shorter-term government debt for $400 billion in longer-term government debt, thus lengthening the maturity of assets held by the central bank over a period of 10 months. This QE operation is called "Operation Twist." The program differed from QE1 and QE2, which were swaps by the Fed of outside money for long-maturity assets. Operation Twist was a swap of government debt of one type for government debt of another type.

Central bankers are not without theory to back up their contention that central bank purchases of long-maturity assets will make long-term interest rates go down. There exist "portfolio balance" models from the 1960s that work very simply. In those models, there are assumed to be demand functions, akin to the demand functions for goods that we learn about in introductory economics, but these are demand functions for assets rather than goods. Basically, portfolio balance theory tells us that, if the central bank decreases the supply of some asset held by the public, then the price of that asset must rise so that the market clears. Applied to long-maturity government bonds, for example, the theory says that, if the central bank conducts a QE operation in which it buys long-term government bonds, reducing the supply of those bonds held in the private sector, then long-term bond prices must go up. If the price of a bond goes up, a bond-purchaser must pay more today for the same claim to payoffs in

the future, which implies that the interest rate on the bond goes down. Thus, portfolio balance theory says that QE makes long-term interest rates go down.

But is portfolio balance theory any good? Is it immune to the Lucas critique for example? Well, unfortunately not. The modern theory of banking and financial economics tells us that assets are malleable objects, quite unlike goods and services. Assets can be transformed in various ways by banks and other financial intermediaries. For example, a bank can transform long-maturity, risky, and illiquid assets into short-maturity, safe, and liquid liabilities which are then held in the private sector. Such transformations change entirely how we should think about asset markets as opposed to goods markets.

Once we take account of the malleability of assets and asset transformation done by financial intermediaries, we can get quite different implications for the effects of QE. Indeed, as discussed in this chapter, QE may not matter at all in a liquidity trap.

Since the Fed began its QE programs, macroeconomists have been collecting data on the effects of QE, and attempting to draw conclusions concerning the effects on market interest rates of QE activity. At a conference at the Federal Reserve Bank of St. Louis in June 2011,[11] several academic papers were presented on the topic. A summary presentation by James Bullard, President of the St. Louis Federal Reserve Bank,[12] provides a central banker's defence of QE, and a good summary of the evidence.

There are two types of empirical evidence relating to QE. The first is provided by an "event study." Event studies are common among researchers studying financial markets. The basic idea is to determine the specific date at which a financial policy changed, and then look at how asset prices move from that date forward. In the case of QE, we can determine the date at which a particular QE intervention was announced, and then follow the course of interest rates, for example, after that date, to determine the effects of QE.

Why do event studies focus on the date of the announcement of a policy rather than the date of actual policy implementation? The reason is that if, for example, QE acts to increase the price of long-term government bonds, then once the policy is announced, all financial market participants understand that bond prices will go up on the day the policy is implemented. But then these same participants could make a profit by buying bonds today, which will force up prices today. This works its way back all the way to the announcement date. Thus, if QE works as advertised, interest rates should decline when the policy is announced, even if that announcement date precedes the policy implementation date by a long time.

There are at least three problems with event studies. The first is that it may be difficult to date the "event." In the case of QE, financial markets had a lot of advance information that the Fed was contemplating QE, and there was much speculation about how large the program would be. In fact it could be the case that, if QE in fact reduces interest rates, but financial market participants expect a bigger program than the one announced, interest rates would go up rather than down on the day of the announcement.

A second problem is that there may be major changes in other key economic factors that occur around the time of the policy announcement. These other factors could confound the effects of QE, for example, and contaminate the study.

Finally, a third problem relates to the Lucas critique. The fact that interest rates go down at the time

of a QE announcement may have nothing to do with the mechanism by which central bankers imagine QE has its effects. For example, financial market participants may think that a purchase of long-term assets by the central bank signals something about policy in the future, for example about the date in the future when the central bank will increase its short-term interest rate target above zero. If QE acts as a signal in this way, it would matter for changes in long-term interest rates at the time of the policy announcement.

In addition to event studies, macroeconomists have studied the effects of QE using standard statistical techniques, principally regression analysis. Under this approach, the analyst attempts to explain how long-term interest rates move over time by including in the regression analysis everything that might seem to be an important factor in explaining these interest rates. Then, the analyst can evaluate the explanatory power of central bank asset purchases relative to other factors in interest rate determination, and determine whether QE is actually statistically significant. Such analysis can be useful in describing the data, but is no substitute for a complete modelling exercise that permits a structural analysis that is immune to the Lucas critique.

In conclusion, very little is known about the effects of QE, in spite of the unprecedented and massive QE interventions conducted in the United States by the Fed. This is a very important topic of research, and much more needs to be done to come up with good macroeconomic models of QE, and good methods for measuring its effects.

---

[11]See research.stlouisfed.org/conferences/qe.

[12]See research.stlouisfed.org/econ/bullard/pdf/Bullard_QE_Conference_June_30_2011_Final.pdf.

Chapter Summary

- Money has three functions in the economy—it is a medium of exchange, a store of value, and a unit of account.

- The key measures of money are the monetary aggregates, which are the sums of quantities of assets having the functions of money. The narrowest measure of money includes only currency in circulation outside of banks, while broader measures of money include deposits at financial institutions.

- The monetary intertemporal model builds on the real intertemporal model of Chapter 9 by including supply and demand in the market for money. An important element of the monetary intertemporal model is the transactions constraint, which states that purchases by consumers and firms must be financed with cash on hand and by using credit cards.

- The demand for money is determined by first determining the equilibrium price and quantity of credit card balances. Credit balances are supplied by banks.

- The real demand for money increases when real income increases, since more money is required to execute more transactions when GDP is higher.

- The real demand for money falls when the nominal interest rate increases, as this increases the opportunity cost of holding money, so that households use less money and use alternatives to money, such as credit cards, more in making transactions.

- In the monetary intertemporal model, money is neutral in the sense that an increase in the level of the money supply leaves real variables—employment, output, consumption, the real interest rate, the real money supply, and the real wage—unaffected and causes only a proportionate increase in all money prices.

- In the monetary intertemporal model, a short-run decrease in total factor productivity leads to an increase in the price level, which is consistent with evidence from Canadian historical episodes when the relative price of energy increased.

- Shifts in money demand can occur because of new information technologies, changes in government regulations, changes in the perceived riskiness of banks, and changes in the hour-to-hour or week-to-week circumstances of the banking system.

- Money demand shifts can be a particular problem for monetary policy, especially if monetary policy is guided by monetarist principles.

- Nominal interest rate targeting by the central bank is preferred to money supply targeting when shifts in money demand are important.

Key Terms

neutrality of money: Money is neutral if a change in its level has no real effects and causes only a proportionate increase in the price level.

medium of exchange: A property of money; a medium of exchange is accepted in transactions for the sole reason that it can, in turn, be exchanged for other goods and services.

store of value: A property of money that is shared with other assets that permit current goods and services to be traded for future goods and services.

unit of account: The object in an economy in which prices and contracts are denominated.

monetary aggregates: These are measures of the money supply; each is the sum of a number of different types of assets in the economy.

outside money: Identical to the monetary base.

Bank of Canada: The central bank in Canada.

single coincidence of wants: A situation in which two people meet and one person has what the other wants.

double coincidence of wants: A situation in which two people meet and the first person has what the second person wants and the second has what the first wants.

nominal bond: A bond for which the payoff is defined in terms of money.

nominal interest rate: If R is the nominal interest rate on an asset, then if 1 unit of money is exchanged for a given quantity of the asset in the current period this quantity of the asset pays off $1 + R$ units of money next period.

inflation rate: The rate of change in the price level.

Fisher relation: A condition stating that $1 + r = [(1 + R)/(1 + i)]$, where r is the real interest rate from the current period to the future period, R is the nominal interest rate from the current period to the future period, and i is the rate of inflation between the current period and the future period.

neutral: Describes a government policy that has no real effects.

helicopter drop: Milton Friedman's thought experiment, which corresponds to an increase in the money supply brought about by transfers.

open market operation: A purchase or sale of interest-bearing government debt by the central bank.

open market purchase: An open market operation in which interest-bearing government debt is purchased by the central bank, increasing the money supply.

open market sale: An open market operation in which interest-bearing government debt is sold by the central bank, decreasing the money supply.

seigniorage: Revenue generated by the government through printing money.

inflation tax: Inflation arising when the government prints money to extract seigniorage; this effectively taxes the private sector.

classical dichotomy: A situation in an economic model where real variables are determined by real factors, and the money supply determines only the price level.

money growth rate targeting: A rule adopted by the central bank to conduct monetary policy so that some monetary aggregate adheres as closely as possible to a constant growth rate path over time.

monetarist: An adherent of ideas shared by Milton Friedman, who argued for money supply targeting as a monetary policy rule.

interest rate targeting: A rule adopted by the central bank to conduct monetary policy so that a short term nominal interest rate comes as close as possible to some pre-specified target value.

bank rate: The interest rate that the Bank of Canada targets in the short run, which is the overnight interest rate at which financial institutions lend to each other.

segmented markets model: A model in which monetary policy actions are nonneutral in the short run because those actions have their first-round effects only on active financial market participants.

monetary policy rules: Relationships between the actions of the central bank and the economic variables that the central bank can observe.

inflation targeting: A monetary policy rule under which policy is conducted so that the inflation rate adheres as closely as possible to a pre-specified target value for the inflation rate.

Taylor rule: A monetary policy rule under which the interest rate target of the central bank should rise if inflation is above its target or if aggregate real economic activity is above its target.

nominal GDP (NGDP) targeting: A monetary policy rule under which the central bank conducts monetary policy so that nominal GDP adheres as closely as possible to a target path for nominal GDP.

arbitrage opportunity: Exists if some financial market participant can buy and sell assets in such a way as to make an immediate profit.

liquidity trap: A state of the world in which the short-term nominal interest rate is zero, and open market operations have no effect on any quantities or prices.

quantitative easing (QE): An attempt by the central bank to lower long-term interest rates by purchasing long-maturity assets when there is a liquidity trap.

yield curve: A plot of the yield to maturity on government debt vs. the time to maturity on that debt.

Questions for Review

1. What are the three functions of money?

2. List three monetary aggregates and the assets that these monetary aggregates include.

3. Why is money used in exchange when people could carry out transactions by trading goods or using credit?

4. How are the real interest rate, the nominal interest rate, and the inflation rate related to one another?

5. What is the real rate of interest on money?

6. What are the alternatives to using currency in transactions, in the monetary intertemporal model?

7. What determines the demand for money in the monetary intertemporal model?

8. What are the effects of an increase in the money supply in the monetary intertemporal model?

9. What are three ways the government could bring about a change in the money supply?

10. Explain how money can be nonneutral in the short run.

11. How can monetary policy act to improve matters in the Friedman-Lucas money surprise model?

12. What are the drawbacks of money growth targeting?

13. Why is it a good idea for the central bank to engage in interest rate targeting?

14. List five monetary policy rules.

15. What happens when monetary policy is subject to the zero lower bound? Is there anything that the central bank can do in such circumstances to affect prices and real economic activity?

Problems

1. In the monetary intertemporal model, show that it is possible to have an equilibrium in which money is not held and only credit cards are used in transactions. Is there such a thing as a price level in this equilibrium? Does monetary policy work? If so, how? Explain your results and what they mean for actual economies.

2. Suppose that the government decides that the use of credit cards is bad and introduces a tax on credit card services. That is, if a consumer or firm holds a credit card balance of X (in real terms), he or she is taxed tX, where t is the tax rate. Determine the effects on the equilibrium price and quantity of credit card services, the demand for money, and the price level, and explain your results.

3. Suppose that the nominal interest rate is zero, that is $R = 0$.
   a. What is the equilibrium quantity of credit card balances?
   b. In what sense does the economy run more efficiently with $R = 0$ than with $R > 0$?
   c. Explain your results in parts (a) and (b). Discuss the realism of these predictions.

4. In the monetary intertemporal model, suppose that the money supply is fixed for all time, and determine the effects of a decrease in the capital stock, brought about by a war or natural disaster, on current equilibrium output, employment, the real wage, the real interest rate, the nominal interest rate, and the price level. Explain your results.

5. A new technological innovation comes on line. What are the current effects on aggregate output, consumption, investment, employment, the real wage, the real interest rate, the nominal interest rate, and the price level? Explain your results, and how they fit the key business cycle facts in Chapter 3.

6. Suppose that there is an increase in the number of ATM machines in service. What are the effects of this innovation on the demand for money and on the price level?

7. Suppose that we allow for the fact that cash can be stolen, but assume that a stolen credit card cannot be used, as it is instantly cancelled, so no one steals credit cards. Determine the effects this has on the quantity and price of credit card balances, the demand for money, and the price level. Explain your results.

8. Suppose, in the Friedman-Lucas money surprise model, that there are money demand shocks and shocks to total factor productivity. Neither private sector economic agents nor the central bank can observe money demand shocks directly. Private sector economic agents cannot observe productivity shocks. However, the central bank can observe productivity shocks. How should the central bank conduct monetary policy? Discuss.

9. Assume that there are no surprises, with all economic agents and the central bank having full information about shocks that are hitting the economy. Suppose that the central bank adopts a nominal GDP target, and interpret this in the model as a goal of maintaining some constant level of nominal GDP.
   a. Suppose that there is an increase in total factor productivity. What should the central bank do in response, given its goal? What are the effects on aggregate variables? Explain.
   b. Now, suppose that there is a positive shift in the money demand function. What should the central bank do now? Determine the effects on aggregate variables. Explain.

13

Business Cycle Models with Flexible Prices and Wages

John Maynard Keynes's *A General Theory of Employment, Interest, and Money*,[1] published in 1936, changed how economists thought about business cycles and the role of government policy. By the 1960s, Keynesian thought had come to dominate macroeconomics. At that time, most macroeconomists accepted Keynesian business cycle models as capturing the behaviour of the economy in the short run. There appeared to be broad agreement that money was not neutral in the short run, and most macroeconomists viewed this nonneutrality as arising from the short-run inflexibility of wages and prices. In Old Keynesian macroeconomic models—the Keynesian models that existed before the 1980s—price and wage inflexibility, and the resulting possibility that all markets may not clear at each point in time, was the key to the mechanism by which shocks to the economy could cause aggregate output to fluctuate. In the Old Keynesian view, the fact that prices and wages are slow to move to clear markets implies that there is a role for monetary and fiscal policy in stabilizing the economy in response to aggregate shocks.

By the 1960s, the main disagreements in macroeconomics were between monetarists and Keynesians. Monetarists tended to believe that monetary policy was a more effective stabilization tool than fiscal policy, but they were skeptical about the ability of government policy to fine-tune the economy; some monetarists argued that the short run over which policy could be effective was very short indeed. Keynesians believed that monetary policy was unimportant relative to fiscal policy and that government policy should take an active role in guiding the economy along a smooth growth path. It may have seemed at the time that all the theoretical issues in macroeconomics had been resolved, in that most everyone agreed that the Old Keynesian model was a satisfactory model of the macroeconomy, and all that remained was for empirical work to sort out the disagreements between monetarists and Keynesians.

This view changed dramatically, however, with the advent of the rational expectations revolution in the early 1970s. Some important early contributors to the rational

---

[1]See J. M. Keynes, 1936, *The General Theory of Employment, Interest, and Money*, Macmillan, London.

expectations revolution were Robert Lucas, Thomas Sargent, Neil Wallace, and Robert Barro. Two key principles coming out of the rational expectations revolution were (1) macroeconomic models should be based on microeconomic principles; that is, they should be grounded in descriptions of the preferences, endowments, technology, and optimizing behaviour of consumers and firms; and (2) equilibrium models (as opposed to models with price and wage inflexibility in which all markets need not clear) are the most productive vehicles for studying macroeconomic phenomena. There was some resistance to following these two principles, but there was wide acceptance, at least of the first principle, by the 1980s. It became clear as well, with respect to the second principle, that equilibrium modelling does not automatically rule out an active role for government policy, and that Keynesian ideas can be articulated in equilibrium models.

In this chapter, we study three models of the business cycle, which were each developed as explicit equilibrium models with optimizing consumers and firms. These models are the real business cycle model, the Keynesian coordination failure model, and a New Monetarist model. Each model differs from the others in terms of what is important in causing business cycles and the role implied for government policy. However, we will show that we can describe each of these models by building on the monetary intertemporal model of Chapter 12 in straightforward ways. For the first two models, we will study each model in turn, examine how well each matches the business cycle facts discussed in Chapter 3, and discuss each model's shortcomings. The last model—the New Monetarist model—will help us to understand some features of the recent financial crisis and recession. Thus, we want to focus on what the New Monetarist Model tells us about financial crises, rather than on what it says about business cycles in general.

Chapter 14 will be devoted to studying a New Keynesian model, which captures the key elements of modern Keynesian thought in a sticky price framework. It is best to treat this model separately, as there are critical differences in how our basic framework operates when we include sticky prices.

Why is it necessary to study several different business cycle models? As we discussed in Chapter 3, business cycles are remarkably similar in terms of the comovements among macroeconomic time series. However, business cycles can have many causes, and fiscal and monetary policymakers are constantly struggling to understand what macroeconomic shocks are driving the economy and what this implies for future aggregate activity. Each business cycle model we study allows us to understand one or a few features of the economy and some aspects of the economy's response to macroeconomic shocks. Putting all of these features into one model would produce an unwieldy mess that would not help us understand the fundamentals of business cycle behaviour and government policy.

Different business cycle models, however, sometimes give contradictory advice concerning the role of government policy. Does this mean that business cycle theory has nothing to say? The contradictory advice that different business cycle models give concerning the role of government policy reflects the reality of macroeconomic policymaking. Policymakers in federal, provincial, and territorial governments and in central banks often disagree about the direction in which policy should move. To make persuasive arguments, however, policymakers have to ground those arguments in well-articulated macroeconomic models. This chapter shows, in part, how we can evaluate and compare macroeconomic models and come to conclusions about their relative usefulness.

The Real Business Cycle Model

Real business cycle theory was introduced by Finn Kydland and Edward Prescott[2] in the early 1980s. Kydland and Prescott asked whether a standard model of economic growth subjected to random productivity shocks (i.e., "real" shocks as opposed to monetary shocks) could replicate, qualitatively and quantitatively, observed business cycles. Kydland and Prescott were perhaps motivated to pursue this question by the observation we made in Chapter 7, and replicate in Figure 13.1, that the detrended Solow residual (a measure of total factor productivity, z) closely tracks detrended real GDP. Thus, productivity shocks appear to be a potential explanation for business cycles.

Recall that many factors can bring about changes in total factor productivity. Essentially, any change implying that an economy can produce more aggregate output with the same factor inputs is an increase in total factor productivity, that is, an increase in z. Factors that increase z include good weather, technological innovations, the easing of government regulations, and decreases in the relative price of energy.

FIGURE 13.1

Solow Residuals and GDP

The Solow residual (the black line), a measure of total factor productivity, tracks aggregate real GDP (the coloured line) quite closely.

Source: Adapted from the Statistics Canada CANSIM database, Series v3860085, v2461119, v3822183, v1078498, and from the Statistics Canada publication *Historical Statistics of Canada*, Catalogue 11-516, 1983, Series D175–189.

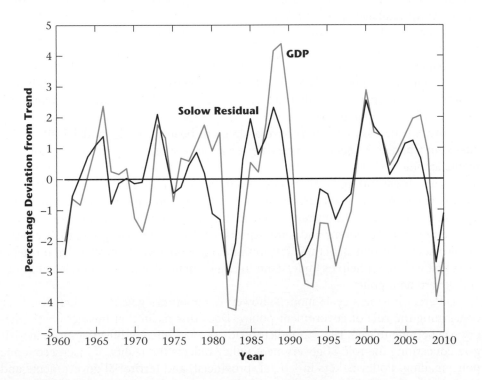

[2]See F. Kydland and E. Prescott, 1982, "Time to Build and Aggregate Fluctuations," *Econometrica* 50, 1345–1370.

The version of the real business cycle model we will study here is the monetary intertemporal model from Chapter 12. Though Kydland and Prescott studied a model where there was no role for money, Thomas Cooley and Gary Hansen showed, in a monetary real business cycle model, that adding money made little difference to the results.[3]

The Solow residual, as observed in Figure 13.1, is a persistent variable. When it is above (below) trend, it tends to stay there. This tells us that total factor productivity shocks are persistent, so that when there is a current increase in z, we would expect future total factor productivity, z', to be higher as well. This implies that in analyzing how the real business cycle model reacts to a total factor productivity shock, we need to combine the results of two different shocks from Chapter 11, a shock to z and a shock to z'.

Now, suppose there is a persistent increase in total factor productivity in the monetary intertemporal model, so that there are increases in z and z', current and future total factor productivity, respectively. In Figure 13.2 we show the equilibrium effects. The increase in current total factor productivity, z, increases the marginal product of labour for each quantity of labour input, so that the labour demand curve shifts rightward from N_1^d to N_2^d in Figure 13.2(a), and this shifts the output supply curve rightward from Y_1^s to Y_2^s in Figure 13.2(b). There are additional effects because of the anticipated increase in future total factor productivity, z'. First, the demand for investment goods increases, as the representative firm anticipates an increase in the future marginal productivity of capital. Second, the representative consumer anticipates that higher future total factor productivity will imply higher future income, so that lifetime wealth increases and the demand for consumption goods goes up. Both these factors will cause the output demand curve Y^d to shift rightward from Y_1^d to Y_2^d.

In equilibrium, in Figure 13.2(b), aggregate output must rise, but it is not clear whether the real interest rate will rise or fall. However, the output demand curve will probably shift less than the output supply curve, since the direct effect of the increase in current total factor productivity on the supply of goods is likely to be larger than the effects of the anticipated increase in future total factor productivity on the demand for goods. Thus, the real interest rate falls, as in Figure 13.2(b), from r_1 to r_2. Current consumption expenditures will then increase because of the decrease in the real interest rate and the increase in lifetime wealth. Current investment rises because of the decrease in the real interest rate and the increase in future total factor productivity. In the money market, in Figure 13.2(c), since equilibrium real output rises and the real interest rate falls, money demand increases, and the nominal money demand curve shifts rightward from $PL(Y_1, r_1)$ to $PL(Y_2, r_2)$. Therefore, in equilibrium, the price level falls from P_1 to P_2. In the labour market, in Figure 13.2(a), the labour supply curve shifts leftward from $N^s(r_1)$ to $N^s(r_2)$ because of the fall in the real interest rate. However, as in Chapter 11, the labour supply curve shifts less than the labour demand curve, since the intertemporal substitution effect on labour supply from the change in the real

[3]See T. Cooley and G. Hansen, 1989, "The Inflation Tax in a Real Business Cycle Model," *American Economic Review* 79, 733–748.

FIGURE 13.2

Effects of a Persistent Increase in Total Factor Productivity in the Real Business Cycle Model

With a persistent increase in total factor productivity, the output supply curve shifts to the right because of the increase in current total factor productivity, and the output demand curve shifts to the right because of the anticipated increase in future total factor productivity. The model replicates the key business cycle facts.

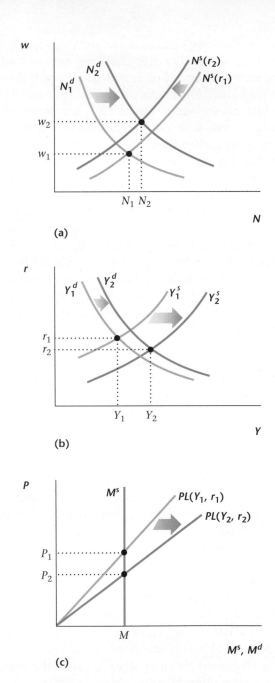

(a)

(b)

(c)

interest rate is relatively small. Hence, current equilibrium employment rises from N_1 to N_2, and the current real wage rises from w_1 to w_2.

In Figure 13.3, we show the response of average labour productivity. Initially employment is N_1 and output is Y_1, and average labour productivity is the slope of AB. After the increase in current and future total factor productivity, employment increases

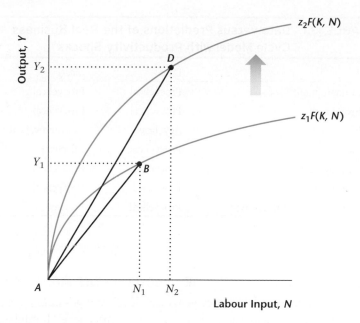

FIGURE 13.3

Average Labour Productivity with Total Factor Productivity Shocks

When output and employment are high, average labour productivity is also high, as in data.

to N_2 and output to Y_2, with average labour productivity being the slope of AD in the figure. Thus, average labour productivity increases. We could have drawn the figure so that employment increased sufficiently that the slope of AD was smaller than the slope of AB. However, Figure 13.3 is consistent with the results from Kydland and Prescott's model, in which N would increase in this circumstance but not enough that Y/N would decrease.

Therefore, as shown in Table 13.1, the real business cycle model qualitatively explains most of the key business cycle regularities. Consumption, investment, employment, the real wage, and average labour productivity are procyclical, both in the model and in the data. Perhaps more importantly, the real business cycle model can also *quantitatively* replicate some important observations about business cycles, as can be shown if a more sophisticated version of this model is put on a computer and simulated. The model can explain the fact that consumption is less variable than output, and that investment is more variable than output. Further, it can approximately replicate the observed relative variabilities in consumption, investment, output, and employment, which were discussed in Chapter 3.[4] As we see in Table 13.1, though, the model does not do well in explaining the behaviour of nominal variables—the price level and the money supply. In the data, the price level is acyclical, but it is countercyclical in the model, and the basic real business cycle model has nothing to say about the behaviour of the money supply. We will discuss this further in the next subsection.

[4]See E. Prescott, 1986, "Theory Ahead of Business Cycle Measurement," *Federal Reserve Bank of Minneapolis Quarterly Review*, Fall, 9–22.

TABLE 13.1 **Data versus Predictions of the Real Business Cycle Model with Productivity Shocks**

	Data	*Model*
Consumption	Procyclical	Procyclical
Investment	Procyclical	Procyclical
Price level	Acyclical	Countercyclical
Money supply	Procyclical	Acyclical
Employment	Procyclical	Procyclical
Real wage	Procyclical	Procyclical
Average labour productivity	Procyclical	Procyclical

REAL BUSINESS CYCLES AND THE BEHAVIOUR OF THE MONEY SUPPLY

In the real business cycle model, money is neutral; level changes in M have no effect on real variables and cause a proportionate increase in the price level. It might seem, then, that the real business cycle model cannot explain two key business cycle regularities from Chapter 3, which are the following:

1. The nominal money supply is procyclical.
2. The nominal money supply tends to lead real GDP.

However, as we will show, the real business cycle model can be made consistent with these two facts through some straightforward extensions.

First, in the real business cycle model, the procyclicality of the nominal money supply can be explained by way of **endogenous money**. That is, in practice, the money supply is not determined exogenously by the monetary authority but responds to conditions in the economy. Endogenous money can explain the procyclicality of money in two ways, supposing that business cycles are caused by fluctuations in total factor productivity. First, if our money supply measure is M1, M2, or some broader monetary aggregate, then part of the money supply consists of bank deposits. When aggregate output increases, all sectors in the economy, including the banking sector, tend to experience an increase in activity at the same time. An increase in banking sector activity will be reflected in an increase in the quantity of bank deposits, and therefore in an increase in M1, M2, and the broader monetary aggregates, and we will observe the money supply increasing when total factor productivity increases. Second, the money supply could increase in response to an increase in total factor productivity because of the response of monetary policy. Suppose that the central bank wants to stabilize the price level, because price level fluctuations are viewed as undesirable by the central bank, for reasons not included in this simple model. When there is a persistent increase in total factor productivity, this will cause an equilibrium increase in Y, and the real interest rate will fall, as we showed above. In Figure 13.4, output increases from Y_1 to Y_2 and the real interest rate falls from r_1 to r_2, so that the nominal money demand curve

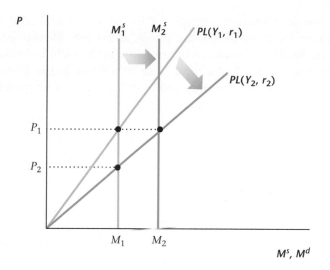

FIGURE 13.4
Procyclical Money Supply in the Real Business Cycle Model with Endogenous Money
A persistent increase in total factor productivity increases aggregate real income and reduces the real interest rate, causing money demand to increase. If the central bank attempts to stabilize the price level, this will increase the money supply in response to the total factor productivity shock.

shifts rightward from $PL(Y_1, r_1)$ to $PL(Y_2, r_2)$. If the central bank did nothing, the price level would fall from P_1 to P_2. However, since the central bank wants to stabilize the price level, it increases the money supply from M_1 to M_2, shifting the money supply curve from M_1^s to M_2^s. As a result, the money supply will be procyclical, as it increases when output increases, in response to the persistent total factor productivity increase. Further, the price level will be acyclical, since the behaviour of the central bank assures that the price level does not respond to productivity shocks. This reconciles the model with all the business cycle facts in Table 13.1.

Fact 2 above, that the nominal money supply tends to lead real GDP, appears to be a particular problem, since this might be viewed as strong evidence that money supply fluctuations cause the fluctuations in real GDP. Indeed, this was the interpretation given to fact 2 by Milton Friedman and Anna Schwartz.[5] However, the weak link in Friedman and Schwartz's interpretation of the data is that **statistical causality** need not tell us anything about true causality. A variable a statistically causes a variable b if current a helps predict future b. For example, every year we observe birds flying south before the onset of winter, and so the flight patterns of birds statistically predict the winter. However, birds flying south do not cause winter; it is the prospect of winter that is causing the birds to fly south.

There is an explanation for the tendency of money to lead output that is analogous to the example of birds flying south for the winter. Productivity shocks could cause money to lead output for two reasons, again through the process of endogenous money. First, the banking sector tends to lead other sectors of the economy, as banks provide loans for production that will occur at a later date. When bank loans increase, so will bank deposits, as a bank borrows by way of bank deposits to finance its lending. Thus, bank deposits will tend to be procyclical and to lead real GDP, and therefore

[5]See M. Friedman and A. Schwartz, 1963, *A Monetary History of the United States, 1867–1960*, National Bureau of Economic Research, Cambridge, MA.

M1, M2, and broader monetary aggregates will tend to lead real GDP. Second, if the monetary authority is trying to stabilize prices, and it uses all available information efficiently, it will be able to predict an increase in output resulting from an increase in z before the output increase is observed. Since an increase in the money supply may take time to affect prices, the monetary authority may want to act on this information before the increase in output and the decrease in the price level actually occur. Thus, money can lead real GDP because of preemptive monetary policy actions.

IMPLICATIONS OF REAL BUSINESS CYCLE THEORY FOR GOVERNMENT POLICY

Now that we know how the real business cycle model works, and have discussed how it fits the data, we can explore what the model implies for government policy. In the basic real business cycle model, there is no role for government stabilization policy. First, level changes in the money supply are neutral, and so attempts to smooth out business cycles through monetary policy actions will have no effect. Second, since all markets clear, and there are no inefficiencies (e.g., distorting taxes or externalities) in the basic model that government policy should correct for, there is also no reason that the government should vary its spending in response to fluctuations in total factor productivity. Government spending can have an effect on output, but the level of such spending should be set according to the appropriate long-run role of the government in providing public goods (goods and services, such as national defence, that cannot or should not be provided by the private sector), not to smooth short-run fluctuations in aggregate GDP. In the basic real business cycle model, business cycles are essentially optimal responses of the economy to fluctuations in total factor productivity, and nothing should be done about them. Given the first fundamental theorem of welfare economics, from Chapter 5, which states that under certain conditions, a competitive equilibrium is Pareto-optimal, if the allocation of resources in the economy is Pareto-optimal, there is no need for the government to intervene, unless we think the government should redistribute income and wealth.

Though there is no role for government in the basic real business model, other, more elaborate versions of this model explain a role for government arising from the need to correct market failures and distortions.[6] For example, in practice, all taxes are distorting. Income taxes distort labour supply decisions because firms and workers face different effective wage rates, and sales taxes distort consumer purchasing patterns because firms and consumers do not face the same effective prices for all goods. Over time, it is efficient for the government to smooth out these distortions, or welfare losses, that arise from taxation. This can tell us that tax rates should be smooth over time, which then implies that the government should let total tax revenues rise in booms and fall in recessions, as tax revenue will increase with income if the income tax rate is constant. This is a kind of countercyclical government policy,

---

[6]See T. Cooley, 1995, *Frontiers of Business Cycle Research*, Princeton University Press, Princeton, NJ.

which may look like it is intended to stabilize output but is actually aimed at smoothing tax distortions.

As well, as in Chapter 5, it is possible to modify the real business cycle model to include a role for spending on public goods, or to include public investment. An argument for countercyclical government spending, for example, might arise from the fact that the opportunity cost of public sector investment—on infrastructure for example—is lower during a recession when private sector total factor productivity is low.

CRITIQUE OF REAL BUSINESS CYCLE THEORY

The real business cycle model clearly does a good job of fitting the key business cycle facts. The theory is internally consistent, and it helps focus our attention on how government policy should act to correct market failures and distortions, rather than on attempting to correct for the fact that prices and wages may not clear markets over short periods of time, as in Old Keynesian models. Models of the New Keynesian variety, which we will study in Chapter 14, rely on a particular kind of private sector market distortion to explain a role for the government in intervening in the macroeconomy.

Real business cycle theory certainly has shortcomings, however, in its ability to explain business cycles. One problem is that the assessment of whether real business cycle theory fits the data is based on using the Solow residual to measure total factor productivity. There are good reasons to believe that there is a large cyclical error in how the Solow residual measures total factor productivity, z, and that the close tracking of detrended GDP by the Solow residual in Figure 13.1 might be accounted for mainly by measurement error. During a boom, the aggregate capital stock is close to being fully utilized. Most machinery is running full-time, and many manufacturing plants are in operation 24 hours per day. Further, the workers who are operating the plant and equipment are very busy. These workers are under pressure to produce output, since demand is high. There are few opportunities to take breaks, and overtime work is common. Thus, workers are being fully utilized as well. Alternatively, in a temporary recession, the aggregate capital stock is not fully utilized, in that some machinery is sitting idle and plants are not running 24 hours per day. Further, during a temporary recession, a firm may not want to lay off workers (even though there is not much for them to do), since this may mean that these workers would get other jobs and the firm would lose workers who have valuable skills that are specific to the firm. Thus, workers employed at the firm during a recession might not be working very hard—they might take long breaks and produce little. In other words, the workforce tends to be underutilized during a recession, just as the aggregate capital stock is. This phenomenon of underutilization of labour during a recession is sometimes called **labour hoarding**.

The underutilization of capital and labour during a recession is a problem for measurement of total factor productivity, since during recessions the capital stock and the labour input would be measured as higher than they actually are. Thus, in terms of measurement, we could see a drop in output during a recession and infer that total factor productivity dropped because the Solow residual decreased. But output may have dropped simply because the quantity of inputs in production dropped, with no change in total factor productivity.

To see how this works, consider the following example. Suppose that the production function is Cobb-Douglas, as we assumed in calculating Solow residuals in Chapter 7. Thus, the production function takes the form

$$Y = zK^{0.3}N^{0.7}, \tag{13.1}$$

where Y is aggregate output, z is total factor productivity, K is the capital stock, and N is employment. Now, suppose initially that $z = 1$, $K = 100$, and $N = 50$, so that, from Equation (13.1), we have $Y = 61.6$, and capital and labour are fully utilized. Now suppose a recession occurs that is not the result of a drop in total factor productivity, so that $z = 1$ as before. Firms still have capital on hand equal to 100 units, and employment is still 50 units, and so measured capital will be $K = 100$ and measured employment will be $N = 50$. However, suppose only 95% of the capital in existence is actually being used in production (the rest is shut down), so that actual capital is $K = 95$. Further, suppose the employed workforce is being used only 90% as intensively as before, with workers actually putting in only 90% of the time working that they were formerly. Thus, actual employment is $N = 45$. Plugging $z = 1$, $K = 95$, and $N = 45$ into Equation (13.1), we get $Y = 56.3$. Now, if we mistakenly used the measured capital stock, measured employment, and measured output to calculate the Solow residual, we would obtain

$$\hat{z} = \frac{56.3}{(100)^{0.36}(50)^{0.64}} = 0.918,$$

where $\hat{z}$ is the Solow residual or measured total factor productivity. Therefore, we would measure total factor productivity as having decreased by 8.2%, when it really had not changed at all. This shows how decreases in the utilization of factors of production during recessions can lead to biases in the measurement of total factor productivity and to biases in how we evaluate the importance of total factor productivity shocks for business cycles.

For a discussion of how real business cycle theory and other theories of the business cycle fit data from the Great Depression, see Macroeconomics in Action 13.1.

A Keynesian Coordination Failure Model

Real business cycle theory is in the classical tradition, in that the basic real business cycle model implies that the government should at best stay out of the way and allow markets to work. However, this does not mean that all theories of the business cycle with flexible wages and prices imply no role for the government in smoothing business cycles. Some modern Keynesians adopt an approach to macroeconomics very similar to that of classical economists, in assuming that prices and wages are fully flexible and that all markets clear. Some of these modern Keynesians explore an idea that we can find in Keynes's *General Theory*, the notion of **coordination failure**. In macroeconomics, coordination failures were first studied rigorously by John Bryant and Peter Diamond in the early 1980s,[7] and later contributions were by Russell Cooper and Andrew John,[8] Jess Benhabib and Roger Farmer,[9] and Roger Farmer and Jang-Ting Guo.[10] The basic idea in coordination failure models is that it is difficult for private sector workers and producers to coordinate their actions, and there exist **strategic complementarities**, which imply that one person's willingness to engage in some activity increases with the number of other people engaged in that activity.

An example of an activity with a strategic complementarity is a party. If Paul knows that someone wants to hold a party, and that only a few other people will be going, he will probably not want to go. However, if many people are going, this will be much more fun and Paul will likely go. Paul's potential enjoyment of the party increases with the number of other people who are likely to go. We might imagine that there are two possible outcomes (equilibria) here. One outcome is that no one goes, and another is that everyone goes. These are equilibria because if no one goes to the party, then no individual would want to go, and if everyone goes to the party, then no individual would want to stay at home. If Paul could coordinate with other people, then everyone would certainly agree that having everyone go to the party would be a good idea, and they could all agree to go. However, without coordination, possibly no one will go.

If we use the party as an analogy for aggregate economic activity, the willingness of one producer to produce may depend on what other producers are doing. For example, if Jennifer is a computer software producer, the quantity of software she can sell depends on the quantity and quality of computer hardware sold. If more is sold, it is easier for Jennifer to sell software, and if Jennifer sells more software, it is easier to sell hardware. Computer hardware and computer software are complementary. Many such complementarities exist in the economy, and different producers find it difficult to coordinate their actions. Thus, there may be **multiple equilibria** for the aggregate economy, whereby output and employment might be high, or output and employment might be low. Business cycles might simply be fluctuations between these high and low equilibria, driven by waves of optimism and pessimism.

---

[7]See Bryant, J. 1983. "A Simple Rational Expectations Keynes-Type Model," *Quarterly Journal of Economics* 98, 525–528, and P. Diamond, 1982, "Aggregate Demand in Search Equilibrium," *Journal of Political Economy* 90, 881–894.

[8]See R. Cooper and A. John, 1988, "Coordinating Coordination Failures in Keynesian Models," *Quarterly Journal of Economics* 103, 441–463.

[9]See J. Benhabib and R. Farmer, 1994, "Indeterminacy and Increasing Returns," *Journal of Economic Theory* 63, 19–41.

[10]See R. Farmer and J. Guo, 1994, "Real Business Cycles and the Animal Spirits Hypothesis," *Journal of Economic Theory* 63, 12–72.

13.1 Business Cycle Models and the Great Depression in Canada

The Great Depression was a unique event in Canadian macroeconomic history, and this unique event was the topic of an article by Pedro Amaral and James MacGee[11] in the *Review of Economic Dynamics*. The authors compared the economic performance of Canada and the United States during the Great Depression and evaluated competing explanations for this performance. Between 1929 and 1933, aggregate output in Canada and the United States was about 40% below the trend established prior to the Great Depression. By the end of the 1930s, Canadian output was still 30% below trend, while U.S. output was 25% below trend. Relative to the average post–World War II recession in Canada or the United States, the length and the size of this decline were very large, and the recovery took an especially long time.

Was the Great Depression essentially a larger-scale version of a recession that otherwise looks much like a typical post–World War II recession, or do standard macroeconomic theories of the business cycle fail to explain the behaviour of the U.S. and Canadian economies during the Great Depression? Amaral and MacGee find that some modern business cycle theories, unlike some traditional ones, help to explain the Great Depression in Canada. Some puzzles remain, however.

The authors first consider a real business cycle explanation for the Great Depression. Total factor productivity in Canada declined sharply at the beginning of the Great Depression and took a very long time to recover, roughly matching the downturn and slow recovery of real output. The authors found that movements in total factor productivity account for about 50% of the decline in output and do well in replicating the slow recovery.

Amaral and MacGee also evaluate sticky wage explanations for the Great Depression. Sticky wages and prices play an important role in Keynesian economics, and we will study a New Keynesian sticky price model in Chapter 14. However, sticky wages have often been cited as a contributing factor to the Great Depression, since there was a large deflation in both Canada and the United States at the time, which would tend to drive up real wages if nominal wages are sticky, thus reducing hiring by firms. Amaral and MacGee find that sticky wages played a small role in the downturn and do not help explain the protracted downturn. Further, they argue, there was an even larger deflation in Canada in 1920–1922 that failed to cause an economic downturn, so it seems hard to believe that deflation was an important contributing factor to the Great Depression.

Amaral and MacGee conclude that there is still much to learn. Although they dismiss conventional channels of business cycle transmission working through trade between Canada and other countries, they argue that there may be unexplored avenues by which trade affects total factor productivity.

---

[11]See P. Amaral and J. MacGee, 2002, "The Great Depression in Canada and the United States: A Neoclassical Perspective," *Review of Economic Dynamics* 5, 45–72.

To formalize this idea in an economic model, we start with the notion that there are aggregate **increasing returns to scale**, which implies that aggregate output more than doubles if all aggregate inputs double. Until now, we have assumed constant returns to scale, which implies that the marginal product of labour is diminishing when the quantity of capital is fixed. Increasing returns to scale at the aggregate level can be

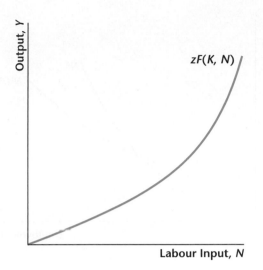

FIGURE 13.5

A Production Function with Increasing Returns to Scale
Strategic complementarities among firms imply that there can be increasing returns to scale at the aggregate level, which can give a convex production function as depicted, where the marginal product of labour increases as the quantity of labour input increases.

due to the strategic complementarities discussed above. We can then have increasing returns to scale at the aggregate level in a situation where, for each individual firm, there are constant returns to scale in production. With sufficient aggregate increasing returns to scale, the aggregate production function, fixing the quantity of capital, can be convex, as in Figure 13.5. Then, since the slope of the production function in the figure increases with the labour input, the marginal product of labour for the aggregate economy will be increasing rather than decreasing. Since the aggregate demand for labour is just the aggregate marginal product of labour schedule, this implies that the aggregate labour demand curve, N^d, can be upward-sloping, as in Figure 13.6.

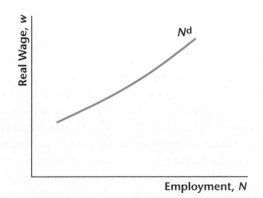

FIGURE 13.6

Aggregate Labour Demand with Sufficient Increasing Returns to Scale
With sufficient increasing returns to scale, the aggregate labour demand curve slopes upward, as the aggregate marginal product of labour increases with aggregate employment.

Source: Adapted from the Statistics Canada CANSIM database, Series v3822650, v735319.

FIGURE 13.7

**The Labour Market in the
Coordination Failure Model**

With sufficient increasing
returns, the labour demand
curve is steeper than the
labour supply curve, which is
required for the coordination
failure model to work.

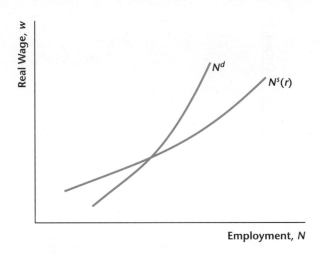

Now, for the coordination failure theory to work, the aggregate labour demand curve must have a greater slope than the labour supply curve, as in Figure 13.7. To repeat the exercise from Chapter 11 where we derived the output supply curve Y^s, suppose that the real interest rate is r_1, with the labour supply curve $N^s(r_1)$ in Figure 13.8(c). Then the equilibrium quantity of employment would be N_1, and output would be Y_1, from the production function in Figure 13.8(b). Therefore, an output–real interest rate pair implying equilibrium in the labour market is (Y_1, r_1) in Figure 13.8(a). Now, if the real interest rate is higher, say r_2, then the labour supply curve shifts rightward to $N^s(r_2)$ in Figure 13.8(c), because workers want to substitute future leisure for current leisure. As a result, the equilibrium quantity of employment falls to N_2, and output falls to Y_2. Thus, another point on the output supply curve in Figure 13.8(a) is (Y_2, r_2), and the Y^s curve is downward-sloping.

THE COORDINATION FAILURE MODEL: AN EXAMPLE

We will now consider a simple example that will show some of the key insights that come from coordination failure models. Suppose that the downward-sloping Y^s curve and the downward-sloping Y^d curve intersect in just two places (though this need not be the case; there could be more than two intersections, or there could be only one), as in Figure 13.9(b). Here, the economy could be in one of two equilibria. In the first, the "bad equilibrium," output is Y_1, the real interest rate is r_1, the price level is P_1, the real wage is w_1, and employment is N_1. In the second, the "good equilibrium," output is Y_2, the real interest rate is r_2, the price level is P_2, the real wage is w_2, and employment is N_2. In a more explicit version of this model, which would have a description of consumers' preferences, consumers would be better off in the good equilibrium, with high output and employment, than in the bad equilibrium, with low output and employment.

Will the economy be in the good or the bad equilibrium? Certainly nothing prevents the latter from arising if everyone is pessimistic, even though everyone prefers the good equilibrium. Similarly, the good equilibrium will arise if everyone is optimistic. In this model, business cycles could result if consumers and firms are alternately optimistic and

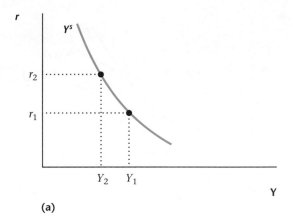

(a)

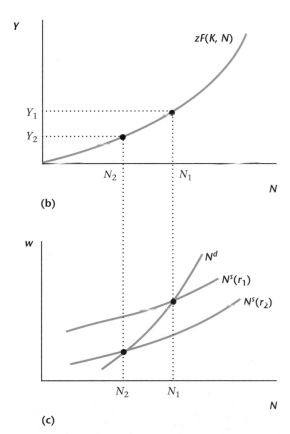

(b)

(c)

FIGURE 13.8
The Output Supply Curve in the Coordination Failure Model
The figure shows the construction of the output supply curve Y^s in the coordination failure model. An increase in the real interest rate shifts the labour supply curve to the right, reducing employment and output.

pessimistic, so that the economy alternates between the good and the bad equilibrium. This seems much like what Keynes referred to as "animal spirits," the waves of optimism and pessimism he saw as an important determinant of investment.

In the coordination failure model, it is possible that extraneous events that are completely unrelated to economic fundamentals (technology, preferences, and

FIGURE 13.9
**Multiple Equilibria in the
Coordination Failure Model**
Because the output supply
curve is downward-sloping
in the coordination failure
model, there can be two
equilibria, as in this example.
In one equilibrium, aggregate
output is low and the real
interest rate is high; in the
other, aggregate output is
high and the real interest rate
is low.

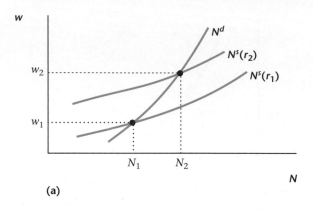

(a)

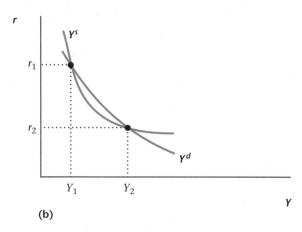

(b)

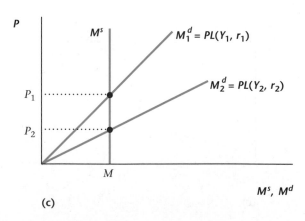

(c)

endowments) can "cause" business cycles. Macroeconomists sometimes call such extraneous events **sunspots**, analogous to the irregular occurrence of dark spots observed on the sun, because a dark spot on the sun does not affect production possibilities, preferences, or available resources (i.e., anything fundamental) on Earth. However, sunspots are in principle observable to everyone. Therefore, if workers and firms all treat the observation of a sunspot as a sign of optimism, then the economy will go to the good equilibrium when a sunspot is observed, and it will go to the bad equilibrium when no sunspot is observed. It will then appear that sunspots are causing business cycles. The behaviour of the stock market is perhaps most indicative of the presence of "sunspot behaviour," in that there is much more variability in stock prices than can be explained by fluctuations in fundamentals (the earnings potential of firms). Alan Greenspan, former chair of the Federal Reserve Board in the United States, once referred to the stock market as being under the influence of "irrational exuberance." Sunspot behaviour in the economy need not literally be driven by sunspots but by events with no connection to anything fundamentally important to preferences, endowments, and technology.

PREDICTIONS OF THE COORDINATION FAILURE MODEL

From Figure 13.9, the good equilibrium has a low real interest rate, a high level of output, a low price level, a high level of employment, and a high real wage. The bad equilibrium has a high real interest rate, a low level of output, a high price level, a low level of employment, and a low real wage. Thus, given the low (high) real interest rate, the good (bad) equilibrium has a high (low) level of consumption and investment. Therefore, if business cycles are fluctuations between the good and bad equilibrium, then, as in Table 13.2, consumption, investment, and employment will be procyclical, and the real wage will be procyclical, just as observed in the data. As well, in Figure 13.10 average labour productivity (the slope of a ray from the origin to the relevant point on the production function) must be procyclical, as it is higher in the good equilibrium than in the bad equilibrium. Further, Roger Farmer and Jang-Ting Guo have shown that a version of the coordination failure model does essentially as well as the real business cycle model in quantitatively replicating U.S. business cycle behaviour.[12]

Just as was the case with the real business cycle model, the Keynesian coordination failure model in this basic example does not replicate the behaviour of nominal

TABLE 13.2 **Data versus Predictions of the Coordination Failure Model**

	Data	Model
Consumption	Procyclical	Procyclical
Investment	Procyclical	Procyclical
Price level	Acyclical	Countercyclical
Money supply	Procyclical	Acyclical
Employment	Procyclical	Procyclical
Real wage	Procyclical	Procyclical
Average labour productivity	Procyclical	Procyclical

[12]See R. Farmer and J. Guo, 1994, "Real Business Cycles and the Animal Spirits Hypothesis," *Journal of Economic Theory* 63, 42–72.

FIGURE 13.10

**Average Labour
Productivity in the
Keynesian Coordination
Failure Model**

In the good (bad) equilibrium,
output is high (low),
employment is high (low),
and average labour
productivity is high (low).

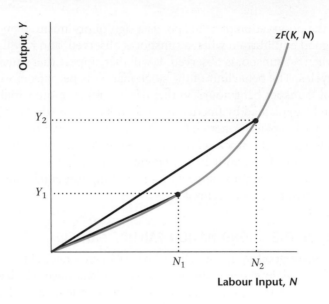

variables that we observe in the data. In particular, the price level is acyclical in the data, but countercyclical in the model, and the basic model does not replicate the procyclical behaviour of the money supply observed in the data.

Though money is neutral in the coordination failure model, as it is in the real business cycle model, the coordination failure model can however explain why the nominal money supply is procyclical. Suppose the money supply fluctuates between M_1 and M_2, where $M_2 > M_1$. Also, suppose that money acts as a sunspot variable; that is, when consumers and firms observe a high money supply, they are optimistic, and when they observe a low money supply, they are pessimistic. Therefore, when the money supply is high the economy will be in the good equilibrium and when the money supply is low the economy will be in the bad equilibrium—people's expectations will be self-fulfilling. Further, the money supply can move in such a way, as in Figure 13.11, that

FIGURE 13.11

**Procyclical Money Supply
in the Coordination
Failure Model**

If the money supply is a
sunspot variable in the
coordination failure model,
then money may appear
to be nonneutral because
people believe it to be. When
the money supply is high
(low), everyone is optimistic
(pessimistic), and output is
high (low). The price level can
be acyclical.

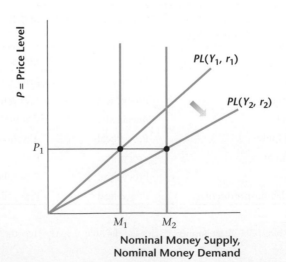

the price level is acyclical. Thus, though money is actually neutral, it can appear to be causing business cycles, and the model can replicate all of the key business cycle facts.

POLICY IMPLICATIONS OF THE COORDINATION FAILURE MODEL

In terms of how they match the data, the coordination failure and real business cycle models are essentially indistinguishable. However, the two models have very different policy implications. In the real business cycle model, decreases in output and employment are just optimal responses to a decline in total factor productivity, while in the coordination failure model, the good equilibrium is, in principle, an opportunity available in the aggregate economy when the bad equilibrium is realized. Thus, if we believed this model, then government policies that promote optimism would be beneficial. For example, encouraging statements by public officials, such as the minister of finance or the governor of the Bank of Canada, could in principle bump the economy from the bad to the good equilibrium.

Policy could also be designed to smooth business cycles or to eliminate them altogether in the coordination failure model. As an example, consider Figure 13.12, in which there are initially two equilibria, a bad equilibrium where the real interest rate is r_1 and the level of output is Y_1 and a good equilibrium where the real interest rate is r_2 and the level of output is Y_2. Then, suppose the government reduces current government spending, G. A decrease in current government spending will reduce the present value of taxes, cause a decrease in current labour supply, and shift the output supply curve to the right, from Y_1^s to Y_2^s in the figure. Further, recall from Chapter 11 that we know that a decrease in G will shift the output demand curve leftward from Y_1^d to Y_2^d. If the government reduces G by just the right amount, then there will be only one equilibrium, where $Y = Y^*$ and $r = r^*$, as in the figure. Effectively, the bad equilibrium gets better and the good equilibrium gets worse because of the decrease in G, and there will be no business cycles. It is not clear whether eliminating business cycles in this manner is advantageous. For example, if in the absence of the decrease in G the economy was in the good equilibrium most of the time, then average welfare

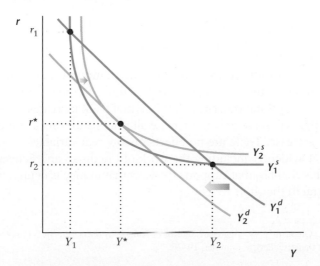

FIGURE 13.12

Stabilizing Fiscal Policy in the Coordination Failure Model

Fiscal policy can stabilize output in the coordination failure model by eliminating multiple equilibria. Here, with a decrease in government spending, the output demand curve shifts to the left and the output supply curve shifts to the right, and this can produce a unique equilibrium where $Y = Y^*$ and $r = r^*$.

could go down when business cycles are eliminated. It could be, however, that there are benefits from reduced uncertainty when business cycles are eliminated, so that even though average output might go down, the benefits from reduced uncertainty from smoothing business cycles could be beneficial.

CRITIQUE OF THE COORDINATION FAILURE MODEL

The key insight of the coordination failure model is that business cycles can result simply from self-fulfilling waves of optimism and pessimism. As mentioned previously, the existence of these self-fulfilling expectations appears to be most evident in the case of the stock market, where it seems difficult to explain the wild gyrations that occur daily as being the result of changes in fundamental economic factors.

However, there are some potential weaknesses in coordination failure theories of the business cycle. First, a critical element of the coordination failure theory is that there exist sufficient increasing returns to scale in aggregate production that the aggregate labour demand curve slopes upward and is steeper than the aggregate labour supply curve. If aggregate production is subject to constant returns to scale or decreasing returns to scale, then this theory is a nonstarter. In practice, the measurement of returns to scale in aggregate production is very imprecise. Some researchers claim to find evidence of increasing returns in the data, but others do not. A good reference for this issue is the work of Harold Cole and Lee Ohanian.[13] At best, the evidence supporting the existence of increasing returns to scale at the aggregate level is weak.

Second, a problem with this model is that the underlying shocks that cause business cycles are expectations, and expectations are essentially unobservable. This makes it difficult to use the theory to understand historical recessions and booms.

For a discussion of how the business cycle theories in Chapters 12 and 13 can be used to make sense of recent business cycle events in Canada, see Theory Confronts the Data 13.1. Also see Macroeconomics in Action 13.2 for a discussion of the role of uncertainty in business cycles.

A New Monetarist Model: Financial Crises and Deficient Liquidity

In Chapter 12, we introduced the monetary intertemporal model, in which money plays a role in the economy in facilitating transactions. In the basic model constructed in Chapter 12, money is neutral, since, if the central bank increases the stock of money in circulation, this will serve only to increase all prices and wages in proportion to the money supply increase. There are no effects on any real variables. However, there is ample empirical evidence, including the work of Friedman and Schwartz mentioned previously in this chapter, that supports the view that money is neutral in the long run, but is not neutral in the short run.

---

[13]See H. Cole and L. Ohanian, 1999, "Aggregate Returns to Scale: Why Measurement Is Imprecise," *Federal Reserve Bank of Minneapolis Quarterly Review*, Summer, 19–28.

| THEORY CONFRONTS THE DATA | **13.1** | *The Four Most Recent Recessions in Canada* |

A problem with real business cycle theory is that it sometimes does not help us understand the underlying causes of business cycles. The Solow residual may fluctuate over time, but what are the causes of these movements in the Solow residual? A case in which the theory helps to explain the data is the 1974–1975 recession in Canada. During this period, we see a drop in the Solow residual in Figure 13.1, which tracks closely a drop in real GDP. Further, in Figure 13.13 we can consider what happened to the nominal money supply during this period. The nominal money supply actually rises above trend in the 1974–1975 recession. Thus, it seems hard to argue that this recession was the result of some nonneutrality of money. In the Friedman-Lucas money surprise model that we studied in Chapter 12, output will fall in the short run when the money supply falls unexpectedly. Other theories of short-run nonneutralities of money may work in quite different ways, but they essentially all have the same implication: an increase in the money stock causes aggregate real output to increase in the short run.

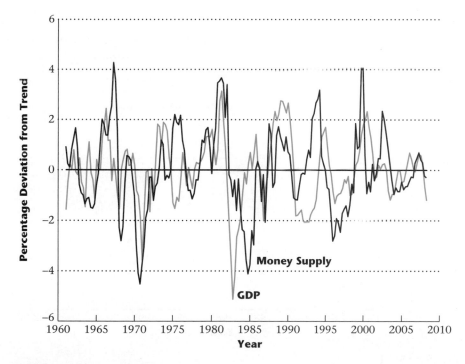

FIGURE 13.13

Deviations from Trend in the Monetary Base and GDP

Monetary factors can be an important in contributing to recessions, and this appears to be have been the case in 1981–1982 and 1990–1992.

Source: Adapted from the Statistics Canada CANSIM database, Series v37145, v1992067.

Leading up to the 1974–75 recession, there was a large increase in the price of imported oil, brought on by actions of the OPEC oil cartel. In Figure 13.14, which depicts the relative price of energy in Canada (with the observation for January 1961 normalized to 100), we see a large increase in this price just prior to the 1974–75 recession. Though this increase in the relative price of energy looks small compared to later changes in this relative price, at the time it was very important. Thus, the 1974–1975 recession seems consistent with real business cycle theory. There was an observable real shock to the economy, which shows up as a decrease in measured total factor productivity, real GDP declined, and the increase in money supply is consistent with money being neutral.

However, suppose that we consider another recession, the one that occurred in Canada in 1981–1982. In Figure 13.1, we again see a large decrease below trend in the Solow residual in 1981–1982, and a somewhat larger percentage decrease in real GDP. In Figure 13.13, there is a decline in the money supply below trend in 1981–1982, but the money supply exhibits a large decrease below trend after the 1981–1982 recession. In 1981–1982 there does not appear to have been any shock

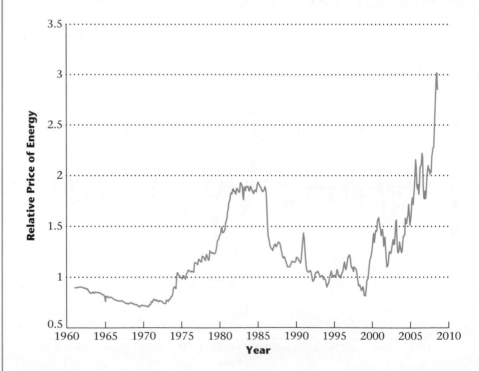

FIGURE 13.14

The Relative Price of Energy in Canada

Sometimes we can associate an increase (decrease) in total factor productivity with a decrease (increase) in the relative price of energy. Large increases in the relative price of energy seem to have contributed to recessions in Canada, particularly the ones that occurred in 1974–75 and (to some extent) 2008–2009.

to the economy that could have caused total factor productivity to fall to the degree it did, as measured by the Solow residual. There was certainly a large increase in the relative price of energy, as we see in Figure 13.14, but this occurred in 1980, and should have had a more immediate effect on aggregate output if this had been the important contributing factor to the 1981–82 recession. However, there is much evidence (not entirely conclusive, though, as we will see in Chapter 14) to indicate that, prior to the 1981–1982 recession, the Bank of Canada tightened monetary policy significantly. This appears to be the likely cause of this recession, though superficially it might appear that a negative productivity shock was the cause.

Next, consider the recession that occurred in Canada in 1990–1992. Note again that in the 1990–1992 period real GDP and the Solow residual drop below trend in Figure 13.1, so that a negative total factor productivity shock is a possibility as an explanation. However, note in Figure 13.13 that the money supply also drops below trend in 1990–1992, and that the money supply decrease actually leads the decrease in GDP. Thus, a negative monetary shock is also a candidate. In Figure 13.14, we see a temporary upward spike in the relative price of energy in 1990, which likely contributed to a decrease in total factor productivity. However, because the energy price increase was temporary, the effect on productivity was likely small. Further, we have other evidence to indicate that the Bank of Canada was very concerned with inflation, around the time of the 1990–92 recession, which supports the conclusion that monetary tightening was a key contributing factor to that particular recession.

Finally, with regard to the most recent recession in Canada, in 2008–2009, this recession is widely attributed to financial factors, originating in the United States. But we cannot rule out some role for total factor productivity in the recession. Figure 13.14 shows an extremely large run-up in the relative price of energy prior to the recession, and Figure 13.1 shows a large drop in measured total factor productivity below trend that coincides with the negative deviation from trend in real GDP. Certainly we cannot blame monetary policy for the recession, as there was a large monetary expansion during 2008–2009, as we see in Figure 13.13.

The drop in total factor productivity during the 2008–2009 recession could, however, just reflect the negative effect of financial market turmoil on aggregate economic activity. One mechanism through which that could work is captured in the Keynesian coordination failure model. Coordination failures can occur in credit markets, for example, due to the fact that, if borrowers are deemed non-creditworthy, then this can be self-fulfilling. A firm may not be able to borrow because lenders think the firm will fail, but the inability of the firm to borrow implies that it will fail. Thus widespread pessimism and uncertainty in credit markets can breed bad outcomes and uncertainty.

Ultimately, the financial crisis provides us with a rich (though, of course, troubling) experience, which will allow macroeconomists to come up with models that fit the data better and are more useful for policy. The models we study in this book go some way in helping us understand the financial crisis, but we can certainly do better.

In the 1960s, most macroeconomists regarded any short-run nonneutralities of money as being the result of frictions in the economy arising from sticky wages and prices. With the rational expectations revolution in the 1970s, however, macroeconomists began to construct flexible-wage-and-price models in which money is not neutral, and which can explain features of aggregate data such as the comovements among nominal and real variables. For example, in the Friedman-Lucas money surprise model we studied in Chapter 12, increases in the money supply will not be neutral if such changes confuse price signals and fool people into working harder. Recently Keynesian ideas have enjoyed a resurgence among academic economists and central bankers, and we will study a New Keynesian sticky price model in Chapter 14, which features a nonneutrality of money and roles for fiscal and monetary policy in correcting economic inefficiencies.

During the recent financial crisis, macroeconomists and policymakers were sometimes at a loss, both in explaining why the crisis was unfolding as it was, and in arriving at well-reasoned policy responses. Some models in conventional use seemed to have come up short, particularly the models widely used by central bankers. This does not mean, however, that macroeconomists need to throw out everything they know and start over, as there is plenty of excellent economics that has been developed over the past 40 years or more that can be brought to bear on current problems.

One branch of macroeconomics, New Monetarist economics, involves the in-depth study of facets of the macroeconomy that are critical for understanding the financial crisis and the recent recession. For example, New Monetarists study the reasons why people hold and trade money and other assets, incentive problems in banking, credit, and financial markets, and the role of central banks. New Monetarist economics is surveyed and developed in some work by Randall Wright and Stephen Williamson.[14] This relatively new and developing area of study in economics introduces new ideas about the role of money, credit, and banking in the macroeconomy, and about how monetary policy works, both in "normal" times and during crises.

Our interest in this section is in understanding some features of the macroeconomy that were of particular importance for the recent financial crisis and recession, and the implications of these features for monetary policy. In the New Monetarist model we study here, money will not be neutral, in general, but there may be circumstances where monetary policy is essentially powerless.

In Chapter 12, we introduced money into our basic intertemporal macroeconomic model, explained the determinants of money demand, and exposited some basic ideas about monetary policy and how it works. In the monetary intertemporal model, money is a liquid asset, in that it is a medium of exchange that is widely accepted in transactions involving goods and services. As such, the money in our model is best interpreted as government-issued currency. Of course, there are many other liquid assets in the

---

[14]S. Williamson and R. Wright, 2010, "New Monetarist Economics: Methods," *Federal Reserve Bank of St. Louis Review* 92, 265–302; S. Williamson and R. Wright, 2011, "New Monetarist Economics: Models," in *Handbook of Monetary Economics*, vol. 3A, B. Friedman and M. Woodford (eds.), Elsevier, pp. 25–96; S. Williamson, 2011, "Liquidity, Monetary Policy, and the Financial Crisis: A New Monetarist Approach," forthcoming in the *American Economic Review*.

economy which play important roles in transactions: government debt, particularly short-term government debt, is widely traded in large financial transactions; reserves at financial institutions—essentially transactions accounts with the Bank of Canada—are used in large financial transactions among these financial institutions during each day through the Large-Value Payments System; and asset-backed securities, particularly in the United States, are key liquid assets in the financial system, and these securities played a key role in the financial crisis.

To keep things simple, we can think of there being two key classes of liquid assets in the economy: currency and financial liquid assets. These financial liquid assets include government interest-bearing debt, reserve accounts of financial institutions with the Bank of Canada, and asset-backed securities, as well as any other assets that banks and other financial institutions can conveniently convert into transactions accounts that are easily traded in financial markets. Like currency, financial liquid assets are important in helping the economy run efficiently. With a large quantity of liquid assets in the financial system, more financial transactions can be executed, credit markets work more efficiently, and real GDP will tend to be higher.

We can express total financial liquid assets in the economy, in units of consumption goods, as

$$a = \frac{B}{P} + k(r).\qquad(13.2)$$

In Equation (13.2), a denotes total financial liquid assets, B is the total outstanding interest-bearing nominal debt of the government (so B/P is the real value of the government debt), and $k(r)$ denotes the quantity of liquid financial assets created by the private sector, where $k(r)$ is a decreasing function of the real interest rate r. Private liquid financial assets are created by banks and other financial institutions. When the real interest rate is lower, this means that there is more lending by banks and other private financial institutions, and therefore a larger stock of private liquid assets that can be used in financial transactions.

Total liquid financial assets, through the financial system, will in general affect the demand for goods and services. Assume that this effect works solely through investment expenditures, as liquid financial assets will have their primary effects through the investment decisions of large firms. Thus, the quantity a in Equation (13.2) can become a positive factor for investment expenditure. However, think of the world as being in two possible states, **adequate financial liquidity** or **deficient financial liquidity**. If a is sufficiently large, then there is adequate financial liquidity, and additional financial liquidity will have no effect on the demand for investment goods. But if a is sufficiently small, then more financial liquidity will increase the demand for investment goods, and less will reduce it.

A REDUCTION IN FINANCIAL LIQUIDITY DURING THE FINANCIAL CRISIS

A useful way to think of one aspect of the financial crisis is that this sent the economy from a state in which there was adequate financial liquidity to one in which there was deficient financial liquidity. This effect was critical to what happened during the financial crisis in the United States, but it was also important in Canada. During the financial crisis, higher uncertainty and new information that the assets backing tradeable securities—particularly mortgage-related assets in the United States—were of much poorer quality than previously thought, had the effect of shifting down the function $k(r)$. There was essentially a reduction in the private economy's capacity to produce financial liquidity.

How would this shift in the $k(r)$ function matter for aggregate economic activity, interest rates, and prices? Given the effect that financial liquidity a has on the demand for goods, our model is a bit more complicated. To make the model amenable to analysis, from Equation (12.12) in Chapter 12 (money supply equals money demand in equilibrium), we can solve for the price level, obtaining

$$P = \frac{M}{L(Y, r)}.$$ (13.3)

Then, substituting for P in Equation (13.2) using Equation (13.3), we get

$$a = \frac{BL(Y, r)}{M} + k(r).$$ (13.4)

Equation (13.4) then tells us that, if we take account of the effects of money demand and money supply on the price level, then financial liquid assets are an increasing function of the nominal quantity of interest-bearing government debt and aggregate real income, and a decreasing function of the real interest rate (since the function k is a decreasing function) and the nominal money supply. Further, since the demand for goods is an increasing function of a when there is deficient financial liquidity, the demand for goods is in turn an increasing function of aggregate real income, and a decreasing function of the real interest rate.

We can then use our monetary intertemporal model in a way consistent with what we have done thus far. The output demand curve is downward-sloping, but including financial liquidity gives us some new effects. If there is deficient financial liquidity, then an increase in B shifts the output demand curve to the right, and an increase in M shifts the curve to the left. For the experiment we are interested in, the negative shift in the $k(r)$ function in the financial crisis acts to reduce the demand for investment goods, and shifts the output demand curve to the left from Y_1^d to Y_2^d in Figure 13.15(b). Then, in Figure 13.15(b), aggregate output falls from Y_1 to Y_2, and the real interest rate decreases from r_1 to r_2. Then, in Figure 13.15(a), the labour supply curve shifts to the left, from N_1^s to N_2^s because of the decrease in the real interest rate. Employment falls from N_1 to N_2, and the real wage rises from w_1 to w_2.

With respect to money demand, since real income falls and the real interest rate also falls, money demand could increase or decrease. In Figure 13.15(c), we show money demand rising, in which case the price level falls, but theory tells us that money demand could decrease, in which case the price level would rise.

What happens to consumption expenditure and investment expenditure as a result of the reduction in private financial liquidity? The decrease in the real interest rate will tend to increase consumption and investment. However, since the initial shock acted

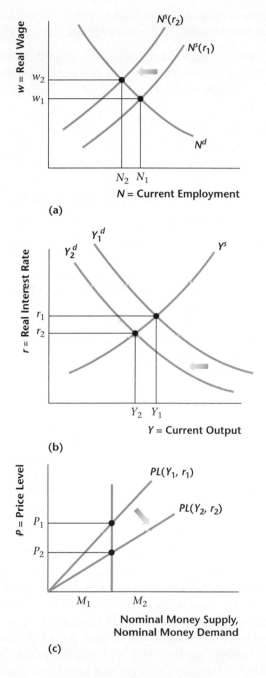

FIGURE 13.15

A Reduction in Financial Liquidity Producing Deficient Liquid Assets
The output demand curve shifts to the left, and there is a decrease in aggregate output and employment. This shock replicates some of the key features of the recent financial crisis.

to reduce investment expenditure, investment will decline. Further, the decrease in real income will tend to reduce consumption, so consumption could rise or fall.

For this experiment, we are more interested in what the model tells us about the recent financial crisis, than with how the model explains typical business cycle events. Therefore, we will not focus on the key business cycle facts from Chapter 3, as we did with the real business cycle model and the Keynesian coordination failure model. Instead, consider some key features of the recent financial crisis and recession:

1. The recent recession had some standard features consistent with the key business cycle facts in Chapter 3: Consumption and investment expenditures fell relative to trend, as did employment and the price level. See Figures 3.9, 3.10, 3.12, and 3.14 in Chapter 3.

2. Though average labour productivity fell in Canada during the recession (see Figure 3.15 in Chapter 3), in the United States average labour productivity increased during the recent recession. Typically average labour productivity falls during a recession.

3. The real interest rate was very low during the recession, and has persisted at a low level since the recession ended.

With regard to the set of standard business cycle facts mentioned in (1) above, Figure 13.15 is consistent with all of them. Consumption in principle may rise or fall in the model, but given a small effect of the real interest rate on consumption, as is consistent with empirical evidence, consumption will decrease in response to the drop in private sector financial liquidity provision. On feature (2) above, Figure 13.15(a) shows a drop in the labour input N which, given that the production function does not shift, implies that average labour productivity increases. This is consistent with what occurred in the United States during the recession, but not with Canadian experience. That suggests that deficient financial liquidity was a problem in the United States during the recession, but not in Canada.

Feature (3) is key to the deficient financial liquidity effect. When financial liquidity is scarce, financial market participants are willing to hold liquid financial assets at very low rates of return. At the margin, liquid financial assets have such a high value in financial transactions that market participants care little about the low rates of return on these assets. In Figure 13.15(b), the real interest rate declines due to the reduction in private financial liquidity provision, consistent with what happened during the financial crisis.

POLICY RESPONSE TO A REDUCTION IN FINANCIAL LIQUIDITY

In Chapter 12 we studied conventional liquidity management through monetary policy, by looking at how policy should respond to the frequent shocks to money demand that occur in financial markets. During normal times, the central bank is continually responding to shocks to the demand for liquidity that show up as shifts in the money demand function. As well, some historical financial panics, for example the banking panics in the United States in the later 19th and very early 20th centuries, and in the Great Depression, featured liquidity shortages that could be captured as positive shifts in money demand in our model. During those financial panics, the demand for government-supplied currency rose, as people withdrew their deposits from banks they no longer trusted.

An appropriate monetary policy response to a conventional liquidity shortage is to increase the money supply to accommodate the increase in money demand.

We learned in Chapter 12 that this can serve to reduce market noise, and clarifies the price signals that individual economic agents receive. Increasing the money supply when money demand increases can also serve to thwart short-run harmful effects on real economic activity that come from other mechanisms than what we studied in the Friedman-Lucas money surprise model.

What is the appropriate monetary policy response to a deficiency in financial liquidity? In Figure 13.16, there is deficient financial liquidity due to a reduction in private financial liquidity provision, which shifts the output demand curve to the left in Figure 13.16(a), from Y_1^d to Y_2^d, with the money demand curve in panel (b) shifting to the right from $PL(Y_1,r_1)$ to $PL(Y_2,r_2)$ (assume as above that money demand increases). What happens if the central bank responds as it would to a conventional liquidity shortage? Indeed, the financial liquidity shortage has at least one feature of a conventional liquidity shortage—an increase in the demand for money—so why not increase the money supply in response? Suppose that the central bank increases the money supply to M_2 through an open market purchase of government bonds. Since B/M falls (B falls and M increases), therefore from Equation (13.4) there will be a reduction in

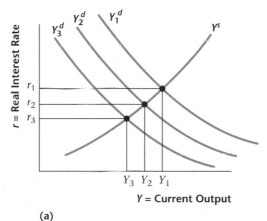

(a)

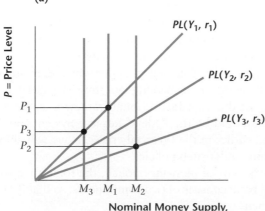

(b)

FIGURE 13.16
Monetary Policy Response to Deficient Financial Liquidity.
Conventional monetary policy "easing" does not work in the usual way. An open market purchase of government bonds reduces output and employment. An open market sale relieves the liquidity deficiency.

financial liquid assets, which shifts the output demand curve even further to the left to Y_3^d in Figure 13.16(a). This causes an additional shift in the money demand curve to the right in Figure 13.16(b), to $PL(Y_3, r_3)$. This has a perverse effect, in that it acts to reduce the quantity of financial liquidity, since the open market purchase reduces the supply of government bonds, and those bonds serve as financial liquidity. A second perverse effect is that the price level can fall because of the money injection, to P_3 in Figure 13.16(b), in spite of the fact that the money supply increased.

The appropriate monetary policy response to the financial liquidity shortage is not an open market purchase of government bonds, but an open market sale. This increases the ratio B/M, which acts to shift the output demand curve to the right. Indeed, the central bank could restore the economy to its original state by reducing the money supply to M_3 in Figure 13.16(b), thus shifting the output demand curve back to Y_1^d in Figure 13.16(a). This is important. Traditional prescriptions for monetary policy may in fact make the problem worse in a financial crisis.

DEFICIENT FINANCIAL LIQUIDITY, EXCESS RESERVES, AND THE LIQUIDITY TRAP

The Bank of Canada normally conducts monetary policy by setting a target for the nominal interest rate at which large financial institutions lend among each other overnight. It then intervenes in financial markets through open market operations so that that this interest rate—the bank rate—comes as close as possible to the Bank's target. Normally, this implies that bank reserves, which are used in large financial transactions during each day, essentially go to zero overnight. Thus, at the end of each financial trading day, the quantity of outside money is essentially all currency and no reserves.

During the recent financial crisis, the Bank of Canada's policy procedures changed from this "normal" mode, as was the case at other central banks in the world. In particular, by April 2009, the Bank had lowered the target for the bank rate to 0.25%, and the interest rate that it set on deposits (reserves) at the Bank was also 0.25%. Normally, this deposit rate is set 1/4% below the target for the bank rate. As well, in April 2009 the Bank began to conduct open market operations so that there would be a significant quantity of reserves held overnight by financial institutions in the system. This ensured that the bank rate would in fact be 0.25%, as financial institutions would have to be indifferent at the end of each day between lending to other institutions overnight and lending to the Bank of Canada by holding reserves. This policy, under which the Bank of Canada's deposit rate determined the bank rate, remained in place until May 2010.

Similar policies, in different institutional frameworks, were carried out by the European Central Bank and by the Federal Reserve System (the U.S. central bank), at the same time and earlier in the financial crisis. As we will show, monetary policy works quite differently under such policies.

With this unusual type of monetary policy, the total quantity of outside money issued by the central bank consists of two components, so that if M is the total quantity of outside money, then

$$M = M_c + M_r,$$

where M_c is currency and M_r is reserves. Suppose there is deficient financial liquidity, so that output demand depends on the quantity of liquid financial assets. However, now we need to include reserves as part of the stock of liquid financial assets, so

$$a = \frac{M_r + B}{P} + k(r) = \frac{(M_r + B)L(Y, r)}{M_c} + k(r), \tag{13.5}$$

where we have used money market clearing, just as in Equation (13.4), to substitute for P in Equation (13.5).

A conventional open market purchase is a swap by the central bank of reserves, M_r, for bonds, B. From Equation (13.5), this has no effect on the total of reserves plus bonds, and therefore no effect on liquid financial assets. Further, since currency M_c remains unchanged, there is no effect in the money market. Therefore, there is no change in any variable in equilibrium.

Thus, a conventional open market purchase under these circumstances is neutral, and does not even change prices. We can then say that there is a liquidity trap, in that reserves and interest-bearing government securities are essentially identical assets, and if the central bank swaps one of these assets for the other, it cannot make any difference. However, note that this is different from the conventional type of liquidity trap discussed in Chapter 12. The conventional liquidity trap occurs when the short-term nominal interest rate is zero, while the liquidity trap we are discussing here could in principle occur for any level of the market nominal interest rate.

The central bank action that matters in this context is not an open market operation, but a change in the interest rate that the central bank pays on reserves or, in Canada, the deposit rate at the Bank of Canada. Provided that the Bank always plans to have a positive supply of reserves in the financial system every night, the interest rate on reserves will determine all short-term interest rates. In Figure 13.17, there is deficient financial liquidity, and initially aggregate real income is Y_1 and the real interest rate is r_1. In the money market in Figure 13.17(b), the nominal stock of currency is initially M_1^c and the price level is P_1. Here, the important thing to note is that the interest rate r and the total quantity of outside money M are set by the central bank. Then, in Equation (13.5), the quantity of liquid financial assets a is endogenous, in that M_r and $M_c = M - M_r$ adjust so that the output demand curve and output supply curve intersect at the interest rate r_1 that the central bank sets.

Next, suppose that the central bank acts to reduce the interest rate on reserves to r_2 in Figure 13.17(a), given deficient liquid financial assets. The output demand curve must then shift to the left, and this happens through a decrease in reserves and an increase in currency, which reduces a in Equation (13.5). As a result, output falls from Y_1 to Y_2 in Figure 13.17(a), and in panel (b) of Figure 13.17 the supply of currency rises from M_1^c to M_2^c.

A deficiency of liquid financial assets thus causes the economy to behave in a perverse way in response to what might be interpreted as an easing in monetary policy. This "easing" occurs through a reduction in the central bank's key policy rate, which is the interest rate on reserves in this instance. But the policy does not "ease," since real output declines, and the price level could even be lower, as in Figure 13.17(b),

FIGURE 13.17

Monetary Policy with Excess Reserves and a Liquidity Trap.

Conventional open market operations have no effect, but an increase in the interest rate on reserves will relieve the deficiency of financial liquidity.

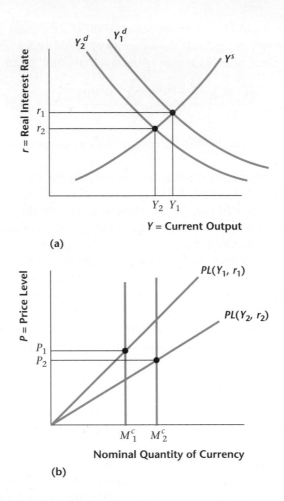

(a)

(b)

because the decrease in the interest rate causes money demand to rise. Thus, the price level could fall if the demand for currency rises sufficiently because of the decrease in the market interest rate. But it is possible for the price level to rise, since the stock of currency is higher and the decrease in real income will reduce money demand.

It is important to note that, if there is deficient financial liquidity, the way that the central bank should relieve the deficiency is to increase the interest rate on reserves, rather than reducing it. Everything will then work in the opposite direction from what is depicted in Figure 13.17, in that bank reserves will rise (because it is now more attractive for financial institutions to hold these reserves), and the quantity of currency will fall. This then works like an injection of the appropriate kind of liquidity by the central bank.

Monetary policymaking is challenging in a modern financial crisis. The deficiency in financial market liquidity that the financial crisis creates means that open market operations can work in the opposite way from what policymakers intend. As well, there can be a liquidity trap, but a perverse one, that has different implications for monetary policy than does a conventional liquidity trap.

Features of the recent recession, including the weak recovery in some parts of the world, particularly the United States and Europe, have generated much interest in the role of uncertainty in the recession, and in previous recessions as well. Aggregate uncertainty can come from the private sector, the public sector, or both.

With respect to the private sector, aggregate economic activity could be depressed because economic agents have observed events that cause them to be more pessimistic about future productivity growth, for example. From Chapter 11, we know that a decline in anticipated future productivity reduces current investment expenditures and current real GDP. An increase in uncertainty can have the same effects, as firms become more cautious and less likely to invest. The recent financial crisis in itself could have caused more uncertainty, as economic agents may have revised their beliefs about the future volatility of the aggregate economy.

The public sector can also generate its own uncertainty. If firms are uncertain about future taxes and future regulatory constraints, these firms could be more reluctant to hire workers or to invest. Also, workers could react to higher uncertainty about future tax rates by working less, or by investing less in their own training.

A recent working paper by Nicholas Bloom, Max Floetotto, and Nir Jaimovich,[15] studies an extension of a real business cycle model that allows for these types of uncertainty. In their model, firms can be uncertain about factors that affect their own productivity, and about factors affecting aggregate productivity. Because it is costly for firms to adjust their capital and labour inputs, a higher degree of uncertainty will cause firms to be cautious, as they do not want to invest more today or hire more workers if they will likely have to reverse these decisions in the future. Thus, recessions tend to be associated with a higher degree of uncertainty in their model.

Bloom, Floetotto, and Jaimovich find strong empirical evidence that increased uncertainty is a regular feature of all recessions, and not only of the most recent recession. Further, an increase in uncertainty will tend to be associated with a lower Solow residual. Thus, some of what we are measuring as decreases in total factor productivity in a recession could actually be a symptom of higher uncertainty.

With respect to uncertainty created by the government, there has been much public speculation about the uncertainty created by economic policymakers, but little empirical evidence to go on. However, two researchers at the Cleveland Federal Reserve Bank, Mark Schweitzer and Scott Shane,[16] find evidence that uncertainty about economic policy has a significant negative effect on the behaviour of small businesses.

Thus, we can say in general that economic uncertainty has been important for business cycle activity, and particularly for the recent recession. The evidence is strong that private sector factors play an important role in aggregate uncertainty. However, while economic policy could potentially create a good deal of uncertainty, there is no overwhelming evidence that it has been important for the recent recession.

---

[15]N. Bloom, M. Floetotto, and N. Jaimovich, 2011, "Really Uncertain Business Cycles," working paper, Stanford University.

[16]M. Schweitzer and S. Shane, 2011. "Economic Policy Uncertainty and Small Business Expansion," *Cleveland Federal Reserve Bank Economic Commentary*, clevelandfed .org/research/commentary/2011/2011-24.cfm.

Chapter Summary

- In this chapter, we constructed three different equilibrium models of the business cycle, and we evaluated these models in terms of how they fit the data, their policy predictions, and their plausibility.

■ The first model studied in this chapter is the real business cycle model, in which business cycles are explained by persistent fluctuations in total factor productivity. The real business cycle model is consistent with all the business cycle facts from Chapter 3, and endogenous money can explain the regularities in the behaviour of the nominal money supply relative to real aggregate output.

■ The basic real business cycle model has no role for government policy, since business cycles are simply optimal responses to fluctuations in total factor productivity.

■ The real business cycle model is not always successful in explaining historical business cycle events, and there are measurement problems in using the Solow residual as a measure of total factor productivity.

■ In the second model, the segmented markets model, consumers do not participate in financial markets, but firms do. Firms are liquidity constrained in hiring labour. An unanticipated increase in the money supply is not neutral, as liquidity-constrained firms hire more labour, output increases, the real wage rises, and the real interest rate falls. The decrease in the real interest rate is a liquidity effect. The price level decreases. The model matches all of the key business cycle facts from Chapter 3 except that average labour productivity is countercyclical in response to unanticipated money shocks.

■ In the segmented markets model, unanticipated changes in the money supply that are not responses to events in the economy are always inefficient, as this just creates uncertainty. However, there can be a role for monetary policy in responding to unanticipated shocks to the economy, if the monetary authority can react to events more quickly than does the private sector.

■ The third model studied here is the Keynesian coordination failure model, which is based on the existence of strategic complementarities giving rise to increasing returns to scale at the aggregate level. This implies that there can be multiple equilibria, and we considered an example in which the model had two equilibria: a good equilibrium with high output, consumption, investment, employment, and real wage, and a low real interest rate and price level; and a bad equilibrium with low output, consumption, investment employment, and real wage, and a high real interest rate and price level. The economy could then fluctuate between these two equilibria, with fluctuations driven by waves of optimism and pessimism.

■ Money is neutral in the Keynesian coordination failure model, but it could be a sunspot variable that produces optimism and pessimism, thus making it appear that money is not neutral.

■ The coordination failure model does as well as the real business cycle model in fitting the data. The role for government policy in the coordination failure model could be to produce optimism, and there may be a role for fiscal policy in smoothing out business cycles.

Key Terms

endogenous money: The concept that the money supply is not exogenous but depends on other aggregate economic variables because of the behaviour of the banking system and the central bank.

statistical causality: When an economic variable a helps predict the future values of an economic variable b, we say that a statistically causes b.

labour hoarding: The process by which firms may not lay off workers during a recession, even though those workers are not as busy on the job as they might be.

coordination failure: A situation in which economic agents cannot coordinate their actions, producing a bad equilibrium.

strategic complementarities: Relationships in which actions taken by others encourage a particular firm or consumer to take the same action.

multiple equilibria: The presence of more than one equilibrium in an economic model.

increasing returns to scale: A situation in which output increases more than proportionally to an increase in factor inputs.

sunspot: An economic variable that has no effect on aggregate production possibilities or on consumers' preferences.

adequate financial liquidity: A state of the world where there are enough liquid assets supplied by the government and the private sector so that financial market trade can occur efficiently.

deficient financial liquidity: A state of the world where financial liquidity is scarce, implying that financial market trade cannot occur efficiently.

Questions for Review

1. What were the two main principles introduced in the rational expectations revolution?

2. Why is it useful to study different models of the business cycle?

3. What causes output to fluctuate in the real business cycle model?

4. Why is money neutral in the real business cycle model?

5. How can the real business cycle model explain the behaviour of the money supply over the business cycle?

6. Should the government act to stabilize output in the real business cycle model?

7. Does the real business cycle model fit the data?

8. What are the important shortcomings of the real business cycle model?

9. Describe an example of a coordination failure problem.

10. What causes business cycles in the coordination failure model?

11. Why is money neutral in the coordination failure model?

12. Does the coordination failure model fit the data?

13. Which is the better macro model, the real business cycle model or the coordination failure model? Explain.

14. What causes deficient financial liquidity?

15. When there is deficient financial liquidity, what happens if the central bank conducts an open market purchase?

16. What is the appropriate monetary policy response to a state of deficient financial liquidity?

17. How does a liquidity trap with interest-bearing reserves and an excess of reserves differ from a conventional liquidity trap?

Problems

1. In the real business cycle model, suppose government spending increases temporarily. Determine the equilibrium effects of this. Could business cycles be explained by fluctuations in G? That is, does the model replicate the key business cycle facts from Chapter 3 when subjected to temporary shocks to government spending? Explain carefully.

2. Suppose temporary increases in government spending lead to permanent increases in total factor productivity, perhaps because some government spending improves infrastructure and makes private firms more productive. Show that temporary shocks to government spending of this type could lead to business cycles consistent with the key business cycle facts, and explain your results.

3. In the real business cycle model, suppose firms become infected with optimism, and they expect that total factor productivity will be much higher in the future.
   a. Determine the equilibrium effects of this expectation.
   b. If waves of optimism and pessimism of this sort cause GDP to fluctuate, does the model explain the key business cycle facts?
   c. Suppose that the monetary authority wants to stabilize the price level in the face of a wave of optimism. Determine what it should do, and explain.

4. Suppose money plays the role of a sunspot variable in the coordination failure model, so that the economy is in the bad equilibrium when the money supply is low and in the good equilibrium when the money supply is high. Explain what the monetary authority could do to make consumers better off. Compare this prescription for monetary policy with the one coming from the segmented markets model, and discuss.

5. In the coordination failure model, suppose consumers' preferences shift so that they want to consume less leisure and more consumption goods. Determine the effects on aggregate variables in the good equilibrium and in the bad equilibrium, and explain your results.

6. In the coordination failure model, suppose there is a permanent increase in government spending. Determine how this will affect output, the real interest rate, employment, the real wage, and the price level in the good equilibrium and in the bad equilibrium. Will real output be more or less volatile over time if there are waves of optimism and pessimism? Explain your results.

7. Suppose a natural disaster destroys some of the nation's capital stock. The central bank's goal is to stabilize the price level. Given this goal, what should the central bank do in response to the disaster? Explain with the aid of diagrams.

8. Suppose that the central bank observes a drop in real GDP, but does not know what caused this drop.
   a. How would the central bank respond if it believed that GDP dropped because of a decline in total factor productivity, and that real business cycle theory is correct?
   b. How would the central bank respond if it believed that GDP dropped because of a wave of pessimism, and that the Keynesian coordination failure model is correct?
   c. Explain your answers to (a) and (b) with the aid of diagrams.

9. Suppose, in the New Monetarist model, that there is deficient financial liquidity. If the fiscal authority were to engineer a tax cut, financed by an increase in the quantity of government debt, with the quantity of outside money held constant, what happens? What does this say about Ricardian equivalence in the New Monetarist model? Discuss.

10. Repeat question 9 for the liquidity trap case where interest is paid on reserves and there are excess reserves held in the financial system. Explain your results and discuss.

11. In the New Monetarist model, suppose that the central bank conducted a "quantitative easing" program, by issuing outside money and exchanging it for privately produced liquid financial assets. What would the macroeconomic effects be? Does it matter if there is a liquidity trap where excess reserves are held in the financial system? If so, why, and if not, why not? Explain.

New Keynesian Economics: Sticky Prices

Keynesian ideas have been with us since Keynes wrote his *General Theory*[1] in 1936. Keynesians argue that wages and prices are not perfectly flexible or "sticky" in the short run, with the result that supply may not equal demand (in the usual sense) in all markets in the economy at each point in time. The implication, as Keynesians argue, is that government intervention through fiscal and monetary policy can improve aggregate economic outcomes by smoothing out business cycles.

Business cycle models based on Keynesian ideas have been very influential among both academics and policymakers, and continue to be so. The basic formal modelling framework underlying these models was developed by Hicks in the late 1930s[2] in his "IS-LM" model, and popularized in Paul Samuelson's textbook in the 1950s. In the 1960s, large-scale versions of these Keynesian business cycle models were fit to data and used in policy analysis.

Since the 1960s, Keynesians have adapted their models and ideas to the newer methods and ideas coming from other schools of thought in macroeconomics. In the 1960s and 1970s, monetarist approaches, represented primarily by the work of Milton Friedman, were in part adopted by Keynesians in what was called the "neoclassical synthesis." In the 1980s, equilibrium models with optimizing consumers and firms, such as the real business cycle model studied in Chapter 13, were influential in the development of Keynesian "menu cost" models, which explained sticky prices as arising from the costs to firms of changing prices.[3] More recently, Keynesian models that have as their core a basic real business cycle framework, but that incorporate sticky prices (and sometimes sticky wages),[4] have been developed. Those who work in this research program call it "New Keynesian Economics," and argue that it represents the newest synthesis of ideas in macroeconomics.

---

[1]See J. M. Keynes, 1936, *The General Theory of Employment, Interest, and Money*, Macmillan, London.

[2]J. Hicks, 1937, "Mr. Keynes and the Classics: A Suggested Interpretation," *Econometrica* 5, 147–159.

[3]L. Ball and N. G. Mankiw, 1994, "A Sticky-Price Manifesto," *Carnegie-Rochester Conference Series on Public Policy* 41, 127–151.

[4]R. Clarida, J. Gali, and M. Gertler, 1999, "The Science of Monetary Policy: A New Keynesian Perspective," *Journal of Economic Literature* 37, 1661-1707; M. Woodford, 2003, *Money, Interest, and Prices*, Princeton University Press, Princeton, NJ.

The primary feature that makes a Keynesian macroeconomic model different from the models we have examined thus far is that some prices and wages are not completely flexible—that is, some are "sticky." That some prices and wages cannot move so as to clear markets will have important implications for how the economy behaves and for economic policy. The New Keynesian model studied in this chapter is essentially identical to the monetary intertemporal model in Chapter 12, except that the price level is not sufficiently flexible for the goods market to clear in the short run. Given the failure of the goods market to clear, the New Keynesian model will have far different properties from the monetary intertemporal model, but constructing the model will be a straightforward extension of our basic monetary intertemporal framework.

Though Keynesian models certainly have some strong adherents, they have many detractors as well.[5] Part of what we will do in this chapter is to critically evaluate the New Keynesian model, just as we evaluated flexible-wage-and-price business cycle models in Chapter 13. We will see how well the New Keynesian model fits the key business cycle facts we discussed in Chapter 3, and we will examine how useful it is for guiding the formulation of economic policy.

In contrast to the monetary intertemporal model in Chapter 12, the New Keynesian model will have the property that money is not neutral. When the monetary authority increases the money supply, there will be an increase in aggregate output and employment. In general, monetary policy can then be used to improve economic performance and welfare. Keynesians typically believe strongly that the government should play an active role in the economy, through both monetary and fiscal policy, and Keynesian business cycle models support this belief. Recall that in the Friedman-Lucas money surprise model discussed in Chapter 12, money is also not neutral; but as we will discuss in this chapter, the role for monetary policy is quite different in the two models.

We take the approach in this chapter that we did in Chapter 12, where we discussed interest rate targeting. Rather than setting up our model as one in which the instrument that the central bank controls is the money supply, we will have the central bank using the market interest rate as its policy target. Most New Keynesian analysis proceeds in this fashion, in a manner consistent with how most central banks behave— in particular, the Bank of Canada targets the bank rate (discussed in Chapter 12) in the short run, and typically considers changing the target for the bank rate eight times per year. As we will show, however, what the central bank controls directly is the money supply, so any target for the market interest rate must be supported with appropriate money supply control. Once we treat the market interest rate as the central bank's policy target, we will eliminate a feature of traditional Keynesian textbook analysis, Hicks's "LM curve," which was included in these traditional models to summarize money demand, money supply, and equilibrium in the money market.

In our New Keynesian model, we will show how active monetary and fiscal policy can smooth out business cycles by reacting to extraneous shocks to the economy. Given well-informed fiscal and monetary authorities that can act very quickly, there

---

[5]See R. Lucas, 1980, "Methods and Problems in Business Cycle Theory," *Journal of Money, Credit, and Banking* 12, 696-715; S. Williamson, 2008, "New Keynesian Economics: A Monetary Perspective," *Economic Quarterly* 94, Federal Reserve Bank of Richmond, 197-218.

is little difference between monetary and fiscal policy in terms of their effects on stabilizing aggregate output. However, the active use of fiscal policy in stabilizing the economy will matter for the division of aggregate spending between the public and private sectors.

The New Keynesian Model

Our New Keynesian model will have very different properties from the basic monetary intertemporal model that we constructed in Chapter 12. However, there is only one fundamental difference in the New Keynesian model, which is that the price level is sticky in the short run and will not adjust quickly to equate the supply and demand for goods.

Why might goods prices be sticky in the short run? Some Keynesians argue that it is costly for firms to change prices, and even if these costs are small, this could lead firms to fix the prices for their products for long periods of time. Consider a restaurant, which must print new menus whenever it changes its prices. Printing menus is costly, and this causes the restaurant to change prices infrequently. Given that prices change infrequently, there may be periods when the restaurant is full and people are being turned away. If menus were not costly to print, the restaurant might increase its prices under these circumstances. Alternatively, there may be periods when the restaurant is not full and prices would be lowered if it were not for the costs of changing prices. The restaurant example is a common one in the economic literature on sticky price models. Indeed, the sticky price models Keynesian worked with in the 1980s were sometimes referred to as **menu cost models**.

In typical New Keynesian models, it is assumed that, among the many firms in the economy, some will change their prices during any given period of time, and some will not. This could be modelled the hard way, by assuming a fixed cost for a firm associated with changing its price. Then, a firm will change its price only when the firm's existing price deviates enough from the optimal price, making it profit-maximizing for the firm to bear the menu cost and shift to the optimal price. An easier approach is to simply assume that a firm receives an opportunity at random to change its price. Every period, the firms that are lucky receive this opportunity and change their prices, while the unlucky firms are stuck charging the price they posted in the previous period.

Whichever way sticky prices are modelled, this tends to lead to forward-looking behaviour on the part of firms. Whenever a firm changes its price, it knows that it may be charging this price for some time into the future, until it can change its posted price again. Thus, in making its price-setting decision the firm will attempt to forecast the shocks that are likely to affect future market conditions and the firm's future profitability. While this forward-looking behaviour can play an important role in New Keynesian economics, we will need to simplify here by assuming that all firms charge the price P for goods in the current period, and that this price is sticky and will not move during the period in response to shifts in the demand for goods.

In Figure 14.1, we display the basic apparatus for the New Keynesian model, which includes the same set of diagrams we used for the basic monetary intertemporal model in Chapter 12, with the addition of the production function. That is, the labour

FIGURE 14.1

The New Keynesian Model
Given the fixed price level P^* and the target interest rate r^*, output is Y^*, determined by the output demand (IS) curve, and the central bank must supply M^* units of money to hit its interest rate target. Firms hire N^* units of labour at the real wage w^*. The natural rate of interest is r_m, and the output gap is $Y_m - Y^*$.

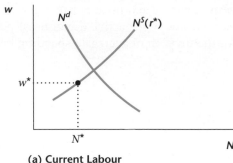

(a) Current Labour

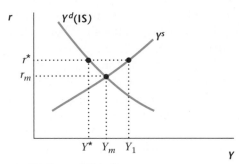

(b) Current Goods

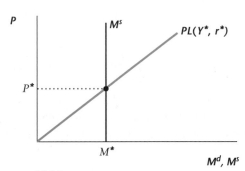

(c) Money

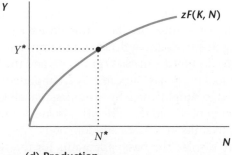

(d) Production

market is in panel (a) of the figure, the goods market in panel (b), the money market in panel (c), and the production function in panel (d).

Now, start with panel (c), the money market. Here, the price level is fixed at P^*, which is the sticky price charged by all firms. Assume that this price was set in the past, and firms cannot change it during the current period. Then, in panel (b), r^* is the interest rate target of the central bank, which we treat as exogenous. Here we assume, as in Chapter 12, that the inflation rate is a constant—zero for convenience—so that the Fisher relation tells us that the nominal interest rate R is identical to the real interest rate r. In practice, we know that central banks typically target a nominal interest rate, which is consistent with what the central bank does in the model, where setting r is the same as setting R.

Given the interest rate target r^*, output is determined by the output demand curve in Figure 14.1(b), so aggregate output is Y^*. Note that, in Keynesian models with sticky prices or wages, in line with the tradition of Hicks, what we have called the output demand curve, Y^d, is typically called the "IS" curve. Thus, we have labelled the output demand curve "Y^d(IS)" in Figure 14.1(b).

Given the level of output Y^* and the interest rate r^*, in the money market in 14.1(c), the quantity of money demanded is $PL(Y^*, r^*)$, so in order to hit its target market interest rate of r^*, given the price level P^*, the central bank must supply M^* units of money. From the production function in panel (d), firms hire the quantity of labour N^* that is just sufficient to produce the quantity of output demanded in the goods market, Y^*. In the labour market in panel (a), the labour supply curve is $N^s(r^*)$, determined by the equilibrium real interest rate r^*. The real wage w^* is the wage rate at which the quantity of labour that consumers are willing to supply is N^*.

A critical feature of the model is that some markets clear, while others do not. The money market clears in Figure 14.1(c), since the central bank needs to supply a sufficient quantity of money, that money demand equals money supply at the central bank's target interest rate r^*, given the fixed price level P^* and the level of output Y^*. The goods market need not clear, however. In panel (b), firms would like to supply the quantity of output Y_1 at the interest rate r^*, but firms actually produce only the quantity demanded, which is Y^*. If firms could, they would lower prices, but prices are rigid in the short run. Note that the quantity of output Y_m is the market-clearing level of output that would be determined in the monetary intertemporal model. The market-clearing interest rate r_m is sometimes referred to as the **natural rate of interest** in the New Keynesian literature. As well, New Keynesians call the difference between the market-clearing level of output and actual level of output, $Y_m - Y^*$, the **output gap**.

In the New Keynesian model, the labour market need not clear in the short run. In particular, in Figure 14.1(a), at the market real wage w^*, firms would like to hire more labour than N^*, but firms know that if they hired more labour they would not be able to sell the larger amount of produced output at the price P^*.

THE NON-NEUTRALITY OF MONEY IN THE NEW KEYNESIAN MODEL

Given our short-run New Keynesian model, we can proceed with an experiment that will illustrate how money fails to be neutral in this model. Keynesian price stickiness is an alternative theory to the Friedman-Lucas money surprise model studied in

Chapter 12 for explaining why changes in monetary policy can have real effects on aggregate economic activity in the short run.

In Figure 14.2, suppose initially that the economy is in a long-run equilibrium with level of output Y_1, real interest rate r_1, price level P_1, employment N_1, and real wage w_1, given the money supply M_1. Then, the central bank lowers its interest rate target to r_2, implying that output increases to Y_2 in Figure 14.2(b), as firms supply the extra output demanded since the price of output is fixed in the short run at P_1. In Figure 14.2(c), money demand shifts to the right from $PL(Y_1, r_1)$ to $PL(Y_2, r_2)$, as real income has risen and the real interest rate has fallen, both of which act to increase money demand. Therefore, to support the lower nominal interest rate target, the central bank must increase the money supply to M_2. In the labour market in Figure 14.2(a), the labour supply curve shifts to the left from $N^s(r_1)$ to $N^s(r_2)$ as a result of intertemporal substitution in response to the lower interest rate. Therefore, the real wage must rise so as to induce consumers to supply the extra labour required to produce the higher level of output.

Another way to view this is that the central bank increases the money supply, which results in an excess supply of money at the interest rate r_1, and so the interest rate falls so as to equate money supply and demand. The decrease in the real interest rate then increases the demand for consumption goods and investment goods, and so firms supply the extra output given that prices are fixed in the short run. Money is not neutral, because the increase in the money supply has real effects; the real interest rate falls, real output increases, the real wage increases, and employment increases. Keynesians think of money as having these real effects through the above-described **Keynesian transmission mechanism for monetary policy**. That is, an increase in the money supply has its first effects in financial markets; the real interest rate falls to equate money demand with the increased money supply, and this acts to increase the demand for goods.

Most Keynesians regard money as being neutral in the long run. Although Keynesians argue that money is not neutral in the short run because of sticky prices (or wages), they also typically accept that prices will eventually adjust so that supply equals demand in the goods and labour markets, in which case money will be neutral, just as in the monetary intertemporal model we studied in Chapter 12.

The Role of Government Policy in the New Keynesian Model

In macroeconomics, some important disagreements focus on the issue of whether the government should act to smooth out business cycles. This smoothing, or what is sometimes referred to as **stabilization policy**, involves carrying out government actions that will increase aggregate real output when it is below trend and decrease it when it is above trend. Using government policy to smooth business cycles may appear to be a good idea. For example, we know that a consumer whose income fluctuates will behave optimally by smoothing consumption relative to income, so why shouldn't the government take actions that will smooth aggregate real income over time? But as we

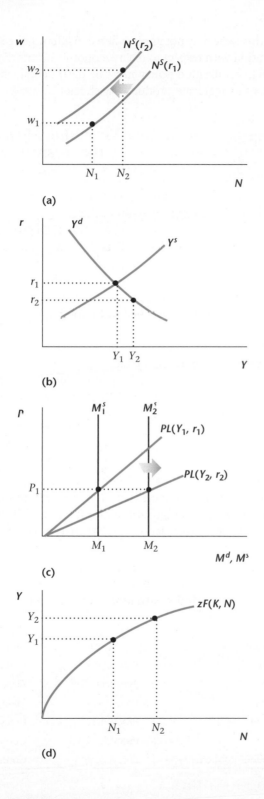

FIGURE 14.2

A Decrease in the Central Bank's Interest Rate Target in the New Keynesian Model
Money is not neutral with sticky prices. A decrease in the interest rate target results in an increase in output, and the central bank must increase the money supply to achieve its interest rate target. Employment, the real wage, consumption, investment, and the money supply all increase.

saw in Chapter 13, this logic may not apply when considering the rationale for government policy intervention with respect to macroeconomic events. For example, in a real business cycle model, stabilization policy must be detrimental, as business cycles are just optimal responses to aggregate productivity shocks.

<table>
<tr><td>THEORY
CONFRONTS
THE DATA</td><td>*14.1*</td><td>*Can the New Keynesian Model under Fluctuations in the Interest Rate Target Explain Business Cycles?*</td></tr>
</table>

Since changes in the central bank's interest rate target can cause output to change in the New Keynesian model, a key prediction of the model is that if the interest rate target fluctuates, so will aggregate output. The model then gives a monetary theory of business cycles. That is, the model predicts that policy-induced fluctuations in the central bank's interest rate target could cause business cycles. As economists, we would then like to ask whether this is a good or bad theory of business cycles. To answer this question, we have to ask how the predictions of the model fit the key business cycle regularities that we outlined in Chapter 3.

In Table 14.1 we show how the predictions of the New Keynesian model with interest rate target fluctuations fits features of the data we examined in Chapter 3. Some features of the model clearly fit the data. For example, when the interest rate target falls and the money supply increases, output increases, which is consistent with the fact that money is procyclical in the data. As well, when the interest rate target falls, this causes investment and consumption to rise, so that investment, I, and consumption, C, are procyclical, as is true for the data. Further, a decrease in the interest rate target causes an increase in employment and the real wage, and so employment and the real wage will be procyclical, as is the case in the data.

However, not all the results fit. Since the interest rate target decrease does not shift the production function, the increase in the level of employment and output must result in a decrease in average labour productivity. Therefore, under fluctuations in the interest rate target, labour productivity is countercyclical, and not procyclical as in the data.

TABLE 14.1   **Data versus Predictions of the Keynesian Sticky Wage Model with Monetary Shocks**

	Data	*Model*
Consumption	Procyclical	Procyclical
Investment	Procyclical	Procyclical
Price level	Acyclical	Acyclical
Money supply	Procyclical	Procyclical
Employment	Procyclical	Procyclical
Real wage	Procyclical	Countercyclical
Average labour productivity	Procyclical	Countercyclical

We conclude that, at least for the time period in Canada we examined in Chapter 3, fluctuations in the central bank's interest rate target may not have been the most important cause of business cycles, if money affects the economy as captured in the New Keynesian model. It is possible, however, that fluctuations in the Bank of Canada's interest rate target, acting through the Keynesian transmission mechanism for monetary policy, made significant contributions (though not the primary ones) to fluctuations in GDP over this period.

We must regard conclusions from Table 14.1 with caution, as in practice the Bank of Canada's interest rate target changes with events in the economy. Bank of Canada policymakers living in the New Keynesian world would come to realize that fluctuations in the Bank's interest rate target could cause output and employment to fluctuate. In circumstances where no other shocks were impinging on the economy, the Bank would have no reason to change its interest rate target, and so we would not observe events where a change in the interest rate target was the obvious cause of a change in output. As we will study in more detail later in this chapter, the Bank might have good reasons to change the interest rate target in response to other shocks to the economy, but then it would be hard to disentangle the effects of monetary policy on real activity from the effects of other shocks.

**THEORY
CONFRONTS
THE DATA** **14.2** *Keynesian Aggregate Demand Shocks
as Causes of Business Cycles*

Though monetary policy shocks in the New Keynesian model may not be able to explain all the key business cycle regularities discussed in Chapter 3, some other shock to the economy might successfully explain observed business cycles in this model. Keynes argued in his *General Theory of Employment, Interest, and Money* that a principal cause of business cycles is fluctuations in aggregate demand. What he appears to have had in mind was shocks to investment, which would be captured here as shifts in the Y^d curve. That is, suppose that firms become more optimistic about future total factor productivity, so that they view the future marginal product of capital as having increased. (Keynes referred to such waves of optimism as being due to the "animal spirits" of investors.) This increases the demand for investment goods and shifts the Y^d curve to the right.

In Figure 14.3, suppose that the economy is initially in long-run equilibrium, with all markets clearing. The level of output is Y_1, the central bank's interest rate target is r_1, the price level is P_1, the money supply is M_1, the real wage is w_1, and the level of employment is N_1. Then, an increase in the demand for investment goods leads to a rightward shift in the Y^d curve from Y_1^d to Y_2^d in Figure 14.3(b). An important factor in determining the effects on the economy will be the central bank's response to this aggregate shock. Here, we will assume that the interest rate target does not change, remaining at r_1. As a result, in Figure 14.3(b), the level of output increases to Y_2, with firms increasing output to meet the increase in demand for goods.

FIGURE 14.3

An Increase in the Demand for Investment Goods in the New Keynesian Model

The output demand curve shifts to the left, with the central bank's target interest rate unchanged. Output, investment, consumption, the money supply, employment, and the real wage all increase. In panel (d), average labour productivity must fall.

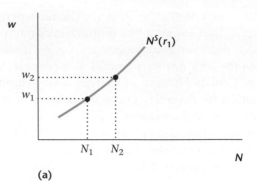

(a)

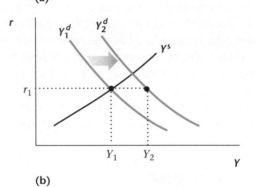

(b)

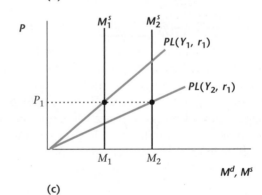

(c)

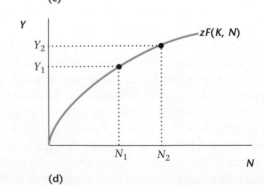

(d)

In Figure 14.3(c), the money demand curve shifts to the right from $PL(Y_1, r_1)$ to $PL(Y_2, r_1)$, due to the increase in real aggregate income. Then, in order for the central bank to meet its interest rate target r_1, it must increase the money supply from M_1 to M_2 so as to accommodate the increase in the demand for money. In Figure 14.3(d), firms must increase employment to N_2 from N_1 so as to produce the higher level of output required to meet the increase in demand for goods. In Figure 14.3(a), this requires that the market real wage increase so that consumers are willing to supply a higher quantity of labour.

Now investment must rise, as the real interest rate is unchanged and firms expect productivity to be higher in the future. Consumption also increases, since real income has risen and the interest rate is unchanged. The price level is sticky in the short run, and therefore unchanged, while in Figure 14.3(d), average labour productivity must fall, since employment and output increase and the production function does not shift.

Table 14.2 summarizes the key business cycle facts from Chapter 3 and the predictions of the New Keynesian model under investment shocks. From Figure 14.3, an increase in output coincides with an increase in investment, an increase in consumption, no change in the price level, an increase in the money supply, an increase in employment, an increase in the real wage, and a decrease in average labour productivity. Therefore, the model fits the key business cycle facts in most respects, but the fact that the model predicts countercyclical rather procyclical average labour productivity is problematic.

TABLE 14.2 **Data versus Predictions of the Keynesian Sticky Wage Model with Investment Shocks**

	Data	*Model*
Consumption	Procyclical	Procyclical
Investment	Procyclical	Procyclical
Price level	Acyclical	Acyclical
Money supply	Procyclical	Procyclical
Employment	Procyclical	Procyclical
Real wage	Procyclical	Procyclical
Average labour productivity	Procyclical	Countercyclical

Keynesians tend to argue that government intervention to smooth out business cycles is appropriate, and the New Keynesian model provides a justification for this argument. We will start by considering a situation where an unanticipated shock has hit the economy, causing the price level to be higher than its equilibrium level in the goods market, as in Figure 14.4. Alternatively, the central bank's interest rate target r_1 is too high, so there exists a positive output gap of $Y_2 - Y_1$ in Figure 14.4 or, in other

FIGURE 14.4

Stabilization Using Monetary Policy

Initially, the level of output is Y_1 given the interest rate target r_1 and the price level P_1. In the long run, the price level will fall to P_2, but the central bank can achieve Y_2 in the short run by reducing the interest rate target to r_2.

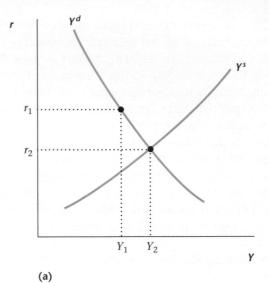

(a)

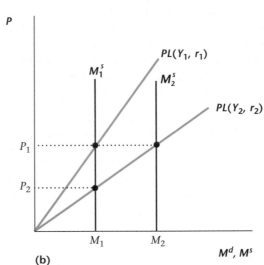

(b)

words, a situation where firms would like to supply more output than is demanded given the price level P_1 and the interest rate target r_1.

Now, after the shock has hit the economy, the allocation of resources is not economically efficient. Recall from Chapter 5 that the first fundamental theorem of welfare economics implies that a competitive equilibrium is Pareto-optimal, but in Figure 14.4 the economy is not in a competitive equilibrium, as initially the quantity of output demanded is not equal to the quantity of output that firms would like to supply. One response of the government to the economic inefficiency caused by the shock to the economy would be to do nothing and let the problem cure itself. Since the price level P_1 is initially above its long-run equilibrium level, with the quantity of goods demanded less than what firms would like to supply, the price level will tend to fall over time.

If the central bank does nothing, this means that it does not change the quantity directly under its control, which is the quantity of money. The money supply remains fixed at M_1, as in Figure 14.4(b). Then, as the price level falls over time, money demand must increase, so the central bank's interest rate target must fall until ultimately, in the long run, the interest rate target is r_2, output is Y_2, and the price level is P_2, as in Figure 14.4. The economy is therefore again in equilibrium and operating efficiently.

Keynesian macroeconomists argue that the long run is too long to wait. In Figure 14.4, suppose alternatively that instead of doing nothing in response to the shock to the economy, the central bank immediately reduces its interest rate target from r_1 to r_2. To hit this lower interest rate target requires that the central bank increase the money supply from M_1 to M_2 in Figure 14.4. This immediately closes the output gap and restores economic efficiency in the short run. The price level is P_1 and the level of output is Y_2.

Note that after the increase in the money supply, the economy is in exactly the same situation, in real terms, as it would have been in the long run had the central bank done nothing and allowed the price level to fall. The only difference is that the price level is higher in the case where the central bank intervenes. The advantage of intervention is that an efficient outcome is achieved faster than if the central bank lets events take their course.

The return to full employment could also be achieved through an increase in government expenditures, G, but with some different results. In Figure 14.5, we show a similar initial situation to Figure 14.4, where initial output is Y_1, which is less than the quantity of output that firms want to supply given the price level P_1 and the interest rate target r_1. Now, suppose that the central bank maintains its interest rate target at r_1, in anticipation that the government fiscal authority will increase government spending to correct the inefficiency problem that exists in the short run. If the government increases government purchases, G, by just the right amount, then the output demand curve shifts to the right from Y_1^d to Y_2^d and the output supply curve shifts to the right from Y_1^s to Y_2^s. (Recall our analysis from Chapter 11, where we analyzed the effects of temporary increases in G.) In Figure 14.5(b), the price level is sticky in the short run at P_1, and the increase in output shifts the money demand curve to the right from $PL(Y_1, r_1)$ to $PL(Y_2, r_1)$, and so to maintain its interest rate target the central bank increases the money supply from M_1 to M_2.

Now, note the differences in final outcomes between Figures 14.4 and 14.5. Recall from Chapter 11 that the entire increase in output from Y_1 to Y_2 in Figure 14.5 is due to the increase in government spending, as the interest rate is unchanged. That is, the fiscal policy response to the shock results in no increase in consumption or investment, with the only component of spending that increases being government spending, with output increasing one-for-one with government spending. After government intervention, output is higher in Figure 14.5 than in Figure 14.4, but with monetary policy intervention, consumption and output are higher in Figure 14.4 than in Figure 14.5 because of the decrease in the target central bank interest rate. Thus, the key differences that fiscal policy intervention makes, relative to monetary policy intervention to stabilize the economy, is that output needs to change more in response to fiscal policy in order to restore efficiency, and the composition of output is different with fiscal policy,

FIGURE 14.5
Stabilization Using
Fiscal Policy
Given the central bank's
interest rate target r_1, an
increase in government
spending shifts the output
demand and supply curves
to the right and restores
efficiency in the short run.

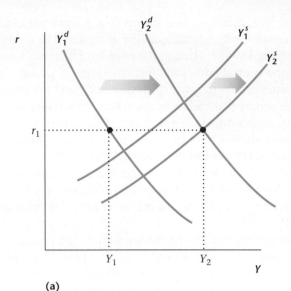

(a)

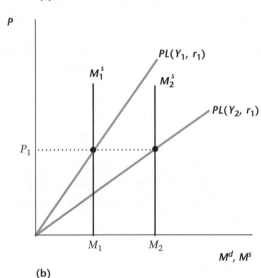

(b)

with a greater emphasis on public spending relative to private spending, compared to what happens with monetary policy intervention.

Whether fiscal or monetary policy is used to smooth business cycles, the Keynesian sticky wage model provides a rationale for stabilization policy. If shocks kick the economy out of equilibrium, because of a failure of private markets to clear in the short run, fiscal or monetary policymakers can, if they move fast enough, restore the economy to equilibrium before self-adjusting markets achieve this on their own. Thus, the important elements of the Keynesian view of government's role in the macroeconomy are the following:

In the Keynesian sticky wage model, we have shown that either fiscal or monetary policy can stabilize the economy. That is, if government spending is set appropriately by the fiscal authority, then full employment can be achieved; and economic efficiency can also be achieved if the monetary authority acts to set its interest rate target appropriately in response to shocks that affect aggregate economic activity. In practice, important imperfections—the policy lags in the formulation and implementation of monetary and fiscal policies—matter critically for the absolute and relative effectiveness of monetary and fiscal policies.

Milton Friedman argued that there are three key lags involved in policymaking: (1) the lag between the need for action and the recognition of this need; (2) the lag between recognition of the need for action and the taking of action; and (3) the lag between the action and its effects.[6] First, policymakers do not have complete information. The National Income and Expenditure Accounts, employment data, and price data are time-consuming to compile, and policymakers in the federal government and at the Bank of Canada have good information only for what was happening in the economy months previously. Second, when information is available, it may take time for policymakers to agree among themselves

concerning a course of action. Third, once policy is implemented, there is a lag before policy has its effects on aggregate economic activity.

The first lag is the same for monetary and fiscal policy. In Canada, economists working at the Bank of Canada and the Department of Finance, and the key leaders who are making decisions on fiscal and monetary policies, have essentially identical information. Further, the governor of the Bank of Canada and the minister of finance consult regularly, as do other officials in the Bank of Canada and the Department of Finance. The key differences between the lags in fiscal and monetary policy lie in the second and third stages.

David Dodge, the previous governor of the Bank of Canada, has been in the somewhat unusual position of being a practitioner of both fiscal and monetary policy. Before being appointed governor in 2001, Dodge served as deputy minister of finance (the top civil service position in the Department of Finance) from 1992 to 1997. Dodge's views on the effectiveness of monetary and fiscal policies in stabilization are nicely articulated in his remarks at a symposium held by the Federal Reserve Bank of Kansas City on August 31, 2002.[7] Dodge feels, in terms of the second stage of the policy lag (the lag between the recognition of action and the taking of action), that

1. Private markets fail to operate smoothly on their own, in that not all wages and prices are perfectly flexible, implying that supply is not equal to demand in all markets, and economic efficiency is not always achieved in a world without government intervention.

2. Fiscal policy and/or monetary policy decisions can be made quickly enough, and information on the behaviour of the economy is good enough, that the fiscal or monetary authorities can improve efficiency by countering shocks that cause a deviation from a full-employment equilibrium.

In Macroeconomics in Action 14.1, we discuss the problem of stabilization policy in the face of real-world lags in the implementation and effects of monetary and fiscal policy.

monetary policy wins out. On the one hand, monetary policy actions can be taken at any time, with decisions made by a small group of people led by the governor of the Bank of Canada, and there is no need for legislative action. On the other hand, Dodge argues that "I can tell you that the great problem here [with fiscal policy] is that temporary measures are both difficult to initiate quickly when the need arises and extraordinarily difficult to stop once the need is past." For fiscal policy action to be implemented requires that recommendations be formulated at the Department of Finance and passed to the minister of finance, following which legislative action needs to be taken by Parliament. All this takes much time and, as Dodge points out, is costly to reverse.

With respect to the third stage, the lag between the action and its effects, Dodge views monetary policy as being somewhat inferior to fiscal policy. He states that "monetary policy ... takes time to work, with the full impact on output normally felt after 12 to 18 months," while "fiscal policy measures could, *in principle*, and under ideal circumstances, shorten the time it takes to move output back to its desired level."

The conclusion is that, even if we believe stabilizing the economy through the use of fiscal and monetary policy is appropriate, as the Keynesian sticky wage model tells us, there is still much that can go wrong. Guiding the economy can be much like trying to steer a car with a faulty steering mechanism; one has to see the bumps and curves in the road well in advance to avoid driving in the ditch or otherwise having a very uncomfortable ride. This is in part why Milton Friedman, among others, has encouraged abstinence from stabilization policy altogether. Friedman argued that well-intentioned stabilization policy could do more harm than good, as the lags in policy could lead to stimulative action being taken when tightening the screws on the economy would be more appropriate, and vice versa.

---

[6]See M. Friedman, 1953, *Essays in Positive Economics*, University of Chicago Press, Chicago, p. 145.

[7]See David Dodge, 2002, "Macroeconomic Stabilization Policy in Canada," remarks to a symposium sponsored by the Federal Reserve Bank of Kansas City, Jackson Hole, Wyoming, August 31, available at www.bis.org/review/r020905b.pdf, accessed May 14, 2009.

Total Factor Productivity Shocks in the New Keynesian Model

The New Keynesian Model responds quite differently to shocks to total factor productivity than does the real business cycle model studied in Chapter 13. This different behaviour is important, as we can then use the data to draw conclusions about the relative performance of the two models.

First, consider the response of the New Keynesian model to a positive shock to total factor productivity. In Figure 14.6(a), initially the level of output is Y_1 with the central bank target interest rate r_1, and we have assumed that the economy is initially in equilibrium with output demand curve Y_1^d and output supply curve Y_1^s. In Figure 14.6(b), the price level is P_1, with the price level inflexible in the short run, and the money supply is M_1. In Figure 14.6(c), the initial production function is $z_1 F(K, N)$ and, given the level of output Y_1, employment is N_1.

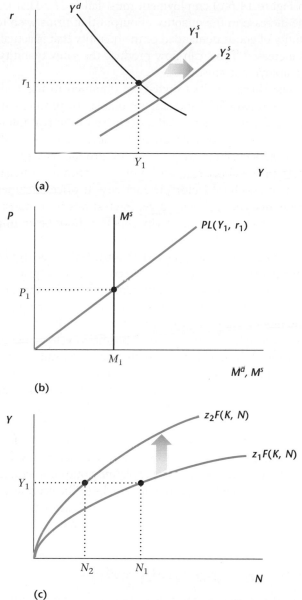

FIGURE 14.6
An Increase in Total Factor Productivity in the New Keynesian Model
An increase in total factor productivity shifts the production function up and shifts the output supply curve to the right. Output does not increase, as there is no increase in the demand for goods in the short run. Firms can produce the same quantity of output with less labour, and they reduce employment.

Now, if total factor productivity increases from z_1 to z_2, then the production function shifts up to $z_2 F(K, N)$ in Figure 14.6(c), and the output supply curve shifts to the right from Y_1^s to Y_2^s in Figure 14.6(a). Supposing that the central bank's interest rate target remains unchanged, output remains at the level Y_1, as output is demand-determined in the goods market. Therefore, after the productivity shock a positive output gap opens up, since output is below its equilibrium level. Given that there is no change in the interest rate or in output, the money demand curve does not shift, and so there are no changes in Figure 14.6(b). However, given that the level of output is unchanged, in Figure 14.6(c) employment must fall to N_2. That is, since the price level is sticky, the increase in the quantity of output that firms wish to supply has no effect on the quantity of goods demanded or the quantity that is actually produced. As productivity has increased, firms can now produce the same quantity of output with less labour, and employment must fall.

We can contrast these results to what we obtained in the real business cycle model in Chapter 13, in which an increase in total factor productivity resulted in an increase in output and employment, and a decrease in the real interest rate and the price level. Given our assumptions, productivity shocks in the New Keynesian model do not produce business cycles as we know them. Productivity shocks will not cause output to fluctuate in the short run, and will only produce a negative correlation between employment and total factor productivity. If price stickiness is important, and the central bank does not move its target interest rate in response to productivity shocks (this is important), then productivity shocks cannot be an important cause of business cycles.

What do the data tell us about this issue? Jordi Gali[8] has argued that statistical evidence supports the idea that, when the U.S. economy is hit by a positive productivity shock, employment declines in the short run. This would appear to be consistent with the New Keynesian model and inconsistent with the sticky wage model and the real business cycle model. However, this is not the end of the story. V. V. Chari, Ellen McGratten, and Patrick Kehoe[9] simulate a real business cycle model on the computer, producing some artificial data, which they then treat in the same way that Gali treated his actual data when he did his statistical tests. They get the same results as did Gali, but Chari, McGratten, and Kehoe know that their data come from a real business cycle world. This makes Gali's results seem suspicious. Further, we need to explain why the Solow residual is positively correlated with real output, as we saw in Figure 13.1 in Chapter 13. The real business cycle model provides an explanation for that fact, that is, that the Solow residual is a measure of total factor productivity, and that fluctuations in total factor productivity are important in explaining output fluctuations. The onus is on New Keynesians to explain how particular shocks to the economy, other than productivity shocks, can make the Solow residual move with aggregate output. Obviously, the debate about which business cycle model best fits reality is far from over.

The liquidity trap and sticky prices

In Chapter 12, we discussed the zero lower bound on the market nominal interest rate and the implications of this for both the conventional liquidity trap and monetary policy. Recall that the nominal interest rate cannot go below zero because of financial market arbitrage—if the nominal interest rate were negative, it would be possible for financial market participants to make enormous profits by borrowing at the market

---

[8]See J. Gali, 2004, "Technology Shocks and Aggregate Fluctuations: How Well Does the RBC Model Fit Postwar US Data?" *NBER Macreconomics Annual* 2004, 225-228.

[9]V. V. Chari, E. McGratten, and P. Kehoe, 2006, "A Critique of Structural VARs Using Real Business Cycle Theory," working paper, University of Minnesota and Federal Reserve Bank of Minneapolis.

interest rate and holding cash. The zero lower bound presents a problem for a New Keynesian monetary policymaker, as the economy could be in a state such as the one depicted in Figure 14.7, where aggregate output, Y_1, is less than the efficient level of output, so that there is a positive output gap, but the interest rate $r = 0$, so it is not possible for the central bank to lower its interest rate target and close the output gap.

As in Chapter 12, when the market interest rate hits the zero lower bound, money demand is essentially infinitely elastic at the current price level, which is P_1 in Figure 14.7(b). In this circumstance there is a liquidity trap, in that an increase in the money supply will do nothing, since an open market operation—a swap by the central bank of outside money for government bonds—is a swap of two assets that are essentially identical when the interest rate is zero. However, though monetary policy is powerless under these circumstances to close the output gap, fiscal policy still works, just as portrayed in Figure 14.5.

During the recent financial crisis, key central banks in the world did not lower their nominal interest rate targets all the way to zero, but got very close to it. For example, the Bank of Canada reduced the bank rate as low as 0.25%, and the policy rate for the U.S. Federal Reserve System went to a range of 0.0%–0.25%. But all that was keeping

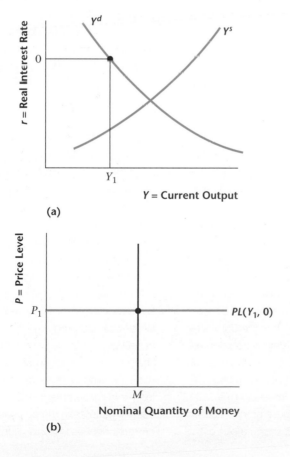

(a)

(b)

FIGURE 14.7

A Liquidity Trap at the Zero Lower Bound

Monetary policy cannot close the output gap, as the central bank's interest rate target cannot go below zero. Increasing the money supply will do nothing as the demand for money is perfectly elastic at the price level *P*.

The model presented in this chapter is a simplification of New Keynesian models that are used by economists and central bankers. Those models have a more elaborate dynamic structure than we have shown here, and typically include a monetary policy rule that explains how the central bank's nominal interest rate target evolves over time. Recall that we studied monetary policy rules in Chapter 12, and one of the policy rules under discussion was the *Taylor rule*, named after John Taylor, currently at Stanford University.

The Taylor rule is included in most New Keynesian models, and versions of it have been successfully fit to the data. One such version is described in a newsletter from the Federal Reserve Bank of San Francisco, by Glenn Rudebusch.[10] Rudebusch's Taylor rule, which comes from fitting the behaviour of the U.S. Federal Reserve System to the data, takes the form

$$R = 2.1 + 1.3\pi - 2.0gap,$$

where R is the central bank's nominal interest rate target, π is the inflation rate, and *gap* is the output gap, measured here as the difference between the unemployment rate and trend unemployment. This Taylor rule says that, if the inflation rate were to increase by one percentage point, then the central bank should tighten by increasing the target nominal interest rate by 1.3 percentage points. However, if the unemployment rate were to increase by one percentage point relative to trend, then the central bank should ease by reducing the target nominal interest rate by 2.0 percentage points.

Suppose that we examine how Rudebusch's Taylor rule fits the behaviour of the Bank of Canada. We will look only at the behaviour of the Bank after 1991, when formal inflation targets were adopted. Though Bank of Canada officials typically speak on the record as if they care only about controlling inflation, they may in fact care about influencing real activity in the economy, in part because of the influence of Keynesian ideas. Figure 14.8 shows a plot of the

actual bank rate (the Bank of Canada's target rate) over the period 1991–2011, and the bank rate predicted by Rudebusch's Taylor rule. The rule in fact fits the data for Canada reasonably well. However, what Rudebusch says the Bank of Canada should do is not quite what the Bank does. During the early 1990s Rudebusch would have called for an easier monetary policy, and from 2000–2008 for a tighter policy.

An interesting feature of Figure 14.7 is that, at the time in early 2009 when the bank rate reaches its lowest value of 0.25%, the Rudebusch recommendation would be to have a negative bank rate. Indeed, the predicted bank rate from the Rudebusch Taylor rule is about –3.5% at its lowest. Of course, we know that the nominal interest rate cannot be negative, that is, this is a circumstance in which a recommended policy is thwarted by the zero lower bound—the liquidity trap case.

So what is to be done in a case like this? As was discussed in this chapter, the central bank has no power to ease policy through a reduction in its target interest rate, so one possibility is for the central bank to do nothing and let fiscal policy take the lead. But there are other policies the central bank might pursue other than changes in its policy rate, particularly during a financial crisis. One such policy is for the central bank to step into its role as lender of last resort to financial institutions, which is part of what the Bank of Canada and other central banks did in the recent financial crisis.

A policy the Bank of Canada did not follow during the financial crisis, except perhaps in a relatively minor way, was quantitative easing (QE), discussed in Chapter 12. However, the Federal Reserve System in the United States implemented very-large-scale QE programs that more than tripled the asset holdings of the U.S. central bank over a three-year period beginning in late 2008. Recall that quantitative easing involves open market purchases of long-term government debt or other long-maturity assets, rather than the purchase of short-term government debt as in conventional monetary policy.

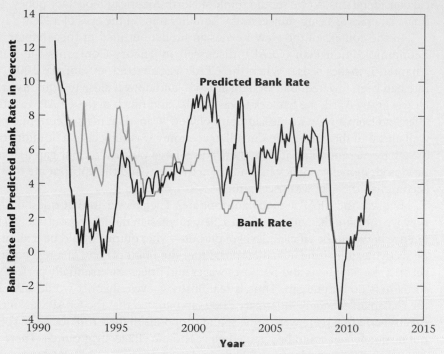

FIGURE 14.8

The Bank of Canada's Target Interest Rate, and Predictions of a Taylor Rule

A Taylor rule fit to U.S. data does a fairly good job of filling the behaviour of the Bank of Canada. Note that the predicted bank rate is negative in 2009. Desired policy, according to the Taylor rule, could not be implemented in 2009 because of the zero lower bound.

Source: Adapted from the Statistics Canada CANSIM database, Series v122530, v1992067, v41690973.

One argument that was used for QE during the financial crisis, particularly among central bankers in the United States, was based on pictures like Figure 14.8. Assuming that monetary policy was being conducted appropriately before the financial crisis, the fitted Taylor rule tells us how the central bank's policy rate should be set in a way consistent with past behaviour. For Canada, Figure 14.8 tells us that, during 2009, the bank rate should have been negative. But the bank rate cannot be negative, so if the Bank could somehow ease policy in another way, that would be appropriate. The Fed, in a situation like the Bank of Canada faced in 2009, decided to implement QE. Fed officials argued that they could reduce long-term interest rates by purchasing long-term assets and thereby reduce the output gap.

What is wrong with that argument? Unfortunately, the New Keynesian models that formed the framework that was guiding many central bankers did not have the financial detail necessary to evaluate the effects of QE, and whether it would work as intended. This is one way in which macroeconomists and policymakers missed the boat. This experience points out the need for more macroeconomic research on central banking and the effects of various kinds of central bank asset purchases on market interest rates and economic activity.

[10]See G. Rudebusch, 2009, "The Fed's Monetary Policy Response to the Current Crisis," www.frbsf.org/publications/economics/letter/2009/el2009-17.html

the Bank and the Fed from taking their policy rates to zero were some minor technical considerations, so we should think of North American monetary policy during the financial crisis as being subject to the liquidity trap, in the eyes of a New Keynesian.

In the context of the New Keynesian model outlined in this chapter, Canada's Economic Action Plan (CEAP), discussed in Theory Confronts the Data 5.3 in Chapter 5, makes sense. When the CEAP was enacted, in January 2009, the bank rate had been lowered, but was still at 1.5%, and not yet close to liquidity-trap range. However, by April, the bank rate was 0.25%, and much of the CEAP was still to take effect, so from a New Keynesian point of view, Canadian macroeconomic policy was well ahead of the curve. The Canadian economy was subject to a liquidity trap, from a New Keynesian point of view there was a large positive output gap that needed to be closed, monetary policy had no room to move, and the appropriate tool to use to accomplish the goal was fiscal policy.

But was the CEAP actually appropriate? The answer to that question hinges on how we measure the output gap. In a New Keynesian model, the output gap is the difference between the efficient level of output—what output would be if all prices were perfectly flexible—and actual output. From the point of view of a real business cycle theorist, for all intents and purposes wages and prices are essentially perfectly flexible, so there is no output gap. Thus, a real business cycle theorist would have looked at the Canadian economy in January 2009, and argued that the CEAP was unnecessary, except perhaps if there were some sound proposals in the CEAP for more spending on public goods that could be justified on economic efficiency grounds. There is further discussion of this in Macroeconomics in Action 14.2.

Criticisms of Keynesian Models

Critics of Keynesian sticky wage and sticky price models argue that these models fall short in several respects. First, as we have already pointed out, the New Keynesian model does not fully replicate the key business cycle regularities, in particular it does not explain why observed average labour productivity is procyclical. Second, critics of New Keynesianism argue that the theory underlying sticky wage and sticky price models is poor or nonexistent. In sticky wage models, it is argued that the nominal wage is fixed because of long-term labour contracts, but the model does not take explicit account of the reasons that firms and workers write such contracts. To properly understand why wages might be sticky and exactly how this matters for macroeconomic activity, we need to be explicit in our theories about the features of the world that are important to labour contracting and to show how a model with such features explains reality. Finally, the predictions of sticky price models do not fit all of the observed features of observed price-setting, as discussed in Macroeconomics in Action 14.3.

Menu cost models were a response to some of the criticisms of Keynesian sticky price models. In menu cost models, firms face explicit costs of changing prices, firms maximize profits in the face of these costs, and the result is that prices are, in fact, sticky and the models have implications much like those of our New Keynesian model. However, menu cost models have certainly not been immune from criticism. Some economists argue that the costs of changing prices are minuscule compared with

Casual observation tells us that some prices appear to be quite sticky. For example, the prices of newspapers and magazines tend to remain fixed for long periods of time. As well, there are some prices that clearly change frequently. The prices of fresh produce change week-to-week in the supermarket, and the prices of gasoline posted by gas stations can change on a daily basis. However, to evaluate the importance of Keynesian sticky price models, it is important to quantify the degree of price stickiness for a broad array of consumer goods. If there is little actual price stickiness for the average good or service in the economy, then price stickiness will be relatively unimportant in contributing to business cycles and the nonneutrality of money. As well, we would like to know whether the pattern of price changes we observe in the economy is consistent with the type of price stickiness that Keynesian theorists typically build into their models.

Until recently, economists had not gathered comprehensive evidence on the nature of price changes across the economy's goods and services. However, Mark Bils and Peter Klenow[11] gained access to U.S. Bureau of Labour Statistics data on the prices of goods and services that was previously unavailable to researchers. Their findings are surprising. Bils and Klenow found that for half of the goods and services in their data set, prices changed every 4.3 months or less, which is a much lower frequency of price changes than indicated by previous studies. While this does not entirely preclude significant effects from the sticky price mechanism for business cycles and the nonneutrality of money, it raises questions about previous results in Keynesian macroeconomics that would have exaggerated Keynesian sticky price effects.

Another feature of the data that Bils and Klenow find is that the rates of change in prices for particular goods and services are far more variable than is consistent with sticky price models. In a typical sticky price model, of the type in common use by Keynesian researchers, a shock to the economy that causes prices to increase will lead to staggered price increases over time, as individual firms do not coordinate their price increases. As a result, the rate of change in the price of an individual good or service should be persistent over time, and not very volatile, but this is not so in the data.

The work of Bils and Klenow points up key faults in the sticky price models typically used in practice. Their work does not definitively resolve issues about the value of Keynesian business cycle models relative to the alternatives, but Bils and Klenow have cast doubt on whether the sticky price mechanism is of key importance in understanding business cycles and how monetary policy works.

---

[11]M. Bils and P. Klenow, 2004, "Some Evidence on the Importance of Sticky Prices," *Journal of Political Economy* 112, 947–985.

the short-run costs of changing the quantity of output. Consider the case of a restaurant. On the one hand, the cost of changing menu prices is the cost of making a few keystrokes on a computer keyboard, and then running off a few copies of the menu on the printer in the back room. Indeed, a restaurant will be printing new menus frequently anyway, because restaurant patrons tend to spill food on the menus. On the other hand, if the restaurant wants to increase output in response to higher demand, it will have to move in more tables and chairs and hire and train new staff. Why would the restaurant want to change output in response to a temporary increase in demand rather than just increasing prices temporarily?

The questions we have raised above help in framing the debate on whether Keynesian sticky wage and sticky price models on the one hand, or flexible-wage-and-price business cycle models on the other, are more useful. As we saw in Chapter 13, flexible-wage-and-price models in general have quite different implications for the role of fiscal and monetary policy than does the New Keynesian model, with the real business cycle model, for example, implying that government intervention is detrimental. However, in the Keynesian coordination failure model (an equilibrium business cycle model) active government stabilization policy could be justified in the absence of sticky wages and prices.

The reader may wonder at this point why we should study different business cycle models that appear to have contradictory implications. The reason is that business cycles can have many causes, and each of the business cycle models we have examined contains an element of truth that is useful in understanding why business cycles occur and what, if anything, can or should be done about them.

This chapter completes our study of the macroeconomics of business cycles in closed economies. We go on in Chapters 15 and 16 to study macroeconomics in an open-economy context.

Chapter Summary

- A New Keynesian model was constructed in which the price level is sticky in the short run and the central bank manipulates the money supply so as to maintain a target interest rate. Otherwise, the model is identical to the monetary intertemporal model of Chapter 12. Price stickiness implies that the goods market and labour market need not clear in the short run, though the money market does clear.

- Monetary policy is not neutral in the New Keynesian model. A decrease in the central bank's target interest rate, brought about by an increase in the money supply, will increase output, employment, consumption, investment, and the real wage.

- Under either monetary policy shocks or shocks to the demand for investment goods, the New Keynesian model replicates most of the key business cycle facts from Chapter 3, but the price level is not countercyclical in the model, and average labour productivity is countercyclical rather than procyclical, as it is in the data.

- Though some markets do not clear in the short run and the economy does not achieve a Pareto-optimal outcome, in the long run prices will adjust so that economic efficiency holds. Keynesians argue that the long run is too long to wait and that better results can be achieved through monetary and fiscal policy intervention in the short run in response to shocks to the aggregate economy.

- Aggregate stabilization through monetary policy has different effects from fiscal policy stabilization. Monetary policy stabilization achieves the same result that would occur in the long run when prices adjust, in terms of real economic variables, but fiscal policy stabilization alters the mix of public versus private spending in the goods market.

- Changes in total factor productivity have very different effects in the New Keynesian model than in the real business cycle model of Chapter 13. In the New Keynesian model, a positive productivity shock has no effect on output in the short run, and employment falls.

- The nominal interest rate cannot fall below zero, which may constrain monetary policy. At the zero lower bound, there is a liquidity trap and monetary policy is ineffective. However expansionary fiscal policy works in a liquidity trap just as it does away from the zero lower bound.

- Some economists find the assumptions made in sticky price and sticky wage Keynesian models implausible, and empirical evidence on the behaviour of individual prices seems inconsistent with some elements of Keynesian models.

Key Terms

menu cost models: Sticky price models with explicit costs of changing prices.

natural rate of interest: The real interest rate that would be determined in equilibrium when all prices and wages are flexible.

output gap: The difference between actual aggregate output and the efficient level of aggregate output.

Keynesian transmission mechanism for monetary policy: The real effects of monetary policy in the Keynesian model. In the model, money is not neutral, because an increase in the money supply causes the real interest rate to fall, increasing the demand for consumption and investment, and causing the price level to increase. The real wage then falls; the firm hires more labour; and output increases.

stabilization policy: Fiscal or monetary policy justified by Keynesian models, which acts to offset shocks to the economy.

Questions for Review

1. Are Keynesian business cycle models still used? If so, what for?

2. What is the key difference between the New Keynesian model and the models studied in Chapter 11?

3. Which markets clear in the New Keynesian model? Which do not?

4. How is monetary policy determined in the New Keynesian model? What is the central bank's target, and what does the central bank control directly?

5. Why is monetary policy not neutral in the New Keynesian model? What are the effects of a change in the central bank's target interest rate?

6. How does the New Keynesian model fit the key business cycle facts from Chapter 3?

7. What happens in the long run in the New Keynesian model?

8. How do Keynesians justify intervention in the economy through monetary and fiscal policy?

9. How does monetary policy stabilization differ from fiscal policy stabilization?

10. Explain the differences in how the New Keynesian model and the real business cycle model respond to changes in total factor productivity.

11. What happens when the money supply increases in a liquidity trap?

12. In the New Keynesian model, does a liquidity trap imply that no economic policy can close a positive output gap?

13. What are the faults of the New Keynesian model?

Problems

1. Suppose government spending increases temporarily in the New Keynesian model.
   a. What are the effects on real output, consumption, investment, the price level, employment, and the real wage?
   b. Are these effects consistent with the key business cycle facts from Chapter 3? What does this say about the ability of government spending shocks to explain business cycles?

2. In the New Keynesian model, suppose that supply is initially equal to demand in the goods market and that there is a negative shock to the demand for investment goods because firms anticipate lower total factor productivity in the future.
   a. Determine the effects on real output, the real interest rate, the price level, employment, and the real wage if the government did nothing in response to the shock.
   b. Determine the effects if monetary policy is used to stabilize the economy, with the goal of the central bank being zero economic efficiency.
   c. Determine the effects if government spending is used to stabilize the economy, with the goal of the fiscal authority being economic efficiency.
   d. Explain and comment on the differences in your results among parts (a), (b), and (c).

3. Suppose that the goal of the fiscal authority is to set government spending so as to achieve economic efficiency, while the goal of the monetary authority is to achieve stability of the price level over the long run. Assume that the economy is initially in equilibrium and that there is then a temporary decrease in total factor productivity. Show that there are many ways in which the fiscal and monetary authority can achieve their separate goals. What could determine what fiscal and monetary policy settings are actually used in this context? Discuss.

4. Some macroeconomists have argued that it would be beneficial for the government to run a deficit when the economy is in a recession, and a surplus during a boom. Does this make sense? Carefully explain why or why not, using the New Keynesian model.

5. In the New Keynesian model, how should the central bank change its target interest rate in response to each of the following shocks? Use diagrams, and explain your results.
   a. There is a shift in money demand.
   b. Total factor productivity is expected to decrease in the future.
   c. Total factor productivity decreases in the present.

6. Suppose that the central bank sets its interest rate target to achieve efficiency in response to temporary shocks to total factor productivity. Using diagrams, determine what the economy's responses will then be to the total factor productivity shocks. How will this differ from what happens in a real business cycle model? Explain your results, and discuss the implications for what the data can reveal about what is the better business cycle model: the real business cycle model or the New Keynesian model.

7. In the New Keynesian model, suppose that in the short run the central bank cannot observe aggregate output or the shocks that hit the economy. However, the central bank would like to come as close as possible to economic efficiency. That is, ideally the central bank would like the output gap to be zero. Suppose initially that the economy is in equilibrium with a zero output gap.
   a. Suppose there is a shift in money demand. That is, the quantity of money demanded increases for each interest rate and level of real income. How well does the central bank perform relative to its goal? Explain using diagrams.
   b. Suppose that firms expect total factor productivity to increase in the future. Repeat part (a).

c. Suppose that total factor productivity increases in the current period. Repeat part (a).

d. Explain any differences in your results in parts (a)–(c), and explain what this implies about the wisdom of following an interest rate rule for the central bank.

8. Suppose, in the sticky price model, that there is deficient financial liquidity, as we studied in Chapter 13, and that there is a positive output gap. What will be the effect of a reduction in the central bank's target interest rate? Construct a diagram, and explain your results. What would the appropriate monetary policy be?

9. Suppose that consumption expenditures and investment expenditures are very inelastic with respect to the real interest rate. What does this imply about the power of monetary policy relative to fiscal policy in closing a positive output gap? Explain your results with the aid of diagrams.

Part 6

International Macroeconomics

Because of globalization—the continuing integration of world markets in goods, services, and assets—international factors are increasingly important for the performance of the domestic economy and for the conduct of fiscal and monetary policy. In this part, we will study models of open economies in which there is trade between the domestic economy and the rest of the world. We will use these models in Chapter 15 to study the benefits from international trade, the effects of changes in world prices and interest rates, the determinants of the current account surplus, and the implications of current account deficits. In Chapter 16, we will examine the role of money in the world economy, the determination of exchange rates, the effects of fixed and flexible exchange rates, and the implications of shocks occurring abroad for domestic business cycles.

15 International Trade in Goods and Assets

Our goal in this chapter will be to extend the models developed in Chapters 5, 9, and 11 so that we can address issues in international macroeconomics. Until now, we have looked at closed-economy macroeconomic issues by using closed-economy models, but for many interesting macroeconomic problems, we must do our analysis in an open-economy context. This chapter will be confined to issues relating to real international macroeconomics. In Chapter 16, we will address the monetary side of international interaction.

International trade is of key importance for Canada, as is reflected by the fact that in 2011, exports of goods and services were 31.1% of GDP, and imports were 32.4% of GDP. Thus, the volume of trade between Canada and the rest of the world is close to three times the volume of trade (as a fraction of GDP) between the United States and its trading partners. Just as trade is important for Canada, international trade in goods and assets has become increasingly important in the twentieth and twenty-first centuries for the world as a whole. This growth in world trade has occurred for two reasons. First, the costs of transporting goods and assets across international boundaries have fallen dramatically, permitting a freer flow of international trade. Second, government-imposed barriers to trade, such as import quotas, tariffs, and restrictions on international financial activity, have been relaxed. A relaxation of trade restrictions was carried out under the General Agreement on Tariffs and Trade (GATT) between 1947 and 1995, when the GATT framework was replaced by the World Trade Organization. Trade restrictions have also been reduced through regional agreements, for example, the Canada–U.S. Free Trade Agreement (1989), the North American Free Trade Agreement (NAFTA) (1994), and the European Union (EU). Given the critical nature of trade for Canada and the increasing importance of trade in the world economy, we must understand its implications for domestic macroeconomic activity.

In this chapter, we will study the importance for domestic aggregate economic activity of trade with the rest of the world in goods and assets. We are interested particularly in how the current account surplus and domestic output, employment, consumption, and investment are affected by events in the rest of the world. Throughout this chapter, we will confine attention to small open-economy models, which are models in which actions by consumers and firms in the domestic economy will have no collective effect on world prices. Some countries are clearly small relative to the rest of the world, such as New Zealand, Singapore, and Luxembourg, and for these countries it is clear that the small open-economy assumption is quite realistic. Canada is also sufficiently small in most respects that for macroeconomic analysis the small open-economy assumption is a good one. However, for large countries, such as the United States, Germany, or Japan, which play a particularly important role in the world economy, the assumption of price-taking on world markets is perhaps less plausible. There are three reasons why using small open-economy models to explain events in large open economies is a useful approach. First, small open-economy models are relatively simple to work with; for example, it is easy to modify closed-economy models so as to construct small open-economy models. Second, many of the conclusions we derive from small open-economy models will be identical to the ones we would obtain in more complicated large open-economy models. Third, as time passes, the small open-economy assumption becomes more realistic for such countries as Germany, Japan, and the United States. Given development in the rest of the world, GDP in these countries relative to GDP in the rest of the world falls, and it becomes a closer approximation to the truth that these countries are price-takers in world goods and asset markets.

In this chapter, we will study three small open-economy models that build, respectively, on the one-period model in Chapter 5, the two-period model in Chapter 9, and the real intertemporal model in Chapter 11. The first model focuses on the determinants of domestic production and consumption of goods, and the volume of trade between the domestic economy and the rest of the world. This model will be used to study how the welfare of domestic consumers can be improved through free trade in goods with the rest of the world, and to study the effects of changes in world prices on domestic consumption, production, and the volume of trade.

In the second model, there are two periods, so that we can examine the impact of borrowing and lending between the domestic economy and the rest of the world. Here, we are primarily interested in the determinants of the current account surplus and the importance of the current account surplus in domestic policymaking. An important idea is that international borrowing and lending permits the smoothing of aggregate consumption over time for the domestic economy, just as a single consumer can smooth consumption by borrowing and lending.

In the third and final model, we include investment and production, so that we can study the relationships among domestic consumption, output, investment, government spending, and the current account balance. This model is used to examine the relationship between the current account deficit and the government budget deficit, and we can apply this analysis to understanding the observed relationship between the two deficits in Canada. We also will examine the role of investment in determining the current account deficit, and we will address to what extent a current account deficit is good or bad for a nation's welfare.

A Two-Good Model of a Small Open Economy

The first international model we will consider is closely related to the one-period model we constructed in Chapter 5, and the analysis we developed there will also be useful here. However, we will use this international model for quite different purposes—to understand why countries trade and the primary determinants of the volume of trade. This is a model of a **small open economy (SOE)**. The economy is small, in the sense that economic activity in this country does not affect the world prices of goods. That is, the firms and consumers in this economy are both individual price-takers—they treat market prices as being given—and collective price-takers—their collective actions have no effect on the world prices for goods. The economy is also open, in that we will explore the consequences of trade between this economy and the rest of the world. Until now, we have considered macroeconomic models of closed economies where there is no trade with the rest of the world.

In the SOE, two goods are produced and consumed, which we will call good a and good b. From the viewpoint of people in the SOE, the price of good a in terms of good b, denoted by TOT_{ab}, is given. This price is the **terms of trade** or the **real exchange rate**, since TOT_{ab} is the rate at which the residents of the SOE can trade good b for good a on world markets. The model will tell us under what conditions the SOE will import good a and export good b, or export good a and import good b.

Allowing the two goods in the model, a and b, to stand in for all of the goods produced and consumed in the economy is clearly an important simplification. A given country will import and export many different kinds of goods, and so assuming that there are only two goods may seem unrealistic. For many countries, however, the assumption of two broad categories of goods fits the facts of their trade patterns well. For example, New Zealand's exports are primarily agricultural products, and its main imports are manufactured goods. Similarly, Kuwait exports crude oil and imports manufactured goods. For Canada, the story is somewhat more complicated, as we import and export goods that may appear to be the same. For example, a good portion of trade between Canada and the United States is in automobiles. The Ford Motor Company assembles cars in Oakville, Ontario, for export to the United States, and it also builds cars in Detroit, Michigan, for export to Canada. For our purposes, however, it will prove convenient to think of exports and imports as different goods. However, note that most of the trade between Canada and the United States in automobiles is explained by factors quite specific to the nature of production in the auto industry. These factors will be unimportant for the issues we want to address.

The SOE has a production possibilities frontier (*PPF*), which describes the combinations of good a and good b that the SOE can produce, and this *PPF* is depicted in Figure 15.1. The *PPF* is similar to the ones that we constructed in Chapter 5, where we considered the combinations of consumption and leisure that could be produced in a closed economy. We will not formally derive the *PPF* for the SOE in the figure as we did in Chapter 5, but we can give some intuition for why it has the shape that it does. In the SOE, goods a and b are produced by using labour and capital. At point A on the *PPF* in the figure, only good a is produced; at point B only good b is produced. Now, consider what happens if we begin at point *B* and move along the *PPF* toward point *A*. As we do so, more of good *a* is produced, and less of good *b*, with labour and capital being reallocated from production of good *b* to production of good *a*. Since the *PPF* represents combinations of goods *b* and *a* that can be produced *efficiently* in the SOE, when labour and capital are reallocated from production of good *b* to production of good *a*, these factors of production will be those that are most productive at the margin in producing good *a* relative to good *b*. Thus, the *PPF* is not very steep at point *B*, as only a small amount of good *b* is sacrificed at the margin to obtain another unit of good *a*. As we move down the *PPF* from point *B* to point *A*, however, the *PPF* becomes steeper, as the labour and capital reallocated from production of good *b* to production of good *a* become relatively more productive at the margin in industry *b* than in industry *a*, and we need to sacrifice more of good *b* at the margin to obtain another unit of *a*. Recall that the slope of the *PPF* is equal to minus the marginal rate of transformation, which is denoted by $MRT_{a,b}$. The marginal rate of transformation, $MRT_{a,b}$, is the quantity of good *b* that must be forgone in the economy if another unit of good *a* is produced. At point *D* in Figure 15.1, $MRT_{a,b}$ is minus the slope of a tangent to the *PPF*. Thus, as for the *PPF* in Chapter 5, the marginal rate of transformation increases as we move down the *PPF* from point *B* to point *A*. That is, the *PPF* is concave.

The residents of the SOE consume only goods *a* and *b*, and we will assume that we can capture their preferences by using the representative consumer device, as in Chapter 4. That is, there is a representative consumer in the SOE whose preferences are represented by indifference curves, as in Figure 15.2. As we assumed in Chapter 4, the representative consumer prefers more to less and has a preference for diversity, so that the indifference curves in Figure 15.2 slope downward and are convex. Further, goods *a* and *b* are both normal, in that an increase in income, holding prices constant, will imply that domestic consumption of both goods increases.

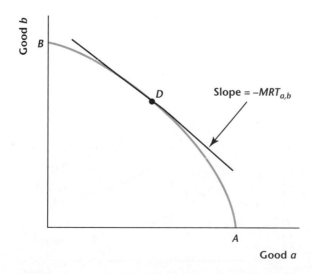

FIGURE 15.1

Production Possibilities Frontier for the SOE

The figure depicts the production possibilities frontier (*PPF*) for the SOE, a small open economy. The slope of the *PPF* is minus the marginal rate of transformation, and the *PPF* is concave.

COMPETITIVE EQUILIBRIUM IN THE SOE WITHOUT TRADE

Now that we know the basic elements of the SOE, given by the production possibilities frontier and the representative consumer's indifference curves, our first goal will be to understand what determines the pattern of trade in the SOE. That is, we want to know what factors determine whether the SOE imports *a* and exports *b*, or vice versa, and how this is important for the welfare of consumers in the SOE.

To show the effects of trade in the SOE, we want to first determine the characteristics of a competitive equilibrium if the SOE could not engage in trade. Just as in Chapter 5, a competitive equilibrium for this economy will be Pareto-optimal, and the competitive equilibrium quantities of goods *a* and *b* produced and consumed are determined by the point at which an indifference curve is tangent to the *PPF*. That is, the competitive equilibrium is point *A* in Figure 15.3. Recall that, at the competitive equilibrium point *A*, the marginal rate of substitution of good *a* for good *b* is equal to the marginal rate of transformation, or

$$MRS_{a,b} = MRT_{a,b},$$

since the marginal rate of substitution is minus the slope of the indifference curve at point *A*, and the marginal rate of transformation is minus the slope of the *PPF* at point *A*. Further, the equilibrium price of good *a* relative to good *b*, or p_{ab}, is equal to minus the slope of a line tangent to the indifference curve and the *PPF* at point *A*. This is because, first, in equilibrium the representative consumer optimizes by setting

$$MRS_{a,b} = p_{ab}. \qquad (15.1)$$

FIGURE 15.2

Indifference Curves of the Representative Consumer in the SOE

The indifference curves of the representative consumer in the SOE are downward-sloping and convex.

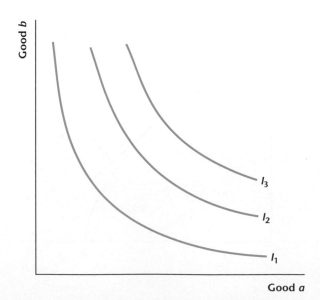

Good b

I_3

I_2

I_1

Good a

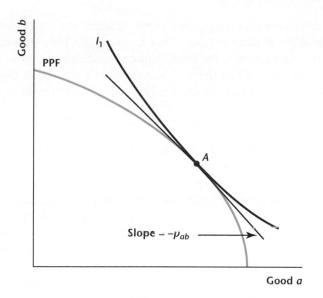

FIGURE 15.3

Equilibrium in the SOE with No Trade

If there is no trade in the SOE, equilibrium is determined by the tangency between the production possibilities frontier and an indifference curve for the representative consumer. In equilibrium, the slope of the *PPF* is equal to minus the price of good *a* relative to good *b*.

Recall from Chapter 4 that consumer optimization implies that a consumer will set the marginal rate of substitution of one good for another equal to the price of one good relative to the other, which implies that Equation (15.1) holds in this model in equilibrium. Second, optimization by firms will imply that

$$MRT_{a,b} = p_{ab}. \tag{15.2}$$

This second condition holds for the following reason. The marginal rate of transformation, $MRT_{a,b}$, tells us how many units of good *b* must be given up to produce one additional unit of good *a*, while p_{ab} is the price that can be received in the market for one unit of good *a* in units of good *b*. If $MRT_{a,b} < p_{ab}$, then a firm could profit by taking capital and labour from the production of good *b* and producing good *a*, whereas if $MRT_{a,b} > p_{ab}$, then a firm could profit by taking capital and labour from the production of good *a* and producing good *b*. Therefore, profit maximization implies that Equation (15.2) holds in equilibrium.

THE EFFECTS OF TRADE ON THE SOE

We now know the characteristics of a competitive equilibrium in the SOE in the case in which there is no trade with the rest of the world. Of course, our objective is to show the determinants of the pattern and volume of trade between the SOE and the rest of the world, and to show how trade affects welfare. Thus, at this stage, we will suppose that the SOE can trade with the rest of the world at world prices given by TOT_{ab}; that is, the relative price of good *a* in terms of good *b* is now determined on world markets, rather than in domestic markets in the SOE. Recall that the SOE is a price-taker on world markets, so that economic activity in the SOE will not affect the terms of trade TOT_{ab}.

Trade opens up consumption opportunities not available to the representative consumer in the SOE in the absence of trade. That is, in equilibrium, the representative consumer need no longer consume the consumption bundle produced in the SOE, as was the case in Figure 15.3. When the SOE can trade with the rest of the world, the terms of trade will determine what is produced. Thus, optimization by firms implies that

$$MRT_{a,b} = TOT_{ab},$$

so that the quantities of goods a and b produced in the SOE are given by point D in Figure 15.4, where the slope of DE is equal to $-TOT_{ab}$. The quantity of good a produced is a_1, and the quantity of good b produced is b_1. To determine what is consumed in a competitive equilibrium with trade, we will think of the consumption bundle produced in the SOE as being an endowment available to the consumer, which will then determine the representative consumer's budget constraint. Essentially, the representative consumer will receive what is produced as income, through wages and the dividends distributed by firms. Then, if the consumer is endowed with a_1 units of good a and b_1 units of good b, and can exchange good b for good a on world markets at the rate TOT_{ab}, the terms of trade, then the representative consumer's budget constraint will be given by

$$TOT_{ab} q_a + q_b = TOT_{ab} a_1 + b_1. \tag{15.3}$$

In the consumer's budget constraint, Equation (15.3), q_a and q_b are the quantities of good a and good b consumed, respectively, and the budget constraint is written in terms of good b. Thus, the quantity on the right-hand side of Equation (15.3) is the representative consumer's income in terms of good b, and the quantity on the left-hand side is the consumer's expenditure on goods a and b, again in units of good b. The budget constraint is then line DE in Figure 15.4.

FIGURE 15.4

Production and Consumption in the SOE with Trade
When the SOE trades with the rest of the world at market prices given by the terms of trade, consumption occurs at point E and production occurs at point D, with the slope of DE equal to minus the terms of trade.

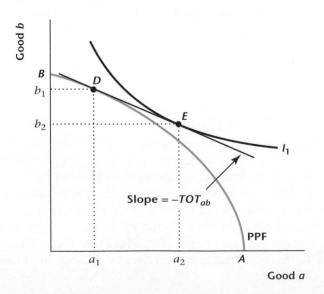

Next, the representative consumer will optimize, just as in Chapter 4, by choosing the consumption bundle where an indifference curve is tangent to his or her budget constraint. In Figure 15.4, the consumer chooses point E, where the quantity of good a consumed is $q_a = a_2$, and the quantity of good b consumed is $q_b = b_2$. In the figure, the SOE will then be an importer of good a and an exporter of good b, since $a_2 > a_1$ and $b_2 < b_1$. The value of imports, in units of good b, is $TOT_{ab}(a_2 - a_1)$, and the value of exports is $b_1 - b_2$. Recalling the definition of the current account surplus from Chapter 2, which is net exports plus net factor payments from abroad, the current account surplus in the SOE, in units of good b, will be the value of exports minus the value of imports (since net factor payments are zero here), which is

$$CA = b_1 - b_2 - TOT_{ab}(a_2 - a_1).$$

But from the consumer's budget constraint, Equation (15.3), we then have $CA = 0$; that is, the current account surplus is zero. This is a one-period model in which the SOE cannot borrow and lend abroad, which implies that the current account surplus *must* be zero in equilibrium. In this model, the value of goods exported will always equal the value of goods imported in equilibrium.

The pattern of trade between the SOE and the rest of the world is determined in part by two factors. The first is the principle of **comparative advantage**. In Figure 15.4, the SOE imports good a and exports good b, so that the SOE tends to have a comparative advantage in producing good b. *Comparative advantage is determined by the slope of the production possibilities frontier.* The steeper the production possibilities frontier, the greater the SOE's comparative advantage in producing good b relative to good a, since more of good b needs to be sacrificed at the margin to produce another unit of good a. A steeper *PPF* will also imply that more of good b is produced and less of good a is produced when the SOE can trade with the rest of the world, and so there will be a tendency to export more of good b.

The second factor that determines the pattern of trade is consumer preferences. Even if the SOE has a strong comparative advantage in producing a good, if the representative consumer has a strong preference for that good, it could be imported rather than exported. The important characteristic of consumer preferences for determining the pattern of trade is the marginal rate of substitution, $MRS_{a,b}$. As $MRS_{a,b}$ increases, the indifference curves of the representative consumer become steeper, and the SOE will have a greater tendency to import good a and export good b.

An important result is that the representative consumer will always be better off with trade than without it. To show this, we will consider two cases. In the first case, the domestic price of good a in terms of good b (when there is no trade) is greater than the terms of trade, as in Figure 15.5. Here, when there is no trade, the consumption bundle produced and consumed is given by point A, but when the SOE is opened up to world trade, production occurs at point B, and the representative consumer chooses point D. The terms of trade are given by minus the slope of the line EF. Note that, with trade, the consumer is on a higher indifference curve; that is, indifference curve I_2 represents a higher level of welfare than indifference curve I_1. In the second case, as in Figure 15.6, the domestic price of good a in terms of good b (when there is no trade)

FIGURE 15.5

An Increase in Welfare when Good *a* Is Imported
When there is no trade, consumption and production occur at point *A*, but when the SOE trades with the rest of the world, production occurs at *B* and consumption at *D*. In this case, good *a* is imported, and welfare is higher with trade, as the representative consumer attains a higher indifference curve.

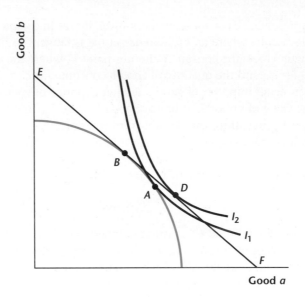

is smaller than the terms of trade. In this case, consumption and production when the economy is closed are at point *A*, but when the economy is open, production occurs at point *B* and consumption at point *D*. Again, the representative consumer's welfare improves with free trade. This result—trade increases opportunities and makes the nation better off—is a fundamental economic principle.

Our model captures the effects of trade on the *average* consumer, showing that trade always makes this average consumer (the representative consumer) better off.

FIGURE 15.6

An Increase in Welfare when Good *b* Is Imported
Here, in contrast to Figure 15.5, good *b* is imported when the SOE can trade with the rest of the world. Trade improves welfare, as the consumer attains a higher indifference curve.

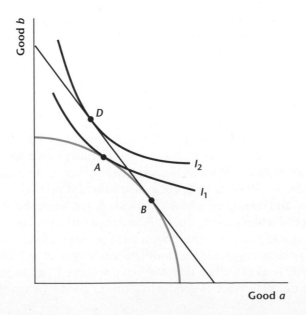

In practice, however, eliminating trade restrictions typically harms some people while benefiting others, though we argue the net effect on welfare is positive. For example, not all Canadian residents were in agreement that the Canada–U.S. Free Trade Agreement (1989) and the North American Free Trade Agreement (NAFTA) were good ideas. NAFTA tended to harm those industries in Canada for which Mexico and the United States had comparative advantages. In those industries, product prices and real wages tended to fall, and workers were displaced. However, in industries for which Canada has a comparative advantage relative to Mexico and the United States, prices and real wages tended to rise, and employment expanded. The fact that someone almost always stands to lose in circumstances in which trade restrictions are relaxed makes it difficult to pass laws that free up international trade. Also, when particular industries in the United States have been harmed by free trade, this has sometimes led to trade disputes with Canada, for example, trade disputes over lumber and agricultural products.

A CHANGE IN THE TERMS OF TRADE: EFFECTS ON PRODUCTION, CONSUMPTION, AND WELFARE

A key macroeconomic shock for an open economy is a change in the price of imports relative to the price of exports, that is, a change in the terms of trade. The terms of trade could move against a country if imports became more expensive relative to exports as, for example, in New Zealand if the prices of manufactured goods were to increase relative to the prices of agricultural goods. In this case, economic welfare would decrease in New Zealand. The terms of trade could also move in favour of a country if imports became cheaper relative to exports. This would happen in Kuwait if there were an increase in the relative price of crude oil, which would increase economic welfare for the residents of Kuwait. As we will show in this section, a change in the terms of trade has similarities to a change in total factor productivity in a closed economy, as considered in Chapter 5. This is because there will in general be income and substitution effects associated with a change in the terms of trade.

In an open economy, changes in the terms of trade will affect domestic production, domestic consumption, exports, and imports. In the model, we must consider the two cases where the terms of trade move against and in favour of the SOE. In the first case, the SOE imports good a before an increase in the terms of trade, and in the second, the SOE initially imports good b. This will matter for the results because of the effects on economic welfare, and because there will be a difference in income effects on consumption of both goods. In the first case, there will be a negative income effect on consumption and in the second case, a positive income effect. Substitution effects work in the same way in each case.

In Figure 15.7 we show the first case, where initially the consumption bundle produced is given by point A, and the initial terms of trade are given by the negative of the slope of a line tangent to point A. The initial consumption bundle is at point B, where this line is tangent to indifference curve I_1. With an increase in the terms of trade, production is at point D, where the terms of trade (minus the slope of a line tangent to the PPF at point D) is higher. Note that production of good a must increase, while production of good *b* decreases, as the relative price of good *a* has risen, encouraging more production of *a* and less of *b*. The new consumption bundle is given by point *E*, where in this case the representative consumer consumes less of good *a* and more of good *b*. In fact, the SOE now imports *b* and exports *a*.

We can separate the effect of the change in the terms of trade on consumption into income and substitution effects. In particular, if we draw a tangent to the initial indifference curve I_1 in Figure 15.7, the slope of which is minus the new terms of trade, then this line will be tangent to I_1 at point *F*, and the substitution effect of the change in the terms of trade is the movement from *B* to *F*. That is, the substitution effect is for consumption of good *a* to decrease and that of good *b* to increase. There is a negative income effect, which is the movement from *F* to *E*. Recall that we assumed that both goods are normal, so that the income effect is for consumption of goods *a* and *b* to decrease.

On net, then, the consumption of good *a* must decrease, and the consumption of good *b* may increase or decrease, depending on the size of the income effect relative to the substitution effect. Production of good *a* increases, and production of good *b* decreases. The quantity of a good imported is given by consumption minus production. Therefore, we can conclude that the quantity of good *a* imported must decrease, as consumption decreases and production increases. For good *b*, however, there is an ambiguous effect on the quantity exported, as production decreases, but consumption may increase or decrease. However, note that if substitution effects dominate income effects, then the quantity of good *b* exported will rise.

In terms of the value of imports and exports, in units of good *b*, the results are ambiguous. The value of imports is

$$\text{Quantity of imports} \times TOT_{ab},$$

FIGURE 15.7

An Increase in the Terms of Trade When Good *a* Is Initially Imported

The terms of trade increase, with the price of good *a* increasing relative to good *b*. When good *a* is initially imported, welfare falls. The substitution effect on consumption is the movement from *B* to *F*, and the income effect is the movement from *F* to *E*. Consumption of good *a* falls, and consumption of good *b* may rise or fall. The production point moves from *A* to *D*.

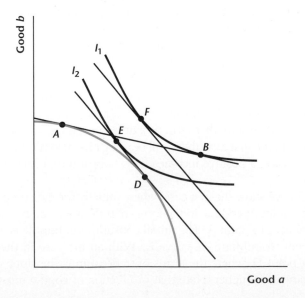

and though we know that the quantity of imports decreases, the terms of trade, TOT_{ab}, increases, and so the product of quantity and terms of trade could either increase or decrease. Since we have already determined that the quantity of good b exported could increase or decrease, we know that the value of good b exported, in units of good b (which is the same thing), could increase or decrease. Though the effects on the value of exports and imports are ambiguous here, we know that there will be no effect on the current account surplus from a change in the terms of trade, since the current account surplus is always zero in this model.

Now consider the second case, in Figure 15.8, where there is an increase in the terms of trade when the SOE initially imports good b and exports good a. Initially, production of goods a and b is given by point A, with consumption at point B. The slope of the line AB is equal to minus the initial terms of trade. When the terms of trade increases, the production point shifts to D, with domestic output of good a rising and output of good b falling, just as in the first case. The representative consumer now chooses point E, with the slope of DE equal to minus the new terms of trade. Here, there is a positive income effect on consumption of goods a and b. Separating the effect of the change in the terms of trade into income and substitution effects, the substitution effect is the movement from B to F, while the income effect is the movement from F to E. As before, the substitution effect leads to an increase in consumption of good b and a decrease in consumption of good a. Here, however, the income effect leads to an increase in consumption of both goods a and b (again, under the assumption that both goods are normal). Therefore, consumption of good b must rise, but consumption of good a may rise or fall.

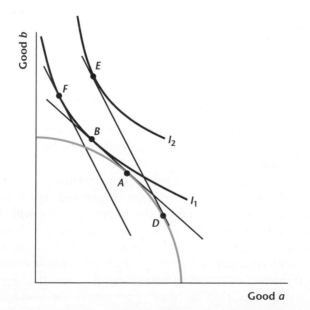

FIGURE 15.8

An Increase in the Terms of Trade When Good *b* Is Initially Imported

An increase in the terms of trade increases welfare when good b is initially imported. The substitution effect on consumption is the movement from B to F, and the income effect is the movement from F to E. Consumption of good a may rise or fall, and consumption of good b rises. Production moves from A to D.

Good a

In the second case, then, imports of good *b* rise, since less is produced and more is consumed as well. Exports of good *a* may rise or fall, since more is produced, but consumption may increase or decrease. What happens to the value of imports and exports is also ambiguous, but again there will be no effect on the current account surplus, which is always zero.

Note that what happens to the representative consumer's welfare differs between the first case and the second. When good *a* is initially imported, and the terms of trade change so that the relative price of good *a* increases, the representative consumer will be worse off. That is, in Figure 15.7, the representative consumer initially chooses a consumption bundle on indifference curve I_1 and chooses a consumption bundle on a lower indifference curve, I_2, when the terms of trade change. This is the case where the terms of trade turn against the SOE, in the sense that the goods that are being sold abroad (good *b*) become cheaper relative to the goods that are purchased abroad (good *a*). In Figure 15.8, however, the change in the terms of trade is favourable to the SOE, in that the representative consumer is on a higher indifference curve after the terms of trade change. In this case, imported goods (good *b*) become cheaper relative to exports, and this is good for economic welfare in the SOE.

Shocks to the terms of trade can be an important cause of business cycles. Macroeconomics in Action 15.1 contains some evidence of the relative importance of shocks to the terms of trade for business cycles in open economies.

A Two-Period Small Open-Economy Model

The previous one-period model is useful for understanding the benefits from trade and the effects of changes in the terms of trade. However, some important issues in international macroeconomics are related to intertemporal choices. In particular, we would like to study the determinants of the current account surplus. We know from Chapter 2 that a current account surplus must always be reflected in an excess of domestic savings over domestic investment and by an increase in the net claims of domestic residents on foreign residents. Thus, to analyze the current account, we need a model in which, at minimum, consumers make borrowing/lending and consumption–savings decisions. A useful model of borrowing/lending and consumption–savings decisions is the two-period model we developed in Chapter 9. Here, we will modify that model by having a single representative consumer, capturing the average behaviour of all domestic consumers, and we will allow borrowing and lending between domestic and foreign residents.

We will suppose that there is a single representative consumer in the SOE and that this consumer lives for two periods, the current and future periods. For the representative consumer, income is exogenous in both periods, with *Y* denoting current real income and *Y'* future real income. The consumer also pays lump-sum taxes to the government of the SOE of *T* in the current period and *T'* in the future period. Since the SOE is a small open economy, the actions of the representative consumer will not affect the world real interest rate, and so we will assume that the consumer in the SOE can borrow and lend as much as he or she wants at the world real interest rate, *r*.

Since the terms of trade cause changes in the makeup of domestic consumption and production, and they affect aggregate economic welfare, shocks to the terms of trade could be sources of business cycles. Indeed, one of the shocks to the economy that we have previously analyzed as a shock to total factor productivity—a change in the relative price of energy—can also be modelled as an adverse change in the terms of trade for most industrialized countries. That is, most industrialized countries are net importers of oil, so if the world price of crude oil increased relative to other world prices, this would imply that the terms of trade had turned against those countries. For example, the large increases in the world price of crude oil that took place in 1973, 1979–1980, 2000–2001, and 2005–2008 were negative terms of trade shocks for Germany, Great Britain, Japan, and the United States, among other countries. For Canada, the effects of an increase in the world price of oil are somewhat more complicated than in these other industrialized countries, in particular because Canada is a net exporter of energy products. Thus, when the world price of oil increases, this is a favourable terms of trade shock for Canada: oil and natural gas production, especially in Alberta, becomes more profitable, and the governments of Alberta and Canada receive higher tax revenues. However, there are negative effects for Canada: energy-using industries, particularly the manufacturing industry centred in eastern Canada, become less profitable. On net, Canada still suffers from an increase in the world price of oil, though the net negative effect on Canadian welfare is smaller than it once was, because Canada's net

exports of energy commodities and products have increased more than sixfold since 1973.[1]

Canada is not as sensitive to changes in the terms of trade as some other countries are, in spite of the fact that exports and imports represent a relatively large fraction of GDP in Canada. Canadian imports and exports have become more diversified across a wide array of goods and services than was once the case. In particular, Canada relies less on exports of raw materials (lumber, metals, wheat) and more on exports of semi-processed and manufactured goods than in the past. In some countries, there is a dependence on one commodity as a major export. For example, Kuwait is primarily an exporter of crude oil, so that fluctuations in the world price of this one commodity can have dramatic effects for the economy of Kuwait.

For all countries of the world, how important are terms of trade shocks for business cycles? Using a real business cycle model, and data from many countries, Enrique Mendoza finds that half of the variability in real GDP is explained by terms of trade shocks.[2] This is a highly significant finding, and it indicates that accounting for shocks from abroad is very important for analyzing business cycles. If attention is confined to a closed-economy analysis of the factors determining business cycles, we lose at least half of the picture.

---

[1] See G. Stuber, 2001, "The Changing Effects of Energy Price Shocks on Economic Activity and Inflation," *Bank of Canada Review*, Summer, pp. 3–14.

[2] See E. Mendoza, 1993, "The Terms of Trade, the Real Exchange Rate, and Economic Fluctuations," *International Economic Review* 36, 101-138.

Just as in Chapter 9, the representative consumer chooses consumption in the current and future periods, C and C', respectively, to make himself or herself as well off as possible given his or her lifetime budget constraint

$$C + \frac{C'}{1 + r} = Y - T + \frac{Y' - T'}{1 + r} \tag{15.4}$$

In Figure 15.9 we show the consumer's lifetime budget constraint as the line AB. Point E is the endowment point, and the representative consumer chooses point D on his or her lifetime budget constraint, which is the point where an indifference curve is tangent to the lifetime budget constraint. In the figure, consumption in the first and second periods is C^* and C'^*, respectively. Private saving in the current period is then given by $S_p = Y - T - C = Y - T - C^*$, and so in the figure the consumer saves a positive amount.

Now, to complete the model, we need to describe the behaviour of the government in the SOE. Government spending in the current and future periods is G and G', respectively, and these quantities are exogenous. The government then sets current and future taxes on the representative consumer, T and T' respectively, to satisfy the government's present-value budget constraint

$$G + \frac{G'}{1 + r} = T + \frac{T'}{1 + r} \tag{15.5}$$

Then, the quantity of government saving is given by $S_g = T - G$, and in this economy where there is no investment, the current account surplus in the current period, from Chapter 2, is

$$CA = S - I = (S_p + S_g) = Y - C - G.$$

FIGURE 15.9

**The Two-Period Small
Open Economy Model**
The representative
consumer's budget
constraint is *AB*, the
endowment point is *E*, and
the consumer chooses
point *D*.

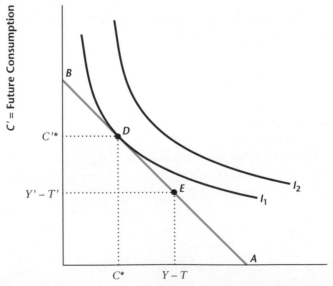

In this model, we are interested in understanding the key factors that affect the current account surplus, *CA*, which are the following:

- *Current period income.* Recall from Chapter 9 that an increase in current income will increase current consumption and future consumption, and current consumption increases by less than the increase in current income, because the consumer wants to smooth consumption over his or her lifetime. Therefore, an increase in Y will lead to an increase in the current account surplus. Because of the consumption-smoothing motive, a country that experiences an increase in current income will save more by lending abroad, and this is reflected in an increase in the current account surplus.

- *Current government spending.* An increase in government spending leads, given the government's present-value budget constraint, Equation (15.5), to an increase by an equal amount in the present value of taxes for the consumer. Therefore, the consumer's lifetime wealth falls by the increase in government spending. We know then that the consumer's current consumption will fall, but by less than the increase in government spending, since the consumer will smooth consumption between the current and future periods. Therefore, the current account surplus will decrease with an increase in government spending.

- *Taxes.* Given the Ricardian equivalence theorem from Chapter 9, changes in taxes will have no effect on aggregate consumption, since consumers simply adjust savings to account for the change in their future tax liabilities. As consumption is unaffected, there will be no effect on the current account surplus. Just as in the closed-economy model in Chapter 9, however, if there are significant credit market imperfections, then a change in current taxes will in general affect current consumption, and this will matter for the trade balance.

- *The real interest rate.* Recall from Chapter 9 that the effect of a change in the real interest rate on current consumption will depend on whether the representative consumer is initially a net borrower or a net lender. If the consumer is a net lender, then current consumption may rise or fall when the real interest rate rises, since there is a positive income effect on consumption, and the substitution effect implies that current consumption falls and future consumption rises. If the consumer is a net borrower, the income and substitution effects work in the same direction, and an increase in the real interest rate will cause a decrease in current consumption. In general, then, if income effects are not too large, an increase in the real interest rate will cause a decrease in current consumption and an increase in the current account surplus.

Production, Investment, and the Current Account

Although the previous model yields useful insights concerning the role of the current account in national consumption smoothing, and some explanations for the behaviour of the current account, we need to understand more completely the relationship between the current account surplus and events in the domestic economy. In this section, we will study a model based on the real intertemporal model in Chapter 11, which includes production and investment behaviour.

| THEORY CONFRONTS THE DATA | **15.1** | *Is a Current Account Deficit a Bad Thing?* |

It may seem that a current account deficit is undesirable, since if a country runs a current account deficit, it is borrowing from the rest of the world and accumulating debt. However, just as for individual consumers, lending and borrowing is the means by which a nation smooths consumption. If a given country runs current account deficits when aggregate income is low, and runs current account surpluses when aggregate income is high, this allows the residents of that country to smooth their consumption over time. This state of affairs is preferable to one where the country always has a current account surplus of zero and consumption is as variable as income.

Thus, there are good reasons for expecting that countries should run current account surpluses in good times and current account deficits in bad times. Government policy aimed at correcting this tendency could be counterproductive. But do countries actually smooth consumption over time as theory predicts? In Figure 15.10 we show the deviations from trend in real GDP and net exports for

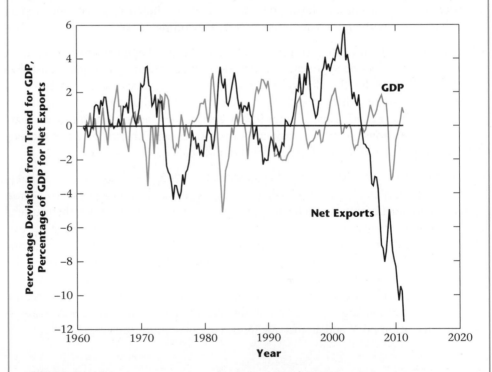

FIGURE 15.10

Deviations from Trend in Net Exports and GDP in Canada, 1961–2011

There does not appear to be evidence of national consumption smoothing for Canada, as deviations from trend in net exports and GDP are negatively correlated. This may be due to synchronization in business cycles across countries.

Source: Adapted from the Statistics Canada CANSIM database, Series v1992060, v1992063, v1992067.

Canada over the period 1961–2011. For real GDP, the deviations are percentage deviations from trend, and net exports are plotted as a percentage of GDP. Note in the figure that there is some tendency for net exports to be above (below) trend when real GDP is below (above) trend, so that deviations from trend in GDP and net exports are negatively correlated. This is the opposite of consumption smoothing, in that Canada tended to export goods and lend more abroad when output was low, and to borrow more abroad when output was high.

Why would the data not exhibit obvious evidence of consumption smoothing when economic theory tells us that nations should smooth consumption by lending (borrowing) abroad when income is high (low)? An explanation may be that the timing and severity of business cycles in the rest of the world and in Canada are similar. For example, the data in Figure 15.10 are consistent with consumption smoothing if, before 1970, output tended to be high (low) in Canada when output was high (low) in the rest of the world, and business cycles were of about the same severity in Canada and in other countries. Then, all countries would want to borrow (lend) at the same times, and interest rates would adjust so that net exports in Canada would be unrelated to GDP. However, after 1970, if business cycles coincided in Canada and the rest of the world, but the upturns and downturns were more severe in the rest of the world, Canada could in equilibrium be lending to other countries when its own output was low and borrowing from other countries when its own output was high.

In this model, just as in the previous one, the SOE faces a given world real interest rate. As in Chapter 11, output supply is given by the upward-sloping curve Y^s in Figure 15.11. Here, however, we assume that goods can be freely traded with foreign countries, and so from the income–expenditure identity, $Y = C + I + G + NX$, the demand for goods also includes net exports, NX. In Figure 15.11, the world real interest rate is r^*, which then determines the domestic demand for consumption goods and investment goods. If total domestic demand, $C + I + G$, exceeds the domestic supply of goods at the world real interest rate, then goods are imported and net exports are negative; and if domestic demand is less than the domestic supply of goods at the world real interest rate, then goods are exported and net exports are positive. The equilibrium quantity of net exports is the quantity NX that implies that the downward-sloping output demand curve, Y^d, intersects the Y^s curve in Figure 15.11 at the world real interest rate, r^*. We have depicted a case in Figure 15.11 where $NX > 0$, that is, if there were no trade in goods with the rest of the world, then the output demand curve would be Y_2^d, to the left of Y_1^d, and the domestic real interest rate would be r_c. In general, it could be that $r^* < r_c$ or $r^* > r_c$. Given the world real interest rate, r^*, the quantity of aggregate output produced in the SOE is Y_1, but in this case the domestic demand for goods, $C + I + G$, is less than Y_1. The domestic demand for goods, $C + I + G$, is sometimes referred to as **absorption**, as this is the quantity of aggregate output that is absorbed by the domestic economy. The quantity NX is then the current account surplus, or net exports. Recall that the current account surplus is net exports plus net factor payments from abroad, but net factor payments from abroad equal zero in this model. In Figure 15.11,

FIGURE 15.11

A Small Open-Economy Model with Production and Investment

The world real interest rate, determined on world credit markets, is r^*. Equilibrium output is Y_1, and there is a current account surplus. If there were no trade, the output demand curve shifts to Y_2^d, and the domestic real interest rate would be r_c.

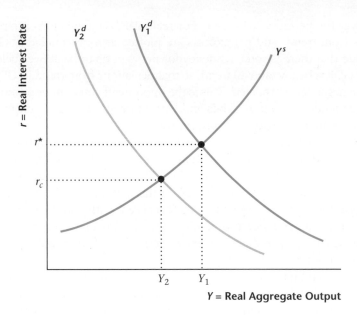

the SOE has a positive current account surplus; that is, $NX > 0$, which implies the SOE is accumulating assets from the rest of the world.

THE EFFECTS OF AN INCREASE IN THE WORLD REAL INTEREST RATE

Since the model here is essentially identical to the real intertemporal model with a real interest rate fixed on world credit markets, it is straightforward to use the model to analyze the effects of particular shocks to the domestic economy. The output demand curve and output supply curve will shift in the same ways in response to shocks as in the real intertemporal model of Chapter 11, with the only modification in the analysis being that NX adjusts so that the output demand curve intersects the output supply curve at the world real interest rate, r^*. The first experiment we will carry out is to look at the effects in the model of an increase in the world real interest rate. Such a change could have many causes; it could result from, for example, a negative total factor productivity shock in other countries (recall our analysis of domestic total factor productivity shocks from Chapter 11).

Suppose, in Figure 15.12, that the world real interest rate increases from r_1 to r_2. Then, the current account surplus increases, causing the output demand curve to shift to the right from Y_1^d to Y_2^d. Domestic investment must decrease, as the real interest rate increases, but domestic consumption may rise or fall, as there is a negative effect from the increase in r and a positive effect from the increase in Y.

These results have the interesting implication that a negative total factor productivity shock abroad, which would *decrease* foreign output and cause the world real interest rate to rise, will also cause an *increase* in domestic output. Therefore, a foreign shock of this sort, when transmitted to the domestic economy, will not cause output in the domestic economy and in the rest of the world to move together.

The effects of the world real interest rate on the current account surplus is related to the "world savings glut," an issue discussed in Macroeconomics in Action 15.2.

A TEMPORARY INCREASE IN GOVERNMENT EXPENDITURE AND THE EFFECTS ON THE CURRENT ACCOUNT AND DOMESTIC OUTPUT

For our second experiment, we will consider the effects of an increase in domestic government expenditure. As we will see, some of the increase in output that occurs in a closed economy is dissipated in an open economy due to the fact that net exports fall. There is more crowding out of spending on domestic goods, and the government expenditure multiplier is smaller in an open economy.

Suppose that G increases. Just as in Chapter 11, there is a negative income effect on leisure for the representative consumer, because of the increase in the present value of taxes, and so labour supply will increase, shifting the output supply curve rightward from Y_1^s to Y_2^s. There is a shift to the right in the output demand curve resulting from the net increase in output demand caused by the increase in G. The current account surplus then adjusts so that the output demand curve ultimately shifts from Y_1^d to Y_2^d (see Figure 15.13). As in Chapter 11, the initial shift in the output supply curve is small relative to the shift in the output demand curve (because the increase in government spending is temporary, so that the effects on lifetime wealth are small). Therefore, the current account surplus must decrease.

Now, relative to what occurred in a closed economy in Chapter 11, where we considered an increase in G, the increase in output is limited by the rightward shift in the output supply curve by the size of the income effect on labour supply of the increase in taxes. Recall in Chapter 11 that there was an additional increase in labour supply due to intertemporal substitution in the closed economy. Therefore, output

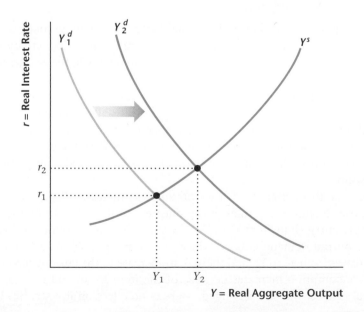

FIGURE 15.12

An Increase in the World Real Interest Rate

An increase in the world real interest rate from r_1 to r_2 causes an increase in output and an increase in the current account surplus.

FIGURE 15.13

**An Increase in Government
Spending**

An increase in current
government spending initially
shifts the output demand
curve and the output supply
curve to the right (the output
demand curve shifts to
a greater extent). Output
increases and the current
account surplus falls.

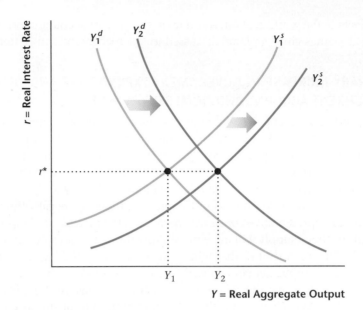

increases by less for a given increase in government spending in an open economy, and the government expenditure multiplier is smaller in the open economy due to the fact that net exports fall. Effectively, some of the increased demand for goods coming from the government sector is satisfied through higher imports. Because the interest rate is unchanged in Figure 15.13, investment does not change, but consumption and net exports both fall.

THE EFFECTS OF INCREASES IN CURRENT AND FUTURE TOTAL FACTOR PRODUCTIVITY

In Chapters 5 and 11, we showed how total factor productivity matters for domestic real aggregate activity. An increase in current total factor productivity in a closed economy increases labour demand, and it leads to increases in the real wage, employment, and output, and a decrease in the real interest rate. An anticipated increase in future total factor productivity increases the current demand for investment goods and consumption goods in a closed economy, and it will increase current aggregate output and the real interest rate. In a small open economy, some of these results are somewhat different, as the real interest rate is determined on the world credit market. We will also be able to determine the effects of total factor productivity shocks on the current account.

Suppose first that current total factor productivity increases. Recall from Chapter 11 that this causes a shift to the right in the output supply curve. In Figure 15.14, the output supply curve shifts from Y_1^s to Y_2^s. Then, the current account surplus increases, shifting the output demand curve to the right from Y_1^d to Y_2^d. As a result, aggregate output increases from Y_1 to Y_2, and there is an increase in the current account surplus. Domestic consumption increases because of the increase in real income, but given that the real interest rate is unchanged, there is no effect on investment. In a closed economy, the real interest rate falls when total factor productivity increases, causing increases in C and I. However, the real interest rate is determined on world markets here, and so an increase in total factor productivity in the domestic economy will have no effect on the real interest rate. Typically, though, different countries will simultaneously experience increases in total factor productivity at the same time, as changes in production technology tend to be transmitted across international borders. Therefore, an increase in total factor productivity domestically would also tend to be associated with a decrease in the world real interest rate and increases in domestic consumption and investment.

Next, suppose an increase in future total factor productivity is anticipated. Recall from Chapter 11 that this implies that the representative firm will expect an increase in the future marginal product of capital, which will cause an increase in the demand for investment goods. Further, the representative consumer will anticipate higher future income as the result of the increase in future total factor productivity, and this will cause an increase in the demand for current consumption goods. The increase in the demand for current consumption and investment goods shifts the output demand curve in Figure 15.15 rightward, but there will be a corresponding decrease in the current account surplus so that demand equals supply for domestically produced goods. In equilibrium, aggregate output remains fixed at Y_1, but the current account surplus then falls.

The above provides a potential explanation for some features of the data. During the 1980s and 1990s there were investment booms in Canada, coupled with trade surpluses. These periods are consistent with the dominant shock being an anticipated increase in future total factor productivity, which is reflected in an increase in investment over these periods of time.

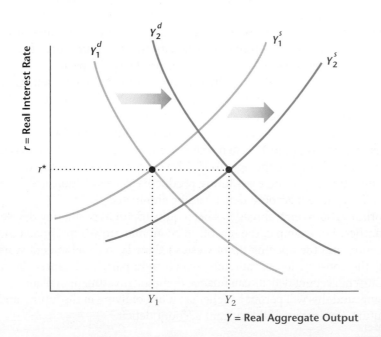

FIGURE 15.14
An Increase in Current Total Factor Productivity
An increase in current total factor productivity shifts the output supply curve to the right. Aggregate output increases, and the current account surplus also increases.

FIGURE 15.15

An Increase in Future Total Factor Productivity

An anticipated increase in future total factor productivity initially shifts the output demand curve.

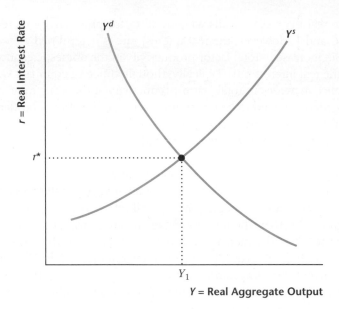

CURRENT ACCOUNT DEFICITS, CONSUMPTION, AND INVESTMENT

We have already discussed how a current account deficit need not be a bad thing, as current account deficits help domestic consumers smooth consumption over time. A current account deficit can also serve another purpose, to finance domestic investment, as was the case when we considered the effects of an anticipated shock to future total factor productivity in the previous subsection. When a country runs a current account deficit so as to finance an increase in domestic investment expenditures, this increases the capital stock and future productive capacity. In the future, the current account deficit can be eliminated because of this higher productive capacity.

In Figure 15.16, the SOE is initially running a current account deficit. The output demand curve is Y_1^d, the output supply curve is Y_1^s, and current output is Y_1. Now, if the current account deficit is financing domestic investment, in the future the capital stock, K, will be higher. This will increase the demand for labour and shift the output supply curve to the right, to Y_2^s. Then, the current account surplus increases, shifting the output demand curve to the right to Y_2^d. Thus, if the current account deficit finances domestic investment, this increases future productive capacity, more goods can be sold abroad, and the current account deficit can be eliminated.

Historically, borrowing abroad has been quite useful in promoting development in some countries. For example, the takeoff in economic growth in Canada in the nineteenth century and the opening up of western Canada to development were spurred in part by the construction of railroads, which were partially financed by borrowing abroad. Current account deficits can finance domestic investment in plants, equipment, and housing, and this will permit a higher standard of living in the future, and possibly cause a future elimination of the current account deficit.

The term "savings glut" appears to have been coined by Ben Bernanke, the current Chair of the Federal Reserve Board in the United States, to refer to the pattern of current account surpluses and level of real interest rates that materialized in the world after 2000.[3] In the United States, net exports and the current account surplus[4] have decreased through most of the period since 1990. Canada has not had the same experience as the United States, but there has been a dramatic decrease in the current account surplus in Canada since the beginning of the recent recession, as can be seen from the graph for net exports (most of the current account surplus) in Figure 15.10. In the world as a whole, a current account deficit in one country has to be matched by current account surpluses in other countries at a given point in time, due to basic accounting principles. A current account deficit in Canada, for example, implies that other countries must be accumulating claims on Canadians, so that the rest of the world must be running a current account surplus relative to Canada. In the world as a whole, the current account surplus must be zero, if we measure it properly.

In 2011, there was wide dispersion across countries in the world in terms of current account surpluses, a situation that some economists refer to as "imbalance," though that word suggests that there is something wrong with this situation, which need not be the case. In absolute terms (not relative to GDP), the largest current account surpluses in the world were for China, Saudi Arabia, Germany, Japan, and Russia. The smallest current account surpluses (all negative numbers, running from smallest to largest) were for the United States, Italy, France, Turkey, and the United Kingdom. Ranking countries by the size of their current account surpluses, China is #1, the United States is #198 (last), and Canada is #190.[5]

In the world as a whole, countries with current account surpluses are lending to countries with current account deficits. Thus, China, Saudi Arabia, Germany, Japan, and Russia are lending countries that are extending credit to borrowing countries such as Canada, the United States, Italy, France, Turkey, and the United Kingdom.

What creates the wide dispersion in current account surpluses in the world? First, a country could be a borrower on world credit markets because of domestic factors. That country could have relatively low income compared to "normal," as is the case for Italy, France, Turkey, and the United Kingdom currently. That country could have relatively high government spending, as is the case in the United States, and Italy currently. That country could have an investment boom, as was the case in the United States since 1990 (a business investment boom followed by a residential construction boom) and before the financial crisis. We know from this chapter that lower aggregate income, higher government spending, and future increases in productivity that increase current investment, all reduce the current account surplus.

Second, a country could be a borrower on world credit markets because the world real interest rate is low, as has been the case since 2000, and even more so since the recent global financial crisis. We know from the last model in this chapter that a drop in the world real interest rate will reduce the current account surplus. Why is the world real interest rate low? Part of the reason is that countries which are lenders on world credit markets, particularly China, are saving a lot. If a country's citizens save more and consume less (for exogenous reasons), this works in a way identical to a decrease in government spending in the last model in this chapter, and acts to increase the current account surplus. When large countries, or many countries, save more, this will cause the world real interest rate to go down. Those saving countries become lenders on the world credit market. The "savings glut" refers to the large increase that has occurred in the world's savings, a large fraction of which is explained by the savings behavior of households in China, which is a very large economy.

The world savings glut which reduced world real interest rates, particularly after 2000, could in part be blamed for the financial crisis that began in the United States and spread worldwide. One of the principal causes of the financial crisis was incentive problems in the U.S. mortgage market, and in the market for sophisticated financial instruments. These incentive problems were accentuated by low

real interest rates, which increased the profit opportunities from financial misbehaviour. Therefore, international borrowing and lending, as reflected in current account surpluses and deficits, can be an important factor in domestic financial developments and for domestic business cycles.

---

[3] See "The World Savings Glut and the US Current Account Deficit," at www.federalreserve.gov/boarddocs/speeches/2005/200503102.

[4] In the United States, the current account surplus and net exports are roughly the same quantity. See Chapter 2 for a definition of the current account surplus.

[5] See www.cia.gov/library/publications/the-world-factbook/rankorder/2187rank.html.

This chapter explored the real macroeconomic implications of having trade in goods and assets among nations. In Chapter 16, we will integrate money into the third model that we studied in this chapter so as to understand the determination of nominal exchange rates, the importance of flexible and fixed exchange rates, and why capital controls are important for macroeconomic activity.

FIGURE 15.16

An Increase in the Capital Stock

The output supply curve shifts to the right, increasing output and potentially eliminating the current account deficit. Thus, investment financed by a current account deficit can eliminate the current account deficit in the long run.

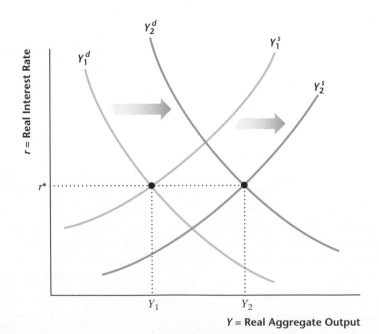

Chapter Summary

- In this chapter we studied the implications of international trade in goods and assets for domestic welfare, output, consumption, investment, and the current account surplus. We constructed three small open-economy models and showed how these models can be used to understand the importance of openness for the domestic economy. In a small open economy (SOE), domestic residents are price-takers with respect to the rest of the world

- The first model is one where two goods, *a* and *b*, are consumed and produced in an SOE. The relative price of good *a* in terms of good *b* is the terms of trade, or the real exchange rate, and this is the rate at which good *b* can be traded for good *a* on world markets.

- The representative consumer in the SOE is always better off by trading on world markets at the terms of trade than by not trading. In equilibrium, domestic production is determined by the condition that the marginal rate of transformation of good *a* for good *b* equals the terms of trade, and domestic consumption satisfies the property that the marginal rate of substitution of good *a* for good *b* equals the terms of trade.

- An increase in the terms of trade, which here means that good *a* becomes more expensive relative to good *b*, always implies that production in the SOE shifts away from production of good *b* and toward production of good *a*. However, whether the consumption of goods *a* or *b* increases or decreases depends on whether the SOE was an importer or exporter of good *a* before the change in the terms of trade and on income and substitution effects.

- The second model we considered was a two-period model of a SOE, where the representative consumer has exogenous income in the current and future periods, and the consumer pays taxes to the government in both periods. Government spending is exogenous in each period, and the government and the representative consumer can borrow and lend in the current period.

- In the model, the current account surplus increases whenever national saving increases. An increase in current income leads to an increase in the current account surplus in equilibrium, an increase in government spending leads to a decrease in the current account surplus, a change in taxes has no effect under Ricardian equivalence, and a change in the real interest rate has an indeterminate effect on the current account surplus.

- Current account deficits need not be a bad thing, as this implies borrowing abroad, which helps domestic consumers to smooth their consumption over time.

- In the third small open-economy model, we allowed for the determination of production and investment, with the domestic economy facing an interest rate determined on world markets. Here, the current account surplus is the difference between consumption and absorption, where absorption is the domestic demand for goods, or consumption plus investment plus government spending.

- An increase in the world real interest rate increases domestic output, reduces absorption, and increases the current account surplus.

- An increase in government spending in the current period increases domestic absorption and decreases the current account surplus. The increase in output is smaller than what occurs in a closed economy.

- An increase in current total factor productivity increases domestic output and increases the current account surplus, whereas an anticipated increase in future total factor productivity causes no change in current aggregate output and reduces the current account surplus.

- A current account deficit that finances investment increases the future capital stock and acts to increase future output and reduces the current account deficit in the future.

Key Terms

small open economy (SOE): An economy that trades with the rest of the world and for which the collective actions of domestic consumers and firms have negligible effects on prices on world markets.

terms of trade: The relative price at which imports trade for exports on world markets.

real exchange rate: The terms of trade.

comparative advantage: How efficient a country is at producing one good relative to another, as compared with the rest of the world. Comparative advantage is determined by the slope of the production possibilities frontier.

absorption: Consumption plus investment plus government expenditures; the quantity of domestically produced goods absorbed through domestic spending.

Questions for Review

1. What is a small open economy?

2. Why is it appropriate to use a small open-economy model to explain events in Canada?

3. In the first model in this chapter, with two goods, what are the conditions that determine production and consumption in the SOE when there is no trade?

4. What are the conditions that determine production and consumption in the SOE when there is trade with the rest of the world?

5. Are the SOE residents better or worse off when they can trade with the rest of the world? Why?

6. If the terms of trade increase and the SOE initially imports good a, what are the effects on consumption and production of goods a and b in the SOE?

7. If the terms of trade increase and the SOE initially imports good b, what are the effects on consumption and production of goods a and b in the SOE?

8. In the second model in this chapter, what are the four determinants of the current account surplus, and how does each of these determinants affect it?

9. Why could it be a good thing for a country to run a current account deficit?

10. What are the effects of an increase in the world real interest rate on output, absorption, and the current account surplus?

11. What are the effects of an increase in government expenditure on output, absorption, and the current account surplus?

12. What are the effects of an increase in current and future total factor productivity on output, absorption, and the current account balance?

13. If an increase in the current account deficit finances an increase in domestic investment, what implications does this have for the future performance of the economy?

Problems

1. Suppose that, in the model in which two goods, a and b, are produced domestically and traded internationally, the representative consumer's preferences change so that the marginal rate of substitution of good a for good b increases for each consumption bundle. That is, the

consumer is now less willing to give up good *a* in exchange for good *b*. Determine the effects of this change in preferences on the production of *a* and *b* in the SOE, on consumption of *a* and *b*, and on the quantities of *a* and *b* imported and exported. Explain your results.

2. Suppose there is an improvement in the technology for producing good *b* in the SOE. This implies that the marginal rate of transformation, $MRT_{a,b}$, increases for each quantity of good *a*. Determine the effects of this technology change on the consumption of *a* and *b*, the production of *a* and *b*, and the quantities of *a* and *b* imported and exported. Explain your results in terms of income and substitution effects, and interpret.

3. The government imposes a quota on imports. Determine the effect of this on production and consumption of goods *a* and *b* in the first model in this chapter. Also determine the effect on the consumer's welfare. Explain your results.

4. Assume a two-period model in which the representative consumer has income of 100 in the current period and income of 120 in the future period and faces a world real interest rate of 10% per period. The consumer always wants to set current consumption equal to future consumption, which implies perfect-complements preferences.
   a. Suppose current government expenditures are 15 and 20 in the future. Determine consumption in the current and future periods and the current account surplus. Draw a diagram to illustrate your results.
   b. Now suppose current government expenditures increase to 25, with everything else unchanged. Again, determine consumption in the current and future periods and the current account surplus, and show these in your diagram.
   c. Explain the difference in your results in parts (a) and (b).

5. Modify the second model in this chapter as follows: Suppose real interest rates are determined on world markets. The government can borrow and lend on world markets at the interest rate *r*, but the representative consumer lends at the interest rate *r* and borrows at the interest rate r^*, which is also determined on world markets. Assume that $r^* > r$, perhaps because of the costs of operating international banks that make loans to consumers.
   a. Suppose r^* increases, with *r* unchanged. Determine the effects on consumption in the current and future periods, and on the current account balance, and explain your results in terms of income and substitution effects.
   b. Now suppose the government cuts current taxes and increases future taxes, holding constant government spending in periods 1 and 2. Assume, before the tax cut is put into effect, that the current account surplus is zero. Determine the effects of the tax cut in period 1 on consumption in periods 1 and 2, the trade balance, and the welfare of the representative consumer. Explain your results.

6. Suppose, as in Chapter 10, that in the second model in this chapter there is limited commitment in the credit relationships between the small open economy and the rest of the world. Some portion of the nation's capital stock, denoted by K^c, is collateralizable on world markets. This collateralizable capital is illiquid in the current period and is valued at price *p* on world markets in the future period. Assume that borrowing by the SOE on world markets is limited by the value of collateralizable wealth in the future period. Now, suppose that *p* falls. How does this affect consumption in the SOE in the present and the future and the current account surplus? Explain your results with the aid of diagrams.

7. Use the third model in this chapter to answer these questions. The government in a small open economy is concerned that the current account deficit is too high. One group of economic advisers to the government argues that high government deficits cause the current

account deficit to be high and that the way to reduce the current account deficit is to increase taxes. A second group of economic advisers argues that the high current account deficit is caused by high domestic investment and proposes taxing domestic investment and returning these tax revenues to consumers as lump-sum transfers.

a. Which advice should the government take if its goal is to reduce the current account deficit? Explain.

b. Is the government's goal of reducing the current account deficit sensible? Why or why not? What will happen if the government takes the advice that achieves its goal, as in part (a)?

8. In Chapter 13, we studied how persistent total factor productivity shocks in a closed economy can provide an explanation for business cycles. In the third model studied in this chapter, determine the effects of a persistent increase in total factor productivity on domestic output, consumption, investment, and the current account surplus. Are the predictions of the model consistent with what you observe in Figure 15.10? Explain why or why not.

9. An interpretation of events after 2000 in the United States is that the current account surplus was negative after 2000 so as to finance domestic investment spending. This investment spending was generated by optimism about future prospects. In 2008, people became much more pessimistic about the future, and investment spending and GDP began to fall. In response, the U.S. government decided to increase government spending in 2009 so as to reduce the negative effect of the decline in investment spending on aggregate economic activity.

a. Use the third model in this chapter to explain exactly how this story works.

b. Will the increase in government spending actually be "stimulative," in that it increases aggregate output by a large amount?

c. Will the increase in government spending have unintended consequences in terms of effects on the current account surplus? Explain carefully, using diagrams.

Money in the Open Economy

Many issues in international macroeconomics can be well understood without the complication of monetary exchange in the picture, as we saw in Chapter 15. However, there are also many intriguing issues in international finance—particularly those involving the determination of nominal exchange rates, the effects of having flexible or fixed exchange rates, the transmission of nominal macroeconomic shocks among countries, the effects of capital controls, and the role of international financial institutions—that we need monetary models to understand. In this chapter, we will build on the third small open-economy model we studied in Chapter 15 to integrate money into a monetary small open-economy model that can address some key issues in international monetary economics.

We will first consider the notion of *purchasing power parity*, or the *law of one price*, which will be a cornerstone of the monetary small open-economy model in this chapter. Purchasing power parity would hold if the prices of all goods in the world economy were equal, corrected for nominal exchange rates, where a nominal exchange rate is the price of one currency in terms of another. Although there are economic forces that result in a long-run tendency toward purchasing power parity, in reality there can be fairly large and persistent deviations from purchasing power parity, some examples of which we will study in this chapter. However, although purchasing power parity may not be the best approximation to reality in the short run, it will prove to be very useful in simplifying the model used in this chapter.

The model we construct and put to work in this chapter builds on the model from Chapter 15 in the sense that the goods markets in the two models are identical. The model of this chapter will also have much in common with the monetary intertemporal model in Chapter 12. In particular, the monetary small open-economy model features a classical dichotomy, in that nominal variables—in this case, the price level and the nominal exchange rate—are determined independently of real variables. Further, money is neutral. This is a useful starting point for international monetary economics, since adding some of the frictions that we considered in the business cycle models of Chapters 13 and 14—sticky prices, New Monetarist frictions, and coordination failures—involves straightforward extensions of this basic framework.

The first experiments we will carry out with the model in this chapter will emphasize the effects of shocks from abroad under flexible and fixed nominal exchange rates. A flexible exchange rate is free to move according to supply and demand in the market for foreign exchange, whereas under a fixed exchange rate the domestic government commits in some fashion to supporting the nominal exchange rate at a specified value. A flexible exchange rate has the property that monetary policy can be set independently in the domestic economy, and the domestic price level is not affected by changes in foreign prices. Under a fixed exchange rate, however, the domestic central bank cannot control its money supply independently, and price level changes originating abroad are essentially imported to the domestic economy. Flexible and fixed exchange rate regimes each have their own advantages and disadvantages, as we will discuss.

Finally, we examine the effects of capital controls on the behaviour of the domestic economy. Capital controls are restrictions on the international flow of assets; such controls tend to dampen the fluctuations that result from some shocks to the economy. However, capital controls are detrimental, in that they reduce economic efficiency.

The Nominal Exchange Rate, the Real Exchange Rate, and Purchasing Power Parity

The model we will work with in this chapter is a monetary small open-economy model, which builds on the third small open-economy model of Chapter 15 and the monetary intertemporal model in Chapter 12. Key variables in this model will be the nominal exchange rate and the real exchange rate, which will be defined in this section. Further, in this section, we will derive the purchasing power parity relationship, which determines the value of the real exchange rate.

In the model in this chapter, just as in the monetary intertemporal model, all domestically produced goods sell at a price P, in terms of domestic currency. Foreign-produced goods sell at the price P^*, in terms of foreign currency. In the model, there is a market for foreign exchange, on which domestic currency can be traded for foreign currency, and we will let e denote the price of one unit of foreign currency in terms of domestic currency. That is, e is the **nominal exchange rate**. Therefore, if a domestic resident holding domestic currency wanted to buy goods abroad, assuming that foreign producers of goods will accept only foreign currency in exchange for their goods, one unit of foreign goods will cost eP^* in units of domestic currency. This is because the domestic resident must first buy foreign currency with domestic currency, at a price of e, and then buy foreign goods with foreign currency at a price of P^*. To give an example, suppose that a book in the United States costs five U.S. dollars, and that the exchange rate between Canadian and U.S. dollars is 1.5 Canadian dollars per U.S. dollar, that is, $e = 1.5$. Then, the cost of the book in Canadian dollars is $1.5 \times 5 = 7.50$.

Since the price of domestic goods in domestic currency is P, and the price of foreign goods in terms of domestic currency is eP^*, the real exchange rate (or the terms of trade), which is the price of foreign goods in terms of domestic goods, is

$$\text{Real exchange rate} \; = \; \frac{eP^*}{P}.$$

Now, suppose it is costless to transport goods between foreign countries and the domestic country and that there are no trade barriers, such as government-set import quotas and tariffs (import taxes). Then, if $eP^* > P$, it would be cheaper to buy goods domestically than abroad, so that foreign consumers would want to buy domestic goods rather than foreign goods, and this would tend to increase P. Alternatively, if $eP^* < P$, then foreign goods would be cheaper than domestic goods, and so domestic consumers would prefer to purchase foreign goods rather than domestic goods, in which case P would tend to fall. Thus, with no transportation costs and no trade barriers, we should expect to observe that

$$P \; = \; eP^*, \tag{16.1}$$

and this relationship is called the **law of one price**, or **purchasing power parity (PPP)**. This relationship is called the law of one price because, if it holds, the price of goods is the same, in terms of domestic currency, at home and abroad. Note that if purchasing power parity holds, then the real exchange rate is 1.

In the real world, we would not in general expect PPP to hold exactly if we measure P and P^* as the price levels in two different countries. Any measure of the price level, such as the consumer price index or the implicit GDP price deflator, includes the prices of a large set of goods produced and consumed in the economy. Some of these goods will be traded on world markets, such as agricultural commodities and raw materials, while other goods will only be traded domestically, such as local services like haircuts. Although we would expect a tendency for the law of one price to hold for goods that are traded internationally, we would not expect it to hold for nontraded goods. For example, crude oil can be shipped at a relatively low cost over large distances by pipeline and in large oil tankers. There is a well-organized world market for crude oil, so that crude oil sells almost anywhere in the world at close to the same price (plus transport costs). However, there is no world market in haircuts, as the cost of travelling to another country for a haircut is in most cases very large relative to the cost of the haircut. The law of one price should hold for crude oil but not for haircuts.

In general, there are strong economic forces that will tend to make market prices and nominal exchange rates adjust so that PPP holds. For example, if PPP does not hold, then even if there are large costs of transporting goods across countries, consumers will want to move to where goods are relatively cheaper, firms will want to move their production where goods are relatively more expensive, and ultimately we would expect PPP to hold over the long run. Unless it is very difficult to move goods, labour, and capital across international borders, purchasing power parity should hold, at least as a long-run relationship. Though PPP may be a poor description of short-run reality, as we will show in Theory Confronts the Data 16.1, and the adjustment to PPP may be quite slow, it will simplify our models considerably to make the PPP assumption, and this simplification will help us focus on the issues of this chapter.

Flexible and Fixed Exchange Rates

In addition to PPP, another important component of the monetary small open-economy model will be the exchange rate regime. As we will show, a key determinant of how the domestic economy responds to shocks, and an important factor for the conduct of domestic monetary and fiscal policy, is the set of rules for government intervention in foreign exchange markets. Roughly speaking, the polar extremes in foreign exchange market intervention are a **flexible exchange rate regime** and a **fixed exchange rate regime**. Currently, some countries conform closely to an idealized flexible exchange rate regime; some fix the exchange rate; and some mix the two approaches.

THEORY CONFRONTS THE DATA **16.1** *The PPP Relationship for the United States and Canada*

A case in which we might expect relatively small deviations from PPP involves the relationship between the United States and Canada. Historically, there has been a high volume of trade between these two countries. The U.S. and Canada signed a free trade agreement in 1989, which was replaced in 1992 by the North American Free Trade Agreement (NAFTA), which included Mexico. An earlier trade agreement was the Canada–U.S. Auto Pact, signed in 1965, which permitted the shipment of autos and auto parts across the Canada–U.S. border by manufacturers. Given the close proximity of Canada and the United States, and natural north–south transportation links, transportation costs between the U.S. and Canada are quite low. Not only are goods easy to move between these two countries, but NAFTA now permits freer movement of labour across the Canada–U.S. border as well. Capital is also relatively free to move between these two countries. Therefore, there are especially strong forces in place in the U.S.–Canada case that would cause us to be surprised if PPP did not apply, at least approximately.

In Figure 16.1 we show the real exchange rate, eP^*/P, for Canada versus the United States for the years 1947–2011. Here, e is the price of Canadian dollars in terms of U.S. dollars, P^* is the Canadian consumer price index, and P is the CPI in the United States. The real exchange rate has been scaled for convenience, so that its value is 100 in January 1956. Purchasing power parity predicts that the real exchange rate in the figure should be constant, but it is certainly not. In the figure, the real exchange rate has fluctuated significantly. The fluctuations are not small short-run fluctuations around a constant value but are more persistent in nature. Indeed, there appears to be no tendency for the real exchange rate to fluctuate more closely around some long-run value after the free trade agreement in 1989. Between 1989 and 2002, the real exchange rate decreased by more than 40%, and then increased by about 30% between 2002 and 2006 before decreasing again. If there are such large deviations from PPP for Canada and the United States, we should expect PPP relationships to be even more loose in the short run between the United States and other countries of the world.

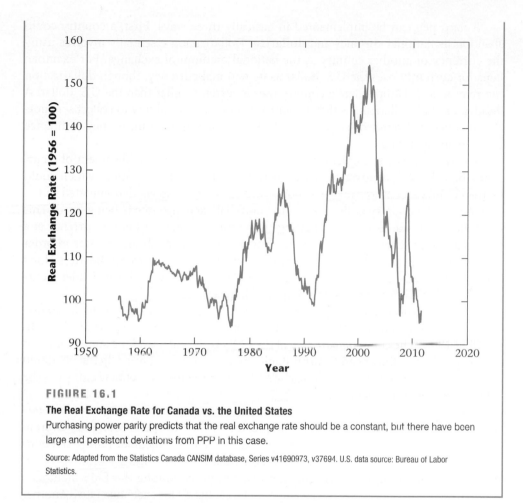

FIGURE 16.1

The Real Exchange Rate for Canada vs. the United States

Purchasing power parity predicts that the real exchange rate should be a constant, but there have been large and persistent deviations from PPP in this case.

Source: Adapted from the Statistics Canada CANSIM database, Series v41690973, v37694. U.S. data source: Bureau of Labor Statistics.

Under a flexible, or floating, exchange rate, there is no intervention by the domestic fiscal or monetary authorities to specifically target the nominal exchange rate, e. If the nominal exchange rate is truly flexible, it is free to move in response to market forces. Some countries with flexible exchange rates are India, South Korea, Brazil, Australia, New Zealand, Canada, and the United States. For reasons we will discuss below, essentially all countries care about short-run movements in their nominal exchange rate, and they will therefore, from time to time, intervene through monetary and fiscal policy to influence the value of the nominal exchange rate, even under a flexible exchange rate regime.

There are several different important fixed exchange rate systems, which can be roughly characterized as **hard pegs** and **soft pegs**. Under a hard peg, a country commits to a fixed nominal exchange rate relative to some other currency for the indefinite future. Under a soft peg, there is no long-term commitment to a particular value for the exchange rate, but the exchange rate can be fixed relative to another currency for long periods, with occasional **devaluations** (increases in the nominal exchange rate e) and **revaluations** (decreases in e).

A hard peg can be implemented in basically three ways. First, a country could abandon its national currency and **dollarize**. Dollarization essentially involves using the currency of another country as the national medium of exchange. For example, Ecuador currently uses the U.S. dollar as its national currency, though dollarization can refer to a situation where a country uses a currency other than the U.S. dollar. A disadvantage of dollarizing is that a country relinquishes its ability to collect seigniorage (a concept discussed in Chapter 12); that is, it cannot print money to finance government spending.

The second way to implement a hard peg is through the establishment of a **currency board**. With a currency board, there is a centralized institution, which could be the country's central bank, that holds interest-bearing assets denominated in the currency of the country against which the nominal exchange rate is being fixed. This institution then stands ready to exchange domestic currency for foreign currency at a specified fixed exchange rate, and it can buy and sell interest-bearing assets in order to carry out these exchanges. A country that currently uses a currency board is Hong Kong, which fixes its nominal exchange rate relative to the U.S. dollar. Under a currency board, a country retains its ability to collect seigniorage.

The third approach to implementing a hard peg is through agreement among countries to a common currency, as in the **European Monetary Union (EMU)**, established in 1999. The common currency of the EMU is the **euro**, and the supply of euros is managed by the **European Central Bank (ECB)**. The rules governing the operation of the ECB specify how the seigniorage revenue from the printing of new euros is to be split among the EMU members.

Soft pegs involve various degrees of commitment to a fixed exchange rate or to target bands for the exchange rate. For example, under the **European Monetary System (EMS)**, which was established in 1979, preceding the EMU, member European countries committed over the short run to target their exchange rates within specified ranges. In this arrangement, coordination was required among the EMS members, and there were periodic crises and changes in target bands for exchange rates. Another soft peg was the **Bretton Woods arrangement**, the rules for which were specified in an agreement negotiated at Bretton Woods, New Hampshire, in 1944. The Bretton Woods arrangement governed post–World War II international monetary relations until 1971. Under Bretton Woods, the United States fixed the value of the U.S. dollar relative to gold by agreeing to exchange U.S. dollars for gold at a specified price. All other countries then agreed to fix their exchange rates relative to the U.S. dollar. This was thus a modified gold standard arrangement. For reasons we will discuss later in this chapter, soft peg arrangements have tended to be unstable, typically collapsing and being replaced by alternative systems—as happened with the EMS and the Bretton Woods arrangement.

A key international monetary institution that plays an important role in exchange rate determination is the **International Monetary Fund (IMF)**, the framework for which was discussed at Bretton Woods in 1944, with the IMF established in 1946. The IMF currently has 185 member countries, and it performs a function in some ways similar to that carried out by a central bank relative to the domestic banks under its supervision. That is, the IMF plays the role of a **lender of last resort** for its member countries, just as a central bank is a lender of last resort for domestic financial institutions (as we will discuss in Chapter 17). However, IMF lending comes with strings attached; typically, the loans are conditional on a member country submitting to a program set up by the IMF, which typically specifies corrective policy actions.

A Monetary Small Open-Economy Model with a Flexible Exchange Rate

Now that we have discussed some of the institutional arrangements governing the determination of exchange rates, we can proceed to work with a monetary small open-economy model in which there is international monetary interaction. This model—in part based on the monetary intertemporal model in Chapter 12—is a small open-economy model that essentially involves adding a money market to the third real small open-economy model in Chapter 15. In this model, we will assume for now that the exchange rate is flexible, and we will study the properties of a fixed exchange rate system in the next section.

In Figure 16.2 we show the goods market for the monetary small open-economy model, which is identical to the goods market for the third real small open-economy model of Chapter 15. The curve Y^d is the output demand curve, which is downward-sloping because of the negative effect of the real interest rate on the demand for consumption and investment goods, and Y^s is the output supply curve, which is upward-sloping because of the intertemporal substitution effect of the real interest rate on labour supply. Just as in Chapter 15, the small open-economy assumption implies

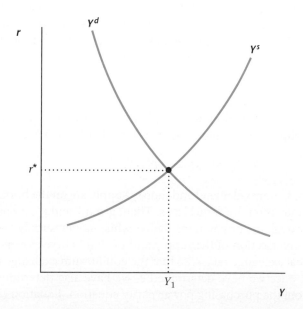

FIGURE 16.2

The Goods Market in the Monetary Small Open-Economy Model
The goods market in this model is identical to the goods market in the real small open-economy model with investment in Chapter 15. The world real interest rate is r^* and equilibrium real output is Y_1.

that domestic firms and consumers are collectively price-takers on world markets. In equilibrium, the income–expenditure identity holds, so that $Y = C + I + G + NX$. Given that the domestic economy is, as a whole, a price-taker on world markets, any output not absorbed domestically as C, I, or G is exported (if net exports are positive) or any excess of domestic absorption over domestic output is purchased abroad (if net exports are negative).

We will assume that purchasing power parity holds, so that

$$P = eP^*, \tag{16.2}$$

where P is the domestic price level, e is the price of foreign exchange in terms of domestic currency, and P^* is the foreign price level. Though we know from above that the PPP relationship typically does not hold in the short run, assuming PPP simplifies our model greatly and essentially implies that we are ignoring the effects of changes in the terms of trade (discussed in Chapter 15), which would cloud some of the issues we want to discuss here. Given the assumption of a small open economy, events in the domestic economy have no effect on the foreign price level, P^*, and so we will treat P^* as exogenous. However, the domestic price level, P, and the exchange rate, e, are endogenous variables. The exchange rate is flexible, in that it is determined by market forces, as we will show below.

Next, we want to determine how the money market works in our equilibrium model. As in Chapter 12, money demand is given by

$$M^d = PL(Y, r^*), \tag{16.3}$$

where $L(Y, r^*)$ denotes the demand for real money balances, which depends positively on aggregate real income, Y, and negatively on the nominal interest rate. Here, recall that the domestic real interest rate is identical to the world real interest rate, r^*, and we are assuming no long-run money growth, so that the domestic inflation rate is zero and the real interest rate is equal to the nominal interest rate given the Fisher relation (recall Chapter 12). Now, given the purchasing power parity relation, Equation (16.2), we can substitute in Equation (16.3) for P to get

$$M^d = eP^*L(Y, r^*).$$

We will take the nominal money supply to be exogenous, with $M^s = M$. In equilibrium, money supply equals money demand, so that $M^s = M^d$, or

$$M = eP^*L(Y, r^*). \tag{16.4}$$

In Figure 16.3, money demand and money supply are on the horizontal axis, while e, the exchange rate, is on the vertical axis. Then, given Y and r^*, money demand M^d is a straight line through the origin in the figure, while money supply M^s is a vertical line at $M^s = M$. The intersection of the supply and demand curves for money then determines the nominal exchange rate, e, so that the equilibrium exchange rate in the figure is e_1. Note that, once we have determined e, we have also determined the domestic price level, P, from the purchasing power parity equation, Equation (16.2).

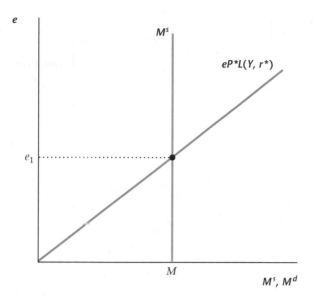

FIGURE 16.3

The Money Market in the Monetary Small Open-Economy Model with a Flexible Exchange Rate
With a flexible exchange rate, and given purchasing power parity, the equilibrium nominal exchange rate is e_1, determined by the intersection of the nominal money supply and nominal money demand curves.

Thus, in this model, the nominal exchange rate is determined by the nominal demand for money relative to the nominal supply of money. Since the nominal exchange rate is a nominal variable, this seems natural. Movements in the exchange rate will be caused either by a shift in money demand or a shift in money supply.

THE NEUTRALITY OF MONEY WITH A FLEXIBLE EXCHANGE RATE

Now that we have set up the model, we can proceed to study its properties. Just as in the monetary intertemporal model we studied in Chapter 12, this model features a classical dichotomy, in that real variables (the level of output, the current account surplus, consumption, and investment) are determined independently of nominal variables (the domestic price level, P, and the nominal exchange rate, e). In Figure 16.3, the nominal exchange rate is determined by the supply and demand for money, and the level of the nominal exchange rate has no bearing on real variables.

If the central bank increases the money supply, say from M_1 to M_2 in Figure 16.4, this has the effect of shifting the money supply curve rightward from M_1^s to M_2^s. In equilibrium, the nominal exchange rate increases from e_1 to e_2, and there is no effect on the level of real output, the real interest rate (which is the real interest rate on world markets, r^*), consumption, investment, or the current account surplus. Since the price of foreign currency has risen in terms of domestic currency, we say that there is a **depreciation** of the domestic currency. Ultimately, since Equation (16.4) implies that, $\dfrac{M}{e} = P^*L(Y, r^*)$ and since P^*, Y, and r^* remain unaffected by the change in the money supply, $\dfrac{M}{e}$ remains unchanged. Thus, the nominal exchange rate increases in proportion to the money supply; for example, if the money supply increased by 5%, the nominal exchange rate would also increase by 5%. Further, since purchasing power parity holds, or $P = eP^*$, and since P^* is fixed, the price level, P, also increases in proportion to the increase in the money supply.

FIGURE 16.4

An Increase in the Money Supply in the Monetary Small Open-Economy Model with a Flexible Exchange Rate

Money is neutral in the monetary small open-economy model with a flexible exchange rate. An increase in the money supply causes the nominal exchange rate and the price level to increase in proportion to the increase in the money supply, with no effect on real variables.

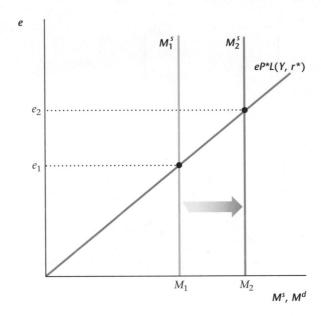

Thus, money is neutral in this model economy with a flexible exchange rate. There are no real effects of an increase in the nominal money supply, but all money prices, including the nominal exchange rate, increase in proportion to the increase in the money supply. Although most macroeconomists adopt the view that money is neutral in the long run in an open economy, there are differences of opinion about the short-run neutrality of money and the explanations for any non-neutralities of money, just as in closed-economy macroeconomics. This model can be extended to incorporate short-run sources of money nonneutralities, such as money surprises, market segmentation (Chapter 12), New Monetarist frictions (Chapter 13), or sticky prices (Chapter 14).

A NOMINAL SHOCK TO THE DOMESTIC ECONOMY FROM ABROAD: P^* INCREASES

We would like to use the monetary small open-economy model to investigate how the domestic economy is affected by events in the rest of the world. The first example we consider is the case of an increase in the price level in the rest of the world, which is essentially an external nominal shock to the domestic economy. We will see that a flexible exchange rate system has an insulating property with respect to increases in the foreign price level. That is, the nominal exchange rate adjusts to exactly offset the increase in the foreign price level, and there are no effects on the domestic price level or domestic real variables. In particular, the temporary foreign inflation resulting from the increase in the foreign price level is not imported to the domestic economy.

Suppose that P^* increases from P_1^* to P_2^*, perhaps because central banks in foreign countries increase the quantity of foreign money in circulation. Then, in Figure 16.5, the money demand curve shifts rightward from $eP_1^*L(Y, r^*)$ to $eP_2^*L(Y, r^*)$. In equilibrium, there will be no effect on real variables, but the nominal exchange rate

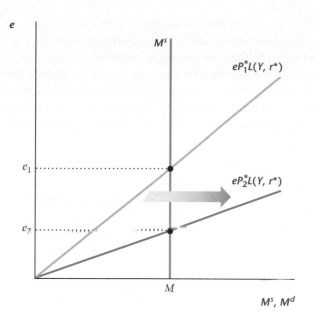

FIGURE 16.5
An Increase in the Foreign
Price Level in the Monetary
Small Open-Economy Model
with a Flexible Exchange
Rate
If the foreign price level
increases, this shifts the
nominal money demand
curve to the right, with the
nominal exchange rate falling
from e_1 to e_2 in equilibrium.
The decrease in the nominal
exchange rate exactly offsets
the increase in the foreign
price level, and there is no
effect on the domestic price
level.

falls from e_1 to e_2, so that there is an **appreciation** of the domestic currency. Since $P = eP^*$, from Equation (16.4) we have

$$\frac{M}{P} = L(Y, r^*),$$

and since M, Y, and r^* remain unchanged, so does P. Therefore, no domestic variables were affected by the price level change in the rest of the world. In particular, the appreciation of the domestic currency was just sufficient to offset the effect of the increase in P^* on the domestic price level. That is, the flexible exchange rate insulated the domestic economy from the nominal shock from abroad. This is certainly a desirable property of a flexible exchange rate regime. Under flexible exchange rates, the domestic price level, and by implication the domestic inflation rate, is determined by the quantity of domestic money supplied by the domestic central bank, and it is not influenced by how monetary policy is conducted by foreign central banks.

A REAL SHOCK TO THE DOMESTIC ECONOMY FROM ABROAD

As an experiment to determine how real domestic variables, the nominal exchange rate, and the price level will respond to a real disturbance transmitted from abroad, we will examine the effects of an increase in the world real interest rate. Such a shock could result, for example, from a decrease in total factor productivity in the rest of the world. (Recall our analysis of the effects of total factor productivity shocks from Chapter 9.) As we will show, a flexible exchange rate cannot shield the domestic economy from the effects of a change in the world real interest rate; the nominal exchange rate appreciates (e falls), and the price level falls.

In Figure 16.6 the world real interest rate increases from r_1^* to r_2^*. The real effects of this are the same as we considered for the third real small open-economy model in Chapter 13. In Figure 16.6(a), the current account surplus increases, shifting the output demand curve to the right until it comes to rest at Y_2^d. Output increases from Y_1 to Y_2 because of the increase in labour supply that results from intertemporal substitution of leisure by the representative consumer. The increase in the real interest rate causes domestic consumption expenditures and investment expenditures to fall, though the

FIGURE 16.6

An Increase in the World Real Interest Rate with a Flexible Exchange Rate
Under a flexible exchange rate, if the world real interest rate increases, this causes real output to rise, and the money demand curve shifts to the right, assuming money demand is much more responsive to real income than to the real interest rate. The nominal exchange rate decreases in equilibrium.

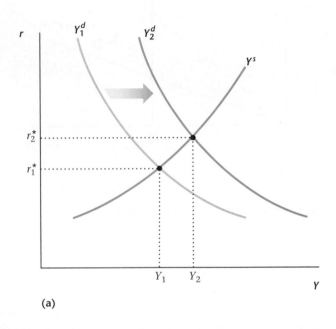

(a)

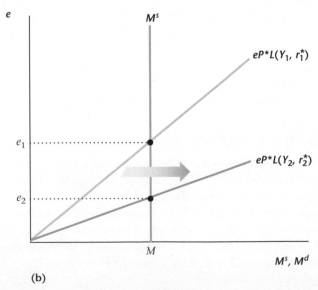

(b)

In 1997, there was a sharp depreciation in nominal exchange rates in East Asia, primarily in Indonesia, South Korea, Malaysia, and Thailand, and these exchange rate depreciations were the first symptoms of what became known as the Asian crisis. From 1996 until the autumn of 1997, the nominal exchange rate (the price of a U.S. dollar in terms of domestic currency) increased by 98.5% in Indonesia, 110.7% in South Korea, 54.4% in Malaysia, and 86.5% in Thailand.[1] What could cause nominal exchange rates to depreciate so dramatically in East Asia over so short a time period? Some answers are provided in a National Bureau of Economic Research working paper[2] by Giancarlo Corsetti, Paolo Pesenti, and Nouriel Roubini (hereafter referred to as CPR).

At the time of the Asian crisis, Indonesia, South Korea, Malaysia, and Thailand were under flexible exchange rate regimes; thus, the model we worked with above should be useful in understanding the large exchange rate depreciation that occurred. The model tells us that a large exchange rate depreciation (a large increase in e) would have to occur because the demand for money fell abruptly or because there was a large increase in the domestic money supply. In our model, money demand could fall because real GDP fell, and so let us first consider the possibility that money demand fell because of a reduction in real GDP in East Asia. This was certainly not the case. Economic growth had been quite strong in East Asia before and during the 1990s. From CPR, the growth rates in real GDP in 1996 for Indonesia, South Korea, Malaysia, and Thailand were 7.98%, 7.10%, 8.58%, and 5.52%, respectively. These rates of growth were very high relative to average growth rates in GDP in other countries, and growth continued to be high for most of these countries in 1997, though lower than in 1996. The exception is Thailand, which had negative real GDP

growth in 1997. In general, though, for these countries money demand would have been *increasing* rather than decreasing because of growth in real GDP, and so this does not seem to explain the large nominal exchange rate depreciations.

To consider a second possibility, the exchange rate depreciations could have been caused during the Asian crisis by rapid growth in the money supply. However, rapid growth in the money supply typically results in a high domestic inflation rate (recall our analysis from Chapter 12), and inflation rates in Indonesia, South Korea, Malaysia, and Thailand, in 1997, from CPR, were 11.62%, 4.45%, 2.66%, and 5.61%, which are certainly moderate relative to the size of the exchange rate depreciations. Thus, money supply growth does not seem to be a potential explanation.

The only other potential explanation could be a dramatic shift in the demand for the currencies of Indonesia, South Korea, Malaysia, and Thailand, and this explanation appears to be in agreement with the analysis of CPR. They argue that these four countries were running large current account deficits prior to the Asian crisis and that these current account deficits were financing investment that would ultimately have poor returns. That is, the domestic financial institutions in these countries were badly regulated, and they were borrowing abroad to make loans to finance domestic investment projects that would ultimately have poor returns. In terms of our analysis of current account deficits from Chapter 15, international lenders became concerned that the large current account deficits in East Asia were not sustainable. That is, to ultimately pay off the foreign debt resulting from large current account deficits, these countries would have to generate large current account surpluses in the future. International lenders to these countries did not appear to believe that the capital stocks in these countries would increase sufficiently to produce high enough future current account surpluses.

The result was a loss in confidence in East Asia on the part of international lenders, who discontinued lending to these countries. Effectively, this loss in confidence works much like a loss in confidence in the domestic banking system. In a domestic banking panic, deposits are withdrawn from banks and converted into domestic currency. In the case of the Asian crisis, the deposits of foreign lenders were withdrawn from East Asian banks and converted into assets denominated in non-East-Asian currencies. This is effectively a fall in the demand for East Asian currencies, and it will result in an exchange rate depreciation, as in our model.

Why was the Asian crisis a crisis? The main risk from the large exchange rate depreciations was

the possibility of a widespread failure of East Asian financial institutions. These institutions were having difficulty borrowing abroad to finance long-term lending, and the exchange rate depreciation implied that the real value of the liabilities of these institutions had increased a great deal relative to the real value of their assets. East Asian financial institutions could then become insolvent and fail. The Asian crisis had temporary and fairly small effects for countries outside of East Asia, in part because of the intervention of the IMF and the world's central banks.

[1]G. Corsetti, P. Pesenti, and N. Roubini, 1998, "What Caused the Asian Currency and Financial Crisis?" working paper, National Bureau of Economic Research.
[2]Ibid.

increase in current income will cause consumption to rise. On net, consumption may rise or fall. Total domestic absorption, $C + I + G$, may rise or fall, but any increase in absorption is smaller than the increase in domestic output, so that the current account surplus rises.

Financial crises are unusual events with large movements in asset prices, including foreign exchange rates. Two such events were the Asian Crisis in the 1990s and the recent global financial crisis. These are discussed, respectively, in Macroeconomics in Action 16.1 and Macroeconomics in Action 16.2.

The nominal effects of the increase in the world real interest rate depend on how the demand for money changes. The increase in the real interest rate causes the demand for money to fall, while the increase in domestic output causes the demand for money to rise. It is not clear whether $L(Y_2, r_2^*) < L(Y_1, r_1^*)$ or $L(Y_2, r_2^*) > L(Y_1, r_1^*)$. However, if real money demand is much more responsive to real income than to the interest rate, then money demand will rise, and the money demand curve in Figure 16.6(b) shifts to the right. In equilibrium, the exchange rate appreciates, with the nominal exchange rate decreasing from e_1 to e_2. As purchasing power parity holds—that is, $P = eP^*$—with P^* constant, P falls in proportion to the decrease in e. Thus, the increase in the world real interest rate leads to an exchange rate appreciation and a decrease in the price level. Clearly, the flexible exchange rate cannot automatically insulate the domestic economy from real shocks that occur abroad. For example, if the central bank wanted to stabilize the price level in the face of the increase in the world real interest rate, it would have to increase the money supply in response to the increase in money demand resulting from the shock.

Why Did the U.S. Currency Appreciate After the Onset of the Global Financial Crisis?

16.2 MACROECONOMICS IN ACTION

When a country experiences a financial crisis, problems in the domestic financial industry typically lead to a flight from the liabilities of domestic financial institutions, and a flight from that country's currency. As for example during the Asian crisis, discussed in the Macroeconomics in Action 16.1, a domestic financial crisis is often associated with an exchange rate depreciation.

In Figure 16.7, we show the trade-weighted exchange rate for the United States, This exchange rate measure is intended to capture the exchange rate of the U.S. currency against all the currencies of the world, with individual foreign exchange rates

weighted in this index according to the importance of the respective countries as US trading partners. The trade-weighted exchange rate is normalized to 100 in January 1997 in the figure. What we observe in Figure 16.7 is a trend decrease in the exchange rate, that is, a U.S. exchange rate depreciation, from 2005 through mid-2008.

A feature of note in Figure 16.7 is that the exchange rate increased by more than 15% from late 2008 to early 2009, at a time when the financial crisis was at its peak. The U.S. nominal exchange rate thus appreciated rather than depreciating during the financial crisis. What is even more puzzling is

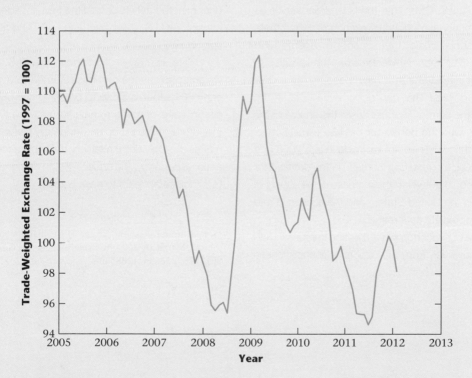

FIGURE 16.7

The Trade-Weighted Nominal U.S. Exchange Rate

There was a trend decrease in the exchange rate from 2005 through mid-2008, and an increase (an appreciation in the U.S. dollar) from late 2008 to early 2009.

that this exchange rate appreciation occurred during a period of time when the quantity of outside money in the United States more than doubled. Given the results from the model in this chapter under a flexible exchange rate, we would expect a large U.S. exchange rate depreciation in response to such a large increase in the domestic money supply. What is going on here? An unusual feature of the United States relative to other countries is that its currency serves essentially as an international medium of exchange. Many transactions in the world, both at the consumer level and among financial institutions, are conducted using U.S. dollars. As well, large quantities of U.S. currency and other U.S. dollar–denominated assets are held outside the United States. Given that the U.S. dollar serves as an international medium of exchange, when there is a financial crisis, then economic agents tend to shift their financial wealth from the liabilities of financial institutions that have become more risky to U.S. dollars. This can occur even if, as in the case of the current financial crisis, the source of the problem was the behaviour of U.S. financial market institutions. Then, for example in late 2008 and early 2009, the resulting increase in the demand for money could outweigh the increase in the supply of money in the United States, and the exchange rate could appreciate as a result.

The U.S. economy need not be immune indefinitely, however, from the effects of financial crises on the value of its exchange rate. World financial market participants are willing to use the U.S. dollar as an international medium of exchange principally because they trust the Federal Reserve System (the "Fed") to manage U.S. monetary policy in a conservative fashion that assures that inflation in the United States will remain low. If the Fed chose to permanently increase the rate of growth in the U.S. money stock, generating a long-run exchange rate depreciation, then foreign residents holding U.S. dollar–denominated assets would suffer losses, and would therefore be reluctant to hold U.S. dollars in the future. Indeed, the Chinese government has been known to make explicit and implicit threats to reduce their holdings of U.S. dollar–denominated assets should the Fed not adequately control the U.S. dollar exchange rate and the inflation rate.[3]

Note in Figure 16.7 how the U.S. trade-weighted exchange rate has returned to a value in early 2012 that is close to pre–financial crisis levels. In spite of some remaining uncertainty about the future of the European Monetary Union, which makes the U.S. dollar relatively desirable as an international currency, the unusually high demand for the U.S. dollars appears to have waned.

[3]See "China Takes Aim at the US Dollar," Wall Street Journal, March 24, 2009, available at online.wsj.com/article/SB123780272456212885.html, accessed June 2, 2012.

A Monetary Small Open-Economy Model with a Fixed Exchange Rate

Now that we have studied how the economy behaves under a flexible exchange rate regime, we will explore how real and nominal variables are determined when the exchange rate is fixed. The type of fixed exchange rate regime we will consider is a type of soft peg, where the government fixes the nominal exchange rate for extended periods of time but might devalue or revalue the domestic currency at some times.

Under the fixed exchange rate regime we model, the government chooses a level at which it wants to fix the nominal exchange rate, which is e_1 in Figure 16.8. The government must then, either through its central bank or some other authority, stand ready to support this exchange rate. For simplicity, we will suppose that the fixed exchange rate is supported through the government standing ready to exchange foreign currency for domestic currency at the fixed exchange rate e_1. To see how this happens, consider the simplified government balance sheet in Table 16.1. This is a consolidated balance sheet for the central bank and the fiscal authority. To support a fixed exchange rate, the government must act to buy or sell its foreign exchange reserves (think of this as foreign currency) for outside money (domestic currency) in foreign exchange markets whenever there are market forces that would tend to push the exchange rate away from the fixed value the government wants it to have. For example, if there are forces tending to increase the exchange rate and thus cause a depreciation of the domestic currency, the government should sell foreign currency and buy domestic currency in order to offset those forces. If there are forces pushing down the exchange rate (appreciation), the government should buy foreign currency and sell domestic currency.

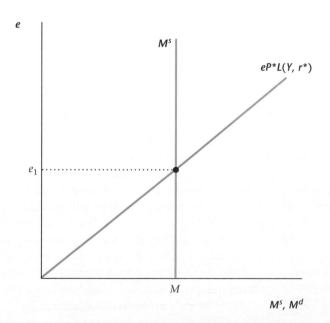

e

M^s

$eP^*L(Y, r^*)$

e_1

M

M^s, M^d

FIGURE 16.8

The Money Market in the Monetary Small Open-Economy Model with a Fixed Exchange Rate
With a fixed exchange rate, the money supply is endogenous. Given the fixed exchange rate e_1, the money supply, M, is determined so that the money supply curve M^s intersects the money demand curve for an exchange rate equal to e_1.

TABLE 16.1   **A Simplified Government Balance Sheet**

Assets	Liabilities
Foreign exchange reserves	Outside money
	Interest-bearing government debt

With a fixed exchange rate, the domestic central bank necessarily loses control over the domestic stock of money. To see this, consider Figure 16.8, where the nominal exchange rate is fixed at e_1. If the domestic central bank attempted to increase the money supply above M, its current value, the effect of this would be to put upward pressure on the exchange rate. Given the tendency for the price of foreign currency to rise in terms of domestic currency as a result, participants in foreign exchange markets would want to trade domestic currency for foreign currency, and the government would have to carry out these exchanges in order to support the fixed exchange rate. This would tend to reduce the stock of domestic money in circulation, and the attempt by the central bank to increase the money supply would be completely undone by actions in the foreign exchange market to support the fixed exchange rate. The money supply would remain at M, with the exchange rate and the domestic price level, P, unchanged. Similarly, if the domestic central bank attempted to engineer a reduction in the money supply below M, this would put downward pressure on the exchange rate, participants in the foreign exchange market would want to exchange foreign currency for domestic currency, and the government would be forced to exchange domestic currency for foreign currency, thus increasing the supply of money. The money supply could therefore not be reduced below M. The implication of this is that, under a fixed exchange rate regime, the supply of money cannot be determined independently by the central bank. Once the government fixes the exchange rate, this determines the domestic money supply.

A NOMINAL FOREIGN SHOCK UNDER A FIXED EXCHANGE RATE

Suppose that the foreign price level increases when the domestic economy is under a fixed exchange rate. In Figure 16.9, P^* increases from P_1^* to P_2^*. As a result, the demand for money shifts rightward from $eP_1^*L(Y, r^*)$ to $eP_2^*L(Y, r^*)$. This increase in the demand for money results in downward pressure on the exchange rate, so that domestic currency becomes more attractive relative to foreign currency. On foreign exchange markets, the government must exchange domestic currency for foreign currency, and this will lead to an increase in the domestic money supply from M_1 to M_2. Since $P = eP^*$, and the exchange rate is fixed, the domestic price level will increase in proportion to the increase in the foreign price level. Thus, under a fixed exchange rate regime, in contrast to the flexible exchange rate regime, the domestic economy is not insulated from nominal shocks that occur abroad. When the foreign price level changes, this price level change is imported, and the domestic price level increases in proportion. Because domestic monetary policy is not independent under a fixed exchange rate, the domestic central bank is forced to adopt the world's inflation rate domestically.

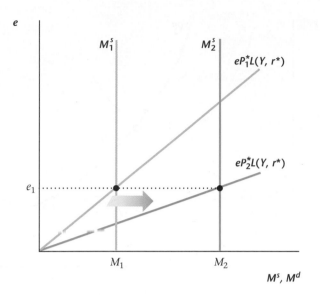

FIGURE 16.9

An Increase in the Foreign Price Level in the Monetary Small Open-Economy Model with a Fixed Exchange Rate
With a fixed exchange rate, an increase in the foreign price level shifts the money demand curve to the right, which causes the domestic money supply to increase. The domestic price level increases in proportion to the increase in the foreign price level.

A REAL FOREIGN SHOCK UNDER A FIXED EXCHANGE RATE

Now we consider the effects of an increase in the world real interest rate from r_1^* to r_2^*, just as we did for the case of a flexible exchange rate. In Figure 16.10(a), as under the flexible exchange rate regime, the real effects of the interest rate increase are an increase in domestic output from Y_1 to Y_2, a decrease in investment, consumption may increase or decrease, and the current account surplus increases. Assuming that the effect of the increase in real income on money demand is much larger than that of the increase in the real interest rate, the demand for money will shift rightward in Figure 16.10(b), from $eP^*L(Y_1, r_1^*)$ to $eP^*L(Y_2, r_2^*)$. Then, with the exchange rate fixed at e_1, the domestic money supply must rise from M_1 to M_2. Since $P = eP^*$ and e and P^* do not change, the domestic price level does not change. Thus, a fixed exchange rate can insulate the domestic price level from real shocks that occur abroad. The same result could be achieved under a flexible exchange rate, but this would require discretionary action by the domestic central bank, rather than the automatic response that occurs under a fixed exchange rate.

EXCHANGE RATE DEVALUATION

Under a fixed exchange rate regime, a devaluation of the domestic currency (an increase in the fixed exchange rate, e) might be a course the government chooses in response to a shock to the economy. In this section, we will show how a temporary reduction in domestic total factor productivity would lead to a reduction in foreign exchange reserves that the government may not desire. In this case, the decrease in foreign exchange reserves can be prevented by a devaluation of the domestic currency. The total factor productivity shock will also cause a decrease in the current account surplus, but the devaluation has no effect in offsetting this current account change.

FIGURE 16.10

An Increase in the World Real Interest Rate with a Fixed Exchange Rate
Under a fixed exchange rate, an increase in the world real interest rate causes an increase in real output and a shift to the right in nominal money demand. The money supply increases to accommodate the increase in money demand, and the domestic price level remains unchanged.

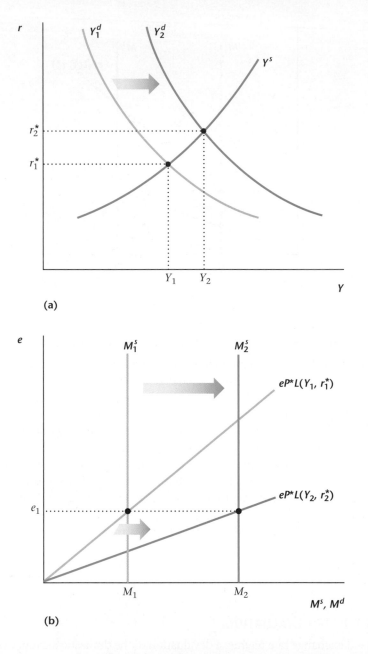

(a)

(b)

Suppose in Figure 16.11 that the domestic economy is initially in equilibrium with the output demand curve Y_1^d and the output supply curve Y_1^s determining domestic output Y_1 in panel (a), given the world real interest rate r^*. In Figure 16.11(b), the exchange rate is fixed at e_1 at first, nominal money demand is initially $eP^*L(Y_1, r^*)$, and the money supply is M_1. Now, suppose that there is a temporary negative shock to domestic total factor productivity. This shifts the output supply curve leftward from Y_1^s to Y_2^s in Figure 16.11(a), as in Chapter 11. The current account surplus falls, shifting

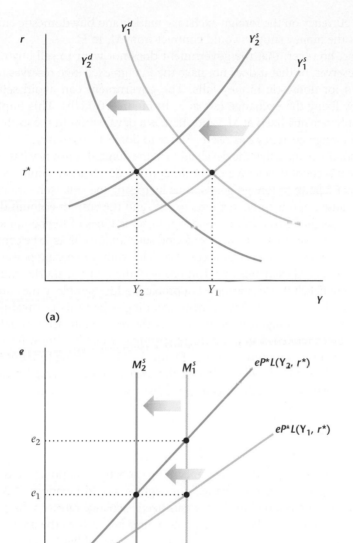

FIGURE 16.11

A Devaluation in Response to a Temporary Total Factor Productivity Shock

A temporary decrease in total factor productivity shifts the output supply curve to the left, reducing output and the current account surplus. The nominal money demand curve shifts to the left. If the government wants to avoid a loss in foreign exchange reserves, it can increase the fixed exchange rate from e_1 to e_2 and devalue the domestic currency.

the output demand curve to the left, until it comes to rest at Y_2^d. In equilibrium, output falls to Y_2, domestic absorption falls because of the decrease in consumption (income falls), and the current account surplus falls. In Figure 16.11(b), the money demand curve shifts leftward to $eP^*L(Y_2, r^*)$ with the fall in real income. If the government were to continue to support the fixed nominal exchange rate at e_1, this would imply, given the fall in the demand for the domestic currency, that the government would have to sell foreign currency on the foreign exchange market and buy domestic currency. This implies that the money supply would contract from M_1 to M_2.

Suppose, however, that the government does not want to sell any of its foreign exchange reserves, or that it does not have the foreign exchange reserves to sell, when the demand for domestic money falls. The government can avoid selling foreign exchange by fixing the exchange rate at e_2 in Figure 16.11(b). This implies that the money supply remains fixed at M_1, and there is a devaluation in the exchange rate, as the price of foreign currency has risen relative to domestic currency.

An important point is that the devaluation of the domestic currency has no effect here on the current account deficit. We might think that a devaluation would make domestic goods cheaper relative to foreign goods, thus increasing the real exchange rate, and that this would cause imports to fall, exports to rise, and the current account deficit to fall. Although this might be true in the short run in some types of Keynesian analysis with sticky prices (but note that there are income and substitution effects to be concerned with, in terms of the effect on the current account deficit), with purchasing power parity there is no effect on the real exchange rate. Ultimately, if the government determined that the current account deficit that results here is a problem—for example, if the current account deficit is caused by excessive government spending—then this is a real problem that should be corrected through real means. That is, the real current account deficit could be reduced through a reduction in government spending, which we know from Chapter 15 can reduce the current account deficit in Figure 16.11(a). Trying to reduce the current account deficit through a devaluation in the domestic currency essentially involves trying to make a real change through nominal means, which cannot work in the long run.

Flexible Versus Fixed Exchange Rates

Governments face important choices concerning exchange rate policy, and a key choice is whether a flexible or fixed exchange rate regime should be adopted. What are the arguments for the adoption of flexible versus fixed exchange rates? In the previous subsections, we have seen that the exchange rate regime affects how the domestic economy is insulated from shocks from abroad. If a country's central bank seeks to stabilize the price level, then our analysis tells us that if nominal shocks from abroad are important, a flexible exchange rate is preferable to a fixed exchange rate—because a flexible exchange rate will absorb a shock to the foreign price level and stabilize the domestic price level. Alternatively, if real shocks from abroad are important, then a fixed exchange rate is preferable to a flexible exchange rate, as this acts to prevent the domestic price level from moving in response to real shocks from abroad; the domestic money supply acts as a shock absorber. Thus, in this respect, whether a particular country should choose a fixed or flexible exchange rate depends on its circumstances. A country might want to move from a fixed to a flexible exchange rate over time, and then back again.

It is sometimes argued that a flexible exchange rate allows the domestic central bank to implement a monetary policy independently of what happens in the rest of the world. In our model, with a flexible exchange rate, the domestic government can set the domestic money supply independently, but with a fixed exchange rate, the money supply is not under the control of the domestic government. However, giving the domestic central bank the power to implement an independent monetary policy is useful only if the central bank can be trusted with this power. Some central banks, such as those in the United States, Canada, and parts of Europe, have excellent track records in controlling the rate of inflation after World War II. In other countries, the track record is not so good. For example, Argentina suffered very high rates of inflation until its nominal exchange rate was fixed relative to the U.S. dollar. If the central bank is weak or having difficulty controlling the domestic money supply, then a fixed exchange rate can be a very important commitment device. If the exchange rate is fixed against the currency of a country with a strong central bank, this implies, given purchasing power parity, that the weak central-bank country essentially adopts the monetary policy of the strong central-bank country. With a fixed exchange rate, the price level of the domestic economy is tied to the foreign price level, which is essentially determined by foreign monetary policy.

In conclusion, there is no clear case for flexible versus fixed exchange rates. For Canada, where the central bank is relatively independent of political pressures and appears to be well focused on controlling inflation, a flexible exchange rate seems appropriate. The Bank of Canada appears to be sufficiently trustworthy relative to foreign central banks that allowing it to pursue a monetary policy geared to Canadian interests seems advisable. However, for other countries, particularly some in Latin America and Africa, a fixed exchange rate regime makes good sense.

Note that there are many long-standing instances of fixed exchange rates that we take for granted. For example, rates of exchange between different denominations of Canadian currency have always been fixed in Canada. Why should it necessarily be the case that five one-dollar coins trade for one five-dollar bill in all circumstances in Canada? This is because the Bank of Canada always stands ready to trade one five-dollar bill for five loonies; essentially, the Bank of Canada maintains fixed exchange rates among different denominations of Canadian currency.

Essentially, all countries maintain fixed exchange rates within their borders. There is a national currency accepted as legal tender, and typically this currency circulates nationally as a medium of exchange, though in some countries foreign currencies, in particular U.S. dollars, circulate widely, as in Canada. What then determines the natural region, or **common currency area**, over which a single currency dominates as a medium of exchange? Clearly, a common currency area need not be the area over which there is a single political or fiscal authority. In Canada, every province has the power to tax provincial residents, but the provinces cede monetary authority to the Bank of Canada. In the European Monetary Union (EMU), member countries maintain their fiscal independence, but monetary policy is in the hands of the European Central Bank (ECB). An advantage of having a large trading area with a common currency is that this simplifies exchange; it is much easier to write contracts and trade across international borders without the complications of converting one currency into another or bearing the risk associated with fluctuating exchange rates. However, in joining a **currency union** such as the EMU, a country must give up its monetary independence to the group. The formation of the EMU has created tensions among EMU members concerning matters that include the choice of the leaders of the European Central Bank, and the monetary policy stance this central bank should take. Britain, which has the world's oldest central bank, the Bank of England, chose not to join the EMU in order to maintain its monetary independence.

Capital Controls

A useful application of the monetary small open-economy model is to the problem of the role of capital controls in the international economy. Capital controls refer broadly to any government restrictions on the trade of assets across international borders. We will show here that capital controls can reduce movements in the nominal exchange rate in response to some shocks under a flexible exchange rate regime, and they can reduce fluctuations in foreign exchange reserves under a fixed exchange rate regime. We will argue, however, that capital controls are in general undesirable, because they introduce welfare-decreasing economic inefficiencies.

THE CAPITAL ACCOUNT AND THE BALANCE OF PAYMENTS

To understand capital controls, we have to first understand the accounting practices behind the **capital account**. The capital account is part of the **balance of payments**, which includes the current account and the capital account. The capital account includes all transactions in assets, where entries in the capital account when a foreign resident purchases a domestic asset are recorded as a positive amount—a **capital inflow**—and entries when a domestic resident purchases a foreign asset are recorded as a negative amount—a **capital outflow**. For example, if a Canadian bank lends to a British firm, this is a capital outflow, as the loan to the British firm is an asset for the Canadian bank. If a U.S. automobile manufacturer builds a new plant in Canada, this is a capital inflow for Canada, and it is part of **foreign direct investment** in Canada. Foreign direct investment is distinct from **portfolio inflows** and **outflows**, which are capital account transactions involving financial assets, including stocks and debt instruments. A helpful rule of thumb in counting asset transactions in the capital account is that the transaction counts as a capital inflow if funds flow into the domestic country to purchase an asset, and as an outflow if funds flow out of the domestic country to purchase an asset.

The balance of payments is defined as the current account surplus plus the capital account surplus. That is, letting BP denote the balance of payments, and KA the capital account surplus, we have

$$BP = KA + CA,$$

where CA is the current account surplus. A key element in balance of payments accounting is that the balance of payments is always zero (though it is not measured as such because of measurement error), so that

$$KA = -CA.$$

Therefore, the capital account surplus is always the negative of the current account surplus. If the current account is in deficit (surplus), then the capital account is in surplus (deficit). We have not discussed the capital account until now for this reason—the capital account surplus is just the flip side of the current account surplus, so that when we know the current account surplus we know exactly what the capital account surplus is.

The balance of payments is always zero, because any transaction entering the balance of payments always has equal and opposite entries in the accounts. For example, suppose that a Canadian firm borrows the equivalent of $50 million in British pounds from a British bank so that it can purchase $50 million worth of auto parts in Britain to ship to Canada. The loan from the British bank will enter as a capital inflow, since the British bank has accumulated a Canadian asset, and so there will be an entry of +$50 million in the capital account for Canada. Next, when the auto parts are purchased and imported into Canada, this will enter as −$50 million in the current account. Thus, in this as in all cases, the net effect on the balance of payments is zero. The offsetting entries associated with a given transaction need not be in the current account and the capital account, but in some cases could be all in the current account, or all in the capital account.

THE EFFECTS OF CAPITAL CONTROLS

In practice, capital controls can be imposed in terms of capital inflows or capital outflows, and they sometimes apply to foreign direct investment and sometimes to portfolio inflows and outflows. For example, restrictions on capital outflows were introduced in Malaysia in 1998 after the Asian crisis, and Chile used controls on capital inflows extensively from 1978 to 1982 and from 1991 to 1998. In both cases, the capital controls were in terms of portfolio inflows and outflows. Countries sometimes also restrict foreign direct investment, which is a control on capital inflows. Controls on foreign direct investment are sometimes put in place because of concern (perhaps misplaced) over the foreign ownership of the domestic capital stock.

What are the macroeconomic effects of capital controls? Essentially, they alter how the domestic economy responds to a shock. For example, suppose that there is a temporary negative shock to domestic total factor productivity under a flexible exchange rate. In Figure 16.12(a), suppose that the output demand curve is Y_1^d and the initial output supply curve is Y_1^s, and assume that initially the current account surplus is zero with output equal to Y_1 at the world real interest rate r^*. In Figure 16.12(b), the initial money demand curve is $eP^*L(Y_1, r^*)$, and the initial nominal exchange rate is e_1, given the nominal money supply, M.

Now, suppose there is a temporary decrease in domestic total factor productivity, which shifts the output supply curve leftward to Y_2^s in Figure 16.12(a). With no capital controls in place, this will imply that the current account surplus falls (with the current account then running a deficit), shifting the output demand curve to the left until it comes to rest at Y_2^d. Real output falls to Y_2 from Y_1, and consumption falls because of the decrease in income. In Figure 16.12(b), nominal money demand shifts leftward to $eP^*L(Y_2, r^*)$, and there is an exchange rate depreciation, with the nominal exchange rate increasing to e_2.

FIGURE 16.12

A Temporary Total Factor Productivity Shock, with and without Capital Controls

With a temporary decrease in total factor productivity, under a flexible exchange rate there is a larger decrease in aggregate output and the current account surplus, and a larger increase in the nominal exchange rate in the case without capital controls.

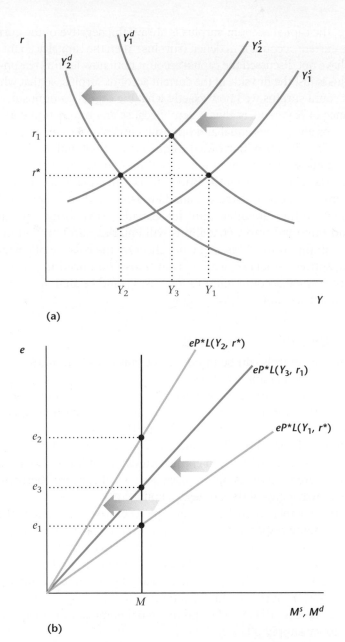

(a)

(b)

Now, assume an extreme form of capital controls in which the government prohibits all capital inflows and outflows. This will imply that the capital account surplus must be zero in equilibrium, and so the current account surplus must be zero as well. With a temporary decrease in domestic total factor productivity in Figure 16.12(a), the domestic real interest rate will rise to r_1, which is above the world real interest rate r^*. In equilibrium, foreign investors would like to purchase domestic assets, as the return on domestic assets is greater than it is in the rest of the world, but they are prohibited from doing so. Thus, in this case, real output decreases to Y_3 in equilibrium. Assuming that money demand is much more responsive to real income than to the real interest rate, the money demand curve shifts to the left in Figure 16.12(b), though by less than it does in the case with no capital controls. The nominal exchange rate rises to e_3.

The results are that the nominal exchange rate increases by a smaller amount when capital controls are in place than when they are not; output falls by a smaller amount; and there is a smaller change in the current account deficit. Thus, capital controls tend to dampen aggregate fluctuations in output, the current account surplus, and the nominal exchange rate resulting from shocks of this type to the economy. If a country is concerned about the effects of fluctuations in the nominal exchange rate under a flexible exchange rate regime (for reasons not modelled here), capital controls will tend to mitigate this problem, at least if the major source of shocks is temporary changes in total factor productivity. However, this solution is quite costly, as it produces an economic inefficiency. As in Chapter 5, the equilibrium allocation of resources is Pareto-optimal in this model in the absence of capital controls. With no capital controls, in this example, the domestic economy would face a lower real interest rate after the total factor productivity shock, and this means that lenders would be worse off and borrowers better off. Though some would win and some would lose from getting rid of capital controls, there would in general be an average gain in welfare.

Under a fixed exchange rate, Figure 16.12(a) still applies, but the money market works as in Figure 16.13. The nominal exchange rate is assumed to be fixed at e_1. Initially, the money supply is M_1, and in the absence of capital controls, the money supply declines to M_2, but with capital controls there will be a decline in the money

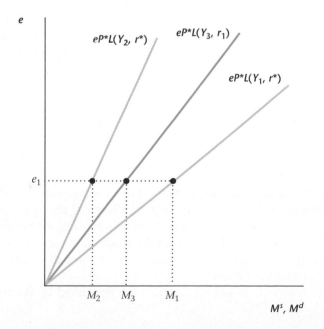

FIGURE 16.13

A Total Factor Productivity Shock under a Fixed Exchange Rate, with and without Capital Controls
Under a fixed exchange rate, capital controls dampen the reduction in the money supply that occurs when there is a temporary decline in total factor productivity.

16.3 Do Capital Controls Work in Practice?

With regard to how capital controls work in practice, we are primarily interested in two questions: (1) Can capital controls be effectively enforced so that they have the intended effects? (2) How large are the economic inefficiencies that capital controls cause? In an article in the *Journal of Economic Perspectives*, Sebastian Edwards sets out to answer these questions by using the example of Chile.[4]

Edwards argues that there is little support by economists for restrictions on capital outflows, but that some economists have pointed to Chile as an example of how restrictions on capital inflows appeared to have worked well. One aim of his article is to dismiss these latter arguments by studying the details of what happened in Chile, where controls on capital inflows were in place from 1978 to 1982 and from 1991 to 1998. These restrictions mainly applied to portfolio inflows of short-maturity securities, and they took the form of reserve requirements on these inflows. That is, if a foreigner purchased short-term interest-bearing Chilean assets (a capital inflow), then a fraction of the value of these assets would have to be held as a non-interest-bearing deposit with the central bank. This had the same effect as a tax on short-term capital inflows, as the non-interest-bearing deposits could otherwise be held in interest-bearing form.

What were the effects of the capital controls in Chile? Edwards finds that apparently many investors learned how to avoid them. Although capital inflows appeared to have shifted somewhat toward longer-term from shorter-term inflows, the shift was not very large, and investors seemed to have found many clever schemes for disguising short-term capital inflows as long-term ones. Edwards argues that the controls had severe effects on small and medium-sized Chilean firms, which faced much higher costs of borrowing.

Edwards's conclusion is that the welfare costs of capital controls are small on average, mainly because the controls are ineffective, but the costs are large for some groups in the population. He argues that capital controls should be phased out in countries where they still exist. However, he argues that in some cases this phaseout should be gradual. The inefficiencies caused by capital controls may in some cases be small relative to the inefficiencies arising from a poorly regulated banking system. If restrictions on capital inflows are relaxed quickly, then domestic banks can borrow abroad more easily to finance domestic lending. However, if domestic banks are improperly regulated (as we will study in more depth in Chapter 17), then they will take on too much risk; and this problem can be exacerbated in a wide-open international lending environment. The relaxation of capital controls sometimes needs to be coupled with improvements in the regulation of domestic financial institutions.

---

[4]S. Edwards, 1999, "How Effective Are Capital Controls?" *Journal of Economic Perspectives* 13, 65–84.

supply only to M_3. Here, fluctuations in the money supply are smaller with capital controls, which implies that foreign exchange reserves will drop by a smaller amount with capital controls. Therefore, with capital controls in place, a government can better support a fixed exchange rate, if exhausting the stock of foreign exchange reserves on hand is potentially a problem without controls. Again, though, capital controls come at a cost in lost economic efficiency.

The practical aspects of capital controls are discussed in Macroeconomics in Action 16.3.

Although there are many more interesting issues to study in international macroeconomics, this chapter ends our discussion of this topic here. In Part 7, we will move on to study topics in money, banking, and inflation, which involve in-depth issues in closed-economy macroeconomics.

Chapter Summary

- We first studied purchasing power parity, or the law of one price, which predicts that prices are equated across countries in terms of the same currency. While there can be large and persistent deviations from purchasing power parity in practice, there are strong economic forces that move prices and exchange rates toward purchasing power parity over the long run. The purchasing power parity assumption is very useful in the model studied in this chapter.

- In the monetary small open-economy model, the real interest rate and the foreign price level are determined on world markets.

- Under a flexible exchange rate, money is neutral, and the domestic economy is insulated from nominal shocks from abroad, in that no real or nominal domestic variables are affected by a change in the foreign price level. The nominal exchange rate moves in equilibrium to absorb completely a shock to the foreign price level. However, the flexible exchange rate does not insulate the domestic price level against real shocks from abroad.

- A fixed exchange rate causes the domestic price level to increase in proportion to an increase in the foreign price level, but the fixed exchange rate regime insulates the domestic price level from foreign real shocks. Under a fixed exchange rate regime, a devaluation of the domestic currency might occur if the government's foreign exchange reserves are depleted. A devaluation raises the domestic price level.

- Whether a flexible exchange rate regime is preferred to a fixed exchange rate regime depends on a country's circumstances, but a flexible exchange rate regime implies that domestic monetary policy can be independent, whereas a fixed exchange rate regime implies that the domestic economy adopts the monetary policy of a foreign central bank.

- Capital controls involve restrictions on capital inflows and outflows, which are items in the capital account, where the asset transactions for a nation are added up. The balance of payments surplus is the sum of the capital account surplus and the current account surplus, and the balance of payments surplus is always zero.

- Capital controls can dampen fluctuations in output, the current account surplus, and the exchange rate (under a flexible exchange rate) or the money supply (under a fixed exchange rate), but these controls reduce economic efficiency. In practice, capital controls appear not to have been very effective, and in this sense they have not had large effects on efficiency.

Key Terms

nominal exchange rate: The price of foreign currency in terms of domestic currency, denoted by e in the model of this chapter.

law of one price: $P = eP^*$, where P is the domestic price, P^* is the foreign price, and e is the exchange rate.

purchasing power parity (PPP): The same thing as the law of one price, except that P is the domestic price *level* and P^* is the foreign price *level*.

flexible exchange rate regime: A system under which a nation's nominal exchange rate is determined by market forces.

fixed exchange rate regime: A system under which the domestic government supports the value of the exchange rate at a specified level in terms of a foreign currency or currencies.

hard pegs: Exchange rate systems under which there is firm commitment to a fixed exchange rate, through either dollarization or a currency board.

soft pegs: Exchange rate systems under which the government commits to a fixed exchange rate for periods of time, but sometimes changes the value at which the exchange rate is fixed.

devaluations: Increases in the price of foreign exchange in terms of domestic currency.

revaluations: Decreases in the price of foreign exchange in terms of domestic currency.

dollarize: For a nation to abandon its own currency and adopt the currency of another country as its medium of exchange.

currency board: An institution that fixes the exchange rate by holding foreign-currency-denominated interest-bearing assets and committing to buying and selling foreign exchange at a fixed rate of exchange.

European Monetary Union (EMU): An organization of European countries, established in 1999, that shares a common currency, the euro.

euro: The currency shared by the members of the EMU.

European Central Bank (ECB): The central bank of the EMU countries.

European Monetary System (EMS): A cooperative exchange rate system in place among European countries from 1979 until 1999.

Bretton Woods arrangement: A worldwide cooperative exchange rate system, in place from 1946 to 1971, under which the price of gold was fixed in terms of U.S. dollars, and there were fixed exchange rates for all other currencies in terms of the U.S. dollar.

International Monetary Fund (IMF): An international monetary institution established in 1946, intended as a lender of last resort for its member countries, which now number 185.

lender of last resort: A centralized institution that lends to economic agents in distress; examples are central banks, which lend to domestic banks, and the IMF, which lends to its member countries.

depreciation (of the domestic currency): A rise in the price of foreign currency in terms of domestic currency.

appreciation (of the domestic currency): A fall in the price of foreign currency in terms of domestic currency.

common currency area: A region over which a single currency dominates as a medium of exchange.

currency union: A group of countries that agree to become a common currency area.

capital account: The component of the balance of payments in which all international asset transactions between the domestic economy and foreign countries are added up.

balance of payments: A system of accounts for a country for adding up all international transactions in goods and assets.

capital inflow: The purchase of a domestic asset by a foreign resident, recorded as a positive entry in the capital account.

capital outflow: The purchase of a foreign asset by a domestic resident, recorded as a negative entry in the capital account.

foreign direct investment: A capital inflow that involves the acquisition of a new physical asset by a foreign resident.

portfolio inflows and outflows: Capital account transactions involving international transactions in financial assets.

Questions for Review

1. Does purchasing power parity hold in practice in the short run? Why or why not? Does it hold in the long run? Why or why not?

2. Which countries in the world have flexible exchange rates? Which have fixed exchange rates?

3. What are the different systems for fixing the exchange rate? Describe how each works.

4. Describe the role of the International Monetary Fund.

5. In the model constructed in this chapter, what are the effects on the domestic economy of an increase in the foreign price level under a flexible exchange rate and under a fixed exchange rate?

6. In the model, what are the effects on the domestic economy of an increase in the world real interest rate under a flexible exchange rate and under a fixed exchange rate?

7. In the model, is money neutral under a flexible exchange rate? Explain why or why not. Can we say that money is neutral under a fixed exchange rate? Explain.

8. Explain why domestic monetary policy is not independent under a flexible exchange rate.

9. What are the effects of a devaluation of the domestic currency under a fixed exchange rate?

10. List the key pros and cons of fixed versus flexible exchange rate regimes.

11. Give two examples of fixed exchange rates within Canada.

12. What are the advantages and disadvantages of a common currency area or currency union?

13. If there is a capital account surplus, what can we say about the current account surplus?

14. Give two examples of countries where capital controls were imposed.

15. What do capital controls imply for the response of the economy to shocks?

16. Are capital controls a good idea? Why or why not?

17. Are capital controls effective in practice? Explain.

Problems

1. Suppose there is a cost to carrying out transactions in the foreign exchange market. That is, to purchase one unit of foreign currency requires $e(1 + a)$ units of domestic currency, where e is the nominal exchange rate and a is the proportional fee. Suppose that a decreases. What will be the equilibrium effects under a flexible exchange rate regime, and under a fixed exchange rate regime? Explain your results.

2. In the equilibrium small open-economy model, suppose that total factor productivity increases temporarily.
   a. If the exchange rate is flexible, determine the effects on aggregate output, absorption, the current account surplus, the nominal exchange rate, and the price level.
   b. Repeat part (a) for the case of a fixed exchange rate. If the goal of the domestic government is to stabilize the price level, would it be preferable to have a fixed exchange rate or a flexible exchange rate regime when there is a change in total factor productivity?
   c. Now suppose that under a flexible exchange rate regime the domestic monetary authority controls the money supply so as to stabilize the price level when total factor productivity increases. Explain the differences between the outcome in this case and what happens in part (b) with a fixed exchange rate.

3. Suppose in the model that government expenditures increase temporarily. Determine the effects on aggregate output, absorption, the current account surplus, the nominal exchange rate, and the price level. What difference will it make if the exchange rate is flexible or fixed?

4. Suppose that better transaction technologies are developed that reduce the domestic demand for money. Use the monetary small open-economy model to answer the following:
   a. Suppose that the exchange rate is flexible. What are the equilibrium effects on the price level and the exchange rate?
   b. Suppose that the exchange rate is flexible, and the domestic monetary authority acts to stabilize the price level. Determine how the domestic money supply changes and the effect on the nominal exchange rate.
   c. Suppose that the exchange rate is fixed. Determine the effects on the exchange rate and the price level, and determine the differences from your results in parts (a) and (b).

5. Consider a country, with a flexible exchange rate, that initially has a current account surplus of zero. Then suppose there is an anticipated increase in future total factor productivity.
   a. Determine the equilibrium effects on the domestic economy in the case where there are no capital controls. In particular, show that there will be a current account deficit when firms and consumers anticipate the increase in future total factor productivity.
   b. Now suppose that the government dislikes current account deficits and that it imposes capital controls in an attempt to reduce the current account deficit. With the anticipated increase in future total factor productivity, what will the equilibrium effects on the economy be? Do the capital controls have the desired effect on the current account deficit? Do capital controls dampen the effects of the shock to the economy on output and the exchange rate? Are capital controls sound macroeconomic policy in this context? Why or why not?

6. Suppose a flexible exchange rate. There is an increase in the degree of uncertainty in credit markets, which affects firms but not consumers, as considered in Chapter 11.
   a. Determine the effects on aggregate output, the price level, the exchange rate, and the real interest rate. Explain your results.
   b. Does this explain features of the financial crisis? Explain.

7. The domestic central bank increases the supply of money under a flexible exchange rate regime, leading to a depreciation of the nominal exchange rate. If the government had imposed capital controls before the increase in the money supply, would this have had any effect on the exchange rate depreciation? Explain your results, and comment on their significance.

8. Suppose that capital controls take the form of a total ban on capital inflows, but all capital outflows are permitted. Also suppose that initially the current account surplus is zero. Determine the effects of a temporary increase in total factor productivity and of a temporary decrease in total factor productivity under a flexible exchange rate. Carefully explain how and why your results differ in the two cases.

Money, Banking, and Inflation

In this Part, we deal with some in-depth topics. In Chapter 17, we study, at a more detailed level, the role of money in the economy, the forms that money has taken historically, the effects of long-run inflation on aggregate activity and economic welfare, and the role of banks and other financial intermediaries in the economy. Then, in Chapter 18 we explain why central banks may cause inflation, even though it is well known that inflation is harmful. We use recent inflation history in Canada as a backdrop in examining the role of central bank learning and commitment in inflation policy.

17

Money, Inflation, and Banking

In the monetary analysis we have done so far in this book, particularly in Chapters 12–14 and 16, we began by determining a demand function for money and showed how this demand function reflects the tradeoffs consumers and firms face between the costs of using alternatives to money, and the interest earnings resulting from economizing on money balances. This allowed us to understand the effects of changes in the quantity of money, the role of money in the business cycle, and the way money influences foreign exchange rates. In this chapter, we want to gain a deeper understanding of the functions of money in the economy to understand the long-run effects of inflation on aggregate economic activity and economic welfare and to study the role of banks and other financial intermediaries in the economy.

In this chapter we first discuss how historical monetary systems worked, and we study the basic role of money in the economy in overcoming the difficulty of carrying out exchange by using only commodities. Then, we return to the monetary intertemporal model developed in Chapter 12 and use this model to study the long-run effects of inflation. Empirically and in our model, long-run inflation is caused by growth in the money supply. We see that higher rates of money growth and inflation tend to reduce employment and output. This is because inflation erodes the purchasing power of money in the period between when labour income is earned and when it is spent. Thus, inflation tends to distort labour supply decisions. We show that an optimal long-run inflation policy for a central bank is to follow a **Friedman rule**, according to which the money supply grows at a rate that makes the rate of return on money identical to the rate of return on alternative assets and drives the nominal interest rate to zero. We discuss why real-world central banks do not appear to follow Friedman rules.

Finally, we examine the role of banks and other financial intermediaries in the economy. A **financial intermediary** is any financial institution that borrows from one large group of people and lends to another large group of people, transforms assets in some way, and processes information. Banks and other deposit-taking financial institutions are financial intermediaries that are of particular interest to macroeconomists for two reasons. First, some of the liabilities that deposit-taking financial institutions issue are included in measures of the money supply and compete with currency as media of exchange. Second, deposit-taking financial institutions interact closely with the central bank and are typically on the receiving end of the first-round effects of monetary policy.

We study a simple model of a bank, the Diamond-Dybvig banking model. This model shows how banks supply a kind of insurance against the need to make transactions by using liquid assets, why bank runs can occur (as happened in some countries in the nineteenth century and during the Great Depression), and why government-provided deposit insurance might prevent bank runs. We discuss the incentive problem that deposit insurance creates for banks.

Alternative Forms of Money

In Chapter 12, we discussed how money functions as a medium of exchange, a store of value, and a unit of account, with the key distinguishing feature of money being its medium-of-exchange property. Though all money is a medium of exchange, historically there have been many different objects that have performed this role. The most important forms of money have been commodity money, circulating private bank notes, commodity-backed paper currency, fiat money, and transactions deposits at private banks. We will discuss each of these in turn.

- *Commodity money.*   This was the earliest money, in common use in Greek and Roman civilizations and in earlier times, and it was typically a precious metal: gold, silver, or copper. In practice, commodity money systems involved having the government operate a mint to produce coins from precious metals, which then circulated as money. Control over the mint by the government was important, since the ability to issue money provided an important source of seigniorage revenue. Commodity money systems had several problems, however. First, the quality of any commodity is difficult to verify. For example, gold can be adulterated with other cheaper metals, so that there is an opportunity for fraud in the production of commodity money. Also, in the exchange of commodity monies, bits could be clipped off coins and melted down, with the hope that this would go undetected. Second, commodity money is costly to produce. For example, gold has to be dug out of the ground, minted, and then reminted when the coins wear out. Third, the use of a commodity as money diverts it from other uses. Gold and silver, for example, can also be used as jewellery and in industrial applications. In spite of these three problems, at the time commodity monies were used there were no good alternatives, mainly because any laws against the counterfeiting of paper currency would have been difficult or impossible to enforce. What may seem paradoxical is that the high cost of producing a commodity money was a virtue. To avoid inflation, the quantity of money must be in limited supply, and one reason that gold and silver functioned well as commodity monies is that they were scarce.

Commodity Money and Commodity-Backed Paper Money: Yap Stones and Playing Cards

A commodity money system that appears unusual on the surface, but has several features common to other commodity money systems, is the exchange of so-called Yap stones on the island of Yap in Micronesia, as studied by the anthropologist William Henry Furness III in 1903.[2]

On Yap, large stones measuring from about 0.3 to 3.7 metres in diameter served as money.[3] The stones were quarried from limestone deposits on another island about 650 kilometres from Yap and transported back by boat. What the Yap stones had in common with other commodity monies, such as gold and silver, was scarcity. It was quite costly in time and effort to create a new stone, and the value of the stones increased with the difficulty of acquiring them, which might include weathering storms on the trip back to Yap. What seems different about the Yap stones as a commodity money is that they were extremely difficult to move around; an attractive feature of gold and silver as commodity monies was that the quantities of it required to make moderate-sized transactions

were extremely portable. However, the islanders did not typically move the Yap stones when transactions were made; they were most often used to make large land transactions and large gifts, but the stones themselves usually stayed put. It was well known to most of the small population of Yap who owned which stones, and a transaction involving one of these stones was public knowledge, but there was no written record of ownership. Thus, it appears that exchange was actually carried out on the island using commodity-backed money. What "changed hands" in a transaction was the record of the ownership of the stone, which was stored in the collective memories of the islanders. The stones were just the backing for the "currency," which was not physical objects at all but an entry in public memory.

Yap stones had much in common with the earliest known paper money used in North America, in New France in 1685. There had been difficulties in keeping coins minted in France in circulation in New France, as the coins were often used in payment

• *Circulating private bank notes:* Before the Bank of Canada was established in 1935, much of the currency in circulation in Canada was issued by Canadian chartered banks. In other countries, monetary systems with private currency issue appeared not to have worked well, as in the United States before 1863. However, the Canadian monetary system before 1935 seemed to have functioned efficiently.[1]

• *Commodity-backed paper currency:* In this type of monetary system, there is government-issued paper currency, but the currency is backed by some commodity, the **gold standard**, for example. Canada operated under the gold standard before 1929. Under the rules of the gold standard, the Canadian government stood ready to exchange currency for gold at some specified price, so that government currency was always redeemable in gold. Effectively this was a commodity money system, but it saved on some of the costs of a commodity money, in that consumers

---

[1]See S. Williamson, 1989, "Restrictions on Financial Intermediaries and Implications for Aggregate Fluctuations: Canada and the United States, 1870–1913," in *NBER Macroeconomics Annual* 1989, 303–340, in Olivier Blanchard and Stanley Fischer (eds.), MIT Press, Cambridge, MA; and B. Champ, B. Smith, and S. Williamson, 1996, "Currency Elasticity and Banking Panics: Theory and Evidence," *Canadian Journal of Economics* 29, 828–864.

for imports from France, and thus left the colony. Therefore, the coins constantly had to be replenished by shipments from France in the form of payments to the troops in New France. In 1685, the shipment of coins was late in arriving from France, and De Meulles, the intendant (governor of the colony) of New France, authorized the issue of playing-card money. De Meulles requisitioned the playing cards in the colony, and the cards were issued, signed by him in different denominations, as payment to the troops. These cards were essentially IOUs, which promised payment in coin when the shipment arrived from France. The playing cards then circulated as a medium of exchange in New France and were subsequently retired as promised. The cards were then issued repeatedly in later years. But ultimately the government of France lost interest in its colony in New France, and the shipments of coins stopped arriving from France in the quantities promised, so that the IOUs the playing cards represented could not be honoured in full. There were problems with inflation, because of the temptation

to issue the playing-card money in excess of the promises the intendant could actually keep.[4]

Like the ownership rights to the Yap stones, playing-card money in New France was a commodity-backed money. However, the New France playing-card monetary system seems to have been less successful than the Yap system, because the commodity backing of the playing-card money was uncertain (because of the inability of public officials to keep their promises), whereas the existence of the Yap stones was well known to essentially everyone on the island of Yap.

---

[2]W. Furness, 1910, *The Island of Stone Money: Yap of the Carolines*, J. P. Lippincott Co., Philadelphia and London.

[3]The Bank of Canada has an impressive Yap stone in the atrium of its building in Ottawa.

[4]For a description and photograph of card money in New France, see "'Card Money' 3 livres, 1749," Currency Museum of the Bank of Canada, Industry Canada, available at collections.ic.gc.ca/bank/english/emar76.htm, accessed July 17, 2003.

---

did not have to carry around large quantities of the commodity (in this case, gold) when they wanted to make large purchases. For two historical examples of commodity-backed currency, see Macroeconomics in Action 17.1.

- *Fiat money:* This is at least part of the monetary system in most modern economies. In Canada, fiat money is the stock of outside money issued by the Bank of Canada, including currency and the deposits of financial institutions held with the Bank of Canada. Fiat money is essentially worthless: for example, most people do not value Canadian currency for its colour or for what is depicted on it. However, fiat money is accepted in exchange for goods. Why? Because people believe others will accept it in exchange for goods in the future. This notion of the value of money supported by belief is intriguing, and it is part of what excites those who study monetary economics.

- *Transactions deposits at private banks:* In Canada, widespread deposit banking and the use of cheques in transactions evolved later in the nineteenth century, and the Canadian financial system (like the financial systems in most developed economies) has evolved to the point where much of the total volume of transactions is carried out through banks. With a chequable bank deposit, consumers can make purchases without the use of fiat money. A cheque is a message that specifies that a given quantity of value is to be debited from the account of the person writing the cheque and credited to the account of the person receiving the cheque. If the accounts of the writer and the receiver are in different banks, the cheque needs to pass through the **cheque-clearing system** for the correct accounts to be debited and credited. Cheque clearing is one mechanism by which banks carry out exchanges with each other. Transactions accounts can also be debited and credited by debit card, which is now a less costly technology than chequing, and much more widespread.

Some readers may be concerned that we have not mentioned credit cards, which entered our monetary intertemporal model in Chapter 12 as a form of money. There is a good reason we have not done this—money and credit are fundamentally different. When a credit card purchase is made, the vendor of goods or services extends credit to the purchaser, and then this credit is transferred to the credit card issuer (e.g., Visa, MasterCard, American Express). The credit extended is not money in the sense that currency or a bank deposit is money, since the issuer of credit cannot use what is effectively an IOU of the purchaser as a medium of exchange. Note, however, that forms of credit, particularly credit cards, are a substitute for money in making transactions, and therefore they are important in terms of how we think about the monetary system, as we showed in Chapter 12.

Money and the Absence of Double Coincidence of Wants: The Roles of Commodity Money and Fiat Money

Now that we know something about what objects have served as a medium of exchange, we will consider in more detail what it means for some object to be a medium of exchange, which is the distinctive function of money. In this section, we will consider a model that formalizes why money is useful as a medium of exchange. This model will help us understand the role of the two simplest types of money: commodity money and fiat money.

A fundamental question in monetary economics is why market exchange is typically an exchange of goods for money (monetary exchange) rather than of goods for goods (barter exchange). Jevons[5] argued that money helped to solve a problem of an **absence of double coincidence of wants** associated with barter exchange. To understand the double-coincidence-of-wants problem, imagine a world where there are many goods, and people are specialized in what they want to produce and consume. For example, suppose person *A* produces corn but wants to consume wheat. If person *A* meets another person *B* who has wheat, that would be a single coincidence of wants, since *B* has what *A* wants. However, *B* may not want corn in exchange for her wheat. If *B* wanted to consume corn, there would be a double coincidence of wants,

---

[5]See S. Jevons, 1910, *Money and the Mechanism of Exchange*, 23rd ed., Kegan Paul.

since *A* wants what *B* has and *B* wants what *A* has. Barter exchange can only take place if there is a double coincidence. Now, searching for a trading partner is costly in time and resources (e.g., hauling corn from place to place looking for a double coincidence of wants), particularly if there are many goods in the economy, so that there are many would-be sellers to search among. It would be much easier if, in selling corn, person *A* needs to satisfy only a single coincidence of wants, that is, find a person who wants corn. This would be the case if everyone accepted some particular object. Then, in selling corn in exchange for wheat, all person *A* would need to do is sell corn for this particular object in a single-coincidence meeting, then sell the particular object for wheat in another single-coincidence meeting. The "particular object" would then be money.

To see how this might work, consider the following simple economy, depicted in Figure 17.1. The example is from the work of Nobuhiro Kiyotaki and Randall Wright,[6] who formalized Jevons's notion of the role of money by using modern dynamic methods. There are three types of people in this economy. Type I people consume good 1 and produce good 2; type II people consume good 2 and produce good 3; and type III people consume good 3 and produce good 1. There are many people of each type in the economy, and everyone lives forever, with people meeting each other pairwise and at random each period. That is, each person meets one other person each period, and that other person is someone he or she bumps into at random. If the people in this economy each produce their good, and then wait until they meet another person with whom they can engage in a barter exchange, everyone will wait forever to trade, since

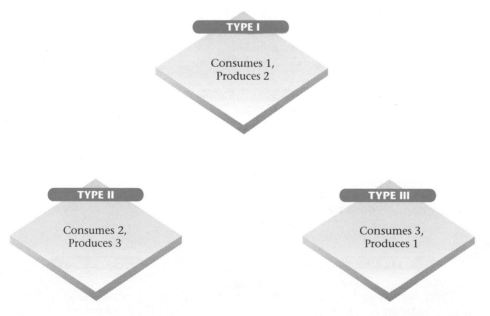

FIGURE 17.1

An Absence-of-Double-Coincidence Economy

In the model there are three types of people. A type I person consumes good 1 and produces good 2; a type II person consumes good 2 and produces good 3; and a type III person consumes good 3 and produces good 1.

TYPE I
Consumes 1, Produces 2

TYPE II
Consumes 2, Produces 3

TYPE III
Consumes 3, Produces 1

---

[6]See N. Kiyotaki and R. Wright, 1989, "On Money as a Medium of Exchange," *Journal of Political Economy* 97, 927–954.

this economy has an absence of double coincidence of wants. This is the simplest type of example where there are no possible pairwise meetings where a double coincidence of wants occurs.

How might trade be accomplished here? One solution would be for people to use a commodity money. Suppose, for example, that good 1 can be stored at a relatively low cost. Then good 1 might be used as a commodity money, in that type II people accept good 1 in exchange for good 3 when meeting type III people. Why does type II accept good 1 even though it is not something he or she consumes? This situation occurs because type II knows that type I will accept good 1 in exchange for good 2 (this is a double-coincidence trade). Good 1 in this example is then a commodity money—a medium of exchange—as it is accepted in exchange by people who do not ultimately consume it. We show the equilibrium patterns of trade in Figure 17.2.

Another solution to the absence-of-double-coincidence problem would be the introduction of a fourth good, fiat money, which no one consumes but which is acceptable to everyone in exchange for goods. A possible equilibrium pattern of exchange is shown in Figure 17.3. Here, when types I and II meet, II buys good 2 with money; when I and III meet, I buys good 1 with money; and when III and II meet, III buys good 3 with money. Thus, money circulates clockwise in Figure 17.3, and goods are passed counterclockwise.

For this model to say something interesting about the conditions under which commodity money would be useful, and when fiat money would be better than commodity money, we would have to introduce costs of counterfeiting, the resource costs of producing commodity money, and so forth. This would be quite complicated to do. However, this simple model captures the essentials of the absence-of-double-coincidence problem and why this helps to make money socially useful in promoting exchange. Barter exchange is difficult, in fact impossible, in this example, unless individuals accept objects that they do not consume. That is, a medium of exchange—money—is essential in

FIGURE 17.2

Good 1 as a Commodity Money in the Absence-of-Double-Coincidence Economy

Given the absence-of-double-coincidence problem, one solution is to have good 1 serve as a commodity money. A type II person accepts good 1 even though he or she does not consume it. Good 1 is held by type II until he or she can exchange it for good 2 with a type I person.

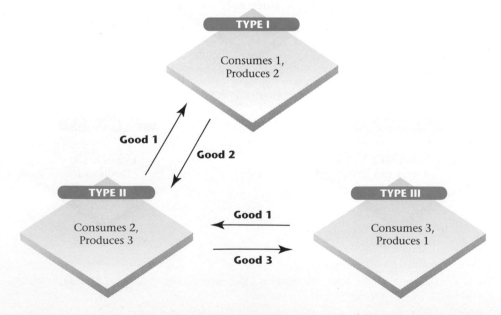

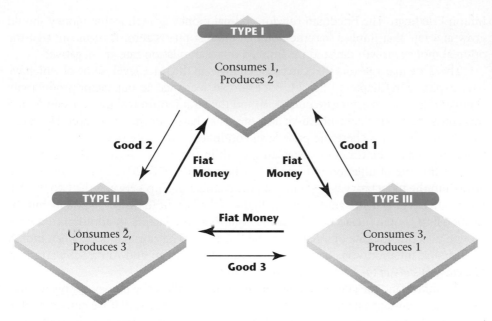

FIGURE 17.3
Fiat Money in the Absence-of-Double-Coincidence Economy
The double-coincidence problem can be solved if the people in this economy all accept fiat money. Money circulates clockwise in the figure, while goods are passed counterclockwise.

allowing people to exchange what they do not want for what they want, and it therefore increases welfare. In fact, in this example the institution of money is a Pareto improvement (recall our discussion from Chapter 5), since it increases welfare for everyone over what it would be otherwise.

Long-Run Inflation in the Monetary Intertemporal Model

The institution of monetary exchange matters for the determination of real macroeconomic quantities and contributes in important ways to economic welfare in modern economies. Once this institution is in place, however, the money supply can change in ways that have no consequences at all for real macroeconomic variables or for welfare. Though short-run monetary non-neutralities might arise because of money surprise or segmented markets (studied in Chapter 12), New Monetarist frictions (Chapter 13), or sticky prices (Chapter 14), in the long run money is neutral (as we showed in Chapter 12), in that a one-time level increase in the stock of money only changes prices in proportion and has no long-run effects on real variables.

Though money is neutral in the long run, in that a change in the level of the money supply has no long-run real effects, permanent changes in the growth rate of the money supply are not neutral. For example, a permanent increase in the rate of growth in the money supply will ultimately cause the inflation rate to increase permanently. Using the monetary intertemporal model we constructed in Chapter 12, we are able to show why money growth and inflation are costly in terms of lost aggregate output and the misallocation of resources. Further, we determine an optimal prescription for monetary growth, often referred to as the Friedman rule for monetary policy, after

Milton Friedman. The Friedman rule for optimal money growth is that money should grow at a rate that implies that the nominal interest rate is zero. It turns out that the optimal money growth rate and the implied optimal inflation rate are negative.

There are many factors that can cause changes in the price level, some of which we have explored in Chapters 12 to 14. For example, a change in total factor productivity changes equilibrium aggregate output, Y, and the equilibrium real interest rate, r, and this shifts the money demand curve and causes a change in the price level. However, sustained inflations, where the price level continues to increase over a long period of time, are usually the result of sustained growth in the money supply. In Figure 17.4 we plot the rate of inflation in Canada for the period 1956–2011 against the rate of growth in the monetary base. There is a positive relationship between the two, in that the positively sloped straight line in the figure is the best fit to the set of points, but the relationship is quite noisy, which reflects that there are factors in addition to money growth affecting the rate of inflation in the short run. The causal link between money growth and inflation was emphasized by Milton Friedman and Anna Schwartz in *A Monetary History of the United States: 1867–1960*.[7]

To understand the effects of long-run inflation, we allow the money supply to grow forever at a constant rate in the monetary intertemporal model that we constructed in Chapter 12. We suppose that the government permits the money supply to grow by

FIGURE 17.4

Scatter Plot of the Inflation Rate versus the Growth Rate in the Monetary Base for Canada, 1956–2011

Clearly, these two variables are positively correlated, but there is a lot of noise around the straight line that is the best fit to the points in the scatter plot.

Source: Adapted from the Statistics Canada CANSIM database, Series v37152, v41690973.

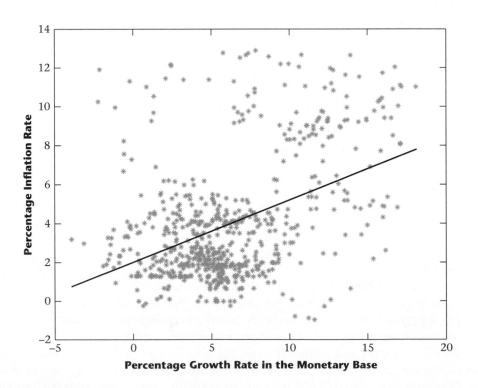

[7]M. Friedman and A. Schwartz, 1960, A Monetary History of the United States 1867–1960, Princeton University Press, Princeton N.J.

making lump-sum transfers to consumers each period, with the money supply growing according to

$$M' = (1 + x)M, \qquad (17.1)$$

where M' is the future money supply, M is the current money supply, and x is the growth rate of the money supply from the current period to the future period. For simplicity, we suppose that the economy looks exactly the same in every period, in that total factor productivity, real government spending, and consumer preferences are identical in every period. The only exogenous variable that changes over time is the money supply, which grows according to Equation (17.1). This implies that all of the endogenous variables in the model, except the price level, remain the same for all time. That is, the real wage, employment, aggregate output, the real interest rate, and the inflation rate are constant for all time. In the current period, money supply is equal to money demand in equilibrium, and so from Chapter 12 we have

$$M = PL(Y, r + i). \qquad (17.2)$$

Recall from Chapter 12 that, on the left-hand side of Equation (17.2), M is the nominal money supply and, on the right-hand side of Equation (17.2), $PL(Y, r + i)$ is nominal money demand. From the Fisher relation, recall that $r + i$ (the real interest rate plus the inflation rate) is equal (approximately) to the nominal interest rate. It must also be the case in equilibrium that money supply is equal to money demand in the future period, so that

$$M' = P'L(Y', r' + i'), \qquad (17.3)$$

where P' is the price level in the future period, Y' is future aggregate output, r' is the future real interest rate, and i' is the future inflation rate. Then, from Equations (17.2) and (17.3), we have

$$\frac{M'}{M} = \frac{P'L(Y', r' + i')}{PL(Y, r + i)} \qquad (17.4)$$

But in equilibrium, aggregate output, the real interest rate, and the inflation rate remain constant over time, which implies that $Y' = Y$, $r' = r$, and $i' = i$. This then gives $L(Y', r' + i') = L(Y, r + i)$, so that the real demand for money is the same in the future and current periods. Then, from Equation (17.4), we get

$$\frac{M'}{M} = \frac{P'}{P},$$

so that the growth rates of the money supply and the price level are the same in equilibrium. This implies, from Equation (17.1), that the inflation rate is given by

$$i = \frac{P'}{P} - 1 = \frac{M'}{M} - 1 = x$$

so that the inflation rate is equal to the money growth rate. The equality of the money growth rate and the inflation rate is special to this situation in which real variables remain constant over time. From Equation (17.4), if the real demand for money changes over time, so that $L(Y', r' + i') \neq L(Y, r + i)$, then the money growth rate is not equal to the inflation rate. However, it is still true that the inflation rate will increase as the money growth rate increases. Note that, in reality, real income grows over time, which causes the demand for money to grow over time. If the money supply and real income grow at constant rates over time, the rate of inflation will be lower than the rate of money growth.

We want to determine the effects of an increase in x on output, the real interest rate, employment, and the real wage in the monetary intertemporal model. To do this, we first need to understand how inflation affects labour supply and the demand for current consumption goods in this model. Recall from Chapter 12 that in the monetary intertemporal model, some consumption goods are purchased by using money acquired by the representative consumer before the goods market opens and that the consumer receives his or her wage income after goods are purchased, so that wage income must be held in the form of money before it is spent in the future period. Just as in Chapter 9, when the representative consumer optimizes, he or she sets the marginal rate of substitution of current consumption goods for future consumption goods equal to $1 + r$ or

$$MRS_{C,C'} = 1 + r. \tag{17.5}$$

As well, assuming current wages cannot be spent on consumption goods until the future period, the effective real wage for the consumer is $\dfrac{Pw}{P'}$, which is the current nominal wage divided by the future price level. Therefore (recall Chapter 4), when the consumer optimizes, he or she sets the marginal rate of substitution of current leisure for future consumption equal to $\dfrac{Pw}{P'}$ or

$$MRS_{l,C'} = \frac{Pw}{P'} \tag{17.6}$$

Now, because Equations (17.5) and (17.6) tell us how the consumer substitutes at the optimum between current and future consumption and between current leisure and future consumption, we can derive from these two equations a marginal condition for substitution at the optimum between current leisure and current consumption. That is, at the optimum it must be the case that

$$MRS_{l,C} = \frac{MRS_{l,C'}}{MRS_{C,C'}} = \frac{Pw}{P'(1 + r)},$$

from Equations (17.5) and (17.6). Therefore, from the Fisher relation in Chapter 12, we have

$$MRS_{l,C} = \frac{w}{1 + R}, \tag{17.7}$$

where R is the nominal interest rate. To understand the marginal condition, Equation (17.7), it helps to run through how the consumer would substitute between current consumption and current leisure, which is roundabout because of the transactions constraint. If the consumer wants to supply one extra unit of time during the current period as labour, he or she earns additional real wages of w, which then must be held over to the future period, when their value in terms of future consumption goods is $\dfrac{Pw}{P'}$. To consume more current goods, the consumer can borrow against this amount in the credit market (not with a credit card—this only helps finance consumption within the period) before he or she arrives in the goods market. The real quantity that can be borrowed is $\dfrac{Pw}{P'(1+r)} = \dfrac{w}{1+R}$, which then must be the relative price of current leisure for current consumption.

Given Equation (17.7), a higher nominal interest rate, R, causes substitution away from consumption goods and toward leisure. Equation (17.4) then tells us that, from the approximate Fisher relation $R = r + i$, given the real interest rate, r, and the real wage, w, and assuming that substitution effects dominate income effects, an increase in the inflation rate, i, causes substitution from consumption goods to leisure.

In Figure 17.5 we show the effects in the current period of an increase in the money growth rate from x_1 to x_2, which takes place for all periods and is anticipated by everyone. In equilibrium the inflation rate in every period then increases from x_1 to x_2, given our analysis above where we showed that the money growth rate equals the inflation rate in equilibrium. The increase in the inflation rate causes substitution by the representative consumer from consumption goods to leisure. This causes the labour

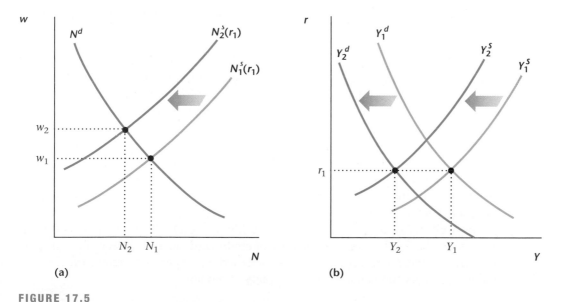

(a)

(b)

FIGURE 17.5

The Long-Run Effects of an Increase in the Money Growth Rate

An increase in the money growth rate increases the inflation rate, which shifts the labour supply curve to the left, the output supply curve to the left, and the output demand curve to the left. The real wage rises, employment falls, and output falls. The real interest rate may rise or fall, but for simplicity we show the case where it stays constant.

supply curve to shift to the left in Figure 17.5(a), which in turn shifts the output supply curve to the left in Figure 17.5(b). As well, because the consumer substitutes away from consumption goods, the output demand curve shifts to the left in Figure 17.5(b). Now, in Figure 17.5(b), it is not clear whether the real interest rate rises or falls. For simplicity, we show the case where the output demand and output supply effects on the real interest rate just cancel, so that the real interest rate does not change. This also implies that investment and the capital stock are unaffected (assume that we are in a steady state where the capital stock is constant over time), which also greatly simplifies matters.

In Figure 17.5, in equilibrium output falls from Y_1 to Y_2, employment falls from N_1 to N_2, and the real wage rises from w_1 to w_2. In the figure the real interest rate remains constant, so that investment expenditures are unaffected, but consumption must fall as real income has decreased. From the approximate Fisher relation, we have $R = r + i$, where R is the nominal interest rate. Therefore, because r is constant and i increases from x_1 to x_2, the nominal interest rate increases by the amount of the money growth rate increase (the **Fisher effect**; in the long run, an increase in the inflation rate is reflected one-for-one in an increase in the nominal interest rate). Also, given equilibrium in the money market,

$$\frac{M}{P} = L(Y, r + i), \tag{17.8}$$

real output, Y, has decreased, r is the same, and i has increased; therefore, real money demand on the right-hand side of Equation (17.8) has decreased, and so the current real money supply on the left-hand side of Equation (17.8) must also decrease. Higher money growth and inflation causes consumers and firms to hold a smaller quantity of real cash balances in equilibrium.

Though money is neutral in this economy, in that a change in the level of the money supply has no real effects, a change in the growth rate of the money supply is not neutral. If a change in the money growth rate had no real effects, we would say that money was **superneutral**. However, money is not superneutral here, as an increase in the money growth rate leads to decreases in consumption, output, and employment. These effects occur because higher money growth leads to higher inflation, which affects the consumer's decisions concerning how much to work in the current period and how much and what to consume. Higher inflation increases the nominal interest rate, which is the opportunity cost of holding money for transactions purposes. As a result, the household economizes on money balances. The resulting costs of inflation are lost output and consumption.

As well, recall from Chapter 12 that a higher nominal interest rate causes an increase in the equilibrium real quantity of credit card balances in equilibrium. This is costly, as there are real resource costs associated with operating credit card systems, and it represents another super-nonneutrality of money.

OPTIMAL MONETARY POLICY: THE FRIEDMAN RULE

At this point, we would like to demonstrate the key economic inefficiencies that result from inflation, and then show how these inefficiencies can be corrected by the appropriate long-run monetary policy. Recall from Chapter 5 that economic efficiency is achieved when the allocation of resources in an economy is Pareto-optimal, that is, when there is no way to rearrange production or the allocation of goods so that someone is better off and no one is worse off. A key condition for Pareto-optimality that we derived in Chapter 5 was that the marginal rate of substitution of leisure for consumption must be equal to the marginal rate of transformation of leisure for consumption, that is

$$MRS_{l,C} = MRT_{l,C}. \tag{17.9}$$

This condition holds at the Pareto optimum because it is efficient for the rate at which the consumer is just willing to substitute leisure for consumption to be equal to the rate at which leisure can be converted into consumption goods using the production technology. In this model, as in the model of Chapter 5, the marginal rate of transformation of leisure for consumption is equal to the marginal product of labour, MP_N. In a competitive equilibrium, profit maximization by the representative firm implies that $MP_N = w$, so it is also true in a competitive equilibrium that

$$MRT_{l,C} = w. \tag{17.10}$$

Therefore, substituting for w in Equation (17.7) by using Equation (17.10) gives

$$MRS_{l,C} = \frac{MRT_{l,C}}{1 + R}. \tag{17.11}$$

Therefore, because Equation (17.11) holds in competitive equilibrium in this model, Equation (17.9) does not hold, and so the competitive equilibrium is not Pareto-optimal, in general, as long as the nominal interest rate is positive, or $R > 0$. That is, a positive nominal interest rate drives a wedge between the marginal rate of substitution and the marginal rate of transformation, thus creating an inefficiency. The fact that the nominal interest rate is positive implies that too much leisure is consumed, too little output is produced, consumption is too low, real money balances are too low, and too large a quantity of resources is used in operating the credit card system.

We know that an increase in the money growth rate, x, causes an increase in the nominal interest rate, so that higher money growth, which is associated with higher inflation, implies a larger wedge separating the marginal rate of substitution from the marginal rate of transformation. If the money growth rate and inflation were reduced, then it appears that this would promote economic efficiency, but what would be the best money growth rate for the government to set? Clearly, if the nominal interest rate were reduced to zero, then the marginal rate of substitution would be equal to the marginal rate of transformation in Equation (17.11). What is the money growth rate, x, that would drive the nominal interest rate to zero? Because in equilibrium the nominal interest rate is $R = r + x$, if $R = 0$ then it is optimal for the money growth rate to be $x = -r$. Because the real interest rate is positive ($r > 0$), then at the optimum, $x < 0$ and the money supply decreases over time. Further, if the money supply is decreasing over time, there is **deflation**, because the inflation rate is $i = x = -r$. Thus, it is optimal for the government to generate a deflation that continues forever, implying that the nominal interest rate is zero in every period.

The fact that the optimal monetary policy drives the nominal interest rate to zero is of prime importance in understanding why this policy works to maximize welfare. A positive nominal interest rate on bonds and time deposits implies that consumers and firms economize too much on money balances in favour of holding time deposits (and indirectly, through banks, holding government bonds). The consumer also consumes too small a quantity of goods and too much leisure. If the nominal interest rate is driven to zero through deflation, giving money a higher real return, then consumers and firms become indifferent between holding time deposits and money, and this is optimal.

This type of optimal deflationary monetary policy is called a *Friedman rule*, after Milton Friedman.[8] In practice, the Friedman rule means that the nominal interest rate on riskless securities should always be zero. This does not mean that all nominal interest rates should be zero (this would be impossible), but that the nominal interest rate on short-term government debt (e.g., Treasury bills) should be zero. The Friedman rule is probably the most robust policy conclusion that comes from monetary economics, but it is a policy that essentially no central bank currently follows or ever has followed. No central bank pursues long-run deflation as a goal, and no central bank advocates pushing the nominal interest rate to zero over the long term (though the Japanese central bank set nominal interest rates at essentially zero in the 1990s, and the U.S. Federal Reserve System has set its target nominal interest rate at essentially zero since late 2008). Thus, it may be that central banks are doing something wrong, that our model leaves out some important aspect(s) of the problem at hand, or that inflation just does not matter much.

To pursue the last explanation, one possible reason central banks do not follow the Friedman rule is that at low levels of inflation, say below 10% per annum, the gains from reducing inflation are very small. Indeed, Thomas Cooley and Gary Hansen conclude that, in a monetary model similar to the one we have studied here, the welfare loss from an inflation rate of 10% per annum is about 0.5% of consumption for the average consumer, and the welfare loss from a monetary rule with 0% inflation versus the Friedman rule rate of deflation is about 0.14% of consumption for the average consumer.[9]

Though most macroeconomic models tell us that the welfare losses from moderate inflations are quite small, the costs of extremely high rates of inflation—that is, **hyperinflations**—are clearly very large. Some prominent hyperinflations occurred in Austria, Hungary, Germany, and Poland in the early 1920s following World War I. For example, the inflation rate in Austria averaged 10 000% per annum between January 1921 and August 1922. Typically, hyperinflations occur because the government is unwilling or unable to finance large government outlays through taxation or borrowing, and so it must resort to seigniorage. For example, the German hyperinflation following World War I occurred in part because the German government financed large war reparations to other European countries by printing money at a very high rate.

---

[8]See "The Optimum Quantity of Money," 1969, in M. Friedman (ed.), *The Optimum Quantity of Money and Other Essays*, Hawthorne, NY: Aldine Publishing, pp. 1–50.

[9]See T. Cooley and G. Hansen, 1989, "The Inflation Tax in a Real Business Cycle Model," *American Economic Review* 79, 733–748.

Should the Bank of Canada Reduce the Inflation Rate to Zero or Less?

172

MACROECONOMICS
IN ACTION

Our monetary intertemporal model tells us that the optimal rate of inflation is negative, which implies that the Bank of Canada should engineer a rate of growth in the money supply that would give permanent deflation. However, as we pointed out, no central bank appears to have attempted to bring about a deflation. Currently, the Bank's target for the inflation rate is 2% per year. At most, some policymakers are willing to recommend that the inflation rate be reduced to zero, so that the price level will remain constant over time. Does this imply there is something missing in the monetary intertemporal model in terms of the costs and benefits of inflation? Could the optimal inflation rate be higher than zero? S. Rao Aiyagari makes a case that the costs of reducing the inflation rate to zero would exceed the benefits.[11] In making his argument, Aiyagari appeals to some of the costs of inflation contained in our monetary intertemporal model, but he considers other costs and benefits of inflation as well.

First, as in our model, Aiyagari argues that a cost of inflation arises because the nominal interest rate is positive, which causes people to economize too much on money balances. He points out that some of these costs can be eliminated if interest is paid on some of the components of the money stock. A practice in Canada that is different from what occurs in many other countries (including the United States) is that the Bank of Canada pays interest on the component of outside money balances (reserves) held by financial institutions as deposits at the Bank. The payment of interest on reserves is good for economic efficiency. Indeed, if a central bank could pay interest on currency as well as reserves, then this could implement the Friedman rule. However, it seems impractical for interest to be paid on circulating currency.

Although the costs of inflation are very small, as Aiyagari argues, the short-run costs of reducing the inflation rate might potentially be large. Keynesian economists argue that price and wage stickiness can cause short-run decreases in aggregate output if the Bank of Canada were to reduce money supply growth to bring about a reduction in inflation, as we studied in Chapter 14. As well, if the private sector doubts the Bank's resolve to reduce inflation, this can cause a short-run drop in aggregate activity until the Bank proves it is serious, an issue we will address in Chapter 18. Given these potentially large short-run costs, Aiyagari concludes that a reduction in the inflation rate to zero would not be worthwhile, but that relaxing regulations on the financial sector—for example, in countries where interest is currently not paid on bank reserves—would certainly be beneficial.

[11]See S. R. Aiyagari, 1990, "Deflating the Case for Zero Inflation," *Federal Reserve Bank of Minneapolis Quarterly Review*, Summer, 2–11.

The key to stopping a hyperinflation, as Thomas Sargent points out, is gaining control over fiscal policy by reducing the government deficit.[10]

Another reason that central bankers are wary of deflation and low nominal interest rates is that these have been characteristics of poorly performing economies. For example, there was deflation and very low nominal interest rates in the United States during the Great Depression, in the 1990s in Japan, and during the recent financial

---

[10]See "The Ends of Four Big Inflations," 1993, in T. Sargent (ed.), *Rational Expectations and Inflation*, 2nd ed., New York: Harper Collins, pp. 43–116.

crisis in the United States and elsewhere. Keynes argued that at a low nominal interest rate, there could be a **liquidity trap**. That is, if the nominal interest rate on government securities is zero, then money and government securities are essentially identical assets. If the central bank attempts to increase the money supply through an open market sale of government securities when the nominal interest rate is zero, this will have no effect, since the central bank is simply exchanging one type of asset for another identical asset. Perhaps central bankers fear a liquidity trap, but the logic of the Friedman rule tells us that a liquidity trap is actually a good place to be. We discussed liquidity traps in more detail in Chapters 12 and 14.

Macroeconomics in Action 17.2 discusses the practical aspects of inflation control for central banks.

Financial Intermediation and Banking

The purpose of this section is to study the place of banking in the monetary system. Earlier in this chapter we discussed the historical importance of currency issued by private banks and how, in modern economies, much of transactions activity takes place by using bank deposits. The role that banks and other financial intermediaries play in the economy is intimately related to the properties that different assets have, and so in the following subsection we discuss the characteristics of assets and their economic importance.

PROPERTIES OF ASSETS

The four most important properties of assets are rate of return, risk, maturity, and liquidity; we will discuss each of these in turn.

- *Rate of return:* The rate of return on an asset is the payoff on the asset over some specified period of time divided by the initial investment in the asset, minus one. For example, the one-period rate of return, r_t^a, on an asset bought at price q_t in period t, sold at price q_{t+1} in period $t + 1$, with a payout (say a dividend on a stock) of d in period $t + 1$, would be

$$r_t^a = \frac{q_{t+1} + d}{q_t} - 1.$$

Everything else held constant, consumers prefer assets that bear higher rates of return.

- *Risk:* In modern finance theory, the risk that matters for a consumer's behaviour is the risk an asset contributes to the consumer's entire **portfolio**, where a portfolio is the entire set of assets the consumer holds. For example, a set of stocks might be quite risky on an individual basis, since their rates of return fluctuate a great deal over time. However, when all these stocks are held together in a well-diversified portfolio, the entire portfolio may not be very risky. For instance, holding all your wealth in shares of Joe's Restaurant might be quite risky, but holding shares in all the restaurants in town might not be very risky at all. Even though diversifying a portfolio by holding many different assets reduces risk, because the rates of return on some assets can go up while other rates of return go down, there is a limit to the risk reduction that can be gained from diversification. Risk that cannot be diversified away is aggregate or macroeconomic risk, and it is the amount of this **nondiversifiable risk** present in a particular asset that matters for economic behaviour. Here, we will assume that consumers are **risk-averse**, so that, everything else held constant, a consumer will prefer to hold assets with less nondiversifiable risk.

- *Maturity:* Maturity refers to the time it takes for an asset to pay off. For some assets, maturity is a straightforward concept. For example, a three-month Treasury bill is a security issued by the Canadian government that pays its face value three months from the date of issue, and so maturity in this case is three months. For some other assets, however, this is not so clear, as in the case of a long-maturity bond. Many bonds provide for coupon payments, which are amounts the bearer receives at fixed intervals until the bond matures, when it pays its face value.

  Thus, a 30-year bond that provides for coupon payments at monthly intervals does not have a maturity of 30 years, but something less than that, since the payoffs on the asset take place during the 30-year period until all payoffs are received. All other things held constant, a consumer will prefer a short-maturity asset to a long-maturity asset. Short-maturity assets imply more flexibility in meeting unanticipated needs for funds, and even if a consumer is certain the funds will not be needed until far into the future (e.g., suppose the consumer is saving for a child's education), it is possible to meet this need by holding a string of short-maturity assets rather than a long-maturity asset.

- *Liquidity:* The final asset characteristic is liquidity, which is a measure of how long it takes to sell an asset for its market value and of how high the costs are of selling the asset. Since money is widely acceptable in exchange and can therefore essentially be sold for its market value instantaneously, it is the most liquid asset. A good example of an illiquid asset is a house, which can often take weeks to sell, with a high transaction fee paid to an intermediary—the real estate agent—to find a buyer. Liquidity is important to an asset holder, since investors face uncertainty about when they want to purchase goods or assets. For example, consumers may face unforeseen expenses, such as medical bills, or they may want to take advantage of an unanticipated investment opportunity. All else held constant, consumers prefer more liquidity to less liquidity.

FINANCIAL INTERMEDIATION

Now that we know something about the properties of assets, we can examine the role of financial intermediaries in the monetary system.

A financial intermediary is defined by the following characteristics:

1. It borrows from one group of economic agents and lends to another.
2. The group of economic agents it borrows from is large and so is the group it lends to. That is, a financial intermediary is well diversified.
3. It transforms assets. That is, the properties of its liabilities are different from the properties of its assets.
4. It processes information.

Examples of financial intermediaries are insurance companies, mutual funds, and depository institutions. The economic role these intermediaries play is intimately related to their four defining characteristics. Consider depository institutions as an example. Depository institutions include chartered banks, mortgage and trust companies, credit unions, and caisses populaires. These institutions exist in part because of difficulties in getting together ultimate borrowers and ultimate lenders. To see why this is so, consider how the borrowing and lending done by a depository institution would take place in the absence of this institution. An individual wanting to borrow to purchase a house, for example, would have to first find a lender willing to lend him or her the funds to make the purchase. Even if the potential borrower were well known to the potential lender, the potential lender may not have good information on the potential borrower's ability to repay the loan, and some time and effort would have to be forgone to acquire this information. Further, given that the loan required is sizeable, the potential borrower might have to approach several potential lenders to finance the purchase, and each of these would have to incur information costs to ascertain the riskiness of the loan. Now, supposing the loan is made, each of the lenders would bear some risk, given that there is always some chance the borrower will not repay. Further, unless the lenders had the means to enforce the contract, the borrower might try to abscond without repaying, even though he or she could repay. Finally, after the loan is made, it would be difficult for the lender to sell the loan to someone else should he or she require funds on short notice. That is, the loan is illiquid, in part because it has a long maturity. In fact, given the high value of the loan relative to the potential borrower's income, the maturity of the loan may be so long that few potential lenders would want to tie up funds for this length of time.

To summarize, there are six potential problems with direct lending from ultimate lenders to ultimate borrowers, without the benefit of a financial intermediary:

1. Matching borrowers with lenders is costly in time and effort.
2. The ultimate lenders may not be skilled at evaluating credit risks.
3. Because several lenders would often be required to fund any one borrower, there would be replication of the costs required to evaluate credit risk.
4. Because lenders economize on information costs by lending to few borrowers, lending will be risky.
5. Loans will tend to be illiquid.
6. Loans will tend to have longer maturities than lenders would like.

Without financial intermediaries, few loans would be made, and the only lending would be to the least risky borrowers. However, in our running example, consider what a depository institution can do to alleviate the above six difficulties. First, the depository institution is a well-defined place of business, and people know where to go if they want to borrow or lend, and so this eliminates the search costs involved in getting borrowers and lenders together. Second, the depository institution specializes in evaluating credit risks, and so can do this at a lower cost per loan than an unspecialized individual. That is, there are economies of scale in acquiring information. Third, because the financial intermediary pools the funds of many lenders, it can avoid the replication of costs that occurs with direct lending. Fourth, because the financial intermediary is well diversified with respect to both its assets and liabilities, it can transform risky, illiquid, long-maturity assets into relatively safe, liquid, short-maturity liabilities.

Taking a depository institution specializing in mortgage lending as an example, each mortgage may be risky, illiquid, and of long maturity. However, because the depository institution holds many mortgages (it is well diversified on the asset side of its balance sheet), the payoff on the bank's entire asset portfolio will be relatively predictable, since the fraction of mortgage loans that default should be predictable. Further, even though all the assets of the depository institution are illiquid and of long maturity, the institution's liabilities can be liquid and of short maturity because of the diversification of its liabilities. That is, suppose that the depository institution has many depositors, all holding transactions accounts. An individual depositor could decide to make withdrawals and deposits or to make debit card transactions at random times, but the behaviour of depositors as a group will be predictable. Thus, though a transactions deposit is highly liquid and has as short a maturity as the depositor could wish for, the institution can make highly illiquid and long-maturity loans on the basis of its ability to predict the aggregate behaviour of a large number of depositors.

THE DIAMOND-DYBVIG BANKING MODEL

This banking model was developed in the early 1980s by Douglas Diamond and Philip Dybvig.[12] It is a simple model that captures some of the important features of banks and helps to explain why bank runs might occur (as they did historically in some countries) and what role the government might have in preventing bank runs.

In the model, there are three periods: 0, 1, and 2. There are N consumers, where N is very large, and each consumer is endowed with one unit of a good in period 0, which can serve as an input to production. The production technology takes one unit of the input good in period 0 and converts this into $1 + r$ units of the consumption good in period 2. However, this production technology can also be interrupted in period 1. If interruption occurs in period 1, then one unit of consumption goods can be obtained for each unit of the good invested in period 0. If production is interrupted, then nothing is produced in period 2.

A given consumer might want to consume early, in period 1, or to consume late, in period 2. However, in period 0, individual consumers do not know whether they are early or late consumers; they learn this in period 1. In period 0, each consumer knows that she or he has a probability t of being an early consumer and probability $1 - t$ of being a late consumer, and in period 1, tN consumers learn that they are early consumers and $(1 - t)N$ consumers learn that they are late consumers. We have $0 < t < 1$. For example, if $t = 1/2$, then a consumer has equal probabilities of being an early or a late consumer, as if consuming early or late were determined by the flip of a coin.

The production technology captures liquidity in a simple way. That is, using the production technology is much like investing in a long-maturity asset that could be

---

[12]D. Diamond and P. Dybvig, 1983, "Bank Runs, Liquidity, and Deposit Insurance," *Journal of Political Economy* 91, 401–419.

sold with some loss before it matures. For a consumer, the possibility that he or she might consume early captures the idea that there exist random needs for liquid assets, that is, unforeseen circumstances when transactions need to be made. In practice we make many transactions over the course of a day or a week, and not all of these transactions are anticipated. For example, we might see a book in a store window and want to purchase it, or we might be caught in an unexpected rainstorm and need to buy an umbrella.

Whether consumption takes place early or late, the utility (or pleasure) that the consumer receives is given by $U(c)$, where U is a utility function and c is consumption. The utility function is concave, as in Figure 17.6, because the **marginal utility of consumption** declines as consumption increases. The marginal utility of consumption, MU_c, is given by the slope of the utility function. For example, in Figure 17.6 the MU_c when $c = c^*$ is given by the slope of a tangent to the utility function at point A.

Given the world that an individual consumer lives in here, he or she needs to make decisions under uncertainty in period 0. In economics, a productive approach to modelling consumer choice under uncertainty is to assume that a consumer maximizes expected utility, which here is

$$\text{Expected utility} = tU(c_1) + (1-t)U(c_2),$$

where c_1 is consumption if the consumer needs to consume early, and c_2 is consumption if the consumer is a late consumer. That is, expected utility is a weighted average of utilities that occur if the particular events happen (early or late consumption), where the weights are the probabilities that the particular events occur, which in this case are t and $1 - t$, respectively.

We can represent a consumer's expected utility preferences in terms of indifference curves, with c_1 (early consumption) on the horizontal axis and c_2 (late consumption) on the vertical axis in Figure 17.7. As in Chapters 4 and 9, these indifference curves are

FIGURE 17.6

The Utility Function for a Consumer in the Diamond-Dybvig Model

The utility function is concave, and the slope of the function is the marginal utility of consumption, MU_C.

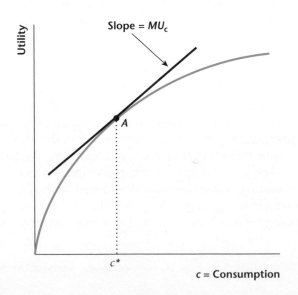

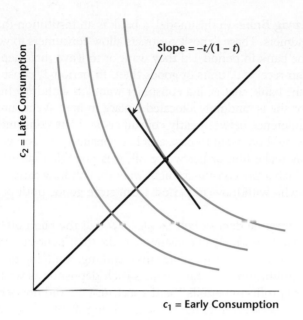

FIGURE 17.7

The Preferences of a Diamond-Dybvig Consumer The figure shows the indifference curves for a Diamond-Dybvig consumer, who has preferences over early consumption and late consumption.

downward-sloping and convex. The marginal rate of substitution of early consumption for late consumption for the consumer is given by

$$MRS_{c_1,c_2} = \frac{tMU_{c_1}}{(1-t)MU_{c_2}}, \qquad (17.12)$$

where MRS_{c_1,c_2} is minus the slope of an indifference curve in Figure 17.7. When $c_1 = c_2$ so that early consumption and late consumption are equal, we have $MU_{c_1} = MU_{c_2}$ (if consumption is the same, the marginal utility of consumption must also be the same). From Equation (17.12) we have

$$MRS_{c_1,c_2} = \frac{t}{(1-t)} \qquad (17.13)$$

when $c_1 = c_2$. Therefore, in Figure 17.7, an important property of the indifference curves is that, along the line $c_1 = c_2$, the slope of each of the indifference curves is $\frac{-t}{1-t}$.

Now, suppose that each consumer must invest independently. On his or her own, what would a consumer do? Clearly, he or she invests all of his or her one unit of endowment in the technology in period 0. Then, in period 1, if he or she is an early consumer, he or she interrupts the technology and is able to consume $c_1 = 1$. If he or she is a late consumer, then the technology is not interrupted and the consumer gets $c_2 = 1 + r$ in period 2 when the investment matures. What we would like to show is that a bank can form that allows all consumers to do better than this.

A Diamond-Dybvig Bank In this model, a bank is an institution that offers deposit contracts to consumers. These deposit contracts allow consumers to withdraw c_1 units of goods from the bank in period 1 if they want or to leave their deposit in the bank until period 2 and receive c_2 units of goods then. In period 1, consumers are served in sequence by the bank; that is, if a consumer wants to withdraw his or her deposit in period 1, he or she is randomly allocated a place in line. We assume that the bank cannot tell the difference between early consumers and late consumers. Although an early consumer would not want to pose as a late consumer by not withdrawing early, as this could only make him or her worse off, it is possible that there might be circumstances in which a late consumer might want to withdraw early. We suppose that a late consumer who withdraws in period 1 can store goods until period 2 and then consume them.

What determines the deposit contract (c_1, c_2) that the bank offers? We suppose that there is one bank in which all consumers make their deposits and that this bank behaves competitively. There is free entry into banking, implying that the bank earns zero profits in equilibrium. The bank makes each depositor as well off as possible, while earning zero profits in periods 1 and 2, because if it did not behave in this way, then some other bank could enter the market, offering an alternative deposit contract, and attract all consumers away from the first bank. Because all consumers deposit in the bank in period 0, the bank has N units of goods to invest in the technology in period 0. In period 1, the bank must choose the fraction x of the investment to interrupt so that it can pay c_1 to each depositor who wants to withdraw at that time. Supposing that only early consumers show up at the bank to withdraw in period 1, we must have

$$Ntc_1 = xN, \tag{17.14}$$

or the total quantity of withdrawals equals the quantity of production interrupted. Then, in period 2, the quantity of uninterrupted production matures, and this quantity is used to make payments to those consumers who chose to wait, who we are supposing are only the late consumers. Then, we have

$$N(1 - t)c_2 = (1 - x)N(1 + r). \tag{17.15}$$

That is, the total payout to the late consumers (on the left-hand side of Equation (17.15)) is equal to the total return on uninterrupted production (on the right-hand side of Equation (17.15)). If we substitute in Equation (17.15) for x by using Equation (17.14) and simplify, we get

$$tc_1 + \frac{(1 - t)c_2}{1 + r} = 1, \tag{17.16}$$

and Equation (17.16) is like a lifetime budget constraint for the bank that governs how the deposit contract (c_1, c_2) can be set by the bank. We can rewrite the bank's lifetime budget constraint in slope–intercept form as

$$c_2 = -\frac{t(1 + r)}{1 - t}c_1 + \frac{1 + r}{1 - t}, \tag{17.17}$$

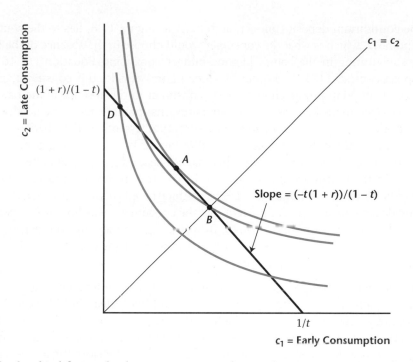

FIGURE 17.8

The Equilibrium Deposit Contract Offered by the Diamond-Dybvig Bank
Point A, where there is a tangency between the bank's lifetime budget constraint and the consumer's indifference curve, is the equilibrium deposit contract. Point B would have equal consumption for early and late consumers, and point D is what the consumer could achieve in the absence of the bank.

and the bank's lifetime budget constraint is depicted in Figure 17.8; in the figure, points A, B, and D lie on the constraint. The constraint has a vertical intercept of $\frac{1+r}{1-t}$, which is the maximum payout to late consumers if the bank does not interrupt any of its production, and the horizontal intercept is $\frac{1}{t}$, which is the maximum amount that could be withdrawn by early consumers in the case where all production is interrupted by the bank. The slope of the bank's lifetime budget constraint is $\frac{-t(1+r)}{1-t}$. The equilibrium deposit contract offered by the bank is at point A in Figure 17.8, where an indifference curve for the consumer is tangent to the bank's lifetime budget constraint. The equilibrium deposit contract has two important properties:

1. The equilibrium deposit contract, at point A in Figure 17.8, lies to the northwest of point B, which is the point on the bank's lifetime budget constraint where the bank's payouts to early and late consumers are the same. We know from above that at point B the marginal rate of substitution of early consumption for late consumption is $\frac{-t}{1-t}$, and so an indifference curve running through point B is less steep than the lifetime budget constraint of the bank. Therefore, A must lie to the northwest of B in the figure. The importance of this observation is that late consumers consume more than early consumers, given the equilibrium deposit contract; that is $c_2 > c_1$. Thus, if all other late consumers do not withdraw, any individual late consumer prefers not to withdraw in period 1. A late consumer is not tempted to pose as an early consumer if other late consumers do not do this.

2. The equilibrium deposit contract, at point A in Figure 17.8, lies to the southeast of point D, which is what the consumer would choose in the absence of the bank. By substituting in the bank's lifetime budget constraint, Equation (17.16), the deposit contract $(1, 1 + r)$ (point A in the figure) satisfies this constraint, so that the consumption profile chosen by the consumer in the absence of the bank is a choice open to the bank as well. To guarantee that point D lies to the northwest of point A in the figure requires an extra assumption, essentially that there is enough curvature in the utility function depicted in Figure 17.6. Without getting into the technical details concerning why this makes sense, we simply assume here that D lies to the northwest of A in the figure. The reason this is important is that it guarantees that $c_1 > 1$ and $c_2 < 1 + r$, so that there is a sense in which the bank provides insurance against the event that the consumer needs liquidity in period 1 to make a transaction (to consume). By accepting the banking contract, the consumer is able to consume more in period 1 than he or she could otherwise, at the expense of lower consumption in period 2.

The Diamond-Dybvig bank has some of the properties of financial intermediaries that we mentioned above. Although it does not lend but instead holds assets directly and does not process information, the bank in this model borrows from a large number of depositors (it is well diversified), and it carries out an asset transformation. The fact that the bank is well diversified is important for its role in transforming assets. That is, because the bank holds the deposits of a large number of depositors, the number of depositors who want to withdraw is predictable, and so the bank need only interrupt that fraction of production required to satisfy the withdrawal needs of the early consumers. The bank holds illiquid assets and is able to convert these assets into liquid deposits, providing depositors with a type of insurance against the need for liquid assets.

Bank Runs in the Diamond-Dybvig Model The fact that the Diamond-Dybvig bank supplies consumers with insurance against the need for liquidity also leaves the bank open to bank runs. Given the banking contract at point A in Figure 17.8, where $c_1 > 1$ and $c_2 < 1 + r$, there is a *good equilibrium* in which each early consumer lines up at the bank to withdraw his or her deposit in period 1, each late consumer waits to withdraw until period 2, and everyone is happy. Given these circumstances, no late consumer has the incentive to withdraw in period 1, as $c_2 > c_1$ at point A in Figure 17.8, so withdrawing early would only make a late consumer worse off. However, suppose that a late consumer believes that all other late consumers will go to the bank to withdraw in period 1. Because all early consumers withdraw in period 1, the individual late consumer then believes that everyone else will go to the bank in period 1. Because $c_1 > 1$ at point A in Figure 17.8, even if the bank liquidates all of its assets in period 1, which yields the quantity N in consumption goods, it cannot satisfy total withdrawal demand, which is $(N - 1)c_1$ (recall that N is large, so that $(N - 1)c_1 > N$ at point A in the figure). Thus, the individual late consumer is faced with two choices. First, he or she could run to the bank and hope to get a place close to the front of the line, in which case he or she gets c_1, while risking the chance of being too close to the rear of line, in which case he or she gets nothing. Second, he or she can choose to wait until period 2 to withdraw, in which case there would definitely be nothing left. Therefore, the choice is clear; if a late consumer anticipates in period 1 that everyone else will run to the bank to withdraw their deposit, he or she will want to do it as well. Thus, there is a *bad equilibrium*, which is a **bank run**. Everyone runs to the bank in period 1; some consume c_1, but others consume nothing. This outcome is no better for some consumers (the early consumers who manage to get to the bank before it runs out of funds) and is worse for everyone else than the good equilibrium.

The Diamond-Dybvig model, thus, has multiple equilibria, much like the Keynesian coordination failure models we studied in Chapters 6 and 13. Multiple equilibria are used here to explain why bank runs have occurred historically. Bank runs have never been an important phenomenon in Canada. However, in the United States before the establishment of the Federal Reserve System (the central bank of the U.S.) in 1914, there were recurring **banking panics** during the national banking era (1863–1913). During these panic episodes, which were typically triggered by the failure of a large financial institution or institutions, there were large deposit withdrawals from banks that sometimes appeared to be contagious. As well, widespread bank runs occurred during the Great Depression in the United States. The Diamond-Dybvig model provides an explanation for why an otherwise sound bank could experience a bank run and fail. According to the logic of the model, because a bank provides a liquidity transformation service to consumers, this leaves it open to bank runs. Because bank deposits are liquid, if all depositors show up at the bank in the anticipation that the bank will fail, then their expectations are self-fulfilling, and the bank will indeed fail.

DEPOSIT INSURANCE

A potential solution to the problem of bank runs is government-provided deposit insurance. In the Diamond-Dybvig model, if the government steps in and guarantees each depositor that they will receive the quantity c_2 given by the banking contract at point A in Figure 17.8, then no late consumer would have a reason to run to the bank. This leaves aside the question of who the government will tax if it has to make good on its deposit insurance guarantees. However, in the model, the bad equilibrium will never occur with deposit insurance in place, so the government will never have to make any payouts related to its insurance program. The model tells us that promises by the government can serve to prevent a bad outcome.

In Canada, the **Canada Deposit Insurance Corporation (CDIC)** is a Crown corporation that insures deposits at chartered banks and trust and loan companies up to $100 000 per depositor. The CDIC was established in 1967, which was much later than deposit insurance arrangements were introduced in some other countries. For example, the United States introduced deposit insurance during the 1930s Great Depression. One reason deposit insurance appeared later in Canada than in some other countries, is that Canada did not experience the episodes of widespread bank failures and banking panics that occurred, for example, in the United States in the late nineteenth and early twentieth centuries and during the Great Depression. (See Macroeconomics in Action 17.4.)

MACROECONOMICS
IN ACTION

17.3

The Financial Crisis in the United States: Banks, Non-bank Financial Intermediaries, Too-Big-to-Fail, and Moral Hazard

The United States has a colourful history of financial crises and governmental responses to those crises. The repeated banking panic episodes of the National Banking Era, following the Civil War, resulted in the *Federal Reserve Act* (1913), and the establishment of the Federal Reserve System (the "Fed") in 1914. The failure of about one-third of U.S. banks during the Great Depression led to legislation that introduced deposit insurance and the separation of banking and stock market activity in the United States. In the late 1980s, the savings and loan crisis (the failure of many savings and loan depository institutions due to excessive risk-taking) led to reforms of deposit insurance and bank regulation. These are only some examples of an at-times-chaotic U.S. financial and banking history.

The intervention by the U.S. Treasury and the Fed in the financial system beginning in the fall of 2008 was unprecedented in scale. The two key interventions were: (1) the *Emergency Economic Stabilization Act* of 2008 (EESA) and (2) a more-than-doubling of the stock of outside money by the Fed. The ESSA gave the Treasury considerable discretion to allocate up to $700 billion through the Troubled Asset Relief Program (TARP). Ultimately, intervention through this program amounted to an injection of funds to banks and other financial intermediaries in exchange for federal government equity participation in those financial institutions. The increase in the stock of outside money by the Fed was used to purchase large quantities of assets not typically found on the Fed's balance sheet, including loans to non-bank financial intermediaries and mortgage-backed securities.

What financial crisis was the U.S. Treasury and the Fed responding to, and what were its causes? The crisis had the following elements:

1. In most countries of the world where organized mortgage lending exists, most mortgage loans are made by banks which hold and service the loans until they mature. The mortgage market in the United States is unusual. Currently, most mortgages in the U.S. are originated by brokers who negotiate the terms of the loan with the borrower, and who then sell the loan to another financial institution. This institution could be a government agency, such as FNMA or FHLMC ("Fannie Mae," the Federal National Mortgage Association and "Freddie Mac," the Federal Home Loan Mortgage Corporation, respectively) which finances purchases of mortgages by issuing debt, or a private financial intermediary that repackages these mortgages as mortgage-backed securities. A mortgage-backed security is an asset that is a claim to the payoffs (or some part of the payoffs) on an underlying portfolio of mortgages. Mortgage-backed securities are tradeable on financial markets. With financial innovation, mainly after 2000, mortgage originators began lending to increasingly risky borrowers in the so-called subprime mortgage market. The financial institutions that purchased these mortgages and repackaged them as mortgage-backed securities, and the rating agencies that certified the quality of the mortgage-backed securities, seemed assured that the underlying mortgages were sound, or at least that their payoffs were very predictable, given the diversification involved. However, the prices of houses began to fall widely across the U.S. in 2006, and this lead to a large increase in the default rates on subprime mortgages. These mortgages appeared not to be so sound after all, and it became clear that there were severe incentive problems in the mortgage market— mortgage brokers were doing a poor job of screening borrowers, as they would be well paid for their work whether the mortgages ultimately paid off or not, and someone else would be left holding the bag.

The practice of securitizing mortgages has grown in Canada recently. However, securitization in Canada does not appear to be prone to the same kinds of severe incentive problems as existed in the United States prior to the financial crisis.

2. Some investment banks that were heavy investors in mortgage-backed securities were carrying on activities that looked much like conventional banking. These investment banks would purchase mortgage-backed securities, and finance these purchases through a sequence of short-term repurchase agreements, which are short-term collateralized loans. In these repurchase agreements, it was the mortgage-backed securities themselves that served as collateral for the loans. This type of financial intermediation looks somewhat like what a bank does, as the assets on the investment banks' balance sheets were long-maturity, while the liabilities were short-maturity. A difference from a conventional bank is that mortgage-backed securities are by nature liquid—they can be sold at any time on organized markets. However, the assets held by a traditional bank are illiquid.

3. An important recent financial innovation was the credit default swap, which is essentially insurance on a debt contract. Suppose for example that Lehman Brothers (a now-defunct investment bank) issued debt in order to purchase mortgage-backed securities. Someone, say the holder of this debt, could purchase a credit default swap at some price from American International Group (an insurance company), for example. If Lehman Brothers were to default on its debt, then American International Group would guarantee the specified payoffs on the debt for the debtholder who had purchased the credit default swap. Holding the credit default swap in conjunction with the underlying debt essentially insures the debt-holder against the event that the debt-issuer defaults. However, someone could purchase a credit default swap and not hold the underlying debt, and thus be taking a bet on whether the debt-issuer would default.

4. Once it became clear (for most investors, mainly in 2008) that the ultimate payoffs on subprime mortgages were not going to be as high as expected, the mortgage-backed securities which represented packages of these mortgages fell in price. Investment banks such as Bear Stearns and Lehman Brothers found it increasing difficult to borrow short-term to finance their holdings of mortgage backed securities, so that there was pressure to sell these securities. This further reduced the market prices of mortgage-backed securities, and ultimately led to the failure of Lehman Brothers in the fall of 2008. Once Lehman Brothers had failed, financial market participants learned that American International Group (AIG) was the issuer of a large quantity of credit default swaps which would have to be paid out. At this point, there was the potential that AIG could fail, along with some other large financial institutions, including investment banks and the largest U.S. banks, principally Citigroup and Bank of America. It was in this context that the U.S. Treasury and the Fed intervened in such a massive way.

What was the rationale for this dramatic policy intervention, and what were the alternatives? It will be useful to frame the arguments in terms of (1) the interventionist view; and (2) the laissez-faire view.

The interventionist view is perhaps best summarized in Fed Chairman Ben Bernanke's speech at the August 2009 Policy Conference at Jackson Hole, Wyoming.[13]

Bernanke argued that the financial intervention by the Treasury and the Fed was essentially staving off a repeat of the Great Depression. According to Bernanke, there were elements of the financial crisis that looked much like a Diamond-Dybvig bank run, though in this case the run was on non-bank financial institutions that were not protected by deposit insurance. Indeed, the liabilities of these institutions were not deposits, but typically short-term repurchase agreements. However, the argument is that a flight of lenders from short-term lending was much like a bank run or classic liquidity crisis. At risk, according to Bernanke, was the whole financial sector, through interrelationships of borrowing, lending, and elaborate financial arrangements that were difficult for anyone to understand in full. Should one large financial institution fail, the others would soon follow, according to the interventionist view. The correct response to the problem, in the Fed's view was: (1) to intervene in conventional ways through open market operations, reducing short-term nominal market interest rates essentially to zero; (2) to lend generously by way of the Fed's "discount window," not only to banks, but to other financial institutions; (3) to have the Fed act essentially as a mortgage banker, issuing outside money and holding mortgage-backed securities.

The other piece of financial intervention, the TARP funds authorized through the ESSA, was another means to prevent the failure of large financial institutions. By "recapitalizing" banks and other financial institutions with government funds, it was thought that banks would begin lending more (lending in credit markets tightened dramatically in mid to late 2008), and the failure of these large financial institutions would be forestalled.

The laissez-faire view is that the Fed and the Treasury overdid their intervention. This appears to be the view held by some policymakers in the Federal Reserve System. In the laissez-faire view, some intervention in response to the crisis may have been called for, but the Fed should have restricted its activities to conventional types of central bank intervention—lending exclusively to banks, and open market operations in short-term government securities. According to this view, activities such as the purchase of mortgage-backed securities by the

Fed are at best ineffective and at worst misallocate credit in the economy. Laissez-faire economists would argue that large financial institutions should be allowed to fail. If not, serious moral hazard problems set in—these institutions come to expect that they can take on large amounts of risk, reap the benefits when times are good, and let taxpayers make up the difference when times are bad. Indeed, one could view the whole financial crisis as stemming from the too-big-to-fail doctrine. Large financial institutions engaged in some very risky activities knowing that, in the seemingly unlikely event that house prices should fall, setting off a chain reaction of defaults on credit arrangements, that the government would intervene and bail out the losers. These large institutions were then ultimately correct in their assumptions about how the federal government and the Fed would behave.

Which view is correct, the interventionist view or the laissez-faire view? It is impossible to know for sure, without re-running history in the absence of the massive policy interventions. It currently appears (as of March 2012), that the U.S. economy is on its way (perhaps too slowly) to recovery. Ben Bernanke insists that his astute intervention prevented a second Great Depression, and the Obama administration in the U.S. appears to agree, as Bernanke has been appointed to a second four-year term as Fed Chairman. Holders of the laissez-faire view do not agree. One could argue that, if financial intervention had been more modest, and large financial institutions had been permitted to fail, the 2008–2009 recession may have been somewhat more severe, but that the long-term costs of the too-big-to-fail doctrine and ensuing moral hazard problems easily outweigh this short-term cost in terms of lower real GDP.

---

[13]See www.federalreserve.gov/newsevents/speech/bernanke20090821a.htm.

Canada and the United States are in many ways economically similar, but they have very different banking systems.[14] The two countries have also had very different historical experiences with banking panics and bank failures, and this represents a challenge to the Diamond-Dybvig banking model.

While the United States has a unit banking system, with thousands of small banks that typically serve small geographical areas, along with a few large banks, Canada has a branch banking system, with only a handful of commercial banks that branch nationally. On the one hand, the United States has had a network of regulations designed to keep banks small, and it is relatively easy to open a new bank. On the other hand, in Canadian banks are typically not prevented from becoming large, and it requires federal legislation for a bank to obtain a charter and open for business.

United States banking history has many episodes of widespread bank failures and banking panics, as we have discussed. There were recurrent banking panics during the National Banking era in the United States, from 1863 to 1913. The Federal Reserve System, established in 1914, was supposed to correct the institutional problems that caused banking panics, but missteps in monetary policy in the Great Depression contributed to a situation in which about one-third of U.S. banks failed between 1929 and 1933.

Before the establishment of the Bank of Canada, in 1935, there were no banking panics of note in Canada. Canada was a latecomer to deposit insurance, introducing it in 1967, but in spite of this there were few bank failures before that time. No commercial banks failed in the Great Depression in Canada, and the most recent bank failure before 1985 was the failure of the Home Bank in 1923. The most recent commercial bank failures were those of the Northland Bank and the Canadian Commercial Bank in 1985. From January to August 2009, about 80 banks failed in the United States, while there were zero failures in Canada.

Why have the experiences with bank failures and panics been so different in Canada and the United States? This seems hard to explain using the Diamond-Dybvig banking model, in which bank runs arise simply because banks are performing a useful intermediation service; in this sense U.S. banks and Canadian banks are no different. The evidence points to two factors (not included in the Diamond-Dybvig banking model), that appear to be important in explaining these differences between the United States and Canada. First, in the period before 1935, much of the circulating currency in Canada was issued by commercial banks (see the discussion earlier in this chapter). This private currency was viewed by the public as being quite safe. At times of the year when the demand for currency was particularly high (typically during the fall harvest) relative to bank deposits, it was easy for the chartered banks to convert deposit liabilities into notes in circulation by printing more notes to issue when depositors chose to withdraw. In periods of high demand for currency in the United States between 1863 and 1913, a panic could result, but this was averted in Canada because of the note issuing ability of Canadian commercial banks. Bank failures are also averted in Canada by the fact that Canadian banks are relatively large and well diversified geographically. One of the reasons for the failures of the Northland Bank and Canadian Commercial Bank in 1985 was that these banks did most of their lending in one western province of Canada, which exposed them to the risks associated with local shocks. In this case the local shock was a sharp drop in the prices of oil and natural gas that caused a reduction in local asset prices, resulting in borrowers at these banks defaulting on their loans. Small U.S. banks, which are typically not well diversified geographically, are exposed to the same kind of risk and, thus, are more likely to fail than a well-diversified Canadian branch bank.

One might think that the negative effects of the too-big-to-fail doctrine would be in evidence in Canada, with its large banks, but there appears to be no history in Canada of the government or the central bank propping up ailing banks. Indeed, Canada's banking system is viewed as one of the world's safest. Why? In Canada, banks are regulated differently. First, Canada does not have the confusing, conflicting, and overlapping regulatory structure involving several different financial regulators that the United States does. Second, Canadian banks are in some ways more tightly regulated (though they have more flexibility in terms of how they offer financial services). In particular, entry into the banking system is more difficult in Canada, and banks are required to hold higher levels of capital in Canada than in the United States. Canadian regulations, while they reduce competition among Canadian banks, give these banks a larger cushion against losses, and make them fundamentally sounder.

---

[14]The material here relies heavily on S. Williamson, 1989, "Restrictions on Financial Intermediaries and Implications for Aggregate Fluctuations: Canada and the United States, 1870–1913," in *NBER Macroeconomics Annual 1989*, O. Blanchard and S. Fischer (eds.), NBER, Cambridge, MA; and B. Champ, B. Smith, and S. Williamson, 1996, "Currency Elasticity and Banking Panics: Theory and Evidence," *Canadian Journal of Economics* 29, 828–864.

An argument for deposit insurance is that it can prevent the failure of an otherwise sound depository institution. Suppose, for example, that there is no deposit insurance. Because a depository institution has highly illiquid assets, it is not possible for it to quickly liquidate its loans when there is heavy unexpected demand for withdrawals. Therefore, suppose that depositors lose faith in a depository institution, perhaps because other depository institutions have failed, and these depositors do not have good information on the quality of the institution's assets. From an individual depositor's point of view, even if he or she still believes the bank is sound, if other depositors are running to the bank to withdraw their deposits, he or she will want to run to the bank to withdraw as well. It then could become optimal for all depositors to run to the bank, resulting in a failure of the bank to satisfy all its depositors because of the illiquidity of its assets. This bank failure is a self-fulfilling phenomenon, and it need not have occurred.

Now, supposing that there is deposit insurance, all depositors know that their deposits are safe, even if the bank should fail. The fact that a few depositors choose to withdraw their deposits therefore need not trigger a run on the depository institution. In this view, deposit insurance can prevent incipient banking panics.

The main cost of deposit insurance is that it creates a **moral hazard** problem. Moral hazard arises in essentially all insurance situations, because the insured individual will tend to take less care in preventing the event against which he or she is insured. For example, if the owner of a car is completely insured against damages to his or her car, he or she may take less care in driving in parking lots, and may therefore be more likely to have an accident. It is difficult for the insurance company to correct for this problem, because the amount of care taken by the driver of the car is hard to observe. Moral hazard can explain the existence of deductibles in insurance contracts, which require the insured party to bear the cost of small losses.

For a depository institution, moral hazard arises because deposit insurance encourages the depository institution to take on more risk. This happens because the riskiness of the bank's assets is difficult to observe, and with deposit insurance the depositors have no interest in whether the depository institution is risky. Therefore, though deposit insurance can prevent the failures of sound depository institutions that might occur because of self-fulfilling panics, it could produce more failures because of the increased riskiness of banks. Thus, the existence of deposit insurance requires that the regulators of depository institutions impose restrictions on depository institution activities to ensure that these institutions do not take on too much risk. In Macroeconomics in Action 17.3, moral hazard is discussed in more detail, as it relates to the recent U.S. financial crisis.

This completes our study of money, banking, and central banking in this book. In the next chapter, we will examine some topics in unemployment and inflation.

Chapter Summary

- Money functions as a medium of exchange, a store of value, and a unit of account. Historically, the objects that have played the role of money are commodity money, circulating private bank notes, commodity-backed paper currency, fiat money, and transactions deposits at private banks.

- We considered a simple model capturing the absence-of-double-coincidence-of-wants problem that can exist in barter economies where people only have goods to trade. In the model, commodity money or fiat money can overcome the double-coincidence problem by providing a universally acceptable medium of exchange.

- The monetary intertemporal model from Chapter 12 was used to study the effects of long-run inflation. A higher money growth rate causes an increase in the rate of inflation, an increase in the nominal interest rate, and decreases in output, consumption, and employment.

- A positive nominal interest rate represents a distortion that drives a wedge between the marginal rate of substitution of leisure for consumption and the marginal rate of transformation of leisure for consumption.

- An optimal long-run monetary policy in the monetary intertemporal model is for the central bank to follow a Friedman rule, whereby the money growth rate and the inflation rate are equal to minus the real interest rate. This implies that the nominal interest rate is zero at the optimum.

- In the Diamond-Dybvig banking model, a bank provides its depositors with insurance against the event that they need liquid assets to make transactions. The bank converts illiquid assets into liquid deposits.

- In the Diamond-Dybvig model, there is a good equilibrium in which all early consumers withdraw their deposits from the bank early and all late consumers withdraw late. There is also a bad equilibrium (a bank run) in which all consumers choose to withdraw early, and the bank fails. The bank run equilibrium can be prevented through government-provided deposit insurance.

- There is a moral hazard problem associated with deposit insurance, in that an unregulated bank with insured deposits takes on too much risk.

Key Terms

Friedman rule: An optimal rule for monetary policy whereby the money supply grows at a rate that implies a zero nominal interest rate.

financial intermediary: Any financial institution that borrows from one large group of people and lends to another large group of people, transforms assets in some way, and processes information.

gold standard: An arrangement whereby a country stands ready to exchange its money for gold at a fixed price.

cheque-clearing system: The system that allows for debiting and crediting of the appropriate bank deposit accounts when a cheque deposited in a bank is written on an account in another bank.

absence of double coincidence of wants: A situation in which there are two would-be trading partners, but it is not true that each has the good the other wants.

Fisher effect: The one-for-one increase in the nominal interest rate resulting from an increase in the rate of inflation.

superneutral: Describes money in the situation where a change in the money supply growth rate has no real effects.

deflation: Decrease in the price level over time.

hyperinflation: Situation where the inflation rate is extremely high.

liquidity trap: A situation where, if the nominal interest rate is zero, then open market operations by the central bank have no effect.

portfolio: A collection of assets.

nondiversifiable risk: Risk that an individual cannot diversify away by holding a large portfolio of assets.

risk-averse: Describes an individual who does not like risk.

marginal utility of consumption: The slope of the utility function, or the marginal increase in utility (happiness) resulting from a one-unit increase in consumption.

bank run: A situation in which a bank's depositors panic and simultaneously attempt to withdraw their deposits.

banking panics: Situations in which bank runs are widespread.

Canada Deposit Insurance Corporation (CDIC): A Crown corporation that insures deposits at banks and trust and loan companies up to $100 000 per depositor.

moral hazard: The tendency of insured individuals to take less care to prevent a loss against which they are insured.

Questions for Review

1. What are five forms that money has taken historically?

2. What do Yap stones and the playing-card money of New France have in common? What is different about these two forms of money?

3. How does an absence of double coincidence of wants make money socially useful?

4. What are the effects of an increase in the money supply growth rate in the monetary intertemporal model?

5. What are the costs of inflation?

6. Should the monetary authority manipulate the money supply to hold the price level constant over time?

7. Why don't real-world central banks follow the Friedman rule?

8. List four properties of assets and explain why these properties are important.

9. What are the four defining characteristics of a financial intermediary?

10. What are three types of financial intermediaries?

11. What is unusual about depository institutions relative to other financial intermediaries?

12. In the Diamond-Dybvig banking model, why does a consumer do better by depositing in a bank rather than by investing on his or her own?

13. What features of real-world banks does a Diamond-Dybvig bank have?

14. Why are there two equilibria in the Diamond-Dybvig banking model? How do the two equilibria compare?

15. How can bank runs be prevented?

16. Explain what moral hazard is and why and how deposit insurance induces a moral hazard problem.

Problems

1. Consider the absence-of double-coincidence economy depicted in Figure 17.1. Determine who would trade what with whom if good 2 were used as a commodity money. Explain your results.

2. As an alternative to the economy depicted in Figure 17.1, suppose that there are three types of people, but now the person who consumes good 1 produces good 3, the person who consumes good 2 produces good 1, and the person who consumes good 3 produces good 2.
   a. Determine who trades what with whom if good 1 is used as a commodity money, and compare this with what happens when good 1 is used as a commodity money in the economy in Figure 17.1. Explain.
   b. Determine who trades what with whom if fiat money is used in exchange and commodity money is not used. Explain.

3. In the monetary intertemporal model, suppose the central bank issues money in exchange for capital and rents this capital out to firms each period, thus earning the market real interest rate r on the capital. Over time, as the central bank earns interest on its capital holdings, it uses these returns to retire money from the private economy. What are the long-run effects? Is the outcome economically efficient? Explain your results.

4. Suppose in the monetary intertemporal model that the government can pay interest on money, financing this interest with lump-sum taxes on consumers. If the nominal interest rate on money is the same as the nominal interest rate on bonds, determine the effects in the model, illustrating this in a diagram. Explain your results.

5. Suppose that firms and consumers are concerned about theft, so they are willing to use credit cards for some of their transactions even if the nominal interest rate is zero. Further, suppose that the more currency that consumers and firms use, the more people are encouraged to steal, as theft is now more profitable. How would the Friedman rule for monetary policy be altered under these circumstances?

6. Consider the following assets: (i) a work of art; (ii) a Treasury bill; (iii) a share in Microsoft; (iv) a loan to a close relative; (v) a loan to General Motors. For each asset, answer the following questions:
   a. Does the asset have a high rate of return or a low rate of return (on average)?
   b. Is the asset high-risk or low-risk?
   c. Is the asset a long-maturity asset or a short-maturity asset?
   d. Is the asset highly liquid, less liquid, somewhat illiquid, or highly illiquid?
   e. Explain why the asset has the above four properties.
   f. Which of the properties of money (medium of exchange, store of value, unit of account) does the asset have? Would we consider it money and why or why not?

7. In the Diamond-Dybvig banking model, suppose that the banking contract includes a suspension of convertibility provision according to which the bank allows only the first tN depositors in line in period 1 to withdraw their deposits. Will there still be a bank-run equilibrium? Carefully explain why or why not.

8. Alter the Diamond-Dybvig model in the following way. Suppose that there are two assets, an illiquid asset that returns $1 + r$ units of consumption goods in period 2 for each unit invested in period 0, and a liquid asset that returns one unit of consumption goods in period 1 for each unit invested in period 0. The illiquid asset production technology cannot be interrupted in period 1. The model is otherwise the same as outlined in this chapter.
   a. Determine a consumer's lifetime budget constraint when there is no bank, show this in a diagram, and determine the consumer's optimal consumption as an early consumer and as a late consumer in the diagram.
   b. Determine a bank's lifetime budget constraint, show this in your diagram, and determine the optimal deposit contract for the bank in the diagram. Are consumers who deposit in the bank better off than in part (a)? Explain why or why not.
   c. Is there a bank-run equilibrium? Explain why or why not.

9. In the Diamond-Dybvig banking model, suppose that, instead of a bank, consumers can trade shares in the production technology. That is, each consumer invests in the production technology in period 0. Then, if the consumer learns that he or she is an early consumer in period 1, he or she can either interrupt the technology or can sell their investment at a price, p. A consumer who learns that he or she is a later consumer in period 1 can purchase shares in investment projects at price p and can interrupt his or her production technology in order to acquire the goods required to buy shares.
   a. Determine what p is in equilibrium and what each consumer's quantity of early and late consumption is, in a diagram like Figure 17.8.
   b. Do consumers do better or worse than they would with a banking system? Do they do better than they would with no banks and with no trading in shares?
   c. Explain your results.

10. Explain how moral hazard arises in each of the following situations:
    a. A mother promises her daughter that she will help her with her homework during the coming school year, but only if the daughter has difficulty with her homework.
    b. An individual's house is insured against damage by fire for its full value.
    c. An individual is appointed to manage an investment portfolio for a group of coworkers.
    d. The same individual in part (c) is appointed to manage the investment portfolio, and the government guarantees that all investors in the group will receive a 5% return per year. That is, the government will make up the difference if the return on the portfolio falls below 5% in a given year.

Inflation, the Phillips Curve, and Central Bank Commitment

Recently, the inflation rate has been quite low in Canada. Using the rate of growth in the implicit GDP price deflator as a measure of inflation, the quarterly inflation rate, at annual rates, has been mainly in the 0% to 5% range, and an inflation rate in excess of 10% was last seen in Canada in the early 1980s. Further, Canada has never had a hyperinflationary episode on the order of the 10 000% inflation rate experienced in Austria in 1921–1922, or the 20 000% inflation rate in Argentina in 1989–1990. Inflation is of little public concern currently in Canada, and Canadians have been able to avoid some of the truly calamitous experiences with inflation of other countries.

From Chapter 17, we know some of the economic costs of inflation, which arise from the distortions inflation causes in intertemporal rates of return. Long-run inflation causes the public to hold an inefficiently low aggregate stock of real money balances, and it reduces aggregate output and employment below their efficient levels. The costs of inflation are certainly obvious to anyone who has lived through a hyperinflation. Significant public concern can even arise about inflation during relatively moderate inflations, such as what occurred in Canada during the 1970s, when the average inflation rate was below 10%.

If it is widely recognized that inflation is undesirable, why then do governments let it happen? In some circumstances, it is clear that inflation results from problems associated with fiscal policy. Indeed, essentially all hyperinflations can be traced to the existence of large government budget deficits. A government may have high expenditures, perhaps because it must fight a war. However, the public may be unwilling to pay for these expenditures through taxation, or the government may be unwilling to increase taxes. As a result, the government may resort to printing money to finance the government deficit. Moderate inflations, though, need not result from high government budget deficits and the necessity of resorting to the inflation tax. For example, the moderate inflation in Canada in the 1970s was not associated with large government budget deficits, and would not have generated much seigniorage. So what motivated the Bank of Canada to increase the money supply at a high rate and cause what appeared to be excessive inflation? In this chapter, we use a version of the Friedman-Lucas money surprise model to evaluate two explanations for the behaviour of the Bank of Canada in the post-1960 period.

The post-1960 inflation will serve as a convenient example to illustrate some principles concerning the causes of inflation.

The Friedman-Lucas money surprise model, studied in Chapter 12, provides an explanation for the **Phillips curve**, which is the sometimes-observed short-run positive relationship between the inflation rate and real aggregate economic activity. In Canadian data, the Phillips curve is readily discernible during some time periods, while during other periods it is not. The Friedman-Lucas money surprise model is a useful aid in understanding why we should sometimes observe a Phillips curve, and sometimes not. The model tells us that the Phillips curve is an unstable relationship that shifts with the inflation rate that the private sector expects.

Two competing explanations for the behaviour of the Bank of Canada over the post–World War II period are the "central bank learning story" and the "central bank commitment story." In the central bank learning story, high inflation in the 1970s was caused by a lack of knowledge on the part of the Bank of Canada concerning how the economy works. Once the Bank of Canada understood, by the early 1980s, that higher inflation could not permanently increase aggregate output, it acted quickly to reduce inflation. In the central bank commitment story, high inflation in the 1970s was caused by an inability of the Bank of Canada to commit to not using surprise inflation to increase output in the short run.

Ultimately, we will conclude that central bank commitment was probably not an important element in recent Canadian inflation history. However, this does not mean that commitment is unimportant for central banks in all countries and under all circumstances. Indeed, as we will discuss, central bank commitment appears to have been critical in controlling inflation in Hong Kong since 1983.

The Phillips Curve

In the 1950s, A. W. Phillips noticed, in data for the United Kingdom, that there was a negative relationship between the rate of change in nominal wages and the unemployment rate.[1] Other researchers found that such a relationship existed in data for other countries. Further, since the rate of change in nominal wages is highly positively correlated with the rate of change in other money prices, and the unemployment rate is highly negatively correlated with the deviation of aggregate economic activity from trend, it should not be surprising that if there is a negative correlation between the rate of change in nominal wages and the unemployment rate, there will also be a positive correlation between the inflation rate and the deviation of aggregate economic activity from trend. Indeed, the term *Phillips curve* has come to denote any positive correlation between aggregate economic activity and the inflation rate. For our purposes, it will be convenient to define the Phillips curve to be a positive relationship between the rate of inflation and the deviation of real aggregate output from trend. If we let Y^T denote

---

[1]See A. W. Phillips, 1958, "The Relationship between Unemployment and the Rate of Change of Money Wages in the United Kingdom, 1861–1957," *Economica* 25, 283–299.

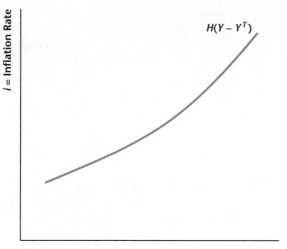

FIGURE 18.1

The Phillips Curve

This is an idealized Phillips curve, which is a positive relationship between the inflation rate and the deviation of aggregate real output from trend.

trend real aggregate output and Y denote actual real aggregate output, then a Phillips curve is described by the relationship

$$i = H(Y - Y^T),$$

where i is the inflation rate and H is an increasing function. We depict this relationship in Figure 18.1.

It is important to recognize that there are models other than the Friedman-Lucas money surprise model that imply a Phillips curve relationship. Indeed, recently developed New Keynesian models, discussed in Chapter 14, typically imply a Phillips curve relationship, which comes about because of the price-setting behaviour of firms in response to the shocks hitting the economy. In New Keynesian theory, $Y - Y^T$ is the "output gap," which is the difference between efficient aggregate output and actual aggregate output, and trend real aggregate output would then be a measure of efficient output.[2]

Is there a clear Phillips curve relationship in Canadian data? That depends on what time period we examine. Figure 18.2 shows a scatter plot of the inflation rate in Canada versus the percentage deviation from trend in real GDP, for 1962–2011. The scatter plot shows no discernible Phillips curve, but it is possible to subdivide the whole time period into subperiods, and detect Phillips curve relationships for these subperiods. What that analysis shows, however, is that the Phillips curve shifts over time, and its slope changes.

In Figure 18.2, we show five Phillips curve relationships, fit respectively to the data for 1962–1969, 1970–1979, 1980–1989, 1990–1999, and 2000–2011. For 1962–1969 and 1970–1979, the slope of the Phillips curve is relatively small, making it appear, if

---

[2]Trend output is often used in the Keynesian literature as a measure of efficient output. There are good reasons to think that this might be a poor approach to capturing efficient output, but for our purposes it would be very difficult to come up with a good measure of the output gap.

FIGURE 18.2
The Shifting Phillips Curve: Inflation Rate vs. Percentage Deviation from Trend in Aggregate Real GDP
The Phillips curve shifts over time. Later Phillips curves represent a less favourable tradeoff between inflation and aggregate output.

Source: Adapted from the Statistics Canada CANSIM database, Series v1992067, v1997756.

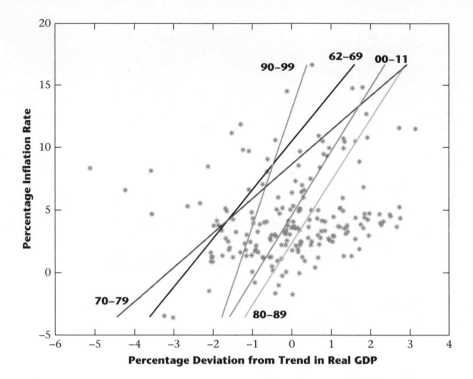

we looked only at the data for 1962–1979, that there is a significant tradeoff between inflation and aggregate output in the data. A policymaker who could observe only the 1962–1979 data might be led to believe that the economy could perform at a much higher level of aggregate activity if people were willing to pay the price of a little more inflation.

However, the Phillips curves estimated from the data for 1980–1989, 1990–1999, and 2000–2011, represent a downward shift from the earlier Phillips curves. Also, the tradeoff is not as favourable, that is, these later Phillips curves are much steeper, particularly the one for 1990–1999.

The Friedman-Lucas Money Surprise Model and the Phillips Curve

Now that we have studied empirical Phillips curve relations for Canada and uncovered the important characteristics of the relationship between cyclical aggregate economic activity and inflation, our goal is to construct a version of the Friedman-Lucas money surprise model that we will use to understand this data. The idea behind the money surprise model was described by Milton Friedman in 1968 and later worked out explicitly by Robert Lucas.[3] Again, note that it is possible to do a similar analysis with some New Keynesian models, related to the sticky price New Keynesian model studied in Chapter 14. Under some kinds of shocks to the economy, New Keynesian models will have similar policy implications to the Friedman-Lucas money surprise model.

The money surprise model works as follows. We will suppose that by controlling money supply growth, the central bank can control the inflation rate, so we will think of the inflation rate as the central bank's policy variable. In the money surprise world, workers have imperfect information about all of the prices in the economy, since there are goods that they buy infrequently (e.g., shoes and refrigerators). Thus, any worker knows his or her own nominal wage but can only make an inference about what his or her real wage is, because he or she does not know the price level with precision. If the central bank brings about a surprise increase in the inflation rate, then a given worker's nominal wage will also tend to increase at a higher rate. However, the worker only sees an increase in his or her nominal wage and does not realize in the short run that the inflation rate has also increased. Therefore, each worker mistakenly believes that he or she has experienced an increase in his or her real wage, and therefore (assuming the substitution effect on the quantity of labour supplied dominates the income effect) increases the quantity of labour supplied. As a result, the surprise increase in the inflation rate will cause an increase in the aggregate quantity of labour supplied and in aggregate output. According to the money surprise model, surprise increases in inflation cause increases in aggregate output above trend.

The Friedman-Lucas money surprise model can be summarized by the simplified relationship

$$i - i^e = a(Y - Y^T),\tag{18.1}$$

where i is the actual inflation rate, i^e is the expected inflation rate, or the inflation rate perceived by the private sector, a is a positive constant, Y is aggregate output, and Y^T is trend aggregate output.[4] Equation (18.1) states that there is a positive relationship between the deviation of the inflation rate from what it is expected to be, and the deviation of real output from trend. This relationship arises because real output will deviate from trend in the model only if the central bank increases the growth rate of the money supply in a surprise way, causing a surprise increase in the inflation rate. We can rewrite (18.1) as

$$i = i^e + a(Y - Y^T),\tag{18.2}$$

which is a Phillips curve relationship, graphed in Figure 18.3. Note that when $Y = Y^T$, we have $i = i^e$. That is, if workers are not surprised by the current inflation rate, then output is equal to its trend value.

---

[3]See M. Friedman, 1968, "The Role of Monetary Policy," *American Economic Review* 58, 1–17; and R. Lucas, 1972, "Expectations and the Neutrality of Money," *Journal of Economic Theory* 4, 103–124.

[4]There are dangers in representing the Friedman-Lucas money surprise model by Equation (18.1). For example, the constant a in general will depend, as Lucas pointed out, on particular features of central bank behaviour. However, for what we want to accomplish in this chapter, there will not be much harm in using (18.1) as a reduced form for the Friedman-Lucas money surprise model.

FIGURE 18.3

Model Phillips Curve Relationship

This is a linear Phillips curve relationship, from the version of the Friedman-Lucas money surprise model used in this chapter. When the inflation rate is equal to the expected inflation rate, then output is equal to trend output.

Jones: AS_t !

$$\overline{\pi}_t = \overline{\pi}_t^e + \overline{v}\,\tilde{Y}_t^2 + \overline{o}$$

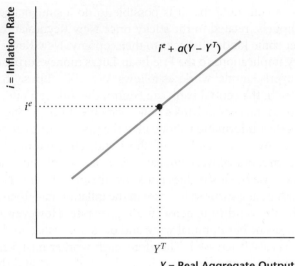

Y = Real Aggregate Output

From (18.2), the position of the Phillips curve depends on i^e, the expected inflation rate. In Figure 18.4 we show the effects of an increase in the expected inflation rate from i_1^e to i_2^e. As a result, the Phillips curve shifts up, by the change in the expected inflation rate, $i_2^e - i_1^e$. This provides an explanation for why the Phillips curve is difficult to find in the data over some periods of time. If the expected inflation rate fluctuates significantly, so that there are frequent sizeable shifts in the Phillips curve, we may observe no discernible Phillips curve relation, as in Figure 18.2.

FIGURE 18.4

The Effects of an Increase in the Expected Inflation Rate

The increase in i^e shifts the Phillips curve up.

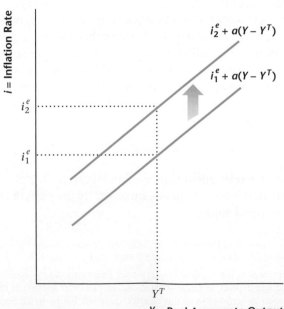

Y = Real Aggregate Output

Understanding the Behaviour
of the Inflation Rate in Canada

The reduction in the inflation rate in Canada from the early 1980s through the late 1990s is viewed as an important success in the implementation of monetary policy by the Bank of Canada. If it was so clear to the Bank of Canada early in the 1980s that the high inflation rate at that time was too costly and should be reduced through reduction in money growth, why was inflation not reduced earlier, and why did the inflation rate increase in the 1970s? We will consider two possible answers to this question, which we call the "central bank learning story" and the "central bank commitment story."

The Central Bank Learning Story   In the late 1950s and the 1960s, the Bank of Canada became aware of the existence of the Phillips curve, through the work of A. W. Phillips and others. The Bank may have become convinced, even though a good theory was not yet available to explain the existence of the Phillips curve, that it represented a stable relationship between the rate of inflation and the level of real aggregate output.

Now, to determine how the Bank of Canada would behave if it operated under the belief that the Phillips curve was stable, we need a device for representing the goals of the central bank. In general, a central bank should be concerned with the welfare of private citizens, though of course there is nothing to guarantee this, since central bank decision makers are guided by their own selfish motives, such as career advancement and the acquisition of more power. We will assume, however, that the framers of the acts of Parliament governing the Bank of Canada's behaviour understood how to correctly align the selfish goals of the Bank of Canada officials with the public good. Then, assuming that the Bank of Canada's goal is to maximize public welfare, it must decide how to further this goal indirectly by controlling some observable economic variables. For our purposes, we will suppose that the Bank of Canada has indirect policy goals relating to inflation and aggregate output. First, there is some inflation rate, i^*, that is regarded as optimal by the Bank. Some economic models tell us that i^* should be minus the real interest rate (the Friedman rule; see Chapter 17), though in practice many central banks appear to behave as if $i^* = 0$ or $i^* > 0$ but small. If $i > i^*$, the Bank of Canada views more inflation as being more costly, so that less inflation is preferred to more. However, if $i < i^*$, then more inflation is preferred to less. In addition, the Bank always prefers more aggregate output to less, as higher GDP is assumed to be preferred by the public.

We can then represent the Bank of Canada's preferences over inflation and aggregate output by indifference curves, as in Figure 18.5. When $i > i^*$, the Bank is happier if inflation falls and output increases, and when $i < i^*$, it is happier when inflation rises and output increases. Further, the indifference curves capture a preference for diversity: they are concave when $i > i^*$ and convex when $i < i^*$. That is, as we move up and to the right along a particular indifference curve where $i > i^*$, output is rising and the inflation rate is rising. The slope of the indifference curve falls because the higher the inflation rate, the smaller the increase in the inflation rate the Bank is willing to tolerate for a given increase in aggregate output. However, when $i < i^*$, as we move down the indifference curve and the inflation rate falls, the Bank is willing to tolerate smaller decreases in the inflation rate for a given increase in output.

FIGURE 18.5

The Bank of Canada's Preferences over Inflation Rates and Output

The figure shows indifference curves for the Bank of Canada, capturing the Bank's preferences over output and inflation. The inflation rate, i^*, is optimal for the Bank, and the Bank always prefers more output to less. If $i < i^*$, then the Bank prefers more inflation to less, and if $i > i^*$, the Bank prefers less inflation to more.

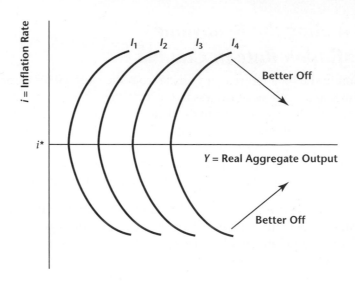

In Figure 18.6 we show the Phillips curve relationship (18.2) along with the Bank of Canada's indifference curves. If the Bank treats the Phillips curve as a fixed relationship, then it thinks that it can simply choose the point on the Phillips curve that best suits it. Therefore, if we suppose that the indifference curve that passes through point A, where $i = i^e$ and $Y = Y^T$, is steeper than the Phillips curve at point A, then the Bank is willing to increase the money supply growth rate so as to surprise workers with a higher-than-expected inflation rate and generate a level of aggregate output above trend output Y^T.

FIGURE 18.6

The Bank of Canada Exploits the Phillips Curve

Facing a Phillips curve that it believes to be stable, the Bank of Canada optimizes by choosing point B, where an indifference curve is tangent to the Phillips curve.

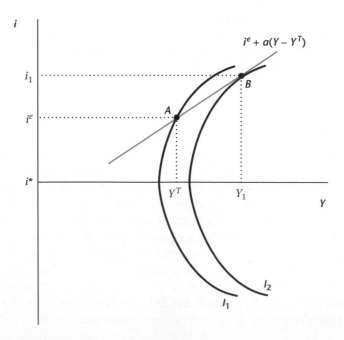

That is, the optimal choice for the Bank of Canada is point B, where an indifference curve is just tangent to the Phillips curve. At B, the inflation rate is i_1 and the level of aggregate output is Y_1. Note that $i_1 > i^e$, so that the actual inflation rate is greater than what is expected by the private sector, and $Y_1 > Y^T$, so that output is above trend.

This will not be the end of the story, since the public is being fooled at point B in Figure 18.6. If the Bank of Canada attempts to hold output permanently at Y_1, then the public will eventually learn that the actual inflation rate is higher than what they perceived, and they will revise upward their expected inflation rate. In Figure 18.7, the Bank of Canada initially chooses point A on Phillips curve PC_1, but as the public observes that the actual inflation rate is higher than the expected inflation rate i_1^e, the expected inflation rate is revised upward, say to i_2^e. This then implies that the Phillips curve shifts up to PC_2, and the Bank will now choose point B, where again the public sector is fooled, since the actual inflation rate is still higher than the expected inflation rate, i_2^e. Again, the public will eventually catch on and will revise upward the expected rate of inflation. Ultimately, the economy will come to rest at point D, where $i = i^e = i_3^e$, so that public expectations about inflation prove to be correct, and the Bank has no incentive at point D to change money growth so as to change the inflation rate.

After experiencing the movement from point A to point D in Figure 18.7, and also after reading Friedman and Lucas's work,[5] the Bank now realizes that the Phillips curve is not a stable relationship and that it shifts with changes in expected inflation. This implies that there is no long-run tradeoff between inflation and aggregate output; in the long run, when the public is not fooled, output will always settle down to its trend

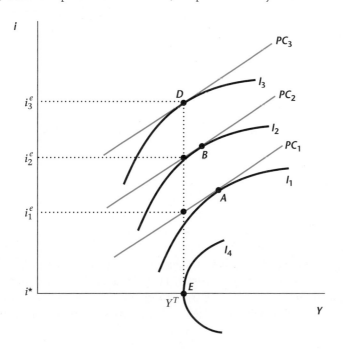

FIGURE 18.7

The Bank of Canada Attempts to Increase *Y* Permanently

If the Bank of Canada attempts to increase *Y* above Y^T permanently, then initially it chooses *A*; but an upward revision in i^e shifts the Phillips curve up, so that the Bank chooses *B* on the Phillips curve PC_2. Ultimately, the economy comes to rest at *D*, where $i = i^e$ and $Y = Y^T$.

[5]See M. Friedman, 1968, "The Role of Monetary Policy," *American Economic Review* 58, 1–17; and R. Lucas, 1972, "Expectations and the Neutrality of Money," *Journal of Economic Theory* 4, 103–124.

level, Y^T. Once the Bank realizes this, it will not optimize by choosing a point along the upward-sloping short-run Phillips curve but will choose the optimal inflation rate given that the long-run level of output will be Y^T. Therefore, once the Bank of Canada understands the theory correctly, it will want to set the money growth rate so that $i = i^*$, and the economy will in the long run be at point E, after expected inflation adjusts downward again.

This story fits the data in Figure 18.2 in the following sense. During the 1960s and the early 1970s, the Bank of Canada felt that it could exploit a stable Phillips curve, which produced outcomes like the movement from point E to points A and B in Figure 18.7, but by 1980 the Canadian economy was in a position like point D. By then, the Bank understood what was happening, and began the move from D to E in Figure 18.7.

This is a sanguine view of central banking in Canada, since it reflects the attitude that the Bank of Canada will learn from its mistakes and act fairly quickly to correct them. In this view, the inflation of the 1970s was an experiment gone wrong, and an event that is not likely to be repeated. In the central bank learning story, the Bank of Canada is fundamentally sound in that it has the ability to absorb new economic thinking, to efficiently make sense of the new data it is constantly receiving, and to use all this information to make better decisions. See Macroeconomics in Action 18.1 for a discussion of the somewhat different approach to controlling inflation followed in New Zealand.

The Central Bank Commitment Story   The second possible explanation for the reduction in inflation that occurred over the 1980s and 1990s in Canada is the central bank commitment story. The theory behind central bank commitment and inflation was first exposited by Kydland and Prescott,[6] who did the first work on the **time consistency problem** in macroeconomics. The fundamentals of the time consistency problem can be explained through a simple example. A teacher is giving a one-semester course in macroeconomics, and his or her goal is to make sure that the students in the class learn as much as possible. The students want to get high grades but with as little effort as possible, since they have other things to do with their time than learning macroeconomics. If there is a final exam in the course, the students will work hard to get good grades; they will learn, and their teacher will be happy.

However, a problem is that the teacher does not like to grade exams. He or she can promise at the beginning of the semester to give a final exam, but by the end of the semester the students will have learned the course material anyway, in expectation of having to write an exam. Therefore, the teacher need not give the exam, as his or her goal has been accomplished, and he or she can avoid the work of grading exams. The plan made at the beginning of the semester to give a final exam is not time-consistent. That is, when the time comes to have the exam, the teacher has no incentive to give it.

However, the students are not stupid. They understand the teacher's motives and recognize that he or she has no incentive to give a final exam, even if he or she has promised to do so. They will therefore not learn anything. Thus, the outcome is that

---

[6]See F. Kydland and E. Prescott, 1977, "Rules Rather Than Discretion: The Inconsistency of Optimal Plans," *Journal of Political Economy* 87, 473–492.

the students do not learn, and the teacher does not give the final exam. The teacher would prefer to have to grade the exam and have the students learn than not to grade the exam and have no learning, and so the outcome is clearly bad.

Essentially, there is a commitment problem here. A better outcome would be achieved if the teacher could tie his or her hands at the beginning of the semester by somehow committing to giving the final exam. Of course, in practice such commitment is achieved through university rules that bind the teacher to carrying out the promises made in the course outline distributed at the beginning of the semester.

An analogous problem exists for the Bank of Canada if we make some modifications to our model. Suppose that each period there is a game being played between the private sector and the Bank of Canada. At the beginning of the period, the private sector chooses the expected rate of inflation, i^e. Then, the Bank chooses the rate of money growth, which effectively involves determining i. Thus, given i^e, the Bank chooses i, satisfying the Phillips curve relationship

$$i - i^e = a(Y - Y^T)$$

so as to be as well off as possible. However, since the public sector is forward-looking and understands the motivation of the Bank of Canada, it must be true in equilibrium that the public cannot be fooled—that is, $i = i^e$. The assumption that $i = i^e$ is a version of the **rational expectations hypothesis**, which states that economic agents do not make systematic errors; that is, they use all information efficiently. In this case, using information efficiently means the public sector understands the Bank of Canada's preferences over output and inflation, and uses this information efficiently to predict how the Bank will behave.

In Figure 18.8, since $i = i^e$ in equilibrium, this implies that $Y = Y^T$ in equilibrium. Therefore, if the Bank of Canada could commit in advance to an inflation rate, it would

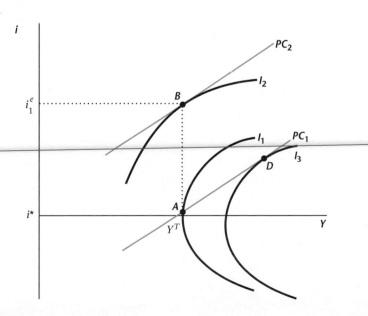

FIGURE 18.8

The Commitment Problem
If the Bank of Canada could commit to an inflation rate, it would choose i^*, and the equilibrium would be at *A*. However, without commitment, the equilibrium is at *B*, where inflation is too high, and where an indifference curve is tangent to the Phillips curve at $i = i^e$ (rational expectations holds).

Before reductions in the inflation rate occurred in New Zealand in the late 1970s, this country experienced inflation that was relatively high among developed countries. The average inflation rate in New Zealand between 1977 and 1986 was 13% per year—much higher than in Canada, for example (see Figure 18.8). However, the inflation rate in New Zealand was reduced to 3.3% per year in the 1990–1992 period and to 2.3% in the 1993–1996 period. In part, this reduction in inflation was brought about through changes in the legal structure within which the Reserve Bank of New Zealand (RBNZ)—the central bank of New Zealand—was constrained to operate, as discussed in a working paper by Michael Hutchison and Carl Walsh.[7]

The changes in the rules governing the operation of the RBNZ were enacted in the *RBNZ Act* in December 1989, which went into effect in February 1990. Under the *Act*, "the primary function of the Bank [the RBNZ] is to formulate and implement monetary policy directed to the economic objective of achieving and maintaining stability in the general level of prices." This statement of the goals of the central bank is quite restrictive, since left out are any Keynesian-type objectives, such as "full employment" or "sustained growth," goals that often find their way into the language of central bankers. Given that the objective of the RBNZ as defined by the *RBNZ Act* is to achieve price stability, how should this be done? The Act also specifies that the finance minister (a cabinet member in the government of New Zealand) will negotiate a Policy Target Agreement (PTA) with the governor of the RBNZ at the beginning of the governor's term of office. This PTA will specify explicitly what price stability means,

in terms of numerical objectives, for the governor's term. These objectives are then publicly announced. Should the governor be judged by the prime minister of New Zealand to have failed to meet the goals set out in the PTA, he or she can be removed from office.

In practice, the PTAs that have been negotiated consist of explicit inflation targets. For example, the first PTA agreed to under the *RBNZ Act* specified a target range for the inflation rate of 0%–2% per annum to be achieved by December 1992. As mentioned above, the *Act* appears to have been very successful in meeting its intended goal of reducing inflation in New Zealand. Inflation targeting in this instance seems to have been much more successful than was the targeting of monetary aggregates in some countries in the 1970s and 1980s.

The rules in the *RBNZ Act* governing the operation of New Zealand's central bank put an unusual amount of structure on monetary policy relative to what governs most central banks in the world. For example, although the Bank of Canada sets inflation rate targets, the governor of the Bank of Canada would not be fired by the prime minister for failing to meet those targets. New Zealand was highly innovative in central banking by setting up explicit objectives and penalties for its central bank. Other central banks, including the Bank of Canada and the Bank of England, have since introduced inflation targeting, though in a less restrictive structure than in New Zealand.

---

[7]See M. Hutchison and C. Walsh, 1998, "Disinflation in New Zealand," working paper, University of California, Santa Cruz.

The world's central banks have resorted to several different means to show that they are committed to controlling inflation. During the 1970s and 1980s, many central banks announced explicit targets for the growth of monetary aggregates, and currently several central banks, including those of Canada, New Zealand, and Britain, have inflation targets. One device for tying the hands of the central bank is the introduction of a currency board. A prominent jurisdiction with a currency board is Hong Kong.

As was discussed in Chapter 16, a currency board is one way to operate a fixed exchange rate system. Under a currency board some governmental authority, which could be the central bank, stands ready to buy and sell domestic currency for some foreign currency at a fixed rate. All domestic currency is backed one-for-one by safe assets (including interest-earning assets) denominated in the foreign currency. If the currency board is run properly, there is no risk of the governmental authority running out of foreign exchange. Typically, a country adopting a currency board fixes its foreign exchange rate relative to the currency of a country with sound monetary policy. This is because, as we studied in Chapter 16, in the long run a country under a fixed exchange rate adopts the inflation rate of the country against which the currency is pegged.

In Hong Kong, the exchange rate was fixed at 7.8 Hong Kong dollars per U.S. dollar in October 1983, and it has remained at that value since then.[8] The currency board in Hong Kong is operated by the Hong Kong Monetary Authority (HKMA), though there is a sense in which the Hong Kong system is not a pure currency board. This is because the HKMA commits to sell U.S. dollars at a fixed rate against Hong Kong dollars, but there is no commitment to buy U.S. dollars at a particular rate. As well, the rules by which the HKMA operates are not written into law; there is only an implicit commitment to continue the currency board into the future.

The HKMA has been quite successful in controlling inflation. While the inflation experience of Hong Kong has not been identical to that of the United States since 1983, the difference between the Hong Kong inflation rate and the U.S. inflation rate from 1983–2003 was not great. The HKMA was able to maintain its fixed exchange rate through the Asian crisis of 1997, with some changes made in the system in 1998. Recently, Hong Kong may have been too successful in reducing inflation, in that there was a deflation from 1998–2002, with the consumer price index falling by 12% over that period.[9] Although this might be consistent with a Friedman rule (see Chapter 17), and thus be optimal, some would argue that deflation of this magnitude is excessive.

Hong Kong's success story in controlling inflation under a currency board was not repeated in Argentina. There, the currency was pegged against the U.S. dollar in 1990 and supported by a currency board. Initially there was success, with inflation reduced from triple-digit rates in the 1980s to single-digit rates in the 1990s. However, under the pressure of out-of-control fiscal policy, the currency board was abandoned in January 2002. Thus, a currency board is not a simple recipe for establishing the commitment to control inflation.

---

[8]See S. Gerlach, 2003, "Monetary Operations of Hong Kong's Currency Board," working paper, Hong Kong Institute for Monetary Research.

[9]See Tony Latter, "Hong Kong's Currency Board Today—The Unexpected Challenge of Deflation," available at www.info .gov.hk/hkma/eng/currency/link_ex/index.htm.

choose $i = i^*$, and the equilibrium would be at point A. However, if $i^e = i^*$, then the Phillips curve running through point A is PC_1, and the Bank will then choose point D, where $i > i^e = i^*$; so point A is not an equilibrium. In equilibrium, the Bank's indifference curve must be tangent to the Phillips curve where $i = i_1^e$. That is, the equilibrium point will be at B on Phillips curve PC_2. Note that point A is strictly preferred by the Bank to B, but A cannot be achieved because of the Bank's inability to commit in advance.

Kydland and Prescott interpreted this exercise as indicating that central bank discretion is dangerous and that there is something inherently wrong with letting central banks make decisions on an ad hoc basis. The solution to the lack of commitment problem, in their view, is to tie a central bank's hands by imposing some rule to govern monetary policy that would prevent the central bank from using discretion. One such rule for monetary policy, advocated by Milton Friedman and adopted in the 1970s by many central banks in the world, including the Bank of Canada, was money growth rate targeting. However, increasing instability in the relationships among monetary aggregates, prices, and real activity, which occurred in the 1980s, led to the abandonment of money growth rate targeting in favour of inflation targeting by the Bank of Canada. Inflation targets for monetary policy have been in place in Canada since 1992. Whether these targets represent a firm commitment is debatable. They could easily go the way of money growth targets if the Bank of Canada does not like the outcomes.

A problem with the central bank commitment story is that it does not explain the run-up in inflation in the 1970s or why inflation decreased in the 1980s and 1990s. Did the Bank of Canada suddenly lose its ability to commit in the late 1960s and then find it again in the early 1980s? This seems unlikely. Further, as Robert Barro and David Gordon have argued,[10] if the Bank of Canada is playing a repeated game with the private sector, then its long-term reputation becomes important, and the long-run equilibrium can be point A in Figure 18.8. That is, the Bank understands that if it attempts to use surprise inflation to generate more aggregate output in the short run, then it will destroy its reputation for producing low inflation. Therefore, a long-run equilibrium can exist at point A in Figure 18.8, since the Bank understands that if it loses its reputation, then the equilibrium will be at point B forever.

Of course, if we accept the importance of the Bank of Canada's concern for its reputation in determining its behaviour, we have to ask what it was about the 1970s that made the Bank of Canada willing to lose its reputation for low money growth and low inflation at the time.

In summary, several arguments cast doubt on the central bank commitment story as an explanation for recent Canadian inflation history. It seems that commitment issues are probably not very important for the behaviour of the Bank of Canada. The central bank learning story seems to give a more plausible account of the run-up in inflation in the 1970s and the subsequent decline in the inflation rate in the 1980s and 1990s. However, see Macroeconomics in Action 18.2 for a discussion of the importance of commitment in the case of Hong Kong.

---

[10]See R. Barro and D. Gordon, 1983, "A Positive Theory of Monetary Policy in a Natural Rate Model," *Journal of Political Economy* 91, 589–610; and R. Barro and D. Gordon, 1983, "Rules, Discretion and Reputation in a Model of Monetary Policy," *Journal of Monetary Economics* 12, 101–121.

Chapter Summary

- The Phillips curve relationship studied here is a positive relationship between the inflation rate and the deviation of real aggregate output from trend.

- For some periods, a Phillips curve can be observed in Canadian data, but the Phillips curve shifts over time, and its slope changes.

- We used a version of the Friedman-Lucas money surprise model to explain these facts. In the version of the Friedman-Lucas money surprise model we use, the deviation of real aggregate output from trend is positively related to the difference between the actual and expected inflation rates.

- If the Bank of Canada generates a surprise increase in money growth, leading to a surprise increase in inflation, this causes an increase in labour supply, employment, and real output. The money surprise model predicts that the Phillips curve is unstable, as it shifts with changes in the expected rate of inflation.

- In Canada, the rate of inflation was moderate during the 1960s, increased substantially in the 1970s, and then declined over the 1980s and 1990s. We considered two possible explanations for this.

- The first explanation for recent Canadian inflation experience was the central bank learning story, whereby the Bank of Canada discovered the existence of the Phillips curve in the 1960s and, assuming the Phillips curve was stable, attempted to exploit this relationship in the 1970s. However, the increased inflation in the 1970s did not generate permanently higher output, and it became clear to the Bank that there was no long-run tradeoff between output and inflation.

- Higher inflation simply shifts up the Phillips curve relationship as expected inflation adjusts upward. Once the Bank of Canada discovered that there was no long-run tradeoff between output and inflation, it could then, in the early 1980s, focus solely on the goal of reducing inflation.

- The second explanation for recent Canadian inflation history is the central bank commitment story. According to this story, high inflation is caused by the inability of the central bank to commit to a policy of not generating surprise inflation in an attempt to exploit the short-run Phillips curve.

- The central bank learning story provides a more plausible explanation than the central bank commitment story for the path followed by the Canadian inflation rate, as it seems difficult to argue that the Bank found it difficult to commit in the 1970s, but easy to commit itself otherwise.

Key Terms

Phillips curve: A positive relationship between the rate of inflation and the level of aggregate economic activity.

time consistency problem: A situation that occurs when it proves optimal to abandon a previously announced plan.

rational expectations hypothesis: Hypothesis asserting that economic agents do not make systematic errors and that they use information efficiently.

Questions for Review

1. Why is the "Phillips curve" so called?

2. The Phillips curve relationship examined in this chapter is a positive relationship between what two variables?

3. How did the observed Phillips curve change over time?

4. Explain how the Friedman-Lucas money surprise model works.

5. What is the relationship that summarizes the Friedman-Lucas money surprise model in this chapter?

6. When real aggregate output is equal to trend output, what is the inflation rate equal to?

7. What is the effect of an increase in expected inflation on the Phillips curve?

8. Describe the course of the inflation rate in Canada from 1962 until late 2008.

9. What are two possible explanations for the Canadian inflation rate history after 1962?

10. Why can the central bank have an incentive to increase the inflation rate if it believes that the Phillips curve is stable?

11. Can the Bank of Canada permanently increase the level of aggregate output? Explain why or why not.

12. Why will the inflation rate be high in the long run if the central bank cannot commit itself?

13. Explain why, if the central bank is concerned about its reputation, inflation can be low in the long run.

14. Which is a more satisfactory explanation of recent Canadian inflation: the central bank learning story or the central bank commitment story? Why?

Problems

1 Suppose that the private sector does not have rational expectations but instead follows an "adaptive expectations" scheme. That is, the private sector's expected inflation rate is what the inflation rate was last period. Show in a diagram how the inflation rate and output move over time if the initial inflation rate is the optimal rate i^*, and then the central bank acts to exploit the Phillips curve. Explain your results.

2 Suppose that the economy is in a long-run equilibrium where the inflation rate is greater than the optimal rate, i^*, and then the central bank acts to reduce the inflation rate to i^*.
   a. Suppose that the central bank decides to take drastic action and reduces the inflation rate within one period to i^*. Also, suppose that the private sector has adaptive expectations, so the current expected inflation rate is last period's actual inflation rate. Show in a diagram the path real aggregate output and the inflation rate take over time.
   b. Now suppose that the central bank takes the drastic strategy in part (a), but that the private sector has rational expectations, so that $i = i^e$. Again, show in a diagram the path followed by output and the inflation rate over time.

c. Now suppose that the central bank takes a gradual strategy of reducing the inflation rate in a number of steps to i^*. Under a gradual strategy, show what differences there are between adaptive and rational expectations for the path of output and the inflation rate over time.

d. Explain your results in parts (a)–(c), and comment on what light this sheds on Figure 18.2.

3 Suppose that the inflation rate is higher than i^*, that the central bank announces it will reduce the inflation rate, and that it actually proceeds to do this. Answer the following:

a. Suppose that the private sector believes the central bank announcement. What are the effects on the inflation rate and real output? Show this in a diagram.

b. Suppose that the private sector does not believe the central bank announcement. What are the effects on the inflation rate and real output now? Show this in a diagram.

c. Explain your results in parts (a) and (b).

4 (Warning: This is challenging.) Suppose that the central bank is in a repeated relationship with the private sector. If the inflation rate is $i = i^*$ and output is $Y = Y^T$, then suppose the reward to the central bank in each period is u_1. If consumers anticipate $i^e = i^*$, then the one-period reward the central bank receives from fooling consumers with $i > i^e$ is u_2, and we will have $i > i^e = i^*$. When the central bank cannot commit and expectations are rational, then the reward the central bank gets is $u_3 < u_1$ with $i = i^e = i_1$ i^* and $Y = Y^T$. Now, suppose that the government anticipates that if it deviates from $i = i^*$, then it will totally lose its reputation and consumers will anticipate $i = i_1$ forever after, so that the government will receive a reward of u_3 forever after. That is, suppose the central bank has two alternatives, which are (a) set $i = i^*$, forever receiving reward u_1, and (b) cheat for this period, receiving reward u_2, implying that the reward will be u_3 in every future period. Suppose that the central bank discounts the future at the rate r.

a. Show that it is an equilibrium for the government to choose $i = i^*$ forever if

$$u_1(1 + r) - u_3 \geq r\, u_2.$$

b. Interpret the condition in part (a).

c. Show that, as r becomes small, the condition in part (a) must hold, and explain this.

MATHEMATICAL APPENDIX

This appendix provides more formal treatments of some of the models in the book, and it is intended for students with a knowledge of calculus and more advanced algebraic techniques who want to study some of the topics of this book in more depth. The appendix assumes an understanding of mathematical methods in economics at the level of Alpha C. Chiang's *Fundamental Methods of Mathematical Economics*, 3rd ed. (New York: McGraw-Hill, 1984). We will proceed by working through results for selected models from selected chapters.

Chapter 4: Consumer and Firm Behaviour

Chapter 4 dealt with the representative consumer's and representative firm's optimization problems in the closed-economy one-period model. We will set up the consumer's and firm's problems and derive the main results of Chapter 4 formally.

THE REPRESENTATIVE CONSUMER

The representative consumer's preferences are defined by the utility function $U(C, l)$, where C is consumption and l is leisure, with $U(\cdot, \cdot)$ a function that is increasing in both arguments, strictly quasiconcave, and twice differentiable. These properties of the utility function imply that indifference curves are downward-sloping and convex, and that the consumer strictly prefers more to less. The consumer's optimization problem is to choose C and l so as to maximize $U(C, l)$ subject to his or her budget constraint—that is,

$$\max_{C, l} U(C, l)$$

subject to

$$C = w(h - l) + \pi - T,$$

and $C \geq 0$, $0 \leq l \leq h$, where w is the real wage, h is the quantity of time the consumer has available, π is dividend income, and T is the lump-sum tax. The above problem is a constrained optimization problem, with the associated Lagrangian

$$L = U(C, l) + \lambda[w(h - l) + \pi - T - C],$$

where λ is the Lagrange multiplier.

We will assume that there is an interior solution to the consumer's problem where $C > 0$ and $0 < l < h$. This can be guaranteed by assuming that $U_1(0, l) = \infty$ (i.e., the derivative of the utility function with respect to the first argument goes to infinity in the limit as consumption goes to zero), and $U_2(C, 0) = \infty$. These assumptions imply that $C > 0$ and $l > 0$ at the optimum. In a competitive equilibrium we cannot have $l = h$, as this would imply that nothing would be produced and $C = 0$. Given an interior solution to the consumer's problem, we can characterize the solution by the first-order conditions from the problem of choosing C, l, and λ to maximize L. These first-order conditions are (differentiating L with respect to C, l, and λ, respectively, and setting each of these first derivatives equal to zero)

$$U_1(C, l) - \lambda = 0, \tag{A.1}$$

$$U_2(C, l) - \lambda w = 0, \tag{A.2}$$

$$w(h - l) + \pi - T - C = 0. \tag{A.3}$$

In (A.1) and (A.2), $U_i(C, l)$ denotes the first derivative with respect to the ith argument of $U(\cdot, \cdot)$, evaluated at (C, l). From Equations (A.1) and (A.2), we can obtain the condition

$$\frac{U_2(C, l)}{U_1(C, l)} = w, \tag{A.4}$$

which is the optimization condition for the consumer that we showed graphically in Chapter 4, Figure 4.5. Equation (A.4) states that the marginal rate of substitution of leisure for consumption (on the left-hand side of the equation) is equal to the real wage (on the right-hand side) at the optimum. For our purposes, we can rewrite Equation (A.4) as

$$U_2(C, l) - wU_1(C, l) = 0, \tag{A.5}$$

and then (A.3) and (A.5) are two equations determining the optimal choices of C and l given w, π, and T.

In general, we cannot obtain explicit closed-form solutions for C and l from (A.3) and (A.5) without assuming an explicit form for the utility function $U(\cdot, \cdot)$, but we can use comparative statics techniques to determine how C and l will change when any of w, π, or T change. To do this, we totally differentiate (A.3) and (A.5), obtaining

$$-dC - wdl + (h - l)dw + d\pi - dT = 0, \tag{A.6}$$

$$[U_{12} - wU_{11}] dC + [U_{22} - wU_{12}] dl - U_1 dw = 0. \tag{A.7}$$

In Equation (A.7), U_{ij} denotes the second derivative with respect to the ith and jth arguments of $U(\cdot, \cdot)$. It will prove useful to write (A.6) and (A.7) in matrix form, as

$$\begin{bmatrix} -1 & -w \\ U_{12} - wU_{11} & U_{22} - wU_{12} \end{bmatrix} \begin{bmatrix} dC \\ dl \end{bmatrix} = \begin{bmatrix} -(h - l)dw - d\pi + dT \\ U_1 dw \end{bmatrix}. \tag{A.8}$$

Then, we can solve for the derivatives of interest by using Cramer's rule.

First, consider the effects of a change in dividend income π. Using Cramer's rule, from (A.8) we get

$$\frac{dC}{d\pi} = \frac{-U_{22} + wU_{12}}{\nabla}, \tag{A.9}$$

$$\frac{dl}{d\pi} = \frac{U_{12} - wU_{11}}{\nabla}, \tag{A.10}$$

where

$$\nabla = -U_{22} + 2wU_{12} - w^2U_{11}.$$

Now, ∇ is the determinant of the bordered Hessian associated with the constrained optimization problem for the consumer, and the quasiconcavity of the utility function implies that $\nabla > 0$. This, however, does not allow us to sign the derivatives in (A.9) and (A.10). Our assumption from Chapter 4 that consumption and leisure are normal goods is equivalent to the conditions $-U_{22} + wU_{12} > 0$ and $U_{12} - wU_{11} > 0$. Thus, given normal goods, we have $\frac{dC}{d\pi} > 0$ and $\frac{dl}{d\pi} > 0$, so that the quantities of consumption and leisure chosen by the consumer increase when dividend income increases. It is straightforward to show that $\frac{dC}{dT} = -\frac{dC}{d\pi}$ and $\frac{dl}{dT} = -\frac{dl}{d\pi}$, so that the effects of a decrease in taxes are equivalent to the effects of an increase in dividend income.

Next, we can derive the effects of a change in the real wage, again using Cramer's rule to obtain, from (A.8),

$$\frac{dC}{dw} = \frac{wU_1 + (h - l)(-U_{22} + wU_{12})}{\nabla}, \tag{A.11}$$

$$\frac{dl}{dw} = \frac{-U_1 + (h - l)(U_{12} - wU_{11})}{\nabla}. \tag{A.12}$$

Now, assuming that consumption is a normal good, we have $-U_{22} + wU_{12} > 0$, and since $\nabla > 0$ and $U_1 > 0$ (utility increases as consumption increases), we know from (A.11) that $\frac{dC}{dw} > 0$, so that consumption increases when the real wage increases. However, we cannot determine the sign of $\frac{dl}{dw}$ from (A.12), and this is because of the opposing income and substitution effects of a change in the real wage on leisure. It is possible to separate algebraically the income and substitution effects in Equation (A.12) by determining the response of leisure to a change in the real wage, holding utility constant. This gives a substitution effect, which can be expressed as

$$\frac{dl}{dw}(subst) = \frac{-U_1}{\nabla} < 0,$$

so that the substitution effect is for leisure to fall and hours worked to rise when the real wage increases. This implies that, from (A.12), the income effect is

$$\frac{dl}{dw}(inc) = \frac{dl}{dw} - \frac{dl}{dw}(subst) = \frac{(h - l)(U_{12} - wU_{11})}{\nabla} > 0,$$

assuming that leisure is a normal good, which implies that $U_{12} - wU_{11} > 0$. Therefore, the income effect is for leisure to increase when the real wage increases. In general, without putting additional restrictions on the utility function, we do not know the sign of $\frac{dl}{dw}$.

THE REPRESENTATIVE FIRM

We assumed in Chapter 4 that the production function for the representative firm is described by

$$Y = zF(K, N^d),$$

where Y is output, z is total factor productivity, $F(\cdot, \cdot)$ is a function, K is the capital stock, and N^d is the firm's labour input. The function $F(\cdot, \cdot)$ is assumed to be quasiconcave, strictly increasing in both arguments, homogeneous of degree one or constant-returns-to-scale, and twice differentiable. We also assume that $F_2(K, 0) = \infty$ and $F_2(K, \infty) = 0$ to guarantee that there is always an interior solution to the firm's profit maximization problem, where $F_2(K, N^d)$ is the first derivative with respect to the second argument of the function $F(\cdot, \cdot)$, evaluated at (K, N^d). The firm's profit maximization problem is to choose the labour input N^d so as to maximize

$$\pi = zF(K, N^d) - wN^d,$$

subject to $N^d \geq 0$, where π is the difference between revenue and labour costs, in terms of consumption goods. That is, the firm solves

$$\max_{N^d} \left[zF(K, N^d) - wN^d \right] \tag{A.13}$$

The restrictions on the function $F(\cdot, \cdot)$ imply that there is a unique interior solution to problem (A.13), characterized by the first-order condition

$$zF_2(K, N^d) = w, \tag{A.14}$$

which states that the firm hires labour until the marginal product of labour $zF_2(K, N^d)$ equals the real wage, w.

We can determine the effects of changes in w, z, and K on labour demand N^d through comparative statics techniques. Totally differentiating Equation (A.14), which determines N^d implicitly as a function of w, z, and K, we obtain

$$zF_{22}dN^d - dw + F_2\, dz + zF_{12}dK = 0.$$

Then, solving for the appropriate derivatives, we have

$$\frac{dN^d}{dw} = \frac{1}{zF_{22}} < 0,$$

$$\frac{dN^d}{dz} = \frac{-F_2}{zF_{22}} > 0,$$

$$\frac{dN^d}{dK} = \frac{-zF_{12}}{zF_{22}} > 0.$$

We can sign the above derivatives since $F_{22} < 0$ (the marginal product of labour decreases as the quantity of labour increases), $F_2 > 0$ (the marginal product of labour is positive), and $F_{12} > 0$ (the marginal product of labour increases as the capital input increases). These are restrictions on the production function discussed in Chapter 4. Since $\frac{dN^d}{dw} < 0$, the labour demand curve is downward-sloping. Further, $\frac{dN^d}{dz} > 0$ and $\frac{dN^d}{dK} > 0$ imply that the labour demand curve shifts to the right when z or K increases.

Problems

1. Suppose that the consumer's preferences are given by the utility function $U(C, l) = \ln C + \alpha \ln l$. Determine the consumer's choice of consumption and leisure and interpret your solutions.

2. In the consumer's choice problem, show that at least one good must be normal.

3. Suppose that the firm's production technology is given by $Y = zF(K, N) = zK^\alpha N^{1-\alpha}$, where $0 < \alpha < 1$. Determine the firm's demand for labour as a function of z, K, α, and w, and interpret.

4. Suppose that the firm's production technology is given by $Y = z \min (K, \alpha N)$, where $\alpha > 0$. As in problem 3, determine the firm's demand for labour as a function of z, K, α, and w, and interpret.

Chapter 5: A Closed-Economy One-Period Macroeconomic Model

Here, we will show formally the equivalence between the competitive equilibrium and the Pareto optimum in the one-period model, and then determine, using comparative statics, the equilibrium effects of a change in government spending and in total factor productivity.

COMPETITIVE EQUILIBRIUM

In a competitive equilibrium, the representative consumer maximizes utility subject to his or her budget constraint, the representative firm maximizes profits, the government budget constraint holds, and the market on which labour is exchanged for consumption goods clears. From the previous section, the two equations describing consumer optimization are the budget constraint, (A.3), or

$$w(h-l) + \pi - T - C = 0, \tag{A.15}$$

and condition (A.5), or

$$U_2(C, l) - wU_1(C, l) = 0. \tag{A.16}$$

Optimization by the representative firm implies (A.14), or

$$zF_2(K, N^d) = w, \tag{A.17}$$

and profits for the firm are

$$\pi = zF(K, N^d) - wN^d. \tag{A.18}$$

The government budget constraint states that government spending is equal to taxes; that is,

$$G = T. \tag{A.19}$$

Finally, the market-clearing condition is

$$h - l = N^d, \tag{A.20}$$

or the supply of labour is equal to the demand for labour. Equations (A.15)–(A.20) are six equations that solve for the six endogenous variables C, l, N^d, T, π, and w, given the exogenous variables z and G. To make this system of equations more manageable, we can simplify as follows. First, using Equations (A.18)–(A.20) to substitute for π, T, and N^d in Equation (A.15), we obtain

$$C = zF(K, h - l) - G. \tag{A.21}$$

Then, substituting in Equation (A.17) for N^d using Equation (A.20), and then in turn for w in (A.16) using Equation (A.17), we obtain

$$U_2(C, l) - zF_2(K, h - l)U_1(C, l) = 0. \tag{A.22}$$

Equations (A.21) and (A.22) then solve for equilibrium C and l. Then, the real wage w can be determined from (A.17), after substituting for N^d from (A.20), to get

$$w = zF_2(K, h - l). \tag{A.23}$$

Finally, aggregate output is given from the production function by

$$Y = zF(K, h - l).$$

PARETO OPTIMUM

To determine the Pareto optimum, we need to ask how a fictitious social planner would choose consumption and leisure so as to maximize welfare for the representative consumer, given the production technology. The social planner solves

$$\max_{C, l} U(C, l)$$

subject to

$$C = zF(K, h - l) - G.$$

To solve the social planner's problem, set up the Lagrangian associated with the constrained optimization problem above, which is

$$L = U(C, l) + \lambda[zF(K, h - l) - G - C].$$

The first order conditions for an optimum are then

$$U_1(C, l) - \lambda = 0, \tag{A.24}$$

$$U_2(C, l) - \lambda z F_2(K, h - l) = 0, \tag{A.25}$$

$$zF(K, h - l) - G - C = 0. \tag{A.26}$$

From Equations (A.24) and (A.25), we obtain

$$U_2(C, l) - zF_2(K, h - l)U_1(C, l) = 0. \tag{A.27}$$

Now, note that Equations (A.26) and (A.27), which solve for the Pareto-optimal quantities of leisure l and consumption C, are identical to Equations (A.21) and (A.22), so that the Pareto-optimal quantities of leisure and consumption are identical to the competitive equilibrium quantities of leisure and consumption. As a result, the competitive equilibrium and the Pareto optimum are the same thing in this model, so the first and second welfare theorems hold.

Note also that Equation (A.27) can be written (suppressing arguments for convenience) as

$$\frac{U_2}{U_1} = zF_2,$$

which states that the marginal rate of substitution of leisure for consumption is equal to the marginal product of labour (the marginal rate of transformation) at the optimum.

COMPARATIVE STATICS

We would like to determine the effects of changes in G and z on equilibrium C, l, Y, and w. To do this, we totally differentiate Equations (A.26) and (A.27), obtaining

$$-dC - zF_2 \, dl + F \, dz - dG = 0,$$

$$(U_{12} - zF_2U_{11}) \, dC + (U_{22} + zF_{22}U_1 - zF_2U_{12}) \, dl - F_2U_1 \, dz = 0.$$

Then, putting these two equations in matrix form, we get

$$\begin{bmatrix} -1 & -zF_2 \\ U_{12} - zF_2U_{11} & U_{22} + zF_{22}U_1 - zF_2U_{12} \end{bmatrix} \begin{bmatrix} dC \\ dl \end{bmatrix} = \begin{bmatrix} -Fdz + dG \\ F_2U_1dz \end{bmatrix}. \tag{A.28}$$

Using Cramer's rule to determine the effects of a change in government spending, G, from (A.28) we then get

$$\frac{dC}{dG} = \frac{U_{22} + zF_{22}U_1 - zF_2U_{12}}{\nabla};$$

$$\frac{dl}{dG} = \frac{-U_{12} + zF_2U_{11}}{\nabla},$$

where

$$\nabla = -z^2F_2^2U_{11} + 2zF_2U_{12} - U_{22} - zF_{22}U_1.$$

Here, ∇ is the determinant of the bordered Hessian associated with the social planner's constrained optimization problem, and the quasiconcavity of the utility function and the production function guarantees that $\nabla > 0$. To sign the derivatives above, note that in equilibrium $zF_2 = w$, from (A.17). This then implies, given our assumption that consumption and leisure are normal goods, that $U_{22} - zF_2U_{12} < 0$ and $-U_{12} + zF_2U_{11} < 0$ (recall our discussion from the previous section); since $F_{22} < 0$ (the marginal product of labour declines as the labour input increases), we have $\frac{dC}{dG} < 0$ and $\frac{dl}{dG} < 0$, so that consumption and leisure decline when government purchases increase, due to negative income effects. For the effect on the real wage w, since $w = zF_2(K, h - l)$, we have

$$\frac{dw}{dG} = -zF_{22}\frac{dl}{dG} < 0,$$

and so the real wage decreases. For the effect on aggregate output, since $Y = C + G$, we have

$$\frac{dY}{dG} = \frac{dC}{dG} + 1 = \frac{-z^2F_2^2U_{11} + zF_2U_{12}}{\nabla} > 0,$$

as leisure is assumed to be normal, implying $zF_2U_{11} - U_{12} < 0$.

Now, to determine the effects of a change in z, again we use Cramer's rule in conjunction with (A.28), obtaining

$$\frac{dC}{dz} = \frac{-F(U_{22} + zF_{22}U_1 - zF_2U_{12}) + F_2^2zU_1}{\nabla};$$

$$\frac{dl}{dz} = \frac{-F_2U_1 + F(U_{12} - zF_2U_{11})}{\nabla}.$$

Here, since consumption is a normal good, $U_{22} - zF_2U_{12} < 0$, and given $F_{22} < 0$, $F > 0$, and $U_1 > 0$, we have $\frac{dC}{dz} > 0$ and consumption increases with an increase in total factor productivity, as we showed diagrammatically in Chapter 5, Figure 5.9. However, we cannot sign $\frac{dl}{dz}$, as there are opposing income and substitution effects. We can separate out the income and substitution effects on leisure by determining the response of leisure to a change in z holding utility constant. This will give a substitution effect, which is

$$\frac{dl}{dz}(subst) = \frac{-F_2 U_1}{\nabla} < 0,$$

so that the substitution effect is for leisure to decrease and employment $(h - l)$ to increase. The income effect of the change in z is then

$$\frac{dl}{dz}(inc) = \frac{dl}{dz} - \frac{dl}{dz}(subst) = \frac{F(U_{12} - zF_2 U_{11})}{\nabla} > 0,$$

since leisure is a normal good. Therefore, an increase in z has a positive income effect on leisure.

Problems

1. For the closed-economy one period model, suppose that $U(C, l) = \ln C + \beta l$, and $F(K, N) = zK^\alpha N^{1-\alpha}$, where $\beta > 0$ and $0 < \alpha < 1$. Determine consumption, employment, output, leisure, and the real wage in a competitive equilibrium, and explain your solutions.

2. For the closed-economy one-period model, suppose that $U(C, l) = \min(C, \beta l)$, and $F(K, N) = \alpha K + \delta N$, where $\beta > 0$, $\alpha > 0$, and $\delta > 0$. Determine consumption, employment, output, leisure, and the real wage in a competitive equilibrium, and explain your solutions. Also draw a diagram with the consumer's preferences and the production possibilities frontier, and show the competitive equilibrium in this diagram.

Chapters 7 and 8: Economic Growth

In this section we will work out explicitly the effects of changes in the savings rate, the labour force growth rate, and total factor productivity on the steady state quantity of capital per worker and output per worker in the Solow growth model. Then, we will determine the golden rule for capital accumulation in the Solow model. Finally, we will develop a growth model where consumption–savings decisions are made endogenously. In solving this model, we will introduce dynamic programming techniques, which will prove useful later in this appendix.

EXPLICIT RESULTS FOR THE SOLOW GROWTH MODEL

Recall from Chapter 7 that the aggregate quantity of capital in the Solow growth model evolves according to

$$K' = (1 - d)K + I, \tag{A.29}$$

where K' is future period capital, d is the depreciation rate, K is current period capital, and I is current period investment. In equilibrium, saving is equal to investment, and so $sY = I$, where s is the savings rate and Y is aggregate income. Further, the production function is given by $Y = zF(K, N)$, where z is total factor productivity and N is the labour force, so that substituting in Equation (A.29), we have

$$K' = (1 - d)K + szF(K, N). \tag{A.30}$$

Then, dividing the right-hand and left-hand sides of Equation (A.30) by N, using the relationship $N' = (1 + n)N$, which describes labour force growth, with N' denoting the future labour force and n the population growth rate, and rewriting in the form of lowercase variables that denote per-worker quantities, we have

$$k' = \frac{szf(k)}{1 + n} + \frac{(1 - d)k}{1 + n}. \tag{A.31}$$

Equation (A.31) then determines the evolution of the per-worker capital stock from the current period to the future period, where k is the current stock of capital per worker, k' is the stock of future capital per worker, and $f(k)$ is the per-worker production function.

In the steady state, $k' = k = k^*$, where k^* is the steady state quantity of capital per worker, which, from (A.31), satisfies

$$szf(k^*) - (n + d)k^* = 0. \tag{A.32}$$

Now, to determine the effects of changes in s, n, and z on the steady state quantity of capital per worker, we totally differentiate Equation (A.32), getting

$$[szf'(k^*) - n - d]dk^* + zf(k^*)\, ds - k^*\, dn + sf(k^*)\, dz = 0. \tag{A.33}$$

Then, solving for the appropriate derivatives, we obtain

$$\begin{aligned}
\frac{dk^*}{ds} &= \frac{-zf(k^*)}{szf'(k^*) - n - d} > 0, \\
\frac{dk^*}{dn} &= \frac{k^*}{szf'(k^*) - n - d} < 0, \\
\frac{dk^*}{dz} &= \frac{-sf(k^*)}{szf'(k^*) - n - d} > 0.
\end{aligned} \tag{A.34}$$

Here, capital per worker increases with increases in s and z, and decreases with an increase in n. We get these results since $szf'(k^*) - n - d < 0$ in the steady state. Since output per worker in the steady state is $y^* = zf(k^*)$, for each of these experiments steady state output per worker moves in the same direction as steady state capital per worker.

In the steady state, the quantity of consumption per worker is

$$c^* = zf(k^*) - (n + d)k^*.$$

Now, note that when the savings rate changes, the response of consumption per worker in the steady state is given by

$$\frac{dc^*}{ds} = [zf'(k^*) - n - d]\frac{dk^*}{ds}.$$

Though $\frac{dk^*}{ds} > 0$, the sign of $zf'(k^*) - n - d$ is ambiguous, so that consumption per worker could increase or decrease with an increase in the savings rate. The golden rule savings rate is the savings rate s_{gr} that maximizes consumption per worker in the steady state. The golden rule steady state quantity of capital per worker solves the problem

$$\max_{k^*} [zf(k^*) - (n + d)k^*];$$

letting k_{gr}^* denote this quantity of capital per worker, k_{gr}^* solves

$$zf'(k_{gr}^*) - n - d = 0,$$

and then s_{gr} is determined from (A.32) by

$$s_{gr} = \frac{(n + d)k_{gr}^*}{zf(k_{gr}^*)}.$$

For example, if $F(K, N) = K^\alpha N^{1-\alpha}$, where $0 < \alpha < 1$ (a Cobb-Douglas production function), then $f(k) = k^\alpha$, and we get

$$k_{gr}^* = \left(\frac{z\alpha}{n + d} \right)^{\frac{1}{1-\alpha}},$$

$$s_{gr} = \alpha.$$

Problem

1. Suppose in the Solow growth model that there is government spending financed by lump-sum taxes, with total government spending $G = gY$, where $0 < g < 1$. Solve for steady state capital per worker, consumption per worker, and output per worker, and determine how each depends on g. Can g be set so as to maximize steady state consumption per worker? If so, determine the optimal fraction of output purchased by the government, g^*, and explain your results.

OPTIMAL GROWTH: ENDOGENOUS CONSUMPTION–SAVINGS DECISIONS

In this model, we will relax the assumption made in the Solow growth model that the savings rate is exogenous, and allow consumption to be determined optimally over time. The model we develop here is a version of the optimal growth theory originally developed by David Cass and Tjalling Koopmans.[1] In this model, the second welfare theorem will hold, and so we can solve the social planner's problem to determine the competitive equilibrium. We will set the model up as simply as possible, leaving out population growth and changes in total factor productivity, but these features are easy to add.

There is a representative infinitely long-lived consumer with preferences given by

$$\sum_{t=0}^{\infty} \beta^t U(C_t), \tag{A.35}$$

where β is the subjective discount factor of the representative consumer, with $0 < \beta < 1$, and C_t is consumption in period t. Throughout, t subscripts will denote the time period. The period utility function $U(\cdot)$ is continuously differentiable, strictly increasing, strictly concave, and bounded. Assume that $\lim_{C \to 0} U'(C) = \infty$. Each period, the consumer is endowed with one unit of time, which can be supplied as labour.

The production function is given by

$$Y_t = F(K_t, N_t),$$

[1]See D. Cass, 1965, "Optimum Growth in an Aggregative Model of Capital Accumulation," *Review of Economic Studies* 32, 233–240; and T. Koopmans, 1965, "On the Concept of Optimal Growth," in *The Econometric Approach to Development Planning*, North Holland, Amsterdam.

where Y_t is output, K_t is the capital input, and N_t is the labour input. The production function $F(\cdot, \cdot)$ is continuously differentiable, strictly increasing in both arguments, homogeneous of degree one, and strictly quasiconcave. Assume that $F(0, N) = 0$, $\lim_{K \to 0} F_1(K, 1) = \infty$, and $\lim_{K \to \infty} F_1(K, 1) = 0$.

The capital stock obeys the law of motion

$$K_{t+1} = (1 - d)K_t + I_t, \tag{A.36}$$

where I_t is investment and d is the depreciation rate, with $0 \le d \le 1$, and K_0 is the initial capital stock, which is given. In equilibrium, we will have $N_t = 1$ for all t, and so it will prove convenient to define the function $H(K_t)$ by $H(K_t) \equiv F(K_t, 1)$. The resource constraint for the economy is

$$C_t + I_t = H(K_t), \tag{A.37}$$

or consumption plus investment is equal to the total quantity of output produced. It is convenient to substitute for I_t in (A.37) using (A.36) and to rearrange, obtaining a single constraint

$$C_t + K_{t+1} = H(K_t) + (1 - d)K_t; \tag{A.38}$$

we can think of the resources available in period t to the social planner on the right-hand side of Equation (A.38) as being period t output plus the undepreciated portion of the capital stock, which is then split up (on the left-hand side of the equation) between period t consumption and the capital stock for period $t + 1$.

The social planner's problem for this economy is to determine consumption and the capital stock in each period so as to maximize (A.35) subject to the constraint (A.38). Again, the solution to this problem is equivalent to the competitive equilibrium solution. The social planner solves

$$\max_{\{C_t, K_{t+1}\}_{t=0}^{\infty}} \sum_{t=0}^{\infty} \beta^t U(C_t), \tag{A.39}$$

given K_0 and (A.38) for $t = 0, 1, 2, ..., \infty$.

Now, the problem of solving (A.39) subject to (A.38) may appear quite formidable, as we need to solve for an infinite sequence of choice variables. However, dynamic programming techniques essentially allow us to turn this infinite-dimensional problem into a two-dimensional problem.[2] To see how this works, note from the right-hand side of (A.38) that the current capital stock K_t determines the resources that are available to the social planner at the beginning of period t. Thus, K_t will determine how much utility the social planner can give to the consumer from period t on. Suppose that the social planner knows $v(K_t)$, which is the maximum utility that the social planner could provide for the representative consumer from period t on. Then, the problem that the social planner would solve in any period t would be

$$\max_{C_t, K_{t+1}} \left[U(C_t) + \beta v(K_{t+1}) \right]$$

subject to

$$C_t + K_{t+1} = H(K_t) + (1 - d)K_t.$$

---

[2] For more detail on dynamic programming methods in economics, see N. Stokey, R. Lucas, and E. Prescott, 1989, *Recursive Methods in Economic Dynamics*, Harvard University Press, Cambridge, MA.

That is, the social planner chooses current period consumption and the capital stock for the following period so as to maximize the sum of current period utility and the discounted value of utility from the next period on, subject to the resource constraint.

Now, since the problem of the social planner looks the same in every period, it will be true that

$$v(K_t) = \max_{C_t, K_{t+1}} \left[U(C_t) + \beta v(K_{t+1}) \right] \tag{A.40}$$

subject to

$$C_t + K_{t+1} = H(K_t) + (1-d)K_t. \tag{A.41}$$

Then, Equation (A.40) is called a *Bellman equation*, or *functional equation*, and it determines what $v(\cdot)$ is. We call $v(K_t)$ the *value function*, as this tells us the value of the problem at time t to the social planner, as a function of the *state variable* K_t. Given the assumptions we have made, there is a unique function $v(\cdot)$ that solves the Bellman equation. There are some circumstances where we can obtain an explicit solution for $v(\cdot)$ (see the problem at the end of this section), but in any case the dynamic programming formulation of the social planner's problem, (A.40) subject to (A.41), can be convenient for characterizing solutions, if we assume that $v(\cdot)$ is differentiable and strictly concave (which it is here, given our assumptions).

We can simplify the problem above by substituting for C_t in the objective function (A.40) using the constraint (A.41), getting

$$v(K_t) = \max_{K_{t+1}} \left\{ U[H(K_t) + (1-d)K_t - K_{t+1}] + \beta v(K_{t+1}) \right\}. \tag{A.42}$$

Then, given that the value function $v(\cdot)$ is concave and differentiable, we can differentiate on the right-hand side of (A.42) to get the first-order condition for an optimum, which is

$$-U'[H(K_t) + (1-d)K_t - K_{t+1}] + \beta v'(K_{t+1}) = 0. \tag{A.43}$$

Now, to determine $v'(K_{t+1})$, we apply the envelope theorem in differentiating Equation (A.42), obtaining

$$v'(K_t) = [H'(K_t) + 1 - d]U'[H(K_t) + (1-d)K_t - K_{t+1}];$$

then, we update one period, and substitute for $v'(K_{t+1})$ in (A.43), getting

$$\begin{aligned} -U'[H(K_t) + (1-d)K_t - K_{t+1}] + \beta[H'(K_{t+1}) + 1 - d]U'[H(K_{t+1}) \\ + (1-d)K_{t+1} - K_{t+2}] = 0. \end{aligned} \tag{A.44}$$

Now, it can be shown that, in this model, the quantity of capital converges to a constant steady state value, K^*. Equation (A.44) can be used to solve for K^* by substituting $K_{t+1} = K_t = K^*$ in (A.44), which gives, after simplifying,

$$-1 + \beta[H'(K^*) + 1 - d] = 0, \tag{A.45}$$

or

$$H'(K^*) - d = \frac{1}{\beta} - 1$$

in the optimal steady state. That is, in the optimal steady state, the net marginal product of capital is equal to the subjective discount rate of the representative consumer.

In the model, the savings rate is given by

$$s_t = \frac{I_t}{Y_t} = \frac{K_{t+1} - (1 - d)K_t}{H(K_t)},$$

and so in the steady state the savings rate is

$$s^* = \frac{dK^*}{H(K^*)}.$$

In this model, since the savings rate is optimally chosen over time, choosing a "golden rule savings rate" makes no sense. Indeed, note that the steady state optimal savings rate in this model does not maximize steady state consumption. Steady state consumption would be maximized for a value of the steady state capital stock, K^*, such that $H'(K^*) = d$, but this is different from the optimal steady state capital stock determined by (A.45).

Problem

1. In the optimal growth model, suppose that $U(C_t) = \ln C_t$, and $F(K_t, N_t) = K_t^{\alpha} N_t^{1-\alpha}$, with $d = 1$ (100% depreciation).

   a. Guess that the value function takes the form $v(K_t) = A + B \ln K_t$, where A and B are undetermined constants.

   b. Substitute your guess for the value function on the right-hand side of Equation (A.42), solve the optimization problem, and verify that your guess was correct.

   c. Solve for A and B by substituting your optimal solution from part (b) on the right-hand side of Equation (A.42) and equating coefficients on the left and right-hand sides of the equation.

   d. Determine the solutions for K_{t+1} and C_t as functions of K_t, and interpret these solutions.

Chapter 9: Two-Period Model

In this section we will formally derive the results for individual consumer behaviour, showing how a consumer optimizes by choosing consumption and savings over two periods, and how the consumer responds to changes in income and the market real interest rate.

THE CONSUMER'S OPTIMIZATION PROBLEM

The consumer has preferences defined by a utility function $U(c, c')$, where c is current-period consumption, c' is future consumption, and $U(\cdot, \cdot)$ is strictly quasiconcave, increasing in both arguments, and twice differentiable. To guarantee an interior solution to the consumer's problem, we assume that the marginal utilities of current and future consumption each go to infinity in the limit as current and future consumption go to zero, respectively. The consumer chooses c and c' to maximize $U(c, c')$ subject to the consumer's lifetime budget constraint—that is,

$$\max_{c, c'} U(c, c')$$

subject to

$$c + \frac{c'}{1 + r} = y + \frac{y'}{1 + r} - t - \frac{t'}{1 + r},$$

where y is current income, y' is future income, t is the current tax, and t' is the future tax. The Lagrangian associated with this constrained optimization problem is

$$L = U(c, c') + \lambda \left(y + \frac{y'}{1 + r} - t - \frac{t'}{1 + r} - c - \frac{c'}{1 + r} \right),$$

here λ is the Lagrange multiplier. Therefore, the first-order conditions for an optimum are

$$U_1(c, c') - \lambda = 0, \tag{A.46}$$

$$U_2(c, c') - \frac{\lambda}{1 + r} = 0, \tag{A.47}$$

$$y + \frac{y'}{1 + r} - t - \frac{t'}{1 + r} - c - \frac{c'}{1 + r} = 0. \tag{A.48}$$

Then, in (A.46) and (A.47), we can eliminate λ to obtain

$$U_1(c, c') - (1 + r)U_2(c, c') = 0, \tag{A.49}$$

or, rewriting (A.49),

$$\frac{U_1(c, c')}{U_2(c, c')} = 1 + r,$$

which states that the intertemporal marginal rate of substitution (the marginal rate of substitution of current consumption for future consumption) is equal to one plus the real interest rate at the optimum.

For convenience, we can rewrite (A.48) as

$$y(1 + r) + y' - t(1 + r) - t' - c(1 + r) - c' = 0. \tag{A.50}$$

Then, Equations (A.49) and (A.50) determine the quantities of c and c' the consumer will choose given current and future incomes y and y', current and future taxes t and t', and the real interest rate r.

COMPARATIVE STATICS

To determine the effects of changes in current and future income and the real interest rate on current and future consumption and savings, we totally differentiate Equations (A.49) and (A.50), obtaining

$$[U_{11} - (1 + r)U_{12}]dc + [U_{12} - (1 + r)U_{22}]dc' - U_2 dr = 0,$$

$$-(1 + r)dc - dc' + (y - t - c)dr + (1 + r)dy + dy' - (1 + r)dt - dt' = 0;$$

these two equations can be written in matrix form as

$$\begin{bmatrix} U_{11} - (1 + r)U_{12} & U_{12} - (1 + r)U_{22} \\ - (1 + r) & - 1 \end{bmatrix} \begin{bmatrix} dc \\ dc' \end{bmatrix} = $$

$$\begin{bmatrix} U_2 dr \\ -(y - t - c)dr - (1 + r)dy - dy' - (1 + r)dt - dt' \end{bmatrix}. \tag{A.51}$$

First, we will determine the effects of a change in current income y. Applying Cramer's rule to (A.51), we obtain

$$\frac{dc}{dy} = \frac{(1 + r)[U_{12} - (1 + r)U_{22}]}{\nabla},$$

$$\frac{dc'}{dy} = \frac{(1 + r)[-U_{11} + (1 + r)U_{12}]}{\nabla};$$

where

$$\nabla = -U_{11} + 2(1 + r)U_{12} - (1 + r)^2 U_{22}.$$

Given our restrictions on the utility function, ∇, which is the determinant of the bordered Hessian associated with the consumer's constrained optimization problem, is strictly positive. Further, assuming current and future consumption are normal goods, we have $U_{12} - (1 + r)U_{22} > 0$ and $-U_{11} + (1 + r)U_{12} > 0$, and so $\frac{dc}{dy} > 0$ and $\frac{dc'}{dy} > 0$. Thus, an increase in current income causes increases in both current and future consumption. Saving in the current period is given by $s = y - c - t$, so that

$$\frac{ds}{dy} = 1 - \frac{dc}{dy} = \frac{-U_{11} + (1 + r)U_{12}}{\nabla} > 0,$$

since the assumption that goods are normal gives $-U_{11} + (1 + r)U_{12} > 0$. Therefore, saving increases in the current period when y increases.

To determine the effects of a change in future income y', we again apply Cramer's rule to (A.51), getting

$$\frac{dc}{dy'} = \frac{1}{1 + r} \frac{dc}{dy} > 0,$$

$$\frac{dc'}{dy'} = \frac{1}{1 + r} \frac{dc'}{dy} > 0,$$

so that the effects of a change in y' are identical qualitatively to the effects of a change in y, except that the derivatives are discounted, using the one-period discount factor $\frac{1}{1 + r}$. The effect on saving is given by

$$\frac{ds}{dy'} = -\frac{dc}{dy'} < 0,$$

and so saving decreases when future income increases.

Finally, to determine the effects of a change in the real interest rate r on current and future consumption, we again apply Cramer's rule to (A.34), getting

$$\frac{dc}{dr} = \frac{-U_2 + [U_{12} - (1 + r)U_{22}](y - t - c)}{\nabla},$$

$$\frac{dc'}{dr} = \frac{(1 + r)U_2 - [U_{11} - (1 + r)U_{12}](y - t - c)}{\nabla}.$$

The signs of both of these derivatives are indeterminate, because the income and substitution effects may be opposing. As above, we can separate the income and substitution effects by determining the responses of c and c' to a change in r holding utility constant. The substitution effects are

$$\frac{dc}{dr}(subst) = \frac{-U_2}{\nabla} < 0,$$

$$\frac{dc'}{dr}(subst) = \frac{(1 + r)U_2}{\nabla} > 0,$$

so that the substitution effect is for current consumption to decrease and future consumption to increase when the real interest rate increases. The income effects are

$$\frac{dc}{dr}(inc) = \frac{dc}{dr} - \frac{dc}{dr}(subst) = \frac{[U_{12} - (1 + r)U_{22}](y - t - c)}{\nabla},$$

$$\frac{dc'}{dr}(inc) = \frac{dc'}{dr} - \frac{dc'}{dr}(subst) = -\frac{[U_{11} - (1 + r)U_{12}](y - t - c)}{\nabla}.$$

Here, the assumption that goods are normal gives $U_{12} - (1 + r)U_{22} > 0$ and $U_{11} - (1 + r)U_{12} < 0$, and so given this assumption the signs of the income effects are determined by whether the consumer is a lender or a borrower, that is, by the sign of $y - t - c$. If the consumer is a lender, so that $y - t - c > 0$, then the income effects are for current consumption to increase and future consumption to decrease. However, if $y - t - c < 0$, so that consumer is a borrower, then the income effect is for current consumption to decrease and future consumption to increase.

Since saving is $s - y - c - t$, the effect on savings of a change in the real interest rate is determined by the effect on current consumption, namely,

$$\frac{ds}{dr} = -\frac{dc}{dr}.$$

Problems

1. Suppose that $U(c, c') = \ln c + \beta \ln c'$, where $\beta > 0$. Determine consumption in the current and future periods for the consumer, and interpret your solutions in terms of income and substitution effects.

2. Suppose that $U(c, c') = \ln c + \beta \ln c'$, where $\beta > 0$, and assume that the consumer lends at the real interest rate r_1, and borrows at the interest rate r_2, where $r_1 < r_2$. Under what conditions will the consumer be (i) a borrower, (ii) a lender, (iii) neither a borrower nor a lender? Explain your results.

Chapter 11: A Real Intertemporal Model with Investment

There is not much to be gained from analyzing the model developed in this chapter algebraically. It is possible to linearize the model so as to make it amenable to an explicit solution, but to do analysis with this linearized model requires a good deal of tedious algebra. For this chapter, we will confine attention to a formal treatment of the representative firm's investment problem.

The current and future production functions for the firm are given, respectively, by

$$Y = zF(K, N) \tag{A.52}$$

and

$$Y' = z'(K', N'), \tag{A.53}$$

where Y and Y' are current and future outputs, respectively, z and z' are current and future total factor productivities, K and K' are current and future capital stocks, and N and N' are current and future labour inputs. The capital stock evolves according to

$$K' = (1 - d)K + I, \tag{A.54}$$

where d is the depreciation rate and I is investment in capital in period 1. The present value of profits for the firm is

$$V = Y - I - wN + \frac{Y' - w'N' + (1 - d)K'}{1 + r}, \tag{A.55}$$

where w is the current real wage, w' is the future real wage, and r is the real interest rate. We can substitute in (A.55) for Y, Y', and K' using (A.52)–(A.54) to obtain

$$V = zF(K, N) - I - wN + \frac{z'F[(1 - d)K + I, N'] - w'N' + (1 - d)[(1 - d)K + I]}{1 + r}. \tag{A.56}$$

The objective of the firm is to choose N, N', and I to maximize V. The first-order conditions for an optimum, obtained by differentiating Equation (A.56) with respect to N, N', and I, are

$$\frac{\partial V}{\partial N} = zF_2(K, N) - w = 0, \tag{A.57}$$

$$\frac{\partial V}{\partial N'} = \frac{z'F_2[(1 - d)K + I, N'] - w'}{1 + r} = 0, \tag{A.58}$$

$$\frac{\partial V}{\partial I} = -1 + \frac{z'F_1[(1 - d)K + I, N'] + 1 - d}{1 + r} = 0. \tag{A.59}$$

Equations (A.57) and (A.58) state, respectively, that the firm optimizes by setting the marginal product of labour equal to the real wage in the current period and in the future period. We can simplify Equation (A.59) by writing it as

$$z'F_1[(1 - d)K + I, N'] - d = r, \tag{A.60}$$

or the firm chooses investment optimally by setting the future net marginal product of capital equal to the real interest rate, given N'. To determine how changes in z', K, d, and r affect the investment decision, given future employment N', we totally differentiate (A.60), getting

$$z'F_{11}dI + z'(1 - d)F_{11}dK + F_1dz' - (z'KF_{11} + 1)dd - dr = 0.$$

Then, we have

$$\frac{dI}{dr} = \frac{1}{z'F_{11}} < 0,$$

so that investment declines when the real interest rate increases;

$$\frac{dI}{dK} = d - 1 < 0,$$

so that investment is lower, the higher the initial capital stock K;

$$\frac{dI}{dz'} = \frac{-F_1}{z'F_{11}} > 0,$$

so that investment increases when future total factor productivity increases; and

$$\frac{dI}{dd} = \frac{z'KF_{11} + 1}{z'F_{11}},$$

which has an indeterminate sign, so that the effect of a change in the depreciation rate on investment is ambiguous.

Problem

1. Suppose that the firm produces output only from capital. Current output is given by $Y = zK^\alpha$, and future output is given by $Y' = z'\,(K')^\alpha$, where $0 < \alpha < 1$. Determine investment for the firm, and show how investment depends on the real interest rate, future total factor productivity, the depreciation rate, and α. Explain your results.

Chapter 12: A Monetary Intertemporal Model

Here, we will develop an explicit cash-in-advance model and show some of the implications of this model that we derived more informally in Chapter 12. The model will in some ways be simplified relative to the monetary intertemporal model of Chapter 12, but this will allow a clearer derivation of the results.

In the cash-in-advance model there is a representative consumer, who lives forever, and has preferences given by the utility function

$$\sum_{t=0}^{\infty} \beta^t [U(C_t) - V(N_t)], \tag{A.61}$$

where β is the subjective discount factor, with $0 < \beta < 1$, C_t is consumption in period t, N_t is labour supply in period t, $U(\cdot)$ is a strictly increasing and strictly concave function with $U'(0) = \infty$, and $V(\cdot)$ is a strictly increasing and strictly convex function with $V'(0) = 0$. Assume that $U(\cdot)$ and $V(\cdot)$ are twice continuously differentiable.

For simplicity we will not have capital or investment in the model, to focus on the key results, and the production function will be given by

$$Y_t = zN_t, \tag{A.62}$$

where Y_t is output in period t, and z is the marginal product of labour. Note that the linear production function has the constant-returns-to-scale property.

Within any period t, timing works as follows. At the beginning of the period, the representative consumer has M_t units of money carried over from the previous period, B_t nominal bonds, and X_t real bonds. Each nominal bond issued in period t is a promise to pay one unit of money in period $t + 1$, and each real bond issued in period t is a promise to pay one unit of the consumption good in period $t + 1$. With nominal and real bonds in the model, we can determine explicitly the nominal and real interest rates. A nominal bond issued in period t sells for q_t units of money, while a real bond sells for s_t units of period t consumption goods.

At the beginning of the period, the asset market opens, the consumer receives the payoffs on the bonds held over from the previous period, and the consumer can exchange money for nominal and real bonds that come due in period $t + 1$. The consumer must also pay a real lump-sum tax of T_t at this time. After the asset market closes, the consumer supplies N_t units of labour to the firm and buys consumption goods on the goods market, but he or she must purchase these consumption goods with money held over after the asset market closes. Consumption goods are sold at the money price P_t in period t. Therefore, the representative consumer must abide by the cash-in-advance constraint

$$P_t C_t + q_t B_{t+1} + P_t s_t X_{t+1} + P_t T_t = M_t + B_t + P_t X_t. \tag{A.63}$$

When the goods market closes, the consumer receives his or her labour earnings from the representative firm in cash. The consumer then faces the budget constraint

$$P_t C_t + q_t B_{t+1} + P_t s_t X_{t+1} + P_t T_t + M_{t+1} = M_t + B_t + P_t X_t + P_t z N_t, \tag{A.64}$$

where M_{t+1} is the quantity of money held by the consumer at the end of the period and z is the real wage in period t, which must be equal to the constant marginal product of labour in equilibrium.

Letting $\overline{M}_t$ denote the supply of money at the beginning of period t, the government budget constraint is given by

$$\overline{M}_{t+1} - \overline{M}_t = -P_t T_t, \tag{A.65}$$

and the government sets taxes so that the money supply grows at a constant rate α. That is, we have $\overline{M}_{t+1} = (1 + \alpha)\overline{M}_t$ for all t. This then implies, from (A.65), that

$$\alpha \overline{M}_t = -P_t T_t. \tag{A.66}$$

Now, it will prove convenient to scale the constraints (A.63) and (A.64) by multiplying through by $\frac{1}{\overline{M}_t}$, and letting lowercase letters denote scaled nominal variables—for example, $p_t = \frac{P_t}{\overline{M}_t}$. Then, we can rewrite (A.63) and (A.64) as

$$p_t C_t + q_t b_{t+1}(1 + \alpha) + p_t s_t X_{t+1} + p_t T_t = m_t + b_t + p_t X_t \tag{A.67}$$

and

$$p_t C_t + q_t b_{t+1}(1 + \alpha) + p_t s_t X_{t+1} + p_t T_t + m_{t+1}(1 + \alpha) = m_t + b_t + p_t X_t + p_t z N_t. \tag{A.68}$$

The representative consumer's problem is to choose C_t, N_t, b_{t+1}, X_{t+1}, and m_{t+1} in each period $t = 0, 1, 2, \ldots, \infty$, to maximize (A.61) subject to the constraints (A.67) and (A.68). We can simplify the problem by formulating it as a dynamic program. Letting $v(m_t, b_t, X_t; p_t, q_t, s_t)$ denote the value function, the Bellman equation associated with the consumer's problem is

$$v(m_t, b_t, X_t; p_t, q_t, s_t) = \max_{C_t, N_t, b_{t+1}, X_{t+1}, m_{t+1}} \left[U(C_t) - V(N_t) + \beta v(m_{t+1}, b_{t+1}, X_{t+1}; p_{t+1}, q_{t+1}, s_{t+1}) \right]$$

subject to (A.67) and (A.68). Letting λ_t and μ_t denote the Lagrange multipliers associated with the constraints (A.67) and (A.68), the first-order conditions for an optimum are

$$U'(C_t) - (\lambda_t + \mu_t) p_t = 0, \tag{A.69}$$

$$-V'(N_t) + \mu_t p_t z = 0, \tag{A.70}$$

$$-q_{t+1}(1 + \alpha)(\lambda_t + \mu_t) + \beta \frac{\partial v}{\partial b_{t+1}} = 0 \tag{A.71}$$

$$-p_t s_t(\lambda_t + \mu_t) + \beta \frac{\partial v}{\partial X_{t+1}} = 0, \tag{A.72}$$

$$-(1 + \alpha)\mu_t + \beta \frac{\partial v}{\partial m_{t+1}} = 0. \tag{A.73}$$

We can also derive the following envelope conditions by differentiating the Bellman equation above and applying the envelope theorem:

$$\frac{\partial v}{\partial b_t} = \lambda_t + \mu_t; \tag{A.74}$$

$$\frac{\partial v}{\partial X_t} = p_t(\lambda_t + \mu_t); \tag{A.75}$$

$$\frac{\partial v}{\partial m_t} = \lambda_t + \mu_t. \tag{A.76}$$

Now, we can use the envelope conditions, (A.74)–(A.76), updated one period, to substitute for the derivatives of the value function in (A.71)–(A.73), and then use (A.69) and (A.70) to substitute for Lagrange multipliers in (A.71)–(A.73), obtaining

$$\frac{-q_t(1 + \alpha)U'(C_t)}{p_t} + \beta \frac{U'(C_{t+1})}{p_{t+1}} = 0, \tag{A.77}$$

$$- s_t U'(C_t) + \beta U'(C_{t+1}) = 0, \tag{A.78}$$

$$\frac{-(1 + \alpha)V'(N_t)}{p_t z} + \beta \frac{U'(C_{t+1})}{p_{t+1}} = 0. \tag{A.79}$$

Next, the market-clearing conditions are

$$m_t = 1, b_t = 0, X_t = 0,$$

for all t. Money demand equals money supply, the demand for nominal bonds equals the zero net supply of nominal bonds, and the demand for real bonds equals the zero net supply of these bonds as well, in each period. Substituting the market-clearing conditions in Equations (A.67) and (A.68), and using Equation (A.66) to substitute for T_t, we obtain

$$p_t C_t = 1 + \alpha, \tag{A.80}$$

$$C_t = z N_t. \tag{A.81}$$

Equations (A.80) and (A.81) state, respectively, that all money is held in equilibrium at the beginning of the period by the representative consumer and is used to purchase consumption goods, and that in equilibrium all output produced is consumed.

Now, there is an equilibrium where $C_t = C$, $N_t = N$, $p_t = p$, $q_t = q$, and $s_t = s$, for all t, and we can use Equations (A.77)–(A.81) to solve for C, N, p, q, and s. We obtain

$$q = \frac{\beta}{1 + \alpha}, \tag{A.82}$$

$$s = \beta, \tag{A.83}$$

$$(1 + \alpha)V'(N) - \beta z U'(zN) = 0, \tag{A.84}$$

$$C = zN, \tag{A.85}$$

$$p = \frac{1 + \alpha}{C}. \tag{A.86}$$

Here, Equations (A.82) and (A.83) give solutions for q and s respectively, while Equation (A.84) solves implicitly for N. Then, given the solution for N, we can solve recursively for C and p from (A.85) and (A.86). Note as well that we can solve for the Lagrange multiplier λ using (A.69), (A.70), (A.80), (A.81), and (A.84), to get

$$\lambda = \frac{CU'(C)}{1 + \alpha}\left(1 - \frac{\beta}{1 + \alpha}\right) = \frac{CU'(C)}{1 + \alpha}(1 - q). \tag{A.87}$$

Now, note that the nominal interest rate is determined by the price of the nominal bond q, as $R = \frac{1}{q} - 1$, so that the nominal interest rate is positive as long as $q < 1$. From (A.82), the nominal interest rate is positive when $\alpha > \beta - 1$, that is, as long as the money growth rate is sufficiently large. Note also that the Lagrange multiplier associated with the cash-in-advance constraint is positive—that is, $\lambda > 0$—if and only if $q < 1$. Thus, a positive nominal interest rate is associated with a binding cash-in-advance constraint. From Equation (A.82), the nominal interest rate is

$$R = \frac{1 + \alpha}{\beta} - 1.$$

The real interest rate is $\frac{1}{s} - 1$; from Equation (A.83), this is

$$r = \frac{1}{\beta} - 1,$$

which is the representative consumer's subjective rate of time preference. Further, the inflation rate is

$$i = \frac{P_{t+1}}{P_t} - 1 = \frac{p_{t+1}\overline{M}_{t+1}}{p_t\overline{M}_t} = \alpha,$$

so that the inflation rate is equal to the money growth rate. Now, from the above, it is clear that the Fisher relation holds, as

$$1 + r = \frac{1 + R}{1 + i}.$$

The effects of money growth on real variables can be obtained by totally differentiating Equation (A.84) with respect to N and α, and solving to obtain

$$\frac{dN}{d\alpha} = \frac{-V'}{(1 + \alpha)V'' - \beta z^2 U''} < 0;$$

thus, employment declines with an increase in the money growth rate, and since $Y = C = zN$ in equilibrium, output and consumption also decline. This effect arises because inflation distorts intertemporal decisions. Period t labour income is held as cash and not spent on consumption until period $t + 1$, and it is therefore eroded by inflation. Higher inflation then reduces labour supply, output, and consumption.

What is the optimal rate of inflation? To determine a Pareto optimum, we solve the social planner's problem, which is to solve

$$\max_{\{C_t, N_t\}_{t=0}^{\infty}} \sum_{t=0}^{\infty} \beta^t [U(C_t) - V(N_t)]$$

subject to $C_t = zN_t$ for all t. The solution to this problem is characterized by the first-order condition

$$zU'(zN^*) - V'(N^*) = 0,$$

where N^* is optimal employment in each period t. In equilibrium, employment N is determined by (A.84), and note that equilibrium employment will be equal to N^* for the case where $\alpha = \beta - 1$. The optimal money growth rate $\beta - 1$ characterizes a Friedman rule, as this implies from (A.82) that the nominal interest rate is zero, and that the inflation rate is $\beta - 1$, so that the rate of return on money is $\frac{1}{\beta} - 1$, which is identical to the real interest rate r. Note also, from (A.87), that the cash-in-advance constraint does not bind when $\alpha = \beta - 1$, since $\lambda = 0$. Thus, a Friedman rule relaxes the cash-in-advance constraint, and causes the rates of return on all assets to be equated in equilibrium.

Problem

1. Suppose in the monetary intertemporal model that $U(C) = 2C^{1/2}$ and $V(N) = (1/2)N^2$. Determine closed-form solutions for consumption, employment, output, the nominal interest rate, and the real interest rate. What are the effects of changes in z and α in equilibrium? Explain your results.

Chapter 17: Money, Inflation, and Banking

A KIYOTAKI-WRIGHT MONETARY SEARCH MODEL

Here, we will develop a version of the Kiyotaki-Wright random matching model, to show how fiat money can overcome an absence-of-double-coincidence-of-wants problem. This model is closely related to the one constructed by Alberto Trejos and Randall Wright in an article in the *Journal of Political Economy*,[3] and it generalizes the model of Chapter 17 to a case in which there are n different goods rather than 3. To work through this model requires an elementary knowledge of probability.

In the model, there are n different types of consumers and n different goods, where $n \geq 3$. Each consumer is infinite-lived and maximizes

$$E_0 \sum_{t=0}^{\infty} \left(\frac{1}{1 + r} \right)^t U_t,$$

where E_0 is the expectations operator conditional on information at $t = 0$, r is the consumer's subjective discount rate, and U_t is the utility from consuming in period t, where $U_t = 0$ if nothing is consumed. Given that the consumer will face uncertainty, we have assumed that he or she is an expected-utility maximizer. A consumer of type i produces good i and consumes good $i + 1$, for $i = 1, 2, 3, \ldots, n - 1$, and a type n consumer produces good n and consumes good 1. Note that if $n = 3$, then this is the same setup as we considered in Chapter 17. In this n-good model, there is an absence-of-double-coincidence problem, as no two consumers produce what each other wants.

Goods are indivisible, so that when a good is produced, the consumer produces only one unit. At $t = 0$, a fraction M of the population is endowed with one unit of fiat money each, and fiat money is also indivisible. Further, a consumer can hold at most one unit of some object at a time, so that at the end of any period a consumer will be holding one unit of a good, one unit of money, or nothing. It is costless to produce a good and costless to hold one unit of a good or money as inventory.

At the end of period 0, each consumer not holding money produces a good, and then he or she holds this in inventory until period 1. In period 1, consumers are matched two-by-two and at random, so that a given consumer meets only one other consumer during period 1. Two consumers who meet inspect each other's goods and announce whether they are willing to trade. If both are willing, they trade, and any consumer receiving his or her consumption good in a trade consumes it (this is optimal), receives utility $u > 0$ from consumption, and produces another good. Then consumers move on to period 2, and so on. No two consumers will meet more than once, since there are infinitely many consumers in the population. We will assume that there are equal numbers of each type of consumer, so that the fraction of the population who are of a given type is $\frac{1}{n}$. Then, in any period, the probability that a consumer meets another consumer of a particular type is $\frac{1}{n}$.

What can be an equilibrium in this model? One equilibrium is where money is not valued. That is, if no one accepts money, then no one will want to hold it and, because of the absence-of-double-coincidence problem, there will be no exchange and everyone's utility will be zero.

---

[3]See A. Trejos and R. Wright, 1995, "Search, Bargaining, Money, and Prices," *Journal of Political Economy* 103, 118–141.

If no one has faith that money will have value in exchange, then this expectation will be self-fulfilling. A more interesting equilibrium is one where everyone accepts money. Here, we will let μ denote the fraction of the population that holds money in equilibrium, V_g will denote the value of holding a good in equilibrium, and V_m will be the value of holding money. Though there are n different goods, the optimization problems of all consumers will be identical in equilibrium, and so the value of holding any good will be the same for each consumer. The Bellman equations associated with a consumer's optimization problem are

$$V_g = \frac{1}{1+r}\left[(1-\mu)V_g + \mu\left(1 - \frac{1}{n}\right)V_g + \mu\frac{1}{n}(V_m - V_g)\right], \tag{A.88}$$

$$V_m = \frac{1}{1+r}\left[(1-\mu)\left(1 - \frac{1}{n}\right)V_m + (1-\mu)\frac{1}{n}(u + V_g) + \mu V_m\right]. \tag{A.89}$$

In Equation (A.88), the value of holding a good at the end of the current period is equal to the discounted sum of the expected payoff in the following period. In the following period, the consumer meets another agent with a good with probability $1-\mu$, in which case trade does not take place, and the consumer will be holding a good at the end of the next period and will receive value V_g. With probability $\mu(1 - \frac{1}{n})$, the consumer meets another consumer with money who does not wish to purchase the consumer's good, and again trade does not take place. With probability $\mu\frac{1}{n}$, the consumer meets a consumer with money who wants his or her good, trade takes place, and the consumer is holding money at the end of the next period. In Equation (A.89), a consumer with money does not trade with another consumer who has money, or with another consumer who has a good that he or she does not consume. However, with probability $(1 - \mu)\frac{1}{n}$ the consumer meets another consumer with his or her consumption good, in which case trade takes place, the consumer gets utility u from consuming the good, and then he or she produces another good.

We can solve for V_g and V_m from (A.88) and (A.89), which give

$$V_g = \frac{\mu(1-\mu)u}{r(1+r)},$$

$$V_m = \frac{(r+\mu)(1-\mu)u}{r(1+r)}.$$

so that

$$V_m - V_g = \frac{(1-\mu)u}{1+r} > 0.$$

Therefore, the value of holding money is greater than the value of holding a good, so that everyone will accept money (as conjectured) in equilibrium. Further, consumers who have money in any period will prefer to hold it rather than producing a good, and so we will have $\mu = M$ in equilibrium.

The values of V_g and V_m are the utilities that consumers receive from holding goods and money, respectively. As $V_g > 0$ and $V_m > 0$, everyone is better off in an economy where money is used than in one where it is not used.

Problem

1. Suppose a search economy with the possibility of double coincidences. That is, assume that when an agent produces a good, that he or she cannot consume it herself. In a random match where two agents meet and each has the good that they produced, the first agent has what the second consumes with probability x, the second has what the first consumes with probability x, and each has what the other consumes with probability x^2.

   a. In this economy, show that there are three equilibria: a barter equilibrium in which money is not accepted, an equilibrium in which an agent with a good is indifferent between accepting and not accepting money, and an equilibrium in which agents with goods always accept money.

   b. Show that x needs to be sufficiently small before having money in this economy actually increases welfare over having barter, and explain this result.

THE DIAMOND-DYBVIG MODEL

There are three periods, 0, 1, and 2, and an intertemporal technology that allows one unit of the period 0 good to be converted into $1 + r$ units of the period 2 good. The intertemporal technology can be interrupted in period 1, with a yield of one unit in period 1 for each unit of input in period 0. If production is interrupted in period 1, there is no return in period 2. Goods can be stored from period 1 to period 2 with no depreciation. There is a continuum of consumers with unit mass, and each consumer maximizes expected utility

$$W = tU(c_1) + (1 - t)U(c_2),$$

where c_1 is the consumer's consumption if he or she consumes in period i for $i = 1, 2$, and t is the probability that the consumer consumes early. Here, t is also the fraction of agents who are early consumers. We assume that t is known in period 0, but consumers do not know their type (early or late consumer) until period 1. Each consumer is endowed with one unit of goods in period 0.

Suppose that there are no banks, but consumers can trade investment projects in period 1, with one project selling for the price p in terms of consumption goods. Then, each consumer chooses to invest all of their goods in the technology in period 0, and in period 1 a consumer must decide how much of the investment to interrupt and how many investment projects to buy and sell. In period 1 an early consumer wants to sell the investment project if $p > 1$ and will want to interrupt the investment project and consume the proceeds if $p < 1$. The early consumer is indifferent if $p = 1$. A late consumer in period 1 wants to interrupt the investment project and purchase investment projects if $p < 1$, chooses to hold the investment project if $p > 1$, and is indifferent if $p = 1$. The equilibrium price is, therefore, $p = 1$, and in equilibrium fraction t of all projects is interrupted in period 1, early consumers each consume $c_1 = 1$ and late consumers consume $c_2 = 1 + r$. Expected utility for each consumer in period 0 is

$$W_1 = tU(1) + (1 - t)U(1 + r).$$

Now, suppose that there is a bank that takes deposits from consumers in period 0, serves depositors sequentially in period 1 (places in line are drawn at random), and offers a deposit contract (d_1, d_2), where d_1 is the amount that can be withdrawn in period 1 for each unit deposited in period 0 and d_2 is the amount that can be withdrawn in period 2 for each unit deposited.

Assume that all consumers deposit in the bank in period 0. Then, the bank chooses (d_1, d_2) and x, the quantity of production to interrupt, to solve:

$$\max_{d_1, d_2, x} [tU(d_1) + (1 - t)U(d_2)] \qquad (A.90)$$

subject to

$$td_1 = x, \qquad (A.91)$$

$$(1 - t)d_2 = (1 - x)(1 + r), \qquad (A.92)$$

$$d_1 \leq d_2. \qquad (A.93)$$

Here, Equation (A.91) is the bank's resource constraint in period 1, (A.92) is the resource constraint in period 2, and (A.93) is an incentive constraint, which states that it must be in the interest of late consumers to withdraw late rather than posing as early consumers and withdrawing early.

Ignoring the constraint (A.93), substituting for d_1 and d_2 using the constraints (A.91) and (A.92) in the objective function (A.90), the first-order condition for an optimum is

$$U'\left(\frac{x}{t}\right) = (1 + r)U'\left(\frac{(1 - x)(1 + r)}{1 - t}\right), \qquad (A.94)$$

with $d_1 = \frac{x}{t}$ and $d_2 = \frac{(1 - x)(1 + r)}{1 - t}$. Equation (A.94) then implies that $d_1 < d_2$ so that (A.93) is satisfied. Further, if we assume that $\frac{-cU''}{U'} > 1$, then (A.94) implies that $d_1 > 1$ and $d_2 < 1 + r$. Thus, under this condition, the bank provides consumers with insurance against the need for liquid assets in period 1, and the bank gives consumers higher expected utility than when there was no bank ($d_1 - 1$ and $d_2 = 1 + r$) if the bank chooses $x = t$.

However, there also exists a bank-run equilibrium. That is, if a late consumer expects all other consumers to run to the bank in period 1, he or she will want to do it as well.

Problems

1. Suppose that consumers can meet and trade in period 1 instead of going to the bank in sequence. Show that, given the banking contract (d_1, d_2), there could be Pareto-improving trades that early and late consumers could make in period 1 that would undo the banking contract, so that this would not constitute an equilibrium. Discuss your results.

2. Show that, if $U(c) = \log c$, then there is no need for a bank in the Diamond-Dybvig economy, and explain this result.

Chapter 18: Inflation, the Phillips Curve, and Central Bank Commitment

In this section we construct a somewhat more explicit version of the model we worked with in Chapter 18 to show some of the results of that chapter more formally.

The first component of the model is the Phillips curve relationship, which captures the key idea in the Friedman-Lucas money surprise model. That is,

$$i - i^e = a(Y - Y^T), \qquad (A.95)$$

where i is the inflation rate, i^e is the private sector's anticipated inflation rate, $a > 0$, Y is aggregate output, and Y^T is trend output. The second component of the model is the preferences of the central bank, which we will represent by supposing that the central bank maximizes $\phi(Y, i)$, where $\phi(\cdot, \cdot)$ is a function. That is, the central bank cares about the level of output and the inflation rate. It is convenient to express $\phi(Y, i)$ as a quadratic function—that is,

$$\phi(Y, i) = \alpha(i - i^*)^2 + \beta(Y - Y^*)^2, \tag{A.96}$$

where α and β are positive constants, i^* is the target inflation rate for the central bank, and Y^* is the target level of aggregate output for the central bank.

Now suppose, according to the central bank learning story, that the central bank treats the anticipated inflation rate i^e as being given, and chooses i and Y to maximize (A.96) given (A.95). Solving this optimization problem, the central bank will then choose

$$i = \frac{\alpha a^2 i^* + \beta i^e - \beta a(Y^T - Y^*)}{\alpha a^2 + \beta}. \tag{A.97}$$

We will then have

$$i - i^e = \frac{\alpha a^2(i^* - i^e) - \beta a(Y^T - Y^*)}{\alpha a^2 + \beta}.$$

In this circumstance, if the central bank had a target level of output that was higher than trend output—that is, $Y^T - Y^* < 0$—then even if $i^e > i^*$, in which case anticipated inflation is higher than the target inflation rate, the central bank may want to have $i > i^e$ so that the private sector is fooled by positive surprise inflation. Ultimately, though, the private sector is not fooled in the long run, so that $i = i^e$, and if the central bank learns this, then it realizes that, from (A.95), it cannot engineer a level of output other than Y^T, and the best strategy for the central bank is to set $i = i^*$.

Under the central bank commitment story, the central bank cannot commit to an inflation rate, and it is playing a game with the private sector. The private sector first chooses i_e, then the central bank chooses i, and in equilibrium $i = i^e$. In this case, Equation (A.97) is the central bank's reaction function, and we can solve for the equilibrium inflation rate by substituting $i = i^e$ in (A.97), getting

$$i = i^* + \frac{\beta}{\alpha a}(Y^* - Y^T);$$

hence, if $Y^* > Y^T$, in equilibrium the inflation rate can be higher than i^*, which is the inflation rate the central bank would choose if it could tie its hands and commit itself to an inflation policy.

Problem

1. Suppose that, instead of expectations being rational, expectations are adaptive. That is, each period the private sector expects that the inflation rate will be what it was the previous period. That is, $i^e = i_{-1}$, where i_{-1} is the actual inflation rate last period. Under these circumstances, determine what the actual inflation rate and the level of output will be, given i_{-1}. How will the inflation rate and output evolve over time? What will the inflation rate and the level of output be in the long run? Explain your results.

INDEX